THE MODERN THEATRE

Readings and Documents

The Modern Theatre

Readings and Documents

Edited by
DANIEL SELTZER
Loeb Drama Center, Harvard University

 Little, Brown and Company
Boston

LIBRARY OF CONGRESS CATALOG CARD NO. 67-17094

FIRST PRINTING

PUBLISHED SIMULTANEOUSLY IN CANADA
BY LITTLE, BROWN & COMPANY (CANADA) LIMITED

PRINTED IN THE UNITED STATES OF AMERICA

"The End of Tragedy: Pleasure, The Universal, and The Purgation of The Passions of Fear and Pity" from
Francis Fergusson's Introduction to *Aristotle's Poetics*. Introduction copyright © 1961 by Francis Fergusson.
Reprinted by Permission of Hill and Wang, Inc.

"Comedy," copyright © 1951 by Christopher Fry, is reprinted by permission of the author. (This essay was
published initially in *The Adelphi* of November 1950 in England, and subsequently appeared in *Vogue* of January
1951, and in *Tulane Drama Review* of March 1960.)

"Jokes and the Species of the Comic" is reprinted from *Jokes and Their Relation to the Unconscious* by Sigmund
Freud. Translated from the German and Edited by James Strachey, by permission of W. W. Norton & Company,
Inc., and Routledge & Kegan Paul Ltd. (London). Copyright © 1960 by James Strachey.

"The Dramatic Illusion" is reprinted with the permission of Charles Scribner's Sons from *Feeling and Form*,
pages 301-313, 314-323, 324-325, by Susanne K. Langer. Copyright 1953 Charles Scribner's Sons.

"Alienation Effects in Chinese Acting" by Bertolt Brecht is from *Brecht on Theatre*, translated by John Willett.
Copyright © 1957, 1963, and 1964 by Suhrkamp Verlag (Frankfurt am Main). Translation and notes © 1964 by
John Willett. Reprinted by permission of Hill and Wang, Inc., and Methuen and Co. Ltd. (London).

"Why the Cherry Orchard?" by Jean-Louis Barrault is from *The Theatre of Jean-Louis Barrault*, translated by
Joseph Chiari. First published by Flammarion (Paris) under the title *Nouvelles Réflexions sur le Théâtre*. English
translation first published and © 1961 by Barrie and Rockliff (London). Reprinted by permission of Hill and
Wang, Inc., Barrie and Rockliff, and Editions Flammarion.

"The Moscow Art Theatre" is reprinted with the permission of Charles Scribner's Sons from *Immortal Shadows*,
pages 15-19, by Stark Young. Copyright 1948 Charles Scribner's Sons.

CONTENTS

PART THREE ✒ THE DIRECTOR

❦ INTRODUCTION

Although collections of documents are never substitutes for live performance, they can indicate ways in which new views of creativity are really part of a continuing process originating in the past. An understanding of the past as the foundation for new experimentation is in itself a valuable form of conservation — ignored, particularly in the theatre, to one's peril. The achievements of a new sensibility require perspective. They may be kept in balance, and perhaps continually renewed, by the thoughts of such artists of the theatre as those represented in the following pages.

In studying the craft of the truly original artist — of any period — one discovers him immersed in the details of his heritage; yet, at the same time, he becomes more and more involved with that revolutionary approach or technique which is to be his particular contribution. The reshaping of an art form may be seen as a series of vivid observations, both theoretical and "practical"; the artists of each age add to the sequence their own perceptions of reality and ways in which that reality may be captured in stage terms.

We should try to use such perceptions creatively — remembering, modifying, perhaps (ultimately) rejecting — all the while recording something possibly useful for the future. An actor's stage business, his vocal style, his bearing in this or that role, are only the more obvious examples of such preservation and continuity. His approach to his art, his feelings about a specific script, his understanding — limited or not — of his own personality's relevance to a role: these too, properly understood, can sustain a *new* way, a new set of insights.

Similary useful are the observations of those committed to a particular theory of drama or specific theatrical practice. Such theoreticians may be playwrights or directors themselves (as are many included in this book), but others, whose thoughts are equally valuable, may never in their lives have stood upon a stage. The title of the last section of documents in this volume — "The Creative Audience" — implies the editor's belief that the creative act of drama involves those who deeply perceive the effectiveness of a play as well as those who perform it. Contributors to the dramatic experience of the future, then, be they student actors, designers, or directors, or their teachers, or members of a creative audience (the

Elizabethans went straight to the point when they addressed their audiences and readers, simply and honestly, as "Understanders"), can determine for themselves, as they study important documents, a general approach to this ranging yet specialized art.

The documents included in this book have been found helpful in many ways in the context of one university and its theatre. The tastes and preferences of the editor may be held accountable for the inclusion of most selections; these also stand behind certain omissions, of course—although limitations of space and copyright have also helped to shape the table of contents. On the whole, however, the documents included here represent the editor's view of the forms of plays and their effectiveness (set forth sometimes in theory but pertaining always to practice), of players and their artifice, of the purposes and potentials of stage direction, of the major scenic components in drama, and of the emotions and intellects of creative spectators. The group of documents may be used in whole or in part, for support or for useful disagreement, for specific reading relative to a particular play or *genre,* or for a background of varying approaches to many plays from many periods. The criterion for inclusion, however, remains a potential usefulness in undertaking the phenomenon of performance itself.

The documents may be described, roughly, as belonging to the "modern" period. The reason is twofold. First, the "classic" documents—from Aristotle's *Poetics* to Lessing's *Hamburg Dramaturgy*—are usually available in full texts. It has been thought advisable in this collection, therefore, to present a number of modern commentaries on, and reactions to, such basic documents. Such commentaries frequently stimulate new trains of ciritical thought, sometimes appropriate to the study of specific plays or methods of performing them. Secondly, the selections included here set forth important thoughts about plays and the theatre which—although indicating alteration and metamorphoses of taste and opinion over the last seventy-five years—can be organized to throw light upon each other or to parallel patterns of thought begun in the reading of any single text.

Part One, containing theoretical documents, is the most inclusive for it sets forth basic ideas implicit in the more "practical" gatherings that follow. But the goal of this volume is not to offer anthologized materials in specific categories that attempt to be exhaustive or definitive; rather, the editor has tried to present a varied group of writings, each one pertinent to a number of approaches to the understanding of dramatic theory. The *suggestive* qualities of each piece, then, have been important criteria for inclusion.

Thus, one might study different critics' views of the same production or of the dramatic type represented by that production (the views of each critic being equally responsive, equally "creative," yet representing sharply contrasting approaches to theatrical action or mood) and then proceed, perhaps, to historical and theoretical examination. The practical observations of Jouvet, for example, might be supplemented with the probing theoretical essays of Frye and Freud. Drama as a social force might be studied from viewpoints of Herbert Blau, Peter Brook, and Bertolt Brecht. Stanislavski's germinal ideas on the actor's imagination, part of the famous "method," may be seen in practical working terms in the director's score for the climactic episodes of *The Sea Gull* but should be compared to the apparently similar but actually contrasting approach of Michael Chekhov.

A number of selections in different parts of the volume deal with stage reality itself—how one perceives in theatre an illusion of the "real" world. The views of Saint-Denis and Coquelin should be compared; both are distinguished by practical application in the theatre but are separated from each other by decades of professional development, and each reveals the theatrical context of its period. These in turn might be examined in relation to the work of Elia Kazan, derived from the Moscow archetype yet greatly altered (and greatly influential in the modern theatre), and finally set in juxtaposition to the stern assessment of some dangers in the "method" as described by Michael Redgrave.

Gielgud's detailed notes to *King Lear* rehearsals under Granville-Barker should be compared to production discussions of Barrault and Stanislavski; the practical results of theory are both greater and fewer than one might have anticipated. Views of form and style, ranging from Fergusson to Dürrenmatt, may be contrasted in approach and application to those of Ionesco or Langer—and related afterwards, perhaps, to the practical observations by Tynan of Sir Laurence Olivier and his rehearsals of *Othello*.

Many selections in this volume refer to specific plays, but all admit application to more than one script. A principle in gathering these pieces has been to place under several headings perceptions about drama that represent, as a whole, a general and introductory yet sophisticated view of the total experience of theatre. While the four sections following the theoretical opening are concerned with drama as practical experience, only rarely are they purely technical. The student of theatrical crafts must have at his disposal aids to develop his own philosophy of dramatic experience—a general approach to his art that goes beyond certain detailed techniques (important as such techniques are). Such aids may be found, frequently, in such authoritative and varied voices of our own time as, for example, Robert Edmond Jones and Lee Simonson on the craft of surrounding action with a physical context. The student working with purely literary materials must know, as he approaches drama, that the theatrical experience is not only—perhaps not even basically— verbal; his awareness of theatrical crafts will be helped if they are set forth in a manner pertinent to textual studies but *not* in any orthodox sense to "literary criticism."

This is why some pieces included, for example, in the section on the creative audience—such as Miss Sontag's essay on Weiss's *Marat / Sade,* or Mr. Tynan's notes on the National Theatre rehearsals of *Othello,* or the excerpts from Professor Gombrich's great study of perceptions of reality in painting—are as "theoretical" as they are specifically "critical"; this is why some of the observations by directors deal so often with the nature of dramatic phenomena in general, as well as with practical problems in the exercise of technique. It is hoped that every selection, to some degree at least, is pivotal in its usefulness. Taken together, they represent the editor's feeling that the particular artistic experience of the staged play involves—*must* involve, if it is to be complete—the recognition by the audience through the efforts of actor, director, and designer, of the original "gesture," the first intentions of the playwright.

Implicit in the collection of these writings is an assumption that the perceptions of the theatre and those sometimes reserved to purely scholarly pursuit are not necessarily foreign to each other, that the mystery and creative process of one need not prohibit the fruitful investigations of the other. Individual views of drama more often contrast than corroborate; in fact, many of the most original views of the stage may be some of the most unsystematic ones—the ones to which most exceptions may be taken.

The active process of thought, however, to which all students of drama must be ultimately responsible, can find in the flux of the past the impetus for new endeavors. There is a certain irony, after all, whenever a theory or perception at one time considered revolutionary is included in an anthology. Its connections to tradition and convention (if not already apparent in the living theatre) may then become clear; such theories and perceptions invite their own revision.

Acknowledgements to the various authors, translators, and publishers with whose permission selections are reprinted here appear on the first page of each selection or on the copyright page. The editor also wishes to record his particular gratitude to Mr. Bruce B. Renshaw, Mr. Peter S. Ivers, and Miss Phoebe Lambert who have assisted greatly in the preparation of materials for this anthology.

Cambridge, Massachusetts
November 1966

PART ONE ✍ THEORY

Francis Fergusson

In this brief selection from his Introduction to the *Poetics,* the author describes the general "effects" of full tragedy in a way which indicates one of the great uses of Aristotle — whose ideas serve "as guides in one's own thinking about art." Fergusson illustrates the wonderfully suggestive nature of the original document by referring to the ruminations of young Stephen Daedalus on tragedy and tragic poetry derived in essence from Aristotle; as many critics of the *Poetics* have done, he calls our attention as well to helpful passages in other writings by Aristotle (here, from the *Politics*).

Francis Fergusson, one of the most important creative critics of literature in our own time, has written three vital works dealing with basic human responses to literature — literature either directly of the theatre or pertaining to dramatic modes of thought: *The Idea of a Theater* (1950), *Dante's Drama of the Mind* (1952), and *The Human Image in Dramatic Literature* (1957). He has also written a musical play based on the adventures of Huckleberry Finn and was drama critic for *The Bookman* in the 1930's. He has taught at Bennington, Princeton and is presently University Professor of Comparative Literature at Rutgers.

✒ THE END OF TRAGEDY: PLEASURE, THE UNIVERSAL, AND THE PURGATION OF THE PASSIONS OF FEAR AND PITY

The question why tragedy, with its images of conflict, terror and suffering, should give us pleasure and satisfaction, has been answered in many ways. Aristotle's answers, cautious and descriptive as they are, have interested his readers more than anything else in the *Poetics,* and produced more heated controversies among his interpreters. The appeal of tragedy is in the last analysis inexplicable, rooted as it is in our mysterious human nature, but Aristotle's observations of the effect which tragedy has upon us are as illuminating as anything we have on the subject.

He accepted, to begin with, the Greek notion that the fine arts have no end beyond themselves. The useful arts, shipbuilding, carpentry, and the like, provide transportation or shelter, but a play or a symphony cannot be used for anything but "pleasure." And we have seen that in his introductory remarks Aristotle suggests that the

3

arts give pleasure because they satisfy the instincts, or needs, of "imitation" and of "harmony" and "rhythm."

When we recognize the movement-of-spirit "imitated" in a play or poem, we get the satisfaction of knowledge and understanding. The joy of Romeo when he hears Juliet's voice saying his name, the despair of Macbeth when he sees that his mad race is lost, seem to confirm something we half-knew already. The creatures of the poet's imagination do not literally represent anything in our own experience; it must be that *through* word, character, and situation we glimpse something common to men in all times and places. That is why Aristotle writes, (IX.3): "Poetry . . . is a more philosophical and a higher thing than history: for poetry tends to express the universal, history the particular."

"Harmony and rhythm" must refer, not only to music, but to the accords and correspondences that we enjoy in any beautifully formed work of art. Stephen Daedalus, in Joyce's *Portrait of the Artist as a Young Man*, explaining his own Aristotelian conception of art, offers a general definition of rhythm: "Rhythm is the first formal esthetic relation of part to part in any esthetic whole or of an esthetic whole to its part or parts or of any part to the esthetic whole of which it is a part." Young Stephen's formula is laughably pedantic, but (if one thinks it out) extremely accurate. Stephen's whole discussion shows the right way to use Aristotle's ideas: as guides in one's own thinking about art.

Why do harmony and rhythm please us? We do not know; we can only note that they do. "There seems to be in us a sort of affinity to musical modes and rhythms," says Aristotle (*Politics*, VIII), "which makes some philosophers say that the soul is a tuning, others that it possesses tuning." The notion of the human psyche as itself a harmony and rhythm reappears again and again in our tradition, notably in Shakespeare, who often uses music to suggest the health of the inner being.

Such are the pleasures we find in all the fine arts; but the special quality of our pleasure in tragedy may be more closely defined. It comes, says Aristotle, from the purgation of the passions of fear and pity. At this point Stephen's meditations may help us again: "Aristotle has not defined pity and terror. I have. . . . Pity is the feeling which arrests the mind in the presence of whatsoever is grave and constant in human sufferings and unites it with the human sufferer. Terror is the feeling which arrests the mind in the presence of whatsoever is grave and constant in human sufferings and unites it with the secret cause." Notice that these passions must be stirred by the grave and *constant*. A particular calamity with no general meaning—a street accident for example—does not produce the tragic emotion, but only meaningless pain. Here we meet once more the universality of art: the passions of tragedy must spring from something of more than individual, more than momentary, significance. Moreover, the cause of our terror must be "secret." Tragedy, like the Dionysian ceremonies from which it was derived, touches the dark edge of human experience, celebrates a mystery of our nature and destiny.

It would seem (on thinking over the effects of a few tragedies) that pity and fear *together* are required. Pity alone is merely sentimental, like the shameless tears of soap opera. Fear alone, such as we get from a good thriller, merely makes us shift tensely to the edge of the seat and brace ourselves for the pistol shot. But the masters of tragedy, like good cooks, mingle pity and fear in the right proportions. Having given us fear enough, they melt us with pity, purging us of our emotions, and reconciling us to our fate, because we understand it as the universal human lot.

Aristotle's word for this effect is "purgation" or "catharsis." The Greek word can mean either the cleansing of the body (a medical term) or the cleansing of the spirit (a religious term). Some interpreters are shocked by it, because they do not wish to associate poetry with laxatives and enemas; others insist that Aristotle had the religious meaning in mind. I think it is more sensible to assume that Aristotle did not mean either one *literally:* he was talking about tragedy, not medicine or religion, and his use of the term "purgation" is analogical. There are certainly bodily changes (in our chemistry, breathing, muscular tensions, and the like) as we undergo the emotions of tragedy, and they may well constitute a release *like* that of literal purgation. But tragedy speaks essentially to the mind and the spirit, and its effect is *like* that which believers get from religious ceremonies intended to cleanse the spirit. Aristotle noticed (*Politics,* VIII) that, in religious rituals that he knew, the passions were stirred, released, and at last appeased; and he must have been thinking partly of that when he used the term "purgation" to describe the effect of tragedy.

In the *Poetics* Aristotle does not try to show how the various effects which the art of tragedy aims at, as its "end," are united in an actual play. The pleasures of imitation, harmony, and rhythm; the universal quality of art, and the release and cleansing of the passions, are things he observed, and mentioned in different contexts. But we may, if we like, confirm them in any good tragedy. The effect of *Oedipus Rex,* for example, depends upon its subtle and manifold "rhythm" as Joyce defines the word; upon the pity and fear which are stirred in us, and upon our recognition, at the end, of something both mysterious and universal in Oedipus's fate. Aristotle had a consistent and far-reaching conception of the art of tragedy, and of its end; but his conception only emerges gradually as one thinks over his observations in the light of one's own experience of drama.

Gerald F. Else

This is a short but highly detailed discussion of one of the most difficult and frequently analyzed words in Aristotle's *Poetics.* Much of our understanding, not only of Greek tragedy but of all serious drama, depends upon an appropriate perception of the scope of this term. Professor Else's remarks are taken without abridgement from his *Aristotle's Poetics: The Argument* (1957), a running translation, commentary, and analysis of this basic classical text of theatre practice.

In the observations reprinted here, Else demonstrates one of the beautifully creative uses of detailed, rigorous scholarship. By careful comparison, cross-reference with other works, and clear, conservative thinking, he reveals the real pertinence of the Greek term, *hamartia*—for so many years misunderstood by students and teachers of drama. The clarity of Else's discussion allows exciting application of the term to our understanding of plot structure—relative to the Greek tragedies first of all, but also to Shakespeare, and, in a more general way, to many other areas of drama. In the following discussion, Greek words and phrases translated in context by Professor Else are allowed to stand in the original; otherwise, they are translated and placed in square brackets.

Gerald Else is presently Chairman of the Department of Classical Studies at the University of Michigan; he has taught as well at Harvard and at the State University of Indiana. He is also the author of *The Origin and Early Form of Greek Tragedy* (1965).

⚵ *on* HAMARTIA

... All this is further connected with the difficult and long-debated question what Aristotle means by ἁμαρτία....[1] A majority of the modern commentators and interpreters take the *hamartia* to be an error,[2] although the rival interpretation, that it denotes a moral failing, or at least some degree of moral culpability, still has at least one able defender.[3] Unfortunately the issue has been beclouded by the almost habitual use of the terms "intellectual error" or "error of judgment" on the one side and "moral flaw" on the other. All these phrases, as we shall see, are misleading and beside the point.

Here, as Harsh emphasizes in an important essay on *hamartia*,[4] the question of method comes to the fore. How are we to get at Aristotle's meaning? A thorough semasiological investigation like those of Hey and Phillips (to which Harsh contributes an important supplement from the fifth-century tragedies themselves), pursuing the development of the word from Homer down to Aristotle, would seem to be the answer. But such an investigation will be inconclusive, because ἁμαρτάνειν [to miss one's mark], ἁμαρτία, and their cognates and compounds display such a wide range of meanings — all the way from simple error or failure to "sin," or as close to it as a classical Greek ever comes[5] — that either interpretation of our passage remains possible. The only safe guide is the context of Aristotle's own argument. But by "context" I do not mean the sentence before us

Reprinted by permission of the publishers from Gerald F. Else, *Aristotle's Poetics: The Argument* (Cambridge, Mass.: Harvard University Press).

[1] For a very brief survey of the controversy see Pitcher, *op. cit.* 2-4; in a more general sense J. Volkelt, *Ästhetik des Tragischen*,[3] Leipzig, 1917, 163 ff. ("Die Tragische Schuld"). Aside from the regular commentaries on our passage, *hamartia* is discussed in detail by J. H. Reinkens, *Aristoteles über Kunst, besonders über Tragödie*, Vienna, 1870, 321 ff.; P. Manns, *Die Lehre des Aristoteles von der tragischen Katharsis und Hamartia erklärt*, Karlsruhe, 1883, esp. 25 ff.; P. van Braam, "Aristotle's Use of 'Ἁμαρτία," *CQ* 6 (1912) 266-272; O. Hey, "'ΑΜΑΡΤΙΑ: Zur Bedeutungsgeschichte des Wortes," *Philol.* 83 (1928) 1-17, 137-163; H. Phillips, Jr., "De Vocis ΑΜΑΡΤΙΑ Vi et Usu apud Scriptores Graecos usque ad Annum CCC. ante Christum Natum" (unpubl. Harvard diss.; summary in *Harv. Stud. in Class. Philol.* 44 [1933] 244-246); R. A. Pack, "A Passage in Alexander of Aphrodisias Relating to the Theory of Tragedy," *AJP* 58 (1937) 418-436; *id.*, "Fate, Chance, and Tragic Error," *ibid.* 60 (1939) 350-356; Max Kommerell, *Lessing und Aristoteles*, Frankfurt, 1940, 120-129; P. W. Harsh, " 'Ἁμαρτία Again," *TAPA* 76 (1945) 47-58; K. v. Fritz, "Tragische Schuld u. poet. Gerechtigkeit in d. gr. Trag.," *Studium Generale* 8 (1955) 194-237.

[2] So Bywater, Albeggiani, Rostagni, Valgimigli, Hardy, Gudeman, Sykutris; and, of those mentioned in the preceding note, van Braam, Hey, Kommerell, Pitcher.

[3] Harsh. Phillips and Pack also incline in that direction, and Manns in the last century. Butcher wavers ("error or frailty"). As so often happens, the prevailing conception of *hamartia* among laymen and scholars in other fields is still that of the "moral flaw," which was dominant down through the nineteenth century.

[4] *Op. cit.* 51, 53 n. 24.

[5] See W. C. Greene, *Moira: Fate, Good and Evil in Greek Thought*, Cambridge, 1944, 22, 59-60.

(which tells us nothing about *hamartia* except that it is not the same as wickedness), but the larger nexus of argument to which chapter 13 belongs, namely the analysis of the complex tragic plot. *Hamartia* must be a functional element in a complex plot, otherwise Aristotle would not mention it here.

Once the matter is put this way, another concept springs to mind which is fitted to be the exact converse and complement of *hamartia*: i.e., recognition. Recognition is a change ἐξ ἀγνοίας εἰς γνῶσιν [from ignorance into recognition, revelation]; might not *hamartia* be the ἄγνοια [ignorance] from which the change begins? Moreover tragic recognition, or the best tragic recognition, is a discovery of the identity of a "dear" person, a blood-relative; it follows that the precedent *hamartia* would denote particularly a mistake or error or ignorance as to the identity of that person.

These suggestions will not win much credence by being thus baldly stated. They need to be bulwarked by a demonstration (a) that ἁμαρτία can have this meaning in Aristotle's usage, and (b) that such a concept is actually required by his argument just here. For the first of these two *demonstranda* we must go to three interrelated passages in the *Nicomachean Ethics* and the *Rhetoric*, where Aristotle defines or alludes to the distinctions between voluntary and involuntary action.[6] The first of these is in the third book of the *Ethics*, of which the first three chapters are devoted to a discussion of voluntary (ἑκούσια) and involuntary (ἀκούσια) acts. Aristotle begins in chapter 1, by laying it down that involuntary action is generally considered to have two varieties, that which is forced, βία, and that which is caused by ignorance, δι' ἄγνοιαν. After an analysis of forced actions, he proceeds in chapter 2 to the other class. Here he first clears away the category of actions caused by ignorance but not regretted (i.e., after the error is recognized); they may be called nonvoluntary (οὐχ ἑκών) rather than involuntary (ἄχων). From this first distinction we gather that grief and repentance after the discovery of the error is a reliable, in fact a necessary, index of involuntary action. We can even go further and say that an act done in ignorance which is not followed by repentance upon discovery was not, properly speaking, *caused* by ignorance, since in that case the act might well have been performed anyway, even if the doer had had full knowledge. The distinction between "in ignorance" (ἀγνοοῦντα) and "through ignorance" (δι' ἄγνοιαν), however, is

---

[6] On the connection of these passages with Plato's legislation in book 9 of the *Laws* see below on 14. 53b37-54a9; on Aristotle's theory in general, R. Maschke, *Die Willenslehre im griechischen Recht*, Berlin, 1926, 133-159, esp. 146-147, 150-155; I. Glanville, "Tragic Error," *CQ* 43 (1949) 447-456.

only made explicitly in the next sentence, where Aristotle points out that the cause of an act performed while a man is drunk or in the heat of anger seems to be his drunkenness or his anger, not his ignorance. It is performed, therefore, ἀγνοῶν [in ignorance] but not δι' ἄγνοιαν [because of ignorance].

Now we come to the distinction which most interests us, between acts caused by ignorance of general principles (ἡ χαθόλον [sc. ἄγνοια]) and those caused by ignorance of particulars (ἡ χαθ' ἕχαστα, ἐν οἷς χαὶ περὶ ἃ ἡ πρᾶξις). It is the latter, Aristotle says, that win *pity and forgiveness* (ἔλεος χαὶ σνγγνώμη). This, then, is truly involuntary action: ὁ γὰρ τούτων τι ἀγνοῶν ἀχονσίως πράττει [who unwillingly does something in ignorance of these particulars]. Aristotle goes on to specify the varieties of detail of which the doer may be ignorant. He may not know who he is (although this is ruled out as impossible just below), or what he is doing (e.g., Aeschylus revealed something about the mysteries "because he didn't know it was a secret"), or what or whom he is doing it to; and in some cases he may not be aware what he is doing it with (like the man who thought the spearpoint was buttoned) or how he is doing it (the sparring-partner who knocks out his friend when all he intended to do was to "touch" him). Of these varieties of ignorance, the one which interests us most is *ignorance of the identity of the person with whom the action has to do* (ἐν τίνι πράττει); for we remember that the preferred tragic recognition is of the identity of persons. Surely it is no accident that the example Aristotle cites here is from tragedy (the only one in the list): the case of Merope, who was about to kill her son under the mistaken impression that he was someone else; and that this is precisely one of the instances he singles out for special commendation in the *Poetics,* as making the most effective use of recognition.

The other passage in the *Ethics,* 5. 10. 1135a15-1136a9, elaborates and refines the distinction between voluntary and involuntary with an eye to its application in law. Aristotle begins by laying it down that acts of justice and injustice (διχαιοπραγήματα, ἀδιχήματα) are made such by their voluntary character. A voluntary act is then defined ... as one that lies within a man's power *and* is performed knowingly, not in ignorance of the details involved: μή ἀγνοῶν ... μήτε ὅ ν μήτε ᾧ μήτε οὗ<ἕνεχα>, οἷον τίνα τύπτει ...;[... not in ignorance either of the person acted upon nor of the instrument used nor of the end that will be obtained]; and Aristotle adds, a28 — it is hard to believe that he is not thinking of Oedipus —ἐνδέχεται δὲ τὸν τνπτόμενον πατέρα εἶναι, τὸν δ' ὅτι μὲν ἄνθρωπος ἢ τῶν παρόντων

τις γινώσχειν, ὅτι δὲ πατήρ ἀγνοεῖν [the person struck may be striker's father, and the striker may know that it is a man . . . but not know
that it is his father] . . . Involuntary acts resulting in an injury that is
contrary to reasonable expectation (παραλόγως) are ἀτυχήματα,
accidents; when the injury is not contrary to reasonable expectation
they are ἁμαρτήματα, errors or mistakes.[7] Acts which are voluntary
but not premeditated are ἀδικήματα, acts of injustice; and when pre-
meditation is added they not only are unjust in themselves but make
the doer unjust.[8]

The secondary distinctions here, between accident and mistake
and between the two grades of unjust act, do not concern us. They
are relevant in a court of law, where it is essential (or at least was
considered so at Athens) to fix the precise degree of legal responsibility,[9] but Aristotle gives no sign that he regards them as vital in the
case of tragedy.[10] In the theater our function is not to fix and assess a

[7] The same distinction in [Ar.] Rhet. ad Alex. 5. 1427a27-b1, which adds the interesting point
that ἁμάρτημα and ἀτύχημα, unlike ἀδιχία, are shared by the defendant with the jury and all mankind and therefore give him a claim to forgiveness.

[8] Strictly speaking, this is a distinction between two different relations of the doer to the deed
rather than two different statuses of the deed. An act is an ἀδίχημα if it is a wrong act performed
voluntarily (ἐχών), whether or not it is deliberate; but the doer is unjust only if he does it deliberately. Nevertheless the distinction is parallel to that between mistake and accident because it
depends on the presence or absence, not merely of intent, but of forethought or foresight. —
These distinctions are a direct continuation of Plato's in book 9 of the Laws; see esp. 866d-867b.

[9] Cf. Rhet. 1. 13. 1374b4-10, where the same threefold scheme is presented, and in the same
terms, but where Aristotle points out (b5) that the important thing is not to assess the same penalty
for the three grades of offense. The Rhetoric passage and the one in book 5 of the Ethics are often
cited on all fours with the one in book 3 of the Ethics, as if all three were equally pertinent, and in
all respects, to our problem in the Poetics. — In the field of homicide the Athenians had an elaborate and carefully graded series of five courts, going back at least to the time of Dracon and Solon,
whose chief rationale was something very close to this set of distinctions. See R. J. Bonner and
Gertrude Smith, The Administration of Justice from Homer to Aristotle, 2, Chicago, 1938, 208: "These
courts had been founded, not for the purpose of insuring the prosecution of homicide, but
rather for the purpose of differentiating the types of homicide and thereby procuring for the
slayer, if guilty, a more equitable punishment" (cf. Rhet., loc. cit., for the relation of the distinctions
to "equity," ἐπιείχεια). On the five courts themselves see Bonner and Smith, op. cit. 1, Chicago,
1930, 91-110; J. H. Lipsius, Das Attische Recht und Rechtsverfahren, 1, Leipzig, 1905, 121-133; 2,
1908, 600-619; summary by W. Wyse in L. Whibley, A Companion to Greek Studies[4], Cambridge,
1931, 479-480. Aristotle's ἀδίχημα corresponds to the jurisdiction of the Areopagus over cases of
ψόνος ἐχούσιος, including deliberate murder (ψόνος ἐχ προνοίας) and wounding with intent to
kill (τραῦμα ἐχ προνοίας); his ἁμάρτημα to that of the Palladion over ψόνος ἀχούσιος; and ἀτύχημα
in part to that of the court at the Delphinion over cases of justifiable homicide (ψόνος δίχαιος,
which included accidental killings at the games and of comrades in war), in part to that at the
Prytaneum, which tried cases against animals and inanimate objects which had caused a homicide.
Thus it was necessary to determine the type or degree of guilt, not merely in order to assess the
penalty but to determine which court was competent in the case to begin with.

[10] It is true that Oedipus' act in killing his father was a ἁμάρτημα [misfortune] in the strict sense,
rather than an ἀτύχημα [sin, fault], since in the light of the oracle's warning it could not quite be
said to have happened παραλόγως [unexpectedly]. And conversely we have argued that Aristotle
cannot have regarded a pure accident like the falling of Mitys' staue (9. 52a8) as suitable
material for a tragic plot. But no weight falls on these distinctions and exclusions: it is the contrast between "error" and "wickedness" that counts.

penalty, but to feel pity and fear—and to enjoy whatever pleasure may arise from those emotions. On this point the testimony of the *Ethics* is clear: pity goes to ἁμαρτήματα, acts performed in ignorance of details, and not to ἀδιχήματα (which do indeed imply ignorance, but an ignorance of principles).[11]

It follows that the tragic *hamartia* is an ignorance or mistake as to certain details. It should be, further, a "big" mistake, one pregnant with disaster for the hero. Further still, the finest mistake for the purposes of tragedy, like its correlate the finest recognition, will have to do with the identity of a "dear" person, that is, a blood relative, and will accordingly lead to or threaten to lead to his being slain or wounded. As a component or cause of the complex plot, such a *hamartia* is inherently fitted to arouse our pity—and our "fear," that is, our horror that a man should have killed or be about to kill a "dear one."[12] The discovery is then the counterpart and reverse of the mistake. Here the emotional charge which is inherent in the mistake (not in the ignorance *per se,* but in the horrible deed to which it stands in causal relation) finds its discharge. The *hamartia* represents the reservoir of emotional potential, the recognition is the lightning-flash through which it passes off.

A little reflection shows that the development of such an energy-system is not merely fostered by the complex plot but can only come to proper unfolding there. Mistake-recognition is a "complex" structure by definition, because it signifies a complete and instantaneous reversal, not only of the hero's situation but of all his deepest attitudes and feelings. The hated enemy or casually despised fellow-wayfarer suddenly revealed as the person naturally dearest to him in the whole world: that is the quintessence of "complex" as Aristotle defines it. A simple plot cannot be predicated on ignorance in the hero. Either it will take the turn towards recognition—that is, become complex—or he must remain in ignorance throughout and the action will have no real outcome. In other words, simple plots are necessarily restricted to deeds of horror performed or intended knowingly: the *Agamemnon* or *Medea* plot.

[11] At *E. N.* 3. 2. 1110b29 Aristotle refers to acts caused by wickedness as τὴν τοιαύτην ἁμαρτίαν. This usage, which runs square counter to the definition of ἁμαρτία (ἁμάρτημα) in *E. N.* 5. 10 and *Rhet.* 1. 13, is interesting as an example of the freedom Aristotle always reserves, of using a technical term in a broader (often a popular) sense, even in a technical passage. But it does not alter or invalidate our conclusion.

[12] More exactly, we feel horror because of the nature of the deed, and pity because it is executed or planned in ignorance. The specific concept of "deed of horror stemming from ignorance" thus accounts for the close bond that unites the two emotions in tragedy: a bond which is even closer than that indicated by Aristotle's analysis of the two emotions (*Rhet.* 2), or that found in ordinary life.

From these considerations it follows that *hamartia,* like its cor-relate *anagnorisis,* belongs specifically to the theory of the complex plot, not to the theory of plots in general. And indeed we have already pointed out, quite independently of all this, that chapter 13 is an integral part of the discussion of complex plots which began at the end of chapter 9. Let us recall that ... Aristotle reminded us of the two premises on which his examination and rejection of the various plot-patterns was to be based. The first was that the "most beautiful" plot-structure for tragedy is complex, not simple; the second was that the play must imitate fearful and pitiable things.[13] As the mustering of the modes proceeded we did not notice any appeal to the first principle; all we heard about them was that they did not properly excite pity and fear. Nevertheless both principles must have been involved, since the chosen pattern which emerges at the end is inherently complex as well as pathetic and fearful. If now we look back at μεταβάλλοντας [changing of one's course, throwing into a different position], and μετα πίπτειν [falling from one point to another; fall differently], they are seen to refer not to the tragic μεταβολή [change, transition] in general but to peripety in particu-lar. The implication then is — although Aristotle does not make it explicit — that it is impossible to motivate the fall of the perfectly good man in the manner called for in the definition of peripety: that is, "paradoxically" but logically. Or, to put it another way, one chief reason for the superiority of *hamartia* as the "cause" of the tragic action is that it supplies a plausible reason for the fall of a good (though not perfect) man.

The correlation of *hamartia* and recognition as interdependent parts of the best tragic plot explains everything that Aristotle says about both of them. At the same time it effectively disposes, *ut mihi quidem videtur,* of the "moral flaw" interpretation of *hamartia.* We may debate over which caused the killing of Laius, Oedipus's ignorance or his hot temper,[14] but there can be no argument about what he "recognizes": it is the identity of the man he killed.

It would be interesting, though perhaps profitless, to speculate why this correlation of *hamartia* with *anagnorisis* has not been sug-gested before. No doubt the chief reason is the myopia with which

[13] More precisely, the finest tragedy must have a complex structure, *and that* (χαὶ ταύτην) one which is an imitation of tragic events — as opposed, no doubt, to a complex plot which only imi-tates something that is θαυμαστόν but not tragic.

[14] Actually the methods of the *harmatia*-hunters lead only to absurdity; see C. H. Whitman, Jr., *Sophocles: A Study of Heroic Humanism,* Cambridge, 1951, 22-41 ("Scholarship and Hamartia"), esp. 29-38 (Whitman himself, however, takes it as proved that *hamartia* does mean "moral" flaw in the *Poetics*); similarly W. C. Greene in *Perspectives of Criticism,* Cambridge, 1950, 40-41.

the sequence of Aristotle's argument has been regarded, so that *hamartia* was thought of as a part of the hero's character, or at least of his personal experience, while recognition was purely a technical device, a part of plot.[15] Our findings show that *hamartia* also is a part of the plot. The reason why Aristotle does not call it so, along with peripety, recognition, and *pathos,* is presumably that it may lie outside the action of the play proper, as in the *Oedipus* where the mistake occurred years before.[16] In any case *hamartia,* along with some other major concepts of the *Poetics,* must be brought out of its isolation and seen as an integral part of a single edifice of thought.

[15] There has also been the stumbling block of chapter 12 being interposed between *anagnorisis* and *hamartia*. Even scholars who recognized its spuriousness were unconsciously influenced by its presence and position.

[16] But this may not be a very good reason. There is no *pathos* in the *Oedipus* either, but only a peripety and recognition.

Arthur Miller

Parts of the essay from which the following comments are reprinted were written around the time of the premiere of *Death of a Salesman* (1949), the play that established Miller as a leading playwright of his generation. His work has always been concerned with social responsibilities among men and between mankind and various social institutions. It is natural, therefore, that a major aesthetic interest for Miller has been the criteria for tragic achievement—in art or, for that matter, in life. All of his plays, in one way or another, test the individual statement of an "ordinary" man against the implicit requirements for human greatness, probe human motivations and responses, and show responsibility for evil as well as an effort toward moral action to be among the natural inclinations of men. Miller's observations on tragedy itself, then, are of great importance, as are his comments on the ways in which drama can involve itself with the life of the mind and take on a social responsibility.

In the Introduction to his *Collected Plays,* Miller carefully considers his stand on many subjects; although some of these notes refer to specific plays, they apply, in general, to his entire achievement beginning with *All My Sons* (1947). Miller's two latest plays have been *After the Fall* (1963) and *Incident at Vichy* (1964).

from AN INTRODUCTION TO COLLECTED PLAYS

... Another material, so to speak, of drama is not describable in a word, and has a less direct influence on style. I mention it, however, because it is probably the single most powerful influence on my way of writing and enforces on me a kind of taste and approach to the art which marks these plays. It is necessary, if one is to reflect reality, not only to depict why a man does what he does, or why he nearly didn't do it, but why he cannot simply walk away and say to hell with it. To ask this last question of a play is a cruel thing, for evasion is probably the most developed technique most men have, and in truth there is an extraordinarily small number of conflicts which we must, at any cost, live out to their conclusions. To ask this question is immediately to impose on oneself not, perhaps, a style of writing but at least a kind of dramatic construction. For I understand the symbolic meaning of a character and his career to consist of the kind of commitment he makes to life or refuses to make, the kind of challenge he accepts and the kind he can pass by. I take it that if one could know enough about a human being one could discover some conflict, some value, some challenge, however minor or major, which he cannot find it in himself to walk away from or turn his back on. The structure of these plays, in this respect, is to the end that such a conflict be discovered and clarified. Idea, in these plays, is the generalized meaning of that discovery applied to men other than the hero. Time, characterizations, and other elements are treated differently from play to play, but all to the end that that moment of commitment be brought forth, that moment when, in my eyes, a man differentiates himself from every other man, that moment when out of a sky full of stars he fixes on one star. I take it, as well, that the less capable a man is of walking away from the central conflict of the play, the closer he approaches a tragic existence. In turn, this implies that the closer a man approaches tragedy the more intense is his concentration of emotion upon the fixed point of his commitment, which is to say the closer he approaches what in life we call fanaticism. From this flows the necessity for scenes of high and open emotion, and plays constructed toward climax rather than the evocation of a mood alone or of bizarre spectacle....

From such considerations it ought to be clear that the common tokens of realism and non-realism are in themselves not acceptable as criteria. That a play is written prosaically does not make it a realistic play, and that the speech is heightened and intensified by imagery does not set it to one side of realism necessarily. The underlying poem of a play I take to be the organic necessity of its parts. I find in the arbitrary not poetry but indulgence [*sic*]. (The novel is another matter entirely.) A very great play can be mimed and still issue forth its essential actions and their rudiments of symbolic meaning; the word, in drama, is the transformation into speech of what is *happening*, and the fiat for intense language is intensity of happening. We have had more than one extraordinary dramatist who was a cripple as a writer, and this is lamentable but not ruinous. Which is to say that I prize the poetic above [everything] else in the theater, and because I do I insist that the poem truly be there.

The assumption—or presumption—behind these plays is that life has meaning. I would now add, as their momentary commentator, that what they meant to me at the time of writing is not in each instance the same as what they mean to me now in the light of further experience. Plato, by banning artists from citizenship in his ideal republic, expressed at least a partial truth; the intention behind a work of art and its effects upon the public are not always the same. Worse yet, in his conscious intention the artist often conceals from himself an aim which can be quite opposed to his fondest beliefs and ideas. Those more tempted by an evil, for instance, are more likely to feel deeply about it than those who have only known the good. From this, two ironic propositions logically flow. The first is that a play's "idea" may be useful as a unifying force empowering the artist to evoke a cogent emotional life on the stage, but that in itself it has no aesthetic value, since after all, it is only a means to an end. The second is that since every play means something—even the play which denies all meaning to existence—the "idea" of a play is its measure of value and importance and beauty, and that a play which appears merely to exist to one side of "ideas" is an aesthetic nullity.

Idea is very important to me as a dramatist, but I think it is time someone said that playwrights, including the greatest, have not been noted for the new ideas they have broached in their plays. By new I mean an original idea invented by the playwright, quite as such things are created, if infrequently, by scientists, and occasionally by philosophers. Surely there is no known philosophy which was first announced through a play, nor any ethical idea. No social concept in Shaw's plays could have been much of a surprise to the Webbs and thousands of other Socialists of the time; nor can Ibsen, Chekhov, Strindberg, or O'Neill be credited with inventing any new thoughts. As a matter of fact, it is highly unlikely that a new idea could be successfully launched through a play at all, and this for several good reasons.

A genuine invention in the realm of ideas must first emerge as an abstruse and even partial concept. Be it Christianity, Darwinism, Marxism, or any other that can with reason be called original it has always been the product of proofs which, before they go to form a complete and new concept, require years and often generations of testing, research, and polemic. At first blush a new idea appears to be very close to insanity because to be new it must reverse important basic beliefs and assumptions which, in turn, have been institutionalized and are administered by one or another kind of priesthood with a vested interest in the old idea. Nor would the old idea be an idea at all, strictly speaking, if some goodly section of the population did not believe in it. If only because no dramatic structure can bear the brunt of the incredulity with which any really new idea is greeted, the play form would collapse under the burdens of having to deliver up the mountain of proof required for a new idea to be believed. And this would be true even if the audience were all philosophers — perhaps even truer, for the philosopher requires proofs even more exact than the layman does.

The dramatic form is a dynamic thing. It is not possible to dally in it for reflection. The polemical method, as well as the scientific exposition, the parable, or the ethical teaching, all depend upon a process which, in effect, says, "What you believe is wrong for these reasons; what the truth is is as follows." Tremendous energy must go into destroying the validity of the ancient proposition, and destroying it from an absolutely opposite viewpoint. An idea, if it is really new, is a genuine humiliation for the majority of the people; it is an affront not only to their sensibilities but to their deepest convictions. It offends against the things they worship, whether God or science or money. . . .

If plays have not broached new ideas, they have enunciated not-yet-popular ideas which are already in the air, ideas for which there has already been a preparation by non-dramatic media. Which is to say that once an idea is "in the air" it is no longer an idea but a feeling, a sensation, an emotion, and with these the drama can deal. For one thing, where no doubt exists in the hearts of the people, a play cannot create doubt; where no desire to believe exists, a play cannot create a belief. And again, this springs from the nature of dramatic form and its inevitable dynamism; it must communicate as it proceeds and it literally has no existence if it must wait until the audience goes home to think before it can be appreciated. It is the art of the present tense par excellence. . . .

. . . [O]ne aspect of "Ibsenism" as a technique is the quickest path into that discussion. I have no vested interest in any one form — as the variety of forms I have used attests — but there is one element in Ibsen's method which I do not think ought to be overlooked, let alone dismissed as it so often is nowadays. If his plays, and his method, do nothing else they reveal the evolutionary quality of life. One is constantly aware, in watching his plays, of process, change, development. I think too many modern plays assume, so to speak, that their duty is merely to show the present countenance rather than to account for what happens. It is therefore wrong to imagine that because his first and sometimes his second acts devote so much time to a studied revelation of antecedent material, his view is static compared to our own. In truth, it is profoundly dynamic, for that enormous past was always heavily documented to the end that the present be comprehended with wholeness, as a moment in a flow of time, and not — as with so many modern plays — as a situation without roots. Indeed, even though I can myself reject other aspects of his work, it nevertheless presents barely and unadorned what I believe is the biggest single dramatic problem, namely, how to dramatize what has gone before. I say this not merely out of technical interest, but because dramatic characters, and the drama itself, can never hope to attain a maximum degree of consciousness unless they contain a viable unveiling of the contrast between past and present, and an awareness of the process by which the present has become what it is. And I say this, finally, because I take it as a truth that the end of drama is the creation of a higher consciousness and not merely a subjective attack upon the audience's nerves and feelings. What is precious in the Ibsen method is its insistence upon valid causation, and this cannot be dismissed as a wooden notion.

This is the "real" in Ibsen's realism for me, for he was, after all, as much a mystic as a realist. Which is simply to say that while there are mysteries in life which no amount of analyzing will reduce to reason, it is perfectly realistic to admit and even to proclaim that hiatus as a truth. . . .

[*Death of a Salesman*] was always heroic to me, and in later years the academy's charge that Willy lacked the "stature" for the tragic hero

seemed incredible to me. I had not understood that these matters
are measured by Greco-Elizabethan paragraphs which hold no mention of insurance payments, front porches, refrigerator fan belts,
steering knuckles, Chevrolets, and visions seen not through the
portals of Delphi but in the blue flame of the hot-water heater. How
could "Tragedy" make people weep, of all things?

I set out not to "write a tragedy" in this play, but to show the truth
as I saw it. However, some of the attacks upon it as a pseudo-tragedy
contain ideas so misleading, and in some cases so laughable, that it
might be in place here to deal with a few of them.

Aristotle having spoken of a fall from the heights, it goes without
saying that someone of the common mold cannot be a fit tragic hero.
It is now many centuries since Aristotle lived. There is no more
reason for falling down in a faint before his *Poetics* than before
Euclid's geometry, which has been amended numerous times by
men with new insights; nor, for that matter, would I choose to have
my illnesses diagnosed by Hippocrates rather than the most ordinary graduate of an American medical school, despite the Greek's
genius. Things do change, and even a genius is limited by his time
and the nature of his society.

I would deny, on grounds of simple logic, this one of Aristotle's
contentions if only because he lived in a slave society. When a vast
number of people are divested of alternatives, as slaves are, it is
rather inevitable that one will not be able to imagine drama, let alone
tragedy, as being possible for any but the higher ranks of society.
There is a legitimate question of stature here, but none of rank,
which is so often confused with it. So long as the hero may be said to
have had alternatives of a magnitude to have materially changed the
course of his life, it seems to me that in this respect at least, he cannot
be debarred from the heroic role.

The question of rank is significant to me only as it reflects the
question of the social application of the hero's career. There is no
doubt that if a character is shown on the stage who goes through the
most ordinary actions, and is suddenly revealed to be the President
of the United States, his actions immediately assume a much greater
magnitude, and pose the possibilities of much greater meaning, than
if he is the corner grocer. But at the same time, his stature as a hero
is not so utterly dependent upon his rank that the corner grocer
cannot outdistance him as a tragic figure—providing, of course, that
the grocer's career engages the issues of, for instance, the survival of
the race, the relationships of man to God—the questions, in short,

whose answers define humanity and the right way to live so that the world is a home, instead of a battleground or a fog in which disembodied spirits pass each other in an endless twilight.

In this respect *Death of a Salesman* is a slippery play to categorize because nobody in it stops to make a speech objectively stating the great issues which I believe it embodies. If it were a worse play, less closely articulating its meanings with its actions, I think it would have more quickly satisfied a certain kind of criticism. But it was meant to be less a play than a fact; it refused admission to its author's opinions and opened itself to a revelation of process and the operations of an ethic, of social laws of action no less powerful in their effects upon individuals than any tribal law administered by gods with names. I need not claim that this play is a genuine solid gold tragedy for my opinions on tragedy to be held valid. My purpose here is simply to point out a historical fact which must be taken into account in any consideration of tragedy, and it is the sharp alteration in the meaning of rank in society between the present time and the distant past. More important to me is the fact that this particular kind of argument obscures much more relevant considerations.

One of these is the question of intensity. It matters not at all whether a modern play concerns itself with a grocer or a president if the intensity of the hero's commitment to his course is less than the maximum possible. It matters not at all whether the hero falls from a great height or a small one, whether he is highly conscious or only dimly aware of what is happening, whether his pride brings the fall or an unseen pattern written behind clouds; if the intensity, the human passion to surpass his given bounds, the fanatic insistence upon his self-conceived role—if these are not present there can only be an outline of tragedy but no living thing. I believe, for myself, that the lasting appeal of tragedy is due to our need to face the fact of death in order to strengthen ourselves for life, and that over and above this function of the tragic viewpoint there are and will be a great number of formal variations which no single definition will ever embrace.

Another issue worth considering is the so-called tragic victory a question closely related to the consciousness of the hero. One makes nonsense of this if a "victory" means that the hero makes us feel some certain joy when, for instance, he sacrifices himself for a "cause," and unhappy and morose because he dies without one. To begin at the bottom, a man's death is and ought to be an essentially terrifying thing and ought to make nobody happy. But in a great variety of ways even death, the ultimate negative, can be, and appear to be, an assertion of bravery, and can serve to separate the death of man from the death of animals; and I think it is this distinction which underlies any conception of a victory in death. For a society of faith, the nature of the death can prove the existence of the spirit, and posit its immortality. For a secular society it is perhaps more difficult for such a victory to document itself and to make itself felt, but, conversely, the need to offer greater proofs of the humanity of man can make that victory more real. It goes without saying that in a society where there is basic disagreement as to the right way to live, there can hardly be agreement as to the right way to die, and both life and death must be heavily weighted with meaningless futility.

It was not out of any deference to a tragic definition that Willy Loman is filled with a joy, however broken-hearted, as he approaches his end, but simply that my sense of his character dictated his joy, and even what I felt was an exultation. In terms of his character, he has achieved a very powerful piece of knowledge, which is that he is loved by his son and has been embraced by him and forgiven. In this he is given his existence, so to speak—his fatherhood, for which he has always striven and which until now he could not achieve. That he is unable to take this victory thoroughly to his heart, that it closes the circle for him and propels him to his death, is the wage of his sin, which was to have committed himself so completely to the counterfeits of dignity and the false coinage embodied in his idea of success that he can prove his existence only by bestowing "power" on his posterity, a power deriving from the sale of his last asset, himself, for the price of his insurance policy.

I must confess here to a miscalculation, however. I did not realize while writing the play that so many people in the world do not see as clearly, or would not admit, as I thought they must, how futile most lives are; so there could be no hope of consoling the audience for the death of this man. I did not realize either how few would be impressed by the fact that this man is actually a very brave spirit who cannot settle for half but must pursue his dream of himself to the end. Finally, I thought it must be clear, even obvious, that this was no dumb brute heading mindlessly to his catastrophe.

I have no need to be Willy's advocate before the jury which decides who is and who is not a tragic hero. I am merely noting that the lingering ponderousness of so many ancient definitions has blinded students and critics to the facts before them, and not only in regard to this play. Had Willy been unaware of his separation from values that endure he would have died contentedly while polishing his car, probably on a Sunday afternoon with the ball game coming over the radio. But he was agonized by his awareness of being in a false position, so constantly haunted by the hollowness of all he had placed his faith in, so aware, in short, that he must somehow be filled in his spirit or fly apart, that he staked his very life on the ultimate assertion. That he had not the intellectual fluency to verbalize his situation is not the same thing as saying that he lacked awareness, even an overly intensified consciousness that the life he had made was without form and inner meaning.

To be sure, had he been able to know that he was as much the victim of his beliefs as their defeated exemplar, had he known how much of guilt he ought to bear and how much to shed from his soul, he would be more conscious. But it seems to me that there is of necessity a severe limitation of self-awareness in any character, even the most knowing, which serves to define him as a character, and more, that this very limit serves to complete the tragedy and, indeed, to make it at all possible. Complete consciousness is possible only in a play about forces, like *Prometheus,* but not in a play about people. I think that the point is whether there is a sufficient awareness in the hero's career to make the audience supply the rest. Had Oedipus, for instance, been more conscious and more aware of the forces at work upon him he must surely have said that he was not really to blame for having cohabited with his mother since neither he nor anyone else knew she was his mother. He must surely decide to divorce her, provide for their children, firmly resolve to investigate the family background of his next wife, and thus deprive us of a very fine play and the name for a famous neurosis. But he is conscious only up to a point, the point at which guilt begins. Now he is inconsolable and must tear out his eyes. What is tragic about this? Why is it not even ridiculous? How can we respect a man who goes to such extremities over something he could in no way help or prevent? The answer, I think, is not that we respect the man, but that we respect the Law he has so completely broken, wittingly or not, for it is that Law which, we believe, defines us as men. The confusion of some critics viewing *Death of a Salesman* in this regard is that they do not see that Willy Loman has broken a law without whose protection life is insupportable if not incomprehensible to him and to many others; it is the law which says that a failure in society and in business has no right to live. Unlike the law against incest, the law of success is not administered by statute or church, but it is very nearly as powerful in its grip upon men. The confusion increases because, while it is a law, it is by no means a wholly agreeable one even as it is slavishly obeyed, for to fail is no longer to belong to society, in his estimate. Therefore, the path is opened for those who wish to call Willy merely a foolish man even as they themselves are living in obedience to the same law that killed him. Equally, the fact that Willy's law — the belief, in other words, which administers guilt to him — is not a civilizing statute whose destruction menaces us all; it is, rather, a deeply believed and deeply suspect "good" which, when questioned as to its value, as it is in this play, serves more to raise our anxieties than to reassure us of the existence of an unseen but humane metaphysical system in the world. My attempt in the play was to counter this anxiety with an opposing system which, so to speak, is in a race for Willy's faith, and it is the system of love which is the opposite of the law of success. It is embodied in Biff Loman, but by the time Willy can perceive his love it can serve only as an ironic comment upon the life he sacrificed for power and for success and its tokens.

Christopher Fry

This little essay — itself a masterly *jeu d'esprit* — was first published in 1950 (Fry's latest play, *Curtmantle,* was first performed by the Royal Shakespeare Theatre Company in 1962). At that time, Fry could look back upon a series of successes, all revealing in lively stage terms his own view of a world basically comic, yet touched if not by tragedy then by poignant melancholy.

His fame has grown since 1949 when the remarkably actable *The Lady's Not for Burning* was presented in England and America with John Gielgud and Pamela Brown. *Venus Observed* followed in 1950 (with Olivier) and, in the same year, a translation of Jean Anouilh's *L'Invitation au Château (Ring Round the Moon)*. Fry has also written the religious verse-dramas *The Boy with a Cart* (1937), *The Firstborn* (1947), and *Thor, With Angels* (1948) as well as the one-act comedy, *A Phoenix Too Frequent* (1946). He has managed his own repertory theatre, acted, and taught in various schools — including, at present, the London Academy of Music and Dramatic Art. He remains one of

the few playwrights of any period who has used verse this successfully; to do so in our own time and yet remain — as indeed he is — a
very modern artist, must be considered an achievement of magnitude.

COMEDY

A friend once told me that when he was under the influence of ether
he dreamed he was turning over the pages of a great book, in which
he knew he would find, on the last page, the meaning of life. The
pages of the book were alternately tragic and comic, and he turned
page after page, his excitement growing, not only because he was
approaching the answer but because he couldn't know, until he
arrived, on which side of the book the final page would be. At last it
came: the universe opened up to him in a hundred words: and they
were uproariously funny. He came back to consciousness crying with
laughter, remembering everything. He opened his lips to speak. It
was then that the great and comic answer plunged back out of his
reach.

If I had to draw a picture of the person of Comedy it is so I should
like to draw it: the tears of laughter running down the face, one
hand still lying on the tragic page which so nearly contained the
answer, the lips about to frame the great revelation, only to find it
had gone as disconcertingly as a chair twitched away when we went
to sit down. Comedy is an escape, not from truth but from despair: a
narrow escape into faith. It believes in a universal cause for delight,
even though knowledge of the cause is always twitched away from
under us, which leaves us to rest on our own buoyancy. In tragedy
every moment is eternity; in comedy eternity is a moment. In
tragedy we suffer pain; in comedy pain is a fool, suffered gladly.

Charles Williams once said to me — indeed it was the last thing he
said to me: he died not long after: and it was shouted from the
tailboard of a moving bus, over the heads of pedestrians and
bicyclists outside the Midland Station, Oxford — "When we're dead
we shall have the sensation of having enjoyed life altogether,
whatever has happened to us." The distance between us widened,
and he leaned out into the space so that his voice should reach me:
"Even if we've been murdered, what a pleasure to have been capable
of it!"; and, having spoken the words for comedy, away he went like
the revelation which almost came out of the ether.

He was not at all saying that everything is for the best in the best of all possible worlds. He was saying—or so it seems to me—that there is an angle of experience where the dark is distilled into light: either here or hereafter, in or out of time: where our tragic fate finds itself with perfect pitch, and goes straight to the key which creation was composed in. And comedy senses and reaches out to this experience. It says, in effect, that, groaning as we may be, we move in the figure of a dance, and, so moving, we trace the outline of the mystery.

Laughter did not come by chance, but how or why it came is beyond comprehension, unless we think of it as a kind of perception. The human animal, beginning to feel his spiritual inches, broke in on to an unfamiliar tension of life, where laughter became inevitable. But how? Could he, in the first unlaughing condition, have contrived a comic view of life and then developed the strange rib-shaking response? Or is it not more likely that when he was able to grasp the tragic nature of time he was of a stature to sense its comic nature also; and, by the experience of tragedy and the intuition of comedy, to make his difficult way? The difference between tragedy and comedy is the difference between experience and intuition. In the experience we strive against every condition of our animal life: against death, against the frustration of ambition, against the instability of human love. In the intuition we trust the arduous eccentricities we're born to, and see the oddness of a creature who has never got acclimatized to being created. Laughter inclines me to know that man is essential spirit; his body, with its functions and accidents and frustrations, is endlessly quaint and remarkable to him; and though comedy accepts our position in time, it barely accepts our posture in space.

The bridge by which we cross from tragedy to comedy and back again is precarious and narrow. We find ourselves in one or the other by the turn of a thought; a turn such as we make when we turn from speaking to listening. I know that when I set about writing a comedy the idea presents itself to me first of all as tragedy. The characters press on to the theme with all their divisions and perplexities heavy about them; they are already entered for the race to doom, and good and evil are an infernal tangle skinning the fingers that try to unravel them. If the characters were not qualified for tragedy there would be no comedy, and to some extent I have to cross the one before I can light on the other. In a century less flayed and quivering we might reach it more directly; but not now, unless every word we write is going to mock us. A bridge has to be crossed, a thought has to be turned. Somehow the characters have to unmortify themselves: to affirm life and assimilate death and persevere in joy. Their hearts must be as determined as the phoenix; what burns must also light and renew: not by a vulnerable optimism but by a hardwon maturity of delight, by the intuition of comedy, an active patience declaring the solvency of good. The Book of Job is the great reservoir of comedy. "But there is a spirit in man . . . Fair weather cometh out of the north . . . The blessing of him that was ready to perish came upon me: And I caused the widow's heart to sing for joy."

I have come, you may think, to the verge of saying that comedy is greater than tragedy. On the verge I stand and go no further. Tragedy's experience hammers against the mystery to make a breach which would admit the whole triumphant answer. Intuition has no such potential. But there are times in the state of man when comedy has a special worth, and the present is one of them: a time when the loudest faith has been faith in a trampling materialism, when literature has been thought unrealistic which did not mark and remark our poverty and doom. Joy (of a kind) has been all on the devil's side, and one of the necessities of our time is to redeem it. If not, we are in poor sort to meet the circumstances, the circumstances being the contention of death with life, which is to say evil with good, which is to say desolation with delight. Laughter may seem to be only like an exhalation of air, but out of that air we came; in the beginning we inhaled it; it is a truth, not a fantasy, a truth voluble of good which comedy stoutly maintains.

Northrop Frye

The author of this essay may justly be considered one of the four or five most probing, intellectually creative, and influential critics of this century. The intention of the author here is to present an overview of that whole mode of thought and literature called comic; Frye's firm grasp of all aspects of this subject is nowhere more brilliantly demonstrated. The piece eventually formed part of the background of thought for *The Anatomy of Criticism* (1957), a large work thought by many to be a new *Poetics*, formulating a synoptic view of the range and tools of literary criticism.

Although some critics have disagreed with, or felt themselves unable to participate in, Frye's use of myth, archetype, history, and ritual, none of his readers have failed to respond to his approach with imaginative excitement and intellectual stimulation. Ranging from Menander to Congreve to Shakespeare, Frye's citations are always precise, always suggestive in a new way. He has lectured in many colleges and universities in Canada and the United States and has been for many years Professor of English at the University of Toronto where he has served as Principal of Victoria College since 1959. Frye has written extensively on Shakespeare, Blake, Milton, and many other writers. His interests in music and drama are specific, varied, and derived from practical experience in both.

⚑ THE ARGUMENT OF COMEDY

The Greeks produced two kinds of comedy, Old Comedy, represented by the eleven extant plays of Aristophanes, and New Comedy, of which the best known exponent is Menander. About two dozen New Comedies survive in the work of Plautus and Terence. Old Comedy, however, was out of date before Aristophanes himself was dead; and today, when we speak of comedy, we normally think of something that derives from the Menandrine tradition.

New Comedy unfolds from what may be described as a comic Oedipus situation. Its main theme is the successful effort of a young man to outwit an opponent and possess the girl of his choice. The opponent is usually the father (*senex*), and the psychological descent of the heroine from the mother is also sometimes hinted at. The father frequently wants the same girl, and is cheated out of her by

From *English Institute Essays* (1948), pp. 58-73. Reprinted by permission of Columbia University Press.

the son, the mother thus becoming the son's ally. The girl is usually a slave or courtesan, and the plot turns on a *cognitio* or discovery of birth which makes her marriageable. Thus it turns out that she is not under an insuperable taboo after all but is an accessible object of desire, so that the plot follows the regular wishfulfillment pattern. Often the central Oedipus situation is thinly concealed by surrogates or doubles of the main characters, as when the heroine is discovered to be the hero's sister, and has to be married off to his best friend. In Congreve's *Love for Love,* to take a modern instance well within the Menandrine tradition, there are two Oedipus themes in counterpoint: the hero cheats his father out of the heroine, and his best friend violates the wife of an impotent old man who is the heroine's guardian. Whether this analysis is sound or not, New Comedy is certainly concerned with the maneuvering of a young man toward a young woman, and marriage is the tonic chord on which it ends. The normal comic resolution is the surrender of the *senex* to the hero, never the reverse. Shakespeare tried to reverse the pattern in *All's Well That Ends Well,* where the king of France forces Bertram to marry Helena, and the critics have not yet stopped making faces over it.

New Comedy has the blessing of Aristotle, who greatly preferred it to its predecessor, and it exhibits the general pattern of Aristotelian causation. It has a material cause in the young man's sexual desire, and a formal cause in the social order represented by the *senex,* with which the hero comes to terms when he gratifies his desire. It has an efficient cause in the character who brings about the final situation. In classical times this character is a tricky slave; Renaissance dramatists often use some adaptation of the medieval "vice"; modern writers generally like to pretend that nature, or at least the natural course of events, is the efficient cause. The final cause is the audience, which is expected by its applause to take part in the comic resolution. All this takes place on a single order of existence. The action of New Comedy tends to become probable rather than fantastic, and it moves toward realism and away from myth and romance. The one romantic (originally mythical) feature in it, the fact that the hero or heroine turns out to be freeborn or someone's heir, is precisely the feature that trained New Comedy audiences tire of most quickly.

The conventions of New Comedy are the conventions of Jonson and Molière, and a fortiori of the English Restoration and the French rococo. When Ibsen started giving ironic twists to the same formulas, his startled hearers took them for portents of a social revolution. Even the old chestnut about the heroine's being really the hero's sister turns up in *Ghosts* and *Little Eyolf.* The average movie of today is a rigidly conventionalized New Comedy proceeding toward an act which, like death in Greek tragedy, takes place offstage, and is symbolized by the final embrace.

In all good New Comedy there is a social as well as an individual theme which must be sought in the general atmosphere of reconciliation that makes the final marriage possible. As the hero gets closer to the heroine and opposition is overcome, all the right-thinking people come over to his side. Thus a new social unit is formed on the stage, and the moment that this social unit crystallizes is the moment of the comic resolution. In the last scene, when the dramatist usually tries to get all his characters on the stage at once, the audience witnesses the birth of a renewed sense of social integration. In comedy as in life the regular expression of this is a festival, whether a marriage, a dance, or a feast. Old Comedy has, besides a marriage, a *komos,* the processional dance from which comedy derives its name; and the masque, which is a by-form of comedy, also ends in a dance.

This new social integration may be called, first, a kind of moral norm and, second, the pattern of a free society. We can see this more clearly if we look at the sort of characters who impede the progress of the comedy toward the hero's victory. These are always people who are in some kind of mental bondage, who are helplessly driven by ruling passions, neurotic compulsions, social rituals, and selfishness. The miser, the hypochondriac, the hypocrite, the pedant, the snob: these are humors, people who do not fully know what they are doing, who are slaves to a predictable self-imposed pattern of behavior. What we call the moral norm is, then, not morality but deliverance from moral bondage. Comedy is designed not to condemn evil, but to ridicule a lack of self-knowledge. It finds the virtues of Malvolio and Angelo as comic as the vices of Shylock.

The essential comic resolution, therefore, is an individual release which is also a social reconciliation. The normal individual is freed from the bonds of a humorous society, and a normal society is freed from the bonds imposed on it by humorous individuals. The Oedipus pattern we noted in New Comedy belongs to the individual side of this, and the sense of the ridiculousness of the humor to the social side. But all real comedy is based on the principle that these two forms of release are ultimately the same: this principle may be seen at its most concentrated in *The Tempest.* The rule holds whether the resolution is expressed in social terms, as in *The Merchant of Venice,* or in individual terms, as in Ibsen's *An Enemy of the People.*

The freer the society, the greater the variety of individuals it can tolerate, and the natural tendency of comedy is to include as many as possible in its final festival. The motto of comedy is Terence's "Nothing human is alien to me." This may be one reason for the traditional comic importance of the parasite, who has no business to be at the festival but is nevertheless there. The spirit of reconciliation which pervades the comedies of Shakespeare is not to be ascribed to a personal attitude of his own, about which we know nothing whatever, but to his impersonal concentration on the laws of comic form.

Hence the moral quality of the society presented is not the point of the comic resolution. In Jonson's *Volpone* the final assertion of the moral norm takes the form of a social revenge on Volpone, and the play ends with a great bustle of sentences to penal servitude and the galleys. One feels perhaps that the audience's sense of the moral norm does not need so much hard labor. In *The Alchemist,* when Lovewit returns to his house, the virtuous characters have proved so weak and the rascals so ingenious that the action dissolves in laughter. Whichever is morally the better ending, that of *The Alchemist* is more concentrated comedy. *Volpone* is starting to move toward tragedy, toward the vision of a greatness which develops *hybris* and catastrophe.

The same principle is even clearer in Aristophanes. Aristophanes is the most personal of writers: his opinions on every subject are written all over his plays, and we have no doubt of his moral attitude. We know that he wanted peace with Sparta and that he hated Cleon, and when his comedy depicts the attaining of peace and the defeat of Cleon we know that he approved and wanted his audience to approve. But in *Ecclesiazusae* a band of women in disguise railroad a communistic scheme through the Assembly, which is a horrid parody of Plato's *Republic,* and proceed to inaugurate Plato's sexual communism with some astonishing improvements. Presumably Aristophanes did not applaud this, yet the comedy follows the same pattern and the same resolution. In *The Birds* the Peisthetairos who defies Zeus and blocks out Olympus with his Cloud-Cuckoo-Land is accorded the same triumph that is given to the Trygaeus of the *Peace* who flies to heaven and brings a golden age back to Athens.

Comedy, then, may show virtue her own feature and scorn her own image — for Hamlet's famous definition of drama was originally a definition of comedy. It may emphasize the birth of an ideal society as you like it, or the tawdriness of the sham society which is the way of the world. There is an important parallel here with tragedy. Tragedy, we are told, is expected to raise but not ultimately to accept the emotions of pity and terror. These I take to be the sense of moral good and evil, respectively, which we attach to the tragic hero. He may be as good as Caesar, and so appeal to our pity, or as bad as Macbeth, and so appeal to terror, but the particular thing called tragedy that happens to him does not depend on his moral status. The tragic catharsis passes beyond moral judgment, and while it is quite possible to construct a moral tragedy, what tragedy gains in morality it loses in cathartic power. The same is true of the comic catharsis, which raises sympathy and ridicule on a moral basis, but passes beyond both.

Many things are involved in the tragic catharsis, but one of them is a mental or imaginative form of the sacrificial ritual out of which tragedy arose. This is the ritual of the struggle, death, and rebirth of a God-Man, which is linked to the yearly triumph of spring over winter. The tragic hero is not really killed, and the audience no longer eats his body and drinks his blood, but the corresponding thing in art still takes place. The audience enters into communion with the body of the hero, becoming thereby a single body itself. Comedy grows out of the same ritual, for in the ritual the tragic story has a comic sequel. Divine men do not die: they die and rise again. The ritual pattern behind the catharsis of comedy is the resurrection that follows the death, the epiphany or manifestation of the risen hero. This is clear enough in Aristophanes, where the hero is treated as a risen God-Man, led in triumph with the divine honors of the Olympic victor, rejuvenated, or hailed as a new Zeus. In New Comedy the new human body is, as we have seen, both a hero and a social group. Aristophanes is not only closer to the ritual pattern, but contemporary with Plato; and his comedy, unlike Menander's, is Platonic and dialectic: it seeks not the entelechy of the soul but the Form of the Good, and finds it in the resurrection of the soul from the world of the cave to the sunlight. The audience gains a vision of that resurrection whether the conclusion is joyful or ironic, just as in tragedy it gains a vision of a heroic death whether the hero is morally innocent or guilty.

Two things follow from this: first, that tragedy is really implicit or uncompleted comedy; second, that comedy contains a potential tragedy within itself. With regard to the latter, Aristophanes is full of traces of the original death of the hero which preceded his resurrection in the ritual. Even in New Comedy the dramatist usually tries to bring his action as close to a tragic overthrow of the hero as he can get it, and reverses this movement as suddenly as possible. In Plautus the tricky slave is often forgiven or even freed after having been threatened with all the brutalities that a very brutal dramatist can think of, including crucifixion. Thus the resolution of New Comedy seems to be a realistic foreshortening of a death-and-resurrection pattern, in which the struggle and rebirth of a divine hero has shrunk into a marriage, the freeing of a slave, and the triumph of a young man over an older one.

As for the conception of tragedy as implicit comedy, we may notice how often tragedy closes on the major chord of comedy: the Aeschylean trilogy, for instance, proceeds to what is really a comic resolution, and so do many tragedies of Euripides. From the point of view of Christianity, too, tragedy is an episode in that larger scheme of redemption and resurrection to which Dante gave the name of *commedia*. This conception of *commedia* enters drama with the miracle-play cycles, where such tragedies as the Fall and the Crucifixion are episodes of a dramatic scheme in which the divine comedy has the last word. The sense of tragedy as a prelude to comedy is hardly separable from anything explicitly Christian. The serenity of the final double chorus in the St. Matthew Passion would hardly be attainable if composer and audience did not know that there was more to the story. Nor would the death of Samson lead to "calm of mind all passion spent" if Samson were not a prototype of the rising Christ.

New Comedy is thus contained, so to speak, within the symbolic structure of Old Comedy, which in its turn is contained within the Christian conception of *commedia*. This sounds like a logically exhaustive classification, but we have still not caught Shakespeare in it.

It is only in Jonson and the Restoration writers that English comedy can be called a form of New Comedy. The earlier tradition established by Peele and developed by Lyly, Greene, and the masque writers, which uses themes from romance and folklore and avoids the comedy of manners, is the one followed by Shakespeare. These themes are largely medieval in origin, and derive, not from the mysteries or the moralities or the interludes, but from a fourth dramatic tradition. This is the drama of folk ritual, of the St. George play and the mummers' play, of the feast of the ass and the Boy Bishop, and of all the dramatic activity that punctuated the Christian calendar with the rituals of an immemorial paganism. We may call this the drama of the green world, and its theme is once again the triumph of life over the waste land, the death and revival of the year impersonated by figures still human, and once divine as well.

When Shakespeare began to study Plautus and Terence, his dramatic instinct, stimulated by his predecessors, divined that there was a profounder pattern in the argument of comedy than appears in either of them. At once—for the process is beginning in *The Comedy of Errors*—he started groping toward that profounder pattern, the ritual of death and revival that also underlies Aristophanes, of which an exact equivalent lay ready to hand in the drama of the green world. This parallelism largely accounts for the resemblances to Greek ritual which Colin Still has pointed out in *The Tempest*.

The Two Gentlemen of Verona is an orthodox New Comedy except for one thing. The hero Valentine becomes captain of a band of outlaws in a forest, and all the other characters are gathered into this forest and become converted. Thus the action of the comedy begins in a world represented as a normal world, moves into the green world, goes into a metamorphosis there in which the comic resolution is achieved, and returns to the normal world. The forest in this play is the embryonic form of the fairy world of *A Midsummer Night's Dream,* the Forest of Arden in *As You Like It,* Windsor Forest in *The Merry Wives of Windsor,* and the pastoral world of the mythical sea-coasted Bohemia in *The Winter's Tale.* In all these comedies there is the same rhythmic movement from normal world to green world and back again. Nor is this second world confined to the forest comedies. In *The Merchant of Venice* the two worlds are a little harder to see, yet Venice is clearly not the same world as that of Portia's mysterious house in Belmont, where there are caskets teaching that gold and silver are corruptible goods, and from whence proceed the wonderful cosmological harmonies of the fifth act. In *The Tempest* the entire action takes place in the second world, and the same may be said of *Twelfth Night,* which, as its title implies, presents a carnival society, not so much a green world as an evergreen one. The second world is absent from the so-called problem comedies, which is one of the things that makes them problem comedies.

The green world charges the comedies with a symbolism in which the comic resolution contains a suggestion of the old ritual pattern of the victory of summer over winter. This is explicit in *Love's Labor's Lost.* In this very masque-like play, the comic contest takes the form of the medieval debate of winter and spring. In *The Merry Wives of*

Windsor there is an elaborate ritual of the defeat of winter, known to folklorists as "carrying out Death," of which Falstaff is the victim; and Falstaff must have felt that, after being thrown into the water, dressed up as a witch and beaten out of a house with curses, and finally supplied with a beast's head and singed with candles while he said, "Divide me like a brib'd buck, each a haunch," he had done about all that could reasonably be asked of any fertility spirit.

The association of this symbolism with the death and revival of human beings is more elusive, but still perceptible. The fact that the heroine often brings about the comic resolution by disguising herself as a boy is familiar enough. In the Hero of *Much Ado About Nothing* and the Helena of *All's Well That Ends Well,* this theme of the withdrawal and return of the heroine comes as close to a death and revival as Elizabethan conventions will allow. The Thaisa of *Pericles* and the Fidele of *Cymbeline* are beginning to crack the conventions, and with the disappearance and revival of Hermione in *The Winter's Tale,* who actually returns once as a ghost in a dream, the original nature-myth of Demeter and Proserpine is openly established. The fact that the dying and reviving character is usually female strengthens the feeling that there is something maternal about the green world, in which the new order of the comic resolution is nourished and brought to birth. However, a similar theme which is very like the rejuvenation of the *senex* so frequent in Aristophanes occurs in the folklore motif of the healing of the impotent king on which *All's Well That Ends Well* is based, and this theme is probably involved in the symbolism of Prospero.

The conception of a second world bursts the boundaries of Menandrine comedy, yet it is clear that the world of Puck is no world of eternal forms or divine revelation. Shakespeare's comedy is not Aristotelian and realistic like Menander's, nor Platonic and dialectic like Aristophanes', nor Thomist and sacramental like Dante's, but a fourth kind. It is an Elizabethan kind, and is not confined either to Shakespeare or to the drama. Spenser's epic is a wonderful contrapuntal intermingling of two orders of existence, one the red and white world of English history, the other the green world of the Faerie Queene. The latter is a world of crusading virtues proceeding from the Faerie Queene's court and designed to return to that court when the destiny of the other world is fulfilled. The fact that the Faerie Queene's knights are sent out during the twelve days of the Christmas festival suggests our next point.

Shakespeare too has his green world of comedy and his red and white world of history. The story of the latter is at one point interrupted by an invasion from the comic world, when Falstaff *senex et parasitus* throws his gigantic shadow over Prince Henry, assuming on one occasion the role of his father. Clearly, if the Prince is ever to conquer France he must reassert the moral norm. The moral norm is duly reasserted, but the rejection of Falstaff is not a comic resolution. In comedy the moral norm is not morality but deliverance, and we certainly do not feel delivered from Falstaff as we feel delivered from Shylock with his absurd and vicious bond. The moral norm does not carry with it the vision of a free society; Falstaff will always keep a bit of that in his tavern.

Falstaff is a mock king, a lord of misrule, and his tavern is a Saturnalia. Yet we are reminded of the original meaning of the Saturnalia, as a rite intended to recall the golden age of Saturn. Falstaff's world is not a golden world, but as long as we remember it we cannot forget that the world of *Henry V* is an iron one. We are reminded too of another traditional denizen of the green world, Robin Hood, the outlaw who manages to suggest a better kind of society than those who make him an outlaw can produce. The outlaws in *The Two Gentlemen of Verona* compare themselves, in spite of the Italian setting, to Robin Hood, and in *As You Like It* Charles the wrestler says of Duke Senior's followers: "There they live like the old Robin Hood of England: they say many young gentlemen flock to him every day, and fleet the time carelessly, as they did in the golden world."

In the histories, therefore, the comic Saturnalia is a temporary reversal of normal standards, comic "relief" as it is called, which subsides and allows the history to continue. In the comedies, the green world suggests an original golden age which the normal world has usurped and which makes us wonder if it is not the normal world that is the real Saturnalia. In *Cymbeline* the green world finally triumphs over a historical theme, the reason being perhaps that in that play the incarnation of Christ, which is contemporary with Cymbeline, takes place offstage, and accounts for the halcyon peace with which the play concludes. From then on in Shakespeare's plays, the green world has it all its own way, and both in *Cymbeline* and in *Henry VIII* there may be suggestions that Shakespeare, like Spenser, is moving toward a synthesis of the two worlds, a wedding of Prince Arthur and the Faerie Queene.

This world of fairies, dreams, disembodied souls, and pastoral lovers may not be a "real" world, but, if not, there is something equally illusory in the stumbling and blinded follies of the "normal" world, of Theseus' Athens with its idiotic marriage law, of Duke Frederick and his melancholy tyranny, of Leontes and his mad jealousy, of the Court Party with their plots and intrigues. The famous speech of Prospero about the dream nature of reality applies equally to Milan and the enchanted island. We spend our lives partly in a waking world we call normal and partly in a dream world which we create out of our own desires. Shakespeare endows both worlds with equal imaginative power, brings them opposite one another, and makes each world seem unreal when seen by the light of the other. He uses freely both the heroic triumph of New Comedy and the ritual resurrection of its predecessor, but his distinctive comic resolution is different from either: it is a detachment of the spirit born of this reciprocal reflection of two illusory realities. We need not ask whether this brings us into a higher order of existence or not, for the question of existence is not relevant to poetry.

We have spoken of New Comedy as Aristotelian, Old Comedy as Platonic and Dante's *commedia* as Thomist, but it is difficult to suggest a philosophical spokesman for the form of Shakespeare's comedy. For Shakespeare, the subject matter of poetry is not life, or nature, or reality, or revelation, or anything else that the philosopher builds on, but poetry itself, a verbal universe. That is one reason why he is both the most elusive and the most substantial of poets.

Sigmund Freud

These excerpts from Freud's longer work, *Jokes and Their Relation to the Unconscious* (1905), are among the most important theoretical observations on comedy available to us. Freud had always found interesting the range of motivation for laughter and for "humorous" response—both to the specific stimuli of funny stories as well as to humorous life situations. In these remarks he explores many aspects of the comic directly applicable to theatrical matters in terms of plot structure, combination of characters, or dialogue. His own approach deals with physiological responses as well as the unconscious, with the relation of discovery to understanding, with the responses of children, and with many other materials remarkably useful to students of the stage, whether actors, directors, or playwrights.

As in all of his important writings, Freud's understanding of his subject seems to open the way—intentionally or not—to a deeper grasp on the part of the reader of other related matters. Thus, in the observations reprinted here, we find comments relative to the grotesque in comedy, to situation routines, to the use of masks, to problems of plotting and character, and to question of "timing" in comic dialogue. Each reader will discover something important relating to his own particular interests—probably proving to himself as he does so at least one of Freud's basic hypotheses!

❧ *from* JOKES AND THE SPECIES OF THE COMIC

... We have approached the problems of the comic in an unusual way. It seemed to us that jokes, which are ordinarily regarded as a subspecies of the comic, offer enough peculiarities to be attacked directly; thus we have avoided their relation to the more inclusive category of the comic so long as that was possible, though we have not failed to pick out *en passant* a few hints that might throw light on the comic. We have no difficulty in discovering that socially the comic behaves differently from jokes. It can be content with two persons: a first who finds what is comic and a second in whom it is found. The third person, to whom the comic thing is told, intensifies the comic process but adds nothing new to it. In a joke this third person is indispensable for the completion of the pleasure-producing process; but on the other hand the second person may be absent, except where a tendentious, aggressive joke is concerned. A joke is made, the comic is found—and first and foremost in people, only by a subsequent transference in things, situations, and so on, as well. As regards jokes, we know that the sources of the pleasure that is to be fostered lie in the subject himself and not in outside people. We have seen, too, that jokes can sometimes re-open sources of the comic which have become inaccessible, and that the comic often serves as a façade for a joke and replaces the fore-pleasure which has otherwise to be produced by the familiar technique. None of this precisely suggests that the relations between jokes and the comic are very simple. On the other hand, the problems of the comic have proved so complicated and all the efforts of the philosophers at solving them have been so unsuccessful that we cannot hold out any prospect that we shall be able to master them in a sudden onslaught, as it were, by approaching them from the direction of jokes. Moreover, for our investigation of jokes we brought with us an instrument of which no one else had hitherto made use—a knowledge of the dream-work. We have no similar advantages at our command to help us to understand the comic, and we must therefore expect that we shall discover no more about the nature of the comic than what we have already found in jokes, in so far as they form part of the comic and possess in their own nature certain of its features unchanged or merely modified.

The type of the comic which stands nearest to jokes is the naïve. Like the comic in general, the naïve is "found" and not, like a joke, "made." Indeed, the naïve cannot be made at all, whereas alongside the pure comic we have to take into account the case in which something is made comic—an evocation of the comic. The naïve must arise, without our taking any part in it, in the remarks and actions of other people, who stand in the position of the *second* person in the comic or in jokes. The naïve occurs if someone completely disregards an inhibition because it is not present in him—if, therefore, he appears to overcome it without any effort. It is a condition for the naïve's producing its effect that we should know that the person concerned does not possess the inhibition; otherwise we call him not naïve but impudent. We do not laugh at him but are indignant at him. The effect produced by the naïve is irresistible, and seems simple to understand. An inhibitory expenditure which we usually make suddenly becomes unutilizable owing to our hearing the naïve remark, and it is discharged by laughter. There is no need here for the attention to be distracted, probably because the lifting of the inhibition occurs directly and not through the intermediary of an operation that has been provoked. In this we are behaving like the third person in a joke, who is presented with the economy in inhibition without any effort on his own part.

In view of the insight we have gained into the genesis of inhibitions from following the course of development from play to jokes, it will not surprise us to find that the naïve occurs far the most often in children, and is then carried over to uneducated adults, whom we may regard as childish so far as their intellectual development is concerned. Naïve *remarks* are, of course, better suited for comparison with jokes than naïve actions, since remarks and not actions are the usual form in which jokes are expressed. It is illuminating to find that naïve remarks like those made by children may also be described as "naïve jokes.". . .

Whereas it was a condition for the effectiveness of a joke that both persons should be subject to approximately the same inhibitions or internal resistances, it will be seen that it is a condition for the naïve that the one person should possess inhibitions which the other is without. The apprehension of the naïve lies with the person provided with inhibitions, and he alone obtains the yield of pleasure which the naïve brings about. We have come near to guessing that that pleasure arises from the lifting of inhibitions. Since the pleasure from jokes has the same origin—a core of verbal pleasure and pleasure from nonsense, and a casing of pleasure in the lifting of inhibitions or in the relief of psychical expenditure—this similar relation to inhibition explains the internal kinship between the naïve and jokes. In both of them the pleasure arises through the lifting of internal inhibition.

The psychical process in the receptive person, however, is as much more complicated in the case of the naïve as it is simplified in comparison with jokes in the productive person. (In the case of the naïve, incidentally, our own self invariably coincides with the receptive person, while in the case of jokes we may equally occupy the position of the productive one.) When the receptive person hears something naïve, it must on the one hand affect him like a joke—and our examples give evidence precisely of this—for, as with a joke, the lifting of the censorship is made possible for him by no more than the effort of listening. But only a part of the pleasure created by the naïve can be explained in this way; and even this might be endangered in certain instances—for example, at hearing a naïve piece of smut. We might react to this at once with the same indignation that might be felt against a real piece of smut, if it were not that another factor spares us this indignation and at the same time offers us the more important part of our pleasure in the naïve. This other factor is the condition already mentioned that, in order to recognize the naïve, we must know that the internal inhibition is absent in the producing person. Only when this is certain do we laugh instead of being indignant. Thus we take the producing person's psychical state into consideration, put ourselves into it and try to understand it by comparing it with our own. It is these processes of empathy and comparison that result in the economy in expenditure which we discharge by laughing. . . .

It is only with misgivings that I venture to approach the problem of the comic itself. It would be presumptuous to expect that my efforts would be able to make any decisive contribution to its solution when the words of a great number of eminent thinkers have failed to produce a wholly satisfactory explanation. My intention is in fact no more than to pursue the lines of thought that have proved valuable with jokes a short distance further into the sphere of the comic.

The comic arises in the first instance as an unintended discovery derived from human social relations. It is found in people—in their movements, forms, actions and traits of character, originally in all probability only in their physical characteristics but later in their mental ones as well or, as the case may be, in the expression of those characteristics. By means of a very common sort of personification, animals become comic too, and inanimate objects. At the same time, the comic is capable of being detached from people, in so far as we recognize the conditions under which a person seems comic. In this way the comic situation comes about, and this recognition affords the possibility of making a person comic at one's will by putting him in situations in which his actions are subject to these comic conditions. The discovery that one has it in one's power to make someone else comic opens the way to an undreamt-of yield of comic pleasure and is the origin of a highly developed technique. One can make *oneself* comic, too, as easily as other people. The methods that serve to make people comic are: putting them in a comic situation, mimicry, disguise, unmasking, caricature, parody, travesty, and so on. It is obvious that these techniques can be used to serve hostile and aggressive purposes. One can make a person comic in order to make him become contemptible, to deprive him of his claim to dignity and authority. But even if such an intention habitually underlies making people comic, this need not be the meaning of what is comic spontaneously.

This irregular[1] survey of the occurrences of the comic will already show us that a very extensive field of origin is to be ascribed to it and that such specialized conditions as we found, for instance, in the naïve are not to be expected in it. In order to get on the track of the determining condition that is valid for the comic, the most important thing is the choice of an introductory case. We shall choose the comic of movement, because we recollect that the most primitive kind of stage performance—the pantomime—uses that method for making us laugh. The answer to the question of why we laugh at the clown's

---

[1] [*"Ungeordneten."* In 1912 only, this was misprinted *"untergeordneten,"* "secondary."]—Trans.

movements is that they seem to us extravagant and inexpedient. We are laughing at an expenditure that is too large. Let us look now for the determining condition outside the comic that is artifically constructed — where it can be found unintended. A child's movements do not seem to us comic, although he kicks and jumps about. On the other hand, it *is* comic when a child who is learning to write follows the movements of his pen with his tongue stuck out; in these associated motions we see an unnecessary expenditure of movement which we should spare ourselves if we were carrying out the same activity. Similarly, other such associated motions, or merely exaggerated expressive movements, seem to us comic in adults too. Pure examples of this species of the comic are to be seen, for instance, in the movements of someone playing skittles who, after he has released the ball, follows its course as though he could still continue to direct it. Thus, too, all grimaces are comic which exaggerate the normal expression of the emotions, even if they are produced involuntarily as in sufferers from St. Vitus's dance (chorea). And in the same way, the passionate movements of a modern conductor seem comic to any unmusical person who cannot understand their necessity. Indeed, it is from this comic of movement that the comic of bodily shapes and facial features branches off; for these are regarded as though they were the outcome of an exaggerated or pointless movement. Staring eyes, a hooked nose hanging down to the mouth, ears sticking out, a hump-back — all such things probably only produce a comic effect in so far as movements are imagined which would be necessary to bring about these features; and here the nose, the ears and other parts of the body are imagined as more movable than they are in reality. There is no doubt that it is comic if someone can "waggle his ears," and it would certainly be still more comic if he could move his nose up and down. A good deal of the comic effect produced on us by animals comes from our perceiving in them movements such as these which we cannot imitate ourselves.

But how is it that we laugh when we have recognized that some other person's movements are exaggerated and inexpedient? By making a comparison, I believe, between the movement I observe in the other person and the one that I should have carried out myself in his place. The two things compared must of course be judged by the same standard, and this standard is my expenditure of innervation, which is linked to my idea of the movement in both of the two cases. . . .

The origin of comic pleasure which has been discussed here — its derivation from a comparison of another person with ourself, from the difference between our own psychical expenditure and the other person's as estimated by empathy—is probably the most important genetically. It is certain, however, that it has not remained the only one. We have learnt at one time or other to disregard this comparison between the other person and ourself and to derive the pleasurable difference from the one side only, whether from the empathy or from the processes in ourself—which proves that the feeling of superiority bears no essential relation to comic pleasure. A comparison is [nevertheless] indispensable for the generation of this pleasure. We find that it is made between two cathectic expenditures that occur in rapid succession and are concerned with the same function, and these expenditures are either brought about in us through empathy into someone else or, without any such relation, are discovered in our own mental processes.

The first of these cases—in which, therefore, the other person still plays a part, though no longer in comparison with our own self—arises when the pleasurable difference in cathectic expenditures is brought about by external influences, which we may sum up as a "situation." For that reason, this species of the comic is also known as "the comic of situation." The characteristics of the person who provides the comic effect do not in this case play an essential part: we laugh even if we have to confess that *we* should have had to do the same in that situation. We are here extracting the comic from the relation of human beings to the often over-powerful external world; and so far as the mental processes of a human being are concerned, this external world also comprises social conventions and necessities and even his own bodily needs. A typical instance of the latter kind is provided if, in the middle of an activity which makes demands on a person's powers, he is suddenly interrupted by a pain or an excretory need. The contrast which, through empathy, offers us the comic difference is that between the high degree of interest taken by him *before* the interruption and the minimal one that he has left over for his mental activity when the interruption has occurred. The person who offers us this difference becomes comic to us once again for his inferiority; but he is inferior only in comparison with his earlier self and not in comparison with *us,* for we know that in the same circumstances we could not have behaved otherwise. But it is noteworthy that we only find someone's being put in a position of inferiority comic where there is empathy—that is, where someone else is concerned: if we ourselves were in similar straits we should be conscious only of distressing feelings. It is probably only by keeping such feelings away from ourselves that we are able to enjoy pleasure from the difference arising out of a comparison between these changing cathexes. . . .

Mankind have not been content to enjoy the comic where they have come upon it in their experience; they have also sought to bring it about intentionally, and we can learn more about the nature of the comic if we study the means which serve to *make* things comic. First and foremost, it is possible to produce the comic in relation to oneself in order to amuse other people—for instance, by making oneself out clumsy or stupid. In that way one produces a comic effect exactly as though one really were these things, by fulfilling the condition of the comparison which leads to the difference in expenditure. But one does not in this way make oneself ridiculous or contemptible, but may in some circumstances even achieve admiration. The feeling of superiority does not arise in the other person if he knows that one has only been pretending; and this affords fresh evidence of the fundamental independence of the comic from the feeling of superiority.

As regards making *other people* comic, the principal means is to put them in situations in which a person becomes comic as a result of human dependence on external events, particularly on social factors, without regard to the personal characteristics of the individual concerned—that is to say, by employing the comic of situation. This putting of someone in a comic situation may be a *real* one (a practical joke[2])—by sticking out a leg so that someone trips over it as though he were clumsy, by making him seem stupid by exploiting his credulity, or trying to convince him of something nonsensical, and so on—or it may be simulated by speech or play. The aggressiveness, to which making a person comic usually ministers, is much assisted by the fact that the comic pleasure is independent of the reality of the comic situation, so that everyone is in fact exposed, without any defence, to being made comic.

But there are yet other means of making things comic which deserve special consideration and also indicate in part fresh sources of comic pleasure. Among these, for instance, is *mimicry,* which gives quite extraordinary pleasure to the hearer and makes its object comic even if it is still far from the exaggeration of a caricature. It is much easier to find a reason for the comic effect of *caricature* than for

---

[2] [In English in the original.]—Trans.

that of mere mimicry. Caricature, parody and travesty (as well as their practical counterpart, unmasking) are directed against people and objects which lay claim to authority and respect, which are in some sense *"sublime."*[3]. . .

Caricature, as is well known, brings about degradation by emphasizing in the general impression given by the exalted object a single trait which is comic in itself but was bound to be overlooked so long as it was only perceivable in the general picture. By isolating this, a comic effect can be attained which extends in our memory over the whole object. This is subject to the condition that the actual presence of the exalted object himself does not keep us in a reverential attitude. If a comic trait of this kind that has been overlooked is lacking in reality, a caricature will unhesitatingly create it by exaggerating one that is not comic in itself; and the fact that the effect of the caricature is not essentially diminished by this falsification of reality is once again an indication of the origin of comic pleasure.

Parody and *travesty* achieve the degradation of something exalted in another way: by destroying the unity that exists between people's characters as we know them and their speeches and actions, by replacing either the exalted figures or their utterances by inferior ones. They are distinguished from caricature in this, but not in the mechanism of their production of comic pleasure. The same mechanism is also used for *unmasking,* which only applies where someone has seized dignity and authority by a deception and these have to be taken from him in reality. We have already met with a few examples of the comic effect of unmasking in jokes — for instance, in the story of the aristocratic lady who, at the first onset of her labour-pains, exclaimed "Ah! mon Dieu!" but whom the doctor would not assist till she cried out "Aa-ee, aa-ee!" Having come to know the characteristics of the comic, we can no longer dispute that this anecdote is in fact an example of comic unmasking and has no justifiable claim to be called a joke. It only recalls jokes by its setting and by the technical method of "representation by something very small" — in this case the patient's cry, which is found sufficient to establish the indication for treatment. It nevertheless remains true that our linguistic sense, if we call on it for a decision, raises no objection to our calling a story like this a joke. We may explain this by reflecting that linguistic usage is not based on the scientific insight

---

[3] [The German word here is *"erhaben,"* for which the accepted English translation in aesthetics is "sublime." As, however, it is difficult to apply this rendering in the case of people, we have, where necessary, used the word "exalted" instead.]— Trans.

into the nature of jokes that we have arrived at in this laborious investigation. Since one of the functions of jokes is to make hidden sources of comic pleasure accessible once more, any device that brings to light something that is not manifestly comic may, by a loose analogy, be termed a joke. This applies preferably, however, to unmasking as well as to other methods of making people comic.[4]

Under the heading of "unmasking" we may also include a procedure for making things comic with which we are already acquainted —the method of degrading the dignity of individuals by directing attention to the frailties which they share with all humanity, but in particular the dependence of their mental functions on bodily needs. The unmasking is equivalent here to an admonition: such and such a person, who is admired as a demigod, is after all only human like you and me. Here, too, are to be placed the efforts at laying bare the monotonous psychical automatism that lies behind the wealth and apparent freedom of psychical functions. We came across examples of "unmasking" of this kind in the marriage-broker jokes, and felt a doubt at the time whether these anecdotes have a right to be counted as jokes. We are now able to decide with greater certainty that the anecdote of the echo who reinforced all the assertions of the marriage-broker and finally confirmed his admission that the bride had a hump with the exclamation "And *what* a hump!"—that this anecdote is essentially a *comic* story, an example of the unmasking of a psychical automatism. Here, however, the comic story is only serving as a façade. For anyone who will attend to the hidden meaning of the marriage-broker anecdotes, the whole thing remains an admirably staged joke; anyone who does not penetrate so far is left with a comic story. The same thing applies to the other joke, about the marriage-broker who, in order to answer an objection, ended by confessing the truth with a cry of "But I ask you, who would lend such people anything?" Here again we have a comic unmasking as the façade for a joke, though in this instance the characteristic of a joke is much more unmistakable, since the marriage-broker's remark is at the same time a representation by the opposite. In trying to prove that the people are rich he at the same time proves that they are *not* rich, but very poor. Here a joke and the comic are combined, and teach us that the same remark can be both things at once.

We are glad to seize the opportunity of returning to jokes from

---

[4] "Thus every conscious and ingenious evocation of the comic (whether the comic of contemplation or of situation) is in general described as a joke. We, of course, cannot here make use of this concept of the joke either." (Lipps, 1898, 78.)

the comic of unmasking, since our true problem is not to determine the nature of the comic but to throw light on the relation between jokes and the comic. We have discussed the uncovering of psychical automatism, in a case in which our feeling as to whether something is comic or a joke left us in the lurch. And we will now add another case in which there is a similar confusion between jokes and the comic — the case of nonsensical jokes. But our investigation will show us in the end that as regards this second case the convergence between jokes and the comic can be theoretically accounted for.

In discussing the techniques of jokes we found that giving free play to modes of thought which are usual in the unconscious but which can only be judged as examples of "faulty reasoning" in the conscious is the technical method adopted in many jokes; and about these, once again, we felt doubts whether they possessed the true character of jokes, so that we were inclined to classify them simply as comic stories. We were unable to reach a decision about our doubts because at the time we were ignorant of the essential characteristic of jokes. Subsequently, led by an analogy with the dream-work, we discovered that it lay in the compromise effected by the joke-work between the demands of reasonable criticism and the urge not to renounce the ancient pleasure in words and nonense. What came about in this way as a compromise, when the preconscious start of the thought was left for a moment to unconscious revision, satisfied both claims in every instance, but presented itself to criticism in various forms and had to put up with various judgements at its hands. Sometimes a joke would succeed in slipping on the appearance of an insignificant but nevertheless permissible assertion, another time it would smuggle itself in as the expression of a valuable thought. But, in the marginal case of effecting a compromise, it would give up attempting to satisfy criticism. Boasting of the sources of pleasure at its command, it would appear before criticism as sheer nonsense and not be afraid to provoke contradiction from it; for the joke could reckon on the hearer straightening out the disfigurement in the form of its expression by unconscious revision and so giving it back its meaning.

In what instances, then, will a joke appear before criticism as nonsense? Particularly when it makes use of the modes of thought which are usual in the unconscious but are proscribed in conscious thought—faulty reasoning, in fact. For certain modes of thought proper to the unconscious have also been retained by the conscious — for instance, some kinds of indirect representation, allusion, and so on—even though their conscious employment is subject to considerable restrictions. When a joke makes use of these techniques it will raise little or no objection on the part of criticism; objections will only appear if it also makes use for its technique of the methods with which conscious thought will have nothing more to do. A joke can still avoid objection, if it conceals the faulty reasoning it has used and disguises it under a show of logic . . . But if it produces the faulty reasoning undisguised, then the objections of criticism will follow with certainty.

In such cases the joke has another resource. The faulty reasoning, which it uses for its technique as one of the modes of thought of the unconscious, strikes criticism—even though not invariably so—as being *comic*. Consciously giving free play to unconscious modes of thought (which have been rejected as faulty) is a means of producing comic pleasure; and it is easy to understand this, since it certainly requires a greater expenditure of energy to establish a preconscious cathexis than to give free play to an unconscious one. When, on hearing a thought which has, as it were, been formed in the unconscious, we compare it with its correction, a difference in expenditure emerges for us from which comic pleasure arises. A joke which makes use of faulty reasoning like this for its technique, and therefore appears nonsensical, can thus produce a comic effect at the same time. If we fail to detect the joke, we are once again left with only the comic or funny story. . . .

It is probably right to say that children laugh from pure pleasure in a variety of circumstances that we feel as "comic" and cannot find the motive for, whereas a child's motives are clear and can be stated. For instance, if someone slips in the street and falls down we laugh because the impression—we do not know why—is comic. A child laughs in the same case from a feeling of superiority or from *Schadenfreude:* "You've fallen down, I haven't." Certain motives for pleasure in children seem to be lost to us adults, and instead in the same circumstances we have the "comic" feeling as a substitute for the lost one.

If one might generalize, it would seem most attractive to place the specific characteristic of the comic which we are in search of in an awakening of the infantile—to regard the comic as the regained "lost laughter of childhood." One could then say: "I laugh at a difference in expenditure between another person and myself, every time I rediscover the child in him." Or, put more exactly, the complete comparison which leads to the comic would run: "That is how he does it — I do it in another way — he does it as I used to do it as a child."

Thus the laughter would always apply to the comparison between the adult's ego and the child's ego. Even the lack of uniformity in the comic difference — the fact that what seems to me comic is sometimes a greater and sometimes a smaller expenditure — would fit in with the infantile determinant; actually what is comic is invariably on the infantile side.

This is not contradicted by the fact that, when children themselves are the object of the comparison, they do not give me a comic impression but a purely pleasurable one; nor is it contradicted because the comparison with the infantile only produces a comic effect if any other use of the difference is avoided. For these are matters concerned with the conditions governing *discharge*. Whatever brings a psychical process into connection with others operates against the discharge of the surplus cathexis and puts it to some other use; whatever isolates a psychical act encourages discharge. A conscious attitude to children as objects of comparison therefore makes impossible the discharge that is necessary for comic pleasure. Only when the cathexis is *preconscious* is there an approximation to an isolation such as, incidentally, we may ascribe to the mental processes in children as well. The addition to the comparison ("I did it like that as a child too") from which the comic effect is derived would thus only come into consideration, as far as differences of medium magnitude are concerned, if no other nexus could gain control over the liberated surplus.

If we pursue our attempt to discover the essence of the comic in a preconscious link with the infantile, we must go a step further than Bergson and admit that a comparison need not, in order to produce the comic, arouse old childish pleasures and childish play; it will be enough for it to touch upon childish nature in general, and perhaps even on childish suffering. Here we shall be parting from Bergson but remaining in agreement with ourselves if we connect comic pleasure not with recollected pleasure but once more with a comparison. It may be that cases of the former kind [those connected with recollected pleasure] may coincide with the invariably and irresistibly comic.

Let us at this point review the scheme which we drew up earlier of the various comic possibilities. We remarked that the comic difference was found either

- (*a*) by a comparison between another person and oneself, or
- (*b*) by a comparison entirely within the other person, or
- (*c*) by a comparison entirely within oneself.

In the first of these cases the other person would appear to me as a child; in the second he would reduce himself to a child; and in the third I should discover the child in myself.

[*a*] The first case would include the comic of movement and form, of mental functioning and of character. The corresponding infantile factors would be the urge to movement and the child's inferior mental and moral development. So that, for instance, a stupid person would be comic to me in so far as he reminded me of a lazy child and a bad person in so far as he reminded me of a naughty child. There could only be a question of a childish pleasure lost to adults in the single instance in which the child's own joy in movement was concerned.

[*b*] The second case, in which the comic depends entirely on "empathy," includes the most numerous possibilities — the comic of situation, of exaggeration (caricature), of mimicry, of degradation and of unmasking. This is the case in which the introduction of the infantile point of view proves most useful. For the comic of situation is mostly based on embarrassments, in which we rediscover the child's helplessness. The worst of the embarrassments, the interference by the peremptory demands of natural needs with other functions, corresponds to the child's incomplete control over his bodily functions. Where the comic of situation operates by means of repetitions, it is based on the child's peculiar pleasure in constant repetition (of questions or of being told stories) which make him a nuisance to the adult. Exaggeration, which still gives pleasure to adults in so far as it can find justification with their critical faculty, is connected with the child's peculiar lack of a sense of proportion, his ignorance of all quantitative relations, which he comes to know later than qualitative ones. The use of moderation and restraint, even in the case of permitted impulses, is a late fruit of education and is acquired by the mutual inhibition of mental activities brought together in a combination. Where such combinations are weakened, as in the unconscious of dreams or in the mono-ideism of psychoneuroses, the child's lack of moderation re-emerges.[5]

---

[5] [This point had been brought out already by Freud in a footnote to *The Interpretation of Dreams* (1900*a*), *Standard Ed.*, 4, 268.] — Trans.

We found relatively great difficulties in understanding the comic of mimicry so long as we left the infantile factor out of account. But mimicry is the child's best art and the driving motive of most of his games. A child's ambition aims far less at excelling among his equals than at mimicking the grown-ups. The relation of children to adults is also the basis of the comic of degradation, which corresponds to the condescension shown by adults in their attitude to the life of children. There is little that gives children greater pleasure than when a grown-up lets himself down to their level, renounces his oppressive superiority and plays with them as an equal. This relief, which gives the child pure pleasure, becomes in adults, in the form of degradation, a means of making things comic and a source of comic pleasure. As regards unmasking, we know that it goes back to degradation.

[c] We come up against the most difficulties in finding the infantile basis of the third case, the comic of expectation, which no doubt explains why those authorities who have put this case first in their discussion of the comic have found no occasion for taking account of the infantile factor in the comic. The comic of expectation is no doubt the remotest in children; the capacity to grasp it is the latest to appear. In most of the instances which seem comic to an adult a child would probably feel only disappointment. We might, however, take the child's power of blissful expectation and credulity as a basis for understanding how we appear to ourselves comic "as a child" when we meet with a comic disappointment.

What we have said would seem to suggest a certain probability for a translation of the comic feeling that might run: "Those things are comic which are not proper for an adult." Nevertheless I do not feel bold enough, in virtue of my whole attitude to the problem of the comic, to defend this last assertion with as much seriousness as my earlier ones. I am unable to decide whether degradation to being a child is only a special case of comic degradation, or whether everything comic is based fundamentally on degradation to being a child.[6]

---

[6] The fact that comic pleasure has its source in the "quantitative contrast" of a comparison between small and large, which after all also expresses the essential relation between a child and an adult—this would certainly be a strange coincidence if the comic had no other connection with the infantile.

George Santayana

This short, energetic essay deals with the nature of — and need for — that aspect of comic creation identifiable, since the time of Aristophanes, as excess. Confirmed since the writing of these observations by many anthropologists and social historians, Santayana's essay describes the almost heroic lunacy of the comic spirit when it can avoid the repressions of the reasonable, the legal, the wise. Implicit in his description is the defense of excess in the great comic drama of the world from the Greeks onward; before the men and women of such plays can return to the productive living processes of the reasonable world, their vision must have included some cloud-cuckoo-land which the reasonable world would have found intolerable. It is this vision, and its psychological, verbal, and physical components, that the author — one of the great men of letters of the twentieth century — seeks to describe and, in many specific terms, to defend.

❧ THE COMIC MASK

The clown is the primitive comedian. Sometimes in the exuberance of animal life a spirit of riot and frolic comes over a man; he leaps, he dances, he tumbles head over heels, he grins, shouts, or leers, possibly he pretends to go to pieces suddenly, and blubbers like a child. A moment later he may look up wreathed in smiles, and hugely pleased about nothing. All this he does hysterically, without any reason, by a sort of mad inspiration and irresistible impulse. He may easily, however, turn his absolute histrionic impulse, his pure fooling, into mimicry of anything or anybody that at the moment happens to impress his senses; he will crow like a cock, simper like a young lady, or reel like a drunkard. Such mimicry is virtual mockery, because the actor is able to revert from those assumed attitudes to his natural self; whilst his models, as he thinks, have no natural self save that imitable attitude, and can never disown it; so that the clown feels himself immensely superior, in his rôle of universal satirist, to all actual men, and belabours and rails at them unmercifully. He sees everything in caricature, because he sees the surface only, with the lucid innocence of a child; and all these grotesque personages stimulate him, not to moral sympathy, nor to any consid-

From *Soliloquies in England and Later Soliloquies* (1921) by George Santayana. Reprinted by permission of Constable Publishers (London).

eration of their fate, but rather to boisterous sallies, as the rush of a crowd, or the hue and cry of a hunt, or the contortions of a jumping-jack might stimulate him. He is not at all amused intellectually; he is not rendered wiser or tenderer by knowing the predicaments into which people inevitably fall; he is merely excited, flushed, and challenged by an absurd spectacle. Of course this rush and suasion of mere existence must never fail on the stage, nor in any art; it is to the drama what the hypnotizing stone block is to the statue, or shouts and rhythmic breathing to the bard; but such primary magical influences may be qualified by reflection, and then rational and semi-tragic unities will supervene. When this happens the histrionic impulse creates the idyl or the tragic chorus; henceforth the muse of reflection follows in the train of Dionysus, and the revel or the rude farce passes into humane comedy.

Paganism was full of scruples and superstitions in matters of behaviour or of *cultus,* since the *cultus* too was regarded as a business or a magic craft; but in expression, in reflection, paganism was frank and even shameless; it felt itself inspired, and revered this inspiration. It saw nothing impious in inventing or recasting a myth about no matter how sacred a subject. Its inspiration, however, soon fell into classic moulds, because the primary impulses of nature, though intermittent, are monotonous and clearly defined, as are the gestures of love and of anger. A man who is unaffectedly himself turns out to be uncommonly like other people. Simple sincerity will continually rediscover the old right ways of thinking and speaking, and will be perfectly conventional without suspecting it. This classic iteration comes of nature, it is not the consequence of any revision or censorship imposed by reason. Reason, not being responsible for any of the facts or passions that enter into human life, has no interest in maintaining them as they are; any novelty, even the most revolutionary, would merely afford reason a fresh occasion for demanding a fresh harmony. But the Old Adam is conservative; he repeats himself mechanically in every child who cries and loves sweets and is imitative and jealous. Reason, with its tragic discoveries and restraints, is a far more precarious and personal possession than the trite animal experience and the ancestral grimaces on which it supervenes; and automatically even the philosopher continues to cut his old comic capers, as if no such thing as reason existed. The wiseacres too are comic, and their mask is one of the most harmlessly amusing in the human museum; for reason, taken psychologically, is an old inherited passion like any other, the passion for consistency and order; and it is just as prone as the other passions to overstep the modesty of nature and to regard its own aims as alone important. But this is ridiculous; because importance springs from the stress of nature, from the cry of life, not from reason and its pale prescriptions. Reason cannot stand alone; brute habit and blind play are at the bottom of art and morals, and unless irrational impulses and fancies are kept alive, the life of reason collapses for sheer emptiness. What tragedy could there be, or what sublime harmonies rising out of tragedy, if there were no spontaneous passions to create the issue, no wild voices to be reduced to harmony? Moralists have habitually aimed at suppression, wisely perhaps at first, when they were preaching to men of spirit; but why continue to harp on propriety and unselfishness and labour, when we are little but labour-machines already, and have hardly any self or any passions left to indulge? Perhaps the time has come to suspend those exhortations, and to encourage us to be sometimes a little lively, and see if we can invent something worth saying or doing. We should then be living in the spirit of comedy, and the world would grow young. Every occasion would don its comic mask, and make its bold grimace at the world for a moment. We should be constantly original without effort and without shame, somewhat as we are in dreams, and consistent only in sincerity; and we should gloriously emphasize all the poses we fell into, without seeking to prolong them.

Objections to the comic mask—to the irresponsible, complete, extreme expression of each moment—cut at the roots of all expression. Pursue this path, and at once you do away with gesture: we must not point, we must not pout, we must not cry, we must not laugh aloud; we must not only avoid attracting attention, but our attention must not be obviously attracted; it is silly to gaze, says the nursery-governess, and rude to stare. Presently words, too, will be reduced to a telegraphic code. A man in his own country will talk like the laconic tourist abroad; his whole vocabulary will be *Où? Combien? All right! Dear me!* Conversation in the quiet home will dispense even with these phrases; nothing will be required but a few pragmatic grunts and signals for action. Where the spirit of comedy has departed, company becomes constraint, reserve eats up the spirit, and people fall into a penurious melancholy in their scruple to be always exact, sane, and reasonable, never to mourn, never to glow, never to betray a passion or a weakness, nor venture to utter a thought they might not wish to harbour for ever.

Yet irony pursues these enemies of comedy, and for fear of wearing a mask for a moment they are hypocrites all their lives. Their very reserve becomes a pose, a convention imposed externally, and their mincing speech turns to cant. Sometimes this evasion of impulsive sentiment fosters a poignant sentimentality beneath. The comedy goes on silently behind the scenes, until perhaps it gets the upper hand and becomes positive madness; or else it breaks out in some shy, indirect fashion, as among Americans with their perpetual joking. Where there is no habitual art and no moral liberty, the instinct for direct expression is atrophied for want of exercise; and then slang and a humorous perversity of phrase or manner act as safety-valves to sanity; and you manage to express yourself in spite of the censor by saying something grotesquely different from what you mean. That is a long way round to sincerity, and an ugly one. What, on the contrary, could be more splendidly sincere than the impulse to play in real life, to rise on the rising wave of every feeling and let it burst, if it will, into the foam of exaggeration? Life is not a means, the mind is not a slave nor a photograph: it has a right to enact a pose, to assume a *panache,* and to create what prodigious allegories it will for the mere sport and glory of it. Nor is this art of innocent make-believe forbidden in the Decalogue, although Bible-reading Anglo-Saxondom might seem to think so. On the contrary, the Bible and the Decalogue are themselves instances of it. To embroider upon experience is not to bear false witness against one's neighbour, but to bear true witness to oneself. Fancy is playful and may be misleading to those who try to take it for literal fact; but literalness is impossible in any utterance of spirit, and if it were possible it would be deadly. Why should we quarrel with human nature, with metaphor, with myth, with impersonation? The foolishness of the simple is delightful; only the foolishness of the wise is exasperating.

Friedrich Dürrenmatt

In the autumn of 1954 and the spring of 1955, Dürrenmatt lectured on the theatre in different cities of Switzerland and West Germany. The comments reprinted here are from this lecture which covers — and covers thoroughly — an amazing range of subject matter pertinent not only to students of this dramatist in particular but to students of modern theatre in general — its social, financial, and artistic situations, the goals of its playwrights, its role in the future of any community.

In this lecture, Dürrenmatt refers specifically to many of his own plays but also to works from "classical" and contemporary repertories, to problems of stage design and character, to theories of comedy, to questions of timing and structure. The piece is full of irony as well, for Dürrenmatt is poignantly conscious of the economic and ideological questions that govern choice of plays for performance in various theatres. Here his remarks have special application in North American theatre centers where frequently exists an even greater neglect of the new playwright than that which exists in Europe. It is, therefore, of special importance to have at hand the considered and highly articulate remarks on such a wide range of subject matter by a distinguished and prolific practicing playwright. Dürrenmatt's works for the stage include *The Visit, Romulus the Great, The Marriage of Mr. Mississippi, An Angel Comes to Babylon,* and, most recently, *The Physicists.*

✄ *from PROBLEMS OF THE THEATRE*

... In undertaking to write a play I must first make clear to myself just where it is to take place. At first glance that does not seem much of a problem. A play takes place in London or Berlin, in the mountains, a hospital or on a battlefield, wherever the action demands. But it does not work out quite that way. A play, after all, takes place upon a stage which in turn must represent London, the mountains or a battlefield. This distinction need not, but can be made. It depends entirely on how much the author takes the stage into account, how strongly he wants to create the illusion without which no theatre can exist, and whether he wants it smeared on thickly with gobs of paint heaped upon the canvas, or transparent, diaphanous and fragile. A playwright can be deadly serious about the place: Madrid, the Rütli, the Russian steppe, or he can think of it as just a stage, the world, his world.

How the stage is to represent a given place is, of course, the task of the scene designer. Since designing scenes is a form of painting, the developments which have taken place in painting in

From Preface to *Four Plays* (1965) by Friedrich Dürrenmatt, translated by Gerhard Nellhaus. Reprinted by permission of Grove Press, Inc., and Hope Leresche & Steele (London).

our time have not failed to touch the theatre. But the theatre can really neither abstract man nor language, which is in itself both abstract and concrete, and scenery, no matter how abstract it would pretend to be, must still represent something concrete to make sense, and for both of these reasons, abstraction in scenic design has essentially failed. Nevertheless the "green curtain" behind which the spectators have to imagine the place, the royal chamber, was reinstituted. The fact was recalled that the dramatic place and the stage were not one and the same, no matter how elaborate, how verisimilar the stage setting might be. The fact is the place has to be created by the play. One word: we are in Venice; another, in the Tower of London. The imagination of the audience needs but little support. Scenery is to suggest, point out, intensify, but not describe the place. Once more it has become transparent, immaterialized. And similarly the place of the drama to be shown on the stage can be made immaterial.

Two fairly recent plays which most clearly illustrate the possibility referred to as immaterializing the scenery and the dramatic place are Wilder's *Our Town* and *The Skin of Our Teeth*. The immaterializing of the stage in *Our Town* consists of this: the stage is nearly empty; only a few objects needed for rehearsals stand about—some chairs, tables, ladders and so on; and out of these everyday objects the place is created, the dramatic place, the town, all out of the word, the play, the wakened imagination of the spectators. In his other play Wilder, that great fanatic of the theatre, immaterializes the dramatic place; where the Antrobus family really lives, in what age and what stage of civilization, is never wholly clear; now it is the ice age, now a world war. This sort of experiment may be met quite often in modern drama; thus it is indefinite where in Frisch's play, *Graf Öderland,* the strange Count Wasteland abides; no man knows where to wait for Godot, and in *The Marriage of Mr. Mississippi (Die Ehe des Herrn Mississippi)* I expressed the indefiniteness of the locale (in order to give the play its spirit of wit, of comedy) by having the right window of a room look out upon a northern landscape with a Gothic cathedral and an apple tree, while the left window of the same room opens on a southern scene with an ancient ruin, a touch of the Mediterranean and a cypress. The really decisive point in all this is that, to quote Max Frisch, the playwright is making poetry with the stage, a possibility which has always entertained and occupied me and which is one of the reasons, if not the main one, why I write plays. But then—and I am thinking of the comedies of Aristophanes and the comic plays of Nestroy—in every age poetry has been written not only *for,* but *with* the stage.

Let us turn from these incidental problems to more basic ones. What do the particular problems look like, which I—to cite an author whom I know at least partially, though not fully—have faced? In *The Blind Man (Der Blinde)* I wanted to juxtapose the word against the dramatic place, to turn the word against the scene. The blind duke believes he is living in his well-preserved castle whereas he is living in a ruin; he thinks he is humbling himself before Wallenstein, but sinks to his knees before a negro. The dramatic place is one and the same, but by means of the pretence carried on before the blind man, it plays a dual role: the place seen by the audience and the place in which the blind man fancies himself to be. So also, when in my comedy, *An Angel comes to Babylon (Ein Engel kommt nach Babylon),* I picked for my dramatic locale the city in which the Tower was built, I had essentially to solve two problems. In the first place the stage had to express the fact that there were two places of action in my comedy, heaven and the city of Babylon; heaven, which was the secret point of origin of the action, and Babylon the locale, where that action ran its course.

Well, I suppose heaven could have been simply represented by a dark background to suggest its infinity, but since I wanted to convey in my comedy the idea that heaven was not something infinite, but something incomprehensible and altogether different, I asked for the stage background, the heaven above the city of Babylon, to be occupied entirely by the Great Nebula in Andromeda, just as we might see it through the telescope on Mount Palomar. What I hoped to achieve thereby was that heaven, the incomprehensible and inscrutable, would take on form, gain, as it were, its own stage presence. In this wise also heaven's rapprochement with the earth was to be brought out, reiterating the coming together of the two that is expressed in the action through the angel's visiting Babylon. Thus, too, a world was constructed in which the result of the action, namely the building of the Tower of Babylon, became possible.

In the second place I had to think of how to make the stage represent Babylon, the place in which the action unfolds. I found the idea of Babylon challenging because of its timeliness, its Cyclopean big-city character, its New York look with skyscrapers and slums, and by having the first two acts take place along the banks of the Euphrates I wished to hint at Paris. Babylon, in brief, stands for the metropolis. It is a Babylon of the imagination, having a few typically Babylonian features, but in a modernized parodied version, with its modernities — for instance the convenience of electric street-lights. Of course the execution of the scenery, the building of the stage itself, is a job for the scene designer, but the playwright must always decide himself just what kind of stage he wants.

I love a colourful stage setting, a colourful theatre, like the stage of Theo Otto, to mention an admirable example. I have little use for a theatre that uses black curtains as was the fashion once upon a time, or for the tendency to glory in threadbare poverty which some stage designers seem to aim for. To be sure the word is important above all else in the theatre; but note: above all else. For after the word there are many other things, which also rightfully belong to the theatre, even a certain wantonness. Thus when someone asked me quite thoughtfully with respect to my play *Mississippi,* where one of the characters enters through a grandfather clock, whether or not I thought a four-dimensional theatre possible, I could only remark that I had not thought of Einstein when I did it. It is just that in my daily life it would give me great pleasure if I could join a gathering and astonish those present by coming into the room through a grandfather clock or by floating in through a window. No one should deny us playwrights the opportunity to satisfy such desires now and then at least on the stage, where such whims can be fulfilled. The old argument as to which came first, the chicken or the egg, can be transformed in art into the question of whether the egg or the chicken, the world as potential or as rich harvest, is to be presented. Artists might very well be divided then into those favouring the egg and those favouring the chicken. The argument is a lively one. Alfred Polgar once said to me, it was odd that while in contemporary Anglo-Saxon drama everything came out in the dialogue, there was always much too much happening on the stage in my plays and that he, Polgar, would sometimes like to see a simple Dürrenmatt play. Behind this truth, however, lies my refusal to say that the egg came before the chicken, and my personal prejudice of preferring the chicken to the egg. It happens to be my passion, not always a happy one perhaps, to want to put on the stage the richness, the manifold diversity of the world. As a result my theatre is open to many interpretations and appears to confuse some. Misunderstandings creep in, as when someone looks around desperately in the chicken coop of my plays, hoping to find the egg of Columbus which I stubbornly refuse to lay.

But a play is bound not only to a place, but also to a time. Just as the stage represents a place, so it also represents a time, the time *during* which the action takes place as well as the time *in* which it occurs. If Aristotle had really demanded the unity of time, place and action, he would have limited the duration of a tragedy to the time it took for the action to be carried out (a feat which the Greek tragedians nearly achieved), for which reasons, of course, everything would have to be concentrated upon that action. Time would pass "naturally," everything coming one after the other without breaks. But this does not always have to be the case. In general the actions on the stage follow one another but, to cite an example, in Nestroy's magical farce, *Death on the Wedding Day (Der Tod am Hochzeitstag)*, there are two acts taking place simultaneously and the illusion of simultaneity is skilfully achieved by having the action of the second act form the background noise for the first, and the action of the first act the background noise for the second. Other examples of how time is used as a theatrical device could be easily recalled. Time can be shortened, stretched, intensified, arrested, repeated; the dramatist can, like Joshua, call to his heaven's orbits, "Theatre-Sun, stand thou still upon Gibeon! And thou, Theatre-Moon, in the valley of Ajalon!"

It may be noted further that the unities ascribed to Aristotle were not wholly kept in Greek tragedy either. The action is interrupted by the choruses, and by this means time is spaced. When the chorus interrupts the action, it achieves as regards time—to elucidate the obvious like an amateur—the very same thing the curtain does today. The curtain cuts up and spreads out the time of an action. I have nothing against such an honourable device. The good thing about a curtain is that it so clearly defines an act, that it clears the table, so to speak. Moreover, it is psychologically often extremely necessary to give the exhausted and frightened audience a rest. But a new way of binding language and time has evolved in our day.

If I cite Wilder's *Our Town* once again, I do so because I assume that this fine play is widely known. You may recall that in it different characters turn towards the audience and talk of the worries and needs of their small town. In this way Wilder is able to dispense with the curtain. The curtain has been replaced by the direct address to the audience. The epic element of description has been added to the drama. For this reason, of course, this form of theatre has been called the epic theatre.

Yet when looked at quite closely, Shakespeare's plays or Goethe's *Götz von Berlichingen* are in a certain sense also epic theatre. Only in a different, less obvious manner. Since Shakespeare's histories often extend over a considerable period of time, this time-span is divided into different actions, different episodes, each of which is treated dramatically. *Henry IV*, Part I, consists of nineteen such episodes, while by the end of the fourth act of *Götz* there are already no less than forty-one tableaux. I stopped counting after that. If one looks at the way the overall action has been built up, then, with respect to time, it is quite close to the epic, like a film that is run too slowly, so that the individual shots can be seen. The condensation of everything into a certain time has been given up in favour of an episodic form of drama.

Thus when an author in some of our modern plays turns towards the audience, he attempts to give the play a greater continuity than is otherwise possible in an episodic form. The void between the acts is to be filled; the time-gap is to be bridged, not by a pause, but by words, by a description of what has gone on in the meanwhile, or by having some new character introduce himself. In other words, the expositions are handled in an epic manner, not the actions to which these expositions lead. This represents an advance of the word in the theatre, the attempt of the word to reconquer territory lost a long time ago. Let us emphasize that it is but an attempt; for all too often the direct address to the audience is used to explain the play, an undertaking that makes no sense whatever. If the audience is moved by the play, it will not need prodding by explanations; if the audience is not moved, all the prodding in the world will not be of help.

In contrast to the epic, which can describe human beings as they are, the drama unavoidably limits and therefore stylizes them. This limitation is inherent in the art form itself. The human being of the drama is, after all, a talking individual, and speech is his limitation. The action only serves to force this human being on the stage to talk in a certain way. The action is the crucible in which the human being is molten into words, must become words. This, of course, means that I, as the playwright, have to get the people in my drama into situations which force them to speak. If I merely show two people sitting together and drinking coffee while they talk about the weather, politics or the latest fashions, then I provide neither a dramatic situation nor dramatic dialogue, no matter how clever their talk. Some other ingredient must be added to their conversation, something to add pique, drama, double meaning. If the audience knows that there is some poison in one of the coffee cups, or perhaps even in both, so that the conversation is really one between two poisoners, then this little coffee-for-two idyll becomes through this artistic device a dramatic situation, out of which and on the basis of which dramatic dialogue can develop. Without the addition of some special tension or special condition, dramatic dialogue cannot develop.

Just as dialogue must develop out of a situation, so it must also lead into some situation, that is to say, of course, a new situation. Dramatic dialogue effects some action, some suffering, some new situation, out of which in turn new dialogue can again develop, and so on and so forth.

However, a human being does more than just talk. The fact that a man also thinks, or at least should think, that he feels, yes, more than anything feels, and that he does not always wish to show others what he is thinking or feeling, has led to the use of another artistic device, the monologue. It is true, of course, that a person standing on a stage and carrying on a conversation with himself out loud is not exactly natural; and the same thing can be said, only more so, of an operatic aria. But the monologue (like the aria) proves that an artistic trick, which really ought not to be played, can achieve an unexpected effect, to which, and rightly so, the public succumbs time and again; so much so that Hamlet's monologue, "To be or not to be," or Faust's, are among the most beloved and most famous passages in the theatre.

But not everything that sounds like a monologue is monologue. The purpose of dialogue is not only to lead a human being to a point where he must act or suffer; at times it also leads into a major speech, to the explanation of some point of view. Many people have lost the appreciation of rhetoric since, as Hilpert maintains, some actor who was not sure of his lines discovered naturalism. That loss is rather sad. A speech can win its way across the footlights more effectively than any other artistic device. But many of our critics no longer know what to make of a speech. An author who today dares a speech will suffer the same fate as the peasant Dicaeopolis; he will have to lay his head upon the executioner's block. Except that instead of the

Acharnians of Aristophanes, it will be the majority of critics who descend on the author—the most normal thing in the world. Nobody is more anxious to bash out someone's brains than those who haven't any.

Moreover, the drama has always embodied some narrative elements; epic drama did not introduce this. So, for instance, the background of an action has always had to be related, or an event announced in the form of a messenger's report. But narration on the stage is not without its dangers, for it does not live in the same manner, is not tangible the way an action taking place on the stage is. Attempts have been made to overcome this, as by dramatizing the messenger, by letting him appear at a crucial moment, or by making him a blockhead from whom a report can only be extracted with great difficulties. Yet certain elements of rhetoric must still be present if narration is to succeed on the stage. Stage narratives cannot exist without some exaggeration. Observe, for instance, how Shakespeare elaborates on Plutarch's description of Cleopatra's barge. This exaggeration is not just a characteristic of the baroque style, but a means of launching Cleopatra's barge upon the stage, of making it visible there. But while the speech of the theatre cannot exist without exaggeration, it is important to know when to exaggerate and above all, how.

Furthermore, just as stage characters can suffer a certain fate, so also can their language. The angel that came to Babylon, for example, grows more and more enthusiastic about the earth's beauty from act to act, and hence his language must parallel this rising enthusiasm until it grows into a veritable hymn. In the same comedy the beggar Akki relates his life in a series of *makamat,* passages of a rich and stately prose interspersed with rhymes, refined in grammar, rhetoric, poetic idiom and tradition, that come from the Arabic and flourished a thousand years ago. In this way I try to convey the Arabic character of this personage, his joy in inventing stories and in duelling and playing with words, without at the same time wandering off into another form, the chanson. The *makamat* or anecdotes of Akki are nothing less than the most extreme possibilities offered by his language, and therefore they intensify his being. Through the *makamat* Akki has become all language, and this is just what an author must always strive for, so that there are moments in his plays in which the characters he has created with the written word become living language and nothing less.

A danger lurks here, too, of course. Language can lead a writer astray. The joy of being able all of a sudden to write, of possessing language, as it came over me, for instance, while I was writing *The Blind Man,* can make an author talk too much, can make him escape from his subject into language. To keep close to the subject is itself a great art, achieved only by masterful control of the impetus to talk. Dialogue, like playing on words, can also lead an author into byways, take him unawares away from his subject. Yet ideas flash into his mind again and again, ideas which he ought not resist, even if they disrupt his carefully laid plans. For in addition to being on guard against some of these tempting flashes of ideas, a writer must also have the courage to follow some of them.

These elements and problems of place, time, and action, which are all, of course, interwoven and are but hinted at here, belong to the basic material, to the artistic devices and tools of the craft of the drama. But let me make it clear here and now that I make war upon the notion of "the craft of the drama." The very idea that anyone who makes a sufficiently diligent and steadfast endeavour to achieve something in that art will succeed in the end, or even that this craft can be learned, is a notion we thought discarded long ago. Yet it is still frequently met with in critical writings about the art of play-writing. This art is supposed to be a sound and solid, respectable and well-mannered affair. Thus, too, the relationship between a play-wright and his art is considered by some to be like a marriage in which everything is quite legal when blessed with the sacraments of aesthetics. For these reasons, perhaps, critics often refer to the theatre, much more than to any other form of art, as a craft which, depending on the particular case, has been more or less mastered. If we investigate closely what the critics really mean by "the craft of the drama," then it becomes obvious that it is little else but the sum of their prejudices. There is no craft of the theatre; there is only the mastery of the material through language and the stage or, to be more exact, it is an overpowering of the material, for any creative writing is a kind of warfare with its victories, defeats and indecisive battles. Perfect plays do not exist except as a fiction of aesthetics in which, as in the films, perfect heroes may alone be found. Never yet has a playwright left this battle without his wounds; each one has his Achilles' heel, and the playwright's antagonist, his material, never fights fairly. It is cunning stuff, often not to be drawn out of its lair, and it employs highly secret and low-down tricks. This forces the playwright to fight back with every permissible and even non-permissible means, no matter what the wise exhortations, rules and adages of the masters of this craft and their most honoured trade may say. Best foot forward won't get an author anywhere in the drama, not even his foot in the doorway. The difficulties in writing for the drama lie where no one suspects them; sometimes it is no more than the problem of how to have two people say hello, or the difficulty in writing an opening sentence. What is sometimes considered to be the craft of the drama can be easily learned in half an hour. But how difficult it is to divide a given material into five acts, and how few subjects there are which can be divided that way, how nearly impossible it is to write today in iambic pentameter, those things are hardly ever suspected by the hack writers who can slap a play together any time and without trouble, who can always divide any subject into five acts, and who have always written and still write with facility in iambic pentameter. They really pick their material and their language in the way some critics think this is done. They are not so much amateurs when they talk about art as when they tailor art to their talk. No matter what the material is like, they always fashion the same bath-robe to be sure the audience will not catch cold and that it will sleep comfortably. There is nothing more idiotic than the opinion that only a genius does not have to obey those rules prescribed for writers of talent. In that case I should like to be counted among the geniuses. What I want to emphasize strongly is that the art of writing a play does not necessarily start out with the planning of a certain child, or however else a eunuch thinks love is made; but it starts out with love-making, of which a eunuch is incapable. Though really the difficulties, pains and also fortunes of writing do not lie within the realm of things we mean to talk about or even can talk about. We can only talk about the craft of the drama, a craft that exists only when one *talks* of drama, but not when one writes plays. The craft of the drama is an optical illusion. To talk about plays, about art, is a much more utopian undertaking than is ever appreciated by those who talk the most.

Employing this — really non-existent — craft, let us try and give shape to a certain material. Usually there is a central point of reference, the hero. In theories of the drama a difference is made between a tragic hero, the hero of tragedy, and a comic hero, the hero of comedy. The qualities a tragic hero must possess are well known. He must be capable of rousing our sympathy. His guilt and his innocence, his virtues and his vices must be mixed in the most pleasant and yet exact manner, and administered in doses according to well-defined rules. If, for example, I make my tragic hero an evil man, then I must endow him with a portion of intellect equal to his malevolence. As a result of this rule, the most sympathetic stage character in German literature has turned out to be the devil. The role of the hero in the play has not changed. The only thing that has changed is the social position of the character who awakens our sympathy.

In ancient tragedy and in Shakespeare the hero belongs to the highest class in society, to the nobility. The spectators watch a suffering, acting, raving hero who occupies a social position far higher than their own. This still continues to impress audiences today.

Then when Lessing and Schiller introduced the bourgeois drama, the audience saw itself as the suffering hero on the stage. But the evolution of the hero continued. Büchner's Wozzeck is a primitive proletarian who represents far less socially than the average spectator. But it is precisely in this extreme form of human existence, in this last, most miserable form, that the audience is to see the human being also, indeed itself.

And finally we might mention Pirandello who was the first, as far as I know, to render the hero, the character on the stage, immaterial and transparent just as Wilder did the dramatic place. The audience watching this sort of presentation attends, as it were, its own dissection, its own psycho-analysis, and the stage becomes man's internal milieu, the inner space of the world.

Of course, the theatre has never dealt only with kings and generals; in comedy the hero has always been the peasant, the beggar, the ordinary citizen — but this was always in comedy. Nowhere in Shakespeare do we find a comic king; in his day a ruler could appear as a bloody monster but never as a fool. In Shakespeare the courtiers, the artisans, the working people are comic. Hence, in the evolution of the tragic hero we see a trend towards comedy. Analogously the fool becomes more and more of a tragic figure. This fact is by no means without significance. The hero of a play not only propels an action on, he not only suffers a certain fate, but he also represents a world. Therefore we have to ask ourselves how we should present our own questionable world and with what sort of heroes. We have to ask ourselves how the mirrors which catch and reflect this world should be ground and set.

Can our present-day world, to ask a concrete question, be represented by Schiller's dramatic art? Some writers claim it can be, since Schiller still holds audiences in his grip. To be sure, in art everything is possible when the art is right. But the question is if an art valid for its time could possibly be so even for our day. Art can never be repeated. If it were repeatable, it would be foolish not just to write according to the rules of Schiller.

Schiller wrote as he did because the world in which he lived could still be mirrored in the world his writing created, a world he could build as an historian. But just barely. For was not Napoleon perhaps the last hero in the old sense? The world today as it appears to us could hardly be encompassed in the form of the historical drama as Schiller wrote it, for the reason alone that we no longer have any tragic heroes, but only vast tragedies staged by world butchers and produced by slaughtering machines. Hitler and Stalin cannot be made into Wallensteins. Their power was so enormous that they themselves were no more than incidental, corporeal and easily replaceable expressions of this power; and the misfortune associated with the former and to a considerable extent also with the latter is too vast, too complex, too horrible, too mechanical and usually simply too devoid of all sense. Wallenstein's power can still be envisioned; power as we know it today can only be seen in its smallest part for, like an iceberg, the largest part is submerged in anonymity and abstraction. Schiller's drama presupposes a world that the eye can take in, that takes for granted genuine actions of state, just as Greek tragedy did. For only what the eye can take in can be made visible in art. The state today, however, cannot be envisioned, for it is anonymous and bureaucratic; and not only in Moscow and Washington, but also in Berne. Actions of state today have become *post-hoc* satyric dramas which follow the tragedies executed in secret earlier. True representatives of our world are missing; the tragic heroes are nameless. Any small-time crook, petty government official or policeman better represents our world than a senator or president. Today art can only embrace the victims, if it can reach men at all; it can no longer come close to the mighty. Creon's secretaries close Antigone's case. The state has lost its physical reality, and just as physics can now only cope with the world in mathematical formulae, so the state can only be expressed in statistics. Power today becomes visible, material only when it explodes as in the atom bomb, in this marvelous mushroom which rises and spreads immaculate as the sun and in which mass murder and beauty have become one. The atom bomb cannot be reproduced artistically since it is mass-produced. In its face all man's art that would recreate it must fail, since it is itself a creation of man. Two mirrors which reflect one another remain empty.

But the task of art, in so far as art can have a task at all, and hence also the task of drama today, is to create something concrete, something that has form. This can be accomplished best by comedy. Tragedy, the strictest genre in art, presupposes a formed world. Comedy—in so far as it is not just satire of a particular society as in Molière—supposes an unformed world, a world being made and turned upside down, a world about to fold like ours. Tragedy overcomes distance; it can make myths originating in times imme-morial seem like the present to the Athenians. But comedy creates distance; the attempt of the Athenians to gain a foothold in Sicily is translated by comedy into the birds undertaking to create their own empire before which the gods and men will have to capitulate. How comedy works can be seen in the most primitive kind of joke, in the dirty story, which, though it is of very dubious value, I bring up only because it is the best illustration of what I mean by creating distance. The subject of the dirty story is the purely sexual, which because it is purely sexual, is formless and without objective distance. To give form the purely sexual is transmuted, as I have already mentioned, into the dirty joke. Therefore this type of joke is a kind of original comedy, a transposition of the sexual on to the plain of the comical. In this way it is possible today, in a society dominated by John Doe, to talk in an accepted way about the purely sexual. In the dirty story it becomes clear that the comical exists in forming what is formless, in creating order out of chaos.

The means by which comedy creates distance is the conceit. Tragedy is without conceit. Hence there are few tragedies whose subjects were invented. By this I do not mean to imply that the ancient tragedians lacked inventive ideas of the sort that are written today, but the marvel of their art was that they had no need of these inventions, of conceits. That makes all the difference. Aristophanes, on the other hand, lives by conceits. The stuff of his plays are not myths but inventions, which take place not in the past but the present. They drop into their world like bomb-shells which, by throwing up huge craters of dirt, change the present into the comic and thus scatter the dirt for everyone to see. This, of course, does not mean that drama today can only be comical. Tragedy and comedy are but formal concepts, dramatic attitudes, figments of the aesthetic imagination which can embrace one and the same thing. Only the conditions under which each is created are different, and these conditions have their basis only in small part in art.

Tragedy presupposes guilt, despair, moderation, lucidity, vision, a sense of responsibility. In the Punch-and-Judy show of our century, in this back-sliding of the white race, there are no more guilty and also, no responsible men. It is always, "We couldn't help it" and "We didn't really want that to happen." And indeed, things happen without anyone in particular being responsible for them. Everything is dragged along and everyone gets caught somewhere in the sweep of events. We are all collectively guilty, collectively bogged down in the sins of our fathers and of our forefathers. We are the offspring of children. That is our misfortune, but not our guilt: guilt can exist only as a personal achievement, as a religious deed. Comedy alone is suitable for us. Our world has led to the grotesque as well as to the atom bomb, and so it is a world like that of Hieronymus Bosch whose apocalypic paintings are also grotesque. But the grotesque is only a way of expressing in a tangible manner, of making us perceive physically the paradoxical, the form of the unformed, the face of a world without face; and just as in our thinking today we seem to be unable to do without the concept of the paradox, so also in art, and in our world which at times seems still to exist only because the atom bomb exists: out of fear of the bomb.

But the tragic is still possible even if pure tragedy is not. We can achieve the tragic out of comedy. We can bring it forth as a frightening moment, as an abyss that opens suddenly; indeed, many of Shakespeare's tragedies are already really comedies out of which the tragic arises.

After all this the conclusion might easily be drawn that comedy is the expression of despair, but this conclusion is not inevitable. To be sure, whoever realizes the senselessness, the hopelessness of this world might well despair, but this despair is not a result of this world. Rather it is an answer given by an individual to this world; another answer would be not to despair, would be an individual's decision to endure this world in which we live like Gulliver among the giants. He also achieves distance, he also steps back a pace or two who takes measure of his opponent, who prepares himself to fight his opponent or to escape him. It is still possible to show man as a courageous being.

In truth this is a principal concern of mine. The blind man,

Romulus, Übelohe, Akki, are all men of courage. The lost world-order is restored within them; the universal escapes my grasp. I refuse to find the universal in a doctrine. The universal for me is chaos. The world (hence the stage which represents this world) is for me something monstrous, a riddle of misfortunes which must be accepted but before which one must not capitulate. The world is far bigger than any man, and perforce threatens him constantly. If one could but stand outside the world, it would no longer be threatening. But I have neither the right nor the ability to be an outsider to this world. To find solace in poetry can also be all too cheap; it is more honest to retain one's human point of view. Brecht's thesis, that the world is an accident, which he developed in his *Street Scene* where he shows how this accident happened, may yield — as it in fact did — some magnificent theatre; but he did it by concealing most of the evidence! Brecht's thinking is inexorable, because inexorably there are many things he will not think about.

And lastly it is through the conceit, through comedy, that the anonymous audience becomes possible as an audience, becomes a reality to be counted on, and also one to be taken into account. The conceit easily transforms the crowd of theatre-goers into a mass which can be attacked, deceived, outsmarted into listening to things it would otherwise not so readily listen to. Comedy is a mouse-trap in which the public is easily caught and in which it will get caught over and over again. Tragedy, on the other hand, predicated a true community, a kind of community whose existence in our day is but an embarrassing fiction. Nothing is more ludicrous, for instance, than to sit and watch the mystery plays of the Anthroposophists when one is not a participant.

Granting all this, there is still one more question to be asked: is it permissible to go from a generality to a particular form of art, to do what I just did when I went from my assertion that the world was formless to the particular possibility for writing comedies today. I doubt that this is permissible. Art is something personal, and something personal should never be explained with generalities. The value of a work of art does not depend on whether more or less good reasons for its existence can be found. Hence I have also tried to avoid certain problems, as for example the argument which is quite lively today, whether or not plays ought to be written in verse or in prose. My own answer lies simply in writing prose, without any intention of thereby deciding the issue. A man has to choose to go one way, after all, and why should one way always be worse than another? As far as my concepts of comedy are concerned, I believe that here, too, personal reasons are more important than more general ones that are always open to argument. What logic in matters of art could not be refuted! One talks best about art when one talks of one's own art. The art one chooses is an expression of freedom without which no art can exist, and at the same time also of necessity without which art cannot exist either. The artist always represents his world and himself. If at one time philosophy taught men to arrive at the particular from the general, then — unlike Schiller, who started out believing in general conclusions — I cannot construct a play as he did when I doubt that the particular can ever be reached from the general. But my doubt is mine and only mine, and not the doubt and problems of a Catholic for whom drama holds possibilities non-Catholics do not share. This is so even if, on the other hand, a Catholic who takes his religion seriously, is denied those possibilities which other men possess. The danger inherent in this thesis lies in the fact that there are always those artists who for the sake of finding some generalities to believe in accept conversion, taking a step which is the more to be wondered at for the sad fact that it really will not help them. The difficulties experienced by a Protestant in writing a drama are just the same difficulties he has with his faith. Thus it is my way to mistrust what is ordinarily called the building of the drama, and to arrive at my plays from the unique, the sudden idea or conceit, rather than from some general concept or plan. Speaking for myself, I need to write off into the blue, as I like to put it so that I might give critics a catchword to hang on to. They use it often enough, too, without really understanding what I mean by it.

But these matters are my own concerns and hence it is not necessary to invoke the whole world and to make out that what are my concerns are the concerns of art in general (lest I be like the drunk who goes back to Noah, the Flood, original sin and the beginning of the world to explain what is, after all, only his own weakness). As in everything and everywhere, and not just in the field of art, the rule is: No excuses, please!

Nevertheless the fact remains (always keeping in mind, of course, the reservations just made) that we now stand in a different relationship to what we have called our material. Our unformed, amorphous present is characterized by being surrounded by figures and forms that reduce our time to a mere result, even less, to a mere transitional state, and which give excessive weight to the past as something finished and to the future as something possible. This applies equally well to politics. Related to art it means that the artist is surrounded by all sort of opinions about art and by demands on him which are based not upon his capacities, but upon the historical past and present forms. He is surrounded therefore by materials which are no longer materials, that is possibilities, but by materials which have already taken on shape, that is some definitive form. Caesar is no longer pure subject matter for us; he has become the Caesar whom scholarship made the object of its researches. And so it happened that scholars, having thrown themselves with increasing energy not only upon nature but also upon intellectual life and upon art, establishing in the process intellectual history, literary scholarship, philology and goodness knows what else, have created a body of factual information which cannot be ignored (for one cannot be conscious of these facts and at the same time pretend to be so naïve that one need pay no attention to the results of scholarship). In this way, however, scholars have deprived the artist of materials by doing what was really the artist's task. The mastery of Richard Feller's *History of Berne* precludes the possibility of an historical drama about the city of Berne; the history of Berne was thus given shape before some literary artist could do it. True, it is a scholastic form (and not a mythical one which would leave the way open for a tragedian), a form that severely limits the field for the artist, leaving to art only psychology which, of course, has also become a science. To rewrite such a history in a creative literary manner would now be a tautology, a repetition by means which are not suitable or fitting, a mere illustration of scholarly insight; in short, it would be the very thing science often claims literature to be. It was still possible for Shakespeare to base his Caesar upon Plutarch, for the Roman was not an historian in our sense of the word but a story-teller, the author of biographical sketches. Had Shakespeare read Mommsen he could not have written his Caesar because he would of necessity have lost the supremacy over his materials. And this holds true now in all things, even the myths of the Greeks which, since we no longer live them but only study, evaluate, investigate them, recognizing them to be mere myths and as such destroying them, have become mummies; and these, bound tightly round with philosophy and theology, are all too often substituted for the living thing.

Therefore the artist must reduce the subjects he finds and runs into everywhere if he wants to turn them once more into real materials, hoping always that he will succeed. He parodies his materials, contrasts them consciously with what they have actually been turned into. By this means, by this act of parody, the artist regains his freedom and hence his material; and thus material is no longer found but invented. For every parody presupposes a conceit and an invention. In laughter man's freedom becomes manifest, in crying his necessity. Our task today is to demonstrate freedom. The tyrants of this planet are not moved by the works of the poets. They yawn at a poet's threnodies. For them heroic epics are silly fairy-tales and religious poetry puts them to sleep. Tyrants fear only one thing: a poet's mockery. For this reason, then, parody has crept into all literary genres, into the novel, the drama, into lyrical poetry. Much of painting, even of music, has been conquered by parody, and the grotesque has followed, often well camouflaged, on the heels of parody: all of a sudden the grotesque is there.

But our times, up to every imaginable trick there is, can handle all that and nothing can intimidate it: the public has been educated to see in art something solemn, hallowed and even pathetic. The comic is considered inferior, dubious, unseemly; it is accepted only when it makes people feel as bestially happy as a bunch of pigs. But the very moment people recognize the comic to be dangerous, an art that exposes, demands, moralizes, it is dropped like a hot potato, for art may be everything it wants to be so long as it remains *gemütlich*.

We writers are often accused of art that is nihilistic. Today, of course, there exists a nihilistic art, but not every art that seems nihilistic is so. True nihilistic art does not appear to be nihilistic at all; usually it is considered to be especially humane and supremely worthy of being read by our more mature young people. A man must be a pretty bungling sort of nihilist to be recognized as such by the world at large. People call nihilistic what is merely uncomfortable. Then also people say, the artist is supposed to create, not to talk; to give shape to things, not to preach. To be sure. But it becomes more and more difficult to create "purely" or however people imagine the creative mind should work. Mankind today is like a reckless driver racing ever faster, ever more heedlessly along the highway. And he does not like it when the frightened passengers cry out, "Watch out" and "There's a warning sign! Slow down," or "Don't kill that child!"

What is more, the driver hates it even worse when he is asked, "Who is paying for the car?" or "Who's providing the petrol and oil for this mad journey?," to say nothing of what happens when he is asked for his driver's licence. What unpleasant facts might then come to light! Maybe the car was stolen from some relatives, the petrol and oil squeezed from the passengers, and really not petrol and oil but the blood and sweat of us all; and most likely he wouldn't even have a driver's licence and it would turn out that this was his first time driving. Of course, it would be embarrassing if such personal questions were to be asked. The driver would much prefer the passengers to praise the beauty of the countryside through which they are travelling, the silver of the river and the brilliant reflection of the ice-capped mountains in the far distance, would even prefer to have amusing stories whispered into his ear. Today's author, however, can no longer confine himself with good conscience to whispering pleasant stories and praising the beautiful landscape. Unfortunately, too, he cannot get out of this mad race in order to sit by the wayside, writing the pure poetry demanded of him by all the non-poets. Fear, worry, and above all anger open his mouth wide.

How very nice it would be if we could end now on this emphatic note. It would be a conclusion that could be considered at least partially safe and not wholly impossible. But in all honesty we must ask ourselves at this point if any of this makes sense today, if it were not better if we practised silence. I have tried to show that the theatre today is, in the best sense of the word to be sure, in part a museum, and in part a field of experimentation. I have also tried to show here and there what these experiments are. Is the theatre capable of fulfilling this, its latter destiny? Not only has the writing of plays become more difficult today but also the rehearsing and performing of these plays is harder. The very lack of time results at best in only a decent attempt, a first probing, a slight advance in what might be the right direction. A play that is to be more than a merely conventional piece, that is really to be an experiment, can no longer be solved at the writing desk. Giraudoux's fortune was that he had Jouvet. Unhappily this happens only once or twice. The repertory theatre of Germany can afford less and less to experiment. A new play must be got rid of as quickly as possible. The museum's treasures weigh too heavily in the scales. The theatre, our whole culture, lives on the interest of the well invested intellect, to which nothing can happen any more and for which not even royalties have to be paid. Assured of having a Goethe, Schiller or Sophocles at hand, the theatres are willing now and then to put on a modern piece — but preferably only for a premiere performance. Heroically this duty is discharged, and sighs of relief are breathed all round when Shakespeare is performed next time. What can we say or do? Clear the stages completely! Make room for the classics! The world of the museum is growing and bursts with its treasures. The cultures of the cave-dwellers have not yet been investigated to the nth degree. Let the custodians of the future concern themselves with our art when it is our turn. It does not make much difference then if something new is added, something new is written. The demands made of the artist by aesthetics increase from day to day. What is wanted is the perfection which is read into the classics. And let the artist even be suspected of having taken one step backwards, of having made a mistake, just watch how quickly he is dropped. Thus a climate is created in which literature can be studied but not made. How can the artist exist in a world of educated and literate people? This question oppresses me, and I know no answer. Perhaps the writer can best exist by writing detective stories, by creating art where it is least suspected. Literature must become so light that it will weigh nothing upon the scale of today's literary criticism: only in this way will it regain its true worth.

Susanne Langer

These observations on the aesthetic nature of the phenomenon of drama are taken from Mrs. Langer's longer study, *Feeling and Form* (1953). In the remarks reprinted here, she utilizes several disciplines in formulating an articulate and sensible description of the ways in which dramatic experience differs from other "artistic" experiences and endeavors, as well as of the ways in which it stands unique among the various arts of creating poetry. Of particular importance are her descriptions of the "organic" nature of a play and the ways in which an audience participates in its power of illusion.

Susanne Langer has taught various areas of Philosophy at Radcliffe College, Columbia, the University of Michigan, and at many other colleges and universities in this country; she is presently Professor Emeritus at Connecticut College. Her work has frequently been concerned with the philosophy of art, and, in her investigations represented below, she has gone far to bring the efforts of the interpretive, practicing artist and the theoretical aesthetician into a productive relationship.

✍ *from* THE DRAMATIC ILLUSION

Most theoretical treatments of literature draw their material and evidence as much from drama as from lyric and narrative works. A serious analysis of literary art with only an occasional, passing mention of Shakespeare may have seemed to many readers a curious innovation. The reason for it, however, is simple enough, and has been suggested above: Shakespeare is essentially a dramatist, and drama is not, in the strict sense, "literature."

Yet it is a poetic art, because it creates the primary illusion of all poetry — virtual history. Its substance is an image of human life — ends, means, gains and losses, fulfillment and decline and death. It is a fabric of illusory experience, and that is the essential product of poesis. But drama is not merely a distinct literary form; it is a special poetic mode, as different from genuine literature as sculpture from pictorial art, or either of these from architecture. That is to say, it makes its own basic abstraction, which gives it a way of its own in making the semblance of history.

Literature projects the image of life in the mode of virtual memory; language is its essential material; the sound and meaning of words, their familiar or unusual use and order, even their presentation on the printed page, create the illusion of life as a realm of events — completed, lived, as words formulate them — events that compose a Past. But drama presents the poetic illusion in a different light: not finished realities, or "events," but immediate, visible responses of human beints, make its semblance of life. Its basic abstraction is the act, which springs from the past, but is directed toward the future, and is always great with things to come.

In using common words, such as "event" or "act," as analytic terms, one runs the danger of suggesting far less general concepts, and indeed a variety of them, all equally inadequate to the purpose in hand. "Event," in the foregoing chapters, was used in the sense given it by Whitehead, to cover all space-time occurrence, even the persistence of objects, the repetitious rhythms of life, the occasion of a thought as well as of an earthquake. Similarly, by "act" I mean any sort of human response, physical or mental. The word is commonly used, of course, in more specialized senses. It may mean one of the major divisions of a play — Act I, Act II, etc.; or it may refer to overt behavior, rushing about, laying hands on someone, taking or surrendering an object, and so forth; or it may mean a piece of dissembling, as when one says of a person that he feels one way and acts another. In the general sense here employed, however, all *reactions* are acts, visible or invisible; so in drama, any illusion of physical or mental activity is here called an "act," and the total structure of acts is *a virtual history in the mode of dramatic action*.

An act, whether instinctive or deliberate, is normally oriented toward the future. Drama, though it implies past actions (the "situation"), moves not toward the present, as narrative does, but toward something beyond; it deals essentially with commitments and consequences. Persons, too, in drama are purely agents — whether consciously or blindly, makers of the future. This future, which is made before our eyes, gives importance to the very beginnings of dramatic acts, i.e. to the motives from which the acts arise, and the situations in which they develop; the making of it is the principle that unifies and organizes the continuum of stage action. It has been said repeatedly that the theater creates a perpetual present moment[1]; but it is only a present filled with its own future that is really dramatic. A sheer immediacy, an imperishable direct experience without the ominous forward movement of consequential action, would not be so. As literature creates a virtual past, drama creates a virtual future. The literary mode is the mode of Memory; the dramatic is the mode of Destiny.

The future, like the past, is a conceptual structure, and expectation, even more obviously than memory, is a product of imagination. The "now" created by poetic composition is always under the aegis of some historical vision which transcends it; and its poignancy derives not from any comparison with actuality, but from the fact that the two great realms of envisagement — past and future — intersect in the present, which consequently has not the pure imaginative

---

[1] For example, R. E. Jones in *The Dramatic Imagination*, p. 40, says: "This is drama; this is theatre — *to be aware of the Now.*" And Thornton Wilder, in "Some Thoughts on Playwriting," lists as one of the "four fundamental conditions of the drama" that "its action takes place in a perpetual present time." — "On the stage it is always now." (*The Intent of the Artist*, p. 83.) [Notes throughout are by the author]

form of either memory or prophecy, but a peculiar appearance of its own which we designate as "immediacy" or "now."

In actual life the impending future is very vaguely felt. Each separate act is forward-looking — we put on a kettle expecting it to boil, hand someone a bill and expect to be given change, board a bus with casual confidence that we shall leave it again at an intended point, or board an airplane with somewhat more conscious interest in our prospective exit from its inside. But we do not usually have any idea of the future as a total experience which is coming because of our past and present acts; such a sense of destiny arises only in unusual moments under peculiar emotional stress.

In drama, however, this sense of destiny is paramount. It is what makes the present action seem like an integral part of the future, howbeit that future has not unfolded yet. The reason is that on the stage, every thought expressed in conversation, every feeling betrayed by voice or look, is determined by the total action of which it is a part — perhaps an embryonic part, the first hint of the motive that will soon gather force. Even before one has any idea of what the conflict is to be (i.e. before the "exposition" has been given), one feels the tension developing. This tension between past and future, the theatrical "present moment," is what gives to acts, situations, and even such constituent elements as gestures and attitudes and tones, the peculiar intensity known as "dramatic quality."

In a little-known volume, bearing the modest, impersonal title: *Essays by Divers Hands* (a volume of "Transactions" of the Royal Society of Literature in England),[2] there is a very thoughtful philosophical essay by Charles Morgan, called "The Nature of Dramatic Illusion," in which he seems to me to have both stated and answered the question of what is created in the full-fledged work of dramatic art — the enacted play.

"With every development of dramatic technique," he wrote there, "and every departure from classical structure, the need increases for a new discussion which. . . shall establish for the stage not indeed a formal rule but an aesthetic discipline, elastic, reasoned, and acceptable to it in modern circumstances.

"It is my purpose, then, to discover the principle from which such a discipline might arise. This principle I call the principle of illusion."[3]

---

[2] N. S. Vol. 12, ed. by R. W. Macan, 1933. The article in question covers pp. 61-77.
[3] *Ibid.,* p. 61.

"Illusion, as I conceive it, is form in suspense... In a play form is not valuable *in itself;* only the suspense of form has value. In a play, form is not and cannot be valuable in itself, because until the play is over form does not exist....

"A play's performance occupies two or three hours. Until the end its form is latent in it....

"This suspense of form, by which is meant the incompleteness of a known completion, is to be clearly distinguished from common suspense — suspense of plot — the ignorance of what will happen, ... for suspense of plot is a structural accident, and suspense of form is, as I understand it, essential to the dramatic form itself...

"What form is chosen ... matters less than that while the drama moves *a* form is being fulfilled."[4]

"Fulfilled" is here the key word to the idea of dramatic form. Everything, of course, has a form of some sort: the famous million monkeys playing a million typewriters for a million years, turning out chance combinations of letters, would be rendering countless phonetic forms (though some of these might not encourage pronunciation); similarly, the most aimless conglomerate of events, acts, utterances, or what not, would *produce* a form when taken together; but before such collections were complete (which would be simply when, for any reason, one stopped collecting), no one could imagine their form. There has to be a sense of the whole, some anticipation of what may or even must come, if the production of new elements is to give the impression that "a form is being fulfilled."

Dramatic action is a semblance of action so constructed that a whole, indivisible piece of virtual history is implicit in it, as a yet unrealized form, long before the presentation is completed. This constant illusion of an imminent future, this vivid appearance of a growing situation before anything startling has occurred, is "form in suspense." It is a human destiny that unfolds before us, its unity is apparent from the opening words or even silent action, because on the stage we see acts in their entirety, as we do not see them in the real world except in retrospect, that is, by constructive reflection. In the theatre they occur in simplified and completed form, with visible motives, directions, and ends. Since stage action is not, like genuine action, embedded in a welter of irrelevant doings and divided interests, and characters on the stage have no unknown complexities

[4] *Ibid.*, pp. 70-72.

(however complex they may be), it is possible there to see a person's feelings grow into passions, and those passions issue in words and deeds.

We know, in fact, so little about the personalities before us at the opening of a play that their every move and word, even their dress and walk, are distinct items for our perception. Because we are not involved with them as with real people, we can view each smallest act in its context, as a symptom of character and condition. We do not have to find what is significant; the selection has been made — whatever is there is significant, and it is not too much to be surveyed *in toto*. A character stands before us as a coherent whole. It is with characters as with their situations: both become visible on the stage, transparent and complete, as their analogues in the world are not.[5]

But what really assures the artistic unity Morgan called "form in suspense," is the illusion of Destiny itself that is given in drama, and that arises chiefly from the way the dramatist handles circumstance. Before a play has progressed by many lines, one is aware not only of vague conditions of life in general, but of a special situation. Like the distribution of figures on a chessboard, the combination of characters makes a strategic pattern. In actual life we usually recognize a distinct situation only when it has reached, or nearly reached, a crisis; but in the theater we see the whole setup of human relationships and conflicting interests long before any abnormal event has occurred that would, in actual life, have brought it into focus. Where in the real world we would witness some extraordinary act and gradually understand the circumstances that lie behind it, in the theater we perceive an ominous situation and see that some far-reaching action must grow out of it. This creates the peculiar tension between the given present and its yet unrealized consequent, "form in suspense," the essential dramatic illusion. This illusion of a visible future is created in every play — not only in very good plays, but in everything we recognize as a play, and not as dance, pageantry, or

---

[5] A German critic, Peter Richard Rohden, saw this difference in our understanding of illusory and actual persons, respectively, as something of a paradox. "What," he wrote, "distinguishes a character on stage from a 'real' person? Obviously the fact that the former stands before us as a fully articulated whole. Our fellowmen we always perceive only in fragmentary fashion, and our power of self-observation is usually reduced, by vanity and cupidity, to zero. What we call 'dramatic illusion' is, therefore, the paradoxical phenomenon that we know more about the mental processes of a Hamlet than about our own inner life. For the poet-actor Shakespeare shows not only the deed, but also its motives, and indeed more perfectly than we ever see them together in actual life." (See "Das Schauspielerische Erlebnis," in Ewald Geissler's collection of essays, *Der Schauspieler* p. 36.)

other non-dramatic "theater art."[6] It is the primary illusion of poetry, or virtual history, in the mode peculiar to drama. The future appears as already an entity, embryonic in the present. That is Destiny.

Destiny is, of course, always a virtual phenomenon — there is no such thing in cold fact. It is a pure semblance. But what it "resembles" (or, in the Aristotelian language which has lately been revived, what it "imitates") is nonetheless an aspect of real experience, and, indeed, a fundamental one, which distinguishes human life from animal existence: the sense of past and future as parts of one continuum, and therefore of life as a single reality.

This wide awareness, which we owe to our peculiarly human talent of symbolic expression, is rooted, however, in the elementary rhythms which we share with all other organisms, and the Destiny which dramatic art creates bears the stamp of organic process — of predeterminate function, tendency, growth, and completion. The abstraction of those vital forms by means of art has already been considered in Chapter 4, with reference to primitive design. In every art it is differently achieved; but in each one, I think, it is equally subtle — not a simple reference to natural instances of that form, but a genuinely abstractive handling of its reflection in non-living or even non-physical structures. Literally, "organic process" is a biological concept; "life," "growth," "development," "decline," "death" — all these are strictly biological terms. They are applicable only to organisms. In art they are lifted out of their literal context, and forthwith, in place of organic processes, we have dynamic forms: instead of metabolism, rhythmic progression, instead of stimulus and response, completeness, instead of maturation, fulfillment, instead of procreation, the repetition of the whole in the parts — what Henry James calls "reflection" in the parts,[7] and Heinrich Schenker "diminution,"[8] and Francis Fergusson "analogy."[9] And in lieu of a law of development, such as biology sets up, in art we have destiny, the implicit future.

The purpose of abstracting vital forms from their natural exem-

---

[6] On this point Mr. Morgan might not agree with me. Having stated that "form in suspense" is the dramatic illusion itself, and the suspense of form something "without which drama is not," he speaks elsewhere of the dramatic illusion as a rare experience, "the highest reward of play-going." I do not know whether he uses two concepts or only one, somewhat different from mine.

[7] *The Art of Fiction*, p. 170.

[8] Cf. Chap. 8, p. 129.

[9] *The Idea of a Theater*, p. 104.

plifications is, of course, to make them available for unhampered artistic use. The illusion of growth, for instance, may be made in any medium, and in numberless ways: lengthening or flowing lines, that represent no live creatures at all; rhythmically rising steps even though they divide or diminish; increasing complexity of musical cords, or insistent repetitions; a centrifugal dance; poetic lines of gradually deepening seriousness; there is no need of "imitating" anything literally alive in order to convey the appearance of life. Vital forms may be reflected in any elements of a work, with or without representation of living things.

In drama the *situation* has its own "organic" character, that is to say, it develops, or grows, as the play proceeds. That is because all happenings, to be dramatic, must be conceived in terms of acts, and acts belong only to life; they have motives rather than causes, and in turn motivate further and further acts, which compose integrated *actions*. A situation is a complex of impending acts. It changes from moment to moment, or rather, from move to move, as the directly imminent acts are realized and the future beyond them becomes distinct and fraught with excitement. In this way, the *situation* in which characters act differs from their "environment"—a term with which it is sometimes confused, through the influence of the social sciences that invaded the theater a generation ago and bred a teeming, if shortlived progeny of sociological plays, with a few real dramas among them. The environment wherein characters have developed, and whereby they are stunted or hardened, refined or falsely veneered, is almost always implicit (*almost* always, i.e. except where it becomes a conscious factor of interest to someone in the play). The situation, on the other hand, is always explicit. Even in á vague romantic world like that of Pelléas and Mélisande, removed from all actual history, and so ungeographical that the environment is really just castle walls and a forest, without population (the chorus of women in the death-scene simply springs up *ex nihilo*—there were no inhabitants in the background before, as there are in Shakespeare's castles), the situation that elicits the action is clear.

The situation is, indeed, part of the action; it is conceived entirely by the dramatist, and is given by him to the actors to understand and enact, just as he gives them the words to be spoken. The situation is a created element in the play; it grows to its climax, often branching out into elaborate detail in the course of its development, and in the end it is resolved by the closing of the action. . . .

Drama is more variable, more tolerant of choices made by performing artists, than any other art and mode. For this reason, the "commanding form," which is established by the playwright, must be clear and powerful. It has to govern the crisscross of many imaginative minds, and hold them all—the director, the actors, the designers of sets and lights and costumes—to one essential conception, an unmistakable "poetic core." But the poet must give his interpreters scope, too; for drama is essentially an enacted poem, and if the acting can only duplicate what the lines already effect, there will be unintended redundancy, and an apparent clutter of superfluous elements that makes the total form impure and opaque (such failures of clear conception, not the use of materials "belonging" to other arts, nor bold secondary illusions, are the source of impurity in a work; if the commanding form is organic and its realization economical, the most abnormal materials will be assimilated, the most intense effects of abstracted space, time, or power will become part of the pure dramatic work).

If drama is not made of words as a piece of literature is, how can the poet, who composes only the "lines;" be said to create the commanding form? "Lines" in a play are only the stuff of speeches; and speeches are only some of the acts that make drama.

They are, however, acts of a special sort. Speech is a highly specialized activity in human life, and its image in all modes of poetry, therefore, has peculiar and powerful uses. Verbal utterance is the overt issue of a greater emotional, mental, and bodily response, and its preparation in feeling and awareness or in the mounting intensity of thought is implicit in the words spoken. Speech is like a quintessence of action. Edith Wharton described its relation to the rest of our activities very aptly, when she indicated its use in her own poetic medium, prose fiction: "The use of dialogue in fiction . . . should be reserved for the culminating moments, and regarded as the spray into which the great wave of narrative breaks in curving toward the watcher on the shore."[10]

Mrs. Wharton's metaphor of the wave is more apt than her literal statement, because one naturally thinks of "culminating moments" as rare moments, high points of the story, whereas the culmination of thought and feeling in speech is a frequent occurrence, like the culmination and breaking of each wave in a constant surf.

[10] *The Writing of Fiction,* p. 73.

If, moreover, one contemplates the metaphor a little more deeply, it conveys a further relation of speech to the poetic elements that surround it, namely: that it is always of the same nature as they, subject to the basic abstraction of the mode in which it is used. In narrative it is an event, like all the events that compose the virtual Past—the private events that culminate in "direct discourse," the public events that intersect in the speaker's experience, and those which the speech, as a new event, engenders. In drama speech is an act, an utterance, motivated by visible and invisible other acts, and like them shaping the oncoming Future.

A playwright who writes only the lines uttered in a play marks a long series of culminating moments in the flow of the action. Of course he indicates the major non-verbal acts, but that may be done with the fewest possible words: *enter So-and-so, exit So-and-so,* or such laconic directions as: *dies, they fight, excursions and alarums.* Modern playwrights sometimes write pages of instructions to the actors, even describing the heroine's figure and face, or the style of some character's motions and postures (Strindberg tells the leading actor in *Miss Julia* to look like a half-educated man!). Such "stage directions" are really literary treatments of the story—what Clayton Hamilton called, "the sort of stage-directions which, though interesting to the reader, are of no avail whatever to the actor,"[11] because they do not partake of the dramatic form. Ibsen prefaced his opening scenes with minute descriptions of persons and set; but his greatest interpreters have always made free with them. The lines of the play are the only guide a good director or actor needs. What makes the play the author's work is that the lines are really the highlights of a perpetual, progressive action, and determine what can be done with the piece on stage.

Since every utterance is the end of a process which began inside the speaker's body, an enacted utterance is part of a virtual act, apparently springing at the moment from thought and feeling; so the actor has to create the illusion of an inward activity issuing in spontaneous speech, if his words are to make a dramatic and not a rhetorical effect. As a very interesting German writer, Ferdinand Gregori, expressed it, "Gesture is older than words, and in the actor's dramatic creation, too, it must be their herald. Whether it is visible to

---

[11] *The Theory of the Theatre,* p. 307. A few paragraphs later he remarked on Granville-Barker's plays: "Barker's printed stage-directions are little novels in themselves."

the audience or not, it must always be the pacemaker. Anyone who starts with the words and then hunts for the appropriate gesture to accompany them, lies to the face of art and nature both."[12]

The need of preparing every utterance by some elements of expression and bearing that foreshadow it, has led many theorists and almost all naive spectators to the belief that an actor must actually undergo the emotive experiences he renders—that he must "live" his part, and produce speech and gesture from a genuine passion. Of course the stage-occurence is not his own life, but (according to this view) he must pretend to be the individual he represents, until he actually feels the emotions he is to register. Oddly enough, people who hold this belief do not ask whether the actor must also actually have the motives and desires of his alter ego —that is, whether he must really intend or at least wish to kill his antagonist, or to divulge a secret.

The imputation of bona fide feelings and emotions to the actor on stage would be only a negligible popular error, were it not part and parcel of a broader fallacy—the confusion of theatrical representation with "make-believe," or pretense, which has always led both playwrights and directors to misconceive the relation of the audience to the play, and saddled them with the gratuitous and silly problem of the spectator's credulity.The classic expression of this concern is, of course, Castelvetro's warning in his *Poetics,* published in 1570: "The time of the representation and that of the action presented must be exactly coincident. There is no possibility of making the spectators believe that many days and nights have passed, when they themselves obviously know that only a few hours have actually elapsed; they refuse to be so deceived."[13] Corneille, a generation later, still accepted the principle, though he complained that to limit a dramatic action quite strictly to one room and the time span of a theater visit often "is so awkward, not to say impossible, that some enlargement of place must of necessity be found, as also of time."[14]

An art principle that cannot be fully and wholeheartedly applied, but requires compromises and evasions, should be immediately suspect; yet the principle of making the spectators believe that they are witnessing actual happenings has been accepted down to our

[12] "Die Vorbildung des Schauspielers," in Edward Geissler's collection *Der Schauspieler.* See p. 46.
[13] Reprinted in *The Great Critics, An Anthology of Literary Criticism,* edited by J. H. Smith and E. W. Parks. See p. 523.
[14] *Ibid.,* p. 531. From *A Discourse on the Three Unities.*

own day,[15] and though most theorists have seen its error, it still crops up in contemporary criticism, and — worse yet — in theater practice. We have fairly well recovered from the epidemic of naturalism, the stagecraft that sought to dispense with all artifice, and consequently borrowed living material from the actual world — "drugstore clerks drafted to impersonate themselves in real drugstores transferred bodily to the stage," as Robert Edmond Jones described this sort of dramaturgy. Now it is true that real art *can* be made with such devices; no device in itself is taboo, not even putting stage-beggars in clothes begged from real beggars (Edward Sothern, in his autobiography, recalls his acquisition of one such unalluring treasure). But the theory that a play is a game of "make-believe" designed by the poet, carried on by the actors, and supported by an audience willing to pretend that the stage history is actual, which still persists, and with it its practical counterpart — the principle of deluding the audience, aiding the public "make-believe" by making the play seem as real as possible — is another story.

The whole conception of theater as delusion is closely linked with the belief that the audience should be made to share the emotions of the protagonists. The readiest way to effect this is to extend the stage action beyond the stage in the tensest moments, to make the spectators feel themselves actually present as witnesses of the scene. But the result is artistically disastrous, since each person becomes aware not only of his own presence, but of other people's too, and of the house, the stage, the entertainment in progress. Rosamond Gilder reported such an experience in her comment on Orson Welles' staging of *Native Son;* describing the scene wherein Bigger Thomas is cornered by his pursuers, she said: "Here flashing lights, gunplay, shouting and shooting converge on the stage from balcony and boxes. The theatrical illusion, far from being increased, is shattered, and the scene becomes nothing more than a nineteen-forty-one version of Eliza crossing the ice."[16]

I, too, remember vividly to this day the terrible shock of such a

---

[15] Strindberg, for instance, was convinced that the spectators in the theater let themselves be deluded, tricked into believing or making-believe that what they saw was actual life going on in their presence, and he was seriously afraid of what popular education, and the general enlightenment it was expected to bring, would do to people's credulity. In the famous preface to *Miss Julia* he observes that "the theater has always served as a grammar school to young people, women, and those who have acquired a little knowledge, all of whom retain the capacity for deceiving themselves and being deceived," but that "in our time, when the rudimentary, incomplete thought-processes operating through our fancy seem to be developing into reflection, research, and analysis, the theater might stand on the verge of being abandoned as a decaying form, for the enjoyment of which we lack the requisite conditions."

[16] "Glamor and Purpose," in *Theatre Arts,* May, 1941, pp. 327-335.

recall to actuality: as a young child I saw Maude Adams in *Peter Pan*. It was my first visit to the theater, and the illusion was absolute and overwhelming, like something supernatural. At the highest point of the action (Tinkerbell had drunk Peter's poisoned medicine to save him from doing so, and was dying) Peter turned to the spectators and asked them to attest their belief in fairies. Instantly the illusion was gone; there were hundreds of children, sitting in rows, clapping and even calling, while Miss Adams, dressed up as Peter Pan, spoke to us like a teacher coaching us in a play in which she herself was taking the title role. I did not understand, of course, what had happened; but an acute misery obliterated the rest of the scene, and was not entirely dispelled until the curtain rose on a new set.

The central fallacy in such play production, and in the concept of drama that it assumes, is the total disregard of what Edward Bullough, in an essay that has become deservedly famous,[17] called "psychical Distance." All appreciation of art — painting, architecture, music, dance, whatever the piece may be — requires a certain detachment, which has been variously called the "attitude of contemplation," the "aesthetic attitude," or the "objectivity" of the beholder. As I pointed out in an early chapter of this book,[18] it is part of the artist's business to make his work elicit this attitude instead of requiring the percipient to bring an ideal frame of mind with him. What the artist establishes by deliberate stylistic devices is not really the beholder's attitude — that is a by-product — but a relation between the work and its public (including himself). Bullough terms this relationship "Distance," and points out quite rightly that "objectivity," "detachment," and "attitudes" are complete or incomplete, i.e. perfect or imperfect, but do not admit of degrees. "Distance, on the contrary, admits naturally of degrees, and differs not only according to the nature of the *object*, which may impose a greater or smaller degree of Distance, but varies also according to the *individual's capacity* for maintaining a greater or lesser degree."[19]

He describes (rather than defines) his concept, not without resort to metaphor, yet clearly enough to make it a philosophical asset:

"Distance . . . is obtained by separating the object and its appeal from one's own self, by putting it out of gear with practical needs and ends . . . . But it does not mean that the relation between the self

---

[17] "'Psychical Distance' as a Factor in Art and an Aesthetic Principle," *British Journal of Psychology*, June, 1912.
[18] Chap. 4.
[19] *Op. cit.*, p. 94.

and the object is broken to the extent of becoming 'impersonal' . . . On the contrary, it describes a *personal* relation, often highly emotionally colored, but *of a peculiar character*. Its peculiarity lies in that the personal character of the relation has been, so to speak, filtered. It has been cleared of the practical, concrete nature of its appeal. . . . One of the best-known examples is to be found in our attitude towards the events and characters of the drama. . . ."[20]

This relation "of a peculiar character" is, I believe, our natural relation to a symbol that embodies an idea and presents it for our contemplation, not for practical action, but "cleared of the practical, concrete nature of its appeal." It is for the sake of this remove that art deals entirely in illusions, which, because of their lack of "practical, concrete nature," are readily distanced as symbolic forms. But delusion — even the quasi-delusion of " make-believe" — aims at the opposite effect, the greatest possible nearness. To seek delusion, belief, and "audience participation" in the theater is to deny that drama is art.

There are those who do deny it. There are very serious critics who see its essential value to society not in the sort of revelation that is proper to art, but in its function as a form of ritual. Francis Fergusson and T. S. Eliot have treated drama in this vein,[21] and several German critics have found in the custom of hand clapping a last vestige of the audience participation that is really the public's lost birthright.[22] There are others who regard the theater not as a temple, but primarily as an amusement hall, and demand of drama that it shall please, delude us for a while, and incidentally teach morals and "knowledge of man." Brander Mathews extended the demand for amusement — any or every sort of amusement — to all the arts; but as his renown rests entirely on his dramatic criticism and teaching, his view of "art" is really a view of the theater casually extended to all other realms. "The primary purpose of all the arts is to entertain," said Matthews, "even if every art has also to achieve its own secondary aim. Some of these entertainments make their appeal to the intellect, some to the emotions, and some only to the nerves, to our relish for sheer excitement and for brute sensation; but each of them

---

[20] *Op. cit.,* p. 91. The attitude referred to is, of course, the famous "aesthetic attitude," here treated as an index to the proper degree of distance.

[21] Cf. Francis Fergusson, *The Idea of a Theater.* A book so full of ideas, scholarship and discernment that even in taking issue with it I would recommend it to every reader.

T. S. Eliot, in "A Dialogue on Dramatic Poetry," (in *Selected Essays, 1917-1932*), p. 35, lets "E." say, "The only dramatic satisfaction that I find now is in a High Mass well performed."

[22] E.g., Theodor Wiesengrund-Adorno, "Applaus," *Die Musik,* 23 (1930-31), p. 476; also A. E. Günther, "Der Schauspieler und wir," in Geissler's *Der Schauspieler,* p. 144.

in its own way seeks, first of all, to entertain. They are, every one of them, to be included in the show business."[23]

Here we have certainly two extremes of dramatic theory; and the theory I hold — that drama is art, a poetic art in a special mode, with its own version of the poetic illusion to govern every detail of the performed piece — this theory does not lie anywhere between these extremes. Drama is neither ritual nor show business, though it may occur in the frame of either one; it is poetry, which is neither a kind of circus nor a kind of church.

Perhaps the greatest snare in the course of our thinking about theater is its free trafficking with the standard materials of all the other arts. People are so used to defining each art by its characteristic medium that when paint is used in the theater they class the result as "the painter's art," and because the set requires building, they regard the designer of it as an architect. Drama, consequently, has so often been described as a synthesis of several or even all arts that its autonomy, its status as a special mode of a great single art, is always in jeopardy. It has been treated as essentially dance, by confusion with pantomimic dances that have a dramatic plot; it has been conceived as tableau and pageantry heightened by speech and action (Gordon Craig held that the designer of its visual aspects was its real creator), and as poetic recitation accompanied by gestures, some-times by dance-gestures. This last view is traditional in India, where it is supported by the obvious epic sources of Hindu plays (as usual, finding the source of a phenomenon is supposed to reveal its "real" nature). Hindu aestheticians, therefore, regard drama as literature, and judge it by literary standards.[24] Nietzsche found its origin in "the spirit of music" and consequently regarded its true nature as musi-cal. Thornton Wilder describes it as an exalted form of narrative: "The theater," he writes, "carries the art of narration to a higher power than the novel or the epic poem. . . . The dramatist must be by instinct a story-teller."[25]

But story-telling, narration, is something quite different from story-enactment in a theater. Many first-rate story-tellers cannot make a play, and the highest developments of narration, such as the

[23] *A Book About the Theater,* p. 6.

[24] Cf. Sylvain Lévi, *Le théâtre indien,* p. 257: "They [Indian theorists] are wont to consider drama as the juxtaposition of two arts, which simultaneously pursue their respective ends, namely poetry and mimetic dance. . . . Dance and mummery, stagecraft and scenery combine to heighten the illusion and pleasure by appealing to several senses. Representation, therefore, surpasses reading by a quantitative difference of emotion; there is no qualitative difference between them." See also A. B. Smith, *The Sanskrit Drama,* pp. 294-295.

[25] "Some Thoughts on Playwrighting," p. 86.

modern novel and short story, show devices of their own that have no meaning for the stage. They project a history in retrospect, whereas drama is history coming. Even as performed arts, narration and dramatization are distinct. The ancient rhapsodist, for all his gesticulations and inflections, was not an actor, and today, too, people who are known as good readers of poetry or prose need not therefore have any aptitude for the theater.

The concept of drama as literature embellished with concurrent appeals to the sense of sight is belied most convincingly in the very society where it enjoys its traditional vogue; the fact that in India the classic drama survived as a popular art for centuries after both the Sanskrit and the various Prakrits in which it was composed had become dead languages, understood only by scholars, proves that the stage action was no mere accompaniment, but was instinctively developed by the actors to the point of self-sufficiency, making the precise word meanings of the speeches dispensable; that this drama is, in fact, what Cocteau called "a poetry of the theater," as well as "poetry in the theater."

As for dance, though it probably preceded drama on the boards, and though it uses dramatic plots after its own fashion, it does not give rise to drama—not even to true pantomime. Any direct dramatic action tends to suspend the balletic illusion. The fact that Greek drama arose amidst ritual dancing has led several art historians to consider it as a dance episode; but the dance was, in fact, only a perfect framework for the development of an entirely new art; the minute the two antagonist stepped out of the choric ensemble and addressed not the deity, nor the congregation, but each other, they created a poetic illusion, and drama was born in midst of the religious rite. The choric dance itself was assimilated to the world of the virtual history they presented.

Once we recognize that drama is neither dance nor literature, nor a democracy of various arts functioning together, but is poetry in the mode of action, the relations of all its elements to each other and to the whole work become clear: the primacy of the script, which furnishes the commanding form; the use of the stage, with or without representational scenery, to delimit the "world" in which the virtual action exists; the need of making the scene a "place," so that often the designer produces a plastic illusion that is secondary here, but primary in the art of architecture;[26] the use of music and some-

[26] Cf. Jones, *op. cit.,* p. 75: "The energy of a particular play, its emotional content, its aura, so to speak, has its own definite physical dimensions. It extends just so far in space and no farther. The walls of the setting must be placed at precisely this point."

times of dance to keep the fictitious history apart from actuality and insure its artistic abstraction;[27] the nature of dramatic time, which is "musical" instead of practical time, and sometimes becomes strikingly evident—another secondary illusion in poetry, but the primary one of music. The guiding principle in the use of so many transient borrowed illusions is the making of an *appearance,* not under normal circumstances, like a pretense or social convention, but under the circumstances of the play. Its total emotional tone is like the "palette" of a picture, and controls the intensity of color and light, the sober or fantastic character of the sets, the requirements such as overture, interludes, and what not.

Above all, that emotional tone guides the style of the actors. The actors are the chief interpreters—normally, the only indispensable ones—of the poet's incomplete but commanding creations. An actor does not express his emotions, but those of a fictitious person. He does not undergo and vent emotions; he conceives them, to the smallest detail, and enacts them. . . .

As every act and utterance set down in the poet's script serves to create a perceptible destiny, so all plastic, choreographic, or musical elements that are added to his play in the theater must support and enhance that creation. The dramatic illusion is poetic, and where it is primary—that is to say, where the work is a drama—it transmutes all borrowings from other arts into poetic elements. As Mr. Jones says in *The Dramatic Imagination,* "In the last analysis the designing of stage scenery is not the problem of an architect or a painter or a sculptor or even a musician, but of a poet."[28] It is the painter (or architect, or sculptor) turned poet who understands the commanding form which the author has composed by writing the lines of the play, and who carries this form to the further state of visibility, and it is the actor-poet who takes the whole work—words, setting, happenings, all—through the final phase of its creation, where words become utterances and the visible scene is fused into the occurrence of the virtual life.

Histrionic imagination is the same fundamental talent in the playwright, the leading actors, the performers of even the smallest parts in so far as they are genuine actors, the scene and light designer, the costumer, the light controller, the composer or selector

---

George Beiswanger, in a little article entitled "Opera for the Eye" (*Theatre Arts,* January, 1943, p. 59), makes a similar remark: "Each opera has its own ideal dimensions, and their illusion must be created whether the actual stage be large or small."

[27] Schiller, in his famous preface to *Die Braut von Messina,* called the Greek chorus, which he revived in this play, "a living wall" to preserve the Distance of the work.

[28] P. 77.

of incidental music, the ballet master, and the director who surveys the whole to his satisfaction or despair. The work on which they are engaged is one thing—an apparition of Destiny.

"From the Greeks to Ibsen the actor has represented, by elocution as well as by movement, human character and human destiny.... When drama takes on the abstract character of music or pure dance it ceases to be drama....

"The dramatist ... is a writer, a poet, before he is a musician or a choreographer. Wagner of course showed that many dramatic elements can be embodied in orchestral music; silent movies showed how much can be done with the visual element alone; but if you add Wagner to Eisenstein and multiply by ten you still do not have a Shakespeare or an Ibsen. This does not say that drama is better than music, dancing, or the visual arts. It is different.

"The defenders of the arts of the theater must be infected by the commodities of the theater if they can forget that all 'theater arts' are means to one end: the correct presentation of a poem."[29]

[29] From E. R. Bently, "The Drama at Ebb," *Kenyon Review*, VII, 2 (Spring, 1945), 169-184.

Eugène Ionesco

In his observations reprinted here—taken, in the first instance, from an essay of 1958 and in the second, from a talk delivered at the Sorbonne in 1960—Ionesco describes the situation of *any* new conception of theatre. In "Still About Avant-Garde Theatre," he considers the important matters of idiom, the "popular" audience, and the question of social importance or "topical truth." In the second piece, the question of ideology contained in a play is again considered as well as the subject of theatre criticism.

Ionesco has been for over twenty years the leader of absurdist theatre—centered in Paris but clearly influencing the work of playwrights all over the world since 1945. After leaving an academic life and turning to the stage, Ionesco's first successes were *The Bald Soprano* (1950), *The Lesson* (1951), and *The Chairs* (1952). His later plays have included *Rhinoceros* (1960), *The King Dies* (1963), and *The Airwalker* (1964).

✚ STILL ABOUT AVANT-GARDE THEATRE

What is meant by "avant-garde theatre"? Deliberately or not, great confusion has arisen around these words, mainly owing to prejudice. The expression itself is confusing and the idea that avant-garde theatre is "ridiculous" might even be caused merely by faulty definition. A critic in one of the foreign countries where I have been lucky enough to see my plays acted—favorable, moreover, to my work—still wondered whether this kind of theatre was not after all just a transition, a stage in the development of drama. So that is what avant-garde means: a kind of drama that opens the way to another kind of drama, which will be definitive. But nothing is definitive, everything is just a stage in development, our very lives are essentially transitory: everything is, at one and the same time, the culmination of one thing and the announcement of something else. So one can say that the French theatre of the seventeenth century prepares the way for romantic drama (which is not worth much anyway in France) and that Racine and Corneille are the advance guard of the theatre of Victor Hugo, who himself blazed the trail for what came after and rejected him.

And again: the mechanism governing forward and rear positions is far more complicated than overly-simple dialecticians imagine. There are some productive "avant-garde" movements which arise from opposition to the achievements of preceding generations or, on the other hand, others which are encouraged or facilitated by a reappraisal of sources, of old and forgotten works. Shakespeare is always far more contemporary than Victor Hugo (cited above); Pirandello far more "avant-garde" than Roger Ferdinand; Büchner infinitely more poignant and alive than, for example, Bertholt Brecht and his imitators in Paris.

And this is where matters seem to become clearer: in reality, the avant-garde does not exist; or rather it is quite different from what it is thought to be.

As the avant-garde is, we all agree, revolutionary, it has always been and still is, like most revolutionary movements, a turning back, a reappraisal. The change is only apparent: this "apparentness" is of enormous importance, for it is this that allows (by presenting something new and yet going beyond it) reassessment and restoration of something permanent. For example: the political upheavals that appear at moments when a regime is worn out and "liberalized" – when the structure has weakened to such a point that collapse is anyway imminent, ready to take place, as one might say, unaided – prepare and allow for a strengthening and reconstitution of the social structure according to an archetypal and changeless model: there is a real change on the personal plane, obviously, on the level of superficial conditions, in idiom: that is to say things – identical in essence – assume different names, without modifying the deeper reality or the fundamental pattern of society.

What has really happened? Simply this: authority (which had been relaxed) has tightened up, "order" is re-established, tyranny clamps down again on freedom, the leaders of the State recover their taste and vocation for power with a quiet conscience, for they feel themselves to be invested with a kind of "God's Grace," with an alibi provided by a firm and reliable ideological justification for the cynicism inseparable from power. And there we have the basic hierarchical social structure, clearly reaffirmed and reconstituted, with the king (the political leaders) upheld by dogma and the church (the ideologists, the writers, the artists, the journalists, the propagandists, all back in obedience) and either supported or suffered by the majority – the people (the believers, the faithful or the passive) who are no longer capable of insurrection.

Almost the same thing happens with artistic revolutions, when there is really an attempt at revolution, or a revolutionary experiment coming from the avant-garde. This happens inevitably, of its own accord as you might say, at a moment when certain modes of expression have become exhausted and worn out, when they have deteriorated, when they have wandered too far from some forgotten model. Thus, in painting, the moderns have been able to *rediscover* in the painters we call "primitives" forms that are pure and permanent, the basic laws that govern their art. And this rediscovery, dictated by the history of art where forms and models lose their power – has been made possible thanks to an art, an *idiom* that springs from a reality lying outside history.

It is indeed in the union between the historical and the unhistorical, the topical and the untopical (that is to say the permanent) that we can seek this changeless basic material which we can also succeed in finding, instinctively, in ourselves: without it, any work of art is valueless, it keeps everything alive. So finally I maintain quite fearlessly that the true avant-garde or revolutionary art is that which, boldly setting its face against its own times, looks as if it is *untopical*. By casting off all claim to topicality, it reveals its links with this universal basic material we have already spoken of, and being universal it may be considered classical; but it should be understood that this classicism must be rediscovered by passing through and going beyond the new elements that should permeate this kind of art. Any attempt to return to some sort of "historical" classicism by turning one's back on what is new would only encourage the development of an outdated and academic style. For example: *Endgame* by Beckett, a so-called avant-garde play, is far closer to the lamentations of Job, the tragedies of Sophocles or Shakespeare, than to the tawdry drama known as "committed" or boulevard theatre. Topical drama does not last (by definition) and it does not last for the good reason that people are not truly profoundly interested in it.

It is also worth noting that social changes are not always related to artistic revolution. Or rather: when the mystique of a revolution becomes a regime, it returns to artistic forms (and so to a mentality) that are outmoded, with the result that the new realism is bound up with the mental clichés we call bourgeois and reactionary. Conventionalism repeats itself and the bewhiskered academic portraits of the new reaction are—stylistically—no different from the academic portraits, with or without whiskers, of the bourgeois period which did not understand Cézanne. So we can say, somewhat paradoxically perhaps, *that it is the "historical" which is moribund, and the non-historical which remains alive.*

Chekhov in his drama shows us dying men in a particular dying society; the destruction, as time runs out and gnaws away, of the men of a certain period; Proust too had done this in his novels—and so had Gustave Flaubert in *L'Education sentimentale,* although he showed as a background to his characters not a declining but a rising society. So it is not the collapse or the break-up or the erosion of a social system which is the principal theme, the *truth* of these works: but man eroded by time, his destruction seen at a certain historical moment but true for *all* history; we are *all* murdered by time.

I mistrust pacifist plays, which seem to be showing us that it is war that destroys mankind and that we only die in wartime. This is more or less what one young critic seemed to be saying, obstinately dogmatic, when commenting on *Mother Courage.*

More of us die in wartime: topical truth. We die: permanent truth, not topical yet always topical, it concerns everybody, and so it also concerns people not involved in war: Beckett's *Endgame* is more true, more universal, than Schéhadé's *Histoire de Vasco* (which in no way prevents this play from having high poetic qualities).

Since at first sight "what concerns us all fundamentally" is curiously less accessible than what concerns only some people or what concerns us less—it is obvious that avant-garde plays, whose aim is (I apologize for being so insistent) to rediscover and make known a forgotten truth—and to reintegrate it, in an untopical way, into what is topical—it is obvious that when these works appear they cannot help being misunderstood by the majority of people. So they are not "popular." This in no way invalidates them. The plainest realities are discovered by the poet in silence and solitude. The philosopher too, in the silence of his library, discovers truths difficult to communicate: how long did it take for Karl Marx himself to be understood, and even now can *everyone* understand him? He is not "popular." How many people have succeeded in assimilating Einstein? The fact that only a few people are capable of a clear understanding of the theories of modern physicists does not make me doubt their validity; and this truth that they have discovered is neither invention nor subjective vision, but objective reality, outside time, eternal, and the scientific mind has only just touched the fringe of it. Where we are concerned with an unchanging truth, all we ever do is approach, move away and then draw closer again.

There also exists—as we are meant to be talking about the theatre—a dramatic idiom, a theatrical method of approach, a trail to blaze, if we are to reach a reality that has objective existence: and this trail to blaze (or path to find again) cannot be other than one belonging to the theatre, which will lead to a reality that can only be revealed theatrically. It is what we might agree to call laboratory research.

There is no reason why there should not be drama for *the people* (I am not quite sure who the people are, unless it is the majority, the non-specialists), boulevard theatre, a theatre of propaganda and instruction, composed in some conventional idiom: this is popularized theatre. We must not for this reason prevent the other kind of theatre from continuing its work: a drama of research, laboratory drama, the avant-garde. If it is not taken up by a large public, this in no way means that it is not of vital importance to our minds, as necessary as artistic, literary or scientific research. We do not always know *what use it is*—but as it fulfills a mental requirement, it is clearly quite indispensable. If such drama has an audience of fifty people every evening (and it can have that number) the need for it is proved. This kind of theatre is in danger. Politics, apathy, malice and jealousy are, unfortunately, a dangerous threat on every side to such writers as Beckett, Vauthier, Schéhadé, Weingarten and others, as well as to their supporters.

from REMARKS ON MY THEATRE AND ON THE REMARKS OF OTHERS

... Nowadays there are many dogmas, many dogmatic thinkers: could it be that these dogmatic doctrines now provide the framework for our subjective responses?

I will not suggest that nowadays we do not think. But we think about what a few leading thinkers give us to think about, we think about what *they* think, if we do not think exactly *what* they think, repeating or paraphrasing their thoughts. In any case, it is clear that three or four thinkers have taken the initiative in thought and chosen their own weapons and battleground; and the thousands of other thinkers who believe they think thrash about in the intellectual nets cast by the three others, trapped by the terms in which the latter force them to consider the problem. The problem imposed upon them may have its importance. But there are also other problems, other aspects of reality and the world: and the least we can say of our leading thinkers is that they restrict us to their own more or less doctrinaire, subjective approach, which conceals from us, like a screen, the infinitely varied points of view possible to the human spirit. But to think for oneself, to discover problems for oneself is an extremely difficult thing. It is so much more convenient to find one's nourishment in predigested foods. We are or have been the pupils of this or that teacher. And not only has he taught us, he has influenced us by his own way of thinking, his theories, his subjective view of the truth. In short he has "formed" us. It is chance that has formed us: for if this same chance had sent us to a different school, a different teacher would have fashioned our minds in his own image, and our thinking would doubtless have been of a different kind. I am certainly not suggesting we should reject the basic ideas given to us, or pour scorn on the opinions and solutions chosen by others: anyhow, this is not possible: but we should think out for ourselves the problems we are asked to think about and the terms in which we are asked to think, to try and discover what particular subjective elements there are in ideas presented to us as objective or generally accepted; we should be on our guard and remain free to put our own examiners through our own examination; and only when this has been done accept or reject their point of view. . . .

The "popular" audience of former times used to wait at the end of the show for the actor who had played the part of the villain in order to lynch him. Today it is the author whom the critics crudely identify with his characters.

Also, what the author thinks of his work is often confused with the work itself. An English critic concluded that Arthur Miller was a great author because what Miller said about his own work was interesting: yet the question of his artistic success was not even raised, as though it were of quite secondary importance whether Miller had written plays or not, still less whether they were good or bad.

A teacher in turn gently admonishes me for making out a case, at least in principle, for a terroristic nihilism that I defend with a vigor worthy of a better cause. Yet he says my plays would have less force if they were negative. What does he hold against me then?

Man is alone and in anguish only at certain periods, our own for example, where, goes on the teacher, there is a cleavage that splits society into at least two groups. But does not the character of Hamlet express solitude and anguish? And is not Richard II's cell the prison house of all our solitudes? It seems to me that solitude and anguish especially characterize the fundamental conditions of man. This teacher, who believes that an economic and political revolution will automatically resolve all man's problems, is a utopian. My parrot is more intelligent.

This critic blames me again for wanting to escape from a social framework, for, he says, "every man is part of a certain civilization that nurtures him but," he adds, "does not totally explain him."

My plays were never meant to express anything else: just that man is not simply a social animal, a prisoner of his time, but also and above all, at all times, different in his historical context, identical in his essence. So if we can converse with Shakespeare, Molière and Sophocles, if we understand them, it is because they are in their essence profoundly like ourselves. I find that the humanity of universal man is not general and abstract, but real and concrete; and man "in general" is more real than man limited to his own period, diminished. Several times I have said that it is in our fundamental solitude that we rediscover ourselves and that the more I am alone, the more I am in communion with others; whereas in organized society, which is an organization of functions, man is merely reduced to his function, which alienates him from the rest.

I would add that it is its fictional power that gives a work of art its value, for it is above all fictional, a construction of the imagination; of course one first comes to grips with everything in it that is topical, moral, ideological, etc. . . . but this is grasping the least essential part of it. Is this imaginative structure, built of course with materials drawn from reality, of no real use? There are some who think so. But why should literary construction be less acceptable than pictorial or musical form? Because it is not so easy to use the latter for propaganda purposes: as soon as one makes propaganda of them, on the one hand they change their nature, and on the other they are too obviously revealed as propaganda. In literature, ambiguity is easier.

And if some people do not like constructions of the imagination this does not alter the fact that they exist; they are created because they answer a profound spiritual need.

If there is so much confusion in the appreciation of a work of art, of a play, it is briefly because no one knows exactly what a play or a piece of literature really is. Reread Jean Paulhan's "Short Preface to all Criticism": he will tell you, infinitely better than I can, all the different ways of not knowing.

To sum up then, what have I found particularly annoying in the judgments passed by others? I think what irritated me above all and what continues to irritate me is that I have not been judged on the right issue. I feel I have been judged not by literary critics or by dramatic critics but by moralists. And by moralists I mean fanatical, dogmatic and ideological theologians of every creed. In other words, they beg the question. I am absolutely convinced that it is not this kind of emotional judgment that will finally count. I have also noticed that it is at the time extremely irritating. The subjective moralizing of our contemporaries, caught in a storm of passions of every kind, seems to me not only irritating but also blind and blinding. As for the subjective reactions of posterity, these may prove to be just as inacceptable, so that one really does not know where to look for a solution. However, I hope a time for relatively absolute objectivity, if I may so express myself, will one day come when all the storms have passed.

I am going to try and clarify one or two points. When I declare, for example, that a work of art, a play in this context, should not be ideological, I certainly do not mean one ought not to find ideas or opinions in it. I simply believe it is not the opinions expressed in it that matter. What matters is the flesh and blood of these ideas, their incarnation, their passion and their life.

A work of art cannot have the same function as an ideology, for if it did it would *be* an ideology, it would no longer be a work of art, that is to say an autonomous creation, an independent universe with its own life and its own laws. I mean that a play, for example, finds its own way, explores itself and must use its own methods to make discovery of certain realities, certain fundamental evidence that reveals itself in the process of creative thinking—for this is what writing is—evidence of an intimate nature (which does not prevent it from joining with the intimate evidence of others, so that in this way solitude ends or may end by identifying itself with the community), intimate evidence that is unexpected at the start and surprising for the author himself, often above all for the author himself. Perhaps this means that imagination is revelation, that it is charged with multiple meanings which a narrow and everyday "realism" or a limiting ideology can no longer reveal: indeed, when a work of art is compelled simply to illustrate ideology, it is no longer a creative process, action and surprise; it is known in advance. Realistic or ideological works can do no more than confirm us in or nail us down to previous and too firmly established positions. Too often what is sought in works of literature is defense and illustration, a demonstration of what has already been and so need not again be demonstrated. This cramps the horizon, it is prison or desert, no more unexpected events, and so no more theatre. It therefore leads me to suggest that realism, for example, is false or unreal and that only the imaginary is true. So a living work of art is one that first of all surprises its own author, escapes from him and throws author and public into disarray, putting them in some way at variance with each other. Otherwise creative work would be pointless, for why give a message that has already been given? A work of art is for me an expression of native intuition that owes almost nothing to other people: by creating a world, by inventing it, the creator discovers it for himself.

A dramatist who has too much control over what he is doing, or a poet whose creative work is intended to be a simple demonstration of this or that, ends by writing something self-sufficient, sealed off from greater potentialities. He is no longer a poet, he is a schoolmaster. I profoundly mistrust drama that is called didactic, for didacticism kills art . . . and instruction too: it is no good always hammering away at the same lesson! Ideologists more Stalinist than Stalin himself, and even some eminent playwrights, want to save or educate the world at any price. But we know only too well that when religions speak of the salvation of the soul, what they have in mind above all is the hell surely awaiting souls that rebel against salvation; we also know that when education is mentioned one soon ends up with re-education, and we all know what *that* means! It is pedants of every kind, educators and re-educators, propagandists for all kinds of beliefs, theologians and politicians who finally constitute the oppressive forces against which an artist must struggle. I have thought it my duty on several occasions to insist on the two dangers threatening the life of the mind and of the theatre in particular: the mental sluggishness of the bourgeois on the one hand, and on the other the tyranny of political regimes and movements, in other words opposing manifestations of the bourgeois spirit. And by the bourgeois spirit I mean: conformism from above, from below, from the left and the right, bourgeois as well as socialist unreality, dried-up conventional systems. Unfortunately the worst bourgeois are often the anti-bourgeois bourgeois. And I wonder if art might not achieve that liberation, that re-apprenticeship to a free mind to which we are no longer accustomed, which we have forgotten, but whose loss is felt as much by those who believe themselves to be free without being so (being prevented by prejudice) as by those who believe they are not or cannot be free.

And yet I believe I am right in thinking that the avant-garde would be the very theatre to contribute to this rediscovery of freedom. I should like to say at once that artistic freedom does not by any means indicate ignorance of laws and standards. Freedom of imagination is not flight into the unreal, it is not escape, it is daring and invention. And invention is not evasive or abdication. The paths of imagination are without number and the inventive powers are boundless. On the contrary, the way is barred only when we find ourselves within the narrow confines of what we call some dreary "thesis" or realism, whether it be socialist or not. The latter has already withered, its revelations have faded, it is academic and conventional, it is a prison.

Michel Saint-Denis

The author, now (with Peter Brook and Peter Hall) one of the Directors of the Royal Shakespeare Theatre Company, is one of the most distinguished teachers, writers on theatre, and stage directors in the world. He has held administrative and artistic appointments with the Old Vic in London, with the Comédie Française in Paris, and with the School of Dramatic Art of the Juilliard School of Music, part of Lincoln Center in New York. His experience and understanding of all theatre arts stand behind such observations as those reprinted here, taken from a lecture delivered before the American Shakespeare Festival and Academy.

Essentially, Saint-Denis is discussing the nature of style itself and why the work of one nation — or of one period — must be seen differently and performed differently from that of another nation or century. This is the fundamental question asked by those who must concern themselves with the illusion of reality in stage production; Saint-Denis approaches his own answers from a range of equally viable viewpoints. He considers physical stage plants themselves, the question of language, the nature of individual acting style. Perhaps most important, his over-all approach is humane, remembering the variety of theatres and schools with which he has been associated in his own lifetime — a range of experience to which he refers at the beginning of these comments.

from STYLE AND REALITY

... In 1919 I joined the company of the Théâtre du Vieux Colombier in Paris. Jacques Copeau had just come back from two seasons at the Garrick Theatre in New York. (He had opened the Vieux Colombier in 1913 when he was thirty-three but had had to close it in 1914 owing to the war.) So I was in a position to watch from its beginnings the movement that was to transform the French stage and have upon the European theatre an influence that is not over today; a movement that has proved to be more important than one could have believed even at the time of Copeau's death in 1949. Why was this? What gave such an impulse to this artistic revolution?

To begin with, it was a fight against naturalism as it had been

From *Theatre: The Rediscovery of Style* by Michel Saint-Denis. Copyright 1960 by Michel Saint-Denis. Reprinted with the permission of Theatre Arts Books (New York) and Heinemann Educational Books Ltd. (London).

started in our country by André Antoine. It was also a fight against the survival of romantic rhetoric in the interpretation of the classics, particularly at the Comédie Française. But it had an even broader and deeper purpose which was expressed by Copeau in his manifesto *Un Essai de rénovation dramatique* written in 1913. Reacting against many aspects of the theatre of that time, Copeau wanted to free the stage from cumbersome machinery and showy effects; to concentrate his efforts on the development of a new school of acting; and to give first place and importance to "poets," by which he meant real dramatists, whether of the past or contemporary. It was in this spirit that he wrote at the end of his famous manifesto: *Pour l'oeuvre nouvelle qu'on nous laisse un tréteau nu* (For the work of the future let us have a bare platform).

When at the Vieux Colombier in the spring of 1920 Copeau gave a realistic play written by a "poet," *Le Paquebot Tenacity* by Charles Vildrac, Antoine, the father of French naturalism, who had become a dramatic critic, wrote that he was astonished by the kind of "reality" he saw on the stage. The floor of the stage was made of concrete. There was a proscenium but no footlights, and so no "fourth wall." *Le Paquebot Tenacity* takes place in a seaman's "dive" in a small harbour. There was a door at the back through which the sea was suggested by means of light; there was a counter, three tables and ten chairs. That was all. And Antoine wrote, "The atmosphere is created with an almost unbearable intensity ... The public is no longer seated in front of a picture, but in the same room, by the side of the characters. This extraordinary impression has never before been produced to this extent: such a complete elimination of all 'theatrical elements' makes for detailed perfection in acting."

A little later Copeau gave the most "theatrical" production of *Les Fouberies de Scapin* by Molière, set on a bare platform, built of wood, which was isolated on the concrete stage and violently lit by a large triangle of lights hung above it in full view. The actors played on the platform and around it. Such a disposition called for movement and speed, acting of a really physical kind, but at the same time the actors, exposed on that bare platform, had to give true "reality" to their characterisations. Jouvet, who was little more than thirty, created an old miser of the utmost veracity.

A new reality had been brought to the interpretation of the French classics, a reality that had style, animated by a human, "realistic" truthfulness.

In the autumn of 1921 the school of the Vieux Colombier was opened. The training was most unusual. The students, familiar with the theatre of the Greeks, of the Chinese and Japanese, with the Commedia dell'Arte, used to work most of the time without texts. Very often they wore masks. In fact Copeau used his young pupils as gifted children with whom, away from the influence of the much too normal actors of his company, he wanted to rediscover the secrets of acting, to experiment on new or renewed forms of dramatic expression.

In 1922 Stanislavski came to Paris with the Moscow Art Theatre. They played at the Théâtre des Champs Elysées. There we all went, all the students together, very smart, a little ready to laugh in advance: we were going to see those realists, those naturalistic people, the contemporaries of old Antoine! We saw *The Cherry Orchard* that night and we stopped laughing very quickly. There is a moment in the first act of *The Cherry Orchard* when all the characters return from a trip to Paris, worn out by days and nights in the train. They enter the nursery; Madame Ranevsky pauses to admire and feel the old room, full of memories, and Anya, her young daughter of seventeen, who has been brought up in that nursery, jumps on to a sofa and, crouching on it, is caught up by a fit of that high-pitched laughter which is induced by a combination of tiredness and emotion. And on that piece of wordless acting the audience of two thousand five hundred people burst into applause. Later on in the third act, Olga Knipper Chekhova, the wife of Chekhov, playing Madame Ranevsky, takes a cup of tea from the old servant while she is engaged in talking to someone else. Her hand shakes, she's burnt by the tea, drops the cup which falls on the ground and breaks. Fresh burst of applause. Why? Because the reality of this action was so complete, so untheatrically managed as to be striking even from a distance. It was enough to create enthusiasm. I had the opportunity of asking Stanislavski how he had achieved such balanced and convincing reality. He replied, "Oh it's very stupid. She couldn't get it. We rehearsed for seven months but she still couldn't get it; so one day I told the stage-manager to put boiling water in the cup. And he did." I couldn't help saying—I was twenty-five at the time, (but that man was wonderful)—"Yes, that was stupid." He laughed, "It was absolutely stupid. But you have to do everything, anything, even stupid things, to get what you need in the theatre."

Earlier that evening we had taken Stanislavski to see *Sganarelle ou Le Cocu Imaginaire* at the Comédie Française. It was a traditional production but there was an extraordinary actor in it, Jean Dehelly, already old, who revealed to me what lightness, what virtuosity can be reached by a juvenile in a classical farce. His performance was exquisitely true in its youthful artificiality—like a butterfly. But Stanislavski did not seem to appreciate this kind of acting. When we went out he said, "You see my friends, we had a very good example tonight in that old theatre of what not to do." That was all.

This visit of Stanislavski and his company was of incalculable importance to me. For the first time our classical attitude towards the theatre, our efforts to bring a new reality to acting, a reality transposed from life, were confronted by a superior form of modern realism, the realism of Chekhov. Stanislavski was then at his best; all the great names were in the company; the Russian Revolution was only five years old.

In 1931, after ten years of work and close collaboration with Copeau, I started my own company, La Compagnie des Quinze, at the Vieux Colombier. We rebuilt the stage on the assumption that Copeau had not gone far enough and that his permanent and formal setting was still too open to compromise. The new stage looked like a large room in a palace with visible sources of light in the visible ceiling and walls. Permanent columns would not prevent us from representing the sea, the banks of a river, a battlefield, as well as Lucrèce's bedroom. On the contrary this architectural disposition would emphasise our contempt for ordinary theatrical illusion. In fact, at the time we would have liked to get out of the theatre altogether. I thought seriously of taking a big boxing-hall in Paris, la Salle Wagram, and of playing there on the bare platform in the middle of the audience.

We had worked ten years together. We had developed a lot of possibilities as a company: we were mimes, we were acrobats; some of us could play musical instruments and sing. We could invent characters and improvise. In fact we were a chorus with a few personalities sticking out rather than actors ready to act the usual repertory, classical or modern. We brought to the Parisian theatre a specialised repertory of plays, most of them written by one dramatist, André Obey. We were single-minded. Our plays were of an epic character long before the style became better known. They dealt with broad popular themes; their plots did not turn on the psychological development of the characters. As actors we were sincere and resourceful; on the stage we gave the impression of being free, fresh, and real. A critic in Paris wrote that we brought "nature" back to the artificial theatre-world of that period. We took London by surprise and by storm: maybe our genuine qualities pleased the English even more than they had the French.

During that period, 1931-1935, I directed all the plays—there were about ten—given by the Compagnie des Quinze, and acted in most of them.

In 1935, following the success of my company in London and its slow disintegration, I was asked to establish myself there. I drew up the plan of a school. The kind of actor I wanted was not to be found ready-made. Training and experiment seemed to me more important than the quick gathering together of a company without either meaning or unity. With the effective support of Tyrone Guthrie, the close collaboration of George Devine, and soon the help and friendship of Laurence Olivier, John Gielgud, Glen Byam Shaw, of Peggy Ashcroft, Edith Evans, Michael Redgrave, Alec Guinness, and of "Motley," I opened my first school, the London Theatre Studio, a private school.

And now, on top of my French education I had to begin a new apprenticeship—in the English theatre, in the English themselves (not easy), in Shakespeare (more difficult still). After two years, at the invitation of Tyrone Guthrie, I had the daring to direct *The Witch of Edmonton* at the Old Vic, and a year later, in the same theatre, Laurence Olivier himself in *Macbeth*.

Intimacy with Shakespeare, living in Shakespeare's atmosphere, gradually introduced me to a scale of direction and interpretation infinitely broader than the one I had known in dealing with the French classical repertory. As the years went by I became familiar with Shakespeare's methods of composition, shaped to the architecture of the Elizabethan stage, and with a style of acting in harmony with the lyricism of Shakespeare's great poetical moments as well as with the realism of his popular comedy and farce. I had to follow all the variations of a language of which I tried slowly, painfully, to learn the scansion and to appreciate the rhythm.

In 1938 I had my first experience of realism when I produced *The Three Sisters* by Chekhov with John Gielgud's company.

Immediately after the war, in 1945, I greatly enjoyed producing Sophocles's *Oedipus Rex* with Laurence Olivier who at that time was one of the directors of the Old Vic. It was thanks to him that George Devine, Glen Byam Shaw, and myself succeeded in establishing the Old Vic Theatre Centre and the Old Vic School from 1946-1952. . . .

Finally in 1953 I went back to France. I found again the French classical tradition as it was practised not only by the old masters, Charles Dullin and Louis Jouvet, but by the two new-comers, Jean-Louis Barrault and Jean Vilar, both of whom had followed the classes of Dullin, a disciple of Copeau. I also came into contact with the existentialism of Jean-Paul Sartre, the new atheist humanism of Albert Camus, and the transcendental realism of Ionesco and Beckett. In Paris I watched the success and growing influence of Bertolt Brecht, due I believe, rather to Brecht's qualities as a poet and craftsman than to his support by the Communist Party.

I have had the good fortune in our poor and devastated Europe to have had a great deal to do with theatrical architecture. In 1931, I rebuilt the stage of the Vieux Colombier with André Barsacq. In London I built and equipped two schools (1935 and 1947). In 1950 I contributed to the reconstruction of the Old Vic with the French architect, Pierre Sonrel. With the same architect I built in Strasbourg, between 1953 and 1957, a modern theatre of eight hundred seats as part of an ensemble, where, for the first time in my life, I was able to assemble all the elements of a complete organisation – a small practice theatre, rehearsal rooms, workshops, and stores.

Such is my theatre reality, very quickly and superficially reported, almost reduced to the bare facts. I have been concerned with architecture, with the production of both realistic and classical plays, and with training – three aspects of the theatre closely related to each other. . . .

Some of my students tell me that I am sometimes cruel in my teaching. This would put me in fear of something within myself if I did not know what they mean. It's a certain way I have of working persistently to get what I have in mind; an obstinacy that takes hold of me when my health is good; the passion – that word again – of seeing something happen on the stage, and of creating the conditions which will allow this "something" to happen naturally and continuously and not only by chance and in glimpses. But what is it that should "happen"? What is it I am so eager to see "happen"? Have I ever seen this thing "happen"? Yes, from time to time, and when it does I never forget. That is why I still pursue it. I will try to explain what I mean, although in fact the whole of these four lectures are devoted to this explanation. It is my subject and in rather forbidding words it could be expressed in this way: a study of the conditions in which the interpretation of works of different theatrical styles can possess on the stage the greatest degree of reality.

Every country has its own reality, characteristic of its successive historical periods.

This national reality derives from the nature of the country and its traditions. Sometimes, however, this reality can be of a similar kind in a number of different countries at the same time. That is roughly what is taking place at the present time: with obvious differences between the various countries, realism, generally speaking, is the contemporary style most common to the whole world, and seems to be particularly thriving in its American and Russian forms.

At other times, movements in art, and particularly movements in theatrical art, appear to us like isolated monuments – the Greek theatre, for instance, the Spanish theatre of the Golden Age, the Elizabethan theatre, the Commedia dell' Arte, the classical French theatre of the seventeenth century. The classical theatre of the eighteenth century begins to show features common to all European countries.

I exclude from this picture the theatre of the Far East which has had, and continues to have, increasing influence on us.

The countries of Europe have found a certain individuality as a result of their accumulated traditions, of a super-imposition of periods which form a continuous chain of development; and at the same time they have influenced each other through their similarities as well as their differences.

For a Frenchman or an Englishman, there is a central tradition. It may be said that for the Englishman it is a popular and romantic tradition and that for the Frenchman it is an aristocratic and classical one. But not very far off we can see other traditions at work; the Italian tradition which springs mainly from the Renaissance; the great Spanish tradition which is nearly contemporary, in its origins, with the English; the German which was to develop later.

Another country enters the scene in the nineteenth century – Russia; and finally there is the American civilisation which blossoms particularly in the twentieth century.

The reality of each country is made of its historical personality which is constantly being modified.

The theatre takes part in the expression of that reality which is traditional in the case of old countries or fresh and unconventional in the case of new countries.

But the theatre is an art; and its form depends upon architecture, particularly on the relationship between the auditorium and the stage, on acting, and more than anything else, on the work of the writers.

The theatre's means of expression are forged by the time in which a play is written and performed, and by the contribution of the past.

In each country the theatre addresses itself to the public of its time which in due course will become a "period."

Each period has its own style even though we are not conscious of it as we live. (You know the impression we have today when we look at pictures of 1900, 1910, or even 1925. I can remember 1925 very well and I never thought it would become "a period.") And this style influences everybody. It has an influence on life and it is with that unconscious feeling of the style of our own time in our own country that we turn towards the interpretation of the styles of different periods in different countries.

It is impossible to separate oneself from one's period without danger of death. And it is impossible not to be influenced and supported by the traditions of one's own country.

When an artist gives an interpretation of the works of another period and another country, his interpretation is bound to belong to his own country and his own time. He can try to understand what is past and foreign but it is utterly impossible to capture the spirit of three centuries ago in a foreign land. One day someone rang up Louis Jouvet and criticised his production of a Molière play, saying, "Molière would not have liked that." Jouvet answered, "Have you got his phone number?" So a contemporary artist will give his interpretation of the past from the standpoint of today, on the basis either of traditions which are native to him, or of a knowledge, a feeling, an appreciation, which he has acquired for the reality of past periods and other lands.

On the other hand, what is peculiar to our own time is the speed and violence of the change which has affected every country in the world and tended to unify them. I say it again—in the world of the theatre the common contemporary feature is modern realism.

What is the nature of this realism?

We suffer greatly from doubt and instability. At the same time modern discoveries have given us scientific means of investigation which have created in us an acute need for lucidity and knowledge, a passionate desire to be no longer duped. This astringent attitude forms the essential background of contemporary realism which assumes all kinds of aspects and applies to all sorts of subjects.

Between modern realism and traditional classicism, each with their national colouring, there is a clash; there are also strong reciprocal influences; there may even be the possibility of agreement: that is the important point.

The interpretation of works of the past is often approached with the same kind of anxiety, the same kind of lucidity, the same kind of astringency, which we bring to our comments on the present. In applying this scientific exactness to the examination of reality, and expressing our doubts about the very essence of this reality, we have been led to make an increasingly clear distinction between two kinds of realism. On the one hand we have the deep realism, which studies and expresses the nature of things, the meaning of human life, what happens behind and below appearances; and on the other, we have the realism that is satisfied with the representation of the external, the superficial realism which was called at the beginning of the present century "naturalism." If you will allow me, I would like to make a distinction between "realism," which applies to the art of all times, and "naturalism" which is an ephemeral form of art, belonging to the period of Zola, Ibsen, Strindberg, Antoine, Stanislavski, etc.

From a modern realistic point of view, certain periods in the past are closer to us than others. For instance, the English popular tradition as exemplified by Shakespeare is closer, I believe, to a man today, even to a Frenchman, than French aristocratic art of the seventeenth century as exemplified by the plays of Racine. If the Elizabethan dramatists have become fashionable in France since 1920, is it not because there is some kind of a relationship between modern and Elizabethan "madness"? Is not surrealism evidence of this parentage?

But, in revealing a reality to which we feel related, those ancient periods used means of expression which are at variance with our contemporary custom. This has led us to wonder whether poetry in the theatre, a certain kind of poetry, is not a better instrument with which to penetrate reality than the broken prose of daily speech that is used in most plays.

We have now realised that style, by taking us away from the external forms of reality, from appearances, has itself become a reality, representative of a deeper world. In art the reality of a style has to be appreciated: it cannot be ignored or destroyed. There is a reality of ancient styles which is a part of human reality: a book and a play are as real as a cathedral or a statue, and, even if they are less concrete, they are nonetheless substantial. To have its meaning revealed a classical play must be acted in the reality of its style so far as we can understand and achieve it. You cannot interpret the past in terms of the language and style of today. From your modern standpoint you must assimilate the reality of past styles. There are not two worlds; there is not a world of the modern and a world of the classic theatre. There is only one theatre as there is only one world. But there is a continuity which slowly changes and develops from ancient to modern style. The deeper modern realism becomes in its expression as well as in its subject matter, the more it is possible to say that a modern actor, if he is brought up in a classical tradition which he has properly understood, will be better equipped to bite on modern forms of theatre.

There is a two-way action. The proper realistic approach we have today can be of great benefit to the interpretation of classical works. At the same time, training and practice in the classics is essential to enrich and inspire realism which is otherwise in danger of becoming sensational, sentimental or merely empty.

And to finish, a word about Russia, I told you that I was there in June 1957. I was officially invited with five other French directors and actors to visit the Russian theatre and see it at work in Moscow and Leningrad. We saw fourteen shows in fifteen days. We were very interested in Russian ways of directing, producing and acting; but we were even more anxious to get in touch with the people, to appreciate the conditions in which they lived, to discover something of their "human reality."

I found people in general and theatre people in particular openly expressing their need for contacts with the outside world. They wanted to develop. We heard them say both in private and public, "We are thirty years behind the times in the theatre." And it is true. But why?

For far too long the Russians have been compelled in the name of "socialist realism" to practise exclusively the artistic creed which became official in the thirties — the "Stanislavski system." A system in artistic matters is obviously dangerous. I think that Stanislavski would have been the first to hate the idea that his way of working and of training people should be called a system. The man was the opposite of an intellectual fanatic: he was tall, strong-looking and relaxed. An impression of warmth, goodness, and passion emanated from him. He was a great master of the theatre of his own time and never confined himself to the narrow limits of "naturalism." I believe he would be the first to ask us to reject the system, only taking from it what is good for our time and country, and discarding the rest.

Realism, as I have seen it in Russia, has become academic, comfortable and bourgeois. Admirable in fragments but much of it is congealed.

This time I saw *Three Sisters* done by the Moscow Art Theatre and also an adaptation of Gogol's *Dead Souls* by the same company on tour in Leningrad. *Three Sisters* was what the Russians call a "new production," meaning that it had been produced in 1940 by Nemirovich-Danchenko: and the company included some wonderful actors, but the three actresses playing the sisters were respectively 48, 50, and 52 — which is worse than at the Comédie Française.[1] It was a production of a very high standard, but it was Chekhov simplified both in style and meaning. The simplification of the out-of-door set for the last act was welcome but lacked unity. The play had been speeded up in tempo. Chekhov's famous pauses had been cut or shortened and consequently the "atmospheric" noises, so dear to Stanislavski, were much less noticeable. The poetical values had been damaged in favour of a more optimistic, more clearly constructive meaning. Nostalgic melancholy, even despair, had given way to positive declarations. Vershinin's lines about what is going to happen in "two or three hundred years" had taken on a truly prophetic sense. It was forced. The Russians claimed that at one time before the war their audiences had become bored with Chekhov and that they had had to renew their interpretation. Gogol was much better done. It was given in the original Stanislavski production. There were a lot of scenes with quick changes so that the sets were only sketched and not realistically detailed. Those giant actors, endowed with deep voices, gave full play to robust, colourful characterisations. In my view, one typical blemish did harm to the production. One scene in the play takes place during a storm. It was the most admirable storm! The thunder was unforgettable. And on top of it was the rain. Through the window on the right I could watch the rain go through all its phases: we had fast rain, slow rain, and at the end, remarkably, dripping rain. You could not only hear but *see* the rain, so much so that it was quite impossible to hear or see the play, which is not written in a realistic style.

---

[1] Since those days the Moscow Art Theatre has played *Three Sisters* in London and Paris. The production had the same essential characteristics I had noticed in Moscow but many improvements had been made. In particular the three sisters were played by much younger actresses.

But why did Gogol seem to stand the test of time better than Chekhov?

In spite of all my love for Chekhov, I suggest the reason may be that Gogol has a style which is more objective, more "written," more classical than Chekhov's. It must be difficult to imitate Gogol. But goodness knows, Chekhov is being imitated all the time. The amount of simplified second-rate Chekhov to be seen in London and New York is remarkable—usually leading to a dull mediocrity which is called "life."

But theatre is not life. Theatre comes from life, but theatre is theatre: life in the theatre needs theatrical transposition, in writing and style. . . .

PART TWO ❦ *THE ACTOR*

Constant-Benoit Coquelin

Coquelin, the most famous member of a family of great character actors at the Comédie Française, first appeared in 1860. Living and working almost as often in London as in Paris, he toured Europe and America and in 1900 acted with Sarah Bernhardt. He was considered outstanding in the great comic personalities of Molière but also in roles of a romantic, flamboyant nature — one of his first successes was the title part of Rostand's *Cyrano de Bergerac.*

He wrote *The Art of the Actor* in 1880. It is not a systematic review of the techniques or goals of the actor but, in a brilliant and discursive style, touches — in the excerpts reprinted here — on such matters as the actor's intelligence and its relation to his art, questions of "realism" and style, and the uses of "naturalism." Coquelin stands in the great tradition of French actors, bridging — as he did with ease — the era of classical acting and the modern period.

from THE ART OF THE ACTOR

It is plain that I ask a great deal of the actor, yet a delicate point to determine is whether it is necessary for him to have a great degree of intelligence. There are reasons for and against it.

I have known excellent actors who outside their art were considered, not without cause, to have rather mediocre minds. The fact is that the only intelligence indispensable to the actor is *that of his own art.*

I have read, I do not know where, that the only thing Corot knew in French poetry was *Polyeucte,* and that he had never been able to get to the end of it; this did not prevent him from being himself an admirable poet . . . in painting.

The same thing is true of the actor. He may know nothing of painting, of music, even of poetry, and yet be a very fine actor, and even a poetic actor. It is enough for him to be knowledgeable in his own art, which is something quite different from all these things.

It is, however, quite wrong to belittle the special intelligence of the actor. Faculties which, it is recognised, enable him to move and arouse the enthusiasm of an audience are not negligible, and if it is objected that the author has a great part in his accomplishment, I

From *The Art of the Actor* by Constant-Benoit Coquelin, translated by Elsie Fogerty. Reprinted by permission of George Allen & Unwin Ltd. (London).

recognise it, but I ask that we should recollect how little effect is produced by the finest plays badly acted. How many beautiful lines have called up laughter because they were badly spoken! Finally, taking advantage of an objection I made against myself a little farther back, there are actors in whom the power of characterisation is so strong that they create the most extraordinary, the most living, the most vivid figures from parts entirely conventional, without observation and without grandeur. Of how many plays have we not heard: "What a poor play, but Frédérick was wonderful in it." Into what poor tragedy did Talma breathe the genius and the soul which, vanished, left them what they were in reality: nothing.

It is this creation of living types which constitutes the art of the theatre. It is the most human of all arts, and the supreme pleasure of the stage; that which moves the masses most powerfully and offers to the critical the keenest delight. So to my mind it must remain an *art* —that is to say, it must blend with the expression of truth the fragrance of poetry, the vision of the ideal, and that is why naturalism in the theatre seems to me a fault.

Besides, the public will not have it. It will always jib at crude, violent realism, at obscene ugliness. Even in evil or vile characterisation it demands a gleam of artistry. Paulin-Ménier in his Choppard was terrifying in his debauched realism, but he had just that touch of scampish emphasis which accentuated his personality. "*Well! Here is my head...Not much of a gift I am making you!*" It was a defiance to death itself. It was laughter, it was the gleam!...

No more than I will allow departure from truth under the pretext that it is picturesque, no more do I admit that under pretext of truth we should fall into sordid horror.

I am on the side of nature and against what is naturalistic.

Nature in art; how much could be said on that topic, for in different times and different countries nature is differently understood!

When Garrick came to France he admired our actors very much, but he did not consider them natural enough. I shall be told that that is because they were acting in tragedy, but when Talma appeared he made tragedy natural, and to that he owed his success and his influence.

Was his naturalness that of Garrick? I cannot tell. The genius of the two races is too different; the love of originality is too strong with our neighbours for them always to remain within the true measure of things; in any case, to-day it is we who when we go to see Irving no longer find him near enough to nature. The truth is his nature does not correspond to ours. We would have yet other reservations to make as to the naturalness of the Germans; sentimental beyond measure, and more allied in their philosophical affectations to the "nature" of Diderot and the sentimental school of the later eighteenth century. In their time, we must remember, these too were innovators. That style which seems to us so far from truth they brought into the theatre in the name of nature. And it is the same great name that the Romantics bore on their banner, while we to-day despise as out-of-date their grandiloquence and their thunder-defying attitudes.

These Romantics claimed that they were giving us human drama, mingled laughter and tears, in the place of conventional tragedy; and they gave us *Antony, la Tour de Nesle, Lucrèce Borgia;* with the same good intentions, Baron Taylor collaborated with the exquisite Nodier to produce *Melmoth, l'Homme errant, les Vampires, Honte et Remords, Amour et Étourderie,* etc., etc. Plainly a humanity quite different from that of Voltaire. Actors, following in the steps of the authors, no longer found Talma natural enough. They discovered the method of talking as one talks every day, so as never to be audible; of sitting down and turning one's back to the audience as often as possible. They spoke the lines of Athalie as who should say, "How de do? How are you?" "Heavens, yes," mumbled Abner. "*Yes. I come into his shrine to worship God, the Lord,*" just like that, my cane in my hand, *to celebrate* with you among old pals *the memory of that day where upon Sinai's mount,* if I am not mistaken, *the Law was given us.* My word! *How time has changed since then,* etc. etc. So they flattered themselves that they introduced nature into Racine. By way of retaliation when they were on their own ground — that is to say, in melodrama — emphasis returned to its own. It was no longer, of course, the monotonous tragic purr,[1] but a jolting sublimity, trivial effects breaking through couplets of the most frantic lyricism; antitheses to cut and come again; they never said, "How are you?" but "Give me thy hand that I may clasp it." Profundity was dragged in everywhere; they wore a fatal air, wading in swagger to the top of their jack-boots. It was the day of the swayling plume;[2] the natural-

---

[1] No translation will give the delicious value of "Le ronron tragique." [Notes throughout are those of the translator.]

[2] "*Panache.*" This was the last word of Coquelin's greatest impersonation, Cyrano de Bergerac, at the end of the play of that name, and there it is wisely left untranslated in English versions, for it means the crest on the helmet of knighthood.

ists of to-day, the school of Coupeau would gladly substitute the feather broom.

Permit me to insist, the importance of the subject demands it, if I refuse to believe in art without nature I will not in the theatre have nature without art. Everything must spring from truth; everything must strive towards the ideal. Comedy herself, that good, positive old girl, does she not serve the ideal by lighting up our faults and our vices with the light of her gaiety? If she limited herself to reproducing them brutally in their naked ugliness without relief, without wit, without grace, she would cease to be comedy, for we should cease to laugh.

Terror and pity are the main springs of art, not disgust and horror.

The theatre is a school of manners, not a school of medicine; and besides, pure and photographic reality is impossible in the theatre. If truth can ever seem lacking in verisimilitude it is surely here, under the glare of those lights which shine from below, instead of falling from above, in that enlarging medium which changes the scale of men, of things, even of time.

Only once I was guilty of naturalism—unintentionally—and it is still a source of compunction to me. It was on tour: I had spent the night in the train, rehearsed in the morning, and made some excursion on foot in the afternoon: I was very tired; that night I was playing Annibal in *L'Aventurière*. You know that at the end of the second act Annibal, whom Fabrice has been plying with drink to make him talk, gets tipsy and goes to sleep. I played the drunken scene as usual, neither more nor less, but when it came to sleep, the state I was mimicking seemed so sweet to me, I felt such a longing for it that I allowed myself to be overtaken unawares: I fell to sleep on the stage; right in front of the public! I even went so far, *proh pudor!* as to snore.... It was not according to the stage directions, but the public listened, thought it was all in the part, and that I was putting in a bit of "business." Some of them laughed, others thought it in rather doubtful taste. There were not wanting those who said that I snored without grace, without truth, that I forced the note. Briefly, that it was not natural. Alas! I was indifferent to both applause and blame. I believe a hiss would not have roused me, and when the curtain fell my comrades had some difficulty in calling me back to a sense of reality. My little snooze had in fact done me a great deal of good and I finished the part gallantly.

It was a mistake, however, which might have turned out badly.

Certainly I would not have allowed myself to be led away, supposing I had been timed to wake up before the end of the act; my weakness came from the fact that I knew I had nothing to do but sleep until the curtain came down, and instead of feigning sleep I gave a real performance. It was, I repeat it to my shame, naturalism of the first water. But notwithstanding! since it is well to draw morals from our faults, you see that the spectators thought that sleep badly acted: it seemed to them lacking in reality. That is the story so often verified, of the clown and the peasant. The clown mimicked the cry of a sucking-pig and was applauded. The peasant, having made a bet that he could do the trick as well, hid a real sucking-pig under his cloak, and surreptitiously pinched the animal. It squealed, and he was hissed.

That was because it happened on the boards; the point of view differs according to whether we watch from the sidewalk or from the seats of a theatre. What would you? The pigling no doubt squealed very well, but he squealed without art.

Here we have the error of the naturalists; they always want to make real pigs squeal.

I venture to say that actors who think we can express, and ought to express, only what we ourselves experience, fall into this very same error. Here are the people who should be accused of naturalism; for if it is necessary for them to cry in order to make us cry, logic demands that they should get drunk in order to render intoxication, and in order to act a murder perfectly they should get a hypnotist to suggestionise them into stabbing a comrade—or, if necessary, the prompter. Besides, it always leads to the great danger of appearing unconvincing. If another anecdote is needed to prove my point, I will quote one of which Mr. Edwin Booth is the hero. One night he was playing *The Fool's Revenge* (*Le Roi s'amuse*). The part was one of his best, and he enjoyed playing it. This time he satisfied himself even better than usual; the force of the situations, the pathos of the language worked on him so powerfully that he identified himself completely with his character. Real tears fell from his eyes, his voice was broken with emotion; real sobs choked him, and it seemed to him that he had never played so well. The performance over, he saw his daughter hurrying towards him; she, his truest critic, had been watching the scene from a box, and was hastening anxiously to inquire what was the matter, and how it happened that he had played so badly that night! A valuable confirmation of that famous paradox of Diderot's; the truth according to my mind is that in order to call forth emotion we ourselves must not feel it; and that the actor must in all circumstances remain the absolute master of himself, and leave nothing to chance.

Dissertations on art too often seem to end in mere hair-splitting, and with all my *distinguo* I may not have avoided the danger. But remember what I said above about the magnifying power of the theatre. The footlights exaggerate everything. They modify the laws of space and of time.[3] They gather leagues into so many square yards; they make minutes seem like hours. What seems a mere guiding thread at a reading grows at performance to the thickness of a cable.[4]

Do not let us be afraid, then, of insisting upon fine distinctions. I repeat: Naturalness may differ in kind.

To say a thing is natural does not imply that it is uniform. Two individuals may be completely dissimilar in the expression of their sentiments, yet each may be as sincere and, therefore, as natural as the other.

In France, the natural temperaments of the South and of the North differ absolutely. One must learn to feel these nuances.

Let me add that criticism must be prepared to recognise similar shades of difference in the work of actors. According to their own temperamental peculiarities actors of equal merit may reproduce very different aspects of nature. At first sight you may even find something excessive in the acting of very great artists, something so out of the ordinary that from the point of view of fidelity to nature they compare unfavourably with artists of the second rank. But this is only apparent. Such players give to their creations something of their personal grandeur; that is all. Their naturalness is that of the eagle, not of the domestic hen. But, eagle or hen, no one is above the general laws of art. Truth, proportion, harmony—these are the same for everyone. One more point, and I should like to conclude with it. It requires some explanation in order to make it comprehensible.

As one does not play melodrama on the same lines as comedy, even so Molière must not be produced like Beaumarchais, nor Augier like Meilhac. Every dramatist has his own peculiar mental outlook, his works reveal it, and the actor must reflect it, for he is not merely the interpreter of a single author. Take Dumas Fils, and I am sure you will feel how true this is. Is not every character whom he

[3] This exaggeration is most visible in regard to force; and these three elements, force, time and space, together form the rhythm which the actor has to acquire before he can express himself freely in the theatre; his "sense of the stage."—E. F.

[4] *Une ficelle* is an artificial train of action needed for the plot, but not springing naturally from the action.

creates a kind of missionary, charged with the propaganda of the master's ideas for the benefit of his audience and to obtain as many converts as possible? If that is so, how can you play such parts as you would those of the elder Dumas, for example? These have no desire to demonstrate anything at all; they go their mighty way, nimble, abounding, swift—now caracoling, now pirouetting, always level with the ground, with no other care but to amuse the world and give rein to their imagination. The one romances even in his plays, and makes history serve his purpose in the process. The other theorises, and uses realism as his servant. What intelligence in both of them! What a contrast between the universal animation of the one and the concentrated irony of the other! The Gascon buoyancy of the one and the Parisian acerbity of the other; the words of the father are rockets, the words of the son are bullets. An actor must take account of all this if he does not wish to play *Mlle de Belle-Isle* like *Le Demi-Monde,* and Richelieu like Olivier de Jalin.

These are totally distinct types, each characteristic of the brain that created them. The same thing is true of the more modest characters of Labiche and Scribe. From the brain of their creator they have kept the *accent* of their origin—accent, that indescribable thing by virtue of which, whatever their age, sex or character, the *Canebière* breathes again harmoniously upon the lips of every child of Marseilles.

This accent, the accent of the author, the actor too must have it. It is his business to penetrate deeply enough into his man to find it. It is another form of collaboration, truer and more intimate than that which he undertakes in working out his part and inspiring it with vitality.

I will not speak of the tragedians, not because I have nothing to say: on the contrary, I would gladly insist that they, too, should be played as men of their period. If you are playing in Corneille, do not occupy yourself with an effort to *humanise* him; still less to Latinise him; play him frankly as he saw himself, as a Spaniard of the seventeenth century, as a Norman—that is to say, very nearly a Gascon, more knight than lawyer, a Frenchman in the dawn of the *grand siècle,* only great, perhaps, because of that very dawn: the glorious days when men conspired like Cinna with Montmorency or de Thou, played at politics like Flaminius or Severus, with Retz or Richelieu, intrigued, playing at politics again, with the Émilies of the Fronde; give to your Corneille, in one word, the Cornelian accent. He is a lyrist, spread your wings!

With Racine, in whom I find equal genius (you see, I do not mince matters), furl them again. Human stature has diminished. We are still under Louis XIV, but what is lost in grandeur we have gained in politeness. Good manners rule, but with sobriety; argument takes the place of eloquence. Lyricism has grown elegiac; there are no illusions. Racine's aim is to charm rather than to dazzle. Racine, the most feminine of all our authors, demands to be played with discretion, with delicacy; even Roxana, even Phædra, must keep on the stage the measure the author has imposed upon them in his style. That was how Rachel achieved her triumph.

When you play Molière, take on his breadth, his admirable precision, so indifferent to the mere sparkle of wit, so fascinated, on the contrary, by the broad, open countenance of truth. Take on his gaiety, so completely the natural state of his soul that it becomes most apparent in his latest plays, and that neither sickness nor sorrow can quench that gallant laughter, devoid, whatever men may say, of all admixture of misanthropic bitterness. Speak with fitting breadth that glorious language of comedy, the finest in the theatre.

With Regnard you may take greater liberties. In him fancy often takes the place of observation, but be full of alacrity. Don't be afraid to let that abounding vitality run riot a little; nonchalant and light in pursuit, Rabelais would say, and bold in encounter.

Beaumarchais is something quite different; no sap flowing spontaneously from a naturally joyful soul. Witty, combative, carping, provocative; so rich in all these things that he lavishes them on his characters. That hobbled ass of a Brid'oison, even *he* has wit; poise, audacity, *brass*! that is what you need to play Beaumarchais.

Marivaux saves himself from his intellectuality by his grace. Otherwise it would be overpowering. Nevertheless he is truer than he seems, and it is his expressiveness, by its selective power, which deadens our sense of his gifts of observation, acute as they always are. The comedy of his serving-men, which is a little gross, still seems to me natural and quite in character; forced, it would be deafening, but frank it must be. So it will contrast usefully with that delicate preciosity in the rest of the play, which might grow a little insipid in the long run. Little paths all sown with roses — where the spectators must not be allowed to go to sleep. . . .

I shall be accused of contradiction, at least in regard to Molière and Shakespeare, when on the one hand I declare that I never discover them in their own works, and on the other when I invite all to seek them there and to play them in a certain style. The contradiction is more apparent than real. The personages created by these great men live their own proper and independent lives. Neither Shakespeare nor Molière paint themselves or repeat themselves in their characters. These are men—men whom we know, whom we are going to meet presently in the street. Yet, when we meet them, shall we confound the men of Shakespeare with those of Molière? No. We shall easily differentiate between their creators and restore to each the types that belong to him of right. The fact is, that in their outlook upon all humanity, these geniuses select their types by certain impulses which arise from their own manner of understanding life. Molière goes for the large, sure, frank type; Shakespeare for the type which is extravagant, passionate, unruly. Not only do they so select their characters, but they choose among the thousand traits by which man reveals himself those which seem to them most characteristic, and colour their expression after their own manner. They have the power of creating men, but even more marvellously that of creating the spaces in which they make them live, the atmosphere that fills these spaces, the light that bathes this atmosphere. That is their peculiar genius.

It is this choice of types and of expressions, this diversity of colour and background—all that conforms to the innate constitution of their genius—which constitutes their style, their manner, and by that it is that their personality appears. The foundation is universal, the form belongs to each of them alone. Within the humble course of his powers, the actor must realise something similar to this. He can stamp his individuality on the rôles he interprets, but that stamp must blend with the reality of the character, so that it becomes clear to the spectator only by reflection and by comparison.

In watching him play, it is necessary that the spectator should forget him, and see only the character he represents. He is excellent, and it is a proof of his superiority, when in re-reading the play or in seeing it played by another, the spectator remembers him and cries: "He alone could play that part!"

Who knows? Is it not perhaps because Shakespeare and Molière both belong to our own craft that they understood how to banish their "I" from their works, stamped so profoundly nevertheless with the seal of their genius. Let us study them unceasingly, frail as we are, and above and beyond this (that we may verify and complete ourselves like them), let us never cease to contemplate as they did the eternal, the Divine Comedy in Nature herself.

Konstantin Stanislavski

Stanislavski's pivotal importance in the modern theatre is too great to describe here in detail. His influence among directors, stage designers, actors, and playwrights has been pervasive and, although frequently misinterpreted, is basically among the most affirmative in the history of dramatic activity of any period. These two series of observations are taken from *Building a Character* (published posthumously in 1949) and serve as focal points in a general study of Stanislavski's work. Although they stand as individual essays, they may be useful as starting points in any survey of his writing at large.

Stanislavski had long experience in all areas of theatre work. He acted throughout his career; he directed; he was a distinguished teacher. He was responsible, with Nemirovich-Danchenko, for the founding of the Moscow Art Theatre and, subsequently, for some of its most important productions of Shakespeare, Gogol, and Chekhov. He developed, in the course of many years of teaching and practical experience, his famous "Method" — essentially an intensely practical system for actors desirous of continued imaginative and probing creativity in the projection of their roles. In most of his writings, Stanislavski set up imaginary conversations between a group of acting students and their teacher. In these excerpts, the teacher's "comments" are arranged in a more or less continuous series of observations, deleting most of Stanislavski's interruptions and short comments from the students.

✎ *from PERSPECTIVE IN CHARACTER BUILDING*

... "One half of an actor's soul is absorbed by his super-objective, by the through line of action, the subtext, his inner images, the elements which go to make up his inner creative state. But the other half of it continues to operate on a psycho-technique more or less in the way I demonstrated it to you.

"An actor is split into two parts when he is acting. You recall how Tommaso Salvini[1] put it: 'An actor lives, weeps, laughs on the stage,

---

From *Building a Character* by Konstantin Stanislavski. Copyright 1949 by Elizabeth Reynolds Hapgood. Reprinted by permission of the publisher, Theatre Arts Books (New York).

[1] [The great romantic Italian actor (1829-1916), whose major success was the title role in *Othello*.]

but as he weeps and laughs he observes his own tears and mirth. It is this double existence, this balance between life and acting that makes for art.'

"As you see, this division does no harm to inspiration. On the contrary the one encourages the other. Moreover we lead a double existence in our actual lives. But this does not prevent our living and having strong emotions.

"Do you remember what I told you back in the beginning, when we were working on objectives and the through line of action, about the two parallel lines of perspective?

"The one is the perspective of the role.

"The other is the perspective of the actor, his life on the stage, his psycho-technique while he is acting.

"The stream of *psycho-technique* which I illustrated for you with the *Othello* speech is the line of the *perspective of the actor*. It is close to the *perspective of the role* because it runs parallel with it, the way a foot path may stretch along beside a highway. But at certain moments they may move farther apart when, for one reason or another, an actor is drawn away from the main course of his part by something extraneous and irrelevant to it. Then he loses the perspective of his role. Fortunately our psycho-technique exists for the very purpose of giving ways constantly to attract us back to the true path, just as the foot path will always lead the pedestrian back to the highway." . . .

"I went to the theatre recently to see a five act play . . . [after] the first act I was delighted with the production as well as the acting. The actors gave vivid characterizations, showed much fire and temperament, acted in a special manner which interested me very much. I was curious to see how the play and the acting would develop.

"But after the second act I found they had shown the same thing as in the first. Because of this fact the interest of the audience, as well as my own, suffered a definite decline. After the third act the same thing was repeated to an even more marked degree because the actors plumbed no new depths, their characters were transfixed, there was still the same fiery spirit to which the public was by now accustomed. The same manner of acting by this time had become so routine that it was boring, dull, and at times annoying. By the middle of the fifth act I was unable to take in any more. My eyes were no longer on the stage, my ears were deaf to the lines, my mind was preoccupied with the thought: How can I get out of here unnoticed?

"What is the explanation of this descending scale of impressions gathered from a good play, well acted and produced?"

"Monotony," I ventured.

"A week ago I went to a concert," Tortsov went on. "The same 'monotony' was evident in the music. A good orchestra performed a good symphony. They ended it as they began it, they scarcely altered the tempo or the volume of the sound, there was no shading. It was most boring for the listeners.

"Why did they have no success, this well acted play and this good symphony performed by a good orchestra? Was it not because in both cases they were playing without perspective?

"Let us agree that the word 'perspective' means: the calculated, harmonious inter-relationship and distribution of the parts in a whole play or role.

"This means further that there can be no acting, no movement, no gestures, thoughts, speech, no word, feeling, etc., etc., without its appropriate perspective. The simplest entrance or exit on the stage, any action taken to carry out a scene, to pronounce a phrase, words, soliloquy and so on, must have a perspective and an ultimate purpose (the super-objective). Without those an actor may not so much as say 'yes' or 'no.' Even a tiny phrase taken by itself, has its own brief perspective. A whole thought expressed in a number of clauses is even less able to do without it. A single speech, a scene, an act, a play all need perspective.

"It is customary, in referring to speech, to have in mind the so-called logical perspective. But our practice in the theatre leads us to a broader terminology. We use the descriptions:

1. The perspective of the thought conveyed. This that same logical perspective.

2. The perspective in conveying complex feelings.

3. Artistic perspective, used to add color, vivid illustration to a story or a speech.

"In the first, the perspective used in conveying a thought, logic and coherence play an important part in the unfolding of the thought and the establishing of the relation of the various parts to the whole expression.

"This perspective is achieved with the aid of a long series of key words and their accents which give sense to the phrase.

"Just as we underline this or that syllable of a word, this or that word in a phrase, we have to throw into relief the most important phrase carrying a whole thought, and do the same in a long story, a dialogue, a soliloquy. We follow the same principle of choosing the significant component parts in one large scene, a whole act and so on, the important episodes. Out of it all we evolve a chain of outstanding points which vary among themselves as to their volume and fullness.

"The lines of perspective which are used to convey complex feelings move on the subtextual, inner plane of a role. These are the lines of inner objectives, desires, ambitions, efforts, actions which are grouped, inserted, separated, combined, accented, toned down. Some represent important fundamental objectives and appear in the foreground. Others of medium or minimum value are grouped on a secondary plane, or sink quite into the background, according to the peculiar factors causing the development of the emotions throughout the play.

"These objectives, which go to make up the lines of an inner perspective, are to a large and important degree expressed in words.

"When we come to the laying on of color along the lines of artistic perspectives we again are obliged to adhere to qualities of consecutiveness, tone and harmony. As in paintings, artistic coloring does a very great deal to make it possible to distinguish planes of speech.

"The important parts, which must be filled out most, are most highly colored, whereas those relegated to the background are less vivid in tonal shades.

"It is only when we study a play as a whole and can appreciate its overall perspective that we are able to fit the various planes correctly together, make a beautiful arrangement of the component parts, mold them into harmonious and well rounded forms in terms of words.

"Only after an actor has thought through, analyzed and felt himself to be a living person inside his whole part there opens up to him the long, beautiful, beckoning perspective. His speech becomes, as it were, far-sighted, no longer the myopic vision it was at the start. Against this depth of background he can play out whole actions, speak whole thoughts, rather than be held to limited objectives, separate phrases and words.

"When we read an unfamiliar book aloud for the first time we lack perspective. Moment by moment we have only the immediate action, words, phrases in mind. Can such a reading be artistic and true? Of course not.

"Broad physical actions, the conveying of great thoughts, the experience of wide emotions and passions are made up of a multiplicity of component parts, and in the end a scene, an act, a play cannot escape the necessity of a perspective and an ultimate aim.

"Actors who play a role they have not studied well and thoroughly analyzed are like readers of a complicated, unfamiliar text.

"Such actors have only a dim perspective of the play. They do not understand where they must lead the characters they portray. Often when they play a scene they are familiar with they either do not distinguish or they do not know what lies still unrevealed in the obscure depths of the rest of the play. This obliges them to keep their minds constantly fixed on only the nearest action, the immediate thought expressed, utterly without regard for the whole perspective of the play.

"Take as an illustration of this the fact that some actors who play the part of Luka in Gorki's *The Lower Depths* do not even read the last act because they do not appear in it. As a result they cannot possibly have a true perspective and are unable to play their role correctly. The end hinges on the beginning. The last act is the outcome of the old man's preaching. Therefore one must have one's eyes always trained on the climax and lead all the characters whom Luka affects towards that end.

"In a different way the tragedian who plays the title role of *Othello* knowing the end but without a careful study of the whole play begins to roll his eyes and gnash his teeth in the first act, gloating over the prospect of the murder.

"But Tommaso Salvini was much more calculating than that in working out the plan for his roles. Take *Othello* again. He was always aware of the whole perspective of the play from the moment of his fiery outburst of young passionate love in his first entrance to his supreme hatred as a jealous killer at the end of the tragedy. With mathematical precision and unrelenting consistency, from point to point, he plotted out the evolution of the emotions as they matured in his soul.

"To express this in more understandable terms let me give you another example.

"Let us suppose you are playing *Hamlet,* the most complex role of all in its spiritual coloring. It contains a son's bewilderment over his mother's suddenly transferred love—'or ere those shoes were old' she had already forgotten her beloved husband. In it, too, is the mystic experience of a man who has been afforded a brief glimpse into the world beyond where his father languishes. After Hamlet learns the secret of that other life this one loses its former meaning for him. The role embraces the agonizing recognition of man's existence and the realization of a mission above his strength, on which depends the liberation of his father from his sufferings beyond the grave. For the part you must have the feelings resultant from filial devotion to your mother, love for a young girl, renunciation of that love, her death, the emotions of revenge, horror over your mother's death, of murder, and the expectation of your death after you have fulfilled your duty. Try jumbling up all these emotions on one dish and you can imagine what a hash will result.

"But if you apportion all these experiences along the perspective of the part in logical, systematic and consecutive order, as required by the psychology of such a complex character, and the life of his spirit which unfolds and develops throughout the whole course of the play, you will have a well built structure, a harmonious line, in which the inter-relation of its component elements is an important factor in the gradually growing and deepening tragedy of a great soul.

"Can one project any single part of such a role without bearing in mind the perspective of the whole? If, for example, you do not convey in the beginning of the play Hamlet's deep pain and consternation caused by his mother's frivolity, the famous scene with her later will not be properly prepared.

"If you do not feel the whole impact of the shock Hamlet receives from what the ghost tells him of life beyond the grave, there will be no understanding his doubts, his painful efforts to uncover the meaning of life, his break with his beloved, and all the strange conduct which makes him appear abnormal in the eyes of others.

"Does all this not suggest to you that it is the more incumbent on the actor who plays Hamlet to take care how he plays his first scenes, because so much will be required of him in expanded passion as his part unrolls?

"The result of that kind of preparation is what we call 'acting with perspective.'

"As a part moves along we have, as you might say, two perspectives in mind. The one is related to the character portrayed, the other to the actor. Actually Hamlet, as a figure in a play, has no idea of perspective, he knows nothing of what the future has in store for him, whereas the actor who plays the part must bear this constantly in mind, he is obliged to keep in perspective."

"How is it possible to forget about what is coming when you play a part for the hundredth time?" I asked.

"You cannot and need not do it," explained Tortsov. "Although the character being played should not know what lies ahead, still perspective is neccessary for the part so that he can appreciate more fully each present moment and more fully give himself up to it.

"The future in a part is its super-objective. Let the character keep moving towards it. It will do no harm if the actor meanwhile remembers for a second the whole line of his role. This will only reinforce the meaning of each segment as he lives it and it will pull his attention with increased power.

"Let us suppose that you and Paul are playing a scene between Othello and Iago. Is it not important that you should remember that you, the Moor, only yesterday arrived in Cyprus, were forever united with Desdemona, that you are experiencing the best days of your life — your honeymoon?

"Where else would you get the joyousness necessary to the opening of the scene? It is all the more important because there are so few gay colors in the play. Moreover is it any less important for you to recall for a brief moment that from this scene forward the lucky star of your life will begin to set and that this decline must only gradually become apparent and distinct? There must be a powerful contrast between the present and the future. The brighter the first the darker the second.

"You need that rapid glance into the past and the future in order to make a proper estimate of the present action, and the better you sense its relationship to the whole play the easier it will be for you to focus the full extent of your attention on it.

"Now you have the necessary basis for the perspective of a part," concluded Tortsov.

But I was not satisfied and pressed him further with the question:

"Why does the actor himself have to have that other perspective?"

"His own perspective, as the person playing the role, is necessary to him so that at every given moment while he is on the stage he will be in a position to assess his inner creative powers and ability to express them in external terms, to apportion them and make reasonable use of the material he has amassed for his part. Take that same scene between Othello and Iago. Doubt steals into the former's jealous soul and gradually grows. The actor who plays Othello must remember that he will have to play many more scenes of mounting passion between that point and the end of the play. It would be dangerous for him to break loose in this first scene, to show all his temperament without holding it in reserve for the gradual reinforcement of his unfolding jealousy. To squander his inner powers here would throw the whole role out of proportion. He must be prudent, calculating and always have his eyes on the final, culminating point of the play. "Artistic emotion is weighed not in pounds but in ounces."

"We must not forget one extremely important quality inherent in perspective. It lends a breadth, a sweep, a momentum to our inner experiences and external actions, all of which is of extreme value to our creative achievement.

"Imagine yourself running a race for a prize, but instead of pressing on over a long distance you stopped every twenty paces. If you did this you would never get into your stride or acquire any momentum, and that is enormously important in a race.

"We actors face the same problem. If we stop short at the end of every bit in a role and then start over again with the next we never get up momentum in our efforts, our desires, our actions. Yet we must have it because it prods, stirs, inflames our feelings, our will, thoughts, imagination and so on. You should never spend yourself on a short sprint. You must have the depth, the perspective, the far away beckoning goal in mind.

"What I have said here is equally applicable to the sound of the voice, to speech, gestures, movements, actions, facial expression, temperament and tempo-rhythm. In all these fields it is dangerous to break loose, to squander your all. You must be economical and make a just estimate of your physical powers and means of transposing the character you play into terms of flesh and blood.

"To regulate them you will need not only your inner powers but also the perspective of a dramatic artist.

"Now that you have made the acquaintance of perspective in a play and in a part, think it over and tell me if it does not bear a close resemblance to your old friend the through line of action?

"Of course they are not identical, but there is a kinship between them. The one is the other's closest aid. Perspective is the path through the entire extent of a play, along which the through line of action constantly progresses.

"*Everything happens for the sake of these two elements, perspective and the through line of action. They contain the principal significance of creativeness, of art, of our approach to acting.*"

from SOME CONCLUSIONS ON ACTING

"The method we have been studying is often called the 'Stanislavski system.' But this is not correct. The very power of this method lies in the fact that it was not concocted or invented by anyone. Both in spirit and in body it is a part of our organic natures. It is based on the laws of nature. The birth of a child, the growth of a tree, the creation of an artistic image are all manifestations of a kindred order. How can we come closer to this nature of creation? That has been the principal concern of my whole life. It is not possible to invent a system. We are born with it inside us, with an innate capacity for creativeness. This last is our natural necessity, therefore it would seem that we could not know how to express it except in accordance with a natural system.

"Yet strangely enough, when we step on to the stage we lose our natural endowment and instead of acting creatively we proceed to perform contortions of pretentious proportions. What drives us to do this? The condition of having to create something in public view. Forced, conventional untruthfulness is implicit in stage presentation, in the foisting on us of the acts and words prescribed by an author, the scenery designed by a painter, the production devised by a director, in our own embarrassment, stage fright, the poor taste and false traditions which cramp our natures. All these impel an actor to exhibitionism, insincere representation. The approach we have chosen — the art of living a part — rebels with all the strength it can muster against those other current 'principles' of acting. We assert the contrary principle that the main factor in any form of creativeness is the life of a human spirit, that of the actor and his part, their joint feelings and subconscious creation.

"These cannot be 'exhibited'; they can only be produced spontaneously or as the result of something that has gone before. One can only feel them. All you can 'exhibit' on the stage is the artificial, contrived results of a non-existent experience.

"There is no feeling in that; there is only conventional artificiality, cliché acting."

"But it can also be effective. The public is impressed by it," remarked one of the students.

"I admit that," agreed Tortsov, "but what kind of an impression does it make? The quality of one impression must be distinguished from that of another. Our approach to acting in this theatre is extremely clear on this point.

"We are not interested in hit and run impressions, here today and gone tomorrow. We are not satisfied merely with visual and audible effects. What we hold in highest regard are impressions made on the emotions, which leave a lifelong mark on the spectator and transform actors into real, living beings whom one may include in the roster of one's near and dear friends, whom one may love, feel one's self akin to, whom one goes to the theatre to visit again and again. Our demands are simple, normal, and therefore they are difficult to satisfy. All we ask is that an actor on the stage live in accordance with natural laws. Yet because of the circumstances amid which an actor has to do his work it is much easier for him to distort his nature than to live as a natural human being. So we have had to find means to struggle against this tendency toward distortion—that is the basis of our so-called 'system.' Its purpose lies in destroying inevitable distortions and in directing the work of our inner natures to the right path which is carved out by stubborn work and the proper practices and habits.

"This 'system' should restore the natural laws, which have been dislocated by the circumstances of an actor's having to work in public, it should return him to the creative state of a normal human being.

"But you will have to be patient," Tortsov went on. "It will take several years even if you watch yourself carefully for these things you have been striving for to mature and blossom. By then, when you have the opportunity to go off in a false direction, you will find that you cannot do it, the essentially right way will be so firmly rooted in you."

"But great artists act by the grace of God and without all these elements of a creative state!" I objected.

"You are mistaken," countered Tortsov instantly. "Read what it says in *My Life In Art*. The more talent the actor has the more he cares about his technique, especially with regard to his inner qualities. A true creative state while on the stage, and all the elements that go to compose it, were the natural endowment of Shchepkin, Ermolova, Duse, Salvini. Nevertheless they worked unremittingly on their technique. With them moments of inspiration were almost a natural state. Inspiration came to them by natural means almost every time they repeated a role, yet all their lives they sought an approach to it.

"There is all the more reason why we, of more meagre endowments, should seek it. We ordinary mortals are under the obligation of acquiring, developing, training in ourselves and by ourselves each one of the component elements of a creative state on the stage. It takes us a long time and much hard work. Still we must never forget that the actor who has nothing more than capacity will never be a genius, whereas those whose talents may be more modest, if they will study the nature of their art, the laws of creativeness, may grow into the class of those who are akin to the geniuses. The 'system' will facilitate that growth. The preparation it gives an actor is not something to be laughed at: its results are very very great!"

"But, oh, how hard it all is!" I groaned. "How can we ever take it all in!"

"Those are the doubting reactions of impetuous youth," said Tortsov. "Today you learn something. Tomorrow you think you can already be letter perfect in technique. But the 'system' is not a hand me down suit that you can put on and walk off in, or a cook book where all you need is to find the page and there is your recipe. No, it is a whole way of life, you have to grow up in it, educate yourself in it for years. You cannot cram it into yourselves, you can assimilate it, take it into your blood and flesh, until it becomes second nature, becomes so organic a part of your being that you as an actor are transformed by it for the stage and for all time. It is a system that must be studied in parts and then merged into a whole so that it can be understood in all its fundamentals. When you can spread it all out before you like a fan you will obtain a true grasp of its entirety. You cannot hope to do this all at once. It is like going to war: you must conquer the territory bit by bit, consolidate your gains, keep in contact with your rear communications, expand, make further gains before you can speak of final conquest.

"In the same way we go about conquering our 'system.' In our difficult task the gradual quality and the training in it are of enormous help. They allow us to develop each new means we learn to a point of automatic habit, until it is organically grafted into us. In its initial stages each new factor is an obstacle, it draws off all our attention from other more important matters," Tortsov continued his description. "This process does not wear away until it is quite assimilated, made our own. Here again the 'system' is of great assistance. With each new means once conquered a part of our burden is eased and our attention is freed for concentration on more essential matters.

"Piecemeal the 'system' enters into the human being, who is also an actor, until it ceases to be something outside of him and becomes incorporated in his own second nature. To begin with we find this difficult, just as a year old baby finds it difficult to take his first steps, and is appalled by the complicated problem of controlling the muscles in his still wobbly legs. But he no longer thinks of this a year later when he has already learned to run, play and jump.

"A virtuoso on the keyboard also has his moments of difficulty and is aghast at the complexity of a certain passage. A dancer finds it extremely taxing in his early training to distinguish among all the various complicated, involved steps.

"What indeed would happen should he, when he comes to a public performance, still be obliged to be conscious at every movement of hand or foot, of his exact muscular action? If that is the case then the pianist or the dancer has proved he is not capable of doing the required work. It is out of the question to recall each touch of the fingers on the keys during a long piano concerto. Nor can a dancer be consciously aware of the movements of all his muscles throughout a whole ballet.

"S. M. Volkonski stated this felicitiously when he said: 'The difficult should become habitual, the habitual, easy, the easy, beautiful.' To accomplish this requires unrelenting, systematic exercise.

"That is why the virtuoso pianist or dancer will hammer away at a passage or a 'pas' until it is fixed forever in his muscles, until it has been converted into a simple, mechanical habit. Thereafter he never needs to give another thought to what in the beginning was so difficult to learn.

"The unfortunate and dangerous part of it, however, is that habits can also be developed in the wrong direction. The more often an actor appears on the stage and acts in a theatrical, untrue way and not according to the true dictates of his nature, the farther he will move away from the goal we seek to achieve.

"It is an even sadder fact that this false state is so much easier to acquire and make a habit of.

"I should like to hazard a guess as to the relative results of this fact. I should say that for every performance an actor gives of the wrong sort it takes him ten performances on the right basis to rid himself of its deleterious effects. Nor should you overlook the fact that public performance has still another effect, it tends to fix a habit. So that I should add: ten times of rehearsing in the wrong creative state equal in their bad influence one public performance.

"Habit is a two-edged sword. It can do great harm when badly used on the stage and be of great value when proper advantage is taken of it.

"It is essential to work on the system step by step when you are learning to establish the right creative state by forming trained habits. This is not so difficult in practice as it seems in theory. You must, however, not be in a hurry.

"There is also something worse which obstructs an actor's work." This brought fresh fears to our minds.

"It is the inflexibility of the prejudices some actors have. Almost as a rule, since there are few exceptions to it, actors do not admit that laws, technique, theories, much less a system, have any part in their work. Actors are overwhelmed by their 'genius' in quotation marks," Tortsov said, not without irony. "The less gifted the actor the greater his 'genius' and it does not allow him to make any conscious approach to his art.

"Such actors, in the tradition of the handsome matinee idol Mochalov, gamble on 'inspiration.' The majority of them believe that any conscious factor in creativeness is only a nuisance. They find it easier to be an actor by the grace of God. I shall not deny that there are times when, for unknown reasons, they are able to have an intuitive emotional hold on their parts and they play reasonably well in a scene or even in a whole performance.

"But an actor cannot gamble his career on a few accidental successes. Because they are lazy or stupid these actors of 'genius' convince themselves that all they have to do is 'feel' something or other in order to have the rest take care of itself.

"But there are other occasions when for the same inexplicable and capricious reasons 'inspiration' does not turn up. Then the actor, who is left on the stage without any technique, without any means of drawing out his own feelings, without any knowledge of his own nature, plays not by the grace of God well, but by the grace of God poorly. And he has absolutely no way of getting back on to the right path.

"The creative state, the subconscious, intuition—these are not automatically at one's beck and call. If we can succeed in developing the right approaches to them, they can at least protect us from making the old mistakes. It seems obvious where we should start.

"But actors, like most people, are slow to see where their real interests lie. Think how many lives are still lost from sickness, although talented scientists have discovered specific cures, inoculations, vaccines, medicines! There was an old man in Moscow who boasted that he had never ridden in a train or spoken over a telephone. Humanity searches, it undergoes unspeakable trials and tribulations to discover the great truths, to make great discoveries, and people are so reluctant even to stretch out their hands and take what is freely offered them. That is an absolute lack of civilization!

"In the technique of the stage, and above all in the domain of speech, we see the same sort of thing. Peoples, nature itself, the best brains of the scholars, poets who rank as geniuses, have over the centuries contributed to the formation of language. They did not invent it, like Esperanto. It sprang from the very heart of life. It has been studied for generations by scholars, it has been refined, polished by poetic geniuses like Shakespeare and Pushkin—the actor has only to take what is prepared for him. But he will not swallow even a predigested food.

"There are some lucky ones who, without benefit of any study, have an intuitive sense of the nature of their language, and they speak it correctly. But they are the few, the rare cases. The overwhelming majority of people speak with scandalous slovenliness.

"Look at the way musicians study the laws, the theory of their art, the care they take of their instruments, their violins, cellos, pianos. Why do dramatic artists not do the same? Why do they not learn the laws of speech, why do they not treat their voices, their speech, their bodies with care and respect? Those are their violins, cellos, their most subtle instruments of expression. They were fashioned by the greatest genius of all craftsmen—the magician Nature.

"Most people in the theatre are unwilling to understand that accident is not art, that you cannot build on it. The master performer must have complete control of his instrument, and that of an artist is a complex mechanism. We actors have to deal not just with a voice the way a singer does, not just with hands like a pianist, not just with the body and legs like a dancer. We are obliged to play simultaneously on all the spiritual and physical aspects of a human being. To gain mastery over them requires time and arduous, systematic effort, a program of work such as we have been pursuing here.

"This 'system' is a companion along the way to creative achievement, but it is not a goal in itself. You cannot act the 'system': you can work on it at home, but when you step out on to the stage cast it aside, there only nature is your guide. The 'system' is a reference book, not a philosophy. Where philosophy begins the 'system' ends.

"Reckless use of the 'system,' work that is done according to it but without sustained concentration, will only drive you away from the goal you seek to reach. This is bad and can be overdone. Unfortunately this is often the case.

"A too emphatic, exaggerated care in the handling of our psychotechnique can be alarming, inhibiting, can lead to an overcritical attitude, or result in a technique used for its own sake.

"To insure yourselves against falling into these undesirable bypaths you should do your initial work only under the constant, careful supervision of a trained eye. . . ."

Louis Jouvet

Jouvet, one of the great actors of modern France, began his rise to fame when, with Charles Dullin, he became a leading disciple of Jacques Copeau, director of the Théâtre Vieux Colombier. Since World War I, Jouvet's roles have covered the entire range of dramatic literature, including the great ambiguous character parts of Molière as well as many important roles in the plays of Giraudoux. His production of Molière's *Dom Juan* in 1948 may remain his most famous enterprise, produced after nearly a year of rehearsals and many more years of thought and preparation. He died in 1951, admired by members of his profession and by audiences throughout Europe. The observations reprinted here are from his thoughtful, artistic autobiography *Réflexions du comédien* — and it is worth noting this appellation which Jouvet humbly sought for himself.

❧   COMEDIAN AND ACTOR

We must first of all make a technical distinction between actor and comedian, terms that are used interchangeably in common parlance. The actor c n only play certain roles; he distorts the others in line with his personality. The comedian, however, can play all roles. The actor takes a part, the comedian is taken by it. Garrick was a comedian: he was able to interpret tragic and comic roles with the same power and the same truthfulness. The confusion in everyday speech may be explained by the fact that the line of demarcation between comedian and actor is never strictly defined. We call attention to this difference from the very outset so that we may explain the workings of the acting profession; but there are actors who are comedians and comedians who are actors.

A tragedian is always an actor, that is, an interpreter whose personality is so strong and so unmistakable that pantomime — even when it plays a large part in his role — always leaves him in possession of his personality.

Pantomime is a human instinct present from the earliest childhood. Hence, the perfect comedian would be one who developed this instinct to its maximum. In any event, we must study the calling

"Comedian and Actor" by Louis Jouvet (Joseph M. Bernstein, trans.) is reprinted from *Actors on Acting* by Toby Cole and Helen Krich Chinoy, © 1949, 1954 by Toby Cole and Helen Krich Chinoy. Used by permission of Crown Publishers, Inc.

and profession of comedian from the human point of view. The qualities of adaptation in a human being, oriented and directed toward a definite goal, make the professional comedian.

The chief difference between the comedian and the actor lies in this pantomime, which is not so extensively developed in the actor as in the comedian. The way in which an artist interprets a role — the process by which he succeeds in building up his characterization — determines how much of an actor or comedian he is. The actor substitutes himself for the character, the comedian operates by means of penetration and insinuation.

When to the instinct for pantomime is added a persistent need for escape and incarnation, there is a calling. This calling usually reveals itself very early and authoritatively; and it must overcome the idea that the comedian's profession is a shameful one. But we may also discern in this calling a very intense desire to please — in a sense, a mania for sociability. A true comedian practices a manner of living. The theatre is more than a profession — it is a passion.

It is hard to formulate rules for the profession, except for several laws of technique. There are several reasons for this: 1. It is an empirical profession. 2. The comedian is an intrumentalist who is his own instrument. Only one other kind of artist, the singer, is virtually in the same position. 3. The study of the theatre is a comparative science which proceeds from the notion of collectivity. There are three kinds of actors, all tightly interdependent: the actor-*author,* the actor-*comedian,* and the *audience* actor. We must always bear in mind the process of osmosis that goes on among these three elements. 4. Exercising the comedian's profession is a perpetual adaptation. Theatrical art, more of an improvisation than any other art, reflects the atmosphere of a period and is subject to the laws of fashion. Hence whatever indications we may give have only a relative value.

A Comedian is Commissioned by the Audience

The mechanism of the comedian's calling is explained by the origins of drama, which is a collective manifestation. Among primitive peoples, for example, a whole tribe begins to dance spontaneously in order to express its sentiments. Then there comes a moment in which one dancer takes precedence over the others and performs more remarkably because he is endowed with more powerful magnetism than his fellows. Gradually the others drop out; and he dances alone in their midst. In a sense he is inspired and sustained by all his companions who have become the audience. He is the soloist, commissioned by the mass.

Similarly in ancient days, an inspired individual got up on a cask or some boards; the jokester of his group, he began to talk or sing. The others did not listen to him right away, but then they encouraged him. The audience sat down and waited, and the "commissioned" individual found out how to respond to them. A dramatic theme was created and the profession of comedian was born. We see this same phenomenon in children's games. At first all the youngsters participate, then one child draws apart. He becomes the protagonist. The others group themselves around him, listen, and spontaneously recapture the state of mind of the first audiences in the ancient world—the circle and the circus.

There are no rules in the theatre when there is a personality. Nevertheless, this "sustaining" of the actor indicates that the play exists and develops to the extent that the audience collaborates with it. When those who serve the theatre are no longer "delegated" or "commissioned," the play has no meaning.

PHYSICAL GIFTS

Beauty, power, nobility, resonant voice, gestures, and bearing are the first gifts of the comedian. He must acquire flawless articulation, dramatic sensibility, the understanding of a script, and the ability to project it on the stage; he must know how to dress and make himself up, and he must learn how to combine these qualities in a harmonious way. In France, we have had comedians who fulfilled these requirements: Lekain and Mounet-Sully.

One may arrive at a certain degree of excellence in the profession without possessing all the foregoing qualities. Personal gifts must, from the very beginning of one's studies, be confirmed by signs of progress and by medical check-up (physical resistance, the state of the lungs and throat, etc.).

The comedian must train his physique by means of sports. Although he need not indulge in acrobatics as the Romans did or the modern Russian comedians do, yet he must render his body flexible enough for every kind of movement called for in the script.

In training his voice, the comedian must first *pitch* it as singers do; then he must get to know its exact register. Once he has acquired a good diction, he must study elocution. In the seventeenth century, that constituted almost the entire art of the comedian. For a long time acting, properly speaking, was reserved to pantomimists and actors of the *commedia dell' arte*. Once when he was asked his advice, Henry Irving said: "Speak clearly!" He answered all such questions with this motto: "Speak clearly!" and added: "Be human."

Elocution demands perfect enunciation, clear pronunciation, and correct speech. Then comes the correcting of accents and the work of intonation. But the basis of this art, like that of dancing and singing, is *breathing*. Only long, painstaking, and regular work will give the perfect diction that is the first quality of a comedian.

Gesture is another language—a universal language. The comedian must strive to be as accurate in gestures as he is in intonation. A Greek proverb speaks of "talking improperly with one's hands." Walking across the stage is one of the first and most important difficulties. During rehearsals of each new play, the comedian must work hard to get "in the swing" of the piece, to become part of the stagesetting and atmosphere. And "knowing a part to one's fingertips" often demands long study.

It goes without saying that a comedian must know how to dress and move about in costumes of the most varied types and periods. Knowing his facial traits and the effects he can achieve by them, he must learn how to alter them by the art of make-up, in which he must have some notions of painting, lighting, and even physiology.

THE SCRIPT

Emotion must create and guide gesture. Emotion is the share of sensibility contributed by an actor in reciting a script and in bringing it to the stage. The comedian must know how to think through a script—that is, how to visualize it in dramatic terms after receiving definite impressions from his reading of it. As Paul Claudel says: "The script has a savor and substance; it is a source of nourishment." One must be able to size up the plot and the dramatic situation of a play. "A role is a blank page on which one writes first of all one's emotions," says Stanislavsky. Then, depending on whether the interpreter is an actor or a comedian, he tries out the part during rehearsals and finds the proper harmony with his cast.

There are scripts that are hard to play by speaking them—which is the whole art of the modern comedian. The value of our classical plays lies in the fact that they can be both spoken and played. A fine text constantly stimulates the performer and bears repeating. The actor who depends on the script must similarly be able to stimulate the audience. The script engenders emotion, dramatic sensibility, and also a way of listening (a very important quality to which attention is rarely paid). Scripts are of neccessity composed with an eye to the dramatic qualities of the performer: either the author in writing his play had a definite actor in mind or the actor naturally corresponds to a part—that is, what is called in the language of the theatre a *type*.

The list of these types has changed with changing periods of the drama. The types in the mystery-plays of the Middle Ages were very different from those in the classical Greek theatre. Later, in the *commedia dell' arte,* one finds the most complete list of these types. In Shakespeare's theatre they were individualized, with women's parts taken by men. In Molière's theatre the types were better defined. Eighteenth-century tragedy marked a further evolution and melodrama required a series of special types.

These were the types in tragedy: first roles, princes, second roles, kings, third roles, confidants. The women included queens, princesses old and young, confidants. In comedy: the outstanding first role, *jeune premier,* third roles and *raisonneurs,* noble fathers, judges, old men, valets; first comic, second comic, servants, walk-ons. The women: heroines, *ingénues,* coquettes, *jeunes premières,* character-parts, *soubrettes,* peasants, servants.

A comedian can play several types. An actor usually sticks to a single kind of role.

In our own day the list of types is quite eclectic and it is difficult to classify them accurately. Authors' creations give rise to types; but actors with strong personalities, reacting in turn on literature, create secondary types.

HARMONY WITH THE AUDIENCE

After finding the proper harmony with his cast, the actor must achieve harmony with the audience. To attain this is a difficult matter for, as instrument and instrumentalist, he cannot see himself, judge himself, or hear himself, and he is playing in an ensemble. Before going out on the stage, the actor must cultivate an "inner silence" and at the same time bring about a physical deconcentration. But once on the stage, the comedian must be able to put himself in the second state and control himself.

CONTROL OF THE EMOTIONS

Control of the emotions is a delicate problem which, despite numerous controversies, has not yet been settled. Must the comedian who moves the audience be himself moved? As a matter of fact, the question is badly put. There are only individual cases. Got used to say: "The actor must be dual . . . that is, as the performer plays and feels, a kind of reasoning being must remain vigilantly within him, by his side . . . a regulator, as they say in mechanics."

This statement, which sums up the sentiments of all experienced actors, seems to disprove Diderot's famous *Paradoxe*. Works on the acting profession are so infrequent that as soon as a genuine writer composes one, it becomes a kind of document to which everyone refers — even the comedians. Diderot was not himself a comedian; he could not experience and understand the mysterious process of the movements that quicken the actor on the stage. Diderot the writer knew a great deal about performances and back-stage incidents and wrote some splendid comments on life in the theatre. But in reading him we must never forget the title of his work: it is a *paradox.*

Does not this dualism, which Diderot considered paradoxical, exist in every man who, even as he speaks with one of his fellow-men, retains his free powers of reasoning? This dualism also concerns the audience. Someone should also write a *Paradox of the Spectator.* Like all paradoxes, Diderot's is a preconceived state of mind. It is neither a criticism nor a theory, but an enigmatic way of discoursing.

The actor's fear of "stage fright" (which some actors have never been able to overcome) is an added ingredient, a kind of preparation for anaesthesis on the stage and for the grace of inspiration without which there is no great comedian. Mounet-Sully alluded to this grace when, leaving the stage one evening, he said: "Tonight the god did not come."

On the stage and in the presence of an audience, the comedian must remember that he must not only portray a character, he must also be that character and feel his feelings. He must acquire a safety mechanism which then arouses emotions. Thus he will retain the original rhythm of the work; and his personal magnetism will get across the footlights, where it will be felt by the expectant audience.

The Magnetic Field

By virtue of the fact that it has entered a theatre and gathered to wait for the curtain to rise, the audience has already created a magnetic field. If its expectations are disappointed or if, in the course of the performance, the actor's personal magnetism disappears, the audience gets a sense of alienation. It is enough for one actor to be "out of tune" for the play to be ruined or to stop dead.

Every human being has a specific gravity. Before an audience one may say that the comedian has a density—the quality of his presence. The comedian must learn to make use of this dynamism, this kind of *aura* that surrounds him. This presence is of course greater in an actor than in a comedian. The impression of self-sufficiency which certain actors sometimes give is an excess of personality. The same is true of the sense of authority on the stage. Other things being equal, this authority is much greater in an actor than in a comedian; or at least it is not achieved by the comedian except at specific moments when he is in perfect possession of his role.

The shyness and timidity felt by many performers, far from harming them, may be useful and even necessary. Human beings may be divided into inhibitionists and exhibitionists, according to the way in which they externalize their sentiments. An inhibitionist actor is not on the same level as the character he has to interpret. In order to raise himself to the level of his role, he must exploit this "insecurity," which will tend to diminish as he goes on. One cannot become a true professional unless one learns how to utilize this feeling of shyness and fearfulness. As the actor plays a piece, his insecurity disappears, his self-consciousness decreases. His sensibility lessens, but his power of execution gains.

"The actor enters into the work of art with his entire being, his face, his features, his voice, etc., and his task is to identify himself completely with the role he represents. In this connection the poet has the right to demand of the actor that he really put himself completely into the role given him, without adding anything on his own, and that he behave as the creative writer conceived and developed the part. The actor must be in a sense the instrument on which the author plays, a sponge which is soaked in all the colors and makes them unalterable. . . .

"The tone of his voice, his manner of reciting, his gestures and physiognomy—all his outer and inner manifestations—demand an originality in conformity with the specific role.

"Indeed, the actor as a living human being has his innate originality with regard to his voice, his external appearance, and the expression on his face—he is forced either to suppress this originality in order to express a universal passion or a known type, or to harmonize the various facets of his role with the traits that have been strongly individualized by the writer."—(Hegel.)

Harley Granville-Barker

Granville-Barker's name has been associated with almost every progressive movement in theatre — in England and, many times, in America — during the first half of this century. His work as an educator in theatre, as a director (both represented elsewhere in this volume), as playwright, and as a scholar of Shakespeare, was always important; he never addressed himself to anything superficially, and his influence has been profound. He was responsible for much of Shaw's early success; he articulated, with William Archer, the first demand heard in England for a National Theatre. He was a director of great technical skill and enormous good taste, and his influence in Shakespeare studies has gone far to unite purely academic interests with the demands of the stage.

In this essay, Granville-Barker writes of that most intangible quantity — and quality — the personality of the professional actor and its values to audiences and playwrights. Never condescending, he discusses such personality, with its dangers and virtues, as a promisingly creative instrument.

from THE HERITAGE OF THE ACTOR

... The dramatist demands personality; an indefinable thing, and, alas, he is seldom content with the concrete specimen of it that he gets. It is amusing to watch him at rehearsal while he sees the characters growing quite unlike his own innocent idea of them. If he is altogether a novice, the fascination of seeing them live and move is usually sufficient compensation. But novelists turned playwrights are apt to be agonised by the phenomenon. Experience — and a little sympathy with the difficulties of the actor — will teach them how what is essential may be kept alive and true to the play's purpose if incidentals are not rigidly insisted on. Does the author refuse to admit any such division? Authors, grown expert enough in the whole business to instruct each actor to a nicety, have been known to do so. They make their choice, then, between the letter and the spirit, and they may find that by insistence upon the letter they have — for sensitive auditors at least — taken away the very life of the play's performance. . . .

From *The Quarterly Review,* No. 476 (July 1923). Reprinted by permission of John Murray (Publishers) Ltd. (London).

If an art may have a policy it would seem as if the first thing needful were the envisaging of what the drama can do unapproachably, of what it can be at its best that neither kindred arts nor pseudo-arts can be. For in this must lie its strength to face a future, however ambiguous. Its history has been marked by defections, from which, in some ways it has gathered strength. Dancing and music deserted, to set up on their own account as ballet and opera. Drama on the whole does better without them. Certainly, late in the 17th century it struck up one doubtful alliance with the scenic art, by which it has benefited a little and suffered a lot; the Artist (with a capital A) being a difficult partner to keep in his place, once he has scented the footlights, and an appeal to the thing seen being ever the simplest to make. Four boards and a passion, it has been said, are all the equipment that drama needs, and it is a saying to be taken to heart. Here are the things that drama has never surrendered; her unrivalled riches. First, the fellowship set up between actors and audience on the strength of the fellowship of imagination between the actors themselves. Next, the power of the spoken word. And in these two things the power and the quality of the art must lie....

If this is the dramatist's day, he will be wise to consider the actor, not as a mere appendage to his work, but as its very life-giver. Let him realise that the more he can learn to ask of the actor the more will he gain for his play. But asking is giving. He must give opportunity.

An author may have a thesis to expound or an exciting story to tell. A pamphlet will serve him for one and a novel for the other; or if the matter be all excitement, there is, as aforesaid, the cinema. A play has far other, far wider, artistic purposes. Aristotle laid it down — with that positiveness which in an ancient Greek is supposed, for some reason, to silence all argument — that dramatic action must not be thought of with a view to the representation of character, that the incidents and plot are the end of a tragedy; and the end is the chief thing of all. To prove this, apparently, he further remarks that without action there cannot be a tragedy (which is obviously true), but that there may be without character. In some logical sense, no doubt, there may — and a very dull affair it would be. But perhaps wise playwrights do not read their Aristotle, lest they should be in danger of having to differ from him. For they will remember that every great play of the last three centuries and more holds its place in virtue of character and not of plot. Why do we go to see a play that we really like again and again? (And return visits are the test; in music, in painting, in drama.) Not to have the story re-told us, however ingeniously it may be told. It is the elucidation of character that does not pall; and it is in this—all virtuosity, all that is learnable allowed for—that the actor's art finds its final task and its true achievement. As with the actor, so with the playwright; construction and the rest of it are as learnable as is good speaking and the tricks of painting the face; but either he can create men and women in terms of dramatic action or he cannot. And nothing else finally counts. He need not, however, with Ibsen, disdain to think of them as parts to be played. That was in its time, perhaps, a wholesome protest against the actor's egoism. But it has become—frankly—a piece of snobbery and no more. For now as always it is the power of the actor, adopting the speech and action of the author's imagining, to elucidate the character in the terms of his own personality that gives the thing that apparent spontaneity of life which is the drama's peculiar virtue.

We speak most appropriately of *reviving* an old play; and new actors do in a very real sense give it new life. The fact that (if it has been, to begin with, vitally conceived) it is capable of being interpreted in the terms of another set of personalities (as indeed it may be to some degree variously treated by the same actors time after time) is the chief reason why we can go back to it, not merely as we go back to a familiar novel or poem, but often to receive—though expectancy is rash—a fresher, more vivid enjoyment than that which it first gave us. It is said in the theatre that no actor ever quite fails as Hamlet. That is truer than it sounds; moreover, it goes far to tell us why Hamlet is the most popular play in the world, not so much with actors, who can indeed fail quite sufficiently in it to be chary of the risk, but with the ever-changing, never-changing public. Popular plays are plays that "act well." And the better a play and the better a part the more can an actor find to do in it, and the greater variety of acting will it accommodate. . . .

The beauty of sublimated human emotion; that is the beauty which properly pertains to drama. Without this and its complements of wit and humour, drama will die, and neither brains in the playwright nor the splashing of paint will avail to save it. But there is no need whatever to suppose that the technique of the modern play of verisimilitude is outworn or that its gains to the dramatist must be abandoned in a search for beauty and emotional power. And the gain to drama itself will be entire if the actor can be brought to contribute more largely from his own peculiar resources, the resources of human emotion. Not how to stifle or supersede this in the name of his own new freedom, but how to employ it to new and to subtler purpose should be the dramatist's problem. But—this must be recognised—it is the problem of a partnership. It will not be solved under the tyranny of dramatist or actor. In the lack of a fruitful recognition of this the scene designer has come thrusting in where really he has no business. His interference has resulted in a most beneficent improvement of bad scenery into good. But, if it is to be a question of the development of drama itself—no, no; let him mind his paint-pots.

We may sense what is wrong, yet wisely be chary of dogmatising upon its putting right. Certainly it is futile to request dramatists to give actors better chances of acting, to turn out plays containing such and such ingredients in such and such proportion—as if the making of plays were one with the making of puddings or pills. And the actor's practical difficulty—once he forswears the ideal of a tame dramatist who will make him a play as his cook makes him puddings—is that he must act what he finds to act. Once in a while arises the actor-dramatist who, like Molière, continues in both crafts. There are modern instances; in America, William Gillette; in France, at this moment, Sacha Guitry. Their work is noticeable, if for nothing else (and, Molière on his pedestal apart, it is often noticeable for a great deal else), for the nice adjustment of the play's content to the actor's opportunity. Otherwise, it may be no more in the best plays than in the worst—if by "best" is implied a rounded completeness—that the actor will be able to explore the sheer possibilities of his art as the theatre of the new illusion defines it. He could more often, strangely enough, find the occasion in plays in which the dramatist has himself been impatient of the form chosen and has surcharged it with thought or with feeling. It is, in fact, to the dramatist's experiments in the enlargement of his own art that the actor should look for the development of his.

One practical difficulty immediately arises. The theatre, as we know it, provides small opportunity for experiment of any sort. There is always the audience to be thought of, naturally not interested in the art's future, but expecting the entertainment offered to be both rounded and complete, however smooth, however bare with repetition the ways of it may be worn. In the event the public does have to put up with a good deal of experimenting. Playwrights and actors both are encouraged to give their 'prentice hands practice at its expense to an extent that must make musicians, for instance, disciplined to a hard technical training, simply green with envy. They profit—though Heaven knows the theatre does not—by the public's ignorance of an art which it sets out nevertheless to enjoy. A pity that there should be no more encouragement of true experimenting, by the art's masters, not its 'prentices. For, of all the arts, drama can live least in the light of theory. The dramatist may project his play in imagination pretty completely; the individual actor can at best say what he means his performance to be; few will be rash enough to forecast an exact result for any free and fruitful collaboration of a whole company of actors with the dramatist and among themselves.

We are back to our first admission that this final process of the putting of the play on the stage is a very incalculable thing. And incalculable it must to some extent remain if its chief aim is to be the endowing of the play with anything we are to call life; for the term will escape æsthetic definition. We must join company with the musical critic who, in similar case, disposed of all argument by saying, "I know a good tune when I hear it." But no one who—with critical faculties equipped against mere fraud—has seen a play brought fully and freely to life on the stage, will ever again mistake the sham thing for the real; or ever again, one would suppose, be content with the sham; or, it is to be hoped, ever again, knowing the difference between the two, begrudge the actor his full share in the credit of the life-giving process.

What, then, is the actor's case; what should he claim from the modern drama; what has he to offer? The dramatist's chief gain from the theatre of the new illusion and the conventions which belong to it, has been—at the price of some limitation of his power to project things in the doing—a great extension of resource in picturing things as they are. There was more need, as well as more scope, for physical action upon the older stage, even as there was for the spell-binding sway of verse. But by the new illusion the attention of an audience can be focussed upon the smallest details without either words or action being used to mark them, light, darkness, and silence can be made eloquent in themselves, a whole gamut of effectiveness has been added. It has brought new obligations—of accuracy, of sincerity, of verisimilitude in general, as we have noted. Then gain and loss both must be reflected in the actor's opportunity. His chances of doing are curtailed; in their stead new obligations of being are laid upon him. Can he not turn them to his profit?

One is tempted to imagine a play — to be written in desperate defiance of Aristotle — from which doing would be eliminated altogether, in which nothing but being would be left. The task set the actors of it would be to interest their audience in what the characters *were,* quite apart from anything they might *do;* to set up, that is to say, the relation by which all important human intimacies exist. If the art of the theatre could achieve this it would stand alone in a great achievement. . . .

Englishmen are not glib, but the essential strength of poetic speech is a tradition with them. By which one does not mean, of course, that they lisp in numbers, or imply that on formal occasions they cannot be academically dull. But in the natural speech of the people there is often that power of expression and concentration of meaning which is the essence of poetry, even though the form be prose. And great English writers, from Shakespeare to Hardy, have known how to sublimate it and make it memorable. The speech of the Wessex peasant is not Mr. Hardy's invention, nor did Dickens conjure Sam Weller and Mr. Peggotty out of the void. And for as forceful a passage as any in "Cymbeline," turn to the gaoler's philosophy of hanging and his "O the charity of a penny cord!" Indeed, whether it be in form of verse or prose, Shakespeare (once he shook free of the fashionable affectations of his time and but for falling later into some affectations of his own) did but take the common speech of the people of one class and another as material for his magic.

And this seems certain. All dramatic dialogue needs to have something of this particular quality of poetry in it. It must be dynamic speech. Poetry and drama are organically akin even when they seem sundered both by subject and method. They are notably alike in this, for instance, that they call for economy of effect. Consider how short is even the longest play in comparison with a novel. The mere words of many an excellent part could be written with a fine pen on a postcard. The literary man's failure at playwriting is due, nine times out of ten, to his dialogue being so obviously but a convenient means by which he tells his story and of no further value to the play; it is therefore of no value to the actor at all. If dialogue does not serve three purposes at least, to advance the story, to exhibit the one character and provoke the exhibition of another, it fails of its primary purpose, and the play will go floundering. Further, and most importantly, it must be charged with emotion.

This lacking, the actor—unless he take matters so into his own hands that the play disappears in the process—is helpless.

And one may hazard an assertion that the modern dramatist's failure to provide due opportunity for his actors is oftenest this: he has discovered no sufficient substitute for the poetry and rhetoric in which lay the acting strength of the old plays. He may write excellent sense, and the audience, hearing it, will yet remain profoundly uninterested. Is the actor to blame? No; dramatic dialogue needs other qualities before it can be made to carry conviction. There is no solution, needless to say, in the dressing up of the play in poetic phrasing or the provision of a purple patch here and there. One must choose a medium and stick to it; only so can illusion be sustained. But the old dramatists did put into the hands—or, rather, into the mouths—of their actors a weapon of great, of magical power, by which, with little else to aid them, they could subdue their hearers to every illusion of a mimic world. Useless to-day to imitate its form, to fancy the strength lay in that. The essentials of it must be sought and somehow found. When found they are recognisable enough. Take any play and read two pages aloud. There can be no mistake. Tested by the living voice, either the language has life in it or it has not. A difficult medium, no doubt, to master, the prose of common speech which shall yet have the power of poetry. But it is what the actor asks if he is to command belief in his world of make-believe.

To put it in a phrase then; if the actor is to come to his own in the new drama, something the dynamic equivalent of poetry must be given to him as material for his share of the work. Nor is this too hard a saying. The dramatist's task—and the actor's coming after him—is the building up and exhibition of human character, the picturing of men's natures in the intimacies of their working. To this extent it is essentially a poet's task and the means to it are essentially those a poet seeks. A play's content may be what you will, matter for nothing but laughter; its dialogue may take any form whatever, from poetical imagery to the cracking of jokes. But it will be a good play or a poor one, a living thing or dead, in so far as we are brought to accept its inhabitants as fellow-creatures or left indifferent to them. This is true of high tragedy, and even the clown in the pantomine appeals to some innocent knavery in our hearts that would find it great fun to steal sausages, and to wield a red-hot poker that was not too hot.

And magic is needed; the power of the spoken word is a magic power. But the art of the theatre is not a reasonable art. A play's dialogue is an incantation, and the actors must bewitch us with it. They must seem, now to be the commonest sort of folk, now superhuman, and the form of their talk must fit them. But for all appearance, it must ever be of a trebly-distilled strength. It must have this power of poetry in it. It must be alive with more than the mere meaning of words. In content and in form the modern dramatist has much advanced his art. But still, too often, the worthiest plays will leave us cold, respectful, when we should be deeply moved, or paying them instead of laughter a tolerant smile. What is wrong? This, for one thing, I suggest. The dramatist of the new dispensation has yet, as a rule, to learn both what to ask of his actors and how best to help them to answer the demand.

Michael Redgrave

These candid and sharply direct observations contain some of Mr. Redgrave's reactions to the uses of the Stanislavski "Method," particularly in New York several years ago. His own deeply felt principles of the actor's responsibilities emerge as well, however, and he makes very clear the distinctions between Stanislavski's intentions in the planning of his "Method" and some of the transformations it has undergone in the hands of certain teachers, directors, and actors. Other details of Redgrave's point of view are articulated in the course of his larger observations. His own vast experience on stage and in films provides energy and scope in this short essay which appeared in a longer work on acting entitled *Mask or Face*.

Redgrave has acted a variety of roles in Shakespeare and Chekhov as well as in a wide range of plays from modern and classical repertories. His own abilities range from high style comedy to intense modern naturalism, from the towering heroes of Shakespearean tragedy to heroes of modern film romance. The authority of his position in the theatre is unquestioned.

⚓ *from* TO BE ME OR NOT TO BE ME

... What is often forgotten is that Stanislavski did not intend his system to be used consciously and intellectually except when the actor, while in process of creating a performance, senses some break in its continuity. He then instinctively will stop and try to find out what has gone wrong. This may take time, and if the secret does not disclose itself from a re-examination of part of the scene or all of it, it may be necessary to re-examine the structure of the rôle and its relation to the play. It may even be necessary to re-examine the play. This is often the moment when lines or scenes are cut, rewritten or added. It is the moment when Gilbert Miller thinks that what the play needs is a different chandelier in Act ii.

For all these adjustments except the last the old system can be invaluable in that in provides a sort of catechism. Its technical terms — its "units" and "objectives" and "super-objectives" — sound a little cold and arthritic in the English translation, but a catechism is after all a "solemn interrogation" and Stanislavski's is a very thorough one.

Another point which is forgotten because of the myopic way in which the system is for the most part used is that Stanislavski, at any rate in his later years, expressly instructed his actors to be prepared to *act* and to discover the "truth" of their acting through the doing of it. They were not taught to insist that they must "feel" everything before they did it.

This last is where the latest manifestation of the Method, the one from the Actors' Studio in New York, is notoriously heretical and which, together with several other distortions of Stanislavski's precepts — not all inviolable by any means — is one of the causes of the widespread criticism of the Actors' Studio in New York. This queasiness with what is undeniably a remarkable and potent, but I think limited, influence seems not yet to be guessed at in London.

If at this point I mention that I have for years been "on the record" as a champion of the New York Actors' Studio, I hope it will not seem that I am protesting too much. For in truth I have always been one of its more half-hearted champions. When I wrote of it a few years ago I was mourning the passing of the London Theatre

From *Mask or Face: Reflections in an Actor's Mirror* by Michael Redgrave. Copyright 1958 by Michael Redgrave. Reprinted with the permission of Theatre Arts Books (New York) and Heinemann Educational Books Ltd. (London).

Studio, cut off by the war; and of the Old Vic School, closed because the Governors of the Old Vic had to choose between closing that or possibly having to close the Old Vic itself for lack of funds. The cost of preserving the Old Vic School and the Young Vic, and of continuing the teaching in England of Michel St. Denis, who had been offered the Comédie Française at the end of the war but who chose to remain in London with his colleagues of the London Theatre Studio, among whom were Mr. Glen Byam Shaw and Mr. George Devine, was — so St. Denis informed me at that time — a mere three to four thousand pounds a year, or the cost of presenting a "one-set," "straight" play. These schools did an incalculable amount of good work, as the talents of many of our best young actors, directors and designers still prove. They were the most thorough theatre schools outside Russia; thorough and imaginative. Of course I am only going on what I have been told or have read about Russia, and it is another guess, a wishful one perhaps, when I say that some of our older established English Schools such as the R.A.D.A. are now less conventional, less unreluctantly débutantish than they were. But in 1953 it did not look like it, and I expressed the wish that, bereft of anything like the London Theatre Studio, we had here something like the New York Actors' Studio, where trained actors could take, from time to time, a "refresher course."

Well, now we have it. The young directors of the London Studio, according to the report in *The Times* of August 29th, and other sources, are at pains to point out that there are several differences between the handling of their classes and Mr. Lee Strasberg's method in New York:

"A typical meeting is attended by about 20 members; an arbitrator . . . invites groups of two or three to take the floor and submit some prepared work to general scrutiny. Scenes are rarely improvised ('it encourages slickness') . . ."

I do not understand what is meant by improvisation encouraging slickness. The capacity to improvise is part of the stock-in-trade of the actor's craft. Any actor who is frightened of it must be frightened only by the word itself or by his fear of being cut off from his main source of supply: the author's text. Any actor, even the most timid, is improvising at the very first day of rehearsal and some of these first-day improvisations become set. They may sometimes deteriorate, but they are often true. The actor may improvise — on a given theme, of course — long after the first night. New inflexions, new business can be invented or refined or altered, within the framework of the production, long after the fiftieth performance. No two performances are identical, just as no interpretation or production can ever truly be said to be "definitive." A production or a painting can be the last and best of a line, but it cannot be definitive until the line is over the boundary, and the boundaries of art, especially interpretative art, are fluid, constantly changing, and the demarcations are all but imperceptible. I suggest that Irving's interpretation of *The Bells* may be one of the few examples of the "definitive" in theatrical art.

"Reading from script is banned" says the same report. All right. "Exercises remote from human experience (imitating a cash register for instance) have been allowed to remain in New York." Sensible, and quite suitable. "So has autocratic discipline," the report continues; "the arbitrator acts merely as a chairman."

Pause here (I think to myself) and wonder whether this is an implied criticism of Mr. Strasberg or perhaps the modesty of the young directors-chairmen-arbitrators of the London branch. Both? One? Or neither? But in any case, is it a good thing? Even the most democratic chairmen must retain something of autocratic discipline, or they would cease to discharge their function. Still, we may give them the benefit of the doubt about this and assume that it is their modesty, combined perhaps with youth and inexperience.

But having granted that, we may well be taken aback by what *The Times* describes as their "declared intention to undermine the existing styles of acting in the English theatre."

Not standards, we note, not "some existing styles," but styles.

Well, first of all, it is extremely difficult to lay a finger on what is meant by styles in acting, for when you come to analyse them you find that acting styles are actors' styles, invented and imposed, empirically, by a few actors in their time and grafted from one generation to another. It is not difficult to trace a history of English styles in acting Shakespeare, for instance, but it cannot be done without mentioning, apart from such reformers as Granville-Barker and William Poel, the names of actors and actresses. Our "style" of acting Restoration drama narrows itself to comparatively few players, but many of them still living, for Restoration drama was only restored to us within living memory, thanks largely to the now defunct Phœnix Society. At the comedy of Humours our race of eccentrics has always excelled, and we are adept at amusing ourselves (and others when we perform it) with a kind of entertainment in which the players, like some water insects, seem to be supported only by surface-tension.

Why should anyone want to "undermine" these things, such as

they are and not without honour? It would be easy here to make a list of names, writers and players, plays, past and present, adding: "Our own, and not such poor things neither." Would it not be pertinent to inquire what styles the London Actors' Studio from New York intends to mould to replace them?

Mr. Ben Gazzara, interviewed by Miss Dilys Powell, who asked him what would the Method do for Shakespearean acting, replied "with a smile" that it would slow it up. I like him for that, but he should have added "to a standstill." How, I would like to know, would the Method help an actress to play Millament, where the character as well as the wit is almost entirely contained in the phrasing? Wondrous as it would be to have a film record of Edith Evans' performance in that rôle, nine-tenths of it is conveyed and the essence captured in the recordings she has made. If we need some propping-up (not undermining) in our Restoration style, which we do, for it is more manner than style with most of us, we should turn to the Brecht actors rather than the Actors' Studio. When Miss Ruth Gordon dazzled London in *The Country Wife* at the Old Vic over twenty years ago she possessed the character completely, while at the same time standing so well outside it that she seemed to be sitting in the audience's lap. Indeed Miss Gordon, though she could break our hearts with her realistic Mattie in *Ethan Frome*, might well have been one of Brecht's favourite actresses.

It would be fitter, perhaps, and a shade more dignified, to leave the "declared intentions" of the London Actors' Studio to echo briefly in an insular silence. To judge from the columns of *The Times,* no one here seems perturbed, except Mr. Giles Playfair, and he writes from Massachusetts. But I have spent the better part of the last two theatrical seasons in New York and I think the threat deserves a little more attention than a huffy, British aloofness. One cannot be sure, even in *The Times* (alas!) that the phrase "undermine the existing styles" is verbatim, but it has the typical nihilistic ring. . . .

. . . I think never before, in the history of either country, has anyone declared his intention of changing, or undermining, the other's style of doing anything. (Except, of course, in Big Business.) It is a bold claim, but is it a futile one? There would be many in New York who would say it is by no means impotent and point with despair to what has happened in their own theatre where, around a small group of brilliant and talented actors, has arisen a much larger group of hangers-on who possess little of their talent. There is a cult of the inarticulate, the violent and the selfish.

Individually most of them are engaging to meet. There is a certain amount of cultivated rudeness, designed to draw attention, but one remembers that pleasant manners and a neat appearance have at no time or place been considered the hallmarks of genius. They are tremendous workers, for an actor has to work hard in a theatre where over ninety-two per cent are unemployed. The worst that is said of them individually is the phrase which seems to have been coined for them: "crazy mixed-up kids!"

It is when you come to work with them that you come up against an obstinacy which is like a brick wall covered with foam mattress. Many of them will go to dancing classes (to get into musicals), take singing lessons (for the same reason) as well as acting classes. But mention the word "technique," mention the "voice" as apart from a voice that will get you a job in a musical, mention almost any of the accepted terms if you dare. All that they want to know about is feeling. By this they mean *their* feeling, and very subjective and "off-beat" that feeling can be. . . .

It is justly levelled against English actors that they have too much facility, and a very strong case could be brought against what an English critic has called the "effortless, impactless" style of some of our "surface-tension" actors when they find themselves out of their depth in the wrong kind of play. In New York, to give a good first reading is to lay oneself open to being thought a "radio actor." To avoid this grave charge, a great deal of artificial fumbling and inarticulacy, punctuated by long pauses, can go on. . . .

Such betrayals of the author's word, which should be the actor's bond, are not the sole property of the Actors' Studio nor of New York. You will find them elsewhere, if you look for them. But the extraordinary self-righteous justification of them is, I think, more noticeable in New York, where the discipline, when it is bad, is somewhat worse than the worst in England. You could, if you wished, defend them by saying that the treachery is deliberate and therefore preferable to the *laissez-faire,* happy-go-lucky, lax standards which here and there obtain in the English theatre. You could point to half a hundred plays, from *Golden Boy* to *A View from the Bridge* where team work and fidelity to the text have gone handsomely hand in hand. I would agree. I would agree that Julie Harris is a fine actress and Marlon Brando a remarkable actor. I would believe them willingly if they told me that they owe as much to the Actors' Studio as the Actors' Studio owes to them; but the fact remains that they would have been remarkable whatever studio or school of acting they had attended.

What the Actors' Studio aims to achieve is not, immediately, results. Its aim is to allow the actor, in Stanislavski's phrase, "to work with himself." That is an excellent idea. It is also excellent that the Studio should be exclusive, selecting its students by a rigorous standard. It is remarkable and enviable that such opportunity as it gives should be given without fees or dues. Much as I distrust the idea that the actor should be encouraged in free and frank criticism of each other's experiments I cannot help admiring the courage of it. (The late James Dean is reported to have been unable to attend class for several weeks after his initiation.) But I also cannot help remembering that this ruthless and often exhibitionist kind of criticism is said to have been one of the causes of the disruption of the American Group Theatre in the thirties. "At times, there was an invisible silent slaughter going on among the Group actors," says Mr. Harold Clurman, one of their leading spirits and their historian, in his brilliant book *The Fervent Years,* ". . . At night I was wakened by solicitous telephone calls from some actor who couldn't sleep because of another actor's performance and by day I received friendly letters from fellow workers advising me on how I might overcome the defects in my latest productions, listing them with remarkable patience."

The Group was, without doubt, the most remarkable phenomenon of the modern American theatre, creating a style of its own, an ensemble which has seldom if ever been surpassed, and a number of very remarkable actors and directors, and giving scope to some playwrights. I am sure that Mr. Lee Strasberg, who was one of its leaders, would not claim that the Actors' Studio has yet equalled these achievements. He would almost certainly remark that these things are not what the Actors' Studio is for. "The work at the Studio does not aim at results." Nevertheless, some plays have emerged from the Studio, notably *A Hatful of Rain* and *End as a Man* (both now filmed). I wonder what Mr. Strasberg thinks of these, to my mind, crude melodramas, so eccentrically, so egocentrically, performed. I am not alone in thinking that the New York production of the former was a trunkful of tricks and anyone who has seen the film of the latter and can praise it for its ensemble playing had better stick to Mr. Emlyn Williams as Dickens.

Mr. Lee Strasberg possesses enormous theatrical erudition and evidently, when on the job, a remarkable personality. Like many born teachers he is not notably a doer. He is a catalyst. What he releases in a genuine and remarkable talent is genuine and better than remarkable. What happens to the less gifted is sometimes fortunate, often factitious. The third-rate remain, in the end, third-rate. That, I suppose, is the pattern of all teaching. The silk purse and the sow's ear, the brick and the straw remain constants.

Yet one of Mr. Strasberg's favourite dicta is that if the first-rate would work with the persistency of genius it may seem to equal genius, and that with the same ratio of application the fifth can elevate itself to the first-grade. It is a humdrum-sounding dictum but it has the lustre of a truth. Why then does it seldom seem to be fulfilled among the student-practitioners of the Actors' Studio? For the same reason—it would be easy and obvious to say—that most geese and ugly-ducklings cannot turn into swans. However hard they try, it sooner or later becomes evident to them that it is not of what is in their stars but of what is not in themselves.

The chance, the hope-around-the-corner, the lottery aspects of life light up the world of the theatre with the spasmodic brilliance of the latest *marquee* sign. The frontier of the theatre is, of all the arts, the easiest to cross. There are no guards to turn you back; no one drives any one else out of the enchanted forest, except a few skirmishers who, having lost their way early, turn angrily on those at their heels and shout about "restricted entry."

The actors at the Actors' Studio, whose work, as I have said, is not for immediate results, are encouraged to turn ever inwards onto their own personal problems. The "psycho-technique" of Stanislavski, by which he tried to make the "sub-conscious function naturally" through the "grammar" of playing which he attempted to codify, is all too frequently abandoned and freeplay is given to the subjective, the personal and the odd. No matter how irrelevant to the scene being played, the actor's quirks and quiddities are explored to see if they make dramatic material suitable for him.

For Mr. Strasberg is a "deviationist" from the original "Method" especially where "emotive memory" is concerned.

"Do you think" Stanislavski asks his (imaginary) student "that it would be wise for an actor to give himself up to such spontaneous emotions as that?" "Time is a splendid filter" he has previously remarked "for our remembered feelings—besides it is a great artist. It not only purifies, it transmutes even painfully realistic memories into poetry." The student asks if such spontaneous emotions are never desirable. The teacher replies that on the contrary they are most desirable, but that these direct, powerful and vivid emotions do not make their appearance on the stage in the way we think. They flash, but they do not last. They are often irrelevant to the matter in hand.

"The unfortunate thing about them is that we cannot control

them, they control us. Therefore we have no choice but to leave it to nature and say: 'If they will come, let them come!' We only hope that they will work with the part and not at cross purposes to it.''

We should not laugh at the earnest endeavour to act an inanimate object, such as a typewriter, or the other exercises in sense-and-emotion-memory. I even wish, in a perverse kind of way, that I had seen the actor who gave an exercise as Richard II in prison based on his fear of rats. We should not laugh, for the reason that any experiment, if sincerely conducted, may conceivably find a grain of truth among the chaff. The danger is that what is seized on and preserved, in this passionate quest for originality, is not the essential but the decorative, or even the waste product.

The essence of a work of art is found in its form, content or style. This is not an age of style. It is an age where texture matters more than form. The texture, taste, touch, the tang of a thing mean more, or rather sell better, than a sense of style. "Style" has become a dirty word, like "sincerity."

But style, like sincerity, has not lost its head nor its sense of direction. Symmetry mysteriously remains symmetry, and symmetry and style have a mathematical or logical cohesion which texture, tang and touch can never have. Style courts inevitability. The other things rush to embrace the unexpected and achieve only ornament.

I can pay Mr. Strasberg no greater compliment than to say that I wish him the same kind of brilliantly talented pupils which he, and another iconoclastic genius, Mr. Gordon Craig, deserve. But by the nature of things there will be very few of them. I hope that their talents are not only brilliant but have as much of the indestructible as it is possible for talent short of genius to possess. They may find what it is which the Actors' Studio is seeking and it may be something more elevating and less obscurantist than is now visible. Yes, and more truthful.

To the less indestructible I can only recommend a strict and arduous, however pedestrian course in what is already known about acting.

The first thing that is known is that you must be prepared to get up and do it. If you can't do that because you know you will make mistakes, you had better pack up. To use an adage so hoary that it is almost new: it is like trying to milk a he-goat with a sieve.

Cézanne, in a letter to Roger Marx, says: "To my mind, one should not substitute oneself for the past, one has merely to add a new link." One supposes that the Actors' Studio actress who last summer essayed her first Juliet (in New York's Central Park) has heard of the French impressionists, for she has been reported to exclaim: "I see the part in pastels and they want me to play it in oils!" She was gently and justly rebuked by someone who said: "But it's written in oils!" Anyway, she got up and did it and, from what I have read, with some success.

🐝

Edward Gordon Craig

Craig, the son of the great actress, Ellen Terry, was one of the most important voices in the development of modern stage design in this century. His own life was intimately involved with the theatre in all its aspects, and his conception of the actor as but a part of a huge machine, superintended by a master-designer, master-producer, has been criticized. On the other hand, there is no feeling of condescension in his remarks on the stature of the actor and his responsibilities. Rather, they are praise of the intelligence of a great actor, fully in command of his own artifice. His own long associations with, and memories of, Henry Irving stand behind the last pages of these excerpts. If somewhat naive in tone, Craig's knowledge of actors and their abilities was precise and backed by much experience, and his praise of Irving is probably in large part justified.

Craig designed important productions in Florence, Berlin, London, and Moscow, but most of his influence has stemmed from his vast writings on the theatre, particularly about new approaches to theatre design.

🐝 *from ON THE ACTOR*

As a man he ranks high, possesses generosity, and the truest sense of comradeship. I call to mind one actor whom I know and who shall stand as the type. A genial companion, and spreading a sense of companionship in the theatre; generous in giving assistance to

younger and less accomplished actors, continually speaking about
the work, picturesque in his manner, able to hold his own when
standing at the side of the stage instead of in the centre; with a voice
which commands my attention when I hear it, and, finally, with
about as much knowledge of the art as a cuckoo has of anything
which is at all constructive. Anything to be made according to plan
or design is foreign to his nature. But his good nature tells him that
others are on the stage besides himself, and that there must be a
certain feeling of unity between their thoughts and his, yet this
arrives by a kind of good-natured instinct and not through knowledge, and produces nothing positive. Instinct and experience have
taught him a few things (I am not going to call them tricks), which he
continually repeats. For instance, he has learned that the sudden
drop in the voice from forte to piano has the power of accentuating
and thrilling the audience as much as the crescendo from the piano
into the forte. He also knows that laughter is capable of very many
sounds, and not merely Ha, Ha, Ha. He knows that geniality is a rare
thing on the stage and that the bubbling personality is always
welcomed. But what he does not know is this, that this same bubbling
personality and all this same instinctive knowledge doubles or even
trebles its power when guided by scientific knowledge, that is to say,
by art. If he should hear me say this now he would be lost in
amazement and would consider that I was saying something which
was finicking, dry, and not at all for the consideration of an artist. He
is one who thinks that emotion creates emotion, and hates anything
to do with calculation. It is not necessary for me to point out that all
art has to do with calculation, and that the man who disregards this
can only be but half an actor. Nature will not alone supply all which
goes to create a work of art, and it is not the privilege of trees,
mountains and brooks to create works of art, or everyhing which
they touch would be given a definite and beautiful form. It is the
particular power which belongs to man alone, and to him through
his intelligence and his will. My friend probably thinks that Shakespeare wrote Othello in a passion of jealousy and that all he had to
do was to write the first words which came into his mouth; but I am
of the opinion, and I think others hold the same opinion, that
the words had to pass through our author's head, and that it was
just through this process and through the quality of his imagination and the strength and calmness of his brain that the richness of
his nature was able to be entirely and clearly expressed, and by no
other process could he have arrived at this.

Therefore it follows that the actor who wishes to perform Othello, let us say, must have not only the rich nature from which to draw his wealth, but must also have the imagination to know what to bring forth, and the brain to know how to put it before us. Therefore the ideal actor will be the man who possesses both a rich nature and a powerful brain. Of his nature we need not speak. It will contain everything. Of his brain we can say that the finer the quality the less liberty will it allow itself, remembering how much depends upon its co-worker, the Emotion, and also the less liberty will it allow its fellow-worker, knowing how valuable to it is its sternest control. Finally, the intellect would bring both itself and the emotions to so fine a sense of reason that work would never boil to the bubbling point with its restless exhibition of activity, but would create that perfect moderate heat which it would know how to keep temperate. The perfect actor would be he whose brain could conceive and could show us the perfect symbols of all which his nature contains. He would not ramp and rage up and down in Othello, rolling his eyes and clenching his hands in order to give us an impression of jealousy; he would tell his brain to inquire into the depths, to learn all that lies there, and then to remove itself to another sphere, the sphere of the imagination, and there fashion certain symbols which, without exhibiting the bare passions, would none the less tell us clearly about them.

And the perfect actor who should do this would in time find out that the symbols are to be made mainly from material which lies outside his person. . . .

. . . [D]o not forget that the very nearest approach that has ever been to the ideal actor, with his brain commanding his nature, has been Henry Irving. There are many books which tell you about him, and the best of all the books is his face. Procure all the pictures, photographs, drawings, you can of him, and try to read what is there. To begin with you will find a mask, and the significance of this is most important. I think you will find it difficult to say when you look on the face, that it betrays the weaknesses which may have been in the nature. Try and conceive for yourself that face in movement — movement which was ever under the powerful control of the mind. Can you not see the mouth being made to move by the brain, and that same movement which is called expression creating a thought as definite as the line of a draughtsman does on a piece of paper or as a chord does in music? Cannot you see the slow turning of those eyes and the enlargement of them? These two movements alone contained so great a lesson for the future of the art of the theatre, pointed out so clearly the right use of expression as opposed to the wrong use, that it is amazing to me that many people have not seen more clearly what the future must be. I should say that the face of Irving was the connecting link between that spasmodic and ridiculous expression of the human face as used by the theatres of the last few centuries, and the masks which will be used in place of the human face in the near future.

Try and think of all this when losing hope that you will ever bring your nature as exhibited in your face and your person under sufficient command. Know for a truth that there is something other than your face and your person which you may use and which is easier to control. Know this, but make no attempt yet awhile to close with it. Continue to be an actor, continue to learn all that has to be learned, as to how they set about controlling the face, and then you will learn finally that it is not to be entirely controlled.

I give you this hope so that when this moment arrives you will not do as the other actors have done. They have been met by this difficulty and have shirked it, have compromised, and have not dared to arrive at the conclusion which an artist must arrive at if faithful to himself. That is to say, that the mask is the only right medium of portraying the expressions of the soul as shown through the expressions of the face.

Michael Chekhov

This essay, taken from Chekhov's longer teaching volume *To the Actor,* deals with one of the fundamental problems of the acting student—but pertains as well to a basic technical challenge to the practicing professional actor. The question of making tangible on stage the vagaries and associated memories of the imagination concerned Stanislavski whose approach contrasts with that of Chekhov and with the goals of many other teachers of the techniques of acting.

Michael Chekhov, nephew of the playwright, was a member of the Moscow Art Theatre during Stanislavski's period of influence but achieved his own fame as an actor, director, and teacher on the Continent and in England. In 1936, he founded the Chekhov Theatre Art School in England while, at the same time, continuing his own acting which included films made both in Germany and the United States. He took up residence in America where contact with a younger generation supplemented his long acquaintance with men and women of the theatre in Europe. Here, his active influence continued until his death in 1955.

from IMAGINATION AND INCORPORATION OF IMAGES

Not that which is *inspires the creation, but that which* may *be; not the* actual, *but the* possible.

—RUDOLF STEINER

It is evening. After a long day, after much work and many impressions, experiences, actions and words—you let your tired nerves rest. You sit quietly with your eyes closed. What is it that appears out of the darkness before your mind's eye? You review the faces of people you've met during the day, their voices, movements, their characteristic or humorous features. You run again through the streets, pass familiar houses, read the signs. Passively, you follow the motley images of you memory.

Unnoticed by yourself you step back over the boundaries of today, and in your imagination slowly arise visions of your past life. Your forgotten and half-remembered wishes, daydreams, life's aims, successes and failures appear as pictures before your mind. True, they are not so faithful to the facts as the recollections of the day just passed. Now they are, in retrospect, slightly changed. But you still recognize them. With your mind's eye you now follow them with greater interest, with more awakened attention, because they *are* changed, because they now bear some traces of imagination.

But much more happens. Out of the visions of the past there flash here and there images totally unknown to you! They are pure products of your *Creative Imagination.* They appear, disappear, they come back again, bringing with them new strangers. Presently they enter into relationships with one another. They begin to "act," to "perform" before your fascinated gaze. You follow their heretofore unknown lives. You are absorbed, drawn into strange moods, atmospheres, into the love, hatred, happiness and unhappiness of these imaginary guests. Your mind is now fully awake and active. Your own reminiscences grow paler and paler; the new images are stronger than they. You are amused by the fact that these new images possess their own independent lives; you are astonished that they appear without your invitation. Finally these newcomers force you to watch them with greater poignancy than the simple pictures of everyday memory; these fascinating guests, who made their appearance from nowhere, who live their own lives full of emotions, awaken *your* responsive feelings. They force you to laugh and to cry with them. Like magicians, they call up in you an unconquerable desire to become one of them. You enter into conversations with them, you now see yourself among them; you want to act, and you do so. From a passive state of mind the images have uplifted you to a *creative* one. Such is the power of imagination.

Actors and directors, like all creative artists, are well acquainted with this power. "I am always surrounded by images," said Max Reinhardt. The whole morning, wrote Dickens, he sat in his study expecting Oliver Twist to appear. Goethe observed that inspiring images appear before us of their own accord, exclaiming, "Here we are!" Rafael saw an image pass before him in his room and this was the Sistine Madonna. Michelangelo exclaimed in despair that images pursued him and forced him to carve their likenesses out of rocks.

But although Creative Images are independent and changeable within themselves, although they are full of emotions and desires, you, while working upon your parts, must not think that they will come to you fully developed and accomplished. They don't. To complete themselves, to reach the degree of expressiveness that would satisfy you, they will require your active collaboration. What must you do to perfect them? You must ask questions of these images, as you would ask questions of a friend. Sometimes you must even give them strict orders. Changing and completing themselves under the influence of your questions and orders, they give you answers visible to your inner sight. Let us take an example:

Suppose you are going to play Malvolio in *Twelfth Night*. Suppose you want to study the moment when Malvolio approaches Olivia in the garden, after having received a mysterious letter which he supposes to be "from her." Here is where you begin to ask questions such as "Show me, Malvolio: how would you enter the gates of the garden and with a smile move toward your 'sweet lady?'" The question immediately incites the image of Malvolio to action. You see him in the distance. Hastily he hides the letter under his cloak, to produce it later with triumphant effect! His neck stretched, his face deadly serious, he looks for Olivia. Here she is! How the smile distorts his face! Didn't she write to him, "Thy smiles become thee well . . ."? But his eyes, do they smile? Oh, no! They are alarmed, anxious and watchful! They peer from behind the mask of a madman! His concern is his pace, his beautiful walk! His yellow, cross-gartered stockings seem fascinating and seductive to him. But what is that? Maria! This intrusive creature, this plague is here, too, watching him out of the corner of her mischievous eye! The smile fades from his face, he forgets his legs for a moment and his knees bend slightly, involuntarily, and the whole figure betrays his not-so-youthful body. Hatred new flashes in his gaze! But time is short. His "sweet lady" awaits! Signs of love, of passionate desire, must be given to her without delay! Tighter his cloak, faster his walk, nearer to her he goes! Slowly, secretly, seductively a little tiny corner of "her" letter appears from under his cloak. . . . Doesn't she see it? No! She looks at his face. . . . Oh, the smile! It has been forgotten, and now it turns on when she greets him with:

"How now, Malvolio!"

"Sweet lady, ho, ho!"

"Smilest thou? . . ."

What was this little "performance" Malvolio offered you? It was his first answer to your question. But you may feel dissatisfied. It does not seem right to you; the "performance" left you cold. You ask further questions: Should not Malvolio at this moment be more dignified? Was not his "performance" too much of a caricature? Was he not too old? Would it not better to "see" him as rather pathetic? Or maybe at this moment, when he believes he has achieved the aim of his whole life, he reaches the point where his mind is shaken and he verges on madness. Maybe he should bear more resemblance to a clown. Shouldn't he be even more old and undignified? Shouldn't his lecherous desires be stressed more? Or perhaps his appearance would be enhanced if he made a rather humorous impression. What if he looked like a naïve and rather innocent child? Is he entirely bewildered or still able to keep his senses under control?

Many questions like these may arise in your mind while you are working upon a part. Here your collaboration with the image begins. You guide and build your character by asking it new questions, by ordering it to show you different variations of possible ways of acting, according to your taste (or the director's interpretation of the character). The image changes under your questioning gaze, transforms itself again and again until gradually (or suddenly) you feel satisfied with it. Thereupon you will find your emotions aroused, and the desire to act flares up in you!

By working this way you will be able to study and create your character more profoundly (and more quickly, too); you will not be relying only on ordinary thinking instead of "seeing" these little "performances." Dry reasoning kills your imagination. The more you probe with your analytical mind, the more silent become your feelings, the weaker your will and the poorer your chances for inspiration.

There is no question that cannot be answered in this way. Of course, not all questions will be answered immediately; some are more intricate than others. Were you to ask, for instance, what the *relationship* is between your character and the others in the play, the right answer would not always come at once. Sometimes hours, even days, are required before you "see" your character in these different relationships.

The more you work upon your imagination, strengthing it by means of exercises, the sooner a sensation will arise within you which you can describe as something like this: "The images which I *see* with the mind's eye have their own psychology, like the people surrounding me in my everyday life. However, there is one difference: In everyday life, seeing people by their outer manifestations alone and not seeing behind their facial expressions, movements, gestures, voices and intonations, I might misjudge their inner lives. But it is not so with my creative images. *Their* inner lives are completely open for me to behold. All their emotions, feelings, passions, thoughts, their aims and innermost desires are revealed to me. Through the outer manifestation of my image — that is to say, of the character I am working upon by means of my imagination — I *see* its inner life." . . .

The more developed your imagination through systematic exercises, the more flexible and fleeting it becomes. Images will follow images with increasing rapidity; they will form and vanish too hastily. This may result in your losing them before they can kindle your feelings. You must possess enough will power, more than you normally exert in everyday activities, to keep them before your mind's eye long enough for them to affect and awaken your *own* feelings.

And what is this additional will power? It is the power of concentration.

I anticipate your asking: "Why should I take such pains to develop my imagination and apply it to work upon modern, naturalistic plays when all the characters are so obvious and easy to comprehend; when the lines, situations and business provided by the author take care of everything?" If that is your question, permit me to take issue with it. What the author has given you in the form of a written play is *his* creation, not yours; he has applied *his* talent. But what is *your* contribution to the writer's work? To my understanding, it is, or should be, the discovery of the psychological depths of the characters given you in the play. There is no human being who is obvious and easy to comprehend. The true actor will not glide over the surfaces of the characters he plays nor impose upon them his personal and unvarying mannerisms. I know perfectly well that that is the widely recognized and practiced custom in our profession today. But, for whatever impression it may make upon you, let me take the liberty of expressing myself unrestrainedly on this point.

It is a crime to chain and imprison an actor within the limits of his so-called "personality," thus making of him an enslaved laborer rather than an artist. Where is his freedom? How can he use his own creativeness and originality? Why should he always appear before his audiences as a puppet compelled to make the same kind of movements when the strings are pulled? The fact that modern writers, audiences, critics and even actors themselves have become habituated to this degradation of the actor-artist does not make the charge less true or the evil less execrable.

One of the most disappointing results stemming from this accustomed treatment of the actor has been that it makes him a less interesting human being on the stage than he invariably is in private life. (It would be infinitely better for the theater if the opposite prevailed.) His "creations" are not worthy of himself. Using only his mannerisms, the actor becomes *unimaginative;* all characters become the same to him.

To create, in the real sense, means to discover and show *new* things. But what novelty is there in the stilted mannerisms and clichés of the fettered actor? The deeply hidden, and nowadays almost completely forgotten, desire of every true actor is to express himself, to assert his ego, through the medium of his parts. But how can he do it if he is encouraged, more often required, to resort to his mannerisms instead of his creative imagination? He can't because the creative imagination is one of the main channels through which the artist in him finds the way to express his *own,* individual (and therefore always unique) interpretation of the characters to be protrayed. And how is he going to express his creative individuality if he does not or cannot penetrate deeply into the inner life of the characters themselves by means of his creative imagination? . . .

Sigmund Freud

Although written in 1904, this essay did not appear until 1942. It contains some of the first theories advanced by Freud on this controversial subject and is of special interest in terms of various approaches to the techniques of acting, to methods of teaching, and to contrasting styles of illuminating a character's psychological development in a play, Freud's approach to his subject pertains to a conception of the hero in tragedy but is equally relevant to many stage personalities from all periods of playwriting. The essay is also of importance in dealing with an audience's perceptions of character traits on stage.

PSYCHOPATHIC CHARACTERS ON THE STAGE

If the function of the drama, as has been assumed since Aristotle, is to excite pity and fear, and thus bring about a "catharsis of the emotions," we may describe this same purpose a little more fully if we say that the question is one of opening up sources of pleasure and enjoyment from within our affective life, just as wit and the comic do from within the sphere of the intellect, through the action of which

From *The Psychoanalytic Quarterly,* Vol XI, No. 4 (1942), pp. 459-464. Reprinted by permission of The Psychoanalytic Quarterly, Inc.

many such sources had been made inaccessible. Certainly the release of the subject's own affects must here be given first place, and the enjoyment resulting therefrom corresponds on the one hand to the relief produced by their free discharge, and on the other, very likely, to the concomitant sexual stimulation which, one may suppose occurs as a by-product of every emotional excitation and supplies the subject with that feeling of a heightening of his psychic level which he so greatly prizes. The sympathetic witnessing of a dramatic performance fulfils the same function for the adult as does play for the child, whose besetting hope of being able to do what the adult does, it gratifies. The spectator at the play experiences too little; he feels like a "Misero, to whom nothing worth while can happen"; he has long since had to moderate, or better direct elsewhere, his ambition to occupy a central place in the stream of world events; he wants to feel, to act, to mold the world in the light of his desire—in short, to be a hero. And the playwright-actors make all this possible for him by giving him the opportunity to identify himself with a hero. But they thus spare him something also; for the spectator is well aware that taking over the hero's rôle in his own person would involve such griefs, such sufferings and such frightful terrors as would almost nullify the pleasure therein; and he knows too that he has but a single life to live, and might perhaps perish in a single one of the hero's many battles with the Fates. Hence his enjoyment presupposes an illusion; it presupposes an attenuation of his suffering through the certainty that in the first place it is another than himself who acts and suffers upon the stage, and that in the second place it is only a play, whence no threat to his personal security can ever arise. It is under such circumstances that he may indulge in the luxury of being a hero; he may give way unashamedly to suppressed impulses such as the need for freedom in religious, political, social or sexual respects, and may let himself go in all directions in each and every grand scene of the life enacted upon the stage.

These are prerequisites for enjoyment, however, which are common to several forms of creative art. Epic poetry subserves above all the release of intense but simple feelings—as does, in its sphere, the dance; the epic poem may be said to make possible the enjoyment in particular of the great heroic personality in his triumphs; drama, however, is supposed to delve deeper into emotional possibilities, to manage to transform even the forebodings of doom into something enjoyable, and it therefore depicts the embattled hero rather with a masochistic satisfaction in succumbing. In fact, one might characterize drama by this very relation to suffering and misfortune, whether as in the play mere apprehension is aroused and then allayed, or as in tragedy actual suffering is brought into being. The origin of drama in sacrificial rites (goat and scapegoat) in the cult of the gods cannot be without appositeness to this meaning of drama; it assuages as it were the beginning revolt against the divine order which decreed the suffering. The hero is at first a rebel against God or the divine; and it is from the feeling of misery of the weaker creature pitted against the divine might that pleasure may be said to derive, through masochistic gratification and the direct enjoyment of the personage whose greatness nevertheless the drama emphasizes. This is the Prometheus attitude of man, who in a spirit of petty compliance would be soothed for the time being with a merely momentary gratification.

All varieties of suffering are therefore the theme of drama, which promises to create out of them pleasure for the spectator; whence arises the first condition which this art form must fulfil, that it shall cause the spectator no suffering, and that it must know how to compensate by means of the gratifications which it makes possible for the pity which it arouses — a rule against which modern dramatists have particularly often been offenders. But this suffering is soon restricted to mental anguish only, for nobody wants to witness physical suffering who knows how soon the bodily sensations thus stimulated put an end to all mental enjoyment. He who is ill has but one desire: to get well, to get over his condition; the doctor must come with his medicine; the arresting of the play of fantasy must cease — that arrest which has spoiled us to the extent of letting us extract enjoyment even out of our suffering. When the spectator puts himself in the place of the sufferer from physical illness, he finds nothing within himself of enjoyment or of psychological give and take; and it is on this account that a person physically ill is possible on the stage only as a property, but not as the hero — excepting as some particular psychic aspect of illness is susceptible of psychic elaboration, as for example the abandoning of the sick Philoctetes, or the hopelessness of the sick in the plays of Strindberg.

Mental suffering we recognize, however, chiefly in relation to the circumstances out of which it has developed; hence drama requires an action from which this suffering derives, and begins by introducing to the audience this action. It is only an apparent exception that such plays as *Ajax* and *Philoctetes* present mental suffering as already in existence, for because of the familiarity of the matter to the audience the curtain always rises in the Greek drama in the middle of the play, as it were. Now, it is easy to define the conditions which this action must fulfil. There must be a play of contending forces; the action must contain within itself a striving of the will and some opposition thereto. The first and most grandiose fulfilling of these conditions was exemplified in the struggle against divinity. It has already been said that the essence of this tragedy is revolt, with dramatist and spectator taking sides with the rebel. The less that is then ascribed to the divine, the more accrues to the human element, which, with ever increasing insight, is made responsible for suffering; and so the next struggle, that of the hero against the social community, becomes the social tragedy. Still another fulfilling of these conditions is seen in the struggle between men themselves, that is, the character drama, which contains within itself all the characteristics of the agon, and, enacted preferably between outstanding personalities freed from the restrictions of human institutions, must accordingly have more than one hero. Combinations of these two are of course perfectly permissible, in the form of a struggle on the part of the hero against institutions of which strong characters are the embodiment. The pure drama of character is lacking in the sources of enjoyment afforded by the theme of rebellion, which in social plays, such as those of Ibsen, is again as powerfully to the fore as in the historical plays of Greek classical times. If religious, character and social drama differ from one another chiefly with respect to the arena in which the action takes place from which the suffering has its origin, we may now follow the drama to still another arena, where it becomes the psychological drama. For it is within the soul of the hero himself that there takes place an anguished struggle between various impulses—a struggle which must end, not with the downfall of the hero, but with that of one of the contending impulses, in other words, with a reunuciation. Every combination of this situation with that in the earlier type of drama, that is the social and the character drama, is of course possible in so far as social institutions evoke just such an inner conflict, and so on. It is here that the love drama belongs, in so far as the suppressing of love— whether on the score of the mores, the conventions or the conflict, familiar from opera, between "love and duty"—forms the starting point for an almost endless variety of conflictual situations, as infinite in their variety as the erotic daydreams of mankind. The possibilities multiply still further, however, and the psychological drama becomes the psychopathological, when the source of the suffering which we are to share and from which we are to derive pleasure is no longer a conflict between two almost equally conscious motivations, but one between conscious and repressed ones. Here the precondition for enjoyment is that the spectator shall also be neurotic. For it is only to him that the release and, to a certain extent, the conscious recognition of the repressed motivation can afford pleasure, instead of making merely for unacceptance. In the non-neurotic this will meet only with unacceptance, and will induce a readiness to repeat the act of repression, for in his case the latter has been successful. The repressed impulse is kept in complete counter-balance by the original force of repression. In the neurotic, on the other hand, repression is by way of failing; it is unstable, and requires ever renewed effort, an effort which is spared by recogni-tion. It is only in the neurotic that such a struggle exists as can become the subject of drama; but in him also the dramatist will create not only the pleasure derived from release but resistance as well.

The foremost modern drama of this kind is *Hamlet,* which deals with the theme of a normal man who, because of the particular nature of the task enjoined upon him, becomes neurotic—a man in whom an impulse hitherto successfully repressed seeks to assert itself. *Hamlet* is distinguished by three characteristics which seem of importance to our discussion: 1) that the hero is not psychopathic, but becomes so only in the course of the action we are going to witness; 2) that the repressed desire is one of those that are similarly repressed in all of us, the repression of which belongs to an early stage of our individual development, while the situation arising in the play shatters precisely this repression. Because of these two features it is easy for us to recognize ourselves in the hero. For we are victims of the same conflict as is he; since "he who doesn't lose his reason under certain provocations has no reason to lose." 3) But it appears to be one of the prerequisites of this art form that the struggle of the repressed impulse to become conscious, recognizable though it is, is so little given a definite name that the process of reaching consciousness goes on in turn within the spectator while his attention is distracted and he is in the grip of his emotions, rather than capable of rational judgment. In this way resistance is definitely reduced, in the manner seen in psychoanalytic treatment, when the derivatives of the repressed ideas and emotions come to conscious-ness as a result of a lessening of resistance in a manner denied to the repressed material itself. And indeed the conflict in *Hamlet* is so deeply hidden that at first I could only surmise it.

Possibly it is because of the disregarding of these three requisite conditions that so many other psychopathic characters become as useless for the stage as they are for life itself. For the sick neurotic is to us a man into whose conflict we can obtain no insight (empathy) when he presents it to us in the form of the finished product. Conversely, if we are familiar with this conflict, we forget that he is a sick man, just as when he becomes familiar with it he himself ceases to be sick. It is thus the task of the dramatist to transport us into the same illness — a thing best accomplished if we follow him through its development. This will be particularly needful when the repression is not already existent in ourselves and must therefore be effected *de novo* — which represents a step beyond *Hamlet* in the utilization of neurosis upon the stage. Where the full-blown and strange neurosis confronts us, in real life we call the physician and deem the person in question unsuitable as a stage figure.

In general, it may perhaps be said that the neurotic liability of the public, and the art of the dramatist in making use of resistances and supplying forepleasure, alone determine the limits of the utilization of abnormal characters upon the stage.

Otto Fenichel

Fenichel was one of the most influential and original psychoanalysts of modern times. He studied and taught psychoanalysis and medicine in Vienna, Berlin, and Los Angeles and organized (in Berlin) a highly original method concerned with study groups for training younger analysts. His untimely death in 1946 cut short an immensely productive career during which he had been concerned invariably with deeply ranging human problems and specifically with writing and teaching.

Fenichel had always been interested in those materials of his field that shed light on the problems of artists; his essay on actors and acting, most of which is reprinted here, presents short case summaries and inferences drawn scientifically from these summaries. Pertinent particularly to the student of the modern theatre are his observations on acting methods (defined, interestingly, as "intuitive" and of the "Stanislavski school"), on "test action" as a way to describe playing and acting, and on the general relationships between the personalities of actors and the roles from which they derive most satisfaction in playing.

⚘ *from ON ACTING*

. . . SUMMARY OF THE UNCONCIOUS AIMS OF "ACTING"

1. It affords a certain erogenous satisfaction of an exhibitionistic nature. (This satisfaction has to remain at a minimum. If it is more intense, it will disturb the actor's performance.)

2. Direct narcissistic satisfaction from applause, an outwardly provided increase of self-esteem. The success on the stage is needed in the same way as milk and affection are needed by the infant.

3. Narcissistic satisfaction from a sense of magical influence on the audience. This influence may be directed towards compelling the audience to applaud, towards threatening the audience, or at least showing the actor's own superiority and power, which—as can generally be said wherever the "will to power" is strong—is needed for soothing anxiety, probably in an apotropaic way. From our general knowledge about exhibitionism, we may assume that this anxiety is mostly castration fear.

How are these aims of acting approached? By *playing parts*. What is "playing"? What is a "part"?

All languages state that the actor "plays." There must be a deep connection between actors acting on the stage and children playing games. The playing of "parts" certainly also assumes a dominant rôle in children's games.[1] Thanks to Freud,[2] we know what the psychology of children's play is. Playing is a process of learning while developing the ability to master the outer world. The primitive game is repetitive. It serves the purpose of achieving a belated mastery of highly

From *The Psychoanalytic Quarterly*, Vol XV, No. 2 (1946), pp. 148-154, 154-156, 157-158, 158, 160. Reprinted by permission of The Psychoanalytic Quarterly, Inc.

[1] *Cf.* Klein, Melanie: *Personification in the Play of Children.* Int. J. Psa., X, 1929.

[2] Freud: *Beyond the Pleasure Principle.* New York: Boni & Liveright, 1922. *Cf.* Also the summary by Waelder, Robert: *The Psychoanalytic Theory of Play. Psychoanalytic Quarterly,* II, 1933.

cathected impressions. What was endured passively is done over again in play in an active manner, until the child has become familiar with the qualities and quantities involved. The more highly developed game is anticipatory. It creates tensions which *might* occur, but, at a time and in a degree which is determined by the participant himself, and which therefore is under control. Such playing is an anti surprise measure. Both these types of "playing" are also represented in acting on the stage. More frequently the actor acts by assuming emotions which he does not have but which he might have; or he displaces tensions, which he once experienced in his past, onto imaginary persons and abreacts "unmastered" tensions in identification with them. "Abreaction" is a term which originated in the world of the theater (Aristotle). Thus acting provides for the actor either a belated getting-rid of anxieties, or a defensive anticipation of possible future anxieties.

An actress-patient who was very much afraid of all her emotions, frigid also in her sexual life, always tense and on guard, changed immediately on the stage. Identified with her part, she could permit herself to give in to emotions.

In his "part" the actor shows himself, but not as he really is. Indeed in pretending to be somebody else, he does not show himself; he conceals himself. The importance of this point is demonstrated by the actress-patient described. Her exhibitionism, usually inhibited, was permitted to express itself under the conditions that she actually did not show herself, but some other character created by an author.

But that cannot be entirely true. A good actor actually reveals himself. He cannot play an emotion he has not experienced. The good actor *believes* that he plays his parts, actually he plays himself.

Something very similar may be observed in certain neurotic characters. People of this type sometimes give an ungenuine, affected impression. Analysis of what they are pretending reveals that they actively play at what they are afraid of experiencing passively and in an overwhelming manner. There are many variations of such pretending, the extreme represented by those habitual liars whose lies in the analysis turn out to be confessions of what they have actually experienced.[3]

Certainly the actor does not play himself as he actually is, but

[3] *Cf.* Deutsch, Helene: *Über die pathologische Lüge (Pseudologia phantastica).* Int. Ztschr. f. Psa., VIII, 1922, pp. 153-167, and Fenichel, Otto: *Zur Ökonomik der Pseudologia phantastica.* Int. Ztschr. f. Psa., XXIV, 1939, pp. 21-32.

rather as he might have developed under different circumstances. Wittels has described "phantoms," fantasied personalities, which in everybody's mind play a certain rôle as ideals or possibilities for their own development, and which influence their actual behavior.[4] Although objection may be made to describing these "phantoms" as if they were independent intrapsychic personalities, it cannot be denied that everybody has fantasies and daydreams about how he would like to be, about rôles which he would or would not like to assume under certain circumstances. If an actor's "phantom" fits his part, we say: "The part suits him." The good actor is characterized by the high multiplicity of his "phantoms."

To my knowledge, there are two schools of acting. One school believes only in "intuition," with the actor so in sympathy with his part that he feels the suitable emotions, and also in this way the correct expression of his emotions. The Stanislavski school, on the contrary, stresses extremely detailed study of the actor's expressions. Nothing can be improvised, and the effect is achieved by an exact knowledge of how any detail of intonation or movement influences the audience. According to our clinical studies, the truth lies in between these two extremes. The first school is right in so far as the actor's emotions have to be really felt by him in order to be impressive. The second school has in its favor the view not only that "having emotions" is not identical with being able to express them in an impressive way, but that acting technique has to be learned like any other technique. There may be a drop of truth in the old James-Lange theory that mimicry of an affective expression may secondarily produce the affect itself.

Playing, like thinking, is a test-action: repeating the overwhelming past, and anticipating the possible future. The emotions of the actor are test-emotions. It has often been stressed that the pleasure of the spectator in a tragedy is based on the fact that he knows that the cruelty he witnesses is "but a play." This is much truer of the actor himself. He may welcome the opportunity to act as if he were cruel because he knows that in reality he is not cruel. What he does not know, and what he should not know if he is to be a good actor, is that in a sense it is real and genuine cruelty that he feels in this rôle.

---

[4] The "phantoms" are developed under the influence of real experiences and represent earlier identifications, not necessarily identifications with real objects but also with objects as the child saw them, or as the child would have liked them to be. *Cf.* Wittels, Fritz: *Unconscious Phantoms in Neurotics. Psychoanalytic Quarterly*, VIII, 1939, pp. 141-163.

Playing a part is making test-identifications. The earliest test-identification was probably the priests' identification with God. This identification too (like the identification of the believer with the priest who imitates God) was possible because the imitator felt simultaneously the infinite distance between himself and what he imitated, in the same way that the playing child imitates the serious actions of adults.[5]

Does this mean the best actor would be a character who has not developed an actual marked personality, but who is ready to play any part given him, who has no ego, but is rather a bundle of identification possibilities? Some great actors have been of this type, and did on the stage what Caligula did in life.[6] But it is not all necessarily so. Certainly there are actors who have well integrated personalities. They are not well integrated only in those parts of their personalities involved in their work. They are Caligulas on the stage, but not in life.

We can now better understand some types of failure on the stage. If a part somehow comes too close to painful emotions in the actor's unconscious, if he tends to become aware that the pretended emotions of his rôle also have reality values to him, then he can no longer successfully act the part. He is faced with the immediate necessity of further repression of the emotions, and becomes incapable of acting.

If the magic influence of the audience, which the actor unconsciously strives for, threatens to become too real so that the whole performance loses its "play" character, the actor will fail. Certainly the average actor does not use his playing directly to affect his audience as Hamlet uses the players. His only conscious aim is applause. His wish for reassurances against castration fear, or of "charming" the audience, remains unconscious.

Acting on the stage is endangered by the same two dangers which threaten the "double-edged character" of children's play. The pleasure in playing turns into displeasure if the intended "mastery" fails and the playing gets out of control. The fearsome loss of control may involve the player himself (he might become for good the animal he pretended to be), or the audience (he might charm or destroy it in an irreparable way).

---

[5] The imitation of idealized persons often represents an attempt to "try out" their ways of feeling, without losing the knowledge of the "trial" character. The "test" character of such limited "identifications" in the service of some purpose of the ego, differentiates imitation from full indentification, which takes place unconsciously and independently from the ego's wishes.

[6] Sachs, Hanns: *Caligula*. London: Elkin Mathews & Marrot, Ltd., 1931.

Let us consider the "magic influence" upon the audience to which reference has been made and ask of what this influence actually consists.

Sachs, following Freud, developed a well-known general theory about the unconscious processes within the artist.[7] By presenting his work, which unconsciously represents an expression of repressed instinctual wishes, derivations of the œdipus complex, the artist induces in his public a participation in the forbidden wishes through acceptance and praise of his work. To see that the public accepts the artistic expressions of his unconscious guilt-laden impulses is for him a belated approval of them and removes or decreases his feelings of guilt about them. After having withdrawn from reality into day-dreaming, the artist finds his way back from daydreaming to society by *inducing* an audience to participate in his guilt.

While this applies to all artists, it is especially true for the actor. It is the unconscious aim of all acting to make the audience feel the same emotions that the actor displays. The spectators go to the theater with the tacitly acknowledged intention of identifying themselves with the actors' portrayals. The theater remains the realm of the infantile "ocular identification."[8] The actor seeks to induce the audience's participation and approval of the commission of the deeds which he, under the guise of pretense, would like to commit. If he succeeds, he feels less guilty.

That the audience is compelled to give up its spontaneity to accept hypnotically what the actor suggests (possibly through the "omnipotence of gestures"),[9] gives the actor a satisfying feeling of superiority and of having the audience dependent on him. Actually, he is dependent upon the audience. He has become an actor because he feels guilty unless he can draw the reassuring applause his narcissism requires. The actor needs the audience for the same reason that the audience needs the actor: both get reassurances against guilt feelings which make possible otherwise forbidden discharges of instinctual tension by mutual participation. In a good theatrical performance (as in ancient worship) actor and audience feel, "We do it together." The audience, knowing it is "only a play," loses its fear of the deed, and the actor (likewise the author), secure in the same knowledge, loses his feeling of guilt through the approval of

[7] Sachs, Hanns: *The Creative Unconscious.* Cambridge: Sci-Art Publishers, 1942.

[8] *Cf.* Fenichel, Otto: *The Scopophilic Instinct and Identification.* Int. J. Psa., XVIII, 1937, pp. 6-34.

[9] Ferenczi, Sándor: Stages in the Development of the Sense of Reality. In *Contributions to Psychoanalysis.* Boston: Richard G. Badger, 1916.

the brothers (audience) which releases him, the hero, of his loneliness. The magic induction is in the last analysis a *seduction* to participation in a repetition of the œdipus. . . .

The actor prepares by long preliminary work for the night when he will charm everybody. If he succeeds, a pleasure which has been forbidden to him hitherto will become accessible again. The work of the actor may be compared with the mechanisms of sexual forepleasure and end-pleasure. Rehearsals are usually very strenuous and painful and arduous. They are nevertheless, pleasurable by reason of a mounting anticipatory tension straining towards the end-pleasure of the opening night for release.

The movie actor is cheated of this end-pleasure, but acting for the films gives the actor an exceptional narcissistic satisfaction. The actor cannot feel with his audience, but he can actually be a spectator of his own performance. But other pleasures, and especially the specific end-pleasure are denied him. He feels frustrated. He is deprived of the unique experience of a *unio mystica* with the audience, and of the satisfaction of performing a complete part from the beginning to the end of the plot. The endless repetition of incoherent scenes is all rehearsal, and the only pleasure is anticipation of the satisfaction not of an actor, but at most of a spectator. The essential pleasure of the actor to bring "disjected membra" together, and to present them as a whole, is partly shifted to the director.[10] I was not surprised to find that those few motion picture actors I had the opportunity to analyze were longing to return to the stage. The films have many possibilities for the expression of modern needs and for providing the abreaction of the audience, which the stage never had. The actor is worse off. The knowledge that millions will see him is no reparation for the direct applause of hundreds.

If the actor succeeds, he has fewer guilt feelings, and if he has fewer feelings of guilt, he feels privileged to indulge more freely his instinctual pleasure and seeks greater sexual freedom. That society actually grants him such privileges, more or less, is connected with the peculiar position of the artist in bourgeois society. The artist is still regarded as nearer to God, and enjoys the privileges of the priest. As is well known, the privileges accorded the artist are very ambivalent in intent. The actor is privileged, but he remains some-

[10] It would be interesting to compare the psychology of the scenario writer, who is furnished the complete plot of a story and prepares the script from it, with the psychology of the playwright.

what beyond the pale of "honest" society. He sins publicly and thereby exculpates the others (though he, subjectively, has also the striving of being himself exculpated). Like the whore, he is held in contempt but secretly envied.[11] . . .

The unconscious aims of the magic influence, which the actor tries to convey to his audience, and which has the value of exculpating him, are mainly two: seduction to participate in the actor's guilt, and the craving to gratify passive oral needs by any means, including if necessary, destruction or "castration" of the audience.

In the plots in which theater is used to wring an actual confession of guilt from a spectator, as in Hamlet, or in Schiller's Cranes of Ibicus, not a repressed instinct but a suppressed feeling of guilt and expectation of punishment is mobilized. This, too, to a certain extent, seems to be a component of all theater. Pity and fear have to be provoked, and the evocation of fear—the fear of God who was imitated by the acting priests—was certainly one of the main aims of the primeval theater. Not alone fear, but certainly also hope of salvation was aroused; otherwise the audience would have fled in panic and would not have remained true to God. Seduction and intimidation were both achieved by means of magical gestures. This combination of seduction and intimidation is the essential content of all totem festivals, initiation rites, religious rites, and theatrical performances. It states in effect: "You are given permission for instinctual satisfactions (or you are given your narcissistic indulgence), but only if you fulfil our conditions. And do not forget that you will be dreadfully punished if you transgress these conditions."

Not only has the spectator to be given protective reassurances ("it is only a play") if the attempted seduction is to succeed, but the actor, too, has to deny dangers which are believed to be connected with his seducing and imitating activity. He wants to seduce, or charm, or even to destroy the spectator, but not in such a manner or to a degree that might provoke the spectator to turn against him. The actor has to make sure that the audience remains dependent on him. The more he doubts inwardly its dependence on him, the more urgent his need for outer proofs of it. Seeking applause, as the actor invariably does, he denies to himself and others that he actually is dependent on the spectators. . . .

---

[11] *Cf,* Kris, Ernst and Kurz, Otto: *Die Legende vom Künstler* Vienna: Krystallverlag, 1934.

Exhibitionism in general, and acting in particular, have a deep connection with the castration complex. There many ways in which the "charm" of acting may serve the purpose of denying castration or any possibility of it, or of denying that castration is a danger, and influencing the audience to give some equivalent reassurance. . . .

A discussion of the psychology of the actor should not fail to include comment about the typical actor's neurosis, stage fright.[12]

The general cause of stage fright is to be found in the double-edged character of all the psychological mechanisms we have discussed. The reassurance which theatrical performance unconsciously promises the actor is not always achieved. Stage fright occurs when the unconscious motives of the actor threaten to become conscious (when the "play" threatens to become "real"). Instead of participating in the actor's guilty misdeeds, the audience may turn against him and become the representative of the punishing super-ego. And stage fright has a special quality; it is the specific fright of an exhibitionist: shame. Unconsciously, it is the shame of an inferiority (being castrated), which to cover has been the chief motivation in the choice of acting as a profession. The shame may derive in addition from the threat of display of unconscious intentions hidden in the acting, of sexual tendencies (œdipus), and of primitive destructive impulses to obtain, by deception, gratification of the narcissistic demands. Shame and anxiety arise from the dread of being exposed as a sham, of having expropriated something, of adorning oneself with borrowed plumes. The playing of a part on the stage is moreover a source of potential shame because of the real dependency of the actor who tries to make believe that the others are dependent on him.[13]

✍

[12] I do not remember any published case of the psychoanalysis of stage fright. There is a great deal of literature about the related symptoms such as fear of examinations and erythrophobia: Blum, Ernst: *Zur Psychologie von Studium und Examen.* Int. Ztschr. f. Psa., XII, 1926, pp. 400-412. Feldmann, S.: *Über Erröten. Beitrag zur Psychologie der Scham.* Int. Ztschr f. Psa., VIII, 1922, pp. 14-34. Flugel, J. C.: *The Examination as Initiation Rite and Anxiety Situation.* Int. J. Psa., XX, 1939, pp. 275-286. Jones, Ernest: Pathology of Morbid Anxiety. In *Papers on Psychoanalysis.* Baltimore: Wm. Wood & Co., 1913. Stengel, Erwin: *Prüfungsangst und Prüfungsneurose.* Ztschr. f. Psa. Pädagogik, X, 1936.

[13] Compulsive mechanisms of actors have unconsciously the meaning of ensuring that acting is only "playing" to overcome stage fright. "Getting stuck" may express the resistance against any tendency which was supposed to find an outlet in the acting. It may also have the much more specific meaning of "getting stuck" before the castrated state, which one had intended to play, is achieved; and/or "getting stuck" *in* the castrated state.

John Gielgud

One of the greatest Shakespearean actors of all time, Gielgud transcribed the notes reprinted here during conferences with Harley
Granville-Barker who directed *King Lear* in 1940. These notes tell us
much about Granville-Barker's direction, of course, as well as Gielgud's understanding of motive and reaction as he studied the role.
Of special interest are Gielgud's obvious concern with ensemble
playing (he never neglects to note the interpretive concerns of fellow
actors), specific details of movement that relate directly to development of character, and — always an aspect of classical acting for which
Gielgud has been famous — the "scoring" of the part: small (or large)
vocal inflection, modulation almost in musical terms, and notation
of tempo and pacing.

Ever since his first popular success in 1932 (*Richard of Bordeaux*),
John Gielgud has stood among the first two or three actors in the
English language. Although his appearances have been for the most
part in the classical repertory (from Shakespeare to the great comedies of the Restoration), he has directed many modern plays, has had
considerable success in Chekhov, and has retained a lively and
creative interest in new drama of all kinds. His Hamlet and Lear, his
Prospero, Leontes, Richard II, and Angelo rank among the most
influential Shakespearean interpretations of the century; it is for the
nobility, the musical clarity, and meaningful projection of such roles
that he remains justly famous.

❧ *REHEARSAL NOTES ON* KING LEAR

After the death of Granville-Barker in 1946 I searched in vain for
my rehearsal copy of *King Lear* in which I had hastily scribbled many
of his hints on tone, motives and technical delivery of lines. Shortly
before beginning to study the play again for Stratford-on-Avon in
1950, I was lucky enough to find the missing copy in a neglected
corner of a drawer. Here are the majority of the notes. I add them in
the hope that they may bring to others (as they do so vividly to me)
an echo of the exactness which Barker showed in his criticism and
guidance, and his understanding of every mood and nuance in the

From *Stage Directions*, by John Gielgud. © Copyright 1963 by John Gielgud. Reprinted by
permission of Random House, Inc., and Heinemann Educational Books Ltd. (London).

part of Lear. Here are the notes exactly as I scribbled them down at the time.[1]

Act I. Scene I

[Lear enters ceremoniously from the side carrying a huge staff which he uses to walk with. Reaching the centre of the stage, on his way to the throne, which commands the stage up centre, he suddenly stops, and striking the staff impatiently on the floor, raps out his first command to Gloucester – then he gives the staff to an attendant and mounts the throne. Pleased. Happy.]

Line

102   *Nothing will come of nothing.*   First note of danger.

106   *How now, Cordelia, mend your speech a little.*   Grind.
                                                     Intimidation.

124   *By the sacred radiance of the sun.*   Big without ponging (actor's slang for hamming).

131-2 *The barbarous Scythian.*   Oath over, sulk over this. Descending passage.

139   *I loved her most.*   Justify himself.

152   *With reservation of an*   He thinks this disposes of the whole
         hundred knights.   thing, lean back, happy as at opening.

178   *Kent, on thy life, no more.*   Dead quiet. Turn. Stare at him.

197   *Since thou hast sought to make us*   Everyone must listen.
         break our vow.   Write this down.

205   *If on the tenth day following.* – Get a note of this (to secretary).

[After exit of   Lear – complete change – smooth, courtly,
   Kent.]   charming, anger vanished.

[To Burgundy.]   Irony, smooth, cruel about Cordelia, urbanity, very ironic, schoolmaster showing up dunce.

[To France (whom he liked).]   More respect, genuine. Don't look at Cordelia again.

289   *Nothing. I have sworn,*   Real, sulky. Big Ben striking. Pass by
         I am firm.   exit, cut her dead.

---

[1] These notes were recorded by Sir John in his copy of the play – an edition now no longer available. The line numbers here given refer to Professor Sisson's edition of *The Complete Works of William Shakespeare* (Odhams, London 1954). There are slight differences between the edition used by Barker and Professor Sisson's, but it was thought advantageous to leave the line as studied by the actor.

515   *The jewels of our father*   Cordelia weeps *not* for the behaviour
         with washed eyes.   of Lear, but because of the kindness
                                     of France in accepting her.

ACT I. SCENE IV

[With Kent in disguise. Robust, jolly, give and take, enjoy sparring.
Sing, genial, throw things about (gloves, whip, etc.). Boots off, shoes
on, nuisance. Suddenly checked by the insolence of the knight, continue gloves, etc., mechanically, sudden stop.]

68   *Thou but rememberest me of*   I saw it, felt it, can't be really
          mine own conception.   so.

85   *Do you bandy looks*   Take cloth from table, strike him across
          with me?   the face. Stand quite still, hands on hips.
                               Terrific. Kent trips Oswald. Roars with
                               laughter.

[At entrance of Fool.] Sit him by me, give him food. Immensely fond, sweet to him. Eat and drink heartily. Show him
off to Kent.

112   *Take heed sirrah, the whip.*   Not too fast. Encourage Fool to go
                                        on, buy it. This will be a good one
                                        I expect.

No welcome from Goneril. Suddenly notices her. Take it in.

225   *Are you our daughter?*   Blank.

232   *Does any here know me?*   Danger—end of careless exterior.
                                   Gasps. Feeling. Speech nothing.

243   *Your name, fair gentlewoman.*   Bite. During her speech store
                                         it up—hold back.

262   *Darkness and Devils.*   Crash. Pause between sentences.

[Entrance of Albany.]   More reason. Down towards her. See
                         her. Find it.

285   *Oh, Lear, Lear, Lear.*   Let go. The curse sudden, surprise the
                                  audience.
                                  Speak nicely to Albany, going, then
                                  down to her. Strange, not loud.
                                  Deadly. Ride it.

304   *Sharper than a serpent's tooth.*   Climax. Move backwards
                                            from her.

305   *Away, away.*   Will not go back on it. Slow exit.
       [Sudden   Broken speech in contrast to former scene.
       reappearance.] Change after "What's the matter sir?" See
                       Goneril. Burst into tears. Not too much. Not
                       repeat the curse.

Act I. Scene V

[Represents the journey from Goneril's castle to Gloster's.]

[At entrance.]   Touch of the ruler. Characteristic. Quick, not
thinking of what he says. Walks continually to
and fro. Stop suddenly—deep walk *I did her
wrong* stop again.

33/4   *Be my horses ready?*   Shout. Move about.

38   *Because they are not eight?*   Angry. Heard it before.

40   *Monster ingratitude.*   Walk again.

43   *How's that?*   Sudden.

46   *O let me not be mad.*   Now afraid *inside*. Simple.

50   *Come boy.*   Sustained exit. Use Fool as focal point in the
scene throughout.

Act II. Scene IV

[Arrival at Gloster's Castle.] Pace at which you left. Start
again.

[At entrance.] Puzzled but confident.

7   *Ha?*   Turn. Very slow, very outraged.

15   *What's he that hath so much*   Deadly. Exchange with Kent in
thy place mistook?   the stocks. Pride hurt. Superb.

25   *Thou durst not do it.*   Slow rhythm. Dignity offended. Too
indignant to be angry.

[During Kent's speech.] Absorb the insult.

118/9   *My breath and blood.*   Recover, then hysteria again.

123   *We are not ourselves.*   (As he felt just now himself.)

128   *Death on my state.*   Sudden rage.

133   *Duke and's wife.*   More than temper.

136   *I'll beat the drum.*   Deepest round this point.

139   *O me, my heart.*   Physical. Entirely new voice. Quick. Then
stand still. Pay no attention to the Fool.
Closed eyes, hand to head.

Entrance of Cornwall and Regan. Begin right down.

145   *Good morrow to you both.*   No greeting. Cold.

147   *I am glad to see your highness.*   Don't notice this.

148   *Regan I think you are.*   Tender, just. (In his heart he knows.)

156/7   *Thou'lt not believe with how depraved a quality.*   Literal.

161   *Say how is that?*   Stern, suspicious.

167   *My curses on her.*   Then control it.

182   *Never, Regan.*   Definite. Then a bit petty and distracted,
not deliberate.

190   *You nimble lightnings.*   Rash mood. Burble.

196   *No Regan thou shalt never have my curse.*   Exhausted by the
                                            rage. Tender silly.

200   *'Tis not in thee.*   Fear that he may be wrong. (You didn't mean
                              it, did you?)

     [Does not take in Goneril's arrival till her appearance, turns to
door, and sees her suddenly. Then sees Kent too again.]

210   *Who put my man i' the stocks?*   King.

221   *Who comes here? O heavens.*   Knowledge gradually growing,
                                   more moved than ever.

222   *If you do love old men?*   Noble, becoming helpless.

228   *O Regan, wilt thou take her by the hand?*   Dignity. Slow.

237   *You! Did you?*   Utter Contempt. Period.

249   *The hot-blooded France that dowerless*   Paint it, then off again.
     took our youngest born.

253   *Slave and sumpter.*   Preposterous.

256   *I prithee daughter do not make me mad.* Physical. Real. Turn swift.

260   *Or rather a disease that's in my flesh.*   Rash mood. Then suffer
                                  in the head.

292   *I gave you all.*   Very big. To the front. Bewildered. Not as
                                 fast as their speeches.

299   *These wicked creatures yet do look well-*   (Goneril better than
     favour'd.   Regan.) Tremble.

310   *O reason not the need.*   Drop it right down. Ironic feeling.
                                    Dignity.

320   *You see me here, you gods.*   Sink on to bench. Simple.
                                    Crouching attitude.

326   *Stain my man's cheeks.*   Collapse here. Rash mood suddenly.
                                    Human, broken old man, futile. Sud-
                                    denly   looks   at   them.   Wipe   eyes.
                                    Then   up   and   totter   off   but   more
                                    firmly at the end for the horses.

            Self-devouring   rages. Physical   symptoms   which   he
            ignores.

     Act III. Scene II
     [*1st Storm Scene*]
     Tune in. Pitch voice. Low key. Oratorio. Every word im-
personal.

21   *Here I stand, your slave.*   Simpler. Voice down, then up. Keep
                                  still. Feet.

54   *Let the great gods.*   Full value. Point to the audience.

66/7   *I am a man more sinn'd against than sinning.*   Simple. Clasp
                                          head.

[GOING MAD]

87   *My wits begin to turn.* Real not pitiful.

89   *Where is this straw my fellow.* Kind, next lines casual, make little of them.

Listen tenderly to the Fool, cloak round him (*how nicely you sing*). Hold on to the edge of security. Leave stage on a high, unfinished note.

Act III. Scene IV
[*2nd Heath Scene*]

MAD now. Strange Walk. Strange Voice. Living in purely metaphysical world. At entrance. Distant, dignified.

17   *The tempest in my mind.* Point to head. Move away from them all. Words tumbling out.

24   *O Regan, Goneril.* Climax. See it all in a circle. Vision.

27   *O, that way madness lies.* Horror. Then drop it.

30   *Prithee, go in thyself.* Kind. Stoop to touch the Fool.

34   *I'll pray (and when I have prayed) then I'll sleep.* Away to thought. Kneel in mire. Hands folded conventionally.

The Fool's scream turns him off his head. Leans back on knees. Look through cage—fingers in front of face.

57   *Didst thou give all to thy daughter.* Is that all? Face each other. Still.

72   *Have his daughters brought him to this pass.* Sad dignity. Pity now new.

78   *Now all the plagues.* Just *too* dignified. (Explain to me.)

87   *Judicious punishment.* (Quite right.)

97   *What hast thou been?* Too interested. Listen to his answer and nod approval.

115   *Why thou wert better in thy grave.* Speak to no one. Full value. Now faster.

123   *Off you lendings.* Rash mood suddenly back. Afterward slow, still, stare vacantly.

139   *How fares your grace?* Curious silence.

After Gloster enters. Still Important. King. Walk round stage with Edgar talking to him.

171   *First let me talk with this philosopher.* Wave Gloster aside. Keep step with Edgar.

Fantastic bowing and pantomine.

199   *Come, let's in all.* Still grand.

207   *Come, good Athenian.* Very courteous. Get him again by the arm.

At the end of scene, nod in approval, march off in same
rhythm as we walked before.

ACT III. SCENE VI
[*Hovel*]
Very odd and mysterious. Gradual disintegration.

11   *A King. A King.*   Indignant.

20   *It shall be done.*   Action does not begin till here. Firm.
Sudden move. Swinging stool in hand.

31   *The foul fiend haunts poor Tom.*   Stand aghast. Lunatic for
the first time. Paler and
paler in voice.

37   *I'll see their trial first.*   Stop them dancing.

40   *You are o' the commission.*   Bow, conduct him to place. He
is counsel for the prosecution.

53   *She cannot deny it.*   Very reasonable.

60   *Why hast thou let her 'scape?*   Tiny, trembling, old man,
childlike, tottering about.

66   *The little dogs and all.*   Piteous. In Kent's arms.
Equal value to real and imagined characters, whole scene
QUIET.

84/5 *You, sir, I entertain you for one*   Exhausted courtesy to Edgar.
of my hundred.

Sink onto bench. Lie down. Poke head out again between
imaginary curtains. Then lie again hand under cheek.

ACT IV. SCENE VI
[*Dover Cliff*]
Happy King of Nature. No troubles. Tremendously digni-
fied. Branch in hand, like staff in opening scene, walk with it.

Line

113   *Give the word.*   Nice. Applaud Edgar as he says "Pass."

117   *Ha! Goneril with a white beard.*   Frightful pain. Rub head.

125   *Go to, they are not men o' their word.*   Sad. All away from
the others but don't
move about.

130   *Ay, every inch a King.*   Direct answer, change from sad mood.

134   *Die for adultery? No.*   Light.

137   *Let Copulation thrive.*   Almost jolly. Swing staff above head.

137   *For Gloster's bastard son.*   Special.

141   *To't Luxury, pell mell.*   Comedy.

142   *Behold yond simpering dame.*   Horrid.

146   *The fitchew nor the soiled horse.*   Words.

148   *Down from the waist.*   Intimate. Quicker. Build speech.

159   *Let me wipe it first.*   Real. Physical. Comfortable with Gloster.

163   *Do thy worst blind Cupid.*   Coy.
      Then different key, tone, pace.

169   *Read.*   Very cross.

172/3 *Your eyes are in a heavy case.*   Joke.

186   *Thou rascal Beadle.*   Vision. Begin to get excited. Quicker.
      Bursts of feeling. Flow on.

199   *Get thee glass eyes.*   A bit impatient with him.
      After boots are off, sudden relief. Recognize Gloster slowly,
      comforting him (*I will preach to thee*).

212   *When we are born.*   Serio-comic.

213   *This, a good block.*   Very light.

217   *Kill, kill.*   Build to revenge. End of scene for feeling.

220   *No rescue what! A prisoner?*   Panic. Then light, helpless.

226   *This would make a man a man of salt.*   Empty chatter.

ACT IV. SCENE VII
[*Awakening*]
Sit in profile in chair. Hands in lap. Make them up again.

55   *You do me wrong.*   A bit sulky.

60   *You are a spirit I know.*   Puzzled.

62   *Where have I been?*   Real. Don't anticipate.

64   *I should even die with pity.*   A bit cross.

68/69 *Would I were assured of my condition.*   Troubled. Keep it up.
      Not conscious of surroundings.

87   *Be your tears wet?* Lift her head.   ⎧ He hears the voice he
                                            ⎪ knows, but fears so
95   *Do not abuse me.* Strong.   ⎨ terribly she may not be
                                            ⎩ Cordelia.

102   *You must bear with me.*   Cheerful. End. Come off it.
      Rise as if from throne. Soft dignity at exit.

ACT V. SCENE III
[*Going to prison*]

10   *Come let's away to prison.*   Delighted. Really happy. Dance
                                     the whole speech like a polka.
                                     Music up and down. Variety.
      Exit hand in hand with her, triumphant.

ACT V. SCENE III
[*Death*]

308   *Howl, howl.*   Take time. Dreadful.

308   *O you are men of stone.*   Anger. Hold them off.

328   *Prithee away.*   Strong.

331   *I killed the slave.*   (You know.)

334   *I have seen the day.*   Jolly. Stand firm above her body.

336   *I am old now.*   Sudden break.
       Forget Cordelia in passage with Kent.

345/6 *He's dead and rotten.*   Suddenly sad.

351   *You are welcome hither.*   Careless. Shake hands. Move
                                   away. Wander about at back of
                                   stage.
       Find the body again. The rope round her neck.
       Crouch by her. Kneel.

375   *Pray you, undo this button.*   Real, then a cry.

376   *Look on her.*   Joy.

PART THREE ✒ THE DIRECTOR

Tyrone Guthrie

In these observations on the role and function of the director, Guthrie, one of the most versatile members of his profession, sets forth a description of those intangible qualities of control and attraction necessary for smoothly rendered rehearsals and interpretive communication. Autocratic in general conception, details of Guthrie's approach to directing remain, nevertheless, fundamentally humane; if he does not aim for democracy in the rehearsal room, he achieves the basic generosity of ensemble work.

Guthrie's experience with the classical repertory, with modern drama, musical comedy, and grand opera is ranging and unique in scope. At the Old Vic, the Shakespeare Festival in Stratford, Ontario, with his own new company in the Minnesota Repertory Theatre, and, presently, with directorial engagements in New York and other major cities, Guthrie has impressed audiences at home and abroad with both his originality of conception and control of convention.

from THE DIRECTOR

. . . And now, what does the director do?

He bears to the preparation of a play much the same relation as an orchestral conductor to the rehearsal of a symphony. But the symphony is performed by the conductor with each member of the orchestra playing under his leadership. He does not play the leading part. He does more. He interprets, shapes, guides, inspires the entire performance.

The theatrical director's work ends before the first performance. It is his duty to prepare the work; but when the time has come to show it to the public, the performance goes forward without him. Theoretically, each actor in rehearsal is no more than an instrument in a concerted performance. But in practice the actor has infinitely more technical latitude and a far more creative task than the orchestral player.

This is because the script of a play reveals so much less of its author's intention than does the score of a symphony. This may seem paradoxical, because every literate person can read the text of a play whereas to be able to read a full symphonic score is an accomplishment.

But, once you have mastered the business of reading it, the musical score will indicate in precise terms the pace, pitch, and rhythm of the sounds which are to be heard; how a melody is organized, and a phrase shaped; the logic of counterpoint and harmonic progression. From these instructions an interpreter can deduce, not with precision, but with only moderate margin of error, the color of the different sounds required, the balance of instrumental tone, the relation of one musical statement to others and to a whole work; all sorts of technical and interpretative deductions which enable a conductor, even if he is merely competent and industrious, to recreate a great deal of a composer's intention.

But now consider the text of a play.

Take a single speech from *Hamlet:* "To be or not to be." The text gives a precise indication of its syntax, and in broadest and simplest terms, its rhythm. The pace, pitch, stress, melody of the speech must be invented by the actor. Much of its meaning, and hence many indications as to how to speak it, can be deduced by study of the rest of the work. But this study makes far more severe demands upon the intelligence, feelings, intuition and education of the actor than are ever made upon an orchestral musician.

It must, of course, be admitted that the technique required of a violinist, for instance, demands long training and endless practice; whereas a well-graced actor, with a voice which is naturally well-produced, can play Hamlet with comparatively little technical drudgery. But the intellectual and intuitive demands made upon the actor, because of the incomplete indications to be derived from a play's text—these are what make his work creative and interesting. It is to reinforce, but not to supplant, his own intelligence and intuition that he principally needs a director.

It can readily be seen that a great complicated masterpiece like *Hamlet* needs a director more than a neat little comedy of modern manners in a conventional, naturalistic style. The latter hardly needs any artistic direction. Someone must choose the actors, plan the set, make practical arrangements of various kinds. In most plays of this kind the choreography, if such it can be called, is very simple. Actors enter through one door to indicate that they have come from the street; from another if they have come from kitchen or bedroom; meals occur round a table; love scenes on the sofa; hostesses plump cushions; guests light cigarettes, exchange elegant badinage and forward the plot in a series of almost preordained postures; so rigid are the conventions of this kind of piece. And yet the moment someone with a spark of originality, a quirk of invention, gets to work on the actors, sets them in unconventional positions, cracks the old gags in a new way, how much more lively is the result!

For *Hamlet* or any of the masterpieces, or for any play which is not in an obviously familiar style and whose interpretation is not clearly charted and signposted, much more is required of a director.

First, he must decide what he thinks the play means—to him. The meaning of any work of art is subjective. It is not what the author thinks it means. If the objective meaning of a work of art were known, there would be no point in its existence. It exists merely to suggest many ways in which an undefined truth may be approached. Every interpretation is subjective. Some will be nearer to objective truth than others, but not on that account necessarily more interesting or of wider appeal than others.

To face the fact that your own interpretation of a work of art is consciously and flagrantly subjective always seems to be regarded as an arrogant attitude. But I think the truer view is that an interpretative artist can only make his own comment upon the work which he endeavors to interpret, and that to do so humbly is the only possible attitude to the "creator" (or, more truly, the expressor) of the "original" idea.

Throughout my own career I have been critized for impertinently attempting to express my own subjective, and admittedly limited, comment upon the masterpieces which I have been privileged to direct.

I consider such criticism misplaced. I know perfectly well that my comment upon *Oedipus Rex, Hamlet* or *All's Well That Ends Well* is not the final, any more than it is the first, interpretation of these works. My collaborators and I have merely added one more comment to the vast corpus of criticism, admiration, revulsion, reverence, love and so on, with which a masterpiece of human expression is rightly surrounded.

Performance in the theatre seems to me the right way to make such comment upon works which were written in dramatic form, which exist as the raw material for performance. Shakespeare, for instance, wrote his plays, often in a hurry, for a specific group of players. So little was he interested in the plays as literature that there is no record of their being printed, or published, during his lifetime. And when, shortly after his death, his two friends Heminge and Condell endeavored to get together the texts of his plays for publication, they could only find prompt scripts full of errors, omissions and, we may be sure, "improvements," added in rehearsal or performance.

Scholars have performed service of inestimable value in the elucidation of textual difficulties and in the discussion of many problems, primarily in the literary and intellectual fields. But there are limits to the usefulness of purely intellectual and literary criticism of works which are intended to be realized in theatrical terms. . . .

. . . [H]ow is [the director's] intention to be achieved, once he has decided how a play is to be interpreted?

Many of the important decisions are taken before the actors begin to rehearse.

Their interpretation will be enormously conditioned by the casting. If A, B and C are to play Othello, Iago and Cassio while X and Y are Desdemona and Emilia, before a single rehearsal has been called, it is fairly clear what the general attempt of a director will be in this particular production.

Conferences with those who are to design and make the scenery and dresses will determine how a play shall look. A good director will not dictate to his collaborators in these departments, but they will look to him for general lines of guidance. For instance, in a classical play he must indicate the period, the scenic convention required; some general direction about color, about the "key" of this scene and that. Even the simplest modern comedy in the most obviously realistic single interior set demands that he state where the doors, windows, fireplace and furniture be placed; whether the curtains are to be cottagey or grand. A wise director will know how much, or how little, direction or suggestion to give. Some designers like to work, as it were, on ruled lines; to others a wink or a nudge is as good as three columns of closely typed instruction. It is vital that the designer's creative talents be encouraged, not frustrated; equally vital that other, and possibly more important, aspects of a production are not butchered to make a designer's holiday. With dominant designers this sometimes happens, particularly in our era, when what is seen tends to attract more interest than what is heard.

But while the general shape and feeling of the production will have been settled before the actors assemble for the first rehearsal, nevertheless it is from now on that the most vital and interesting work of interpretation is done.

How can a director communicate his ideas to the cast?

It is usually better to attempt this by implication rather than explication. There is a method of direction, more prevalent in America, Germany and Russia than in Britain, which believes in giving long talks, and in encouraging long discussions among the cast about the meaning of a play and the process of its interpretation.

This may lead to great results in plays which depend upon teamwork and upon achieving a precise and subtle counterpoint between one voice, one movement and another—such plays as those of Chekhov. But, if the process is to succeed, it must essentially be slow and thorough. The voices of the shy and unimportant persons should be heard as well as the more assertive. At the Moscow Art Theatre, where a permanent company, each member of which is like a member of a family, studies one production over a period of many months, the method of discussion probably works excellently. In London or New York, a hastily assembled group of strangers works for three or four weeks. In such conditions the discussion method is likely to be unfruitful.

This is not entirely to disregard the value of discussion. Far from it. But I regard it as an adjunct to, rather than a substitute for, other work. And, where time is severely limited, the discussions ought to be conducted out of working hours.

In all conditions, the lecture method seems to me a bore, an expression of the director's egotism rather than a practical plan of action. Of course the director must from time to time express theoretic ideas about the work in hand. But such expression should be brief and rare. Naturally, there can be no hard and fast rules. No one in his five wits would rehearse *Three Men on a Horse* in the Spirit of the Moscow Art Theatre preparing *Uncle Vanya,* or by similar methods.

In the preparation of *Hamlet,* for instance, it is essential for the director and leading actor to be in the closest accord. But such accord should have been reached before the rehearsals begin. It is not necessary for the actors who play Barnardo or the Second Gravedigger, or who shout offstage that Laertes shall be King, to know all the considerations which govern the production. It is boring for them to sit around while director and leading actor thrash out theoretical ideas about the Oedipus complex, the meaning of this line, the importance of that move. And in the time available for rehearsing any play with which I have ever been connected, it is out of *all* question that the smaller fry should air their views at rehearsal.

They are naturally entitled to views and to express such views to the director when they are relevant to their own parts, but not otherwise, and not publicly.

Of course the contribution of the smaller parts is an important ingredient of the dish. But it is largely determined by the casting. For instance, in *Hamlet* it is possible to use the gravediggers as comic relief. It is also possible, and in my opinion more interesting, to have them make a simple but serious comment on the transitory nature of human existence—"passsing through nature to eternity." It is possible to make this comment and still be amusing. The casting of the gravediggers largely determines the comment which their scene makes, the style in which it is made, and the weight it carries.

What concerns them can be explained to any actor-gravediggers of ordinary capacity in a few seconds. Their cooperative suggestions can be made during the rehearsal of their scene. They do not have to be present at all the discussion of the far more complex scenes between Hamlet and Ophelia, Hamlet and his mother, the Ghost, Claudius and even Polonius.

If attendance of the whole company is compulsory at rehearsals of scenes which do not concern them, the production, rather than being more closely integrated, is far more likely to be disrupted by the boredom and disaffection of the smaller-part players.

In theory, a director should not instruct his actors in the detailed playing of their parts. General aspects of a scene or a speech must be directed. It must be explained why this passage must go fast in order to contrast with a slow passage preceding or following; how this scene must be underemphasized in order that more emphasis may fall elsewhere. The focus of attention must be directed. The audience has to be shown where, at a given instant, it must look; to what, at a given instant, it must listen. Naturally there are many technical devices to do this. All of them depend upon the directed cooperation of the actors.

But, in addition to this, every actor depends upon a director for criticism or advice. Even the greatest and most proficient performer will pay attention to the advice of a director he trusts. It would be highly absurd if a director were to try to teach an actor far better qualified than himself how to play a scene or to speak a speech—if I, for instance, were to offer to teach Laurence Olivier. But Laurence Olivier will look to me for technical criticism and suggestion: "Try this a bit faster. Don't pause there." And the actor will depend upon the director to implement in practice theoretical points upon which, in discussion, they will have previously agreed; that such a scene shall be played for comedy; that such a scene shall be dark and shadowy; that emphasis shall be placed here, or there; that the climax of a scene be made in this way or that.

But frequently, with the less gifted or intelligent or experienced actors, the director must coach the performer, show him where to breathe in a speech, which word to stress, when to move, when to keep still.

It is always a sign of failure when a director makes an actor copy him. The failure may be the actor's: there are some so dull that they can only imitate. Far more often it is a failure of communication on the director's part.

He should be able to indicate a move, an inflection or other piece of expression; and the actor should be able to see the idea and express it in his own terms, not by a literal copy. Such indications can be verbal. But nearly all directors find it far quicker and more vivid to sketch the idea in acted terms; and I believe that, provided the actor is confident that such a sketch is not offered as a model which he must slavishly copy, he will find it immensely more helpful than a verbal disquisition. The *how* and the *why*, incidentally, seem rarely to be verbally definable or logically separable.

While a good director may often offer helpful criticism and valuable coaching or supply interesting, even thrilling, interpretative ideas, perhaps his most useful contribution to the work of rehearsal is not "artistic" at all, but consists of being a good chairman.

It is in this capacity that he arranges the agenda of each day's work, sets the pace and determines the amount of time devoted to this or that. Above all, it is principally from the director that a rehearsal takes its tone, derives its atmosphere.

Even in factory work this matter of tone or atmosphere is important. A good foreman, just and vigilant, who makes no favorites among his subordinates, who commands their trust and respect, creates an atmosphere in which work gets done pleasantly and easily. The preparation of a play is like factory work in that the product is the result of cooperative effort. It differs from factory work in that frequently the workers have to reveal themselves in an uninhibited way which, in the wrong atmosphere, could easily be embarrassing, even disgraceful. Directors must try to create an atmosphere in which efficiency is maintained to create a finished product by an ineluctable dateline, and in which, at the same time, all sorts of strange, intimate, and often uncouth images can be created, all sorts of emotional experiments conducted, without embarrassment or self-consciousness.

This is not perhaps so hard to do as it sounds. Efficiency is supported by the excellent discipline which normally prevails in a theatrical company; first, because actors are usually doing what they want very much to do; and, second, because there are always more actors than jobs. They know that if they are a nuisance they will find it very hard to get work. Then, too, a suitable atmosphere is not too hard to create because most actors are exhibitionists, not only unafraid, but delighted, to tear off the veils which convention drapes around many aspects of our human nature, and to which persons of another temperament cling with the desperate modesty of virginity unlawfully assailed.

It is the strange paradox of acting that the more a person disguises himself in another character, the more, to a discerning eye, does he reveal his own. Actors know this about one another. It makes them tolerant of much that, especially in sexual matters, society at large regards with a very puritan eye; and, in consequence, society is apt to think of actors as "odd" and even "loose." Perhaps I have lived too much in their company to be very detached, but it is not my experience that actors are odder or looser than any other group of people, plumbers, say, or clergymen. They are, perhaps, a little more inclined to admit to kinds of looseness which plumbers endeavor to deny, to flaunt oddities which clergymen not always successfully conceal.

Actors are also artists in the sense that they approach a subject with analytical detachment, trying to apprehend the nature of the material which they must interpret, just as a painter analyzes the proportion, texture and coloring of a model and with no more emotional involvement than the surgeon feels for the inert lump on the table under the lights.

The director, then, is partly an artist presiding over a group of other artists, excitable, unruly, childlike and intermittently "inspired." He is also the foreman of a factory, the abbot of a monastery, and the superintendent of an analytic laboratory. It will do no harm if, in addition to other weapons, he arms himself with the patience of a good nurse, together with the voice and vocabulary of an old-time sergeant-major.

The all-important thing for a director is not to let rehearsals be a bore. The chief practical means to this end is to keep people busy, not to keep them waiting around with nothing to do. This is largely a matter of sensible planning—the factory department. It is also a matter of seeing that work proceeds at a good brisk pace, not at that of the slowest wits. Better to rush the dullards off their feet than to bore and frustrate the brighter spirits.

Again I do not wish to oversimplify. There is far more to directing than just not being a bore. But I have so often seen men and women who have so much to offer in the way of intelligent and sensitive appreciation of a text, who have so much knowledge and wisdom to pass on to actors, but who simply cannot make a rehearsal "go with a swing," and therefore simply cannot infuse the proceedings with the vitality and good will which can bring anything into being....

Konstantin Stanislavski

Reproduced herewith are the notes and drawings in Stanislavski's notebook for his production of Chekhov's *The Sea Gull* at the Moscow Art Theatre. Numbers in the text correspond to those carrying directorial notation; footnotes pertain to alterations in the script made by Stanislavski and inserted by the editor of his notebook, S. D. Balukhaty.

Stanislavski called his notebooks the director's "scores," and the sort of illuminating direction or character description we find in this document makes the musical term relevant. Of special interest are the highly detailed notes for physical movement; the fully *rendered* effect of a Stanislavski production was no accident. We know from several of his letters that Chekhov did not always approve of many of Stanislavski's directorial ideas, but such texts as these leave no doubt of the thorough technical competence and deeply creative effort that was lavished on such productions. The portion of the full score reproduced here begins mid-way in Act IV and continues through the climactic episodes of the play to the final curtain.

❧ from THE DIRECTOR'S NOTEBOOK for THE SEA GULL

A melancholy waltz is played behind the scenes.[1]

Miss Arkadina: The students gave me an ovation. Three baskets of flowers, two bouquets, and look at that! *(Takes a brooch off her dress and throws it on the table.)*[82]

Shamrayev: Ah, now that is something![2] [83]

Masha: [84] Fifty!

Dorn: [85] Did you say fifty?

Miss Arkadina: I wore a lovely dress... Say what you like, but I do know how to dress.[86]

Pauline: Konstantín's playing again. Poor boy, he's unhappy.

Shamrayev: They've been going for him in the papers, I see.

Masha: Seventy-seven! [87]

Miss Arkadina: Why worry about it? [88]

Trigorin: He's unlucky, poor fellow. Seems quite unable to find his own individual style. He writes such queer stuff, so vague. At times it almost reminds you of the ravings of a lunatic. Not one living character!

Masha: Eleven! [89]

Miss Arkadina *(looking round at* Sorin*)*[90]: Are you bored, Peter dear? *(A pause.)*[91] He's asleep.

Dorn: State Councillor Sorin is peacefully asleep.

Masha: [92] Seven! Ninety!

Trigorin: [93] Do you think I'd ever have written anything, if I'd lived in a country

82. Throws the brooch on the table.
83. A pause. Shamráyev takes brooch and examines it in the light of the candle. The game halts for a little while. Shamráyev turns the brooch round and round before the light of the candle, while the rest look on. A pause.
  *The Pause:** wind, rain, rattling of windows, from the distance the sound of the piano (played by Konstantín). The pause lasts ten seconds.
84. Masha in a very mournful and even more monotonous voice.
85. Dorn interrupts his humming (he has just started a waltz tune) to ask his question.
86. *Another pause.** Miss Arkádina speaks very vivaciously. A pause of five seconds.
87. In a still more mournful monotonous voice.
88. Again in a very cheerful voice.
89. The same monotonous voice.
90. Miss Arkádina repeats the phrase a few times—the last time very loudly (to waken Sorin) in a long drawn out sing-song: "Pe-e-e-ter dea-ea-ea-r!" Dorn comes to her help and shouts, "Mr. Sorin!"
91. A pause during which Sorin's head bends lower and lower. He begins to snore. A pause of five seconds. All turn round to look at Sorin.

[1] Stage direction crossed out by Stanislavsky. (S.B.)
[2] In black ink on margin: "A pause." (S.B.)
*Underlined in ink. (S.B.)

house like this, by a lake? I'd have conquered this mania of mine and spent all my days fishing.

MASHA: [94] Twenty-eight!

TRIGORIN: To catch a ruff or a perch, why, that's my idea of heaven!

DORN: Well, and I believe in Konstantín. There's something in him! Yes, there's something in him! He thinks in images, his stories are vivid, brilliant. They affect me strongly. A great pity, though, he doesn't seem to have any definite aim. He produces an impression, and that's all. But you can't go far by merely producing an impression.[95] Are you glad your son's a writer Miss Arkádina?

MISS ARKADINA: I'm ashamed to confess it, doctor, but I haven't read any of his things yet. I can never find the time.

MASHA: [96] Twenty-six!

KONSTANTIN *comes in quietly and goes to his desk.*

SHAMRAYEV (*to* TRIGORIN): I forgot to tell you, Mr. Trigórin. We've still got something here of yours.

TRIGORIN: Oh? What? [97]

SHAMRAYEV: You remember the seagull Konstantín shot down some time ago? Well, you asked me to have it stuffed for you.[98]

TRIGORIN: Did I? I don't remember. (*Thinking.*) No, I don't remember.

MASHA: Sixty-six! One!

KONSTANTIN (*flings open the window and listens*):[3] [99] How dark it is! I wonder why I'm feeling so restless! [100]

MISS ARKADINA: Konstantín, dear, shut the window! There's an awful draught.

KONSTANTIN *closes the window.*[101]

MASHA: Eighty-eight!

92. Again the same monotonous, dead voice.
93. Pointing at the window he is just looking at.
94. Again in the same voice.

95. Dorn is humming. Sorin snores.

96. The same voice.

97. A pause. Effects of Sorin's loud snoring. Miss Arkádina and Dorn sing in parts. Konstantín crosses over to his writing desk.
98. A pause.
99. Speaks at his writing desk, looking at the window.
100. Crosses over to the window and opens it. A pause, during which Masha calls the numbers.
101. Miss Arkádina covers her neck with one hand and waves with the other in the direction of Konstantín, who closes the window and goes back to the writing desk.
102. Miss Arkádina shouts in a loud voice and claps her hands. Dorn echoes her in a thin falsetto. Shamráyev *à la Silva* in a bass. This noise awakens Sorin who wipes his mouth and, still half awake, seems at a loss to know where he is.

[3] Stage direction crossed out by Stanislavsky. (S.B.)

TRIGORIN: My game, ladies and gentlemen.

MISS ARKADINA (gaily):[102] Bravo! Bravo!

SHAMRAYEV: Bravo!

MISS ARKADINA:[103] What marvellous luck that man has! He always wins. (Gets up.)[104] Now let's go and have something to eat. Our great man hasn't had any lunch today. We'll carry on with the game after dinner. (To her son.)[105] Leave your manuscripts, dear. Let's go in to dinner.

KONSTANTIN: I don't want to, mother. I'm not hungry.

MISS ARKADINA: As you wish, dear. (Wakes SORIN.) Dinner, Peter, dear! (Takes SHAMRAYEV'S arm.) Let me tell you about the marvellous reception I had in Kharkov.

PAULINE puts out the candles on the table; then she and DORN wheel the chair. All go out by door on left;

KONSTANTIN alone remains on the stage, sitting at his desk.[4]

KONSTANTIN (preparing to write; runs through what he has written already):[106] I've talked so much about new forms, but I can't help feeling that little by little I'm lapsing into clichés myself. (Reads) "The poster on the wooden fence, announced... A pale face, framed by dark hair"... Announced, frame—it's so trite! [107] (Crosses it out.) I'd better begin where the hero is awakened by the patter of rain and cross out the rest. The description of the moonlight evening is too long and much to precious. Trigórin has his methods all nicely worked out. He finds it easy. The neck of a broken bottle gleaming on the mill-dam, the black shadow of the water-

N.B. I would make Masha —all during this scene (even during the speeches of the other characters) go on calling the numbers, any numbers (irrespective of what the others say); for otherwise we get a very awkward situation on the stage, an artificial situation which occurs on the stage every time during a game of cards, dominoes, etc., namely, the game stops to give the characters time to make their speeches. This is neither life-like nor true. Let Masha go on calling the numbers without paying attention to what the others are saying.

103. Gives her hand to Trigórin to kiss.

104. At that moment Yakov enters and whispers respectfully in Miss Arkádina's ear.

105. All get up. Miss Arkádina goes up to Konstantín and Sorin—and wheels the bath-chair, Shamráyev helping her. Pauline puts out the candles. Exeunt talking...*

106. A very long pause.† Sound effects of wind and rain. Animated conversation in the dining room (voices of Miss Arkádina, Shamráyev, and Dorn louder than any other). Clatter of dishes, Konstantín, without bending his back, writes.

107. Tears up the page and throws it down.

108. A pause of ten seconds —then a knock at the window (on the window-pane). Konstantín raises his head and listens. A pause of five seconds. Knocking repeated. Konstantín crosses over to the window and looks out of it.

109. Opens the french window—noise of wind and rain

---

[4] Stage direction crossed out by Stanislavsky. (S.B.)

* Here the page of Stanislavsky's notes is torn off.

† Underlined in ink. (S.B.)

wheel — and there's your moonlight night all ready for you. But I have to bring in the tremulous light, the gently twinkling stars, and the distant strains of the piano dying away in the still, scented air ... Oh, it's dreadful! *(A pause.)* New forms! No! I'm coming more and more to believe that it isn't old or new forms that matter; what matters is that one should write without thinking about forms at all; what matters is that whatever one has to say should come straight from the heart! *(There's a knock at the window nearest to the desk.)* [108] What's that? *(Looks out of the window.)* Can't see a thing ... *(Opens french window and looks out into the garden.)* Someone ran down the steps. *(Calls.)* Who's there? [109] *(Goes out into the garden; he can be heard walking rapidly on the terrace; presently he comes back with* NINA.*)* [110] Nina! Nina!

NINA *lays her head on his chest and sobs softly.*

KONSTANTIN *(moved):* [111] Nina! Oh, my darling, it's you — you. I had a feeling you'd come. All day I've been so awfully restless. *(Takes off her hat and cloak.)* Oh, my darling, my precious darling, so you've come! Don't let's cry, don't! [112]

NINA: There's someone here.

KONSTANTIN: There's no one, no one.

NINA: Lock the doors. Someone may come in.

KONSTANTIN: No one will come in.

NINA: I know your mother's here. Please, lock the doors ... [113]

KONSTANTIN *(locks the door on right, going*

rushes into room. The door slams to, noise of wind and rain persists, though not so loud. Konstantín can be heard shouting outside the french window a few times, "Who's there?" Then one hears him utter a sudden cry. For the next five seconds everything is quiet. At last rapid steps are heard on the terrace, the french window opens, a gust of wind. Konstantín enters, dragging Nina, wrapped in her cloak, almost by force into the room. The door slams noisily.

110. At the french window Nina falls on Konstantín's chest. A pause. Nina sobs. The sound of a church-bell in the distance; in the dining-room Miss Arkádina's and Shamráyev's laughter.

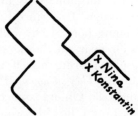

111. Konstantín covers her hands with kisses.

112. He raises her head, takes off her wet kerchief, looks at her, and cannot recognize her: so much has she changed. A pause. Laughter in the dining-room. Nina looks up in alarm in the direction of the dining-room.

113. He turns the key in the door on the left (sound of the key being turned), shuts the door of the dining-room, places a chair against it, and crosses over to Nina; then he tells her that he has placed a chair against the door. While Konstantín is closing the door, Nina is watching him from behind a corner.

to door on left): There's no lock on this [114] door. I'll put [115] a chair against it. *(Puts an arm-chair against the door.)* Don't be afraid. No one will come in.[116]

Nina *(scanning his face intently)*: Come, let me look at you. *(Looking round the room.)* Warm, nice ... This used to be a drawing-room before. Do you find me much changed?

Konstantin: Oh, Nina, it's strange to be seeing you again. Why wouldn't you let me see you? Why haven't you come all this time? I know you've been living here almost a week ... I've been to your hotel several times a day. I stood under your window like a beggar.

Nina: I was afraid you might hate me. Every night I dream that you look and look at me and don't recognize me. Oh, if only you knew! Ever since I returned I've been coming here ... to walk by the lake. I've been near the house many times, but I couldn't bring myself to go in. Let's sit down. *(They sit down.)*[117] Let's sit and talk and talk. Oh, it's so nice here, cosy, warm ... Listen, how the wind howls! There's a passage in Turgenev—"Happy is he who on a night like this has a roof over his head, a warm corner—" I'm a seagull—no, that's not what I was going to say. *(Rubs her forehead.)* I'm sorry—what was I saying? Oh, yes. Turgenev. "And may the Lord help all homeless wanderers." ... Never mind. *(Sobs.)*[118]

Konstantin: Nina, darling, there you go again ... Nina!

Nina: It's nothing. I feel much better now ... I haven't cried for two years. Late last night I went to see if our stage was still in the park. Well, it turned out it was still there. Then I cried for the first time for

114. The word "this" is crossed out by Stanislavsky and the word "that" substituted for it.

115. Changed by Stanislavsky to "have put."

116. Nina takes off her cloak or coat with the help of Konstantin. In the dining-room—general conversation and sounds of knives and forks behind the door (subdued noise). Having taken off her cloak, Nina runs all over the stage, looking round and, at the same time, afraid that she might be seen from the dining-room. She runs over to the hot stove and warms herself by it. Konstantin follows her round. Both are standing by the stove, looking at each other.

117. They go over to the rocking chair. Nina sits down on it, while Konstantin picks up the footstool, which had been placed for Sorin, puts it beside the rocking chair and sits down at Nina's feet. On the way, Konstantin snatches up a rug from Sorin's bed and wraps it round Nina. He takes Nina's hands in his and gazes into her eyes.

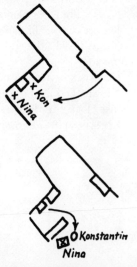

two years, and I felt much better, my heart grew lighter. See? I'm not crying any more. *(Takes his hand.)* And so you're a writer now ... You — a writer, and I — an actress ... It seems we're right in it now, the two of us ... Oh, I used to be so happy! I'd wake up like a child, bright and early, as merry as a lark. I loved you. I dreamt of fame. And now? Early tomorrow morning I shall have to leave for Yeletz. Travel third class — with peasants. And in Yeletz the better class tradesmen will pester me with their attentions. Life is sordid.

KONSTANTIN: Why are you going to Yeletz?

NINA: I've an engagement there for the whole winter. I shall have to go soon.

KONSTANTIN: Oh, Nina, I cursed you, hated you, tore up your letters and photographs, but every minute I was conscious that I belonged to you, that my heart was yours for ever. I find it impossible, Nina, to stop loving you. Ever since I lost you and my stories began to appear in print, life has been unbearable to me. I suffered agonies, agonies ... It was as though I were an old man of ninety. I prayed for you to come back, I kissed the ground you had walked on. Wherever I looked, I saw your dear face, your sweet smile, which brought so much sunshine into the best years of my life ...

NINA *(bewildered)*: Why does he talk like this? Why does he talk like this?

KONSTANTIN: [119] I am alone in the world, Nina. I have no one whose affection might warm me. I'm cold, cold, as though I lived in some underground dungeon, and everything I write is dry, harsh, gloomy. Please,

118. Laughter in the dining-room. (This is a very clumsy stage effect, but it never misses with an audience. I do not, of course, insist on it.)

119. (Konstantín seizes her hand ecstatically and covers it with kisses. Nina tries to free her hand and turns away so that he should not see her face. Konstantín is drawn to her more and more.)*

* Stanislavsky's note has been crossed out with a black pencil, evidently by Nemirovich-Danchenko. (S.B.)

stay Nina, I implore you! Or let me go away with you!

NINA *quickly puts on her hat and cloak.*[120]

KONSTANTIN: Nina, why? For God's sake —*(Looks at her as she puts her things on; a pause.)*[121]

NINA: My cab is waiting for me at the gate ... Don't see me out, please. I'll find my way alone ... *(Bursts into tears.)*[122] Could you give me some water, please?[123]

KONSTANTIN *(gives NINA a glass of water)*: Where are you going now?

NINA: To the town. *(Pause.)*[124] Is your mother here?[125]

KONSTANTIN: Yes, she's here ...[126] Uncle was taken ill on Thursday, so we wired her to come.[127]

NINA: Why did you say that you kissed the ground on which I'd walked? I deserve to be killed. *(Bends over the table.)* Oh, I'm so tired! I want to rest—rest! *(Raises her head.)*[128] I'm a seagull. No, that's not it. I'm an actress. Yes![5] *(Hearing MISS ARKADINA and TRIGORIN laughing, she listens for a minute, then runs to the door on left and looks through the keyhole.)* So he's here too ... *(Returning to KONSTANTIN.)* Oh, well—it doesn't matter.[129] No, he didn't believe in the theatre. He was always laughing at my dreams, and little by little I stopped believing in them and lost heart ... Besides, I had the worries of love to cope with, jealousy, constant anxiety for my little one ... I grew trivial, cheap. And I acted badly ... Didn't know what to do with my hands, how to stand on the stage, how to control my voice. Oh, you've no idea what it feels like to know that you're acting abomin-

120. Nina runs across the whole length of the stage to the french window and puts on her hat and cloak there. Konstantin follows her.

121. No pause here under any circumstances.

122. She opens french window to go out (noise of the wind rushing into the room). Then she stops—leans against the jamb of the door and bursts into sobs. Konstantin, who is leaning against the lamp-post, stands motionless, gazing at Nina. Whistling of wind from the open door. "Could you give me some water, please?" spoken between her sobs.

123. Konstantin walks off slowly (the jug of water is near the mirror in the front of the stage), pours some water into a glass (sound of glass knocking against jug), and gives it to her. A pause. Nina drinks. (Conversation in the dining-room.)

124. Nina wipes her tears with a handkerchief and smothers her sobs. Konstantin stands motionless, glass in hand, leaning against the lamp-post, staring lifelessly at one point. This is where he really dies.

125. Nina speaks restraining her sobs.

126. A pause. (Conversation in the dining-room.)

127. A pause.

128. A pause. Nina leans her head weakly against the door. Both stand as though rooted to the ground for about ten seconds, Trigorin's voice is heard clearly. Nina, stung to the quick, straightens herself. She listens, then takes a few steps towards the dining-room.

129. Nina sinks into a chair (by the card table, where

---

[5] The words "I'm a seagull. No, that's not it. I'm an actress. Yes." are crossed out by Stanislavsky. (S.B.)

ably!¹³⁰ I'm a seagull—no, that's not it. Remember you shot a seagull? A man came along, saw it, and—just for the fun of it—destroyed it ... An idea for a short story ... No, I don't mean that ... *(Rubs her forehead.)*¹³¹ What was I saying? I was talking about the stage. Well, I'm different now ... I'm a real actress now. I enjoy my acting. I revel in it. The stage intoxicates me. I feel that I am—peerless. But now, while I've been here, I've been walking about a lot and thinking—thinking—and feeling that the powers of my mind and soul are growing stronger every day ... Now I know, now I understand, my dear, that in our calling, whether we act on the stage or write, what matters is not fame, nor glory, nor the things I used to dream of. No. What matters is knowing how to endure. Know how to bear your cross and have faith. I have faith, and it no longer hurts so much. And when I think of my calling, I'm no longer afraid of life.

KONSTANTIN *(sadly)*:¹³² You have found your path in life. You know which way you are going. But I am still whirled about in a maze of dreams and images, without knowing what it is all about or who wants it. I have no faith, and I do not know what my calling is.¹³³

NINA *(listening)*: Sh-sh—I'm going. Goodbye. When I'm a famous actress, come and see me in a play. Promise? And now ... —*(Presses his hand.)* It's late. I can hardly stand on my feet— I'm worn out—famished ...

KONSTANTIN:¹³⁴ Won't you stay and have some supper? Please, do ...

NINA: No, thank you. I can't. I can't. Please, don't see me off. I'll find my way alone ... My cab isn't far from here ... So

Shamráyev sat). Konstantín is still standing motionless with the glass in his hand. Nina freezes in one pose. She does not seem to be addressing anybody in particular, but seems to be speaking to herself, her gaze fixed on one point.

130. Propping up her elbow on the table, she puts her weary head on her hand. She is exhausted.

131. Sits up.

132. Without altering his pose. Talks in a dead voice, without life, without hope.

133. A pause of ten seconds. (A sudden noise in the dining-room: two or three chairs being pushed back. Nina jumps to her feet and runs to the door.)

134. His last hope.

she brought him with her? Oh well, it doesn't matter really. When you see Trigórin don't say anything to him ... I love him. I love him more than ever. An idea for a short story. I love him. I love him passionately. I love him to distraction.[135] Oh, how beautiful everything was before, my dear. Remember? What a bright, glorious, happy life! Our feelings for each other were like sweet, exquisite flowers ... Remember? ... *(Recites.)* [136] "Men, lions, eagles and peacocks, horned stags, geese, spiders, silent fish that inhabit the water, starfish, and creatures no eye can see—all living things, all living things, all living things, having completed their round of sorrow, are extinct. For thousands and thousands of years the earth has borne no living creature upon it, and this poor moon lights its lamp in vain. No longer do the cranes waken in the meadow with a cry, and in the lime groves the drone of May-beetles is heard no more" ... *(Embraces* KONSTANTIN *impulsively and runs out through the french window.)* [137]

KONSTANTIN *(after a pause)*: I hope no one sees her in the garden and tells mother about it. It's sure to upset mother. *(During the next two minutes* KONSTANTIN *tears up all his manuscripts and throws them under the desk; then he unlocks the door on right and goes out.)*

DORN *(trying to open the door on left)*: Extraordinary! The door seems to be locked. *(Enters and puts armchair in its place.)* An obstacle race!

Enter MISS ARKADINA *and* PAULINE, *followed by* YAKOV *carrying a tray with bottles, and* MASHA; *then* SHAMRAYEV *and* TRIGÓRIN.

MISS ARKADINA: [138] Put the claret and the beer for Mr. Trigórin here on the

135. Opens french window to go: howling of wind and noise of rain louder than ever.

136. The whole of Nina's speech is made to the accompaniment of the howling of the wind.

137. Once again she leans against the jamb of the door and bursts out crying. A pause of ten seconds, during which can be heard the distant tolling of a church-bell (as in Act I during the performance of Konstantín's play—a rather stale stage effect!). She gives him a quick hug and runs off. One half of the door slams (a pane breaks, so powerfully did the wind slam it), then the other half of the french window shuts; the footsteps on the terrace die away. Noise of the wind, tolling of church-bell, knocking of night-watchman, a louder burst of laughter in the dining-room. For fifteen seconds Konstantín stands without moving, then he lets fall the glass from his hand (this, too, is rather a cheap stage effect!). Konstantín crosses slowly over to the writing desk. Stops. Goes up to where his manuscript lies, picks it up, holds it for a moment in his hand, then tears it up. Sits down, picks something up and tries to read it, but tears it up after reading the first line. Falls into a reverie again, rubs his forehead disconsolately, looks round as though searching for something, gazes for a moment on the heap of manuscripts on his desk, then starts tearing them up with slow deliberation. Gathers up all the scraps of paper and crosses over to the stove with them (noise of opening stove door). Throws the scraps of paper into the stove, leans against it

table, please. We can have our drinks while we play. Come on, sit down everybody, please.

PAULINE *(to* YAKOV*)*: Bring the tea at once, Yakov.

PAULINE *lights the candles. They all sit down to the card table.*

SHAMRAYEV *(leading* TRIGORIN *to the bookcase)*: Here's the thing I mentioned to you before ... *(Takes out the stuffed seagull.)* Your order, sir.[139]

TRIGORIN *(gazing at the seagull)*: Don't remember! *(After a moment's thought.)* Don't remember! *A shot behind the scenes on the right; they all start.*

MISS ARKADINA *(frightened)*: What was that?

DORN: It's nothing. I expect something must have gone off in my medicine-chest. Please, don't be alarmed. *(Goes out at door on right and returns in half a minute.)*[140] Just as I thought. A bottle of ether has gone off. *(Hums.)* "Once more before thee I stand enchanted——"[141]

MISS ARKADINA *(sitting down to the table)*:[142] Heavens, what a fright it gave me! It reminded me how—*(Covers her face with her hands.)* Oh dear, for a moment everything went black before my eyes ...

DORN *(turning the pages of the magazine, to* TRIGORIN*)*:[143] There was an article published here about two months ago—a letter from America—and I meant, incidentally, to ask you about it—*(Puts his arm round* TRIGORIN'S *waist and leads him to the footlights.)*[144]—as I'm rather interested in this question. *(Lowering his voice, in an undertone.)* Get Miss Arkádina away from here somehow.[145] You see, Konstantín has shot himself.[146]

Curtain.

with his hand, looking for some time at the flames devouring his works. Then he turns round, something occurs to him, he rubs his forehead, then crosses over to his desk quickly and opens a drawer. He takes out a bundle of letters and throws it into the fire. Walks away from the stove, ponders for a second, looks round the room once more—and walks out thoughtfully, unhurriedly.

Sound of chairs being pushed back and of loud, merry conversation in the dining-room. The dining-room door begins to give. They knock at the door, shouting, "Konstantín!" A pause. There is no reply. Someone presses hard against the door, which gives a little and stands ajar. Dorn pokes his head through. Miss Arkádina comes in, humming a tune; then she catches hold of Dorn, whirls him round amid general laughter, waltzing with him to the front of the stage.

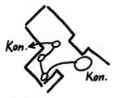

138. Speaks gaily to Yakov and goes to resume her seat at the card table. Pauline lights two candles. Masha collects the lotto cards. Shamráyev and Trigórin walk over to the bookcase. All, except Trigórin and Shamráyev, sit down.

(notes continued)

139. Shamráyev takes out the seagull and holds it in front of Trigórin. A very important pause (those at the card table should do nothing that might distract the attention of the audience from Trigórin and Shamráyev). Trigórin looks a long time at the seagull, shakes his head, repeats twice, "I don't remember,"—a pause of five seconds. A shot is heard. All start, the ladies even uttering a frightened cry, turn to where the sound of the shot came—a pause of five seconds. Miss Arkádina gets up, wants to go out, but Dorn, realizing what has happened, stops her and speaks.

140. Dorn goes out—a pause of ten seconds—a tableau. They freeze into immobility, afraid to breathe. Miss Arkádina remains in the same pose as when she got up. Something comes crashing down off stage (noise of a falling chair). Dorn enters quickly, stops at once and spruces himself up. They all stare at him. For a second he looks disconcerted at Miss Arkádina, who, like the rest, does not take her eyes off him. Dorn changes the expression of his face before the eyes of the audience.

141. A general sigh of relief. Dorn has now regained full control of himself. He starts humming a tune, as though nothing had happened, and crosses over to the mirror. He pours himself out a glass of water, his hands shaking a little. When nobody can see him, his face again expresses concern and shock.

142. Miss Arkádina again sinks into her chair and, leaning against the table, buries her face in her hands. She sits like that for some time; then she takes out a handkerchief and fans herself. In the meantime Trigórin crosses over to the writing desk, where he stops, turning the pages of the magazine. Shamráyev walks over to the card table.

143. Dorn, who, unperceived by the rest, is observing Miss Arkádina, goes up to Trigórin.

144. Gives Trigórin, who has begun to read the magazine, a push, making a sign which only Trigórin can see. Calls him aside. Trigórin gets up in surprise. Dorn again looks at Miss Arkádina; then he takes Trigórin to the front of the stage.

145. A short pause (to keep the audience in suspense). Dorn throws another glance at Miss Arkádina.

146. Trigórin is terribly shocked: he looks stunned. Dorn wags a minatory finger at him. "Keep quiet!" and starts humming again, as though nothing untoward has happened. Then he goes out into the room where Konstantín shot himself.

Masha's monotonous voice, calling the numbers of the lotto, and Miss Arkádina's soft humming (in a gay voice). Trigórin, shaken and pale, walks over to the back of Miss Arkádina's chair where, however, he stops dead, for he cannot summon enough courage to break the terrible news to her.

Curtain.

Entrances of all

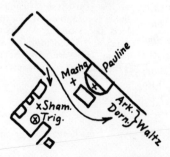

Dorn's Exit

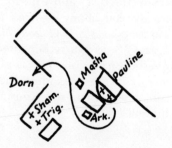

Return of Dorn

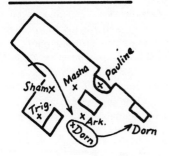

Dorn crosses over to Trigorin

Dorn calls Trigorin aside

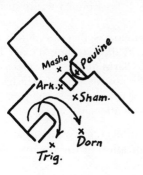

Finale

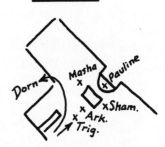

Jean Vilar

In this important essay, Vilar reconsiders the fundamental relationship between the playwright and those who render the playwright's creation. He raises the age-old yet vital question of the relative importance of verbal and visual components in drama and does so in the practical terms of a remarkably successful director. His references to figures of importance in contemporary theatre in Europe—Artaud, Dullin, Barrault, Craig, Jouvet—all serve his general argument and all derive, of course, from personal professional contact or practical knowledge of theatre history.

Vilar, appointed producer in 1947 of the now-famous Avignon Festival and, in 1951, director of the Théâtre National Populaire in Paris, is as excellent an actor as a director; his range of talents may account for the appealing directness of his total approach to his art as presented here. Vilar has played (among many roles) Becket, in a great production of Eliot's *Murder in the Cathedral,* the title roles of Shakespeare's *Richard II* and *Macbeth* and of Molière's *Dom Juan.* His early associations with Copeau and Dullin were of great importance to him, and he now stands as one of the vital influences in current European theatre.

✹ THE DIRECTOR AND THE PLAY

"An Alarming Egg White"

Under the date of December 4, 1900, Jules Renard wrote in his diary:

> *Hernani* at the Comédie Francaise.—Mounet-Sully gives himself *five or six blows in the chest every minute* and then, feeling it's not full measure, adds two or three more. He barks like a seal, widens the opening of a digestive tract, drags up his nostrils to an eye which is of an alarming egg white. Either he can't be heard or he's yelling, but all in all there are some fifty lines which he utters like a god.

This performance of Hernani was not subject, it would appear, to any over-all idea or clearly motivated utilization of the theatre. In a word, it had not been *directed.*

Exciting and inevitable is the admission that these devastatingly precise lines of Jules Renard's on the art of a great actor underline either the need for a unified conception and for an order that is at once particular and general, or their entire uselessness, in accordance with one's belief in the virtues or in the ill effects of play direction. For indeed, had *Hernani* been in the hands of a director worthy of the name, Mounet-Sully and his divinely uttered fifty lines would have been sacrificed, I will not say in the interest of a better, but of a more homogeneous performance—the spasmodic genius of one man would have been sacrificed to a more uniform and all-embracing dramatic interplay.

In our day, I notice that without exception every actor working in

From *Yale French Studies,* III, 1 (1949), pp. 13-26. Translated by Richard R. Strawn. Reprinted by permission of Kraus Reprint Corporation, Richard R. Strawn, and Kenneth Cornell.

an art theatre looks for the guidance of a director. The spirit of the stage has, it is to be feared, abandoned the actor's soul for the director's and fundamentally it is this strange creature, who may be an actor and appear on the scene but who will not, when he is director exclusively, who must clarify the play with his intelligence and the treasures of his sensibility. In our day, from one end to the other of a play's production, the major role no longer rests with our Mounet-Sullys and our Sarah Bernhardts, but is more or less frankly allotted to the directors. It will be understood that this is no part of my personal esthetic, but merely the confirmation of what some twenty or thirty years of theatrical history invite us to assert.

Kill Them Off?

This brings us, at least in my opinion, to the most ticklish problem in the contemporary theatre: *yes or no, should this director fellow be assassinated—yes or no, is the directing of a play a reprehensible activity?* I think that each one of us connected with the theatre should pronounce on the matter unreservedly. Not with the proud intention of making known his personal opinion, but because it seems to me urgently necessary to discover what the new theatre, after having weighed all that has been done so far, intends to do and is capable of doing.

The True Poets of Our Age

For my part, I will advance the following proposition: *the truly creative figures in the theatre during the last thirty years are not the dramatists, but the directors.*

It gives me no pleasure to say so. I say so because it appears to me that the achievement of Charles Dullin, with his researches and his public successes and failures, is more instructive than that of the contemporary dramatists he has produced or started on their way. This search for and this confirmation of a theatrical style by Dullin, via the plays of Pirandello, adaptations of Aristophanes, the rediscovery of Balzac, and so on, which the approval or indifference of the public and of the elite has ratified, to my way of thinking is more significant of our times than the halting philosophy or commonplace style of the contemporary dramatists whose plays he staged.

I am convinced, furthermore, that Jouvet's style, clear and pure, free of useless fripperies and all too self-conscious graces, by far outranks—whatever he himself may think about it—the feeble dramatic merits of the plays of Jean Giraudoux and Marcel Achard, and the rather cumbersome, radical-socialist witticisms of Jules Romains.

Then, again, we knew perfectly well what we were seeking in Pitoëff's theatre: the secret world of childhood which transforms an object according to our desires, an old chest becoming a royal throne, a length of calico the turban of Sheherezada. At all events, transmutations into something very different from the ill prepared or over-done victuals served up by the *contemporary* writers whose plays he performed.

Finally, I am sorry to have to vex Monsieur Gaston Baty with the assertion that, if any poet haunted the boards of the various theatres he managed, it was not the author of *Maya* or of *Têtes de rechange* or of any number of other plays, it was Gaston Baty himself.

I say this without irony and, once again, without any pleasure. Theatrical history in these last thirty years centers round the names of Copeau, Gémier, Lugné-Poë, Dullin, Baty, Jouvet, Pitoëff, that is to say, round the directors. The years to come may, of course, fail to provide us with *poets of the theatre* possessing their genuineness. So we have lived through an *utterly original theatrical epoch,* unlike any in the past. This originality, let it be recalled, is not limited to the con-temporary French theatre. Reinhardt in Germany, Stanislavski, Meyerhold and others in Russia, Gordon Craig in England, the inspirers of the Yiddish theatre among Jews reveal perhaps even more forcibly the preponderance which the directors have estab-lished over the dramatists.

This evidence is not controverted by the example of Claudel in France, Pirandello in Italy, Synge in England, Chekov in Russia and Lorca in Spain. Each of them has done no more than add another body of work to theatrical history, which has also been enriched by the work of the various directors. Furthermore, history may forget the names of Shaw and Pirandello, for instance, there can be no forgetting the work of the directors, unwritten though it is, any more than we have forgotten the part played by the Commedia dell'Arte in the sixteenth and seventeenth centuries and in the early eighteenth century.

The reason for dwelling a little on these last thirty years of theatrical history has been to put forward, free of all reserve, my first point: *the duality affecting creative activity in the theatre,* a duality which awakens in the director's conscience the dilemma of Hamlet — to be or not to be.

THE LIE

Like my masters in things theatrical, like my elders and my fellows among the directors, I am prepared to affirm that the first thing that matters in the theatre is the author's intention.

Unfortunately this is only a pose, or the reply of a conscientious artist who is either somewhat stupid or, on the contrary, very bright indeed.

To tell you the truth, it's a lie.

To tell you the truth, as rehearsals proceed the strange phenomenon occurs (strange only for those who have not before witnessed the gestation of the written work on the stage), the inevitable phenomenon sets in that the author's face lengthens. Assuredly, his play had developed quite differently in his imagination. What the authors go through may be gauged, with no likelihood of error, by the varying degrees of stupefaction their faces show during rehearsals. Rare in our day is the reaction of Racine, who took the manuscript of his *Andromaque* away from Molière's company and handed it to another.

But we do not propose to deal with the reflections and reactions of the author, while his written work is being made flesh. Here we are concerned with the director, and we must remain so.

THE ORTHODOX HERETIC

The director has been induced to make ever greater demands by these thirty years of theatre history, at least as I have seen fit to summarize them. To each newcomer eager for achievement, they propound the following problems in heresy:

Why should the director bow passively before the thought of another, rather than listen to his own daimon? — Why not treat the *written work* as a scenario? — Why not utilize the written play as a more or less brilliant preliminary draft? — Why not make oneself responsible henceforth for exercising every function in the art of the theatre? — Why not write, oneself, the scenario of the play, rediscover and give fresh luster to all the neglected jewels of the art, those of *writing* and of *rhythm,* of the *characters' credibility and lunacy,* of the *fatefulness of the theme?* Theatre history will not suffer thereby, for we sadly realize that dramatists — it would be audacious to call them poets — were never more utterly and preposterously without two, at least, of this art's privileges, those namely of rhythm and language, in other words of the vehicles of poetry.

And since one cannot help thinking that no age of great dramatic poetry rises spontaneously, since history teaches us that Racine was already implicit in Garnier, and Corneille's oratorical line in Agrippe d'Aubigné, since Molière's verve and poetic mobility were borrowed from travelling shows in fairs and lifted out of his contemporaries' innumerable comedies in verse; — whereas, on the other hand, the very first important works of our new generation obey the authoritarian rules of a dialectic and follow, in their creative activity, the rhythmic cadence of a demonstration, so that these writers of philosophical prose will never restore the magical virtues of the theatre; — since the dramatic poet, if any such there be, has thus failed to create or forge anew his own order and his own disciplines, the director is obviously right in thinking that he may and indeed must *proceed as he himself sees fit,* no matter what the play and whether he or someone else worked out the first draft. For *he* possesses his own order, his disciplines and even his traditions.

WHAT IS TO BE DONE?

This temporary conclusion is evidently highly dangerous. It disposes those who are masters of a technique to cut themselves off from the theatrical community. It disposes them to act in selfish isolation. Their venture is all the more damaging to the truth since it is bound to end in failure.

If I speak at such length of the director's hidden thoughts — shameful thoughts, some would say — it is because in each of my fellows, I believe, there can be found the same desire, the same hypnotic fascination with pushing on to the end of the road — or of their destiny, as I was going to say — and because the fundamental condition of such an artist ultimately imposes a choice between three attitudes. Either he will acquiesce in his enslavement to the thought of another, or he will opt for personal and total creative deployment, or he will give up the profession.

What is to be done? The decision to be an interpreter and nothing more, even interpreter number one, cannot always satisfy our directors: men whose knowledge of and utter absorption in their profession have placed them at the forefront of theatrical activity today. This is all the more true because they have not been or are not in touch with real dramatists, and because their imaginations, sharpened by their unchallengeable awareness that they are the only *initiates* in the whole affair, encourage and even oblige them to create, ultimately, a work that is personal to themselves.

After some thirty to fifty years of play direction looked upon as an original piece of work, the theatre today is in a ramshackle state.

A PROPOSAL

To cure this condition, I have first of all one suggestion to make, the second suggestion being of a social nature. This first proposal, at all events, tolerates no compromise.

Since the fact is established that dramatists have no theatrical sense beyond the exigencies of dialogue, that they are the Rossinis and not the Johann Sebastian Bachs of the spoken theatre; since it is established that the only French dramatic poet in whom we can take pride — I mean Claudel — is a Catholic poet enclosed in a sectarian world which arouses the protest of every other religion, philosophy and belief of modern man; since there are no poets and so many dramatists; since the playwright's function is today exercised effectively by no one at all; since, on the other hand, the initiates and technicians, that is to say, the directors, have sometimes stepped with excellent results outside the limits imposed on them by a *conformist morality* of the theatre, they are the men on whom we must place the crushing burden of the dramatic function. Once this has been agreed upon, they must be harassed no longer, and no attempt should be made to lessen their thirst for the absolute.

And thus our reasoning leads us gradually but inevitably towards agreement, not with Gordon Craig but with Antonin Artaud.

It is certainly no easy matter to accept all the propositions advanced by Artaud in his book *Le Théâtre et son double,* yet how ignore that he recalls the sole valid *raison d'être* for the theatrical work when, for example, he compares the individual and social effects of the plague and the effects the theatre should produce. From Artaud's point of view, which is that of the demiurge, of Aeschylus, Shakespeare, Ford, Strindberg, Büchner and Kleist, restored to its rightful place is that essential element in the theatre (of which we French have been deprived since the time of Racine), *incantation,* which elsewhere, on other continents, rises from the tamtam of Negro religious rites, and from the shamisen and the polyphonic melodies of the oriental theatres; and in the west from the grand organ, the silences, the rhythmic mutterings of the Catholic mass, means and instruments for which the dramatist *who is aware* substitutes the rhythms of his prosody.

Here I will repeat an idea that seems self-evident to me, as it has seemed, every time that Parisian producers have provided me more or less unrestrictedly with the means of producing a play. We are robbed of this *incantatory function* because the creators of drama have been writers, not the priests and intitiates of a theatre to which they have sacrificed every other thought or activity, because the *primary conception* of the work has belonged not to the initiate but to the sermonizer, not to the organizer of the spectacle but to the evolver of dialogue, not to the director but to that distinguished, civilized, fashionable, and often cavalier and sprightly gentleman who proudly flaunts the trivial name of *author*.

THE UNFORTUNATE EXAMPLE OF RACINE

Himself a genuine dramatist, Racine has done immense harm to the dramatic poets who followed him in our theatre's history. He gave them to understand—and provided a certain justification—that he was a man of letters, and that the neighborhood of an ink-bottle, with its reveries and nightmares, was the sole privileged site of dramatic creativity. We know that in actual fact this point of view appeals only to the idler, and that Racine directed the mulish Mademoiselle Champmeslé speech by speech and line by line; that Racine, to borrow a term from the stage manager's vocabulary, was "down stage" and himself directed rehearsals; that he read his plays admirably; that he pointed up, or, to put it better, orchestrated his works by reading them aloud. And if history has not recorded the name of the earliest director of his tragedies from *Andromaque* to *Phèdre*, it is because Racine himself carried out that arduous task.

Incidentally a propos of Racine and by means of his plays, I think the distinction might be drawn between the drama that obeys the laws of magic and incantation (the laws dear to Artaud) and the drama in thrall to hybrid distractions and provoking only transitory stimuli; between that which chants and makes us whole, and that which turns out to be cheerless and leaves us in the like state; between that which first lays hold on our senses and that which is naught but dialogue. For, if need be, Racine's plays sacrifice literal and explanatory clearness to the sonorous incantation of the poetic line; he despises pettifogging proofs and obeys only what is song (lamentations, intonings, sighs and outcries, the melodic chant, etc.); and, finally, he rejects that bastard, emasculated form of the drama: *the dialogue as an exercise in virtuosity.*

ANTONIN ARTAUD

This digression in the company of Jean Racine has enabled us to push ahead—at any rate, so I imagine. For now we can inquire *what means of expression will be used* by the man to whom we have entrusted thus *in abstracto* the fate and fortune of the theatre, that is, by the director. And here Artaud must have his say. He alone offers a solution that, at the least, is valid. "I shall ask," he declares, "this question":

> How can it happen that in the theatre, at all events in the theatre as we know it in Europe, or rather in the west, everything specifically theatrical should be relegated to the background, everything, that is to say, which cannot be put into speech, into words, or, if you will, everything which is not contained in the dialogue? ... Dialogue, a written and spoken thing, does not specifically belong to the stage, but to the book ... I maintain that the stage is a concrete, physical place which asks to be filled and to be let speak its own concrete language ... I maintain that this concrete language, directed to the senses and independent of speech, must satisfy the senses first of all, that there is a poetry of the senses just as there is one of language, and that the concrete language to which I refer is truly of the theatre only to the extent that the thoughts it expresses elude articulate utterance. [Further on he gives a more precise idea of what this poetry is:] Most difficult and complex, it has numerous aspects, before all others the means of expression which can be employed on the stage, such as music, dancing, the plastic arts, pantomime, mimicry, gesture, intonation, architecture, lighting and setting.

This is no utopian view, as is proved by the work of some of our colleagues (Jean-Louis Barrault, Decroux, La Compagnie des Quinze, the directors of Travail et Culture) and by the public success of *La Faim* and of Cervantes' *Numantia,* but it reminds us also that the manifestations of such a drama are rare. In the space of twelve years there can be counted only three or four spectacles which more or less faithfully reflect the ideas Artaud first expounded systematically. But such intermittent productivity, it seems to me, makes of the theatre a privileged art, such as it was, if nowhere else, in fifth-century Greece. (At that time the theatre became a public spectacle only three times a year, for the Leneae, at the end of January, for the City Dionysia, at the end of March, and for the Rural Dionysia, in late December.)

This art of the theatre is not so strange as one might think. I have noted that it has found the favor of large audiences. But perhaps its history should be briefly told. The technique of the play director was born, I believe, when Copeau withdrew to Burgundy with the first Vieux Colombier company, which included Jouvet and Dullin. Since that time, every serious school has had an improvisation class in which are studied the composition of the outlines serving as a basis for improvisation (our *authors* would talk of the plot), the grammar and on occasion the vocabulary, so to speak, of gesture, the proper control of the body and the breath, and the development of the plastic imagination. In our era, leaders in the theatre have been more or less obscurely preoccupied with this art, with its quite special exercises and its means of expression. According to Paul Gsell, Gémier used to direct and take part in what were then and for a long time remained exercises in acting only. But Artaud enunciated, in black and white, this fundamental preoccupation of the leader of the company. He finally gave the name of *creation* to what previously had been just a task or a spectacle for the theatre company's personal use only.

SARDOU, OUR CONTEMPORARY

But to go further and try to assay the chances for such a theatre's being able to express itself regularly, means nothing less than running right up against a frightful state of affairs: *the social status of the theatre*. In Paris alone there are some forty theatre buildings which must be "supplied" with shows. To keep at least the actors and stage hands alive, the material actually available must be used. Habit, tradition (even more ineradicable in the privately managed theatres than in the national institutions) and indolence of mind see to it that a genuinely original idea, with every prospect of going over well, is most unlikely to be considered. The consequence is that for the public mind, and even in the eyes of professionals, the theatre can adopt no other devices than those employed in Sardou's day: a plot, the "big scene," bravura passages and dialogue.

For these reasons, for which ignorance or cowardice are to blame, the new conception is lost, at all events in the occident, and dissolved in the structureless goo of the contemporary theatre. It is highly significant—and I say it in all friendliness—that Barrault, the first man to make real and give a poetic meaning to this art, has for the time being gone over to a theatrical style in which the plastic element is merely the obedient servant of the pure word but, like the word, is a traditional expression of theatre. And, lastly, this art, as the ideas of Artaud have enabled us to envisage it, cannot be the responsibility and the undertaking of a single man. If the state did not assume the polite and conformist attitude to the theatre that it does, the task might perhaps be accomplished. It is, in my view, the only original human undertaking that has been ventured in many a long year.

What then, is to be done? Conclusion after conclusion reveals how difficult it is to find a means of expression able to satisfy artist and public and able, also, to dovetail easily into the present social set-up.

We workers in the theatre cannot do anything about this state of affairs. The theatre will have the same bored bourgeois countenance just so long as we are satisfied to live under a regime which treats the theatre as an activity no different, legally and socially, from the industrialist's or shopkeeper's; just so long as it fails to take its place at the very core of the community's essential activity which, in our day, is among the people—or, to put it even more plainly, in the factory. Corneille wrote for the great of his time as though he were at their right hand; Racine wrote for Louis XIV, for and at the behest of Madame; Molière wrote for the Contis, and listened to Condé-Don Juan, or for Louis XIV, leader of his people and leader of the ballet.

Let there be no misunderstanding. I do not recommend the revival of Gémier's experiments, and the summoning of the people to a performance of *Oedipus* in the Vélodrome d'Hiver. To restore the popular appeal of the dramatic spectacle, that is a generous idea, but if it were renewed on exactly the same lines, I doubt whether at present it would have much chance of success.

"The Theatre, an Unknown Art Today"

To tell the truth, we are in a confused and *indeterminate* period with regard to the theatre. Most authors have no notion why they use a particular dramatic form. "Because that is how it was handed down to us," they might well reply. Claudel and the directors excepted, do our dramatists take part even in that *permanent revolt of form* which has enabled French painting, these last fifty years, to assemble such treasures? What dramatic work reflecting our lot and the turmoil of our life can, with any seriousness, be compared to the anxious grace of Matisse, to Picasso's tragic forms and the controlled disorder of Braque? Frankly, when one tries to estimate what chance the contemporary theatre has of rediscovering the brilliance and grandeur of the great epochs, there is no escaping the insistent and hence all the more distressing idea that the theatre *is an unknown art in our time.* Metaphysicians and moralists utilize it to explain or test out a philosophical postulate, successful playwrights drape it in reach-me-downs, and poets, finally, smother it with their verbal incontinence. Even those canning industry arts, the cinema and radio, pour it into their containers. One looks back sadly to Aeschylus and Sophocles, who from April to December prepared the performance of *their dramatic poems, based on a simple idea and observing strict rules, the forms and ideas being known to everybody and demanded by everybody, and contributing towards a spectacle to be given once only* — in which man, confronting the gods, was sometimes greater than the gods themselves.

How painful it is, by comparison, for whoever spends weeks and months over the meticulous staging of a contemporary work, to discover in what measure our human condition is scorned, humiliated and often enough simply forgotten, in the theatre! For what is needed and so seldom is found, in our modern drama, is the man who can rise above even the lowest, most abject and most criminal condition imposed on him and, if not master it, at least come to judge it, sing of it (oh, the recitative and chorus of the Greeks, monologues of Racine and of Shakespeare!) and so dominate it. The hero will die in the end, as we well know. But that is of no consequence. He will have unremittingly vanquished the fate that was his. Though drenched in the blood of others, Macbeth is still a hero in whose company we are not afraid to leave the theatre. Walking by our side, he keeps on singing of some victory, of some transcendence of self even in crime, of a certain pride in being a man.

On this matter, I express my point of view as an actor, rather than as a stage director. I am simply trying to arrive at some general ideas on the basis of my acting experience, short as it still is, and, insofar as my sensibility is trustworthy and can judge of the ugly, the commonplace and the false, to show them up again and again.

For example, I would say this: that it is futile to disclose a human being, on the pedestal of the stage, in a clear light and amidst a total silence that the three knocks have solicited, in order to have him enact a mere wordy parody of man or the demonstration of a thought, even of a true one. The first may just as well be presented in a drawing-room, in a club or a bar, and the second in a university lecture room.

The theatre is not the systematic exposition of our state; it is the dithyrambic chant of our profound desires or of our mocking laughter.

I do not think I have lost contact with my subject, the director and the play, by reminding you incidentally that at least two of our directors have given up the art of the theatre for reasons that have hurriedly been qualified as unfathomable. I refer to Copeau's leave-taking and also to Barrault's abandonment of the dumb-show; to the intermittent, disdainful and, as it were, disillusioned activity of Jouvet and Baty; and to the grating irony that Pitoëff displayed in his last years. Our directors have been forced to parody a role that should be sacred. They have been obliged to remain stage directors when they should have been organizers of festivals. Some, and by no means the least among them, have preferred to abandon this travesty of the real thing.

A Paradoxical Solution

Nevertheless the optimists, theatre managers, assert and would have us believe that a light has dawned in the west. This astronomical paradox may be an artistic truth, who can say. And, after all, it is easy to find out, by reading, attending performances of or *putting into rehearsal* those dramatic works the United States have to offer. But the American drama does not come off well under a closer scrutiny. Their theatrical routines are substantial, like everything we get from over there. Too substantial. They have an adroitness and virtuosity reminiscent of Hugo, of an Hugo utilizing modern means of expression. In France, when treating of the problems of man, we used to wear our hearts on our sleeves, in the guise of languishing moonlit plaints, and historical monologues spoken in front of no less historical mausoleums. We took our disillusioned soul for a stroll amidst rural Italian settings, and declared, with no fear of being scoffed at as petty masochists, that suffering held us in thrall. From the poem, the stage had borrowed with greater or lesser skill the atmosphere of the lakes and dales sung by Lamartine. Illustrations were provided of the poet's individual, personal and egoistic moods and of his amorous irregularities, just as today it would appear that the stage is, for some, only a means of illustrating their dialectics. But what is beautiful, in the Cambré of Chateaubriand, already postures too much in the Musset of the Italian period and in the Spanish Hernani. *For the theatre always shows up the artificialities hidden in literature.* When placed on the stage, even in intelligent fashion, facile sentimentality, the trivialities of the daily round and mere abstractions must drop their mask. And that, by the bye, is the reason why the Romantic hero, in our eyes, is not the stage hero Ruy Blas or Hernani, but René and Lucile, not Octave nor Cœlio nor the wordy Chatterton, but Byron the living man.

There's Arsenic in the Cola

In the present-day United States, on the other hand, nearly everything is dealt with, *on the stage,* according to the pseudo-dramatic virtues of arsenic or sub-machine guns, of coca-cola or of the upper-cut. *A priori,* such an outlook might be accepted, but the distressing thing is the feebleness and childishness of the notion, and the facileness of the way it is done. Declamation and the power and nobility of speech are feared or prohibited, and only bare, realistic dialogue is allowed, the kind a stenographer might transcribe from life. The characters are never allowed to achieve any degree of awareness. Now *I think it may be stated that there is no character, in the drama, unless he achieves awareness, the uttermost limits of awareness.* American dramatists employ all their talent and sometimes their subtle artistry (which is greater than is often imagined) in order to avoid this becoming-aware; they do so because they depict so-called ordinary people whose thinking never goes beyond the boundaries of common sense or conventional twaddle. The vital statistics are accurately recorded, it may be, but artistic truth is lacking. What is the use of finding, on the stage, what the cameraman can treat so well when he wants to? The current topic, colloquial speech, they are the cinema's means of expression! Besides it's being quite forgotten — and it is inexcusable of the directors to forget it — that over sixty years ago a Frenchman, Antoine, man of the theatre and employee of the gas company, did or tried to do, with the plays of the Zolaesque school, what the American dramatists Steinbeck, Sherwood, Wilder, Saroyan, Clifford Odets and O'Neill are belatedly giving us: life depicted in accordance with the tenets of Naturalism. Replace the French petty burgess by a cowboy or the murderer of Thérèse Raquin's husband by a Texas bad man, and you change nothing essential. The assertion will be made that means are secondary, that the important thing is to depict man and man's condition, that the goal has been attained if this description moves us; in a word, that modern tragedy and drama have not gambled on what can be achieved through vocabulary, prosody or syntax. But how can anyone declare, without effrontery, that in an art the means of expression are a secondary matter, and within the reach of every-body? Surely it is by his mastery of these means of expression that we distinguish the true dramatist. The style of his writing, or, more precisely, its singing quality (rhythm, cadence, melody) determines his emotive force. For the theatre is a temple where emotion reigns supreme. When a masterpiece is played, the emotional contact between character and audience must be unbroken throughout. It is not born of the idea or (to return to the Americans) of the truthful, realistic tone of the dialogue; nor does it come from faithfulness to the vital statistics or to the identity of the characters (this is the novel's province!). In the theatre, this emotional contact is established by chant, cadence and rhythm. Your willingness to believe and your sensibility may be taken by storm for a moment, but just try sitting through an American play three or four times. At the third performance, if you get that far, you will feel what a young actor will feel some thirty years from now, when he reads today's plays: boredom.

In France, at least for some of us, this matter of the Naturalist drama — and consequently of American plays — has been settled once and for all. Nor am I sure, when I come to think of it, that the Broadway roster of plays will contribute to our artistic heritage anything as astonishingly funny as Courteline's comedies, any thrusts as shrewd as Becque's and Jules Renard's (one a forerunner of the Théâtre Libre, the other sympathetically interested), or any despairing, tragic chant to match that of Strindberg, who was of course influenced by Antoine.

Let us draw some conclusions from what I have been saying. Reflection on the theatre's last thirty years has enabled me, I believe, to advance certain propositions. First, even though dramatic writing often failed to measure up to its task, one achievement remains: that of the directors (though only oral testimony can be given of it). Second, there exists an art form still in its beginnings: that proposed by Artaud in his *Le Théâtre et son double*. And, lastly, it is not overly romantic to believe that another Lorca may rise and compel us to repudiate what I am about to propose. This will be the end and, in some fashion, the aim of these notes. Here it is: the theatre can be the concern of creators and *witnesses* only in those privileged ages when some belief, be it Christian, pagan or atheist, with apparent spontaneity calls forth the voice of the dramatic poet and draws to him the multitude, filled by a common hope.

THE AGE OF THE DESERTERS

It is highly significant that the works which really bear witness to the period extending from the close of the nineteenth century to the war of 1940 are destined to be read, and by individuals, by solitary souls. Poet and novelist address each one of us in isolation, as an individual. As if each of us had an unquenchable thirst for isolation, new arts have been born, radio, cinema and phonograph, which appeal to the imagination of the man who is alone, and try to satisfy his painful, secret need for another way of life. And reading, manifestly an act of withdrawal, is recognized to be the most sought after diversion of modern man, embracing the daily or twice-daily newspaper weeklies and books.

Those who testify for our age have expressed themselves in the novel. To speak of France alone, fifty years of artistic activity have left us only one important body of work (Claudel's, but is he of our day, or of our future?) against the work of novelists such as Zola, Proust, Gide, Roger Martin du Gard and André Malraux. When an actor, who is the universal interpreter, has to choose between the figures offered by the best writers for the theatre and, for example, those of André Malraux' *Man's Fate* and *Man's Hope,* he will resolve to limber up his talents and his human soul by lending them to these characters who represent our day, to the novelist's brothers Garine, Magnien, Kyo Gisors, Tchen, perhaps even to Feral or the extraordinary Clappique.

Thus it *must* be, I believe, if the actor questions himself a little, if he is at all devoted to his craft—if he is unwilling to see his art of acting, his hard life, the years of apprenticeship and ever present hazards of the profession end up in trivial amusement and be at the service of the digestive tract, if he would have the theatre become other than it now is: a rendez-vous for indiscreet divulgations between 9 and 11 p.m.

Returning to the works that bear testimony to our age, I find it perfectly natural that the creator should be cut off from the theatre, and that our great contemporary works should be musical compositions, novels, movies and paintings, any other genre, in short, rather than the theatre and chanted speech. For, without community festivities, no drama can arise.

AN UNEXPECTED, BUT AN INEVITABLE SOLUTION

What is to be done? Shall we remain idle and indifferent? Or try to convince ourselves that one day we shall behold some first performance that will prove altogether exceptional? Shall we haunt the orchestra seats with the disillusioned or weary smile of the critic (to my mind, the man of the theatre whose lot is the least to be envied)? Shall we limit ourselves to the repertory of the old masters, Racine,

Corneille and Molière? Yet must not a man of the theatre be something other than the conservator of a formers age's master-pieces? What is to be done? Shall we abandon the theatre as having no function in our day? To all these questions raised or hinted at in the course of these pages there is, I believe, a single answer, the only possible answer. It cannot be found in the artistic domain.

It is apposite, at this point, to voice anew the platitude: the theatre is whatever society makes it. Each one of us, consequently, is obliged to take his stand on social problems, which inevitably are political problems also. In our profession, the theory of art for art's sake has never been anything but a noble lie. We must come out for and work towards the creation of a new society, radically different from present society, which is poisoned by skepticism and anarchy on the one hand, and by commercial fakery on the other. *We must first build a society, and then perhaps we can construct a worthy theatre.*

Vsevolod Meyerhold

A dynamic figure in the early years of the Moscow Art Theatre, Meyerhold was one of those creative personalities whose work was influenced by his early associations although it may be seen as a vital divergence from them as well. As a producer at the training Studio of the Moscow Art Theatre for Stanislavski, he developed many of the theories expressed in *On the Theatre* — from which these observations are excerpts. These in effect realized many of Craig's notions of "total theatre" in which the actor was only one of many elements and not necessarily the most important. This theory came to be known as "plastic" or "mood" produc-tion, the total abstracted effect being the goal of the director. As will be seen in these comments, he differed on many basic points of theory with his early associates, Stanislavski and Danchenko.

He experimented during his long career with many styles, achiev-ing countless brilliant productions. Although Meyerhold was one of the first artists to support the Revolution, in his later years his approach — and repertory — became less Soviet, and he fell eventually into disfavor. He died in 1943.

✣ from THE NATURALISTIC THEATRE AND THE THEATRE OF MOOD

The Moscow Art Theatre has two visages: the Naturalistic Theatre and the Theatre of Mood. The naturalism of the Moscow Art Theatre is a naturalism borrowed from the Meiningen players. *Accuracy in reproducing nature* is its basic principle. On the stage everything has to be as real as possible—the ceilings, the stucco cornices, the stones, the wallpaper, the little stove doors, the ventilation holes, and so on.

On stage cascades a real waterfall and real rain falls. A little chapel is constructed of real wood, and a house is faced with fine plywood, its double frames stuffed with cotton. The windows covered with frost. All corners of the stage are clearly visible. The fireplaces, tables, and shelves are filled with a great quantity of small objects visible only with binoculars, which will engage the attention of the curious spectator for the entire act. The noise of the round moon creeping along its wire disturbs the audience. Through the window a real ship can be seen in a fiord. Not only rooms are built on stage, but even several stories with real staircases and oaken doors. The stage is cluttered and confusing. There are footlights and many borders. The canvas which represents the sky is hung in a semicircle. In plays calling for a country estate, the floor is covered with papier-mâché dirt. In a word, an effort is made to achieve what Jan Steen attempted in his paintings, namely, to fuse what is painted with what is real. As with Jan Steen, the artist in the Naturalistic Theatre *works in close collaboration with the carpenter, the property man, and the sculptor.*

When performing historical plays, the Naturalistic Theatre conforms to the rule that the stage must be transformed into an exhibit of authentic museum pieces, or at least of exact copies made after period paintings or from photographs. The stage director and designer try to reproduce as exactly as possible the year, month, and day of the play's action, and find it insufficient, for example, that the play takes place simply "in the age of powder." Elaborate hedges, fantastic fountains, overgrown meandering paths, rose gardens, clipped chestnut and myrtle trees, crinolines and capricious coiffures —all these do not satisfy the naturalistic directors. They find it necessary to reproduce exactly the kind of sleeves worn in Louis XV's times, or to speculate how the coiffures during the reign of

From "On the Theatre" by Vsevolod Meyerhold, translated by Nora Beeson, in *Tulane Drama Review*, IV, 4 (May 1960). Reprinted by permission of *Tulane Drama Review* and Nora B. Beeson.

Louis XVI differed from those worn under Louis XV. Such directors do not want to stylize a period, but rather follow a fashion journal of the year, month, and day on which the action occurs.

Thus, the Naturalistic Theatre devised the method of *copying a historical style.* Such a method, naturally, does not observe the rhythmic architectonics of a play such as *Julius Caesar,* for example, with its plastic conflict between two opposing powers. And not one of the directors realized that a synthesis of "caesarism" could never be achieved with a kaleidoscope of realistic scenes and an imitation of historical costumes.

The actors' make-up is *overly realistic* — real faces as we see them in real life, an exact copy. The Naturalistic Theatre considers the face the actor's main expressive tool and consequently overlooks all other means of expression. The Naturalistic Theatre does not know the advantages of plasticity and does not compel its actors to train their bodies. The schools connected with the Naturalistic Theatre do not realize that physical sport should be a basic training, especially for plays such as *Antigone* and *Julius Caesar,* plays which because of their music belong to *another* kind of theatre.

Many excellently made-up faces remain in one's mind, but no postures or rhythmic movements. During a performance of *Antigone* the director somehow unconsciously arranged his actors to resemble frescoes and vase paintings, but he was not able to *synthesize* or *stylize* what he had seen in actual relics; he could only photograph. On the stage before us we could see a series of groupings, like a row of hill tops, but realistic gestures and movements, like ravines, disturbed the internal rhythm of the reproduction.

The actor in the Naturalistic Theatre is extremely nimble at transforming himself, but his methods do not originate from *plastic* action but from make-up and an onomatopoeic imitation of various accents, dialects, and voices. Instead of developing his esthetic sense to exclude all coarseness, the actor's task is to lose his self-consciousness. A photographic sense of recording daily trivia is instilled in the actor. . . .

The Naturalistic Theatre denies that the spectator has the ability to finish a painting in his imagination, or to dream as he does when listening to music. And yet the spectator possesses such an ability. In the first act of Iartsev's play *At the Monastery* the interior of a monastery was shown and the curfew bells were heard. No window was shown on stage, but from the sound of the bells the playgoer imagined a courtyard covered with piles of bluish snow, fir trees as in the paintings by Nesterov, little paths leading from cell to cell, and the golden cupolas of a church. One spectator imagined such a picture, the second another, and the third still another. Mystery had taken hold of the playgoer, transporting him into the world of dreams. In the second act the director had a window showing the courtyard of the monastery but not those cells, those heaps of snow, nor the color of the cupolas. And the spectator was disenchanted and even enraged, for Mystery had disappeared and dreams were abused.

The Naturalistic Theatre consistently and consciously banished from the stage the power of Mystery. During the first performance of *The Sea Gull,* in the first act, one could not see how the actors made their exit from the stage. Running across some boards, they disappeared into a black cloth thicket, into *somewhere* (at that time the designer still worked without the collaboration of the carpenter); but when *The Sea Gull* was given again in a new version, all the stage was clearly visible: a little summerhouse with real cupolas and real columns, and a ravine into which the actors made their exit seen by all. During *The Sea Gull's* first performance, in the third act, a window was at the side of the stage, and no landscape could be seen; when the actors entered wearing galoshes, shaking their hats, shawls and kerchiefs, they conveyed the spirit of autumn, of freezing rain, puddles in the yard and boards squelching in the mud. When the play was restudied on a technically perfected stage, the window faced the audience and showed a landscape. Your imagination was lulled, and you did not imagine anything more than what the actors said about the weather outside. And the departure with horses and bells (the end of the third act in the first version) was only felt on the stage, yet was clearly pictured by the spectator's imagination; but according to the plan of the later performances, the audience had to see the horses with bells as well as the terrace from which the characters departed.

"A work of art can function only through the imagination. Therefore a work of art must constantly arouse the imagination,"[1] not just arouse, but "activate." To arouse the imagination "is a necessary condition of an esthetic phenomenon, and also a basic law of the fine arts. It therefore follows that an artistic work must *not* supply everything to our senses but only enough to direct our imagination onto the right path, leaving the last word to our imagination."[2]

---

[1] Schopenhauer.
[2] Schopenhauer.

"It may be better not so say everything; the spectator himself will do the rest and as a result the illusion will sometimes seem even greater, but to say too much is like pushing and smashing a statue consisting of many little pieces, or like removing the light from a magic lantern."[3]

Somewhere Voltaire said: "*Le secret d'être ennuyeux, c'est tout dire.*"

When the spectator's imagination is not lulled to sleep but stimulated, then art becomes subtle. Why could the medieval plays be performed without any scenery? Because of the lively imagination of the audience.

The Naturalistic Theatre not only denies the playgoer the ability to dream, but even the ability to understand intelligent conversation on stage. All the scenes in Ibsen's plays are submitted to a tedious analysis which transforms the work of the Norwegian dramatist into something boring, dragging, and doctrinaire. Especially in the performance of Ibsen plays the method of the naturalistic stage director is clearly demonstrated. The play is divided into a series of scenes, and each separate part is *minutely analyzed.* This painstaking analysis is applied to the tiniest scenes of the drama. From these various, thoroughly-digested parts the whole is glued together again. This piecing together of the whole from its parts is called the art of the director, but I think the analytical work of the naturalist-director, this pasting together of the poet's, the actor's, the musician's, the painter's, or even the director's work, will never result in a unified whole. . . .

Naturalism introduced a more complex staging technique in the Russian theatre, yet it is the Theatre of Chekhov, the second style of the Moscow Art Theatre, which demonstrated the power of *mood;* without this mood, or atmosphere, the theatre of the Meiningers would have perished long ago. But the development of the Naturalistic Theatre was not aided by this *new mood* originating from Chekhov's plays. The performance of *The Sea Gull* in the Alexandrinky Theatre did not dispel the author's mood, yet the secret was not to be found in the chirping of crickets, the barking of dogs, or in realistic doors. When *The Sea Gull* was performed in the Ermitazh building of the Moscow Art Theatre, the *machinery* was not working perfectly, and *technique* did not yet extend its feelers into all corners of the theatre.

The secret of Chekhov's mood lies in the *rhythm* of his language. This rhythm was felt by the actors of the Art Theatre during the

[3] Leo Tolstoy, "On Shakespeare and on Drama."

rehearsals of the first Chekhov play, was felt because of the actors' love for Chekhov.

The Moscow Art Theatre would never have achieved its second style without the rhythmicality of Chekhov's words; the theatre of mood became its real character and was not a mask borrowed from the Meiningen players.

That the Art Theatre could under one roof shelter the Naturalistic Theatre and the Theatre of Mood was due, I am convinced, to A. P. Chekhov who personally attended the rehearsals of his plays and with the charm of his personality and with frequent conversations influenced the actors, their tastes, and their ideas about the problem of art.

This new kind of theatre was created chiefly by a group of actors known as "Chekhovian actors." They performed all the Chekhov plays and can be considered the originators of the Chekhovian rhythmic diction. Whenever I remember the active part taken by these actors in creating *The Sea Gull's* characters and mood, I understand why I believe so strongly that the actor is the most important element on a stage. Neither the sets, nor the crickets, nor the horses' hoofs on the boards could create *mood,* but only the extraordinary musicality of the performers who understood the rhythm of Chekhov's poetry and could veil his work in lunar mist.

In the first two productions *(The Sea Gull* and *Uncle Vanya)* the actors were perfectly *free* and the harmony was not disrupted. But later, the naturalist-director made the ensembles more important and lost the key to a Chekhov performance. Once the ensembles became important, the work of the actors became passive; but instead of encouraging the lyricism of this *new key,* the naturalistic director created atmosphere with external devices such as darkness, sounds, accessories, and characters, and soon lost his sense of direction because he did not realize how Chekhov changed from subtle realism to mystic lyricism.

Once the Moscow Art Theatre had decided how to produce Chekhov plays, it applied the same pattern to other authors. Ibsen and Maeterlinck were performed "in the manner of Chekhov.". . .

THE FIRST EXPERIMENTS
OF THE CONVENTIONAL THEATRE

The Theatre Studio, heeding the advice of Maeterlinck and Bruisov, was the first theatre to experiment with a conventional, stylized technique. And as the Studio with its production of Maeterlinck's tragedy, *La Mort de Tintagiles,* came very close to realizing the ideals of the Stylized Theatre, it seems to me not out of place to describe the method of work employed by the directors, actors, and painters on this play, and to recount the experiences gained.

In the theatre there always exists a discord between the creative artists who collectively present their work to the public. Author, director, actor, designer, musician, and property man are never ideally united in a collectively-creative work. For that reason I do not feel that Wagner's synthesis of art is possible. Both the painter and the musician are handicapped, the former in a decorative theatre where he is only able to paint scenery for the stage at night instead of for a painting exhibit in daylight, and the latter because his music always plays a subservient role in the dramatic theatre.

Already at the beginning of our work on *La Mort de Tintagiles* the question of creative differences worried me. If the designer or the musician were not able to fit into the total scheme — with each one trying to pull in his direction — then it seemed to me that at least the author, director, and actor should work closely together. But these three, who form the foundation of any theatre, *could join their efforts* only under the conditions existing in the Theatre Studio during the rehearsals of *La Mort de Tintagiles.*

Following the usual practice of "talking" about the play (preceded, of course, by the director being acquainted with everything written about the play), the director and actor then read some poetry by Maeterlinck, fragments from those of his plays which had scenes similar in mood to *La Mort de Tintagiles.* This was done so as not to make the play into an exercise. Each actor in turn read some verses or excerpts. This work was for the actor what a sketch is for the painter, or an exercise for the musician.

Such exercises polished technique; a painter can begin a picture only after technique has been mastered. Not only the director but all those listening made suggestions. This work was aimed at finding how the author "sounded" best. When in this collective work an author's text begins to "sound," then the audience will proceed to analyze the means which convey the style of a given author.

But before giving an insight into our new ideas I want to point out *two methods of directing a play* which in different ways establish the relationship between the actor and the director: one system restrains the creative freedom of both the actor and the spectator, and the other liberates both actor and spectator permitting the latter to use his imagination actively rather than merely to contemplate. These two systems are best understood if the four fundamentals of the theatre—the author, director, actor, and spectator—are graphically represented as follows:

1) A triangle with the apex representing the director, and the bases the author and the actor. The playgoer sees the work of the author and actor through the *work of the director*. (Graphically the "spectator" is at the top of the triangle.) This is one kind of theatre—the "triangular theatre."

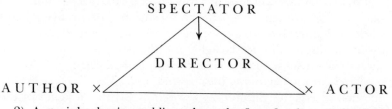

2) A straight, horizontal line where the four fundamentals of the theatre are represented from left to right: author, director, actor, spectator. This is the other kind of theatre—the "straight theatre." The actor freely reveals his soul to the spectator after having incorporated the work of the director, just as the director had incorporated the work of the author.

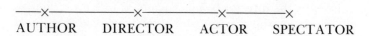

AUTHOR DIRECTOR ACTOR SPECTATOR

In the "triangular theatre" the director, after having discussed his plan in great detail, will rehearse until his conception is simply reproduced, until he hears and sees the play as he had heard and seen it by himself. A symphony orchestra is an example of this "triangular theatre" and the conductor is like the stage director. However, the theatre, architecturally speaking, does not permit the director to use a conductor's stand, and therefore the difference between the methods of a director and a conductor is obvious.

Yes, but it so happens that a symphony orchestra can play without a conductor. Nikisch,[4] for example, performs with an orchestra which he has conducted for many years with hardly a change in its personnel. Some music the orchestra performs year after year. Could not the orchestra bring to life Nikisch's conception without his being on the conductor's stand? Yes, this could happen, yet the audience would nevertheless hear the music as interpreted by

[4] Arthur Nikisch, 1855-1922, for many years the conductor of the Gewandhaus orchestra in Leipzig.

Nikisch. But there is another question—would the music be played exactly the same as if Nikisch had conducted? The performance would have been less good, but we still would have heard Nikisch's interpretation of the piece.

I think a symphony orchestra without a conductor is possible; but it is not possible to draw a parallel between an orchestra without a conductor and a theatre in which the actors perform on stage completely without a director. A symphony orchestra without a conductor is possible, but without rehearsals the audience will not be moved, and an orchestra can only convey the interpretation of this or that conductor. The actor's work must do more than acquaint the audience with a director's conception. An actor can inspire an audience only if he transforms himself into the author and director.

The main virtue of a player in a symphony orchestra is to possess a virtuoso technique and to follow accurately the dictates of a conductor. Like a symphony orchestra, the "triangular theatre" must admit actors with a less individualistic virtuoso technique.

In the "straight theatre" the director takes the part of the author, and makes the actor see his work (author and director are one). After incorporating the author's work by way of the director, the actor comes face to face with the spectator (author and director at the actor's back), and acts *freely* while enjoying the give and take between the two main elements of a theatre—the player and the playgoer. The director *alone* must set the tone and style of a performance so that the "straight theatre" may not become chaotic,[5] and yet the acting will remain free and unrestrained.

The director reveals his *plan* in *talking* about the play. The play is colored by the director's point of view. Captivating the actors with his love for the play, the director infuses them with the spirit of the author. But *after his explanations* all artists have complete independence. Then the director again calls them together to unify the different parts. *He does not want an exact recreation of his conception,* which existed solely to give unity to the whole, but waits for the moment when he can hide in the wings letting the actor either "burn his ship" (if the actor is at odds with the director or with the author, especially when the actor does not belong to the "new School"[6]), or

[5] Alexander Blok (in *Pereval,* 1907) feared that the actors of such a theatre "might burn the ship of the play," but I think differences of opinion occur only when free interpretation is permitted. The danger is removed when the director gives good explanations to the actor, and the latter in turn has really understood his director.

[6] The "triangular theatre" needs actors without individuality but with virtuosity. In the "straight theatre" the individual acting talent is very important, and so a *new school* is needed. A new school is not one in which new techniques are taught, but one which arises only when a new, free theatre is born. *(footnote continued)*

act freely in an almost improvisational manner, of course keeping to the text, but revealing the play to the audience through the prism of the actor's technique which has assimilated both the author's and the director's concepts. *Theatre is acting.*

In the works of Maeterlinck, in his poetry and plays, his introduction to the latest edition, and his little book, *The Treasury of the Humble,* where he speaks of the static theatre, we see clearly that the author did not want to bring horror onto the stage, did not want to annoy the spectator with historical wailing, or make the public recoil in terror. Quite the contrary—he wanted to instill in the spectator a trembling but wise contemplation of the inevitable, to make the spectator weep and suffer but simultaneously move him and bring him to a state of peace and felicity. The basic task which the author sets himself is "to alleviate our sorrows by sowing hope long extinct."[7] Human life with all its passions begins to flow again when the playgoer leaves the theatre, but these passions no longer seem *vain*; life continues with its joys and sorrows, with its obligations, all of which now assume a greater meaning: either we find a way out of the darkness, or learn to endure life without bitterness. Maeterlinck's art is healthy and vivifying. He causes us to contemplate the greatness of Destiny, and his theatre becomes a temple. Not long ago Pastore praised Maeterlinck's mysticism as the last refuge for religious Belgians who did not want to bow to the temporal might of the church yet wanted to retain an independent belief in another world. The solution to religious questions can be found in such a theatre. And once Maeterlinck's work is regarded as a *mystery* not painted in gloomy colors, then his plays become an indefatigable call for life.

I think our predecessors when performing Maeterlinck made a mistake in frightening the spectator without revealing the inevitability of fate. "At the basis of my dramas," wrote Maeterlinck, "is the idea of a Christian God together with the idea of ancient fate." The author perceives people's words and tears as a dull rumble, as if in a deep, bottomless well. He sees people from a great distance, and they seem to him weakly shimmering sparks. And he wants to overhear words of meekness, hope, compassion, and fear, and show the might of that Destiny which controls our fates.

The "straight theatre" grows but once from a school, a single school, just as from each seed grows only one plant. And just as for the next plant a new seed has to be sown, so a new theatre must grow each time from a new school. The "triangular theatre" tolerates many schools, but the task of these schools is to fill vacant positions with a group of candidates who have been trained to imitate the great actors of the established theatres. I am convinced that especially these schools are to be blamed for the lack of real talent on our stages.

[7] Annibal Pastore, "Moris Materlink," *Vestn. inostr. literat.,* Sept., 1903.

We tried in our performances of Maeterlinck to awaken in the spectator the same feelings Maeterlinck tried to arouse. Maeterlinck's plays are mysteries either of hardly perceptible harmony of voices, of quiet tears, of restrained sighs and tremors of hope (as in *La Mort de Tintagiles),* or of ecstasy calling for universal religious belief, for dancing to the sounds of pipe and organ, for a Bacchanalia of the great working of a Miracle (as in the second act of *Beatrice).* Maeterlinck's dramas are "above all a revelation and a purification of the soul. His dramas are of spirits singing *mezza voce* of suffering, love, beauty, and death." Artlessness leading from earth to the world of dreams. Harmony arousing quiet. Or ecstatic joy. These are the spiritual feelings which we brought to Maeterlinck's theatre in our rehearsal studio.

What Muther[8] wrote about Perugino, one of the most charming of the fifteenth-century painters, we likewise wished to say about Maeterlinck: "The contemplative, lyrical nature of his subjects, the quiet grandeur and archaic solemnity of his paintings" can "exist solely in a composition in which the harmony is not marred by one disturbing movement, or one sharp contradiction."

After taking into consideration Maeterlinck's writings and my work with the actors in the rehearsal studio, I intuitively reached the following conclusions:

I. Concerning diction:

> 1. Needed is a cold minting of words, absolutely free from any vibration (tremolo) or weeping. Complete absence of tension or gloom.
>
> 2. The sound must always have support, and the words must fall like drops in a deep well; the clear impact of the drops is heard without the vibration of the sound in space. No indistinctness in the sound, no words with howling endings as when reading "decadent" verses.
>
> 3. A mystic tremor is more forceful than the old-style temperament which was always uncontrolled, externally coarse (swinging of arms, beating of breast and thighs). The inner thrill of the mystic tremor is reflected in the eyes, on the lips, in sounds, in the pronunciation of words; an outer calm during volcanic experiences. And all without tension, lightly.
>
> 4. Spiritual emotions, all their tragedy, are indissolubly connected with form which in turn is inseparable from content, just as content dictates a particular, and no other, form in Maeterlinck.[9]

[8] Richard Muther, 1860-1909, German art historian.
[9] Practice raised a question the answer to which I will not take upon myself, but I only want to propose one: should an actor at first expose the inner content of a role, show bursts of

5. Never fast patter which is permissible only in neurasthenic kinds of plays, in those which have a row of dots. Epic calm does not exclude a tragic experience. Tragic experiences are always majestic.
6. Tragedy with a smile.

I fully understood these intuitive ideas only after reading the words of Savonarola:

Do not think that Mary at the death of her son cried out, walked the streets tearing her hair and acting like a mad woman. She came for her son with meekness and great humility. She undoubtedly cried tears, but from her external appearance she seemed not sad, but simultaneously *sad and joyful*. At the descent from the Cross she was both sad and joyful, absorbed in the secret of the great blessedness of God.

To create an impression on the audience, the actor of the old school shouted, wept, groaned, and beat his chest with his fists. But the new actor must express tragedy like the sad, yet joyful, Mary: externally calm, almost *cold*, without shouts and weeping, without tremulous sounds, yet still profound.

II. Concerning plastic ideas:

1. Richard Wagner with his orchestra provided inner tension; the music sung by the singers seemed insufficiently powerful to convey the inner experiences of his heroes. Wagner called on his orchestra for help, feeling that only an orchestra could reveal Mystery to the audience. In "Drama," likewise, the *word* is not sufficiently strong to bring out the inner meaning. Pronunciation, even good pronunciation, does not mean speaking. It is necessary to seek new ways of expressing the inexpressible, and to reveal what is concealed.

As Wagner makes his orchestra speak about the spiritual experiences of his heroes, so I make plastic movements express inner feelings.

Plastic gestures are not new. Salvini in *Othello* or *Hamlet* always used plastic movements. True, this was also plastic art, but I am not talking about that kind of plasticity. Salvini's gestures closely corre-

---

temperament, and only then clothe his experience with this or that form? Or vice versa? At first we adhered to this method: not to show temperamental outbursts until we had mastered the form. I think this is right. But you will justly complain that form then enchains temperament. No, this is not so. The old, naturalistic actors, our teachers, said: if you don't want to ruin the role for yourself, begin to read it, not out loud, but to yourself, and only when the part begins to sound in your heart, then speak it aloud. To approach a realistic role by silently reading the text, and a nonrealistic part by first mastering the rhythm of the language and movement—that is the only true method.

sponded to the words and their pronunciation. I mean that plasticity which exists aside from words.

What does plasticity aside from words mean?

Two men are holding a conversation about the weather, about art, or about apartments. A third bystander observing them, if he is more or less sensitive, can decide quite accurately who these two men are—friends, enemies, or lovers—from their conversation about subjects which do not reveal their personal relationships. From the way these two conversing men move their hands, take certain poses, lower their eyes, an observer can decipher their relationship, because in talking about the weather or art these two men use gestures which do not necessarily explain their words. And from these movements which are not related to the words, an observer can decide whether friends, enemies, or lovers are conversing.

A director builds a bridge from the spectator to the actor. Following the dictates of the author, and introducing onto the stage friends, enemies, or lovers, the director with movements and postures must present a certain image which will aid the spectator not only to hear the words, but to guess the inner, concealed feelings. And if the director, absorbed in the author's theme, hears the inner music, then he will propose to the actors plastic movements which will enable the spectator to hear this inner music.

Gestures, postures, glances, and silences depict the truthful relationship among people. Words do not tell the whole story. A pattern of movement is needed on the stage which will force the spectator into the position of being a keen observer, just as the third observer of the two talking figures was able to divine their internal thoughts. Words are for hearing, movement for seeing. In this manner the spectator's imagination is aroused by two sensations—the visual and auditory. The difference between the old and the new theatre is that in the latter movement and words are subordinate each to its own rhythm. It does not necessarily follow that movement must never correspond to words. Some phrases need to be illustrated by movement, but this must be as natural as the logical stresses in poetry.

> 2. Maeterlinck's pictures have an archaic quality, as in icons. Arkel, as from a painting by Ambrogio Borgonione. Gothic arches. Wooden statues shining like rose wood. And the actors symmetrically arranged to express holiness, as in a Perugino painting.

"Women, effeminate boys, and languid, gentle old men can best express sweet dreaminess"; this was Perugino's aim. And does it not also express Maeterlinck?

The New Theatre changed the absurd ornateness of the naturalistic theatres into a structural plan based on rhythmic, linear movement and musical harmony of colors.

An iconographic style was used in the sets (since we had not yet abolished scenery altogether). And just as plastic movements were used to bring out inner feelings, so scenery was painted which would not detract from these movements. The spectator's concentration had to be focused on motion; for that reason *La Mort de Tintagiles* used only one backdrop. This tragedy was rehearsed against a background of simple canvas and made a very strong impression because the pattern of the gestures stood out clearly. The play would have been lost had the actors performed in scenery with space and air. Therefore, a decorated panel. But after some experiments with painted panels (as in *Beatrice, Hedda Gabler*), it seemed that they were as unsuitable as the old type of scenery which had blurred movement. In Giotto's paintings nothing marred the smoothness of his lines because he did not adhere to a naturalistic, but rather to a decorative, point of view. But the theatre must not turn toward a "decorative" style (unless treated as in the Japanese theatre).

A decorated panel, like a symphony, has a special function; and if figures are necessary then they should be cardboard puppets, not wax, wood, or cloth. For a painted flat has only two dimensions and demands figures of two dimensions.

The human body and the accessories surrounding it—tables, chairs, beds, and dressers—are all three-dimensional, and therefore a theatre where the actor is the most important factor must be based on the plastic arts and not on painting. A *plastic statuesqueness* should be fundamental to acting.

This was the result of the first cycle of experiments in the New Theatre. The historically-inevitable circle was completed; experiments in stylized staging had raised new ideas concerning the decorative arts in the dramatic theatre.

By rejecting a decorative style, the New Theatre did not negate the new stylized staging nor Maeterlinck's iconographic notions. But the means of expression were architectural rather than painted. All the concepts of a stylized performance were kept inviolate in *La Mort de Tintagiles, Hedda Gabler, Soeur Beatrice,* and *The Eternal Fairy Tale,*[10] but the painter was employed without hindering the actors or the objects.

---

[10] *Vechnaia skazka* by Przybyszewski.

John Gielgud

These observations are a great actor's memories of work with a great director—a director whose rehearsal techniques are not generally known. Although the importance of these comments is the light they throw upon Granville-Barker's procedure and thoughts, it should not go unobserved that the recorder of these details, who played the role of Lear and who effected much that the director could only anticipate, writes with such reticence and humility. Of special interest are Gielgud's memories of Granville-Barker's use of stage convention, of vocal method, of stage blocking and moves; the piece as a whole is a tribute from actor to director which attests to a creative relationship at its best.

GRANVILLE-BARKER REHEARSES KING LEAR

In the ill-fated spring of 1940, just before the Fall of France, Granville-Barker accepted an invitation from Tyrone Guthrie and myself to direct a production of *King Lear* at the Old Vic. The company assembled was a fine one, including as it did Jack Hawkins, Jessica Tandy, Robert Harris, Fay Compton, Cathleen Nesbitt, Lewis Casson, Nicholas Hannen, Stephen Haggard and Harcourt Williams.

Granville-Barker came over from Paris, and spent a week-end making preliminary arrangements with Roger Furse, the designer, and with Lewis Casson, who agreed to undertake the preparatory work of the production. Barker refused to have his name officially announced as director, and only agreed to supervise some rehearsals, using his own preface to the play as a foundation. I went to see him at the Queen's Theatre, and nervously endeavoured to read the part through with him. When I got to the end he remarked: "You got two lines right. Now we will begin to work." He also said: "Lear is an oak. You are an ash. We must see how this will serve you." I left him, deeply apprehensive of my limitations, but with my copy of the text thick with brilliantly suggestive notes.[1]

From *Stage Directions*, by John Gielgud. © Copyright 1963 by John Gielgud. Reprinted by permission of Random House, Inc., and Heinemann Educational Books Ltd. (London).

[1] [These notes are included in Section II, above.]

He came back to London again after rehearsals had already begun and worked with the actors for ten days, but he left after the first dress-rehearsal, and never saw a performance with an audience.

I have often been surprised to find that a very fine theatrical talent does not seem to become rusty through a long period of disuse. It has been suggested that the brilliance of Ellen Terry's work in her middle years may have been deepened and enriched, after her rigorous training as a child actress, by the six years in which she left the theatre and lived privately bringing up her children in the country. Harley Granville-Barker, when I first knew him in the thirties, had not worked professionally in the theatre for twenty years, but he showed no signs, as he resumed work with a company almost completely unknown to him, of any old-fashioned narrowness of outlook or loss of sensitivity. In the very few days in which I had the privilege of working with him, I could see no trace of effort in the use of his superlative gifts—no lack of sureness in his authority, no hint of tentativeness or uncertainty in his approach. From the moment he stepped through the stage-door at the Old Vic, he inspired and dominated everyone like a master-craftsman, and everyone in the theatre recognized this at once.

He had only ten days to work with us on *King Lear*, but they were the fullest in experience that I have ever had in all my years upon the stage. By letter, and at some early conferences, he had already devised a ground-plan for the production, simple patterns of levels and entrances, diagrams showing how the furniture should be placed, and so on. In all these matters he had shown a masterly understanding of the scenic essentials that he felt to be demanded by the text. A few weeks later, when rehearsals had already been held under Lewis Casson and Tyrone Guthrie for some days, he arrived and began to work with the actors, not using any notes, but sitting on the stage with his back to the footlights, a copy of the play in his hand, tortoise-shell spectacles well forward on his nose, dressed in a black business suit, his bushy red eyebrows jutting forward, quiet-voiced, seldom moving, coldly humorous, shrewdly observant, infinitely patient and persevering.

Although he had a very strong conception of how every character should be played, he did not at first try to force his views upon the actors or attempt to discourage their ideas, though he frequently corrected them. He was, as he told me, a great believer in reading the play round a table for a week or more, but on this occasion there was no time for that. His first concern was certainly for the speaking of the verse and the balance of the voices. In dealing with the actors he was quite impersonal, calling everyone by the name of the part they were playing. He neither coaxed nor flattered, but at the same time, though he was intensely autocratic and severe, he was never personal or rude. The actors had immediate respect for his authority. They did not become paralysed or apathetic, as can so often happen when a strong director is not excessively sensitive. They were constantly dismayed, however, by the high standards he continually demanded of them, and by the intense hard work to which he subjected them without showing any appearance of fatigue himself. For, the moment they appeared to begin to satisfy him in one direction, Barker was urging them on to experiment in another. Tempo, atmosphere, diction, balance, character—no detail could escape his fastidious ear, his unerring dramatic instinct and his superb sense of classic shapeliness of line.

And yet he was in no way old-fashioned. He was not afraid to have an actor standing downstage or with his back to the audience. On the other hand, he had none of the modern fear of clichés in the acting of Shakespeare—what is called "ham acting" when it is crudely executed. He encouraged grand entrances and exits centre-stage, a declamatory style, imposing gestures. Only under his subtle hand these theatrical devices became classic, tragic, noble, not merely histrionic or melodramatic, because of the unerring taste and simplicity with which he ordered them.

To my great regret, I never saw him handle supers or drill a crowd scene; indeed, to those of us in the company who had hung on his every word during those short ten days, it seemed something of a disaster that he did not feel free to stay and guide us to the end, either to final victory or defeat. I suppose he was no longer prepared to face the tedious anxieties of the last days before production—the lighting plots, music cues and last-minute adjustments and emergencies, the publicity, photographs and gossip. I think he had ceased to care about the reactions of audiences or the opinions of dramatic critics. The actual working life of the theatre with its petty involvements no longer concerned him. Certainly, he was himself the finest audience and severest critic I have ever set myself to try and please. Praise from him was praise worth waiting for, but it was rare, and often rather implied than stated. "You did some fine things today in that scene" he would say to me, "I hope you know what they were!" and then proceed to read me a long list of my mistakes.

Barker left us to return to Paris, and the production opened without him. Yet for several weeks afterwards I kept receiving postcards and short notes from him, indicating improvements and suggesting details, showing that his mind was not entirely free of his work with us, and that it had even moved him to a reconsidered study of the play.

Incidentally, in the few glimpses which he gave us at rehearsal, he must have been a very fine actor himself, with extraordinary power and repose, though no great range of voice. Of his supremacy as a director no one who had the good fortune to attend those rehearsals can have any possible doubt.

But he loved writing more than the theatre, and Shakespeare perhaps better than either. At least we have the *Prefaces* to comfort us, in some degree at least, for the great man we have lost. He gave so much of his fine early work to the English theatre that one cannot help regretting all it might perhaps have gained over his later years, if only he could have been persuaded to continue working there.

Peter Brook

This essay, written almost twenty years ago by the man who was eventually to direct Weiss's *Marat ... Sade* and Paul Scofield as King Lear, is a manifesto of the most important kind. It states in practical, theatrical terms the artist's belief in the continuity of audiences' perceptions and the viability of a great playwright. It emphasizes the creativity of the audience of any period but emphasizes as strongly the responsibility of a director to the implicit requirements of his text. Those responsibilities, Brook maintains, are to the reality of the playwright's vision in terms that can be perceived by a contemporary audience without doing injustice to the script.

Brook continues to work with increasing pertinence as one of the directors of the Royal Shakespeare Theatre Company in Stratford-on-Avon and in London.

✍ *STYLE IN SHAKESPEAREAN PRODUCTION*

Isolation is a very discredited ambition and complete detachment has almost ceased to be a possibility: it is rare for an historian or a philosopher to escape from the influences of his time, and for the worker in the theatre, whose livelihood depends upon his contact with his audiences, this is impossible. Consequently, however hard a producer or a designer may strive to mount a classic with complete objectivity, he can never avoid reflecting a second period—the one in which he works and lives.

In the centuries since Shakespeare's day, the style of presentation of his plays has closely followed social changes. The Shakespeare tradition which exists today is the result not only of the years of scholarship, on the one hand, and of theatrical development on the other: it is the mirror of all the changes in taste that have come about as English society evolved from the uneasy anarchy of Elizabeth's reign to the stable bourgeois pattern of the Victorian era.

Shakespeare's plays were written in a harsh, vital, virile, pioneering age: they grew out of the atmosphere of adventure, of rebirth that came from the final overthrow of mediævalism by the Renaissance. They were conceived in a world of shifting values, of violent belief and violent disbelief, of individualism, ambition, enterprise, imperialism: they were set on a platform stage in the heart of the audience, and their power lay in their closeness, in this ability to play direct on the fantasy by the force of the acting, by the sweep of the rhetoric, and the vividness of the poetry.

When, in the course of time, England became more ordered, politics less open, diplomacy more subtle, and the entire way of living more urbane, the theatre took a gentler place in people's lives. It moved indoors, the seats became more comfortable, a picture frame arose to form a substantial barrier between the actor's emotion and the spectator—and a discreeter public welcomed this protection. In an age of gallantry, the theatre became decorative; the boy was replaced by the actress; the O of the imagination by the painted cloth; and the uncouth edges of passion softened by the charms of incidental music. When Garrick played Romeo in wig and knee-breeches, the play became eighteenth century, and the Juliet a Beauty of Bath.

From Garrick to Kean, from Macready to Irving, production style

Reprinted by permission of John Lehmann and the author. (This essay originally appeared in *Orpheus,* Vol. I, 1948, pp. 139-146.)

was moulded by social history. As the melodrama houses became popular, as the music halls opened their doors, the groundlings ceased to patronize Shakespeare, and with them some of the fibre went out of his plays. The violence was diminished, the bloodshed reduced, the frankness of language veiled to spare the ears of the new middle-class audience on whom the box-office was coming increasingly to depend. The importance also of the upper classes had diminished: the days were gone since they were the patrons and could call the tune and the aristocratic part of Shakespeare's work — the skilful word-play and the learned pun — became dead-wood. The texts grew shorter, the scenery more opulent. The tragedies of Shakespeare had become shows, ideal for family outings, inseparable companions of the souvenir programme and the chocolate box.

Shakespeare production today is based on a number of axioms whose presence no one even troubles to question. It seems inevitable that the plays should be divided up into acts and scenes, it seems inevitable that the *Midsummer Night's Dream* should have gauzes, ballets and Mendelssohn, that Romeo and Juliet should be middle-aged, that the histories should be played in front of tapestry curtains — red for England, blue for France: it seems inevitable that one should have to change pieces of canvas to indicate to the audience the difference between the outside and the inside of a castle. Yet few people wonder, in fact, few people are aware that the stage directions in their editions of the plays, the eternal "Another part of the battlements," "A forest," were all inserted by eighteenth-century editors. Few people give sufficient consideration to the fundamental difference between a play conceived as one whole poem, written in verse and designed to be played with the sweep and the freedom of verse, and one that is continually broken in line, and converted into a row of static units by the sequence of irrelevantly localising scenery. This realistic scenery has led into a vicious circle. The more elaborate it becomes, the more the sequence of the play has to be broken, and the more the play has to be cut down. It has led to the immense barrier between play and audience that a cliché devotion to period accuracy has created. Poetry is sacrificed to pedantry, and in the meaningless search for historical accuracy, inner reality is smothered by fancy dress.

The greatest mutilation which Shakespeare's plays have suffered is in the attitude of the actors. Through centuries in which actors have been their own managers and producers, the emphasis has not been on plays but on parts. The star actor has cut down all the supporting scenes with their richness of character and background detail, has given smaller parts to indifferent actors and pushed them into insignificent positions. In doing so, he has completely destroyed the balance of the plays, for to Shakespeare each character was of equal importance, and whosoever happened to be speaking at any given moment was for that moment the "lead."

This is the main tradition in Shakespeare production today, and is the tradition to which so many of our scholars and critics have become completely accustomed. It is only by close study of the plays, that one appreciates the astonishing gap between one's preconceptions and the actual text. One discovers how the direct line of tradition from Elizabethan to Victorian has now reached a full stop, and how a century which has, socially, swung back to an atmosphere closer to that of Elizabeth's England than at any point in the last four hundred years, must find a new style and a fresh approach.

One of the greatest possible errors that a producer can make is to believe that a script can speak for itself. No play can speak for itself. If an actor delivers his lines clearly but monotonously, no one will think that he is doing his job well. However, it is still widely believed in this country that the flat and static production is good, whilst the one that uses all the resources of theatre to illuminate the text is said to obscure the play. Indeed, in England, far too large a proportion of intelligent playgoers know their Shakespeare too well. They are no longer capable of going to the theatre with that willingness to suspend disbelief which any naïve spectator can bring. They go coldly, as specialists, to listen to the over-familiar lines, and to watch the actor's treatment of them. It is their influence on the theatre that has led to the type of Shakespeare production that is not uncommon nowadays, cold, correct, literary, untheatrical, winning great praise, but making no emotional impact on the average spectator.

The school of Poel and Granville-Barker rendered a great service to the theatre by its reaction from the excessive elaboration of the His Majesty's style of presentation. However, it went to the other extreme and sought simplicity in retrogression. It believed that the panacea was to go back to the conditions of Shakespeare's day and perform his plays on an Elizabethan stage. It is impossible truly to re-create this inside a modern theatre. To be consistent, one would have to re-create the entire Elizabethan theatre, with its crowd, its noises and its smells. Even supposing one were to achieve a complete reconstruction, one would find that the spirit of Shakespeare had once more slipped away, and that in one's search for the lost Shakespeare one would merely have created a Shakespeare museum.

It is a grotesque over-simplification of the problem to believe that anything can be achieved by going back on the developments of the theatre in the course of the last few hundred years. It is as incongruous as to suggest that the cinema should become silent again, or that classical music should be played on the primitive wind instruments of Mozart's day. Realising this, a number of producers attempt a compromise. Within the pictorial conventions of the present day proscenium, they build a structure that fulfils the necessary geographical qualifications of the Elizabethan stage, and yet can be used and lit as though part of a modern production.

This method falls dangerously between two stools. It aims at freeing the text by turning the set into a formal platform, but it fails to recognise that simply by being inside a proscenium it ceases to be a platform and becomes a picture. The Elizabethan stage was completely undistracting because it was out-of-doors, because it was merely a rostrum jutting out like a pier among the spectators. Its structure was something quite irrelevant, and consequently quite invisible, much as the grey-coated stage-managers who flit to and fro across the stage in a Chinese theatre are completely unnoticed by the audience.

However, no sooner is this same Elizabethan theatre, beam for beam and inch for inch, placed on a modern stage, than it becomes a picture; it ceases to be formal, it suddenly asserts its period, and when the producer still further compromises by using realistic lighting effects, the breakdown of style is complete. The error is very similar in modern-dress productions of Shakespeare. They emanate from the theory that modern clothes, like the contemporary clothes which the Elizabethan actors wore, are completely functional, and thus the least distracting form of costume for a tragedy. However, the Elizabethan actor was playing in his modern clothes on his formal platform stage; actors inside a picture frame are always actors in a period costume, even when the period happens to be the present day. One can not escape from their incongruity, and in the last resort they are less functional and more distracting than the most ornate of dresses.

When an audience enters a theatre, its imagination is completely open. If, as in *Our Town* it finds the curtain up, the stage bare, then the initial anti-pictorial gesture of the production makes it clear that no picture is going to be presented, and that the proscenium is merely an arch over a square of boards on which the actors will seek to create an illusion. Thus in the opening gambit the conventions are established, and the audience's imagination is liberated, leaving it both ready and capable of creating its own pictures. However, if the curtain is lowered, if, when the lights fade and the curtain rises, one sees a structure with period decoration, if the lighting suggests even as elementary an atmosphere as day or night, already the audience has accepted a pictorial convention, and at once surrenders its imagination into the hands of the producer. This imposes a heavy obligation on him not to betray his trust, and if he tries to compromise by allowing the play to be semi-formalised, instead of going all the way pictorially, the audience will feel cheated. It will neither have the satisfaction of exercising its own imagination, nor will it have the thrill of yielding to a continually imaginative and convincing stage illusion. The great percentage of Shakespeare productions that one sees today are dull simply because they make this compromise: sometimes through fear, sometimes through modesty, sometimes through lack of ability the producer fails to fulfil the tacit offer which he has made to the audience.

Musset says that a door must be either open or closed, and we can say with equal simplicity that a production cannot toy with illusion — it must either go all the way or none of it. Both are legitimate, and both can be achieved, but neither can be found by retrogression. It is possible to achieve on the present day stage the formality of the Elizabethan, but only by totally different means. Above all, the means employed must be self-consistent: if the pictorial convention is to be rejected then the curtain must not be used, the lighting and the decorations must at no point suggest whither time or place, period or atmosphere, the stage structure must be made a platform to which they serve the neutral purpose of background and illumination. Similarly, the costumes must be clearly uniforms for actors, satisfying the eye but suggesting neither the past nor the present. Such a technique, like that of the Chinese or Japanese theatre, would make the plays rely exclusively upon the words and the actors, and potentially could give the purest and most æsthetically satisfying renderings of Shakespeare's plays.

Practically speaking, this approach has two great dangers. One is that by placing such complete emphasis on the actor it also imposes upon him a burden that very few casts would be qualified to bear. A large part of the work of every producer is to find external means of supplementing the work of the actor when this cannot rise to the expressive requirements of the moment. If the actor is left on a bare stage with nothing to create a mood for him, and nothing to help him, he must be capable of holding the full attention of the audience every instant by himself. With an ideal company, such a production of Shakespeare could be envisaged. Even then, one would have to take into account the reaction of the audience. The theatre, unlike any other art, is empirical. It has no existence until it exists in front of a spectator, and beyond a certain point it cannot lead further than an audience is prepared to follow. A naked and simplified production of Shakespeare might have great virtue, but it would be of no practical value if it proved to be too rarefied and austere in its idiom for the average person.

Shakespeare is the world's most popular dramatist: his plays have been more played, more translated and more read than those of any other writer. When it then appears that in his own country in the twentieth century he has become one of the least-performed dramatists, it is clear that the method of presentation is at fault. It also follows that popular success must be a very considerable criterion for a Shakespeare production — a production that succeeds is not necessarily good, but one that fails where the appeal of the play has long been established must undoubtedly be on the wrong track.

To communicate any one of Shakespeare's plays to a present day audience, the producer must be prepared to set every resource of modern theatre at the disposal of his text. This text will be obscured by a mass of false traditions, by archaisms, by meaningless references, by out-moded conventions, by the thousand technical differences that the different theatre building of Shakespeare's day dictated. The producer must be able to discriminate between these externals and the essential living heart of the play — the poet's inner dream — for which it is his job to find theatrical correlatives.

In my own production of *Love's Labour Lost* the play was dressed after Watteau — a period 150 years after the play was written. This choice of costume was not dictated by any *a priori* considerations, and historical accuracy was rejected as of supremely little importance. I chose Watteau because the style of his dresses, with its broad, undecorated expanses of billowing satin seemed the ideal visual correlative of the essential sweet-sad mood of this play. In the scenes of the Princess' court, I introduced a chalk-faced, white-clothed zany — a character in no way suggested by any line of the script but who remained to the end as a forlorn, drooping symbol, in period as much Schumann as Shakespeare, of the atmosphere of these scenes. In the more sturdy comedy scenes Dull, the constable, had the bright blue uniform, the eternal truncheon, helmet and string of sausages that symbolises all policemen – Toy Town, Victorian London, Harlequinade or Navarre – and helped to communicate in one glance to the audience the image that springs to mind the moment one reads his name. The congruities and seeming incongruities of this production were all dictated by the expressive requirements of the script, and my claim is that through this fundamental consistency they were bound by one style and acquired their own truth. As innovations, they scandalised the specialists but pleased the public, and when the production was revived a year later they had, it seemed to me, been completely accepted.

In *Romeo and Juliet* the problem was above all to find a modern stagecraft which could give freedom and space to the sweep of the poem. The time for the assumption that *Romeo and Juliet* is a sentimental story to be played against a series of backdrops giving picture-postcard views of Italy must surely be gone. It is a play of youth, of freshness, of open air, in which the sky – the great tent of Mediterranean blue – hangs over every moment of it, from the first brawl in the dusty market to the calm and peaceful cadence in the grave. It is a play of wide spaces, in which all scenery and decoration easily become an irrelevance, in which one tree on a bare stage can suggest the loneliness of a place of exile, one wall, as in Giotto, an entire house. Its atmosphere is described in a single line, "these hot days is the mad blood stirring," and its treatment must be to capture the violent passion of two children lost amongst the Southern fury of the warring houses. Any approach to the play that takes as its starting-point its essentially virile and very Elizabethan spirit soon finds that there is no place for sweetness and sentimentality in the characterisation, in the speaking, in the settings or in the music. I endeavoured to make the Stratford *Romeo and Juliet* essentially 1947 in its approach to the staging, and essentially Elizabethan in atmosphere, and I believe that, in practice, it seemed both true and alive to the theatre-goer who had not over-close acquaintance with the play.

Unlike any other artist, the theatre producer must be continually aware of his audience. He must work to communicate to a specific mass of people, and their immediate reaction is his only measure of success. A production of *The Tempest* that might be good in Moscow could just as well be bad in London, much as the way of interpreting the same play to Norwegians should differ radically from the manner of interpreting it to Latin Americans. The production of *Romeo and Juliet* in Prague which set it in a concentration camp might well seem preposterous outside Czechoslovakia, but in that country at the instant at which it was produced it had a peculiar meaning and poignancy that was the cause of its great success.

The producer is working with three elements: his text, his audience, and his medium, and of these only the first is constant. It is his primary duty to discover every intention of the author and to transmit these with every possible means at his disposal. As the theatre develops, as its shape and geography, its machinery and its conventions change, so production style must change with it. There is no perfect production of any play, nor is there any final one: like a musician's interpretation, its existence is inseparable from its performance. A production is only right at a given moment, and anything that it asserts dogmatically today may well be wrong fifty years from now. The theatre deals with living material and is in an endless state of flux. When a new actor enters a company the treatment of his scenes should be amended; if a play is revived, changes must be made. Any attempt to fix productions by tradition is doomed to lead to the lifeless cul-de-sac of National Theatres.

When Garrick played *Romeo and Juliet* in knee-breeches, he was *right*; when Kean staged *The Winter's Tale* with a hundred Persian pot-carriers, he was *right*; when Tree staged Shakespeare with all the resources of the His Majesty's, he was *right*; when Craig staged his reaction to this he was *right* too. Each was justified in its own time; each would be outrageous out of it. A production is only correct at the moment of its correctness, and only good at the moment of its success. In its beginning is its beginning, and in its end is its end.

Elia Kazan

There is no doubt that such original and flexible directors as Kazan have metamorphosed some of Stanislavski's first intentions in the projection of the famous "Method." On the other hand, such alteration in principle and goal as Kazan develops in such notes as these are, in themselves, important in the history of directorial ideas. Stanislavski's terms are used frequently, sometimes with their original import; the new contexts for these terms make the achievements of such men as Kazan fascinating to the student of theatre history and practice.

Reprinted here are portions of Kazan's notes in preparation for rehearsals of Arthur Miller's *Death of a Salesman* which opened in New York on February 10, 1949. These excerpts represent only a small part of the full notebook and apply mainly to the central character, to analysis of theme, and to a basic directorial approach. Following these entries, printed on facing pages, is a portion of the actual playscript containing Mr. Kazan's annotations for part of Act II, the interview between Willy Loman and Bernard.

from NOTEBOOK MADE IN PREPARATION FOR DIRECTING DEATH OF A SALESMAN

Basic: The play is about Willy Loman.

Basic Style: It is a tragedy, in a classic style, with the drive of an inner inevitability that springs from a single fatal flaw. Willy is a *good* man. He has worth. But he is a Salesman with a Salesman's Philosophy. Therefore he dooms himself.

Basic: This is a story of love—the end of a tragic love between Willy and his son Biff.

Basic: He built his life on his son—but he taught his son wrong. The result: the son crashes and he with him.

Basic: The whole play is about *love*—Love and Competition. The Boy loves him. The only way Willy can give him anything back is thru the $20,000.

Basic: What the audience should feel at the end of this performance is only one thing: Pity, Compassion and Terror for Willy. Every dramatic value should serve this end. This Willy is a fine, tender, capable, potentially useful human. He is just socially mistaught. Society, our present society, is the "heavy"—its current philosophy.

NOTES ON WILLY LOMAN

1). Willy is one vast contradiction, and this contradiction is his downfall. He is a nicer guy than Charley. He is so nice, as someone said once, he's got to end up poor. This makes Charley untroubled and a success, and Willy contradictory, neurotic, full of love and longing, need for admiration and affection, full of a sense of worth-lessness and inadequacy and dislocation *and a failure.*

2) Anxiety, the pressing unrelieved sense of worthlessness and insufficiency for which the salesman compensates, hides and covers up with his line of blarney.

3) Why doesn't he take the job Charley keeps throwing at him? He's got to be employed by a big-shot firm. He can't admit of the humiliation of working for someone who lives next door, and who started just as he did. Everything must be the biggest and the best, and I mean the biggest and the best in terms of beating the other guy.

4) He is torn between an absolute need to believe he is "*vital* in New England" and an absolute knowledge that he is not.

5) His fatal error (this is an Inevitable Tragedy . . . *our* Greek tragedy) is that he built his life and his *sense of worth* on something completely false: the Opinion of Others. This is the error of our whole society. We build our sense of worth not within ourselves but thru our besting others and at the same time having their constant perfect approval. A boy, Biff, must be both pre-eminent and still adored, conquering all and still loved by all. An impossibility!

6) Consequently, he both hates and loves the same people and can neither really love nor really hate anyone. If they perfectly approve of him, they are great. If, on some issue they don't, they are his enemies. . . .

7) A "personality!" Willy has that magical thing with which some people are born. It makes them both pre-eminent, beating all others, and still liked.

Willy: Daydreams. A person "talks to himself," in this case has imaginary conversations with other people, because of some com-pulsive reason. Usually to defend himself, re-enact some scene to prove himself, to *attack* someone that he failed to defend himself against properly in the real world. The FICTION behind each of these imaginary conversations should be found.

Suicide is his only and last desperate means to success . . . also revenge on all people who demeaned his dignity. Suicide solves his problem in the way that he wants it solved. It is his way of proving himself to Biff too, living up to (as he imagines it) the boy's hero-worship of him.

Also the suicide is "an angle," it's the action of a "smart cookie." He's finally in control. It's his way of beating the world that beat him. . . .

Willy is not a retiring, quiet, timid, shrinking man. *N.B. His ideal is Pre-eminence.* His ideal is not to be a little guy. His ideal is to rule the world by selling it. The man himself was violent, tough, loud, fearless (he could handle a meddling cop). He was not a "little man" in the Milquetoast sense. He was explosive. He could raise the roof. Look what he teaches the kids! Self-reliance, Enterprise, Conquest, Beat your neighbor . . . Adventure, Win, Win, Win by your personality, i.e., your natural jungle strength, etc.

And at the end, he wins, *at all costs.* He would and does sacrifice everything to his *ideal.* He really believes it as does all our middle class, and he lives by it.

Willy is haughty, proud — he is dominated by the dream of aggression, competition, pre-eminence. *To end up on top* is a proud thing — even if it seems to be a losing fight with only subjective values.

CHARACTERS IN THE PAST

Ben, *Altogether is in the Past,* is entirely subjective as Willie sees him: the embodiment of Success, Authority, Daring, Manliness, Enterprise, Fearlessness, Self-sufficiency. He is romanticized in Willy's memory and by Willy's necessity — into a God-like figure. He takes his success for granted. He laughs over it, keeps chuckling. Willy talks frantically, a compulsive ardor — then suddenly when Ben touches his arm, he stops, in the middle of a sentence as it were, and then, in due time, Ben speaks his mind in quietness.

Ben (by Willy's romanticized and necessary motive) keeps his own counsel — his mind is always somewhere else on Big things, etc. Ben is amused about his success — Willy is impressed. fierce! frantic, compulsive.

Biff in the Past, is again romanticized in Willy's imagination. Confident, easy, gorgeous, all the kids fawning on him, trying to steal the spotlight from him and no one succeeding. Again, like Ben, self-absorbed with Big things, secret Big things, all in his own mind, contained. Again, when he speaks others are silent. Biff in the past is a stylized figure. Not *as he was* but as Willie sees him retrospectively.

None of these dream figures are actually in the past! They are as much in the present. They are as Willy *needs* to think of them for his own reasons of personal dignity, self-esteem, etc., etc.

Charlie in the past is convenient too for the necessities of Willy's psychology. It's the way he *likes* to think of Charlie, needs to think of

Charlie. Not in the past, necessarily, but as much in the present—
Just Charlie! So Charlie in the past is an embodiment, a comic
embodiment, of all the careless, ambitionless . . . .

Linda in the past is a figure fashioned out of Willy's guilt. Hard
working, sweet, always true, admiring. "I shouldn't cheat on a
woman like that!" Dumb, slaving, loyal, tender, innocent. Patient
with him. Always available for sympathy or even pity.

Actually, i.e., in life, she is much tougher. She has consciously
made her peace with her fate. She has chosen Willy! To hell with
everyone else. She is terrifyingly tough. Why? She senses Willy is in
danger. And she just can't have him hurt.

THEME

Competition is the central fact of our civilization. Willy is compet-
ing with Charlie not only directly but through his sons. He both
admires Bernard and resents hell out of him. Even *hates* him. After
he meets Bernard in Act 2 he goes off talking to himself, asking:
what happened to my boys?

The Problem of Modern Man. The problem is: modern man is *Always
Anxious!* Because he is between two opposite fatal pulls: to best his
neighbor, his brother vs. to be loved by his brother. These are
mutually exclusive, an impossible contradiction. Inevitably it will
end disastrously.

Again this play is about Love and Competition—the two opposing
forces, good and bad, creative and malignant in one Society. Willy
Loman's tragedy is that he is pulled to pieces by these two opposites.

Willy's competitiveness was his *own* which he projects and extends
and tries to achieve thru his son Biff. Thus he ruins Biff's life by
pledging him to an ideal that does not work. Willy should have let
Biff become what he was!!

The Suicide is the last logical piece of competition—his only way of
combining the two opposite principles. He thinks that he fades out at
a moment of love and wins more of Biff's love and at the same time
bests them all through giving Biff $20,000.

Willy built his son's life to lay at rest his own anxiety (success-
anxiety) about himself. He used his son to lay at rest his own
fears . . . and it is this "bad" and selfish need of Willy's that Biff
"betrayed." Willy is not and never is aware of this—he would be left
with nothing if he faced reality (as Biff suggests at the end of the
play).

DIRECTING

It is essential to stick, in your emotional feeling through the play to Willy. Find Willy in you . . . it is the portrait of the soul of a man, at the crash-end of a tragic love for his son Biff, one which leads up (in terms of inner emotional events) to his suicide.

In this play, all movement must come from *Character* impulse. No crosses, etc., with *Energy Substituted for Emotion.* General energy instead of particular emotion. This play has a line which is all down the inside of Willy's spine . . . . this man goes crazy—right before your eyes—and commits suicide and Miller shows you the logic behind this series of acts.

This play takes place in an Arena of people watching the events, sometimes internal and invisible, other times external and visible and sometimes *both.* The world is the world of Willy and the way he sees it. In the end it is completely in his world and his eyes get more and more *glazey* as he talks to the people who exist only within his own mind. The people watching have an emotional relation to Willy, a reaching out to him. But by the end of the play, there is no one there for him to reach out to and he is living entirely within himself. The people watching this spectacle are horrified. The *man* simply isn't with them any more.

Direction and Style: This play is essentially about Willy. Biff's importance is only as the love-object which "failed." But the play describes the *Process*—dramatizes the *Process in Willy's mind.* In doing this all the elements of theatre Magic are *necessary.* Tricks—music—disappearances. That's why the coming down out of the beds is right.

Style: There are no flashbacks!

The only laws of these scenes are the laws of Willy's own mind. And all the figures in Willy's mind are distorted by Willy's *hopes, wishes, desires.* (All these figures are different in Willy's imagination than they are in life. Charley more foolish.)

What they are: DAYDREAMS. And daydreams are an action. What Willy is doing in these daydreams is justifying himself. He knows he's failed and he's living his life over in these daydreams in order to justify himself.

Style: must be an activization in physical equivalents of the events of Willy's mind for the last 24 hours of his life. So it is *all* unrealistic, since it all happens *Willy's way*—as Willy feels it, experiences it.

N.B. The last act of Willy's life is a perfect example—it is a piece of action—not an emotion—it is a *deed,* not a feeling. So all through translate his "suffering consciousness" into *acts.*

Directing: Willy's Actions: It seems to be hard to find actions for Willy. What is a man who is anxious, worried, and swimming in guilt, who is frustrated in his search for pre-eminence, etc. *Doing?* He is defending himself from imagined accusations and insults. He is justifying himself for sins real and imagined. ("I'll make it up to you.") He is excusing himself for things he did and couldn't help. He is overwhelmed by sudden feelings of helplessness and seeking refuge in the sure and unmerited security of his wife. Then he is asserting himself by insulting others. Mocking others, berating others, condemning others and accusing others—all defense through attack! Then suddenly aware of this—"building" himself by generously excusing people who have treated him badly (Biff)— showing off how *big* and generous he is! He is all in all so fragile of self-confidence that he can't stand contradiction on anything—considering it or fearing it a lessening of his position or of his pre-eminence.

Directing: Finding Willy's Actions: Another thing he does is once he gets with someone he lies ("I'll be right up") to get off by himself and "think"—for, finally, the only world where he'll be beyond challenge is in a world of his own making. He feels safest alone.

Directing: This play has to be directed with COMPASSION, which simply means with a quick and intense realization of the PAIN of each of the characters . . . and the real meaning of the "SPINE," which means the living and emotional meaning of the "SPINE." . . .

FROM ELIA KAZAN'S NOTEBOOK, ENTRY DATED DEC. 17, [1948]

This play is a dramatization of the process in the mind of Willy—an interior crisis that takes about twenty-four hours and ends in a suicide. The play dwells within the interior process. All its values and meanings are Willy's. It is time, therefore, to go thru the play with Willy—his processes: his compulsions, defenses, assertions—and get clear the action of this play in the locale where it happens: Willy's consciousness.

Then go thru and match stage activities for the actors, *behavior,* the physicalizations of mental and ideal events, the props, the physical equivalents, the stunts, the active dramatizations of the scene — *all the stage life* which will be the "play" of the *Inner Arena,* the externalizations of the inner life — everything that will make this hidden story lie before our eyes on a stage.

Light rises, on the Right side of the stage, on small table in the reception room of Charlie's office. BERNARD, *now mature, sits whistling to himself. A pair of tennis rackets on the floor beside him and an overnight bag. He is a quiet, earnest, but self-assured young man.* [1] WILLY'S *voice is coming from Right, Upstage now.* [2]*Hearing, he lowers his feet off the table and listens towards upstage. Now* JENNY *comes in, his father's secretary.*

JENNY *(Distressed)*: Say Bernard will you go in the hall and . . . .

BERNARD: What *is* that noise? Who is it?

JENNY: Mr. Loman. He just got off the elevator . . . .

BERNARD *(Gets up)*: Who's he arguing with?

[3] (WILLY *is no longer heard.*)

JENNY: Nobody. There's nobody with him. I can't deal with him any more, and your father gets all upset every time he comes. I've got a lot of typing to do and your father's waiting to sign it. Will you see him?

[4] (WILLY *enters.*)

WILLY: Right under the goal post, boy — *(Sees* JENNY, *gathering his wits.*)

[5] Jenny . . . Jenny . . . good to see you. How're you? Workin? . . . or still honest?

JENNY *(Nervously)*: Fine . . . how've you been feeling?

WILLY: Not much any more, Jenny. Ha, Ha! [6]

1. Willy as he seems to the "outside world!"
2. Bernard is revealed listening to the commotion in the hall. Bernard — a Big Man — looks at his watch all thru. At this moment he is polishing his glasses. Dressed smoothly.
3. A moment of silence plus traffic sounds.
4. Bernard and Willy haven't seen each other for years. Last time their relationship completely different. Both therefor soon begin wondering — what happened — examine each other, etc., etc., etc.

Both men loved Biff. Bernard — behind all his mask can still be touched. He tries to help — has always been *curious,* too, as to what happened to the Boy he loved — and has also had some unanswered questions to ask — if Willy wants to talk "candidly."

Willy, too, is examining something with a *naive* intensity — but something that is vital to him — touches on something that is killing him with guilt.

5. The way a Salesman is supposed to behave with a girl secretary.
6. Willy picks up the tennis rackets.

BERNARD: Hello, Uncle Willy.[7,8]

WILLY (*Almost shocked*): [9] Bernard! Well look who's here!

(*Comes quickly, guiltily to* BERNARD *and warmly shakes his hand.*)

BERNARD: [10] How are you? Glad to see you.

WILLY: What are *you* doing here?

BERNARD: Oh, just stopped by to see Pop; get off my feet until my train leaves. I'm going to Washington[11] in a few minutes.

WILLY: Is he in?

BERNARD: Yes, he's in his office with the accountant. Sit down.

(*They sit*)[12]

WILLY: What're you going to do in Washington?

BERNARD: Oh, just a case I've got there, Willy.

WILLY: That so![13]

(*Noticing the rackets*)

You going to play tennis there?[14]

BERNARD: I'm staying with a friend who's got a court.

WILLY (*Wonderously*): Don't say.[15] His own tennis court. Must be fine[15] people, I bet.

BERNARD: They are, very nice.[16] Dad tells me Biff's in town.[17]

WILLY[18] (*Big smile*): Yeah, Biff's in. Working on a very big deal, Bernard.

BERNARD: [19] What's Biff doing?[20,21]

WILLY: Well, he's been doing very big things in the West. But he decided to

7. He puts them down guiltily.
8. *Inspect* each other.
9. *Willy recovers!*

Willy wouldn't like to be seen by Bernard that way.

Willy has a *whole drama* in his head and in his past with Bernard—he's insulted him 47,000 times behind his back, etc.—and the Boy is a Success! How? Why?

10. *Bernard:* Put him at his ease. A simple social putting someone at his ease; he is light, swift, and social.

11. A gesture similar to Ben's with the watch.

12. *Willy:* Figure out what happened!!??? Bernard is to Willy a mystery, an affront, an insult, a living humiliation.

Bernard: Put him at his ease, help him in a nice simple way. Bernard is proud to be known as the modest fellow.

Bernard offers him a cigarette case. Willy takes it, examines it with awe, hands it back. Bernard opens it, offers cigarette, he shakes his head.

13. Mystery.

14. How did the little schmuck do it?

15. *Willy* invests all these things (a private court) with great drama, mystery, and wonder.

16. *Bernard:* changes subject. Bernard always feels a little uncomfortable squirming under Willy's amazed admiration.

17. *Both* are now figuring out what happened.

Bernard keeps playing with his Phi Beta Kappa key, his glasses, his watch. They smoke, cigarette case, etc.

18. *Willy:* redemption, make it up.

19. *Bernard:* find facts. Bernard knows Willy is lying.

establish himself here. Very big. We're having dinner.[22] Did I hear your wife had a boy?[23]

BERNARD: That's right. Our second.[24]

WILLY: Two boys! — what do you know?

BERNARD: What kind of a deal has Biff got?

WILLY: Well, Bill Oliver — a very big sporting goods man — he wants Biff very badly. Called him in from the West. Long-distance, carte blanche, special deliveries. [25] Your friends have their own private tennis court.

[26] BERNARD: [27] You still with the old firm, Willy?

WILLY: [28] I'm ... I'm overjoyed to see how you made the grade, Bernard — overjoyed. It's an encouraging thing to see a young man, really ... really ... looks very good for Biff ... Very ...[28]

[29]*(He breaks off. Then ...)*
Bernard...[30]

(He is so full of emotion, he breaks off again.)
BERNARD: [31] What is it, Willy?

(Pause)

WILLY *(Small and alone)*: [32] What .... What's the secret?

BERNARD: [33] What secret?

WILLY *(With an embarrassed smile)*: [34] How ... how did you ... ? ... why didn't he ever catch on?

BERNARD: [35] I wouldn't know that, Willy.

WILLY *(Quietly, confidentially, desperately)*: [36] You were his friend, his boyhood friend — There's something I don't understand about it. His life ended after that Ebbets Field game. From the age of seventeen nothing good ever happened to him.

BERNARD: He never trained himself for anything.

Now he begins to wonder the source of it.

20. They are *not talking to each other*. They are *examining each other*. No particular cues — as if speeches are entirely unrelated.

21. What is he *really* doing?

22. Change subject.

23. Willy is *not* a grandfather. He wants it desperately.

24. Offers cigarette here.

25. Change subject.

26. Bernard takes cue — goes behind Willy to get matches, etc.

27. Change subject.

28. *Willy* is bleeding inside. Suddenly can't stand it. Bernard conceals that he thinks Willy is a pathetic fake.

Bernard bows his head and shields his eyes as if he is embarrassed for Willy.

29. *Willy* tries to speak of it. *Can't*. About to cry. Can't speak! Can't speak!

30. *Willy* tenses in his chair and turns out.

31. *Bernard:* to help — he's full of pity.

32. *Willy:* forcing it out.

N.B. He thinks it's some secret. Some magic formula of success! "Sentences that sell," some advice he has failed to give.

33. *Bernard:* help. Gently. Bernard really knows. He *can't look at* Willy, sits on desk with head bowed.

34. *Willy:* just stands there with head bowed ... he can't look at Bernard and ask what he's asking.

35. *Bernard:* avoid. You can't tell a man like Willy the truth ... it would be too cruel.

36. *Willy:* PLEAD. Suddenly direct ... craving to be liberated from his guilt. "I beg you free me from this hell of my guilt." Keep up the "What is it?"

WILLY: But he did, he did. After high school he took so many correspondence courses. Radio, mechanics, television. God knows what, and never made the slightest mark.

BERNARD: [37] Willy, you want to talk candidly? [38]

WILLY: [39] I regard you as a very brilliant man, Bernard. I value your advice.

BERNARD: [40] Oh, the hell with advice, Willy. I couldn't advise you. [41] There's just one thing I've always wanted to ask you. When he was supposed to graduate, and the math teacher flunked him . . .

WILLY: [42] Oh, that son-of-a-bitch ruined his life.

BERNARD: [43] Yeah, but Willy, all he had to do was to go to summer school and make up that subject.

WILLY: [44] That's right, that's right . . .

BERNARD: [45] Did you tell him not to go to summer school?

WILLY: [46] No! I begged him to go. I ordered him to go!

BERNARD: [47] Then why wouldn't he go?

WILLY: Why? [48] Why! Bernard, that question has been trailing me like a ghost for the last fifteen years. [49] He flunked the subject, and laid down and died like a hammer hit him!

BERNARD: [50] Take it easy, Kid. . . .

WILLY: [51] Let me talk to you, I got nobody to talk to. Bernard . . . Bernard, was it my fault? Y'see? — it keeps going around in my mind, maybe I did something to him. I got nothing to give him.

BERNARD: [52] Don't take it so hard. . . .

WILLY: [53] Why did he lay down? [54] What is the story there? — you were his friend.

BERNARD: [55] Willy . . . I remember, it

37. *Bernard:* He's always been curious to find out himself.

38. *Bernard* walks to window to decide whether or not to tell Willy.

39. *Willy:* Pain!!!

40. *Bernard:* still looking out window.

41. *Bernard:* Proceeding, he knows it will hurt. Trying to do what is necessary — a tough gentleman.

42. *Willy:* pop off — defend by attack. But even this far away from his guilt, as Bernard approaches it from a distance as it were, it already is intolerable for Willy. He can't stand it and he defends, as usual, by attack.

43. *Bernard:* Cutting right thru — "don't defend yourself! Please!"

44. *Willy:* beginning to rear defensively.

45. *Bernard:* Point Willy to the truth. So Willy can really look at it.

46. *Willy:* *defending himself.* Guilt!

47. *Bernard* pinning him to it.

48. *Willy:* disliking him.

49. *Willy:* blames Biff to clear himself. Guilt!! — off again like a rocket.

50. *Bernard:* wishes he were out of it.

51. *Willy:* insisting. Demanding.

52. *Bernard:* trying to get out of it. Starts to get away — the watch.

53. *Willy:* insisting. Forces Bernard to speak. Very violent, very dangerous, wild-eyed. He wants to know yet can't face it!! Willy is CRAZY!!!

54. An accusing crazy violent gesture.

55. *Bernard:* telling the truth — there's no way out of it now. laying it on the table — lawyer-like.

was June ... and our grades came out. And he'd flunked math.

WILLY: That son-of-a-bitch ....

BERNARD: No, it wasn't right then. Biff just got very angry, I remember, and he was ready to enroll in summer school.

WILLY: He was?

BERNARD: He wasn't beaten by it at all. But then ...

(Slight pause)

Willy, he disappeared from the block for almost a month. And I got the idea that he'd gone up to New England to see you. Did he have a talk with you then?

(WILLY *stares in silence*) Willy?

WILLY (*Now with the strong edge of resentment against Bernard*): [56] Yeah, he came to Boston. What about it?

BERNARD: [57] Well, just that when he came back ... [58] I'll never forget this ... it always mystified me. Because I'd thought so well of Biff, even though he'd always taken advantage of me. [59] I loved him, Willy, y'know? And he came back after that month and took his sneakers — remember those sneakers with "University of Virginia" printed on them? He was so proud of those, wore them every day. And he took them down to the cellar, and burned them up in the furnace. We started to fight ... punching each other down the cellar ... and crying right through it.

(Slight pause)

I've often thought of how strange it was that I knew he'd given up his life. ... What happened in Boston,[60] Willy?

(WILLY *looks at him as at an intruder.*)

[61] I just bring it up because you asked me.

56. *Willy:* to warn Bernard. Willy very defensive.
57. *Bernard:* forcing himself to once and for all get the whole damned truth out and finish it. He walks around behind through this speech.
58. Proof he is really determined to keep it on the table.
59. Bernard loved Biff. He is almost crying.

60. Not asking it, just saying it.
61. *Bernard:* sees the attack coming — "Don't blame me. You made me tell."

WILLY (*Quite angrily*): [62] Nothing ... what do you mean, "what happened?" What's that got to do with anything?

BERNARD (*Tries to laugh, touches Willy's knee*): [63] Well, don't get sore.

WILLY: [64] What are you trying to do, blame it on me? If a boy lays down is it my fault?

BERNARD (*To calm him*): [65] Now, Willy, don't get ...

WILLY: [66] Well don't ... don't talk to me that way! What does that mean— "What happened?"

(CHARLIE *enters, in vest.*)

CHARLEY: [67] Hey, you're going to miss that train.

62. *Willy:* Attack Bernard—only way out—Mad!!

63. *Bernard:* kid him out of it —a very poor attempt. Miserable. Can't look at him.

64. *Willy:* attack, almost physically.

65. *Bernard:* to calm him. He's beginning to get scared and he certainly regrets the whole thing.

66. *Willy:* same angry challenge. He literally would be fighting him in a moment.

67. *Charley:* has heard, comes in to save the situation.

Jean-Louis Barrault

After several triumphs at the Comédie Française, including the great role of Rodrigue in *Le Cid,* Barrault left that most famous French theatrical institution, opened his own theatre, and formed his own company of actors. His greatest success was the title role in Gide's new translation of *Hamlet.* His direction of Molière, Racine, Corneille, Shakespeare, and other classics, as well as of Claudel and many modern playwrights, his work in films, and guest appearances all over the world have made Barrault's voice one of of the most considerable in his profession today.

Perhaps most pervasive has been his influence as a sensitive yet thoroughly practical force in modern theatre at large in methods of direction, in new ideas for settings, in methods of vocal technique, in the importance of mime, and in general appreciation of literature and music. In these notes he speaks of general matters but, as usual, brings abstractions to life with specific details of production work.

✄ *WITHIN THE EVENT*

> *The public thinks that it chooses its authors; but no. It is the artist who chooses his public. And one is always worthy of the other.*
>
> ANDRÉ GIDE

As I draw nearer to the present time, my reflections, suggested to me by my past most vivid memories, become rarer and rarer and less and less sure.

We cannot judge of an event while living inside it. A certain perspective is necessary if we want to see it properly.

For three seasons we have gone on, that's all.

What we must safeguard above all is the Spirit. I can't say that too often.

It is quite possible that one day in the not too distant future we shall have to draw in a little for economic reasons. Perhaps we shall have to give our performances in a workshop or a studio, or even be a "number" between two films in a cinema. But if we have kept our Spirit, our Ideal intact, if we have stayed faithful to what we love, we shall not have failed.

Perhaps the opposite will happen and one fine day our enterprise will assume vast proportions. On that day more than ever: watch out for the Spirit!

Yes, either development is possible. I have absolutely no idea how the Company will evolve. All I know is that it exists, and that I want to do all I can to ensure it a long life. The external form doesn't really matter, so long, I repeat, as it remains true to itself. There again my master, Charles Dullin, sets an example. Whatever happens to him on the material plane of life, with regard to his art he preserves a novice's freshness of spirit. "One damned thing after another" can befall him, he remains passionately absorbed in an arrangement for a Shakespeare play or a closer interpretation of Molière! What an example of constancy and permanent virginity!

It is possible, like Lugne Poë, to put a play on solely for its literary value and without going to great expense.

It is possible, like Pitoëff, to be sumptous in poverty and noble within a meagre frame.

It is possible, on the other hand (like Max Reinhart), to preserve simplicity and dignity in the midst of vast productions.

From Chapter III in *Reflections on the Theatre* by Jean-Louis Barrault, translated by Barbara Wall. Reprinted by permission of Barrie and Rockliff (London) and Editions Flammarion (Paris).

A lot or a little can be thrown into a production. The important thing is to be *honest* and in tune with the *frame* at one's disposal. . . .

There are a hundred ways of mounting a specific play, but only one way given a particular company and a particular frame.

So the problem should be formulated like this: given a particular company and frame, what is the *one proper* way of mounting a specific play?

Le Soulier de Satin, for example, when played within the frame of the Français and with the cast of the Comédie Française, demanded means other than those required, say, in a small theatre and with a company got together for the occasion; and different again from those required in the courtyard of the Sorbonne with the cast of the Théophilien dramatic society.

I am not sure that an author doesn't show different aspects of himself according to the frame and company serving him. The emblem of the theatre is the Kaleidoscope. . . .

Our activity constitutes a sort of five-point star.
> A. Classical authors.
> B. The Art of Gesture.
> C. The Art of Speech.
> D. Research.
> E. Modern authors.

A. CLASSICAL AUTHORS

The primary function of a classical repertory is to provide *nourishment.*

A good company must be able to interpret the classical theatre.

It is primarily with a view to improving ourselves that we play some of the classics.

The classics provide first and foremost a schooling in style. When we play the classics we have to abandon *naturalism* and yet remain *true* when operating within a particular *tone.* The problem is to find the *tone* and at the same time to remain *true.* The other day I was observing a newspaper-seller. He didn't have to be as it were *present* in his cries because he had found the correct *tone.* If you want to teach someone how to sell papers it is no good telling him to "think carefully about what you're saying." No, he must find the *right tone* and it follows that his cry will produce the *right sound.*

The right tone is the key to style.

There is a Molière tone, a Marivaux tone, a Corneille tone, a Racine tone, a Shakespeare tone, and so on.

And within Molière's plays, for example, there are still further variants of tone. The tone of Amphitryon is musical; the tone of Georges Dandin is realist poetical; the tone of Scapin is almost fishwife, and so on.

The classics, then, improve the style of a company.

A classic is further characterised by its quality of compactness, of *chargedness*. If we divide a picture by an Old Master, say Carpaccio, up into squares and study each square separately we see how loaded the detail is.

In the same way classical dialogue is loaded. Every word is good weight.

The classic demands that we should find the weight of every gesture, every intonation, that we should learn to play *fully,* and capture, in our play, the same sort of chargedness that there is in the text. The interpretation of a part should be divided up into squares, like our picture by Carpaccio, and each section studied for detail; so that the slightest gesture, the most delicate inflection of the voice, may receive its due weight. Its *density.*

If trained like this, a company strikes home and makes a deep impression on the audience.

And side by side with this chargedness, the fountain-head of classical art, the classic teaches *economy.* It makes use of the minimum of means for the maximum yield, and this is because it lives in depth.

Economy is after all less a matter of taste than of concentratedness.

Taste is a tricky and dangerous affair and when discussing economy I prefer to discuss concentratedness rather than good taste.

Before a cat pounces he seems to withdraw into himself; he seems to assemble his resources within himself; dormant. This suggests to me economy in a palpable form.

I remember too the Japanese high-jumpers at the Olympic Games who cleared six and a half feet. Before running almost mechanically towards the bar they too seemed to indulge in a minute's assembling of themselves. They seemed to be lost within themselves. And their leap was all the higher. They skimmed the bar with the maximum of *economy.*

So the classic resists the ravages of Time because of its rightness of tone, its chargedness, its depth and its economy. Because it has gone right to the centre of things, touched the axis. The centre or axis alone is permanent.

The classic starts out from the particular and attains the general.

"Art," says Gide, "lies in painting a particular object with such power that the generality upon which it depends may be grasped."

This is how he makes his own characters. He reveals their general character. He creates the *Function*. The function represents a sort of human type from which depends an infinity of particular people — just as the infinity of points on a circumference depends from one centre.

An actor, by studying the classics, can discover the human type he belongs to, and in that way he can the better serve the characters he is preparing to interpret.

A company versed in the classics is thus easier to cast; and the art of using a company well consists above all in casting it well. If badly cast, a company of good actors can give the appearance of being a bad company. Properly cast, on the other hand, it will give astonishing results. I have known that happen.

Finally, the classical repertory, in its capacity as a crystallised re-creation of mankind, brings us considerable enrichment.

Alas, I am well aware that we do not profit by the experience of others; nevertheless if we knew Shakespeare, Racine and Molière by heart surely we would be the better and the wiser for it.

The poetic perception of Shakespeare, the exacerbated sensibility of Racine, the tragi-comic outlook of Molière — surely these teach us the lesson of things?

That is a summary of the nourishment we can draw from the classics.

Now in what way can a private company serve, in its turn, the classics?

A private company can be useful to the classics because it is a free company. It can look on a classic from an entirely free point of view.

Of course a classic should always be respected. But if it is loved it will automatically be respected. We always respect what we love. And for this very reason it will be respected in the light of love and not in accordance with a list of specifications. A private company can allow itself liberties that a subsidised theatre, custodian of the classical repertory, is denied.

So a private company can shake the classics about a bit at the risk, even, of making mistakes; and yet the shaking brings new life to a classic, spring-cleans it, rejuvenates it.

It also brings *curiosity* to bear on it.

So there can be a mutual exchange of ideas between a private company and a classic, to the benefit of both.

B AND C. THE ART OF GESTURE AND THE ART OF SPEECH

Simultaneously with studying the cream of the Past, the classical repertory, a company should study the art of the Present, and study it to its uttermost limits.

On the extreme left of the art of the theatre stands the art of gesture, or pure mime. On the extreme right stands the art of speech, or pure diction.

We have already given quite enough vent to our preoccupations with these two technical aspects of our art. So we will pass on.

D. RESEARCH

Treasure-seekers dig much and find little.   HERACLITUS

It might well be imagined that by this time every corner of the earth has been explored. No more white blanks on the map of the world.

And yet it appears that there are still some completely unknown regions round about the Orinoco. And that in spite of the march of science and the unconquerable courage and curiosity of some men. So why shouldn't it be the same in the world of the theatre which is after all as old as the earth?

This is the justification for research.

And another thing that justifies it is the fact that the theatre is the art of the Present and that the Present is always *new*.

The study of the classics is a foundation; the study of gesture and diction is a means; the study of the Present, of the ever-new Present, opens up new horizons.

However much a dramatic author may know about man and about the art of using him by voice and gesture, he cannot possibly — because he hasn't the time — drench himself as we do in voice and gesture technique. It follows that he may well overlook some of the resources at his disposal.

And in so far as we can bring light to bear on overlooked resources we can be of service to dramatic authors.

So it is in a "*clinical*" *spirit,* put at the service of modern dramatic authors, that we pursue our researches.

And what enables us to "work at" dramatic art by crooked paths is the fact that we have, as it were, pure material to work with. It is precisely because the means at our disposal are pure and proper to our art that we can allow our approaches to be *crooked*. This was what we were doing in 1935 when we took *As I Lay Dying* as "subject-pretext" for showing up the countless resources there are in the bodily expression of a man. And the same in 1937 when we tested some of our findings in the services of Cervantes' extraordinary classic, *Numantia*.

The same with Knut Hamsun's *Hunger* in 1939.

And our researches were useful to us in 1943, when we produced Claudel's *Soulier de Satin*. Our researches were valuable to some authors.

Valuable when, with André Gide, we attempted the impossible with Kafka's *Trial;* and more recently still with Camus in *L'État de Siège*.

Perhaps for eight authors out of ten who are uninterested in our findings, there are two who will benefit from them. If so, then our ambition in this field is justified.

But I should confess to a personal joy in these researches, too, over and above the joy of perhaps being of use to living authors.

I must confess that I seized upon the plays mentioned above largely so as to see the kind of performance that I have always wanted to see realised on the stage. There is a certain vision of dramatic art that I would like to see as a spectator. As it is a vision that few authors have, I had to try to tackle the job myself in order to give myself the vision I wanted.

So it is to satisfy the spectator in me that I put on certain "shows." And there my ideology could stop.

I am encouraged to press forward along these paths because I was certainly not the only spectator of my kind. (There are many people who have happy memories of *Numantia, Hunger* and *The Trial*.)

But first and foremost, by continuing along these lines, there was a good chance of being useful to the living authors I ought to serve and want to serve.

E. MODERN AUTHORS

Our essential function should be to serve modern authors.

As this section is setting out the very reasons for our existence, it will be brief.

May every author know that we have a place for him. May our state of mind seek to be as broad as possible, as eclectic as possible. We do not seek to be an author's servant, but his server. Salacrou, Gide, Camus and Claudel have already given us excellent opportunities for serving them. No theatre can exist without the authors who "feed" it.

It was Dumas, Hugo, C. Delavigne, Balzac who made the Porte Saint-Martin Theatre.

Capus, Labiche, Meilhac and Halévy, R. de Flers made the Variétés.

Coming nearer to our time, Jouvet knows very well what he owes to Giraudoux; Dullin knows what he owes to Jules Romains and Salacrou.

Nearer still, Barsacq knows what he owes to Anouilh.

As for myself I know what I owe to Salacrou and above all to Claudel. And how many others!

Obviously a theatre can bring much to an author; but that is secondary.

The first "bringing," the one that sets everything going, is the author's.

The author is the CREATOR.

Alongside the authors and the Company, we ourselves dream of forming an intellectual circle round our Company, one that could give us advice if necessary.

Our happiness would be complete if we could bring such a circle into being. A circle, or group, for human communication.

To have ideals in common, to meet together, discuss, sometimes understand each other, give each other the benefit of our knowledge — surely there can be no nobler activity in life.

Christian Bérard, alas, would have been the very spirit of this circle, the symbol of everything I mean by it. . . .

To sum up: from the classics we seek nourishment.

Through the study of gesture and speech we hope to perfect our technique.

By periodic excursions into the unknown we hope to enrich ourselves.

And all *in the service of modern authors.*

That is, it seems to us, our function.

So that is our activity. . . .

Bertolt Brecht

This essay was probably written after Brecht's visit to Moscow in 1935 when he saw a performance by the Chinese actor, Mei Lan-fang, and his company. It is an extraordinarily important expression of some of Brecht's fundamental concerns relating his own political beliefs to practical theory for the theatre. Throughout his career, Brecht was interested in forms of oriental drama; it is important that in this essay, which contains his first use of the term *"Verfremdungseffekt"* ("Alienation effect"), his point of departure and inspiration is the technique of Chinese acting. Also of interest are Brecht's comments on Stanislavski's "Method" which he considered inadequate and incapable of eliciting the correct acting techniques for his own concept of "epic" theatre.

✒ ALIENATION EFFECTS IN CHINESE ACTING

The following is intended to refer briefly to the use of the alienation effect in traditional Chinese acting. This method was most recently used in Germany for plays of a non-aristotelian (not dependent on empathy) type as part of the attempts[1] being made to evolve an epic theatre. The efforts in question were directed to playing in such a way that the audience was hindered from simply identifying itself with the characters in the play. Acceptance or rejection of their actions and utterances was meant to take place on a conscious plane, instead of, as hitherto, in the audience's subconscious.

This effort to make the incidents represented appear strange to the public can be seen in a primitive form in the theatrical and pictorial displays at the old popular fairs. The way the clowns speak and the way the panoramas are painted both embody an act of alienation. The method of painting used to reproduce the picture of "Charles the Bold's flight after the Battle of Murten," as shown at many German fairs, is certainly mediocre; yet the act of alienation which is achieved here (not by the original) is in no wise due to the mediocrity of the copyist. The fleeing commander, his horse, his retinue and the landscape are all quite consciously painted in such a

---

[1] Brecht uses the word "Versuche."

way as to create the impression of an abnormal event, an astonishing disaster. In spite of his inadequacy the painter succeeds brilliantly in bringing out the unexpected. Amazement guides his brush.

Traditional Chinese acting also knows the alienation effect, and applies it most subtly. It is well known that the Chinese theatre uses a lot of symbols. Thus a general will carry little pennants on his shoulder, corresponding to the number of regiments under his command. Poverty is shown by patching the silken costumes with irregular shapes of different colours, likewise silken, to indicate that they have been mended. Characters are distinguished by particular masks, i.e. simply by painting. Certain gestures of the two hands signify the forcible opening of a door, etc. The stage itself remains the same, but articles of furniture are carried in during the action. All this has long been known, and cannot very well be exported.

It is not all that simple to break with the habit of assimilating a work of art as a whole. But this has to be done if just one of a large number of effects is to be singled out and studied. The alienation effect is achieved in the Chinese theatre in the following way.

Above all, the Chinese artist never acts as if there were a fourth wall besides the three surrounding him. He expresses his awareness of being watched. This immediately removes one of the European stage's characteristic illusions. The audience can no longer have the illusion of being the unseen spectator at an event which is really taking place. A whole elaborate European stage technique, which helps to conceal the fact that the scenes are so arranged that the audience can view them in the easiest way, is thereby made unnecessary. The actors openly choose those positions which will best show them off to the audience, just as if they were *acrobats*. A further means is that the artist observes himself. Thus if he is representing a cloud, perhaps, showing its unexpected appearance, its soft and strong growth, its rapid yet gradual transformation, he will occasionally look at the audience as if to say: isn't it just like that? At the same time he also observes his own arms and legs, adducing them, testing them and perhaps finally approving them. An obvious glance at the floor, so as to judge the space available to him for his act, does not strike him as liable to break the illusion. In this way the artist separates mime (showing observation) from gesture (showing a cloud), but without detracting from the latter, since the body's attitude is reflected in the face and is wholly responsible for its expression. At one moment the expression is of well-managed restraint; at another, of utter triumph. The artist has been using his countenance as a blank sheet, to be inscribed by the gest of the body.

The artist's object is to appear strange and even surprising to the audience. He achieves this by looking strangely at himself and his work. As a result everything put forward by him has a touch of the amazing. Everyday things are thereby raised above the level of the obvious and automatic. A young woman, a fisherman's wife, is shown paddling a boat. She stands steering a non-existent boat with a paddle that barely reaches to her knees. Now the current is swifter, and she is finding it harder to keep her balance; now she is in a pool and paddling more easily. Right: that is how one manages a boat. But this journey in the boat is apparently historic, celebrated in many songs, an exceptional journey about which everybody knows. Each of this famous girl's movements has probably been recorded in pictures; each bend in the river was a well-known adventure story, it is even known which particular bend it was. This feeling on the audience's part is induced by the artist's attitude; it is this that makes the journey famous. The scene reminded us of the march to Budejovice in Piscator's production of *The Good Soldier Schweik*. Schweik's three-day-and-night march to a front which he oddly enough never gets to was seen from a completely historic point of view, as no less noteworthy a phenomenon than, for instance, Napoleon's Russian expedition of 1812. The performer's self-observation, an artful and artistic act of self-alienation, stopped the spectator from losing himself in the character completely, i.e. to the point of giving up his own identity, and lent a splendid remoteness to the events. Yet the spectator's empathy was not entirely rejected. The audience identifies itself with the actor as being an observer, and accordingly develops his attitude of observing or looking on.

The Chinese artist's performance often strikes the Western actor as cold. That does not mean that the Chinese theatre rejects all representation of feelings. The performer portrays incidents of utmost passion, but without his delivery becoming heated. At those points where the character portrayed is deeply excited the performer takes a lock of hair between his lips and chews it. But this is like a ritual, there is nothing eruptive about it. It is quite clearly somebody else's repetition of the incident: a representation, even though an artistic one. The performer shows that this man is not in control of himself, and he points to the outward signs. And so lack of control is decorously expressed, or if not decorously at any rate decorously for the stage. Among all the possible signs certain particular ones are picked out, with careful and visible consideration. Anger is naturally different from sulkiness, hatred from distaste, love from liking; but the corresponding fluctuations of feeling are portrayed economically. The coldness comes from the actor's holding himself remote from the character portrayed, along the lines described. He is careful not to make its sensations into those of the spectator. Nobody gets raped by the individual he portrays; this individual is not the spectator himself but his neighbour.

The Western actor does all he can to bring his spectator into the closest proximity to the events and the character he has to portray. To this end he persuades him to identify himself with him (the actor) and uses every energy to convert himself as completely as possible into a different type, that of the character in question. If this complete conversion succeeds then his art has been more or less expended. Once he has become the bank-clerk, doctor or general concerned he will need no more art than any of these people need "in real life."

This complete conversion operation is extremely exhausting. Stanislavsky puts forward a series of means — a complete system — by which what he calls "creative mood" can repeatedly be manufactured afresh at every performance. For the actor cannot usually manage to feel for very long on end that he really is the other person; he soon gets exhausted and begins just to copy various superficialities of the other person's speech and hearing, whereupon the effect on the public drops off alarmingly. This is certainly due to the fact that the other person has been created by an "intuitive" and accordingly murky process which takes place in the subconscious. The subconscious is not at all responsive to guidance; it has as it were a bad memory.

These problems are unknown to the Chinese performer, for he rejects complete conversion. He limits himself from the start to simply quoting the character played. But with what art he does this! He only needs a minimum of illusion. What he has to show is worth seeing even for a man in his right mind. What Western actor of the old sort (apart from one or two comedians) could demonstrate the elements of his art like the Chinese actor Mei Lan-fang, without special lighting and wearing a dinner jacket in an ordinary room full of specialists? It would be like the magician at a fair giving away his tricks, so that nobody ever wanted to see the act again. He would just be showing how to disguise oneself; the hypnotism would vanish and all that would be left would be a few pounds of ill-blended imitation, a quickly-mixed product for selling in the dark to hurried customers. Of course no Western actor would stage such a demonstration. What about the sanctity of Art? The mysteries of metamorphosis? To the Westerner what matters is that his actions should be unconscious; otherwise they would be degraded. By comparison with Asiatic acting our own art still seems hopelessly parsonical. None the less it is becoming increasingly difficult for our actors to bring off the mystery of complete conversion; their subconscious's memory is getting weaker and weaker, and it is almost impossible to extract the truth from the uncensored intuitions of any member of our class society even when the man is a genius.

For the actor it is difficult and taxing to conjure up particular inner moods or emotions night after night; it is simpler to exhibit the outer signs which accompany these emotions and identify them. In this case, however, there is not the same automatic transfer of emotions to the spectator, the same emotional infection. The alienation effect intervenes, not in the form of absence of emotion, but in the form of emotions which need not correspond to those of the character portrayed. On seeing worry the spectator may feel a sensation of joy; on seeing anger, one of disgust. When we speak of exhibiting the outer signs of emotion we do not mean such an exhibition and such a choice of signs that the emotional transference does in fact take place because the actor has managed to infect himself with the emotions portrayed, by exhibiting the outer signs; thus, by letting his voice rise, holding his breath and tightening his neck muscles so that the blood shoots to his head, the actor can easily conjure up a rage. In such a case of course the effect does not occur. But it does occur if the actor at a particular point unexpectedly shows a completely white face, which he has produced mechanically by holding his face in his hands with some white make-up on them. If the actor at the same time displays an apparently composed character, then his terror at this point (as a result of this message, or that discovery) will give rise to an alienation effect. Acting like this is healthier and in our view less unworthy of a thinking being; it demands a considerable knowledge of humanity and worldly wisdom, and a keen eye for what is socially important. In this case too there is of course a creative process at work; but it is a higher one, because it is raised to the conscious level.

The alienation effect does not in any way demand an unnatural way of acting. It has nothing whatever to do with ordinary stylization. On the contrary, the achievement of an A-effect absolutely depends on lightness and naturalness of performance. But when the actor checks the truth of his performance (a necessary operation, which Stanislavsky is much concerned with in his system) he is not just thrown back on his "natural sensibilities," but can always be corrected by a comparison with reality (is that how an angry man really speaks? is that how an offended man sits down?) and so from outside, by other people. He acts in such a way that nearly every sentence could be followed by a verdict of the audience and practically every gesture is submitted for the public's approval.

The Chinese performer is in no trance. He can be interrupted at any moment. He won't have to "come round." After an interruption he will go on with his exposition from that point. We are not disturbing him at the "mystic moment of creation"; when he steps on to the stage before us the process of creation is already over. He does not mind if the setting is changed around him as he plays. Busy hands quite openly pass him what he needs for his performance. When Mei Lan-fang was playing a death scene a spectator sitting next me exclaimed with astonishment at one of his gestures. One or two people sitting in front of us turned around indignantly and sshhh'd. They behaved as if they were present at the real death of a real girl. Possibly their attitude would have been all right for a European production, but for a Chinese it was unspeakably ridiculous. In their case the A-effect had misfired.

It is not entirely easy to realize that the Chinese actor's A-effect is a transportable piece of technique: a conception that can be prised loose from the Chinese theatre. We see this theatre as uncommonly precious, its portrayal of human passions as schematized, its idea of society as rigid and wrong-headed; at first sight this superb art seems to offer nothing applicable to a realistic and revolutionary theatre. Against that, the motives and objects of the A-effect strike us as odd and suspicious.

When one sees the Chinese acting it is at first very hard to discount the feeling of estrangement which they produce in us as Europeans. One has to be able to imagine them achieving an A-effect among their Chinese spectators too. What is still harder is that one must accept the fact that when the Chinese performer conjures up an impression of mystery he seems uninterested in disclosing a mystery to us. He makes his own mystery from the mysteries of nature (especially human nature): he allows nobody to examine how he produces the natural phenomenon, nor does nature allow him to understand as he produces it. We have here the artistic counterpart of a primitive technology, a rudimentary science. The Chinese performer gets his A-effect by association with magic. "How it's done" remains hidden; knowledge is a matter of knowing the tricks and is in the hands of a few men who guard it jealously and profit from their secrets. And yet there is already an attempt here to interfere with the course of nature; the capacity to do so leads to questioning; and the future explorer, with his anxiety to make nature's course intelligible, controllable and down-to-earth, will always start by adopting a standpoint from which it seems mysterious, incomprehensible and beyond control. He will take up the attitude of somebody wondering, will apply the A-effect. Nobody can be a mathematician who takes it for granted that "two and two makes four"; nor is anybody one who fails to understand it. The man who first looked with astonishment at a swinging lantern and instead of taking it for granted found it highly remarkable that it should swing, and swing in that particular way rather than any other, was brought close to understanding the phenomenon by this observation, and so to mastering it. Nor must it simply be exclaimed that the attitude here proposed is all right for science but not for art. Why shouldn't art try, by its *own* means of course, to further the great social task of mastering life?

In point of fact the only people who can profitably study a piece of technique like Chinese acting's A-effect are those who need such a technique for quite definite social purposes.

The experiments conducted by the modern German theatre led to a wholly independent development of the A-effect. So far Asiatic acting has exerted no influence.

The A-effect was achieved in the German epic theatre not only by the actor, but also by the music (choruses, songs) and the setting (placards, film etc.). It was principally designed to historicize the incidents portrayed. By this is meant the following:

The bourgeois theatre emphasized the timelessness of its objects. Its representation of people is bound by the alleged "eternally human." Its story is arranged in such a way as to create "universal" situations that allow Man with a capital M to express himself: man of every period and every colour. All its incidents are just one enormous cue, and this cue is followed by the "eternal" response: the inevitable, usual, natural, purely human response. An example: a black man falls in love in the same way as a white man; the story forces him to react with the same expression as the white man (in theory this formula works as well the other way round); and with that the sphere of art is attained. The cue can take account of what is special, different; the response is shared, there is no element of difference in it. This notion may allow that such a thing as history exists, but it is none the less unhistorical. A few circumstances vary, the environments are altered, but Man remains unchanged. History applies to the environment, not to Man. The environment is remarkably unimportant, is treated simply as a pretext; it is a variable quantity and something remarkably inhuman; it exists in fact apart from Man, confronting him as a coherent whole, whereas he is a fixed quantity, eternally unchanged. The idea of man as a function of the environment and the environment as a function of man, i.e. the breaking up of the environment into relationships between men, corresponds to a new way of thinking, the historical way. Rather than be sidetracked into the philosophy of history, let us give an example. Suppose the following is to be shown on the stage: a girl leaves home in order to take a job in a fair-sized city (Piscator's *American Tragedy*). For the bourgeois theatre this is an insignificant affair, clearly the beginning of a story; it is what one has to have been told in order to understand what comes after, or to be keyed up for it. The actor's imagination will hardly be greatly fired by it. In a sense the incident is universal: girls take jobs (in the case in question one can be keyed up to see what in particular is going to happen to her). Only in one way is it particular: this girl goes away (if she had remained what comes after would not have happened). The fact that her family lets her go is not the object of the inquiry; it is understandable (the motives are understandable). But for the historicizing theatre everything is different. The theatre concentrates entirely on whatever in this perfectly everyday event is remarkable, particular and demanding inquiry. What! A family letting one of its members leave the nest to earn her future living independently and without help? Is she up to it? Will what she has learnt here as a member of the family help her to earn her living? Can't families keep a grip on their children any longer? Have they become (or remained) a burden? Is it like that with every family? Was it always like that? Is this the way of the world, something that can't be affected? The fruit falls off the tree when ripe: does this sentence apply here? Do children always make themselves independent? Did they do so in every age? If so, and if it's something biological, does it always happen in the same way, for the same reasons and with the same results? These are the questions (or a few of them) that the actors must answer if they want to show the incident as a unique, historical one: if they want to demonstrate a custom which leads to conclusions about the entire structure of a society at a particular (transient) time. But how is such an incident to be represented if its historic character is to be brought out? How can the confusion of our unfortunate epoch be striking? When the mother, in between warnings and moral injunctions, packs her daughter's case—a very small one— how is the following to be shown: So many injunctions and so few clothes? Moral injunctions for a lifetime and bread for five hours? How is the actress to speak the mother's sentence as she hands over such a very small case—"There, I guess that ought to do you"—in such way that it is understood as a historic dictum? This can only be achieved if the A-effect is brought out. The actress must not make the sentence her own affair, she must hand it over for criticism, she must help us to understand its causes and protest. The effect can only be got by long training. In the New York Yiddish Theatre, a highly progressive theatre, I saw a play by S. Ornitz showing the rise of an East Side boy to be a big crooked attorney. The theatre could not perform the play. And yet there were scenes like this in it: the young attorney sits in the street outside his house giving cheap legal advice. A young woman arrives and complains that her leg has been hurt in a traffic accident. But the case has been bungled and her compensation has not yet been paid. In desperation she points to her leg and says: "It's started to heal up." Working without the A-effect, the theatre was unable to make use of this exceptional scene to show the horror of a bloody epoch. Few people in the audience noticed it; hardly anyone who reads this will remember that cry. The actress spoke the cry as if it were something perfectly natural. But it is exactly this—the fact that this poor creature finds such a complaint natural—that she should have reported to the public like a horrified messenger returning from the lowest of all hells. To that end she would of course have needed a special technique which would have allowed her to underline the historical aspect of a specific social condition. Only the A-effect makes this possible. Without it all she can do is to observe how she is not forced to go over entirely into the character on the stage.

In setting up new artistic principles and working out new methods of representation we must start with the compelling demands of a changing epoch; the necessity and the possibility of remodelling society loom ahead. All incidents between men must be noted, and everything must be seen from a social point of view. Among other effects that a new theatre will need for its social criticism and its historical reporting of completed transformations is the A-effect.

Peter Brook

In this brief and pungent essay, a brilliant modern director estimates
a way by which modern drama can find an equivalent to the expanse,
richness, and variety of Elizabethan drama. In his context of reference to Brecht and Weiss (and to Artaud and Genet), Brook expounds with powerful directness a theory — or perhaps an approach
to a theory — which may have immense influence in the modern
theatre for years to come.

AN INTRODUCTION TO WEISS'S THE PERSECUTION AND ASSASSINATION OF JEAN-PAUL MARAT... UNDER THE DIRECTION OF THE MARQUIS DE SADE

What's the difference between a poor play and a good one? I think
there's a very simple way of comparing them. A play in performance
is a series of impressions; little dabs, one after another, fragments of
information or feeling in a sequence which stir the audience's perceptions. A good play sends many such messages, often several at a time,
often crowding, jostling, overlapping one another. The intelligence,
the feelings, the memory, the imagination are all stirred. In a poor
play, the impressions are well spaced out, they lope along in single
file, and in the gaps the heart can sleep while the mind wanders to
the day's annoyances and thoughts of dinner.

The whole problem of the theatre today is just this: how can we
make plays dense in experience? Great philosophical novels are
often far longer than thrillers, more content occupies more pages,
but great plays and poor plays fill up evenings of pretty comparable
length. Shakespeare seems better in performance than anyone else
because he gives us more, moment for moment, for our money. This
is due to his genius, but also to his technique. The possibilities of free
verse on an open stage enabled him to cut the inessential detail and
the irrelevant realistic action: in their place he could cram sounds

and ideas, thoughts and images which make each instant into a stunning mobile.

Today we are searching for a twentieth-century technique that could give us the same freedom. For strange reasons, verse alone no longer does the trick: yet there is a device. Brecht invented it, a new device of quite incredible power. This is what has been uncouthly labelled "alienation." Alienation is the art of placing an action at a distance so that it can be judged objectively and so that it can be seen in relation to the world — or rather, worlds — around it. Peter Weiss's play is a great tribute to alienation and breaks important new ground. Brecht's use of "distance" has long been considered in opposition to Artaud's conception of theatre as immediate and violent subjective experience. I have never believed this to be true. I believe that theatre, like life, is made up of the unbroken conflict between impressions and judgments — illusion and disillusion co-habit painfully and are inseparable. This is just what Weiss achieves. Starting with its title, everything about this play is designed to crack the spectator on the jaw, then douse him with ice-cold water, then force him to assess intelligently what has happened to him, then give him a kick in the balls, then bring him back to his senses again. It's not exactly Brecht and it's not Shakespeare either, but it's very Elizabethan and very much of our time.

Weiss not only uses total theatre, that time-honoured notion of getting all the elements of the stage to serve the play. His force is not only in the quantity of instruments he uses; it is above all in the jangle produced by the clash of styles. Everything is put in its place by its neighbour — the serious by the comic, the noble by the popular, the literary by the crude, the intellectual by the physical: the abstraction is vivified by the stage image, the violence illuminated by the cool flow of thought. The strands of meaning of the play pass to and fro through its structure and the result is a very complex form: like in Genet, it is a hall of mirrors or a corridor of echoes — and one must keep looking front and back all the time to reach the author's sense.

One of the London critics attacked the play on the ground that it was a fashionable mixture of all the best theatrical ingredients around — Brechtian — didactic — absurdist — Theatre of Cruelty. He said this to disparage but I repeat this as praise. Weiss saw the use of every one of these idioms and he saw that he needed them all. His assimilation was complete. An undigested set of influences leads to a blur: Weiss's play is strong, its central conception startlingly original, its silhouette sharp and unmistakeable. From our practical experience I can report that the force of the performance is directly related to the imaginative richness of the material: the imaginative richness is the consequence of the amount of levels that are working simultaneously: this simultaneity is the direct result of Weiss's daring combination of so many contradictory techniques.

Is the play political? Weiss says it is Marxist and this has been much discussed. Certainly it is not polemical in the sense that it does not prove a case nor draw a moral. Certainly, its prismatic structure is such that the last line is not the place to search for the summing-up idea. The idea of the play is the play itself, and this cannot be resolved in a simple slogan. It is firmly on the side of revolutionary change. But it is painfully aware of all the elements in a violent human situation and it presents these to the audience in the form of a painful question.

> "The important thing is to pull yourself up by your own hair
> To turn yourself inside out and see the whole world with
>   fresh eyes."

> — Marat

How? someone is bound to ask. Weiss wisely refuses to tell. He forces us to relate opposites and face contradictions. He leaves us raw. He searches for meaning instead of defining one and puts the responsibility of finding the answers back where it properly belongs. Off the dramatist and onto ourselves.

Jean-Louis Barrault

Of all the plays produced by this great actor-director, Chekhov's *The Cherry Orchard* provided one of the deepest challenges to his perception and craft. As Barrault himself observes in this essay, the spirit and tone of the play are alien to the French approach. His approach to this text is a general one, discussing concepts of pacing and action, of character, and society; fundamentally it reveals a moving love for the play itself, a premise demanded by Barrault of himself in all he has undertaken. The subtlety of the production is revealed by the nuance of thought contained in Barrault's preliminary discussion reprinted here.

❧ *WHY* THE CHERRY ORCHARD?

In my opinion, *The Cherry Orchard* is Chekhov's masterpiece; I think that of the four great plays which he has written, this is the one which comes closest to universality and to generalizations which embrace all men. While it reflects striking aspects of the Russian soul it also contains aspects of feelings and thoughts which pertain to all mankind. *The Cherry Orchard* is born from silence, it is a vast pantomime unfolding in the course of two hours and being adorned every now and then with bursts of poetry in the same way as a necklace is livened up here and there with beautiful jewels. It is a setting of brief retorts which frame a very rare silence. *The Cherry Orchard* flows slowly like life; it is a kind of pure spring in which one hears the murmur of souls. Few plays can give such a physical "impression of the passing of time"; this effect is obtained through the fact that starting from silence, the play reproduces most vividly the present; and the theatre is above all the art of the present. In life the present is what is most difficult to get hold of. Therefore it is not surprising that *The Cherry Orchard* should be a play very difficult to grasp; its action takes place in silences, and the dialogues, with the poetic tirades which shine like jewels, are like music only meant to make silence vibrate: silence struggles with time which in front of us or behind our backs continuously transforms the future into past and memory. We say, "Time passes," but what does this mean since time is nothing but action? Should we not say time pushes life as if through a strainer? Thanks to its magic strainer, time turns what is coming to us and does not yet exist concretely, into something finished and which therefore will only exist in memory. Coffee is a solid powder, but the filter strains it through and it becomes a liquid. What is time doing? Oh! it is at work. Ah! what is it working on? It is passing, and it is this mysterious passing or straining which makes our present. Existence is made to vanish by the extraordinary conjurer time. At a certain moment someone in *The Cherry Orchard* says, "You see this card game," and at once one thinks that this card game is life. "Take a card," that is the moment lived. "Look at it, and put it back in the pack"; that, you think, is action in the present. "It's in your pocket and with your handkerchief over it, my dear chap"; the present is past, finished! That's what happens in *The Cherry Orchard*. It is a play about the passing of time; therefore whether the characters are Russian or Japanese does not matter. Like some plays of Shakespeare and Molière it is a play which has universal value and which belongs to all mankind. But just as that English genius has described better than anybody else the approach of madness, and just as French insight is at its best in describing the problems of the human heart, the Russian genius seems to be better fitted than any other to deal with the present or the lived moment. Is Russia not placed astride the east and the west in just the same was as the present is astride the past and the future? Yet the universal values which are found in *The Cherry Orchard* cannot detract from the great homage which is due to the Russian soul for having revealed to us this subtle and profound experience of the passing of time. The structure of this play, which is built on silence and which takes place in the present, is fundamentally musical. The present, of course, is something so elusive, so fast changing, that the author never has enough time to develop a given theme, and so he must always pass on to the next. There is no time to stop, so we pass from an everyday incident to a sentimental sensation, from this sensation to a general thought, from that to a joke, from that to reflections on society, etc., without ever exhausting any one of these moments which are in fact only means of avoiding the danger to which one ceaselessly returns. We are confronted by a succession of moments of torpor interspersed with sharp awakenings and vain attempts to avert a magnetic attraction towards suffering and disaster, in the same way as one tries to keep oneself awake because one is afraid of dying in one's sleep. Each of these unfulfilled and incomplete moments leaves behind a state of anxiety which is really the true subject of the play. One cannot help thinking that if a composer applied these subtle methods of composition to his art, his music would probably be ultra-modern. The themes are no sooner stated than they fade away as if burnt out, and there is an air of incoherence between the various themes which is in fact the result of the most careful and methodical planning. The dramatic movement is extremely subtle, and built as it is on a musical analogy, it is a slow movement.

This is one of the reasons why I like *The Cherry Orchard*. The dramatic tempo of the play is a matter of density and not of velocity, or of speed of acting and unfolding events; it is effective when every instant is filled to capacity. It is often said, and it is even confirmed as far as *The Cherry Orchard* is concerned in the *Dictionnaire des Oeuvres*, that there is very little action in Chekhov. What this really means is that there are no complicated plots or abundance of incidents; but that does not mean that there is no action. Action must not be confused with plot. "Let whatever you do be always simple," said Horace, and Racine added: "Invention consists in making something out of nothing." The action of *The Cherry Orchard* is taut, and it embraces the whole play, for every one of its moments is well filled and has its own density which does not lie in the dialogue but in the flowing life. The subject of the *Three Sisters* could be summed up in the following way: we should like to get to town; will we go to town? we shan't go to town. There is one single catalyser ("the object" as Stanislavski used to describe it) meant to bring about the progress of this simple and unique action: soldiers. In *The Cherry Orchard* the catalyser is the domain which gives the play its title.

Act I   "The cherry orchard" runs the risk of being sold.
Act II   "The cherry orchard" is going to be sold.
Act III "The cherry orchard" is being sold.
Act IV "The cherry orchard" has been sold.

The rest of the play is made up of life itself. The house is asleep in the night, waiting; people arrive, have some coffee, read a telegram, then go to bed. The morning comes, the birds awaken. In small groups, the inmates of the house sit in turn on the same bench, like flights of swallows on the same telegraph wire. Some Jewish musicians pass by, playing; the moon rises; some dancing takes place; another telegram is read, then a few glasses of kvass, a game of cards; five people arrive from town. The time has now come to leave "the cherry orchard"; clothes have to be packed up, furniture has to be brought together; one hears the jingling bells of the horses in the courtyard; the shutters are closed, a last glance at the old walls and all is over. This house, which two hours before was like a pregnant woman about to give birth, is now an icy tomb from which life has fled. This life composed of silences, these mysteriously fleeting themes, this sorrowful and anguished unfolding of the action, confront French actors with entrancing problems. The French actor is used to basing his acting on the text which, in the French theatre, generally contains the action; here in this case, acting must find its basis outside the text. When the action is contained in the text, it unfolds at a quicker tempo than when it is outside the text. The French actor is therefore used to a quick tempo. *The Cherry Orchard* has a slow tempo, even for Russian actors, and besides that, Russian slowness is not the same as French slowness; therefore *The Cherry Orchard* must be produced according to French slowness and not Russian slowness, but this slowness constitutes for French actors an excellent discipline in the art of conveying the density of life. There are few plays more entrancing than this play. There are not many actors who get thoroughly immersed and lost in this play, but when that happens, those who do so live the best moments of their artistic lives. It is the same for a whole cast; *The Cherry Orchard* is one of the few plays in which a whole cast could really get so profoundly lost as to cease to believe that they are in a theatre, and believe on the contrary that this family truly exists and that they are in real life, and such an extraordinary metamorphosis takes place in the name of poetic truth. This play belongs neither to the naturalism of the beginning of the century nor to realism, it belongs to truth, and truth always has two faces, a real one and a poetic one — its appearance and its inner meaning, and that is the basis of poetic realism as in Shakespeare.

These are some of the points I should like to bring out in a production of *The Cherry Orchard,* and I should add that the love I bear to the play is my excuse for the personal way in which I may approach it; true love is better than respect. *The Cherry Orchard* reminds me of a nest of tables which stretch indefinitely one into the other; it starts from any familiar everyday subject, to move to the universal and the general; it is something like a Japanese flower which begins unfolding in a glass of water as soon as the appropriate tablet has been thrown in; it is also a kind of parable, which starting from everyday life rises to the metaphysical plane; it starts from individuals in their own universe and it rises to the general plane where individuals are seen under the angle of universality, and that is what makes it a great play.

Let us have a look at it in detail. In the centre we have a woman full of charm, generous and unconscious to the point of amorality. She represents that type of human being which is weak, passionate, most attractive by the combination of virtue and weakness which makes the true hero. Her heart in her hand, a sinner full of love, distributing her money freely, Liouba is the symbol of humanity, the eternal human being. Around her, there are three men who form the three angles of a triangle and represent the three age-long social currents which never cease to battle against one another. Gaiev personifies tradition, ancient civilization and the old generation; he stands for an age which has lost its vitality, which is now fast fading away, and which one tries to hold back with all the nostalgia of a good thing which has been lost and yet remains worthy of love. At the top of the second angle, we find Lopakine, the son of a moujik, the hard-working business man, proud of his newly acquired strength, and also somewhat ashamed of the imperfections which he still drags about him. He too loves and esteems the age which is just fading away and would like to save it, but social evolution is irresistible and he finds himself more or less compelled to buy "The cherry orchard," symbol of an obsolete world; it is he who has the idea of utilizing it in a modern way, by dividing the property into plots of land for building new houses. He announces in prophetic tones the first revolution which was to break out a year later (we are in 1904). If Gaiev represents the past, Lopakine represents the present. Yet nothing stands still, all things are meant to disappear, that is why Chekhov confronts Lopakine with another character who is the third angle of the triangle, and who is Trofimov, the eternal student. Trofimov has a kind of undeveloped prophetic gift which enables him to tell Lopakine that the present occupiers of his newly built houses will be their owners tomorrow; Trofimov, who is the potential revolutionary, announces the 1917 revolution and the fact that every social revolution is followed by another. We cannot help thinking about the permanent state of revolution of Trotsky.

These various social positions are examined and developed, with a control and a tact which call forth the admiration of the most delicate sensibilities. The social aspect of *The Cherry Orchard* is dealt with by a fairy-like hand and therefore is all the more effective. Like the Chinese methods of acupuncture, the prick is small but the repercussions are of enormous importance and go far beyond the "Russian case." They affect every one of us, both in space and time; it is something that is valid for all men at all times. If the individuals who are studied become sociological cases, sociology then becomes a science which is of interest for the eternal individual. Trofimov explains how this kind of development takes place; he says: "If we wish to begin to live, we must first of all redeem our past and tear ourselves away from it; but one cannot do that without great suffering, and one cannot redeem anything without a frightful and obstinate effort." This sentence is obviously addressed to a whole generation, and to a whole society and also to the religious notion of redemption, but it is also addressed to every individual throughout the ages and in its most general aspects. The human being, like societies and civilizations, comes to life, lives, dies and renews itself. Is it not said that every three weeks all the cells of our body are renewed, and that therefore every three weeks our being is something different from what it was previously? Chekhov deals with three types of human beings: Gaiev the one who is about to disappear, Lopakine the one who is due to replace him in the present, and Trofimov the one who already prepares for the one who will replace Lopakine. They are the past, the present and the future. However attractive our past might be, however much we might cling to it, we must become worthy to receive the future, and in order to be so, we must have the courage to tear ourselves away from our past; it is the price we must pay for the right to live, it is the redemption and the ransom exacted by life; "good night, old life, good morning, new life"; and though the eyes may still be reddened by tears, a new smile begins to break. That's life, and that is the lesson of *The Cherry Orchard*. That is the meaning of the three men who gravitate round Liouba Ranievsky, the moving symbol of humanity on the march, on a plane far above any social plane. *The Cherry Orchard* is neither a realistic play nor a social play; Chekhov is too great a man to tie himself to one single plane; it is the play of a great poet who, owing to the depth of his feelings, and an extraordinary vision, goes beyond the social, which is given the importance that it deserves, to the very sources of existence.

Another lesson which can be learnt from *The Cherry Orchard* is that Chekhov shows us what a true artist is. We rather tend to shun that word because of hypocritical modesty, but we nevertheless know that an artist is a witness for his time and therefore he must try first and foremost to be the servant of justice. We cannot be partisan and just at the same time; a true artist can only be partisan of justice and nothing else; he can only be committed to justice and to nothing else, and such was Chekhov's love of justice that it is said that he was respected and admired by the two camps which existed in the Russia of his time. In *The Cherry Orchard* we love Gaiev and we love the good old days, but we also love Lopakine and would hope to help him to refine himself and to bring to him what he lacks and what at times gives him a sense of shame. At the same time we cannot but approve of the ideas of Trofimov; we regret his slackness, and would ask him to be more realistic in his revolutionary plans. Chekhov's art is an art devoted to justice, therefore to great art, and *The Cherry Orchard* leaves behind it a great feeling of impartiality. Chekhov is an artist because he gives us a lesson of tact, control and above all of restraint. One cannot be a great artist without a strong sense of pudicity. The lack of pudicity can only be excused on the ground of simplicity and candour; but of course one must not confuse restraint and prudishness. Chekhov teaches us the art of economy. One cannot take away anything from *The Cherry Orchard;* whatever could be left out has been left out by the author. One is reminded of Charlie Chaplin's admirable remark about one of his films: "When a work seems finished, you shake it like a fruit tree so as to keep only the fruit which cling solidly to the branches." "Never put anything in a play which is not absolutely necessary," said Racine. With Chekhov the stage directions themselves are important and must be examined with great care; in one of his letters he said: "One finds often in my plays the stage direction: 'through tears,' but that is intended to show the state the characters are in and not the tears." All his characters, like most of Shakespeare's characters, are ambiguous; Lopakine the terrible is also a shy, undecided and good man; Madame Ranievsky, the victim, has also a very passionate nature; Gaiev who represents tradition is lazy; Trofimov, the revolutionary, is a spineless, impulsive character. All Chekhov's characters are complex, they are not wooden, they are all very much alive and with throbbing hearts. *The Cherry Orchard* rests on the heart and that is one of the reasons why I love it—the heart which, as Trofimov says, contains ninety-five senses which go beyond the mind and beyond the five senses which have officially been put at our disposal. It is the heart which puts us in a state of tears when we look back upon our past, and which also pulses on and therefore compels us to face the present and the future. It is the heart which matters, for it is superior to the head which only produces ideas, or to the senses which only produce covetousness; the heart is above all revelation, vision and why not say the word—love, that is to say true knowledge, for as Claudel wisely said, to know is to be born with, or at the same time as, the thing that one knows.

Bertolt Brecht

These notes, discussing general aspects of characterization and staging, are of immense importance to any study of Brecht. They also indicate that special thoroughness typical of a director (or actors) committed to a point of view which is simultaneously an artistic theory and a social stand. Brecht's thoughts on the production of his plays were frequently set forth at length in essays called "models" or general summaries of his thoughts related to the script. In these notes for one of his most famous stage pieces, small production details stand side by side with larger conceptual considerations. The footnotes refer, usually by short quotations, to specific places in the text of *The Threepenny Opera*.

✹ *PRODUCTION NOTES FOR* THE THREEPENNY OPERA

THE READING OF PLAYS

For this opera there is no reason to change the motto which John Gay chose for his own *Beggar's Opera* — "*Nos haec novimus esse nihil.*" As far as the printed form of this work is concerned, it presents scarcely more than the prompt-book of a play that has been unreservedly given over to the theatre. It therefore appeals more to the expert than to the "enjoyer." And it should be said that a transformation of as many spectators and readers as possible into experts is highly desirable — it is also under way.

The Threepenny Opera treats of bourgeois conceptions not only in representing them but also in the *way* in which it represents them. The spectator is shown that portion of real life which he wishes to find presented on the stage, but since, at the same time, he is shown some things which he does not wish to see there, and since also he sees his wishes not only carried out but also criticized (he sees himself not as subject but as object), he is thereby enabled to give the theatre a new function. But because the theatre strenuously resists having its function changed, it is a good thing if the potential spectator *reads* plays which are written not only to be presented in the theatre but

Reprinted from *From the Modern Repertoire* (Series I), Eric Bentley, ed., by permission of the Indiana University Press.

also to change the theatre: he should read them out of mistrust for the theatre. Today we witness the absolute ascendancy of the theatre over dramatic literature. The ascendancy of the apparatus of the theatre is the ascendancy of the means of production. The apparatus of the theatre resists any change in its functions by immediately assimilating such drama as it comes in contact with, eating away from it everything but the most indigestible elements, which appear in performance to be mere eccentricities. The necessity for playing the new drama properly is lessened by the fact that the theatre can, after its own fashion, play anything: it makes everything "theatrical." Of course, there are economic reasons for this.

TITLES AND BOARDS

The boards and/or screens on which the titles of scenes and songs are projected are a primitive attempt at the *"literarisation of the theatre,"* which, along with the literarisation of all such concerns of public interest, must be developed very much further. Literarisation means the combination of what is "embodied" with what is "formulated." It enables the theatre to demonstrate its connection with other forms of intellectual activity.

Against these titles there is the objection, from the standpoint of academic dramaturgy, that the author of the play should include all that is to be said in the action itself, that the work itself must express everything: the spectator, so to say, does not think *over* the matter but *out of* the matter. But this way of subjugating everything to one idea, this passion for driving the spectator in one direction so that he can look neither right nor left, up nor down, is, from the standpoint of the new dramaturgy, to be avoided. Drama, too, can use footnotes. One must be able to turn back to an earlier page. Complex seeing must be practiced. "Thinking above the stream" may be more important than "thinking in the stream."

These boards of ours make possible and indeed compel a new style from the actor. This is *the epic style.* On reading the projections of the boards the spectator takes up the attitude of "watching while smoking." And through this attitude he enforces a better and more intelligent performance, for it is hard to "enthral" a man who is smoking; he is already busy, already entertained.

By such means one might very quickly get a theatre full of dramatic experts, just as one gets stadiums full of sport experts.

Never would spectators permit the actors to fob them off with the miserable little bits of mimicry which nowadays they produce "somehow" with a few rehearsals and no thought! Never would the actors' material be accepted in such a raw state. Since actions which are described on the boards are thereby robbed of direct emotional effect, the actors must give them emphasis in a quite different way.

Unfortunately it is to be feared that the boards, and even permission to smoke, will not suffice to bring the public to a more satisfactory use of the theatre.

THE CHIEF CHARACTERS

The character of Jonathan Peachum must not be reduced to the stock formula of "old miser." He has no regard for money. Since he is suspicious of everything that might awaken hope, money seems a quite inadequate means of defence. He is undeniably a villain, and at that a villain in the sense of the old-fashioned theatre. His crime consists in his conception of the world. This conception of the world is worthy, in all its horribility, to be placed beside the deeds of any of the more notorious criminals, and yet he is only following the "trend of the times" when he regards poverty as a commodity. To give a concrete example: when Peachum takes money from Filch in the first scene, he would never lock it up in a cash-box—he would simply stick it in his trouser pocket. He can be saved neither by this money nor by any other. It is conscientiousness on his part and a proof of his complete desperation that he does not simply throw it away; he cannot throw the least thing away. With ten thousand pounds he would not think otherwise. In his opinion neither his money (nor all the money in the world) nor his head (nor all the heads in the world) can suffice. And this is also the reason why he never works, but walks round the premises, with his hat on his head and his hands in his pockets, just to make sure that nothing is taken away. No one who is really afraid ever works. It is not pettiness on Peachum's part that he chains the Bible to its stand for fear it may be stolen. He never gives a thought to his son-in-law until he has brought him to the gallows, since he cannot even conceive of any personal values that might induce him to change his attitude towards a man who has taken his daughter away. The other crimes of Mackie the Knife interest him only in so far as they provide a means for liquidating him. As for Peachum's daughter, she is like his Bible—nothing more than a means of support. The effect of this is not so much repulsive as shattering. When a man is drowning, his worldly goods in general are of little use to him. But he would welcome a lifebelt.

The actress playing Polly will do well to study Mr. Peachum; she is his daughter.

MacHeath should simply be portrayed by the actor as bourgeois. The bourgeois predilection for robbers is explained by the fallacious premise that a robber is not a bourgeois. This error is fathered by another: a bourgeois is not a robber. Is there then no difference between the two?

Yes. A robber isn't always a coward. The attribute "peaceloving," which is attached to the middle class in the theatre, is applicable here when the business-man MacHeath expresses aversion to spilling blood when it is not absolutely necessary—for carrying on the business. The limitation of blood-spilling to a minimum, its rationalization as a business principle. In moments of emergency MacHeath displays extraordinary skill in fencing. He knows what he owes to his reputation. A certain romanticism, *so long as care is taken that it becomes known,* serves the above-mentioned rationalization. He makes very sure that all the daring, or at least fear-inspiring, deeds of his employees are ascribed to him, and tolerates just as little as a university professor that his assistants should ever put *their* signatures to a piece of work. With regard to women, he impresses them less as handsome than as comfortably situated. The original drawings for Gay's *Beggar's Opera* show a man of about forty, rather undersized but well-built, with a head like a radish, slightly bald, yet not without dignity. He is thoroughly steady, has no humor whatsoever, and his respectability speaks for itself in that his business objective is not so much the robbing of strangers as the exploitation of his own employees. He takes pains to stand in well with the guardians of public security, even when it entails some expense, and all this not merely for his own safety—his practical sense tells him that his own safety and the safety of the present order of society are inextricably bound up together. Any action against the public, such as that with which Peachum threatens the police, would fill Mr. MacHeath with the deepest disgust. In his own eyes, his relations with the ladies of Wapping certainly need an excuse; that excuse, however, is furnished by the peculiar nature of his business. He has taken the opportunity of utilizing a purely business relationship for purpose of pleasure, to which he, as a bachelor, is entitled in moderation; but so far as this intimate side is concerned, he chiefly treasures the regular and pedantically punctual visits to a certain coffee-house in

Wapping because they are a *habit,* and the cultivation and multiplication of habits are the chief aim of his bourgeois existence.

In any case the actor must on no account take these visits to an unruly house as the basis for his characterization of MacHeath. This habit is simply one of the far from rare, though inexplicable, cases of bourgeois daemonism.

MacHeath naturally prefers to meet the sexual requirements of his nature by combining them when he can with certain homely amenities — by sleeping, for example, with women who are not without means. In his marriage he sees an insurance of his business. The nature of his business makes unavoidable his temporary abscence from the metropolis, trivial as he may regard it, and his employees are extremely unreliable. In dreaming of his future, he sees himself, not hanging from the gallows, but standing by the side of a peaceful trout-stream which he can call his own.

The Commissioner of Police, Brown, is a very modern phenomenon. He conceals within himself two very different people: the private citizen and the official. And this is not a schism *in spite of* which he lives, but one *by* which he lives. And in company with him the whole of society. In private he would never lend himself to that which as an official he considers his duty. In private he cannot hurt a fly (and wouldn't need to). Hence his affection for MacHeath is completely genuine. Not even certain monetary advantages deriving therefrom can make it suspect: after all, everything in this life is tainted. . . .

Hints for the Actors

As far as putting the material across is concerned, the spectator should not experience "empathy"; rather there should be a two-way traffic between actor and spectator, for in spite of all strangeness and separateness the actor addresses himself, ultimately, to the spectator. Also the actor should tell the spectator more about the character he represents than is to be found "in his part." He must naturally behave in such a way as facilitates the action, but he must also be able to take into consideration his relationship to events other than those in the plot; he must not serve the plot alone. For example, when Polly is in a love scene with MacHeath, she is not only MacHeath's beloved but also Peachum's daughter, and not only Peachum's daughter but also her father's employee. Her relationship with the spectator must contain her criticism of the spectator's own popular conception of robbers' wives and merchants' daughters.

[1] The actors should avoid portraying the gang as a collection of gloomy individuals with red handkerchiefs round their necks, who frequent low haunts and with whom no respectable man would drink a glass of beer. They are naturally steady, sedate men, some of them inclined to obesity and they are all quite affable outside their profession.

[2] The actors can here show the usefulness of the bourgeois virtues and the intimate connection between the tender emotions and knavery.

[3] Here should be emphasized the brutal energy a man needs in order to create a state of affairs in which it is possible to display the dignity proper to a human being (in this case, a bridegroom).

[4] Here should be represented the "exhibition" of the bride and all her physical attractions at the final moment of reservation. For at the moment when the supply is withdrawn, the demand is driven up to its zenith. The bride is generally desired, and the bridegroom then "makes the running." A thoroughly theatrical proceeding. It should also be shown that the bride eats very little. One often sees the most delicate creatures devour huge meals—but brides? Never.

[5] In the presentation of such things as Peachum's business, the actors need not worry unduly about the progress of the action in the ordinary sense. However, they must depict not a milieu but a series of events. The impersonator of one of these beggars must so enact the process of choosing an effective and suitable wooden leg (trying one, laying it aside, trying another and then returning to the first) that the audience will decide to make another visit to the theatre at just the time when this particular action comes on; and nothing prevents the theatre from announcing such a feature on a "board" upstage.

[6] It is highly desirable that Polly Peachum be regarded by the audience as a pleasant and virtuous girl. Just as she showed in the

---

[1] [Stage Direction, I.2: "...*Half a dozen men come in, carrying carpets, furniture, crockery, etc., and soon the stable is transformed into an over-ornate living-room.*"]

[2] [Stage Direction, I.2: "*The GENTLEMEN place their presents down on the left, congratulate the bride, and report to the bridegroom.*"]

[3] [Note to the Stage Direction for MacHeath, to "*knock (EDE'S) hat from his head,*" as the latter begins to address the bride as "Dear Polly ... "]

[4] [Stage Direction for MacHeath, Polly, and the men: "*They all sit down to the wedding breakfast.*"]

[5] [Note to Stage Direction early in I.3, "*Five men enter,*" to Peachum's shop.]

[6] [At the beginning of II.1, MacHeath discusses with Polly the conduct of the business and sources of income while he is away; the note pertains to this dialogue: "POLLY: And Mac, what about your rooms? Shall I give them up? It would be such a waste to pay the rent! MACHEATH: You seem to think I'm never going to come back. POLLY: What do you mean? You can take them again! ..."]

second scene her entirely unselfish love, now she must display a practical frame of mind without which the former would have been mere frivolity.

⁷ These ladies are in undisturbed possession of their means of production. Hence they must not give the impression of being free. To them democracy cannot offer the freedom which it offers to those whose means of production can be taken away.

⁸ Actors playing MacHeath, who show no qualms at portraying the death struggle, usually object to singing this third verse: they would naturally not reject a *tragic* presentation of sex. But sex in our time undoubtedly belongs to the realm of comedy, for our sexual life is a direct contradiction of our social life, and this contradiction is comic because it can be historically superseded — by another order of society. Hence the actor must present such a ballad humorously. The representation of sex on the stage is very important — partly because it always brings in a primitive materialism. The artificial and transitory nature of all social superstructures also becomes plainly visible.

⁹ This ballad contains, as do others in this work, some lines from François Villon. See also the *Second Finale,* the *Epistle to His Friends,* and *Ballade in Which MacHeath Begs Forgiveness of All.* (*Ballade de Villon et de la Grosse Margot, Ballade intitulée Les Contrediz de Franc-Gontier, Epistre à ses amis, L'épitaphe Villon, Ballade par laquelle Villon crye mercy à chascun* are the relevant French texts.)

¹⁰ This scene is inserted for such actresses of Polly's part as have a gift for comedy.

¹¹ Walking round the cage in a circle, MacHeath can now repeat all the various gaits he has hitherto displayed to the public: the cock-sure step of the seducer, the despairing slouch of the fugitive, the superior tread of self-confidence, etc. In a short space of time he can once again portray all MacHeath's attitudes of the last few days.

¹² At this point, for example, the actor of the Epic Theatre will not

---

⁷ [Stage Direction, opening of II.2: "*A brothel in Wapping. An ordinary early evening. The girls, mostly in their underclothes, are ironing, playing draughts, washing themselves; a peaceful bourgeois idyll. . . .*"]

⁸ [Note to the refrain of *The Ballad of the Fancy-Man,* "That was a time of days now long ago," sung by MacHeath and Ginny Jenny.]

⁹ [Note to *The Ballad of the Pleasant Life,* sung by MacHeath early in II.3.]

¹⁰ [Note to III.2, called *THE BATTLE FOR POSSESSION,* set in the Old Bailey cell in which MacHeath awaits execution.]

¹¹ [Note serving as a direction for the singing of *The Epistle to his Friends*; a Stage Direction in the text notes that this is to be sung "*softly and very quickly.*"]

¹² [Note to line reading for MacHeath, just after the entrance of Matthew and Jacob; the dialogue is: "MACHEATH: Five twenty-five. You've taken your time. JACOB: Well, after all, we had to. . . MACHEATH: After all, after all, I'm going to be hanged, man! . . ."]

strain to aggravate MacHeath's fear of death and make it the dominating effect of the whole act, or the result will be that the subsequent demonstration of *true* friendship is lost upon the audience. (Friendship is only true when restricted. The moral victory of MacHeath's two truest friends will scarcely be lessened by the moral defeat they suffer when they are *not quick enough* in handing over the means of their existence to rescue their friend.)

[13] Perhaps the actor will here find a chance to indicate the following: MacHeath quite correctly realizes that his case is a horrible miscarriage of justice. Indeed, should justice pounce on bandits less infrequently than it does, it would entirely forfeit its present reputation.

ON THE SINGING OF THE SONGS

When he sings, the actor effects a change of function. Nothing is more appalling than when he behaves as though he hasn't noticed that he has left the ground of sober speech and is singing. The three planes — sober speech, oratorical speech, and singing — must always remain separate one from another, and on no account must oratorical speech indicate an intensification of sober speech, or singing an intensification of oratorical speech. Hence, in no case, where words fail for overabundance of feeling, can song be employed. The actor must not only sing but must also show that he is *meant* to be a singer. He is not so much attempting to bring out the feeiings contained in his song (can one offer others food which one has already eaten?) as to reveal those "gestures," which, so to speak, are the habits and usages of the body. To this end it is preferable, when he is studying his part, for him not to use the exact words of the text but current vulgar forms of speech which express the same meaning in slang. As far as melody is concerned, he need not follow it blindly: there is a manner of speaking-against-the-music which can be extremely effective and which comes from an obstinate matter-of-factness, independent of and uninfluenced by music or rhythm. Should he take up the melody, this must be an event, to emphasize which the actor can plainly show his own enjoyment of the melody. It is good for the actor if the musicians are visible. It is also good if the actor makes visible preparations for his song (putting a chair in position, comb-

---

[13] [Note to the following dialogue, as Mr. Brown enters MacHeath's cell to bring him his last meal: "BROWN: Hallo, Mac. Here's your asparagus. Won't you have a little? MACHEATH: Don't trouble yourself, Mr. Brown, there are other people who will do me the last honors."]

ing his hair, etc.). In singing it is particularly important that the manifestor be manifest.

WHY IS MacHEATH ARRESTED TWICE AND NOT ONCE?

The first prison scene is, from the point of view of the German classic drama, a digression. From our point of view it is an example of primitive epic form. It is indeed a disgression if one follows the system of the old dynamic drama, insisting on the primacy of the idea, and making the spectator always wish for one definite end — here, the death of the hero. For thus one, so to speak, creates an ever greater demand for the supply and forces the thought all in one channel to enable the spectator to participate strongly with his feelings; feelings only trust themselves on fully certain ground and cannot tolerate disappointments. Epic dramaturgy, taking its stand on materialism, is less interested in the "investment" of its spectators' feelings. Indeed it knows no goals, only endings. It envisages actions proceeding not only in straight lines but also in curves and even leaps. The "dynamic" drama, taking its stand on idealism, treating of the individual, was, when it began its course (among the Elizabethans), more radical in all decisive points than was, two hundred years later, the classic German drama which substituted the dynamics of the represented individual for the dynamics of representation. (The followers of the followers of the Elizabethans have sunk lower, and now the classic dynamics of representation have fallen before the smart, calculated arrangement of a mass of effects; and the individual, in the process of complete decomposition, with nothing outside himself to feed on, yields on the stage nothing but empty "roles." The late bourgeois novel at least worked out a psychology in order, so it hoped, to analyze the individual — as though he still existed!) The great Elizabethan playwrights were not so self-denying in their choice of material. The sweep of their spade was much wider — in relation, for instance, to events not presented on stage. In their dramas all sorts of external influences play a part. They did not reject such deviations of individuals from their rectilinear course as were caused by "life," but instead used these deviations as dynamic motors. An "irritation" penetrates the individual himself and in him is finally overcome. The whole impress of this drama comes from the accumulation of resistances. The desire for a cheap ideal formula does not yet determine the arrangement of the substance. Something of Baconian materialism is in this drama: the individual himself still has flesh and blood and struggles against all formula. Now, wherever there is materialism, there arise epic forms in drama. In comedy, which has always been more materialistic, a "lower" form, they are most frequently apparent. Today, when man must be regarded as "the totality of social relationships," the epic form is the only one which can comprehend those processes that are the dramatist's material for a comprehensive picture of the world. Man, even physical man, can only be understood through the processes in which and by which he exists. He must be considered as the object of one experiment after another conducted by society. The new drama presents these experiments. To this end it must show connections and relationships on all sides. It needs "static" and has a tension which controls all its individual components. The scenes charge each other with tension. (Epic form is therefore anything but a revue-like stringing together of separate "numbers.")

WHY MUST THE KING'S MESSENGER BE ON HORSEBACK?

This work is a representation of bourgeois society (and not only of the underworld, of the "disreputable"). Bourgeois society has produced a bourgeois world order — and therefore a particular world outlook, without which it could never exist. The arrival of the king's mounted messenger is, as the bourgeois conceives his world, quite indispensable. Mr. Peachum, when he profits financially by the uneasy conscience of society, is using the messenger: what else *could* he use? Theatre people should consider why nothing is more stupid than to do away with the *horse* of the mounted messenger — as nearly all "modernist" directors of this work have done. When a judicial murder is being played it is imperative, in order that the theatre may perform its function in bourgeois society, that the journalist who reveals the innocence of the murdered man should be drawn into court of justice by a swan. For is it not obviously tactless to betray the public into laughing at itself by making the arrival of a mounted messenger an object of merriment? Without the arrival of a mounted messenger in some form or other, bourgeois literature would degenerate into the presentation of actual conditions. The mounted messenger guarantees that one's enjoyment of intolerable conditions shall not be disturbed; he is therefore a *sine qua non* of a literature whose *sine qua non* is non-intervention.

Naturally, the third finale is to be played with absolute seriousness and dignity.

Philip Weissman

Dr. Weissman is presently a psychoanalyst and consultant psychiatrist on the Affiliate Staff of the New York Psychoanalytic Treatment Center. These observations are from a longer study examining various aspects of theatre in terms of psychoanalytic techniques. Those for whom drama is a profession—whether actor, director, playwright, or critic—have always affirmed (and sometimes anticipated) some of the more interesting insights of Freudian approaches. Here one can study the problems of professional directors as seen by a distinguished member of another profession also committed to the close observation of human phenomena. Weissman deals with problems of motivation, childhood reactions, the relations between character traits of directors (in several creative fields) and general artistic creativity, and various other vital subjects as well.

from THE DIRECTOR

... From the examples cited, the following formulations are suggested. The artistic director-to-be, as a child, designs his oedipal structure as one in which he takes the mother's place as heir to her children and their management; the final identification is often related to the idealization of the parents' interests in each other. Most often, as has been illustrated, the mother has an artistic interest or profession and the father's work involves integrating the functions or ideas of a group. More often than not, the father's love for the mother encompasses her appreciation or endowment in the arts. It is likely that the oedipal child subsequently displaces his interest in and envy of the sexual life between his parents onto the aesthetic interest and activities of the parents. This is increased during the postoedipal phase when the parental ego ideals become firmly established in the child's psychic structure. The identification with the ego-ideals derived from the parents' interests and ideals, as well as the sublimation of the child's sexual wishes and rivalry with the father, reinforce the child's own artistic endowment and drives toward a paternally influenced directorial career in a maternally influenced artistic world.

Biographical studies suggest that, when the father has been an actor or performing artist and the mother may or may not have been

From *Creativity in the Theatre,* by Philip Weissman, © 1965 by Philip Weissman, Basic Books, Inc., Publishers, New York. Reprinted with permission.

an actress, the male child more often will have the oedipal roots and resolution toward becoming an actor. It is understood that a child with extraordinary talent for original creating or directing will not be deterred from such a course because his father was a performer or his parents had little artistic endowment. The road might be more difficult because of incompatibility with ego-ideals and the obstructive attitude of the parents.[1] Much of what has been said applies to the male artistic director. The truth is that females rarely become conductors or directors. The female child who identifies with her mother has a more direct outlet in eventually rearing her own children and has less need to redirect such wishes to a directorial substitute.[2]

The oedipal development of the future director, which motivates him toward the role of directing and coordinating the artistic activities of others in a parent-child continuum, enhances and advances his artistic endowment. From the same oedipal ferment, the director is unconsciously motivated to take over the work of a dramatist or composer and bring it out in performance as if it were his own child whom he completely understood and thus may rear as he sees fit. A director, like a teacher, is aided in his work if he has maternal qualities. To transform these psychological ambitions and characteristics into an artistic achievement, the director must have special inherent endowments as well.

A drama director or musical conductor brings the written work of the dramatist or composer into an interpreted existence. Every drama and musical score that is original and artistic must be expressed in terms of aesthetic ambiguity which will permit for a varied and multiple cluster of aesthetic communication to the audience. Hence, no performance of a written work of art can be more than a single interpretation. The greatness of a director depends on his capacities to identify with the creator and to create in performance an optimal and original communication which enhances the author's creation without distorting it.

A director identifies with the contents of the created work and interests himself in communicating its contents. He is more identified with the dramatist or composer than with the audience. He re-

---

[1] Neither of Leonard Bernstein's parents had any musical or artistic endowment. His father bitterly opposed his plan for a musical career (Ewen, 1961). This was accomplished in spite of the unfavorable parental attitude and the absence of a stimulus toward music in the home.

[2] Greenacre has accounted for the absence of original creations by women and the emphasis on the performing arts (1960). The same psychological characteristic of the female castration complex and their capacity for biological creation contributes to the infrequency of female directors, artistic or otherwise.

creates the originator's creative expression. If the director succeeds artistically in his interpretation, he must be endowed with "an intactness of sensorimotor equipment, allowing the building up of projective motor discharge for expressive function."[3] In fact, he is required to have all the additional characteristics that are considered prerequisite for the creative artist. Thus, he must be endowed with greater than usual sensitivity to sensory stimuli; unusual capacity for awareness of relations between various stimuli; basic predisposition to an extraordinary empathy for external animate and inanimate objects. What he need not have is the capacity to create original works of art. In lieu of this, he utilizes his capacity for complete identification with the originator (similar to his identification with his mother) from whence he makes his own artistic contribution as a creator.[4]

Should the director or conductor have the additional good fortune to be endowed with the talent to create his own original works, he will have the advantage of being able to direct the performance of his own works, as well as those of others. Beginning with Shakespeare, the combination of playwright-director in a single person is not an uncommon phenomenon. The combination of composer-conductor is even more frequent, as exemplified by Mendelssohn, Berlioz, Liszt, Wagner, with Bernstein a current example.

The composer or dramatist who lacks the capacity to identify with his creation may well fail when conducting or directing his own works as well as those of others. He fails as director of his own work because once he has created the work it is no longer part of himself and he would need the ability to identify with the creator to perform his own works as well as those of others. Directors often succeed as performers when they have the additional endowment and training in the performing art.[5]

It has already been pointed out that actors often suffer from an undeveloped self-image and intensified conflicts around exhibitionism, whereas the dramatist has the tendency toward enactment (inclusive of acting out), from which he dissociates himself in his capacity as an artist and utilizes its content for his dramas. The

[3] Greenacre, in her study on the childhood of the artist, elaborates the four essential basic endowments of the artist. [Phyllis Greenacre, "The Childhood of the Artist," *The Psychoanalytic Study of the Child,* Vol. 12 (New York: International Univer. Press, 1957), pp. 47-72.]

[4] Bruno Walter says of his contribution to music: "I have made only the music of others sound forth. I have been but a re-creator" (1946).

[5] Toscanini began as a cellist in an opera orchestra. When the conductor became ill and was unavailable, Toscanini was asked to conduct the orchestra; this incident marked the beginning of his career as conductor.

director's maternalistic oedipal wishes and parental characteristics have been described. Theoretically, a given individual may have an inadequate self-image — an exhibitionistic orientation and/or tendencies toward enactment, and/or the typical director's oedipal designs. Such an individual would be expected to be interested in all three aspects of the theater, i.e., actor, director, and dramatist. It would be of interest to determine whether psychobiographical studies of such men as Shakespeare and Molière, who had these three talents, would validate these formulations.

During the creation of a production the director, like the playwright, is regarded by the actors with the same emotional attitudes as children show toward a parent. If the dramatist is deceased or disconnected with the production, he may be regarded by the actors as an unseen immortal god who is consciously or unconsciously represented by the director toward whom these feelings of reverence and respect are transferred.[6] The dramatist-director relationship has many variations. Actual experience and reputation of either the director or the dramatist are often the crucial determinants of the working relationship between them. Thus the young dramatist who is acceptable to the established director, feeling overwhelmed and honored by the opportunity, takes a passive, submissive role in their mutual undertaking. Conversely, the young director who is acceptable to the established playwright approaches his assignment like a dutiful, submissive child. Yet, if he is to succeed as a director or conductor in his own right, it is essential that at the last moment he have his own sense of conviction and capacity for self-assertion to produce the drama or score from his own aesthetic orientation. His aggression must be in the service of his artistic functions.[7]

[6] The paternalism of directors toward a theatrical group extends to the personal lives of the actors. Directors are wont to give parental advice and the most common abuse of this role occurs when directors take on the role of psychoanalyst for the actor. An anecdote illustrating the director's paternalism is told of Tomashevsky, who traveled far and wide throughout the United States with his Jewish group of actors. On the night of a great snowstorm in a small Midwest city, he peered through the curtain to estimate the size of the audience, which was no more than a handful. He turned to the actors gathered about him and said: "Children, America is a wonderful democracy and tonight we are in the majority!"
The extravagant paternalism of Henry Irving has already been described.

[7] A current example in the field of conducting relates to the occasion when Leonard Bernstein, then an unknown assistant conductor, had to replace, on very short notice, the veteran guest conductor, Bruno Walter, at the New York Philharmonic Symphony Orchestra. Bernstein rushed to the bedside of the ailing master, who instructed him as thoroughly as he could in the short time left, how he had intended to interpret the various selections on the program. Bernstein, unnerved, listened as attentively as he could. However, when he stepped on the podium and tapped his baton, he was unable to remember what he had been told and began to conduct as he understood the music. This launched him on a new and brilliant career as an orchestral conductor.

The psychological interplay among the dramatist (creator), director, and actor (performer) may be expressed in a simplified summation. The actor is the child in whom the parentally identified director has instilled the re-created essence of the work of the dramatist — the true parent.

These formulations on the development of the artistic director are offered as hypotheses which require additional validation by future clinical psychoanalytic investigations. The main disadvantage in dealing with the psychology and endowment of the drama director and the musical conductor, as if they were one and the same, is that beyond the features they have in common, the ultimate differences between their art media are not taken into consideration. Music is a nonverbal, auditory means of communication, most often performed on external instruments, with the exception of singers. Drama is verbal and written and, when performed, is spoken and acted. One would expect to find significant differences between the psychology of musicians and theatrical people, determined by the differences in the two art forms, that are beyond the scope of this preliminary investigation.

One vital distinction between the drama director and conductor does belong within the scope of our explorations. The conductor is not only an integral part of the performance but is also most prominently on display. In this sense, he is always functioning in the dual role of performer and director. His body and his mind are his musical instruments. From the vantage of psychology, his exhibitionism and body image are additionally involved, in contrast to the dramatic director, who is not seen.

The justification for the combined investigation of artistic (and nonartistic) directors is that it offers sufficient common findings in early psychological development, particularly in the area of their oedipal design and parental identification, which could be useful in a general understanding of such personalities. It is of some value to have available a pattern of over-all development as one proceeds to the psychoanalytic investigation of the single individual.

PART FOUR ❦ THE SETTING

Robert Edmond Jones

After graduating from Harvard in 1910, Jones worked extensively with Max Reinhardt's vast productions in Berlin; he then returned to America to revitalize conceptions of scene design in this country. His designs for *The Jest, Redemption,* and *Richard III* (with Arthur Hopkins and John Barrymore), many of O'Neill's plays, Nijinsky's ballet of *Til Eulenspiegel,* and a monumental *Oedipus Rex* by Stravinsky at the Metropolitan Opera House stand as landmarks both revolutionary and personal. His faith in the arts of the theatre were always intuitive, even mystical in tone, although based on a long career of intensely practical experience. Jones's testament of his craft—and personal beliefs—is expressed in *The Dramatic Imagination* from which the following excerpts are reprinted. He died in 1954.

A NEW KIND OF DRAMA

In art ... there is a spark which defies foreknowledge ... and all the masterpieces in the world cannot make a precedent.

—LYTTON STRACHEY

In the last quarter of a century we have begun to be interested in the exploration of man's inner life, in the unexpressed and hitherto inexpressible depths of the self. Modern psychology has made us all familiar with the idea of the Unconscious. We have learned that beneath the surface of an ordinary everyday normal casual conscious existence there lies a vast dynamic world of impulse and dream, a hinterland of energy which has an independent existence of its own and laws of its own: laws which motivate all our thoughts and our actions. This energy expresses itself to us in our conscious life in an never-ending stream of images, running incessantly through our minds from the cradle to the grave, and perhaps beyond. The concept of the Unconscious has profoundly influenced the intellectual life of our day. It has already become a commonplace of our thinking, and it is beginning to find an expression in our art.

Writers like James Joyce, Gertrude Stein, Dos Passos, Sherwood Anderson—to name only a few—have ventured boldly into the realm of the subjective and have recorded the results of their

From *The Dramatic Imagination* by Robert Edmond Jones. Copyright 1941 by Robert Edmond Jones. Reprinted with the permission of Theatre Arts Books, New York.

exploration in all sorts of new and arresting forms. The stream-of-consciousness method of writing is an established convention of literature. It is readily accepted by the public and is intelligible to everyone. We find it easier today to read *Ulysses* than to read *Lord Ormont and His Aminta,* and we are no longer bewildered by *A Rose Is a Rose Is a Rose Is a Rose.*

Our playwrights, too, have begun to explore this land of dreams. They are casting about for ways in which to express the activity of the subconscious mind, to express thought before it becomes articulate. They are seeking to penetrate beneath the surface of our everyday life into the stream of images which has its source in the deep unknown springs of our being. They are attempting to express directly to the audience the unspoken thoughts of their characters, to show us not only the patterns of their conscious behavior but the pattern of their subconscious lives. These adventures into a new awareness of life indicate a trend in dramatic writing which is bound to become more clearly understood. But in their search for ways in which to embody this new awareness they have neglected to observe that there has recently come into existence the perfect medium for expressing the Unconscious in terms of the theatre. This medium is the talking picture.

In the simultaneous use of the living actor and the talking picture in the theatre there lies a wholly new theatrical art, whose possibilities are as infinite as those of speech itself.

There exists today a curious misconception as to the essential nature of motion pictures. We accept them unthinkingly as objective transcripts of life, whereas in reality they are subjective images of life. This fact becomes evident at once if we think of some well-known motion-picture star appearing in person on a stage and then of the same star appearing on the screen, a bodiless echo, a memory, a dream. Each self has its own reality, but the one is objective and the other is subjective. Motion pictures are our thoughts made visible and audible. They flow in a swift succession of images, precisely as our thoughts do, and their speed, with their flashbacks — like sudden uprushes of memory — and their abrupt transitions from one subject to another, approximates very closely the speed of our thinking. They have the rhythm of the thought-stream and the same uncanny ability to move forward or backward in space or time, unhampered by the rationalizations of the conscious mind. They project pure thought, pure dream, pure inner life.

Here lies the potential importance of this new invention. A new medium of dramatic expression has become available at the very moment when it is most needed in the theatre. Our dramatists now have it in their power to enlarge the scope of their dramas to an almost infinite extent by the use of these moving and speaking images. Some new playwright will presently set a motion-picture screen on the stage above and behind his actors and will reveal simultaneously the two worlds of the Conscious and the Unconscious which together make up the world we live in — the outer world and the inner world, the objective world of actuality and the subjective world of motive. On the stage we shall see the actual characters of the drama; on the screen we shall see their hidden secret selves. The drama will express the behavior of the characters set against a moving background, the expression of their subconscious mind — a continuous action and interaction.

All art moves inevitably toward this new synthesis of actuality and dream. Our present forms of drama and theatre are not adequate to express our newly enlarged consciousness of life. But within the next decade a new dimension may be added to them, and the eternal subject of drama — the conflict of Man and his Destiny — will take on a new significance.

❧ *from* TO A YOUNG STAGE DESIGNER

A stage setting has no independent life of its own. Its emphasis is directed toward the performance. In the absence of the actor it does not exist. Strange as it may seem, this simple and fundamental principle of stage design still seems to be widely misunderstood. How often in critics' reviews one comes upon the phrase "the settings were gorgeous!" Such a statement, of course, can mean only one thing, that no one concerned with producing the drama has thought of it as an organic whole. . . .

And yet a stage setting holds a curious kind of suspense. Go, for instance, into an ordinary empty drawing-room as it exists normally. There is no particular suspense about this room. It is just — empty. Now imagine the same drawing-room arranged and decorated for a particular function — a Christmas party for children, let us say. It is not completed as a room, now, until the children are in it. And if we wish to visualize for ourselves how important a part the sense of expectancy plays in such a room, let us imagine that there is a storm and that the children cannot come. A scene on the stage is filled with the same feeling of expectancy. It is like a mixture of chemical elements held in solution. The actor adds the one element that releases the hidden energy of the whole. Meanwhile, wanting the actor, the various elements which go to make up the setting remain suspended, as it were, in an indefinable tension. To create this suspense, this tension, is the essence of the problem of stage designing.

The designer must strive to achieve in his settings what I can only call a high potential. The walls, the furniture, the properties, are only the facts of a setting, only the outline. The truth is in everything but these objects, in the space they enclose, in the intense vibration they create. They are fused into a kind of embodied impulse. When the curtain rises we feel a frenzy of excitement focused like a burning-glass upon the actors. Everything on the stage becomes a part of the life of the instant. The play becomes a voice out of a whirlwind. The terrible and wonderful *dynamis* of the theatre pours over the footlights.

A strange, paradoxical calling, to work always behind and around, to bring into being a powerful non-being. How far removed it all is from the sense of display! One is reminded of the portraits of the Spanish noblemen painted by El Greco in the Prado in Madrid, whose faces, as Arthur Symons said, are all nerves, distinguished nerves, quieted by an effort. What a phrase for stage designers to remember! *Quieted by an effort....*

It is to the credit of our designers that they have almost made a fetish of abnegation. But let me remark parenthetically that it is sometimes difficult to go into the background when there is nothing in front of you. These pages are hardly the place in which to perpetuate the centuries-old squabble between playwrights and stage designers... It is enough to say that the jealously still persists and is as corroding in the twentieth century as it was in the seventeenth. The error lies in our conception of the theatre as something set aside for talents that are purely literary. As if the experience of the theatre had only to do with words! Our playwrights need to learn that plays are wrought, not written. There is something to be said in the theatre in terms of form and color and light that can be said in no other way.

The designer must learn to sense the atmosphere of a play with unusual clearness and exactness. He must actually live in it for a time, immerse himself in it, be baptized by it. This process is by no means so easy as it seems. We are all too apt to substitute ingenuity for clairvoyance. The temptation to invent is always present. I was once asked to be one of the judges of a competition of stage designs held by the Department of Drama of one of our well-known universities. All the designers had made sketches for the same play. The setting was the interior of a peasant hut on the west coast of Ireland. It turned out that these twenty or thirty young designers had mastered the technique of using dimmers and sliding stages and projected scenery. They had also acquired a considerable amount of information concerning the latest European developments of stagecraft. Their drawings were full of expressionism from Germany, constructivism from Russia, every kind of modernism. They were compilations of everything that had been said and done in the world of scenery in the last twenty years. But not one of the designers had sensed the atmosphere of the particular play in question.

I recalled for them my memory of the setting for the same play as produced by the Abbey Theatre on its first visit to America. This setting was very simple, far simpler and far less self-conscious than any of their designs. Neutral-tinted walls, a fireplace, a door, a window, a table, a few chairs, the red homespun skirts and bare feet of the peasant girls. A fisher's net, perhaps. Nothing more. But through the little window at the back one saw a sky of enchantment. All the poetry of Ireland shone in that little square of light, moody, haunting, full of dreams, calling us to follow on, follow on.... By this one gesture of excelling simplicity the setting was enlarged into the region of great theatre art.

Now here is a strange thing, I said to the designers. If we can succeed in seeing the essential quality of a play others will see it, too. We know the truth when we see it, Emerson said, from opinion, as we know that we are awake when we are awake. For example: you have never been in Heaven, and you have never seen an angel. But if someone produces a play about angels whose scenes are laid in Heaven you will know at a glance whether his work is right or wrong. Some curious intuition will tell you. The sense of recognition is the highest experience the theatre can give. As we work we must seek not for self-expression or for performance for its own sake, but only to establish the dramatist's intention, knowing that when we have succeeded in doing so audiences will say to themselves, not, This is beautiful, This is charming, This is splendid, but—This is true. This is the way it is. So it is, and not otherwise.... There is nothing esoteric in the search for truth in the theatre. On the contrary, it is a part of the honest everyday life of the theatre.

The energy of a particular play, its emotional content, its aura, so to speak, has its own definite physical dimensions. It extends just so far in space and no farther. The walls of the setting must be placed at precisely this point. If the setting is larger than it should be, the audience gets a feeling of meagerness and hollowness; if smaller, a feeling of confusion and pressure. It is often very difficult to adjust the physical limits of a setting to its emotional limitations. But great plays exist outside the categories of dimension. Their bounty is as boundless as the air. Accordingly we need not think of a stage-setting, in a larger sense, as a matter of establishing space relations. Great plays have nothing to do with space. The setting for a great play is no more subject to the laws of space composition than music is. We may put aside once and for all the idea of a stage-setting as a glorified show-window in which actors are to be exhibited and think of it instead as a kind of symphonic accompaniment or obbligato to the play, as evocative and intangible as music itself. Indeed, music may play a more important role than we now realize in the scenic evocations of the future.

In the last analysis the designing of stage scenery is not the problem of an architect or a painter or a sculptor or even a musician, but of a poet. By a poet I do not mean, of course, an artist who is concerned only with the writing of verse. I am speaking of the poetic attitude.... [A]ll art in the theatre should be, not descriptive, but evocative. Not a description, but an evocation. A bad actor describes a character; he explains it. He expounds it. A good actor evokes a character. He summons it up. He reveals it to us....

The poetic conception of stage design bears little relation to the accepted convention of realistic scenery in the theatre. As a matter of fact it is quite the opposite. Truth in the theatre, as the masters of the theatre have always known, stands above and beyond mere accuracy to fact. In the theatre the actual thing is never the exciting thing. Unless life is turned into art on the stage it stops being alive and goes dead.

So much for the realistic theatre. *The artist should omit the details, the prose of nature and give us only the spirit and splendor*. When we put a star in a sky, for example, it is not just a star in a sky, but a "supernal messenger, excellently bright." This is purely a question of our point of view. A star is, after all, only an electric light. The point is, how the audience will see it, what images it will call to mind. We read of Madame Pitoeff's Ophelia that in the Mad Scene she handled the roses and the rosemary and the rue as if she were in a Paradise of flowers. We must bring into the immediate life of the theatre — "the two hours' traffic of our stage" — images of a larger life. The stage we inhabit is a chamber of the House of Dreams. Our work on this stage is to suggest the immanence of a visionary world all about us. In this world Hamlet dwells, and Oedipus, and great Juno, known by her immortal gait, and the three witches on the blasted heath. We must learn by a deliberate effort of the will to walk in these enchanted regions. We must imagine ourselves into their vastness.

Here is the secret of the flame that burns in the work of the great artists of the theatre. They seem so much more aware than we are, and so much more awake, and so much more alive that they make us feel that what we call living is not living at all, but a kind of sleep. Their knowledge, their wealth of emotion, their wonder, their elation, their swift clear seeing surrounds every occasion with a crowd of values that enriches it beyond anything which we, in our happy satisfaction, had ever imagined. In their hands it becomes not only a thing of beauty but a thing of power. And we see it all — beauty and power alike — as a part of the life of the theatre.

Richard Southern

Southern is a creative teacher of stage history and stage technique; the following remarks are excerpts from one of a series of lectures inaugurating a Rockefeller Lectureship in the Department of Drama at the University of Bristol, England.

The basic conception of the open stage — its potential, its demands upon actors (and the freedom it grants them), its history not only in the Elizabethan public theatres but in architectural aspects of later theatre structures — provide Dr. Southern with a basis for discussion of a vital approach to new drama and modern stage techniques. Southern's understanding of stage technique in general enables him to use his researches in the most creative manner, combining perception of convention with the desire for freedom of expression typical of the working professional. Southern has written extensively on the nature and history of stage practice, including a system of scenery planning in terms of proscenium and sight lines, stage settings, and many other subjects of concern to both amateurs and professionals.

❧ *from* THE RISE OF THE OPEN STAGE IDEA

... The urgent plays of past times fitted their own shape of stage — they did not force themselves to accept a foreign one. The stages they fitted had a certain common factor. Surely it is not illogical to inquire whether this factor common to them, which served their urgency so well, might not also serve well the urgency of those particular plays of to-day which in production rouse a sense of dissatisfaction with the current stage!

Just what the characteristics and limitations of our current stage are, and what is the liberating common factor of this other type of stage — which I have called the open stage — it is the purpose of these papers to find out.

But it is not (I repeat) their purpose to advocate an open stage everywhere, or anywhere where there is no need for it.

Let us not be too precipitate, to begin with, in asking to be told what an "open" stage exactly is. Let us put aside the question-begging word "open" and first see what a *stage* in its simplest form is, and especially how the stage in that simplest form affects an actor upon it.

To do this let us dissect the stage from the theatre, to see what its essential features are when it stands alone. After all, the theatre is only the building put round a stage to supply offices for those concerned with what goes on upon that stage. . . .

This simplest form of stage I may call "the booth stage." I once made an attempt — though it was not an entirely successful one — to represent in a chart the development of stage and theatre structure throughout Europe after the fashion of a genealogical tree, wherein the Hellenistic stage descended from the classical Greek stage and then led to the Graeco-Roman and the Roman, and where the mansion-stage of the Middle Ages led to the simultaneous settings of the sixteenth-century Terentian stages and thence to Mahelot's scenes at the Hôtel de Bourgogne — and so forth; a somewhat artificial attempt that presented me with numerous breaks and failed to be consistently convincing — except on one notable point: one thing did stand out; one form of stage could be tangibly traced at any period and reasonably shown to have an unbroken development, though it was so simple and so adequate for its purpose that it betrayed few signs of the changes of evolution. It was the little strolling-players' stage which is much the same on the Greek mime vases, in the simpler mediaeval fit-ups, in the quack-doctor, or mountebank, stages, the simpler Commedia dell' Arte platforms, the booths of the Victorian fairs, some of the penny gaffs, and the pierrot's home on the sands at any seaside resort to-day.

It was, briefly, a fairly high platform with some sort of curtained booth at the back from which the players came, and with possibly a canopy above, but otherwise generally innocent of further elaboration. It is because of this players' room behind that I name the type the "booth" stage. Now this stage, I believe, has a most fertile contribution to make to the idea of modern theatre.

When we consider the booth stage with the particular intention of finding out just what sort of assistance it gives to the actor and what kind of acting it stands to help, there are fortunately many pictures of scenes of action upon it to help us and we may find them in a variety of periods. Especially suggestive to me among these pictures is one by a German woodcutter, Johann Rassers, from 1574, where a figure dressed as a woman is haranguing the audience from a stage set up in a street. The action of this figure is immensely significant of what I may for the moment call "direct audience-address." She leans forward, one arm raised and the other on her hip, and lets them have it. It is worth studying this figure and its stage.

The background is scenically very simple, but theatrically very sufficient; it is not representational, but it is decorative and it provides an excellent entrance for actors.

The actor is *lifted up* on such a stage—he is eminent. Among these stages a particular feature which stands out is that nearly all are in effect high—like the prow of a ship overhanging the water. They are as a matter of course all three-sided stages with the booth on the fourth side—the back. There are thus always two forward corners, and these are theatrically particularly salient. But we must remember that such stages were commonly watched by a standing (not a sitting) audience, and it is for this reason that they had to be some five to seven feet high.

The actors, then, were well clear of the spectators' heads and they would therefore acquire that strange impressiveness of tilted perspective that C. Lewis Hind so well pointed out as the achievement in Velasquez's portrait of the fat and pompous Alessandro del Boro in Berlin. How to make such a portly figure impressive? Put him on a high stage. Lewis Hind speaks of the picture (see *The Education of an Artist,* chap. xxx) as "that figure of Alessandro del Boro proclaiming magnificently how a Master can *ennoble* his subject. It startled! It fascinated! Never shall I forget my first glimpse of that towering portrait.... Darkly, grossly, arrogantly he poses against the pillar, trampling on the flag of his enemy, standing high, the point of sight at his feet, as if, while still alive, he had stepped into his niche of posthumous fame." Thus also may a character do when an actor brings it into being on an open stage.

It is however no two dimensional-picture of the human figure which the booth stage gives, for the actor stands out from the background and can be notably looked up to, but looked up to, as well, *on three sides.* He can therefore advance all the more impressively into one of those two salient corners and overhang the multitude like a figurehead, or lean over with the impressiveness of a preacher in a pulpit — his arm and eyes sweeping a full semi-circle in his address.

Not only can he be looked up to but also overlooked, from above — and his clearly separate figure, diagonally below us traversing the carpet of the stage floor, is just as theatrically moving. We may see him in this way when, beside the ancient booth stage, we climb an adjacent tree to watch, or look down from an upper-floor window in a nearby house.

Or we may see him in this way in certain other very special circumstances which lead us deep into our subject — that is to say when, after the building of the first English theatre upon so cunning and so inspired a device, James Burbage offers us the vantage point of one of the two galleries. A new experience is open now to playgoers. In such galleries we may see better than ever and partake more fully in the experience of the actor addressing his audience. He may look up and address us directly with a thrown-back head, his white face appealing towards us; he may look out, addressing us vicariously and lowering intensely over the groundlings, but with a breadth of acting that includes us as we lean forward to partake in an address by watching it. This too can be romantic and moving theatre, for to watch intimacy is often to experience it.

On all such stages an actor may come forward and *take* an audience, he may dominate it whether it is at his feet or above his head; and his gestures are broad. There are deep lessons in the art of theatre architecture here. We may touch their fringe now as we watch the booth stage develop into the Elizabethan playhouse. My friend Walter Hodges took the simple theory of the booth stage and gave it a considerable advance.[1]. . .

Hodges' significant suggestion is that Burbage's first English playhouse was made by erecting a galleried auditorium round just this familiar type of stage but retaining the effect of the free-standing platform and its booth behind as entities — as the most vital part and core of the whole structure — not suppressing their character to be a sub-part of a greater, separately envisioned, architectural unity. He claims that the booth-nature of the Elizabethan stage, with all the effect it gave to an actor, should stand forward clear in its integrity in the surrounding embrace of the playhouse galleries — dominating them, not subservient to them or arising from them.

Given this idea of the galleries added round an already designed booth stage, it is easy to see that the upper stage may not have been a mere new development arising from the fortuitous creation of some ranges of spectators' circles, but something that existed before them, perhaps an old feature of the booth stage, and one indeed for which it is easy to find a neighbour parallel in the Rederijker stages of Holland. Thus Hodges conceives the tiring-house façade as a unified feature on its own, evolved on its own with all its details as a proper "scene" to back and furnish an acting-area. . . .

We have, at this point, two contributory streams of thought; first, the eternal booth stage, and second, the Elizabethan theatre which arose deliberately to enclose it. What flavour can we recall of the impression of acting on such a stage when it was enclosed by the galleries of the early theatre?

There is a short passage of Dekker's which so perfectly embodies that commanding spread of attention through the whole house — through the "standings" as well as the two-penny "rooms" — which can be exercised by the striding player on such an open stage, that it becomes a passage almost of revelation about the Elizabethan actor's play with an audience. The actor is apostrophized, in the Prologue of *If It Be Not Good the Devil is in It* (1602), with:

> *Giue me That Man,*
> *Who when the Plague of an Impostumd Braynes*
> *(Breaking out) infects a Theater, and hotly raignes,*
> *Killing the Hearers Hearts, that the vast roomes*
> *Stand empty, like so many Dead-mens toombes,*
> *Can call the Banishd Auditor home, And tye*
> *His Eare (with golden chaines) to his Melody*

[1] C. Walter Hodges, *The Globe Restored* (London, 1953).

The "vast roomes" are the compartments of the great embracing galleries. The actor before them might hold his audience so that they watched him as still as dead men, while he strode the scaffold in their centre.

This matter of *address* — the particular way the actor may direct his scene to the hearers when he has this open stage at his feet, and them around it, is worth expanding in some detail before we go on to consider the development of the booth stage.

The whole matter of this kind of address will rise vividly in the imagination of anyone who can couple an actor's experience of addressing a play-audience in a dark auditorium and through a proscenium frame, with something of the lecturer's experience of addressing a clearly lit audience who gaze now not at a picture but at the lecturer alone. The lecturer is here somewhat in the position of a booth-stage player in a soliloquy, though without make-up and in a lounge suit. To get his show over now he has as it were to gird his loins and come out to them. He needs direct address. He cannot, as the modern actor can, rely on a producer's placing, the picture, and the play. It all depends on him as a person.

Strangely enough, he may come to experience much less stage-fright in such circumstances. He has no longer to remember the eternal restriction of his place in the picture and his place in the lines; but he has to interest his audience directly. You may begin to see how a young actor may often find it difficult to ignore that instinct of direct address and to learn instead to put over his lines as if on the one hand his audience were not there and yet on the other in such a way that they may all fully appreciate every word and point. After such consideration, indeed, it may appear to be a folly to pretend the audience is not in the theatre and watching. Surely the whole craft of acting lies in the assumption that an audience is looking at you! Your acting is the performance of an action for an audience.

Now this estimate of acting the booth stage supports entirely. There is no possibility of a shallow pretence at forgetting the audience. If it's there at all, it's there for certain and around one's feet and around one's brows — a sea and a wall of faces, critical, receptive, what you make it, but your element. . . .

Now what is the real point of all this revival of interest in the Elizabethan stage which we see so widespread to-day in the 1950s? Does it only arise from a commendable desire to perform Shakespeare's plays more faithfully? Or is it composed of a realization that the method of performance itself which the open stage offers is an exciting one, and may perhaps be excellent for some of our own uses? Let us follow the historical fate of the booth stage.

In my own approach as a student to the Elizabethan stage I was for a long time baffled and (to tell the truth) uninterested. I could envision acting as it were "nakedly" on a booth stage, and I could envision something quite different—acting with scenery behind an arch; either idea could arouse fascination. But the Elizabethan stage had neither nakedness nor scene, but a mysterious "study" and a "tarras."

I remember, early in my lecturing, telling the Dean of a London University College at which I was giving a series of talks on scenery, that in effect nothing was known about the Elizabethan stage and that therefore I proposed to devote very little time to it. I remember also the gentle incredulity in his voice as he pointed to the monumental works of Dr. W. J. Lawrence, Sir Edmund Chambers, and others. I therefore suspended my decision and went back to these authorities and read them again.

But I only found afresh that though there was much in the work of the investigators to prompt me yet I was not happy about it all and could not feel my way into the tangle from the scenic angle—the effect which was made on the stage. The Elizabethans are said not to have used scenery; they therefore seemed not my concern nor to offer anything understandable to a research for material for present-day practice. You will see later in how far this was borne out.

Thus, my own research on the Elizabethan stage seemed to come to a dead end at this point. In my study I dropped it and picked up at the Restoration period, for here I had scenery to examine and a kind of show and theatre which seemed more nearly like our own, and thus appeared to be more promising of results suggestive to modern practice.

But I now came across another puzzle about the stage.

In the Restoration, the scenery was often far less important or significant than ours. Some of it was rich, but there was a counter-school of thought whose work we overlook when we concentrate on the evidence of this period for splendid scenic shows. In this other way of procedure the scenery was always set very far away, right at the back of the stage and was probably relatively dimly lit, while the acting generally took place well in front of it on *a very deep forestage*—where the chief candles and the footlights were.

Now a proper and sympathetic understanding of the significance of the use of this deep forestage is not easy at first. Our ideas are obscured by an obsession with our modern stage. We shall find that this forestage really corresponded with the old open stage and had the auditorium round it on three sides as the open stage had the audience round it on three sides. The scenery was at the back where the booth used to be, and was, like it, merely a backing (not a surround) to the action. Unless we realize this we shall not see why the Restoration theatre-men had a very deep forestage, nor why it was that only in England (with its Elizabethan legacy) a forestage of just this type was ever used, nor in fact shall we see what a forestage really is but will continue to suppose it is the front of a "proper" stage.

At this point my picture began to shift and widen. It became clear that investigations might very likely have to turn so far from their original subject of scenery as to embrace something which I had not imagined to be significant at the outset, and which indeed may always have seemed to most a subject of dusty dullness and merely "academic" interest — the subject of the development of the English theatre auditorium — the way the audience sat before a stage. What can this have to do with show presentation?

Once one is prompted to ask this question, the whole subject takes on another life — and an intriguingly interesting life. The theatre as a whole becomes one's concern. And a new vista is opened for our survey in the existence of certain original, early playhouses; notable among them (beside the well-known example at Bristol) being the almost perfect building at Richmond in Yorkshire and the fragile relics at King's Lynn.

It was while investigating King's Lynn that I found myself being pushed back not only to the Restoration but beyond, despite the fact that the theatre there dated only from 1766 — and another piece of the picture dropped into place, for here the only considerable item that remained of the whole thing — stage and auditorium together — was the unity comprising those side-supports and ceiling which were once associated with the forestage.... [I noted during research in 1948 at King's Lynn that there is] good reason to suppose that the canopy...may be derived fairly closely from the Elizabethan canopy...that is to say, the "heavens." ... [I]t will be clear that even in this side avenue of the architectural form of the auditorium we are being led back again to the Elizabethan stage.

I find from my notes on King's Lynn that the steps which took me back were these — I wrote there;

"We may then make this observation — the larger portion of the mid-Georgian stage was incapable of scenic illusion. The area upon which the players principally played was of a purely conventional conception. Its appearance was unrelated to the scenery, and all the actors upon it would be in the atmosphere of the auditorium and not in the atmosphere of the scenery. To drag in a modern phrase, they would be 'out of the picture'.... That the Georgian players used the forestage a great deal is, of course, well known. Something of their relation to the house around them as they stood on the forestage is clear to feel at Richmond. (But the Richmond forestage is later and comparatively shallow.) Nowhere, however, is any conception quite so clearly gained as at King's Lynn of what an individual unity the proscenium-cum-forestage had and what a completely adequate and completely furnished acting-area is presented ... here was a unit adequate in itself—not a mere forward appurtenance of a truer stage behind it. The link with Elizabethan tradition was still tangible."

The forestage was itself a sufficent acting-area, and was the lineal child of the open stage. Scenery was nothing but an indulgence behind it.

In such a way we may begin to feel a more sympathetic approach to the Elizabethan stage—not as the ancestor of a stage with scenery (that has Italian forefathers) but as the begetter of a "furnished acting-area"—that is, a properly appointed acting-place, an area designed exclusively for acting a show upon, and provided with just such particular adjuncts as would aid that acting—without needing scenery....

Peter Larkin

These candid remarks by one of America's most talented younger designers formed part of a preface to a striking exhibit of architectural and stage renderings—hypotheses for new theatres—by eight teams of designers. The plans were reproduced in a book in which Larkin's observations also appeared; they are reprinted here in full.

His stage designs have been seen in New York and in many other cities. He has designed for City Center (*The Wild Duck*) and Stratford, Connecticut (*Hamlet*); in 1952, he designed the ballet of *A Streetcar*

Named Desire in Montreal and, for the National Repertory Theatre in 1964, both *The Sea Gull* and *The Crucible*. Other designs include *Teahouse of the August Moon* (1953), *Ondine* (1954), and *Inherit the Wind* (1955). Mr. Larkin studied at the Yale Drama School (1946-48) and is a member of United Scenic Artists.

ON DESIGN FOR NEW THEATRE

"The trouble with our modern theatre is that it is mechanically perfect. It is far too perfect: its perfection has become tiresome. Interlocking dimmer boxes, stereopticon lenses, false prosceniums, revolving stages, sliding stages. The theatre is like a great throne: a throne with no king."

— ROBERT EDMOND JONES

I have searched my thoughts for some time now to know why all my good artist friends and my good sculptor friends don't have the slightest use for the kind of work that I do, theatre work. Though I know they're an ingrown, contentious, nasty lot, this reaction bothers me. Have theatre workers become those lowest of villains, commercial artists? . . .

The professional theatre is soon going to be in the same predicament that the New Haven Railroad was recently. It will sit there in the mother roc's nest with its beak open, chirping for subsidy.

Why are the professional theatre and the regional theatre further and further apart? Because the regional theatre is growing all the time and Broadway is standing still, and, if it comes down to survival, I will bet on the country mouse rather than on his fat urban cousin.

When talking about new theatre, everyone tends to be glib. Generalities come easily, and pontifical irrelevancies have the ring of sincerity. Seems that it is safe to talk, since it is secretly agreed that the poor thing is dying anyway.

Here are eight theatre projects by architect-designer teams, each working along different lines.[1] Some are city solutions; some are for colleges. Some are all-purpose theatres, others are complexes of theatre buildings. The interesting thing about them is that they all

From "Notes on Theatre Conception and Design" by Peter Larkin in *The Ideal Theatre: Eight Concepts,* pp. 9-10. Reprinted by permission of The American Federation of Arts.

[1] Larkin refers here to designs and renderings contained in the published volume; this essay forms part of the preface and introduction.

tacitly agree that the two-dimensional proscenium theatre is a thing of the past and they look for new theatre performance experiences in three dimensions. Perhaps the flat viewed frieze spectacle has, through vibration of film techniques, lost itself, its own rightful audience. It is certain that the cry for intimacy in performance owes a debt to film — one medium, however, is not another. Why are films made from successful plays or musicals usually bad? Because they are transposed bodily from one medium to another without organization of the material in terms of a new medium.

Plays for new theatres must be developed in the same way. If a three-dimensional plastic experience is created, the plays must be different from what they ever were — bigger in some way. Scene designers on Broadway often design multi-set shows with no waits between scenes, plays which are basically written in film terms. This is not wrong, but the theatre doesn't do that sort of thing well. The author is certainly entitled to want his production to move quickly and easily. He is right in not wanting to wait for scene changes. But some new way of doing this will have to come.

Every one of these projects is trying for a three-dimensional "oneness" of audience-performer relationship. This is not coincidence. Theatre architecture inside and out will become sculpture. But I believe the playwright must begin it. The lure of proscenium is the lure of any toy theatre. Any architect or designer who uses models will tell you that they help him sell his ideas. They do this mostly by intriguing the clients — clients of all ages, 7 to 70. The model trees. The pretty little parked cars. The proscenium weaves the same spell for the adult theatregoer. Nothing does it like peeking in the end of a dark shoe box at actor-puppets, moving crablike across the stage in their Pollach slots. And it has lasted a long time.

The only way the old forms will disappear from theatre production is when they become too expensive to operate. Again, the only way you can get people to use new tools in the theatre is not to give them the old ones.

The proscenium in any thrust stage set-up or arena set-up is a vestige, like the bones in your toes that you don't use any more. It doesn't do any good to build a forestage in front of it, or to surround it with seating. It's still there, and if you are really going to change, you'll have to think of something else.

Scenery as it is now will be going, going, gone soon from the professional theatre. Productions must be made to flow nowadays. The scenery will go, not because anyone wants to change it, but because no one will be able to afford it. Just as the dinosaur became extinct, so will heavily-freighted musicals. Lumber is never a substitute for ideals—construction is not creation. Any new theatre that fobs off turn-tables, elevator traps, full stage wagons, contour curtains as new production techniques is wrong. Someone, for instance, says, let's build a new theatre. Someone else says, we must have a turntable; that's the latest thing. Outside of the fact that it is not the latest thing, it, like all other devices, has as many limitations as the ones it cures. When you have sold your backers or trustees a Glorious Gadget, you are then honor-bound—hell, fire, and damnation—to try and use it every chance you get. What, for instance, is the use of a treadmill 60 feet long, 4 feet wide, that whirs majestically and brings on a table and a chair?

Let's put the money in people.

Just as when you ask someone what a new book is like, he is apt to tell you the plot, if you ask a man what kind of theatre is he building, he will probably start by describing apparatus and dimensions.

These are strange things for a designer to be saying—especially since I have been involved in some particularly large dinasaurs, but it's the way I've come to feel. As I work in the theatre, it seems to me that every kind of theatre piece—a play, opera, whatever—has its own organics—a way of seeing it that is better than any other. Some plays will have more impact when done in certain ways. What if the playwrights and the directors had the choice—as well as cast approval plus script—of what kind of theatre to play in? What if even within the same evening, within the framework of one play, different relationships might occur?

The architect, especially, has a higher responsibility to a theatre building, since so few are built, than to pick consultants like raspberries off a bush and get them to affirm the practicality of a shape and building that he has already decided on. How many regional high schools have gone up in the last 30 years with stages in them, fit only for the graduation exercises, whose responsibility is exactly—the building of a new theatre?

The writer starts theatre.

The author also is a victim of the movies. As he writes his play, he cuts and pans with a vengeance, where before he strove mightily to stick with the classic unities of time and place.

It seems to me that, in many of these projects, the architect and designer are unwilling handmaidens to a big problem.

How can you provide new tools for a new medium, as yet unknown? The cart is way ahead of the horse. I believe that this exhibition [of designs for new theatres and stages] is a challenge to the playwright. If it is not to the playwright, then to some sovereign theatre-thinker who will commission new work done in new ways.

I attended not long ago a meeting at the Ford Foundation in which our finest playwright bawled all the designers out for our prehistoric, creaking old theatre. Why were long scene changes and squeaky casters lousing him up? Why were there no new techniques available to him? It is true our professional theatre hasn't got answers for that. He placed the responsibility on the architect-designer's head. These eight projects [in the exhibit] place some of it back on his. It seems unlikely that he will take his plays out in the country to colleges for their initial production. He is stuck with New York theatres if he stays in New York.

You cannot develop what you believe to be an undiscovered wonder drug and then go looking for a new disease. Designers must not design stage sets but stages, architects not theatre buildings but theatre; and playwrights must stop writing movies and write in a new way for theatre.

I found the other day some material that Robert Edmond Jones had sent to me. He never stopped dreaming about how wonderful the theatre might become. He wrote: "The drama has progressed, as civilization has progressed, from its first aboriginal form, the communal expression of mass emotions, through a great variety of forms which have continually tended to become less and less conventional, more and more naturalistic. The typical play of today is a photographic transcript of actual life. The modern realistic drama with its picture setting—or drama founded on observation and sympathy—has now given place to the motion picture. A new drama is being born—a drama founded not on observation, but on vision— a drama which will be expressed in new conventions of significant form and sound and motion."

🦋

Mordecai Gorelik

The following observations are practical notes by one of our most distinguished teachers and practitioners of stage design. Some of his most important settings were for Group Theatre productions — *Success Story, Golden Boy, Men in White;* he also designed the famous Theatre Guild productions *Processional* and *All My Sons.* Gorelik's teaching experience has ranged back and forth between Europe and America, between the New York theatre industry and film sets for Hollywood. He is conversant with university theatre and with all elements of *avant-garde* techniques and has had personal contact with almost every important European designer of the last thirty years. His comments here range from a short discussion of a play's "atmosphere" to hard specifics of design, from the question of a designer's research to the interesting uses of a small-scale model.

⚓ *from* DESIGNING THE PLAY

. . . The work begins the second time one reads the script. I say the second time, because the designer reads the script the first time just for the joy of reading a good play — if it happens to be good. In passing, it should be noted that some training is necessary for reading plays, even as literature. The lines of dialogue are really only a disguise for the action. One must learn to see back of the written lines, visualizing the *movements* which are taking place, seeing in one's mind the characters and the locale in which they move. The dramatist's stage directions — "a fireplace, left," "she enters, right," do not take the place of one's own imaginative work. . . .

After this preliminary reading the designer analyzes the script with great care. It is not enough to work from the author's description of the setting, no matter how detailed or clearly stated that may be. In fact, many designers deliberately avoid reading the author's directions until later on. Speaking quite seriously, the author must not be taken too literally, and he will not be thankful if he is followed uncreatively. He does not, and should not, want to interfere with the designer's creative work, if this artist knows his business. The designer is a specialist, and may have ideas which the author has overlooked. . . .

If conferences with the dramatist are optional, those with the director are not. The director (who is sometimes the same as the

From "Designing the Play" by Mordecai Gorelik in *Producing the Play,* John Gassner, ed. (Holt, Rinehart and Winston, Inc.: 1953). Reprinted by permission of the author.

producer) is the field marshal of the production. He is responsible not only for the actors' rehearsals but for every production element, including the settings, the technical work, and even the amount of time allotted to scene or light rehearsals. In the inception period, the designer's work does not differ, so far as the scenery is concerned, from that of the director. The designer must see, quite as clearly as the director, how the actors are going to move, what the important scenes are, the "line" of the production, and so on. (The whole point of the production may change if the show acquires a particular leading lady instead of some other leading lady.) Like the director, he must ask himself, "What will this show *say* or *do* to its audiences? How will my settings *help* to say or do it? How will the actors *use* my setting?"

Individual directors vary in their method of talking with designers. A few merely accept any suggestion the designer puts before them. Some sound out the designer until they feel either that he is *en rapport* with the play, or that he is fundamentally removed from it and that someone else should design the settings. Very few directors are prepared for being sounded out by the designer. It may, indeed, be necessary for the latter to take the initiative. I ask a great many questions in order to get my bearings on any show. These questions may be somewhat disconcerting to directors who believe in the "two hearts that beat as one" theory, but in the long run they help to clarify things. The Group Theatre directors would often tell me, "Go ahead and ask your irritating questions. We always get stuck on some of them, but in figuring out the answers we help our own work as well." . . .

DRAMATIC METAPHOR

What is the "atmosphere" of the locale? What quality does it have which makes it an integral part of this play and of no other play? What is the style of the author, what is notable about the historic period of the play or about its geographical location? What is the *dramatic metaphor* of each setting, and of the settings as a whole? What is the presumable history of the locale? What will the actors' movements be like? Will their actions around a table best convey the theme, or is a fireplace or stairway the natural center of the action?

The scene is a dentist's office. Is the dentistry a factor that is important for the story? Or should the point be, merely, that it is the office of a professional man? . . . (See *Rocket to the Moon* by Clifford

Odets.) The scene is a battleship. Is it the heavy steel plates that are important, or the fact that certain tragic events on this ship are taking place on an idyllic summer's day? ... (See *The Sailors of Cattaro* by Friedrich Wolf.) The scene is the home of an Italian fruit peddlar in New York City. The home is not just a box in which the characters knock around. No matter how poor and shabby, it is divided into distinct areas on stage: the cozy corner where the older folks sit and philosophize in armchairs, near a window filled with plants and a canary in a cage. On the other side of the room is the dinner table, where the younger people always seem to gather to carry on their more lively affairs. The steam radiator is the small boy's favorite perch in summer, and sister is always at the family bureau, which she prettifies with imitation flowers from Woolworth's. All these are distinct playing areas, each with its own pathos ... (See *Golden Boy* by Clifford Odets.)

It is the *dramatic metaphor*, probably, which sums up, for each setting, all the thoughts which the designer may have. This metaphor is a piece of dramatic compression. Thus, the attic bedroom of the *Three Sisters* is not only an attic, not only a bedroom, not only a girls' room, not only a European room, not only a room of the period of 1901, not only a room belonging to the gentlefolk whom Chekhov wrote about. On top of all that, and including all that, it may be, for the designer, the scene of a *raging fever*. There is a fire going on outside. The whole house is restless, tossing about in this fire-atmosphere, unable to sleep. People wander about dumbly, or blurt out sudden confidences, as if they were light-headed. The designer shows the fitful reflection of the distant fire on the walls of the room. The beds are surrounded by screens, as they might naturally be, yet the arrangement stresses the idea of a sickbed. The lamp is burning low; next to it a table and chair are heaped with clothes and other objects in disorder ...

Rightly done, the setting has an electric effect on the audience. The audience knows instinctively what the designer is saying; it knows how the designer is describing the room.

In searching for his central dramatic image, the designer should not overlook a possible hint given by the title of the play, since a well-titled play sometimes contains the very essence of the play's meaning. *Desire Under the Elms* is an instance. This title seems clear enough, yet as a designer I found it baffling until it struck me that the phrase "under the elms" ought to be my starting-point. This thought enabled me to escape from the mere naturalism of a farmhouse flanked by elm trees; instead, I conceived of a house under the great, immemorial, spreading elms. A little pencil sketch, some two inches square, was enough to fix this idea; it recorded the silhouettes of two great trees, with a silhouette of a house beneath them.

The metaphor does not have to be spectacular to be effective. One of the best scenes in the movie *The Long Voyage Home,* directed by John Ford, is the brief, transitional shot of the *Glencairn* on the morning after the drunken carouse. We look toward the bow of the *Glencairn.* No sailors are visible. There is a breeze, kicking up spray as the ship plows toward the north. This is *the healing sea*—a metaphor which makes a perfect transition between two important actions on the boat.

As we study the script, we try to penetrate closer and closer to the deepest signifiance of the play. For myself, I usually work from the climactic scenes onward. That is, I try to visualize the most poignant or most striking scenes. I try to understand the dramatic progression in intensity, or the change in quality, from one scene to another. When I know that I have provided for these essential scenes, I make the other scenes fit in. The climactic moments are like the piers of a bridge, on which the cables are afterwards spun. I try, also, to fasten upon a *central scenic motif* for each setting. Does the composition of the room revolve about a door? A table? A view from the window? A color? A texture? Just as the director must find a central action, so the designer must find a central scenic theme related to this action.

An extraordinary amount of pre-vision is required of the designer. His sketches are made, his models and working drawings are half-way finished, about the time the cast begins rehearsal. It will take four weeks before the production as a whole acquires its final meaning; only in the last week of rehearsal, as a rule, will the full significance of the play dawn on the cast and the director, no matter how well thought out the show may be before it starts to rehearse. The process of rehearsal is a voyage of discovery. The director can only set the course and rig the sails; just what he and the cast will eventually create he cannot know for certain. Yet the designer must already have arrived at his artistic destination before his colleagues have set out on their quest.

RESEARCH

. . . Where does one do research? If possible at the very spot where the action is supposed to take place. I have gone, sketch-pad in hand, into copper mines, steel foundries, hospitals, river barges, light-houses, farmhouses, textile factories, police stations, Fifth Avenue mansions, palaces, and hovels. I never travel without going into every kind of place, public or private, into which I can get entry. In order to put dramatic scenes on the stage one must have a richly stored imagination and a background of a million pictures.

Scene design, perhaps more than any other graphic art, demands a wide culture, a life of experience and travel, and of reading. You spend far too much of your income on fine illustrated books. You keep files of clippings taken from magazines and newspapers — pictures of almost everything conceivable. (I started my own file in 1917, and am constantly adding to it.) You keep samples of strange textiles, of wallpapers, of wood veneer, papier-mâché, and metal. You have shelves stocked with merchandising catalogues, including those from Montgomery Ward and Sears, Roebuck. And still you find it necessary to do additional work at the public library. . . .

It is no less vital that the designer know the masterpieces of painting and sculpture. He should be able to detect the kinship of some particular dramatic scene to the work of Renoir, Whistler, Cézanne, Lukas Cranach the Elder, Reginald Marsh, Chagall, Meissonier, Praxiteles, or Hans Arp. The designer who does not have this sort of understanding is professionally illiterate, however gifted he may otherwise be.

MODELS AND BLUEPRINTS

. . . It may seem an anticlimax and rather surprising that one shall make any finished sketches at all, when they come so late in the design process. One reason for the finished sketch is that it remains a record of the work. More immediately important, it sums up, orchestrates, the work that has gone before and helps greatly in solving details of architecture, properties, and painting. It should be added that this method, while craftsmanlike, has the disadvantage of lacking sales value with producers, who want a finished sketch before them from the start, so that they can see what they think they are going to get.

As a rule I start work on the model before I begin drafting, and I never design without making models. I do half my work on the model, working on it as a sculptor does on his clay. I honestly cannot see how a true scene designer can work without models. There are designers who get along without them, but the result tells in the fact that their floor plans are almost always static — a box shape whether for interiors or exteriors, and a type of setting which is fundamentally unrelated to the actors. . . .

Ordinarily I begin the model work, not with the settings, but with the furniture or other large properties, placing these on the model stage area where they are properly in sight lines and of most value to the actors. When the properties are well placed, I start building the settings around them.

The scene designers' models that are displayed in public are usually exhibition models specially built for that purpose; they are made of wood, pressed fibre board or heavy cardboard, and are carefully painted. In everyday practice scenic models are crude paper ones, often uncolored; they are intended only for the eyes of the director and scene builder. Two-ply or three-ply kid finish Bristol paper is well adapted for the working model, especially if it does not have to be colored. It is also possible to use colored paper, heavy cardboard, wood blocks, balsam wood, modelling wax, wall paper, textiles, wire, or any other material that strikes one's fancy. Rubber cement, Scotch tape, heavy glue, and nails serve to fasten the model together.

Once or twice the director escapes from rehearsals long enough to examine the model. Sometimes he brings members of the cast with him, and usually the stage manager calls several times to make written notes while surveying the model. The director's visits are bound to result in some alterations. Furniture is pushed a fraction of an inch here or there. Doors may be taken out, added, or made to exchange places. The scale figure, a piece of cardboard with a human outline, is carried around to all parts of the model. (I have a cardboard figure named John Barrymore who has starred in most of my productions.) The director, with the model before him, gets new ideas for action. Occasionally he sees that he can get along without something he had thought he needed; or he may find that he needs something additional. . . .

Stagecraft and Composition: Pictorial Principles

To the extent that the stage setting resembles a picture, it obeys the laws of painting. It must have pictorial composition, meaning that there is a center of visual interest, to which the other visual elements are related. The center of pictorial composition on stage, aside from the actors, is, logically, the central scenic motif.

If Lee Simonson chose a long, curving ramp as the dominant scenic element of his design for *He Who Gets Slapped,* it was because the action was best played on, or around, the ramp. But in turn the ramp had to become the pictorial center of the design. It had to be designed as the central feature of a painting—which is a somewhat different problem.

This distinction is by no means as fine-spun as it sounds. In order to translate a scenic element into a pictorial element the designer must be aware of a number of pictorial "first principles."

For instance, the principle of *contrast*. Form is defined only by means of contrast—of light and shade, color, or line. When he incorporates a circus ramp into his scenery, the designer must know how the ramp contrasts with surrounding objects in appearance. He must know, also, in what way it contrasts with the figures of the actors in their costumes. The delicacy of the ramp structure may be in contrast with the solidity of the surrounding walls, if the circus is indoors. Or the weight of the ramp may be in contrast to the flimsiness of canvas, if the circus is in a tent. The color of the ramp may be in contrast to the color of the walls, or its curved line may be in contrast to the straight walls. The ramp may be in contrast to the stiff forms and costumes of non-circus people, whereas it may harmonize in line, color, and decoration with the costumes of the acrobats and clowns.

The present writer believes that a significant design can be constructed only on the basis of an essential contrast somewhere in the design, whether in terms of mass, line, color, texture or lighting. A necessary ingredient of drama is a sharp definition of form; and form must have contrast in order to be defined. A playwright cannot write dramatic scenes with nebulous, uncontrasted characters. In the same way a scenic artist cannot create visual drama without visual contrast. (I have sometimes corrected a design that lacked visual significance by checking over every part of the design to see if a contrast had been provided. Sometimes I found the design was monotonous in color, sometimes it lacked contrast between thick and thin, heaviness and lightness, shallowness and depth.)

On the other hand the pictorial composition must have *unity*, as well as contrast. A contrast is significant only when the contrasting elements are fundamentally related in some way. It is not enough to contrast the curved ramp with the straight walls: we must be convinced that such an arrangement is architecturally plausible, for instance. Still, this plausibility may be conveyed in a purely visual manner by pictorial design rather than by factual testimony. For example, the curve may be repeated as a theme in the designs of the posters on the walls; or the straightness of the walls may be repeated in the stanchions lining the ramp. Ramp and walls may be united in color, or through a *balance* of large and small areas. . . .

Lee Simonson

This essay—a full chapter from Mr. Simonson's longer history of stage design, *The Stage is Set*—provides the rare opportunity to observe the perceptions of one highly creative mind describing the influence of another: in this case, one of the most revolutionary and influential thinkers in the world of theatre in our century. Appia, a Swiss, began his work late in the nineteenth century, but the effects of his theory and practice are still being felt; moreover, the full influence of Appia's conceptions—perhaps particularly in terms of lighting—may not yet be realized. Simonson's descriptions of Appia's feelings for music and the Wagnerian "total" music drama are among the best in print, and his survey of the innovator's projects and writings remains unchallenged. The translations made by Simonson of Appia's major works are included herewith; as they are among the few translations in English readily available, they assume a great importance of their own.

Lee Simonson studied Philosophy at Harvard under Santayana and then spent three years in Paris as an art student. His first work as a designer was for the Washington Square Players in New York (1919); here began one of the most productive careers in American professional theatre, leading to work for the Theatre Guild where he was a founder and director as well as a major designer. His accomplishments in many important productions include settings for Wagner's *Ring* cycle at the old Metropolitan Opera House—thus bringing his interest in Appia's theories to fruition. Simonson's talents, of course, are highly independent; their relationship to Appia's earlier work is only one more example of how one major talent informs another, the latter then taking its new course.

✹ *ON THE IDEAS OF ADOLPHE APPIA*

A passionate Wagnerite, music was to Appia, as to Pater, the ideal art to whose condition all the other arts aspired. He found in Wagner's music-dramas of the Niebelungen hoard the key to the scenic artist's liberation. As a philosopher Appia longed for the consolation of the Absolute and found it in a new kind of operatic score, a novel cohesion of music and dialogue; once its secrets had been penetrated, its musical intervals, tonalities, and rhythms deeply felt, these

From *The Stage is Set* by Lee Simonson. Copyright 1932 Harcourt Brace & Company, Copyright 1960 Lee Simonson, Copyright 1963 Theatre Arts Books. Reprinted with the permission of Theatre Arts Books (New York).

could supply an unerring clew to their scenic interpretation, determining not only the form of the stage-setting itself but the movements of the actors within it down to the smallest detail of stage business and the fluctuations of light that illuminated them. As an artist Appia found release in music because its emphasis was emotional rather than factual and so supplied a norm which an artist could approximate until his settings were equally expressive. Stage pictures were to be freed from the necessity of reproducing backgrounds of action; they were to be transfigured until every element in them embodied the emotions that it was to arouse as an integral part of its form, its colour, and its total design. *Ausdruckskraft*—the force of expression, expressiveness—was one of Appia's favourite terms, and became the corner-stone on which most of the later doctrines of theatrical expressionism were reared. "Music finds its ultimate justification in our hearts," he wrote, using that traditional term to summarize the emotional core of our being, "and this occurs so directly, that its expression is thereby impalpably hallowed. When stage pictures take on spatial forms dictated by the rhythms of music they are not arbitrary but on the contrary have the quality of being inevitable."

The theories that elucidated the basic aesthetic principles of modern stage design, analyzed its fundamental technical problems, outlined their solution, and formed a charter of freedom under which scene-designers still practise, appeared in two volumes under two quasi-musical titles: *La Mise en Scène du Drame Wagnérien (The Staging of Wagner's Music-dramas)* and *Die Musik und die Inscenierung (Music and Stage-Setting)*. The first was published in Paris in 1895 as an inconspicuous brochure of fifty-one pages, the second as a full-sized volume, translated from a French script, in Munich in 1899. Neither was ever widely enough read to warrant reprinting, nor has either ever been translated, a fact which immensely aided Gordon Craig in imposing himself as a prophet on the English and American theatre. Both the book and the booklet are now so difficult to procure that they have become collector's items. But their influence was immediately felt, for Appia was that rare combination, a creative artist of exceptional imagination and at the same time a rigorously logical theorist. Many of his ideas are blurred by an appallingly clumsy German translation, which, like most philosophical German, straddles ideas, so that catching their meaning becomes rather like trying to hold a greased pig running between one's legs. Fortunately *Music and Stage-Setting* contained eighteen illustrations of projected settings for Wagner's operas, which embodied Appia's aesthetic principles with such finality that they became a revelation of a totally new kind of stage-setting and stage lighting, then as strange as the outlines of a newly discovered continent at dawn and now so familiar. These drawings revealed a unity and a simplicity that could be made an inherent part of stage-settings in a way that no one had hitherto conceived, Wagner least of all. Practitioners of stage-craft were converted by a set of illustrations to a gospel which most of them never read.

There is in Appia much of the *Schwärmerei* typical of German music, and at times a mouth-filling grandiloquence, a bewildering mixture of philosophic concepts such as "inner reality" and the transcendentalism of German metaphysics, expressed in romantic and mystic imagery (also typically Teutonic) used to beatify Art, Nature, and the Poet. Art is an inner something, eternal, ultimate, hidden behind appearance, another *Ding an sich*, which only a particular kind of poet, like Wagner the creator of music-drama, can clothe with meaning. The demands of Music become a kind of categorical imperative which, if obeyed, will lead to the universal laws of the universal work of art:

> The loftiest expression of the Eternal in Man can only be reborn and forever renew itself in the lap of Music. In return Music demands that we have implicit faith in her. . . . This book was written in the service of Music and for such a mistress no experiment is irrelevant, no labor too great. . . . In order to express the inner reality underlying all phenomena the poet renounces any attempt to reproduce their fortuitous aspects; and once this act of renunciation has taken place the complete work of art arises. . . . Then Wagner appeared. At the same time that his music-dramas revealed a purely expressive form of art, they also confirmed, what we had hitherto dimly sensed, the omnipotent power of music. . . .
>
> Music and music alone can co-ordinate all the elements of scenic presentation into a completely harmonious whole in a way which is utterly beyond the capacity of our unaided imagination. Without music the possibility of such harmony does not exist and therefore cannot be discovered. . . .
>
> Music-drama will become the focus for all our highest artistic accomplishments and will concentrate them like rays of light converging through a lens.

Such prophecies and pronunciamentos resound through Appia's theories, at times with Wagnerian sonority. There are times also when his theories seem the scenario for another music-drama in which the artist-hero, guided by the goddess of Music, will wrest a treasure from its crabbed guardians, not a cursed treasure but a beneficent one whose magic touch is capable of transfiguring not only the artist but the theatre and all the world. Two thirds of *Music and Stage-Setting* are devoted to a lengthy speculation on the future of music-drama. Appia accepts Bayreuth as the ultimate expression of German culture, indulges in an elaborate analysis of French culture, shows how German music can arouse the religious nature of French musicians, how the French artist's sensitiveness to essential form can wean Germans from their instinctive dependence on realism. At Bayreuth, in an international poet's Elysium, the two nations are to conduct jointly a presumably endless cycle of music-dramas which will carry Wagner's original inspiration to the expressionistic heights implicit in his music.

At the same time Appia shows a thoroughly Gallic capacity for objective analysis, which he uses to explain the aesthetic problems of the scene-designer and the technical means available for solving them. Here with amazing directness and clarity he dissects the plastic elements of the stage picture. In doing so he anticipates in detail the present technical basis of stage lighting and outlines precisely the way it has since been used, not only as an indispensable means of unifying stage settings, by suggesting mood and atmosphere, but also as a method of emphasizing the dramatic values of a performance and heightening our emotional response to them. The first hundred and twenty pages of Appia's volume are nothing less than the textbook of modern stage-craft that gave it both a new method of approaching its problems and a new solution.

THE PLASTIC ELEMENTS

The aesthetic problem of scenic design, as Appia made plain, is a plastic one. The designer's task is to relate forms in space, some of which are static, some of which are mobile. The stage itself is an enclosed space. Organization must be actually three-dimensional. Therefore the canons of pictorial art are valueless. The painted illusion of the third dimension, valid in the painted picture where it can evoke both space and mass, is immediately negated when it is set on a stage where the third dimension is real.

The plastic elements involved in scenic design, as Appia analyzed them, are four: perpendicular painted scenery, the horizontal floor, the moving actor, and the lighted space in which they are confined. The aesthetic problem, as he pointed out, is a single one: How are these four elements to be combined so as to produce an indubitable unity? For, like the Duke of Saxe-Meiningen, he was aware that the

plastic elements of a production remained irretrievably at odds if left
to themselves. Looking at the stages about him he saw that the scene-
painter of his day merely snipped his original picture into so many
pieces which he stood about the stage, and then expected the actor to
find his way among them as best he could. The painted back-drop
was the only part of an ensemble of painted scenery that was not a
ludicrous compromise. Naturally the scene-painter was interested,
being a painter, in presenting as many stretches of unbroken canvas
as possible. Their centre of interest was about midway between the
top of the stage and stage floor at a point where, according to the
line of sight of most of the audience, they attained their maximum
pictorial effect. But the actor works on the stage floor at a point
where painted decorations are least effective as painting. So long as
the emphasis of stage setting is on painted decoration, the inanimate
picture is no more than a coloured illustration into which the text,
animated by the actor, is brought. The two collide, they never meet
nor establish any interaction of the slightest dramatic value, whereas,
in Appia's phrase, they should be fused.

"Living feet tread these boards and their every step makes us
aware of how meaningless and inadequate our settings are." The
better the scenery is as painting, the worse it is as a stage setting; the
more completely it creates an illusion of the third dimension by the
pictorial conventions of painting, the more completely an actually
three-dimensional actor destroys that illusion by every movement he
makes. "For no movement on the actor's part can be brought into
vital relation with objects painted on a piece of canvas." Painted
decorations are not only at odds with the actor but also with the light
that illuminates them. "Light and vertical painted surfaces nullify
rather than reinforce each other.... There is an irreconcilable
conflict between these two scenic elements. For the perpendicular,
painted flat in order to be seen, needs to be set so as to catch a
maximum amount of light." The more brilliantly it is lighted, the
more apparent the lack of unity between it and the actor becomes.
"If the setting is so placed as to refract some of the light thrown on it
its importance as a painted picture is diminished to that extent."

For Appia there was no possibility of compromise by keeping
actors away from perspective back-drops where doors reached only
to their elbows, or by warning them not to lean on flimsy canvas cut-
outs down stage. He denied painted simulation of the third dimension a place in the theatre with a finality that gave his analysis the air
of a revolutionary manifesto. He was the first to banish the scenic

painter and his painted architecture from the modern stage. To Appia the actor was *massgebend*—the unit of measurement. Unity could be created only by relating every part of a setting to him. He was three-dimensional, therefore the entire setting would have to be made consistently three-dimensional. The stage setting could have no true aesthetic organization unless it was coherently plastic throughout. Appia's importance as a theorist is due to the consistency and the practicability of the methods he outlined for achieving this result.

One began to set a stage not in mid-air on hanging back-drops, but on the stage floor where the actor moved and worked. It should be broken up into levels, hummocks, slopes, and planes that supported and enhanced his movements. And these were again not to be isolated—a wooden platform draped with canvas here, a block or rock there, planted on a bare board floor, a "chaise-longue made of grass mats." The stage floor was to be a completely fused, plastic unit. Appia in this connection thinks in terms of sculpture. In order to make a model of a stage floor as he described it one would have to use clay. He considered the entire space occupied by a stage setting as a sculpturesque unit. The solidity achieved by setting wings at right angles to each other to imitate the corner of a building seemed to him feebly mechanical. He conceived much freer stage compositions where the entire area could be modelled as a balance of asymmetrical, spatial forms, a composition in three dimensions, that merged imperceptibly with the confining planes that bounded the setting as a whole.

Appia expressed in dogmatic form much of what the Duke of Saxe-Meiningen had demonstrated pragmatically. But in promulgating his theory of a stage setting he completed its unification by insisting on the plasticity of light itself, which no one before him had conceived. He demonstrated in detail, both as a theorist and as a draftsman, how stage lighting could be used and controlled so as to establish a completely unified three-dimensional world on the stage. Appia distinguishes carefully between light that is empty, diffuse radiance, a medium in which things become visible, as fish do in a bowl of water, and concentrated light striking an object in a way that defines its essential form. Diffused light produces blank visibility, in which we recognize objects without emotion. But the light that is blocked by an object and casts shadows has a sculpturesque quality that by the vehemence of its definition, by the balance of light and shade, can carve an object before our eyes. It is capable of arousing us emotionally because it can so emphasize and accent forms as to give them new force and meaning. In Appia's theories, as well as in his drawings, the light which in paintings had already been called dramatic was for the first time brought into the theatre, where its dramatic values could be utilized. Chiaroscuro, so controlled as to reveal essential or significant form, with which painters had been preoccupied for three centuries, became, as Appia described it, an expressive medium for the scene-designer. The light that is important in the theatre, Appia declares, is the light that casts shadows. It alone defines and reveals. The unifying power of light creates the desired fusion that can make stage floor, scenery, and actor one.

Light is the most important plastic medium on the stage.... Without its unifying power our eyes would be able to perceive what objects were but not what they expressed.... What can give us this sublime unity which is capable of uplifting us? Light! ... Light and light alone, quite apart from its subsidiary importance in illuminating a dark stage, has the greatest plastic power, for it is subject to a minimum of conventions and so is able to reveal vividly in its most expressive form the eternally fluctuating appearance of a phenomenal world.

The light and shade of Rembrandt, Piranesi, Daumier, and Meryon was finally brought into the theatre as an interpretative medium, not splashed on a back-drop, as romantic scene-painters had used it, but as an ambient medium actually filling space and possessing actual volume; it was an impalpable bond which fused the actor, wherever and however he moved, with everything around him. The plastic unity of the stage picture was made continuous.

If one looks at reproductions of stage settings before Appia—and the history of stage setting might almost be divided by B.A. as history in general is divided by B.C.—they are filled with even radiance; everything is of equal importance. The stage is like a photograph of a toy theatre; the actors might be cardboard dolls. In Appia's drawings for the first time the stage is a microcosm of the world. It seems to move from "morn to noon, from noon to dewy eve," and on through all the watches of the night. And the actors in it seem living beings who move as we do from sunlight or moonlight into shadow. Beneath their feet there is not a floor but the surface of the earth, over their heads not a back-drop but the heavens as we see them, enveloping and remote. There is depth here that seems hewn and distance that recedes infinitely further than the painted lines converging at a mathematical vanishing point. In attacking the conventions of scene-painting Appia created an ultimate convention. For the transparent trickery of painted illusions of form he substituted the illusion of space built up by the transfiguration that light, directed and controlled, can give to the transient structures of the stage-carpenter. The third dimension, incessant preoccupation of the Occidental mind for four centuries, defined by metaphysicians, explored by scientists, simulated by painters, was re-created in terms of the theatre, made actual. The stage more completely than ever before became a world that we could vicariously inhabit; stage settings acquired a new reality. The light in Appia's first drawings, if one compares them to the designs that had preceded his, seems the night and morning of a First Day.

LIGHT AS THE SCENE-PAINTER

Light was to Appia the supreme scene-painter. "The poet-musician," he declared, "paints his picture with light." Although at one moment Appia announces that his book is dedicated to the service of the goddess of music, at another he says: "It is precisely the misuse of stage lighting with all its far-reaching consequences which has been the chief reason for writing this book in the first place...."

Only light and music can express "the inner nature of all appearance." Even if their relative importance in music-drama is not always the same, their effect is very similar. Both require an object to whose purely superficial aspect they can give creative form. The poet provides the object for music, the actor, in the stage setting, that for light.

In the manipulations of light Appia found the same freedom that, in his eyes, music gave the poet. Light controlled and directed was the counterpart of a musical score; its flexibility, fluidity, and shifting emphasis provided the same opportunity for evoking the emotional values of a performance rather than the factual ones. As music released the mood of a scene, projecting the deepest emotional meaning of an event as well as its apparent action, so the fluctuating intensities of light could transfigure an object and clothe it with all its emotional implications.

Light with its infinite capacity for varying nuances was valuable to Appia for its power of suggestion, which has become for us the distinguishing mark of everything artistic. He points out how in *Das Rheingold* one can give the impression of water through the sensation of depth by keeping the stage dim, filling the scene with "a vague obscurity" where contours are not defined. For *Die Walküre* the open air will be felt only if the summit of a mountain detaches itself clearly against misty distances. The flames of the *Feuerzauber*[1] are not be continued an instant beyond the time allotted to them in the score. Their intensity will be emphasized by contrasting them with "a limpid night sky vaguely pierced by stars." The light in Alberich's cavern, which is illuminated by his forge, is to have an entirely different quality: "The general feeling given will be one of oppression and a lack of light. The proportions of the setting will contribute to this sense of oppressive weight. Reflections of spurts of flame will intermittently illuminate now this detail of the setting, now that one; and the setting itself, in blocking the source of light, will cast shadows that produce an ensemble chaotic in effect of which, it goes without saying, the personages in the scene will be a part." The *Waldweben*[2] in *Siegfried* is to be accompanied by a wavering play of fluttering sunlight and leaf shadows. The forest is to be made with the barest indication of a few tree-trunks and branches. Siegfried will seem to be in a forest because he is tinged in the vaguely green suffusion of light filtering through leaves and bespattered with an occasional sun-spot. The audience will then see a wood even though it does not see all the trees.

The flexibility of stage lighting, as Appia envisaged it, relates it fundamentally to every movement that an actor makes; the whole setting by fluctuations of light and shade moves with him and follows the shifting dramatic emphasis of a particular scene or sequence of scenes. Appia shows how, in the first act of *Siegfried,* Hunding and Siegfried are to be alternately in light and shadow as their respective rôles become more or less important. And he points out also that any portion of a setting — a building, a tree, the background of a room — can actually be brought forth or wiped out as its dramatic importance in the scene increases or diminishes.

Light as Interpreter

Light in Appia's hands became a guiding principle for the designer, enabling him to give to a setting as the audience sees it the same reality that it is supposed to have for the actors in it. In an appendix to *Music and Stage-Setting* he shows in detail how the control of stage lighting makes this possible for a production of *Tristan and Isolda.*

Act II: As Isolda enters she sees only two things: the burning torch set as a signal for Tristan and enveloping darkness. She does not see the castle park, the luminous distance of the night. For her it is only horrible emptiness that separates her from Tristan. Only the torch remains irrefutably just what it is: a signal separating her from the man she loves. Finally she extinguishes it. Time stands still. Time, space, the echoes of the natural world, the threatening torch—everything is wiped out. Nothing exists, for Tristan is in her arms.

How is this to be scenically realized so that the spectator, without resorting to logical reasoning, without conscious mental effort, indentifies himself unreservedly with the inner meaning of these events?

At the rise of the curtain a large torch, stage centre. The stage is bright enough so that one can recognize the actors clearly but not bright enough to dim the torch's flare. The forms that bound the stage are barely visible. A few barely perceptible lines indicate trees.

By degrees the eye grows accustomed to the scene. Gradually it becomes aware of the more or less distinct mass of a building adjoining the terrace. During the entire first scene Isolda and Brangäne remain on this terrace, and between them and the foreground one senses a declivity but one cannot determine its precise character. When Isolda extinguishes the torch the setting is shrouded in a half-light in which the eye loses itself.

Isolda is submerged in this whispering darkness as she rushes to Tristan. During the first ecstasy of their meeting they remain on the terrace. At its climax they approach [the audience]. By almost imperceptible degrees they leave the terrace and by a barely visible flight of steps reach a sort of platform near the foreground. Then, as their desire appeases itself somewhat and only one idea unites them, as we grow more and more aware of the Death of Time, they finally reach the extreme foreground, where—we notice it for the first time —a bench awaits them. The tone of the whole secret, shadowy space surrounding them grows even more uniform; the forms of the terrace and the castle are submerged, even the different levels of the stage floor are hardly perceptible.

Whether because of the contrast of deepened darkness induced by extinguishing the torch, or perhaps because our eye has followed the path that Tristan and Isolda have just trod—however that may be, in any case we feel how softly they are cradled by every object about them. During Brangäne's song the light grows still dimmer; the bodily forms of the people themselves no longer have a distinct outline. Then (page 162, first ff, of the orchestra) suddenly a pale glimmer of light strikes the right side of stage rear: King Mark and his men-at-arms break in. Slowly the cold colourless light of day increases. The eye begins to recognize the main outlines of the stage setting and its colour begins to register in all its harshness. Then as Tristan with the greatest effort at self-mastery realizes that he is after all among the living, he challenges Melot to a duel.

In the setting, cold in colour, hard as bone, only one spot is shaded from the dawning day and remains soft and shadowy, the bench at the foot of the terrace.

This was written in 1899!

I know of no single document in the theatre's history that reveals more completely the rôle that creative imagination plays in staging a play nor one that demonstrates better how inevitably the imagination of a creative artist is specific and concrete. The passage, as well as its continuation and the similar analyses that follow it for the production of the *Ring of the Niebelungen,* are the measure of Appia's genius. In comparison Craig's dark hints and his windy pretensions show him, more than ever, to be an inflated talent. Appia can himself be windy in prognosticating the future of German and French music. But once he focuses upon the theatre he is the master and the master craftsman, completely aware of his methods and materials, certain of how they can be organized, certain too of their effect to the last detail. The semi-obscurity of this second act of Tristan is dictated by a vision where, as in the words of the stage-manager of Mons, all is clarity and light.

The chiaroscuro of Appia's drawings is shadowy like Craig's; its misty envelopments, its dissolving silhouettes and vaporous distances, are characteristically romantic. But this picturesque atmosphere is made an integral part of stage pictures that, instead of dwarfing the actor, are directly related to him as a human being. Despite the shadowy shapes around him the actor remains the centre of our interest, the focus of dramatic emphasis. Appia's stage pictures are not conceived as effects into which the actor is put; they spring from the actor and are complete expressions of his assumed personality and passions. Appia, designing for the opera, evolved a type of stage setting so compact, so directly related to the emotional flux of drama, that he anticipated the development of scenic design in the theatre. Craig, designing for the theatre of the future, made settings so emptily grandiose that they have no future place except in grand opera. Appia staged even fewer productions than Craig did. His contacts with the actual theatre were less frequent. But his sense of the theatre was so concrete, so technically true, that his drawings, like his stage-directions, were capable of being translated to a stage as soon as he had made them.

Light fluctuates in Appia's drawings as it does on the stage of a theatre; it fluctuates on stage settings today as it did in Appia's drawings, and gives to canvas forms just such simplifications of mass and outline as Appia indicated. At one moment or another the lighting of any modern production, whether Jones's *Richard III* or Geddes's *Hamlet,* Reinhardt's *Danton's Death* or Jessner's *Othello* (and I could add the names of a hundred others that I have seen as well as my own), are dramatized with light and shadow in ways that repeat, however much they may amplify, Appia's original methods and effects—the same use of shadows to dignify and to envelop form, to translate emotion into atmospheric moods, to define by suggesting. The modern stage is filled with the light that was always to be seen on land and sea but never in the theatre until Appia brought it there. Craig's belated attempt to emphasize the actor with light against an ambiguous neutral screen, the declaration of Arthur Kahane, Reinhardt's assistant, in 1919, "Lighting is the real source of decoration, its single aim being only to bring the important into light and leave the unimportant in shadow," do nothing more than paraphrase the ideas and the doctrines of Adolphe Appia.

Appia's light-plot is now an accepted part of every modern production. It parallels the plot of a play and is a visual comment upon it as continuous as a musical score. It is separately rehearsed, memorized by the stage-electrician, and is part of the stage-manager's prompt-book. The fewest of its changes are dictated by actual stage-directions, such as the extinguishing of a torch; the vast majority are an accompaniment to action and aim to emphasize the atmospheric qualities of a stage setting in a way that can project variations of dramatic mood and thereby intensify the emotional reaction of an audience.

Appia's supreme intuition was his recognition that light can play as directly upon our emotions as music does. We are more immediately affected by our sensitiveness to variations of light in the theatre than we are by our sensations of colour, shape, or sound. Our emotional reaction to light is more rapid than to any other theatrical means of expression, possibly because no other sensory stimulus moves with the speed of light, possibly because, our earliest inherited fear being a fear of the dark, we inherit with it a primitive worship of the sun. The association between light and joy, between sorrow and darkness, is deeply rooted and tinges the imagery of almost every literature and every religion. It shows itself in such common couplings as "merry and bright," "sad and gloomy." How much less lonely we feel walking along a country road in a pitch-black night when the distant yellow patch of a farm-house window punctures the darkness! The flare of a camp-fire in a black pine forest at night cheers us even though we are not near enough to warm our hands at it. The warmth of the sun or of a flame does of course play a large share in provoking the feeling of elation that light gives us. But the quality of light itself can suggest this warmth effectively enough to arouse almost the same mood of comfort and release, as when, after a dingy day of rain and mist, sunlight strikes our window-curtains and dapples the floor of our room.

Between these two extremes of flaming sun and darkness an immense range of emotion fluctuates almost instantly in response to variations in the intensity of light. The key of our emotions can be set, the quality of our response dictated, almost at the rise of the curtain by the degree and quality of light that pervades a scene. It requires many more moments for the words of the players or their actions to accumulate momentum and to gather enough import for them to awaken as intense and direct an emotional response. And as the action progresses our emotions can be similarly played upon. It was the singular limitation of Appia's temperament that he could find no basis for the interpretation of drama except that dictated by the tempo and timbre of a musical score. His imagination could be stimulated in no other way. But in indicating both theoretically and graphically the complete mobility of stage lighting he has made it possible for any play to be accompanied by a light-score that is almost as directly expressive as a musical accompaniment and can be made as integrally a part of drama as music was in Wagner's music-dramas.

Light Orchestrated

The amazingly concrete quality of Appia's vision is again made apparent by the fact that he predicted the present technical set-up of our stage lighting systems. With nothing more to guide him than the rudimentary systems of his day he understood their inadequacy. He divided light-sources on the stage into two systems — diffused or general light, which merely flooded the stage with an even radiance, called flood-lighting today, and focussed, mobile light, now known as spot-lighting. It was this almost neglected source of light which Appia pointed to as the important one.

Without doubt, as soon as scenery is no longer painted canvas set up in parallel rows, all lighting apparatus will be used in a radically different fashion from what it is today, but the basis of the construction will not change greatly. The mobile [spot-light] *apparatus will be utilized to create plastic light and its mechanical perfection will have to be made the object of the most careful study. In conjunction with the more or less stationary flood-lighting apparatus, screens of varying degrees of opacity will be used; their purpose will be to soften the oversharp definition of light thrown by lamps on parts of*

*the setting or on actors in close proximity to any particular light-source.
But the major portion of the spot-lighting apparatus will be used to break
up light and diversify its direction in every way possible. These lamps will
be . . . of the greatest importance in maintaining the expressive effect of the
total stage picture.*

The development of stage lighting apparatus has followed Appia's
prediction. For a while lamps were moved on bridges above the stage
and literally followed the action of a play. But the spot-light has been
perfected so that it can be equally mobile while its source remains
fixed. Lenses of varying sizes — six or eight inches giving a varying
maximum spread in combination with electric lamps of 250, 500 or
1,000 watts — are focussed to cover overlapping areas or concentrated into a "spot" the size of a face. Each is controlled by a separate
dimmer that regulates its intensity over a range of a hundred fixed
points varying from full to out. For a modern production as many as
a hundred such spot-lights may be in use, each covering a particular
area of the stage floor, hundreds of shafts of light criss-crossing
from iron stanchions at each side of the stage, from one or more
pipes overhead, casting funnels of light of different colours and
intensity which the actor walks into or out of. They are in continual
flux, ebbing and flowing, merging and separating, but always slowly
and subtly enough so that there is never a jump by which a spectator
can become directly aware of the changes that are imperceptibly
taking place before his eyes. He feels their effect before he realizes
that the changes have occurred.

A light-plot of this sort is separately rehearsed and is then known
as a light-rehearsal. For a large production a rehearsal often takes
several days of consecutive work that is an important part of a
designer's job. Conducting a light-rehearsal is very like conducting
an orchestra. Every lamp is a separate instrument carrying its own
thread of symphonic effect, now carrying a theme, now supporting
it. A certain proportion of these lamps are directed at scenery, part
are concentrated on actors' faces. Appia insisted that the "plastic
power of light" was as important for the actor as for the set. He
inveighed against the flattening effect of footlights on actors' faces
and ascribed the overloading of make-up to the fact that an even
brilliance from below wiped out all expression from human features,
whereas focussed light could model faces and carve expression into
them like a sculptor. "But," he adds, "light will not be used merely to
strengthen or to weaken the modelling of a face; rather it will serve

to unite it or to isolate it from the scenic background, in a natural way, depending on whether the rôle of a particular actor dominates a scene or is subordinate to it."

At a light-rehearsal Appia's assertion holds true. Diffused light that merely shows a setting is, as he said, a simple matter. Plastic lighting that dramatizes its meaning is all-important and a matter of complex adjustments. "The difference in intensity between the two kinds of light must be great enough in order to make shadows perceptible; above this minimum an infinite variety of relationship is possible." It is this infinite variety, this continually shifting balance between light-sources, which occupy hours of experiment at light-rehearsals.

Light as Scene-Builder

Appia even envisaged one of the most recent developments of stage lighting—the projected scenery that Craig was astounded to discover at Copenhagen.

Light can be coloured, either by its own quality or by coloured glass slides; it can project pictures, of every degree of intensity, varying from the faintest blurred tonalities to the sharpest definition. Although both diffused and concentrated [spot] light need an object to focus on, they do not change its character; the former makes it more or less perceptible, the latter more or less expressive. Coloured light in itself changes the colour of pigments that reflect it, and by means of projected pictures or combinations of coloured light can create a milieu on the stage or even actual things that before the light was projected, did not exist.

Light became for Appia not only a scene-painter but a scene-builder.

The stage setting will no longer be as now a combination of right-angled flats ... but will rather be arranged for a specific purpose, a combination of varying planes extending into space. This principle gives colour an entirely new meaning; it no longer needs to embody any specific thing on a flat stretch of canvas or to create a factitious reality; it becomes "colour in space," capable of reconciling and combining all the elements of a setting into a simplified whole. ...

These continually changing combinations of colour and form, changing in relation to each other and also to the rest of the stage-setting, provide opportunities for an infinite variety of plastic combinations. They are the palette of the poet-musician.

They are the palette and the chisel of scene-designers today. Appia's vision has made even the third dimension itself completely flexible on the stage. Space is no longer absolute. Distance, as far as the eye of the spectator is concerned, can be created as effectively by the different intensities of intersecting volumes of light as by actual spacing measured in feet. An actor stepping from a brilliant funnel of light into half-shadow may recede far more perceptibly than if he walked fifteen feet up stage through even radiance. The sky beyond the platform of Elsinore can be infinitely remote although it may be almost within reach of Hamlet's outstretched hand at the rampart's rim. Light can contract the deepest stage or extend a shallow one. The heaviest piece of scenery appears flimsy until it reinforced with shadows that suggest its mass and weight and veil the actual material of its linen surface. A designer knows how quickly at light-rehearsal a flood of light from the wrong source can literally blow a setting to pieces, flatten out the heaviest column; an electrician's mistake in bringing on a single extra lamp during a performance can be as disastrous.

For a production of *Don Juan* I made a cathedral of a single column, the silver grille of a *reja,* and a black back-drop. The light had to strike the column principally from stage right, and his supposed funeral, which Don Juan had come to witness, was supposed to take place off stage right so that he faced the principal light-source. The opposite side of the column was left in shadow in order to exaggerate its mass, for, heavy as it was, it was only half the scale of a cathedral pier. Enough light had to be concentrated at the base of the column to illuminate the principal scenes of the act; too much would have destroyed the column's solidity. Just enough light had to spill on to the silver grille to make it gleam, but none could spill too far beyond it, for there was no more than six or eight feet between it and the black back-drop. Even then one sensed the shallowness of this space until I shot a ray of light angled downward, from a point out of sight overhead, so that it seemed a ray coming from an unseen cathedral window. The brilliance of this light-ray was such that by the time the spectator's eye had penetrated it it was slightly dazzled; he could no longer tell whether he was looking into six feet of depth or sixty.

The silhouettes of factories seen through the railroad viaduct in *Liliom* were not more than eight or ten feet back of its opening. The trees on the gauzes of the park scene in the same play were no more than four or five feet apart. Nothing but the balance of light-planes gave them depth and distance and kept them in place so that they seemed hundreds of feet away. It is comparatively easy to light actors to the exclusion of their surroundings, even when they move through a dozen positions in as many minutes, and in the process distort the setting; it is a simple matter to light a setting and obliterate the actors in it. The designer's incessant problem is to keep both in the right relation throughout the course of a play. Nothing but the complex manipulation of light makes a satisfactory solution possible. No scene painted or built through scenic design is completed until it is finally lighted. The designer is today more dependent on the electric filament than he ever was on the brush.

The lighting of the last act of *Elizabeth the Queen* can serve to illustrate how not only the building and painting of a stage setting but even its costuming can be designed almost entirely for their values when lighted. The germ of the scene was the lighting of its final moment: Elizabeth, after Essex had descended the trap-door to his death, was to be seen rigid on her throne-chair, like a bronze statue, staring forever at her fate. Over her head the light was to catch two royal-red banners so that they hung like bloody fangs in the glow of dawn striking through turret windows. Accordingly Elizabeth's gown was made of a copper cloth. But as its metallic brilliance was to be seen only for a final tableau, it was covered with black chiffon stitched to it with a design of black and gold thread almost imperceptible except as its glints gave a sense of encrustation. During most of the act the black film dulled the fabric so that it took no light from Lynn Fontanne's face. The room was an empty cylinder; four narrow windows in an ascending line suggested the spiral ascent of a tower. It was painted in greys and blue, for the turret was to be shadowy with the breath of approaching death. But a fine spatter of dull-red paint was spread on just the portion of the wall behind the throne-chair, invisible until caught by the final light of dawn. The banners overhead were completely lost in shadow at the top of the set. A single candle placed on a chest motivated the general light of the scene. The chest was placed near the trap-door where Essex was to ascend. There were only two areas of light — one around the throne, the other between the chest and the trap-door, at first dim, as no important action took place there for the first part of the act. In each area the light was kept off the walls, raised just high enough to catch the actors' heads. The rest of the stage was in half-shadow. When the players came on to do a scene from *The Merry Wives*, they emerged from shadow only by accident, for they were nothing more than a momentary foil to the queen's mood as she paced back and forth waiting. When the trap-door opened and Essex entered, the lights on it were increased, but the change was imperceptible because none of the added light struck the walls; its slightly increased intensity could not be seen except on Essex's face. During the final colloquy the light grew dimmer everywhere except in the small space where Essex and the queen played their farewell. Just before they parted the blue of night through the windows began to fade to the pink of dawn. As Essex descended, the added light vanished with him, leaving nothing more than a flickering candle. A faint tinge of cold blue light stole up the walls. The light through the slits of windows became brighter, almost red. And as Elizabeth straightened in her chair the first shaft of warm morning sunlight struck full upon her, turning her to bronze and at the same time plucking the banners out of the shadow, turning them into bloody fangs that seemed to drip over the queen's head as the curtain fell.

Legacy

Such a bit of stage lighting is a fraction of Appia's legacy to the modern stage. I do not imply that the designers of this generation read an out-of-print German volume and then rushed into the theatre to apply its precepts. They were already in the air, already being projected by spot-lights, already part of a modern tradition and its technique. Modern designers accepted a torch without knowing who lighted it; our experiments amplified Appia's theories almost before we knew his name, had seen his drawings, or had heard a quotation from his published work. Appia's first two volumes contain the germinal ideas that have sprouted, almost without exception, into the theories of modern stage-craft that we listened to — the necessity of visualizing the mood and atmosphere of a play, the value of presentation as opposed to representation, the importance of suggestion completed in the mind of the spectator, the effectiveness of an actor stabbed by a spot-light in a great dim space, the significance of a "space stage," and the more abstract forms of scenic art.

It was Appia who first said:

Our stage is a vista into the unknown, into boundless space, and this space for which our souls long in order that our imagination can be submerged in it, is given no added value by making our settings part of the structure of the whole theatre building. . . . The Greeks identified the scene of the play with the boundaries of the theatre; we, less fortunate, have extended it beyond that limit. Our drama, thrust into a boundless realm of the imagination, and our roofed-over amphitheatres, into which we are packed, are related only by a proscenium arch; everything beyond it is fictitious, tentative, and bears every evidence of being without any justification except as part of a particular performance.

It was Appia who first emphasized the distinction between the aesthetic values of classic formality and those of modern scenic illusion.

The antique stage was unlike ours, not a hole through which the public was shown in a constricted space the combined effect of an infinite variety of media. Antique drama was the event, the act itself, not a spectacle.

The passage of which these statements are a part gave the cue which prompted our present efforts to dislodge the proscenium arch and to unite the audience with the play by making the stage a part of the auditorium.

It was also Appia who, as a theorist, first insisted on the dominant importance of the director as a dictator controlling every element of a theatrical production.

The man we call director today, whose job consists in merely arranging completed stage sets, will, in poetic [music] drama, play the rôle of a despotic drill-master who will have to understand how much preliminary study stage setting requires, utilize every element of scenic production in order to create an artistic synthesis, reanimate everything under his control at the expense of the actor, who must eventually be dominated. Whatever he does will to a great extent depend upon his individual taste: he must work both as an experimenter and as a poet, play with his scenic materials but at the same time be careful not to create a purely personal formula.

Only an artist and an artist of the first rank can accomplish such a task. He will have to test his own imagination conscientiously in order to free it from every stereotype, above all from anything influenced by the fashion of the moment. But his principal effort as a director will be to convince the individual members of his acting company that only the arduous subjection of their personalities to the unity of the production will create an important result. He will be very like the leader of an orchestra; his effect will be a similarly magnetic one.

This conception of a master artist in the theatre is Craig's "Master of Drama" and, with Appia's contempt for the scene-painter, supplied the theme for Craig's first dialogues on the art of the theatre and most of their subsequent variations.

The art of the theatre today finds its full freedom within the boundaries of Appia's original concepts in a stage setting that is completely plastic—plastic in the sense of being infinitely malleable, plastic also in the sense of being consistently three-dimensional. More recent experiments in production continue to play with our sensations of space and our emotional reactions to projections, either actual or implied, of the third dimension. We accept the dynamic relations of a three-dimensional actor moving through a third dimension, whether constructed or indicated, as the greatest aid that can be given to the expressiveness of a play in performance. Light itself has come to have the character of a form in space. The illumination focussed and projected through the lens of a modern spot-light is a funnel of light that has the shape of a cone. Its outlines, when sharply focussed, are often discernible and are often made part of the pictorial pattern of a stage setting. At one extreme, we make stage space absolute, the stage setting purely architectonic, and depend entirely on the movements of actors, singly or in mass, to create the stage picture. Light then acquires, in our eyes, a classic purity of definition. At the other extreme the stage becomes murkily romantic and the dynamics of light is used to create the illusion of an actual extension of the space played in; it is extended until it seems infinite and is filled with every possible combination of shadowy masses related by atmospheric planes that have every degree of opacity.

Like every other form of scenic effect, modern stage lighting is an illusion. It too deceives the eye. But completely controlled, in the way that Appia indicated, it is the most subtle form of deception yet discovered. It is tactile in effect. The modern stage setting is thereby given unity by evading a conflict between illusions of different kinds. Even at its most vaporous moments a modern setting is three-dimensional, continually relates the actor to the space in which he moves, is an extension of his body as well as a symbolic projection of his state of mind. Our emotional reactions to drama when acted are intensified by an aesthetic emphasis upon extension in space, either reproduced or suggested, expressing dynamic patterns of human beings in action, who move through fluctuating planes of light; and these in turn create a dynamic interplay of contours and forms.

The aesthetics of modern stage setting, like the aesthetics of modern art in general, accepts tactile value as the supreme value and the basis of significant form. In the frame of the theatre, as in the picture-frame, we can find no other test of expressiveness. The modern art of theatrical production, "the art of the theatre," was completely organized, as a medium of expression, when the doctrines that Appia outlined and illustrated were added to the technique of rehearsal and presentation established by the Duke of Saxe-Meiningen's experiments. The unity thus established remains an aesthetic norm. Most of what we call innovation or experiment is a variation of Appia's ideas, deduced from his original premises — the refinements of acting evolved by Stanislavsky, the refinement in the control of electric lighting now being perfected by electrical engineers.

No genuine aesthetic novelty is possible on the modern stage until simulating the third dimension becomes less important to us as an emotional stimulus. For the time being the forces that can contribute to the growth of play-giving as modern art lie outside the theatre's walls.

Abe Feder

These remarks, excerpts from a longer technical essay, are by a leading American lighting designer whose experience ranges from the great production of *Four Saints in Three Acts* in 1934 to his present assignment of design for the lighting plant of the new Kennedy Center for the Performing Arts in Washington, D.C. After an incisive summary of certain important points concerning equipment and technique, Mr. Feder discusses his lighting design for Ibsen's *Ghosts* in a production at New York's Empire Theatre in 1935. Other plays for which he has designed lighting include *The Cradle Will Rock* (1938), *Inherit the Wind* (1955), *Visit to a Small Planet* (1957), *Orpheus Descending* (1957), *Time Remembered* (1957), and *Camelot* (1960). Mr. Feder was the U.S. delegate to the International Theatre Institute sponsored by UNESCO in Paris in 1950, and his innovations in lighting techniques have been useful and influential for many years in this country and abroad.

✤ *from* LIGHTING THE PLAY

... The first thing I discovered at the beginning of my work was the cumbersomeness of available equipment, and I realized that the future of the flexibility in lighting lay in discovering more compact tools. Yet, for a period no real basic changes occurred. Although the equipment took on fancier trimmings, and the design of the borderlights and spotlights took on cleaner lines, basically the lenses and bulbs were the same. However, a revolution was on its way.

First, with the idea borrowed from Germany, the lighting companies designed a *tubular bulb* which burned with its base up. It has the peculiar characteristic of having its filament in the opposite end of the tube, leaving a large empty space of glass between the socket and the filament, to absorb the heat. This bulb made possible a new tool in lighting. We may all remember the old stereopticon machine which projected slides on a white screen. The principle of that instrument appeared in the way the light passed through a series of lenses which converged their beam at the slide and then objectified that through an additional lens at the other end. This new lighting tool used the same principle. It objectified its light source by means of a special reflector, ellipsoidal in shape, and, owing to the construction of the new bulb, required only ⅓ of the light source to be within the curvature of the reflector. The advantage lay in the fact that the beam could be projected in any shape and any direction. Unfortunately, up to now its efficacy has been limited because of the delicacy of its precision adjustment, and its uses have been confined to front light, either from the balcony or from ceiling beams. Furthermore, the character of the light is sharp and very hard.

Then, in Hollywood, the *Fresnel lens* was exploited, helping to supplant the archaic five-foot projectors, with more compact 14-inch Fresnel "incies" (incandescent light sources). The important feature of the Fresnel lens was that by means of a scientific design in curves on a thinner piece of glass, more actual light was emitted from the same light sources. Naturally, this was of tremendous advantage when the intensity of a 1000-watt spot could be achieved with a piece of equipment half its size and half its wattage; and it was a definite step forward in the flexibility of lighting.

The next important development was the *spotlight bulb*. For years

From *Producing the Play,* John Gassner, ed. (Holt, Rinehart and Winston, Inc.: 1953). Reprinted by permission of the author.

attempts had been made commercially to coat the upper half of the inside of a bulb with silver paint and project its beam in one direction. It was not until 1932 that Clarence Birdseye (the frozen food man) was successful in perfecting this process. Subsequently, the major lighting companies, realizing the commercial potentialities, brought out an entire line of spotlight bulbs. These bulbs open up a new horizon for the worker in light in the theatre. The chief advantage of these bulbs is their small size, as one can achieve more flexibility of light sources in the condensed space usually allowed for lighting equipment in most productions. As these lamps began to be used, the bulb companies made variations from intense beam spots to flood reflector bulbs. All of these are valuable for use in lighting.

It is the task of this chapter to view also the future possibility of the newer lighting tools—for example, the *fluorescent tube.* Some years ago there came into use a tube filled with a red neon gas which is now familiar in electric signs. Subsequent gases, such as argon, were developed and also used. Then, out of the laboratories came a new discovery of chemical salts that could be applied to the insides of gas-filled tubes. In the combination, the lighting field acquired a new tool, namely, a brilliant, luminous light source which has no wire filament and emits a high color penetration light. Its physical properties even in its present weak intensities are able to give us a color penetration on materials which reflect their own intensified color. This can readily be seen in any of the shop windows where the fluorescent tube is installed in place of the ordinary type of lighting. The drawback for use in the theatre is the difficulty of control. At the present time the only way of lighting a fluorescent tube is by means of a *shocking coil* which excites the gas between two electric poles within the tube in order to ignite it. This process makes this kind of lighting inflexible, and confines its uses at present to general illumination in places other than the theatre, where absolutely flexible control is necessary.

My primary interest in fluorescent light is what happens to color, because color in the theatre has not begun to touch on the unlimited numbers of tint variations of light and shade that are possible. In the study of painting, red, yellow, and blue are the three basic colors. *In light the three basic colors are red, blue, and green,* which are also spectrum colors. The most important point of all is that our eyes are attuned to the three colors, red, blue, and green,—therefore, giving us a perfect sense of balance in our visual judgment of color in light. The fact to remember in lighting is that except for fluorescent light, all our light sources have tungsten for their filaments. We know that the weaker the light sources, the more yellow the light; the more intense the light sources, the whiter the light. We all forget that any material we use as light filters would naturally be partial to the red side of the spectrum owing to the metal in the filament.

It is important to understand the principle underlying the use of *gelatin*. Gelatin is poured in very thin sheets, mixed with a color dye, and when a piece of this is put in front of a light source, it acts as a filter, cutting out all other spectrum colors except its own value. Prior to gelatin, colored water and colored glass were used. Originally, only primary color gelatins of the most obvious sort were made. In the course of time various workers in light, like painters, began demanding shades and tints which were secondary and tertiary values of the original primaries. Now there are 75 different color gelatins.

As in light-source development, forces outside the theatre were at work which advanced the use of color in the theatre. One was the development of cellophane, whose texture permits more transmission of light than does gelatin and enables color to take on better spectrum values. Unfortunately, cellophane is not fireproof and the colors are limited. Yet in producing the Gertrude Stein opera, I used cellophane colors to light cellophane scenery and the resulting iridescence was definitely responsible for the production's visual quality.

The best technique we have that can approach what fluorescent light does is a method employed called *Whiting Technique*. The development of the technicolor film opened up a new process in the filtering of color, and this type of filter is one of its by-products. The difference in its technique is that the old type stock-color gelatin changes the color of materials. This new type of gelatin, on the other hand, intensifies existing colors in the materials. This is a valuable contribution to lighting because it brings out true color vibrations in materials without a deliberate color change of the whole ensemble. When it was first used in the Federal Theatre in the production of *Pinocchio,* the filter that was partial to red was used with an ordinary follow spotlight on the marionette; the marionette took on a fourth-dimensional quality of a body in space, unlike anything I had ever seen.

There is another color filter to be found in the *Strobile paint technique.* It is a filter which, when used in combination with surfaces painted with Strobile paint, creates a phosphorescent luminosity and is entirely dependent on powerful light intensities. This filter is not used widely in the theatre up to this time because it cuts out too much light.

LIGHTING CONTROL

In summing up our tools of light in the theatre, we come to the most important problem of all — namely, *control.* Electricity, as we all know, is a harnessed force. Its magic lies at a point in its dynamos where it turns from waterfall power to electrical energy, but once that has taken place it is earthbound by wires and conduits, and it is then piped like water to the places where it is needed.

The control of light has the same characteristic as the control of a piano. The layout of the piano keyboard is so arranged that it becomes a servant to the user. The problem of controlling light in the theatre is basically the same. One has to lay out the board control in such a fashion that, with a minimum of movement, the lighting equipment will give the user all the tonalities in light that a piano does in music. (And here the struggle for progress still persists in the commercial theatre.)

Dimming of light was first used in the old gas-lit days by increasing or reducing the flow of gas. With the advent of electricity the dimmer plate was evolved. At first it was a very crude coil device, which acted as a channel for detouring the current of the bulb when dimming it. The next step was in developing maximum and minimum dimming.

The advent of the motion picture theatre proved a great boon to *switchboard control* in lighting. From the early 1920's to the early 1930's the overscaled motion picture theatre stages, with all the fancy, colored light trimmings in the theatre proper, created a demand for some organized method of board control. Although there was no great basic change in the structure of the dimmer apparatus itself, methods of banking the dimmers together in groups with auxiliary master dimming handles were devised. But so large was the actual dimension of these switchboards that the problem of men to handle their controls caused a further step to be taken — namely, *pre-set control.* A device was designed electrically by means of which each circuit switch has three or four little sub-switches. When an entire switchboard through its circuit switches had all been put on the same individual button control, by pressing that button's general master the entire stage could be lit. This method at first left out one very important problem — namely, the pre-setting of dimmers themselves. The first successful installation of the pre-setting of the switch control and dimmer control was in

Radio City Music Hall. The pre-set dimmer control technique was made possible by an entirely different principle of apparatus. The radio industry and its development of various types of tubes opened up the avenue in developing a tube which acted as a transforming device in the construction of a new type of dimmer. This changed the entire panel control to a fraction of its former size; for example, the dimmer board of The Roxy Theatre is 15 feet long by 7 feet high, whereas the entire control of the Radio City Music Hall, which is a much larger stage, is less than 6 feet long, with all the bulk of the apparatus put in some other part of the stage, and all managed by remote control. One immediately realizes the importance of this development to facileness in light. It is now possible through this type of device for entire groups of lights to be controlled by the simple manipulation of a tiny rheostat switch, the size of a radio dial.

In the field of control of lighting for the theatre, the future for resourceful tools is tremendous. What we know of light itself is still in its embryonic stages, but what has been accomplished, despite its crudities, has shown a tremendous stride since the advent of electricity. The future looks bright.

LIGHTING PROCEDURE AND LAYOUT

Although to the rest of the country the Broadway theatre is the standard for theatrical productions, because New York is the haven for leading actors, directors, playwrights, composers, and designers, it is not true that Broadway has the best theatrical conditions for the production of plays. The high price and limited areas of real estate have necessitated very cramped stages, making lighting a difficult problem. Therefore, it may be helpful to describe the procedure for production under these conditions, which are not, however, confined to Broadway. In addition, it may be helpful to illustrate the general approach to lighting a series of plays in a single theatre, where the lighting has to accommodate itself to a great variety of demands without much change. A practical knowledge of lighting equipment and technique should enable us to light plays in different theatres and under different circumstances. Simplifications of method, when these are necessary, are chiefly a matter of experiment and ingenuity. I shall illustrate lighting practice by means of the lighting of *Ghosts* for the Nazimova production in New York.

Lighting Ibsen's "Ghosts." As a painter, having blocked out his composition, finds the key to his mood, so the "worker in light," having laid out his equipment, must find the key to the scenes. In

Ghosts, the entire first act is played on a rainy morning; the second act takes place during the end of the same day, dimming into evening; and the third act is the continuation of that night to dawn.

First Act: It is obvious that, considering the sombreness of the atmosphere, one would choose color tints of light blue and gray, but one must remember that the tragedy of this piece does not reach its height until the middle of the second act. In the first act, Mrs. Alving's happiness is quite apparent in the joy of having her son home with her; so, in spite of the rain, the light on the actors must have a definite warmth of color to give them a visual vitality. In the mechanical execution of the above, it was important to have two qualities of light over the entire acting area: a warm and a cold, which, hung from the front, from the first pipe, and from the side, made it easy to blend the two values at will. The illusion of the fjords in the morning, seen through the windows, upstage left, was created by using color values of the same gray-blue as the inside of the set; the perspective was achieved by the projectors' upstage left shooting shafts of light through the transparent curtains of the conservatory, which acted as a curtain of mist and softened the backdrop.

Second Act: In the second act, as stated in the beginning of the chapter, I used a very simple device to create an illusion in the scene between Mrs. Alving and Oswald. Our eyes are tuned to light intensity as well as color; as the intensity diminishes, there is a natural dilation of the pupils to admit more light. In order to utilize this principle, the best plan is to resort to side-lighting, because it gives the actors a three-dimensional quality; regardless of how much one dims the lamps, the actors will stand out. This was the principle of the big dimdown in the second act. The scene was lit in a high key, with the windows downstage right about the same value as the large bay window up left. From the audience's point of view, the illusion of on-coming darkness was accomplished by reducing the overhead spotlights, and by the lighting outside the fjords dimming into twilight. That left the window downstage right, the predominating source of light in the room, with the vertical tormentor lights giving form to the actors. This shifted the light interest, and concentrated the illusion on the two figures sitting on the couch.

At that moment Oswald confessed to his mother the discovery he had made about himself, that he was doomed to feeble-mindedness. That speech was the cue for the beginning of the dim down, giving to the audience the illusion of two vague forms shrouded in a sea of mist. Then Mrs. Alving got up, walked toward the door (stage left), where the glow from the chandelier was barely visible on her, and went back (upstage left) to the table with a lamp on it. She stood there for a moment, and put on the light. Instantaneously the hook-up[1] of lights from the pipe above and from the balcony front washed in, and the entire scene changed in character, lifting the very action of the piece. She returned to the couch, and put on another lamp there, which automatically switched on that hook-up, and the scene ended with the fire glowing on the curtains in the back.

Third Act: The curtain went up with the lighting the same as we left it at the end of the second act, except that the curtains over the French doors were drawn. All the actors were seated around the table, front stage left, and as the scene progressed, Mrs. Alving and Oswald moved to the couch on stage right, while the other characters made their exits. Here was the most difficult part of the lighting, because the action of the play calls for a sunrise and the big window upstage left has to become visible and bring the morning grayness into the room. To accomplish this, the hookup around the table lamp had to be dimmed, so as to reduce the intensity of that section of the stage and to let the window light come in. This is what I call counterpoint dimming, and it must be so timed as to be imperceptible to the audience. The second this was done, the entire room changed character and the gray light of the bay window predominated the stage, making the hook-up around the couch look dim by comparison.

In the action that followed, Mrs. Alving went back to the lamp, stage left, put that out, and then went to the couch and turned out that lamp. The entire stage was left in a half-light shadowy feeling of darkness, and one heard Oswald's voice asking for the sun. Mrs. Alving rushed to the windows, and pulled open the curtains. The projectors outside the windows, which had been dimming in with the sun projector upstage right, pierced across the couch, etching the side of Oswald's face with all its distortions, and down came the curtain.

The Layout: In the Nazimova production, the set was of the typical box type as shown on p. 375. We hung 22 spotlights with two

---

[1] A hook-up is a simplification for board control of a group of lights, regardless of their location, all directed toward a particular area that we wish to control by means of a master dimmer. For example: as in the case of the above, there were two spotlights on the first pipe, there was one lamp on the balcony front, and one section of foots nearest that part of the stage, all hooked into the little prop lamp, making the board control foolproof.

sections of X-rays on the first pipe. On the front balcony we hung two groups of spotlights of three each. Behind the false portals, on either side of the stage, we stood a vertical pipe, with four lamps on each. To light the two pieces of scenery behind the bay window that simulated the fjords of Norway, we used two sections of X-rays, one above each fjord, and a row of X-rays behind that to light the background. In front of the backdrop, we placed a smaller type of X-ray on the floor to give a pit light effect. The above equipment is what I would consider necessary as a general lighting for this type of production.

In addition to this, we also used the following equipment: There were two types of lighting for the double set of windows downstage right; a powerful projector that had been frosted to give a nondescript north light glow across the room, and a special lamp focused directly across the room to represent the intense glow of the morning sun, which shafted across the couch for the last moment of the play. On downstage left, in back of the double doors leading into the dining room, a baby spot was placed on a high stand, giving the illusion of a glow coming from the chandelier. Upstage left, behind the windows, there was a vertical pipe with two powerful projectors shafting diagonally into the room. The purpose of these two lights was to give the feeling of a misty day, like light coming from an open place in the heavens, casting an eerie glow across the room. On the right side of that window, there was another projector about seven feet off the floor to tie in the lamp on stage right for the morning sunlight. The footlights were in three sections. Because the entire set was in shades of gray, the only device to change the character of the room was by means of using different colors in the "foots."

Two other subtle lighting effects were the illusions of the fire and the river. For the fire, there were two units: one, an oval floor which was masked to glow the back of the bay window; the other, a fire effect machine, which glowed into the room itself and hit the stage wall right. Both of these worked in conjunction with each other. The water effect was made by stretching a piece of cellophane between the two fjords and lighting it from behind with a small strip light. The strip light had two color circuits: a blue green, to give the effect of translucent water; and an orange, which, when dimmed into a glow, gave the feeling of the reflection of dawn lighting the surface of the river. . . .

S. D. Balukhaty

These observations by Professor S. D. Balukhaty (who was responsible for the extremely useful publication of Stanislavski's production notes for Chekhov's *The Sea Gull* at the Moscow Art Theatre) should be read in the light of other documents relative, not only to Stanislavski himself, but to contrasting theories of stage decor (see, for example, Meyerhold's theories as represented elsewhere in this volume). Stanislavski's directorial notes frequently involve setting as well. Balukhaty, in his use of documents relative to Stanislavski's original plans for production, quite justly emphasizes the efforts made to give a highly "realistic" atmosphere to each act setting. One receives, however, the cumulative impression that what was "realistic" then could hardly be so now—nor would one desire the same results today.

✎ NOTES ON STAGE SETTINGS FOR STANISLAVSKI'S PRODUCTION OF THE SEA GULL

During the work on the play particular attention was paid to the sets which had to correspond to the style of the play and, at the same time, help to bring out in the most advantageous way the producer's *mise-en-scènes*. The stage designer was V. A. Simov, who received his general instructions from the directors of the theatre. His task was not only to provide the sets for the park, the house, and the lake, which would introduce the audience into the ordinary domestic life of a well-to-do, though not wealthy, landowner, but also to convey simultaneously to the audience the dominant character of the play, with its highly subtle moods, written, as it were, in half-faded water colours.

A talk with Chekhov at one of the rehearsals did not help the scenic artist very much. "Chekhov," Simov writes in his memoirs, "did not express any opinion (not to me at any rate) about the scenery of *The Sea Gull*. About the lake I was later told that Chekhov's only remark was that 'Well, it is wet'."

The landscape scenery of the First and Second Acts presented the

From *The Sea Gull Produced by Stanislavski*, edited by S. D. Balukhaty, translated by David Magarshack. All rights reserved. Used with permission of the publishers, Theatre Arts Books (New York) and Dennis Dobson (London).

artist with all sorts of difficult problems. He painted it according to the naturalistic, illusory style. The scenery of the First Act, as can be gathered from the artist's statements in his memoirs, did not satisfy Simov, because the park, which by itself produced an excellent impression, did not "harmonise with the fundamental tone of the play." So far as Chekhov was concerned, all he needed was "only a few hints for the clear-cut delineation of a character, costume, scene, etc. It seemed therefore that so far as scene painting was concerned, it, too, had to evolve the same kind of approach in order to achieve the fullest possible harmony with the mood of the play." And Simov cites this illustration: "I remember we wanted to make the moon's ascent to be as like nature as possible: the usual method of raising a round lamp by pushing it higher and higher, adopted on the stage of the Imperial theatres, was too crude to deceive the eye of the spectator. In Chekhov, for example, the whole moonlit night can be felt, as it were, in one single fragment of the moon, which throws its reflection upon the whole scene. So we made the disk of the moon shine through cuts in the canvas and in this way created the illusion of its rising higher and higher in the sky and peeping through the clouds." The directors of the theatre, too, were dissatisfied with the scenery of this act and the artist V. Suryenyanetz was later commissioned to paint it.

More successful and entirely in harmony with Simov's gifts was the scenery of the interiors for Acts Three and Four. According to Simov, the producer had entrusted him with a special task, namely, "to point the contrast between the happy comfort of the genial and agreeable life in the first half of the play and the depressing emptiness, hollowness, and discord in the lives of the people in the play in the last two acts." The mounting of the final act was of particular importance, for it had to bring out the intrinsically cheerless and melancholy atmosphere of the play, characterised by the motif of hopelessness and acceptance of the inevitable. "The room had to bear the stamp of impermanency. Outside it is cold, damp, windy; but there is no warmth in the room, either." According to Simov, the producer was anxious to contrast the period of prosperity with the period of decay, affliction, and adversity. "In the dreary emptiness of the present, the traces of past joys and the long-lost smiles of a former happy existence can still be discerned." This task the artist solved in the following manner: "I began with the furniture, arranging it in every possible way so as to obtain the effect of mental disequilibrium, so that one could see immediately how indifferent the person who lives in that room is to the way the furniture is arranged. If some piece of furniture is in his way, he moves it aside, and does not bother to replace it until someone else finds it is in *his* way. I got the sort of room that made you wish 'to wrap a shawl round you,' as one of the actresses put it."

PART FIVE ✠ *THE*
CREATIVE AUDIENCE

E. H. Gombrich

These excerpts from Professor Gombrich's study of nature of perception in the pictorial arts form the only document in this volume not conceived or written in terms of drama and theatre practice. These observations, however, are among the most important comments on the communicative arts set down in this century. Their application to living drama is direct and highly suggestive; a perception of reality begins in the creative mind of the artist, not in nature itself, and it follows that a recognition of that artistic perception — either by the viewer of a painting or by the members of an audience in a theatre — is itself both a creative act and a phenomenon that establishes the recognizable style of any period. Gombrich's work, then, helps clarify both the nature of persistent stylistic convention and our understanding of "remove" from a work — be that work a picture or a play (or, for that matter, a piece of music, a political poster with a slogan, or a child's apparently capricious combinations of shapes and colors).

Ernst Gombrich is presently Director of the Warburg Institute in London and Professor at the University of London; in addition, he has taught at Cambridge, Harvard, and Oxford. His best known books include *The Story of Art* (1960), *Art and Illusion* — the Mellon Lectures in the Fine Arts (1960) from which the excerpts reprinted here are chosen — and *Meditations on a Hobby Horse* (1963), a collection of essays on art history and the nature and psychology of artistic perception.

⚓ *from* ART AND ILLUSION

> The schematism by which our understanding deals with the phenomenal world . . . is a skill so deeply hidden in the human soul that we shall hardly guess the secret trick that Nature here employs.
> — IMMANUEL KANT, *Kritik der reinen Vernunft*

. . . In his charming autobiography, the German illustrator Ludwig Richter relates how he and his friends, all young art students in Rome in the 1820's, visited the famous beauty spot of Tivoli and sat down to draw. They looked with surprise, but hardly with approval, at a group of French artists who approached the place with enor-

From *Art and Illusion* by E. H. Gombrich, pp. 63-66, 85, 90, 131, 175, 356. The A. W. Mellon Lectures in the Fine Arts, 1956. Bollingen Series XXXV.5. Pantheon Books. Reprinted by permission of the Trustees of the National Gallery of Art (Washington) and the Bollingen Foundation.

mous baggage, carrying large quantities of paint which they applied to the canvas with big, coarse brushes. The Germans, perhaps roused by this self-confident artiness, were determined on the opposite approach. They selected the hardest, best-pointed pencils, which could render the motif firmly and minutely to its finest detail, and each bent down over his small piece of paper, trying to transcribe what he saw with the utmost fidelity. "We fell in love with every blade of grass, every tiny twig, and refused to let anything escape us. Every one tried to render the motif as objectively as possible."

Nevertheless, when they then compared the fruits of their efforts in the evening, their transcripts differed to a surprising extent. The mood, the color, even the outline of the motif had undergone a subtle transformation in each of them. Richter goes on to describe how these different versions reflected the different dispositions of the four friends, for instance, how the melancholy painter had straightened the exuberant contours and emphasized the blue tinges. We might say he gives an illustration of the famous definition by Emile Zola, who called a work of art "a corner of nature seen through a temperament."

It is precisely because we are interested in this definition that we must probe it a little further. The "temperament" or "personality" of the artist, his selective preferences, may be one of the reasons for the transformation which the motif undergoes under the artist's hands, but there must be others—everything, in fact, which we bundle together into the word "style," the style of the period and the style of the artist. When this transformation is very noticeable we say the motif has been greatly "stylized," and the corollary to this observation is that those who happen to be interested in the motif, for one reason or another, must learn to discount the style. This is part of that natural adjustment, the change in what I called "mental set," which we all perform quite automatically when looking at old illustrations. We can "read" the Bayeux tapestry without reflecting on its countless "deviations from reality." We are not tempted for a moment to think the trees at Hastings in 1066 looked like palmettes and the ground at that time consisted of scrolls. It is an extreme example, but it brings out the all-important fact that the word "stylized" somehow tends to beg the question. It implies there was a special activity by which the artist transformed the trees, much as the Victorian designer was taught to study the forms of flowers before he turned them into patterns. It was a practice which chimed in well with ideas of Victorian architecture, when railways and factories were built first and then adorned with the marks of a style. It was not the practice of earlier times.

The very point of Richter's story, after all, is that style rules even where the artist wishes to reproduce nature faithfully, and trying to analyze these limits to objectivity may help us get nearer to the riddle of style. One of these limits we know from the last chapter; it is indicated in Richter's story by the contrast between coarse brush and fine pencil. The artist, clearly, can render only what his tool and his medium are capable of rendering. His technique restricts his freedom of choice. The features and relationships the pencil picks out will differ from those the brush can indicate. Sitting in front of his motif, pencil in hand, the artist will, therefore, look out for those aspects which can be rendered in lines—as we say in a pardonable abbreviation, he will tend to see his motif in terms of lines, while, brush in hand, he sees it in terms of masses.

The question of why style should impose similar limitations is less easily answered, least of all when we do not know whether the artist's intentions were the same as those of Richter and his friends.

Historians of art have explored the regions where Cézanne and van Gogh set up their easels and have photographed their motifs. Such comparisons will always retain their fascination since they almost allow us to look over the artist's shoulder—and who does not wish he had this privilege? But however instructive such confrontations may be when handled with care, we must clearly beware of the fallacy of "stylization." Should we believe the photograph represents the "objective truth" while the painting records the artist's subjective vision—the way he transformed "what he saw"? Can we here compare "the image on the retina" with the "image in the mind"? Such speculations easily lead into a morass of unprovables. Take the image on the artist's retina. It sounds scientific enough, but actually there never was *one* such image which we could single out for comparison with either photograph or painting. What there was was an endless succession of innumerable images as the painter scanned the landscape in front of him, and these images sent a complex pattern of impulses through the optic nerves to his brain. Even the artist knew nothing of these events, and we know even less. How far the picture that formed in his mind corresponded to or deviated from the photograph it is even less profitable to ask. What we do know is that these artists went out into nature to look for material for a picture and their artistic wisdom led them to organize the elements of the landscape into works of art of marvelous complexity that bear as much relationship to a surveyor's record as a poem bears to a police report. . . . The artist will be attracted by motifs which can be rendered in his idiom. As he scans the landscape, the sights which can be matched successfully with the schemata he has learned to handle will leap forward as centers of attention. The style, like the medium, creates a mental set which makes the artist look for certain aspects in the scene around him that he can render. Painting is an activity, and the artist will therefore tend to see what he paints rather than to paint what he sees.

It is this interaction between style and preference which Nietzsche summed up in his mordant comment on the claims of realism:

> *"All Nature faithfully"—But by what feint*
> *Can Nature be subdued to art's constraint?*
> *Her smallest fragment is still infinite!*
> *And so he paints but what he likes in it.*
> *What does he like? He likes, what he can paint!*

There is more in this observation than just a cool reminder of the limitations of artistic means. We catch a glimpse of the reasons why these limitations will never obtrude themselves within the domain of art itself. Art presupposes mastery, and the greater the artist the more surely will he instinctively avoid a task where his mastery would fail to serve him. The layman may wonder whether Giotto could have painted a view of Fiesole in sunshine, but the historian will suspect that, lacking the means, he would not have wanted to, or rather that he could not have wanted to. We like to assume, somehow, that where there is a will there is also a way, but in matters of art the maxim should read that only where there is a way is there also a will. The individual can enrich the ways and means that his culture offers him; he can hardly wish for something that he has never known is possible.

The fact that artists tend to look for motifs for which their style and training equip them explains why the problem of representational skill looks different to the historian of art and to the historian of visual information. The one is concerned with success, the other must also observe the failures. But these failures suggest that we sometimes assume a little rashly that the ability of art to portray the visible world developed, as it were, along a uniform front. We know of specialists in art—of Claude Lorrain, the master of landscape whose figure paintings were poor, of Frans Hals who concentrated almost exclusively on portraits. May not skill as much as will have dictated this type of preference? Is not all naturalism in the art of the past selective?

A somewhat Philistine experiment would suggest that it is. Take the next magazine containing snapshots of crowds and street scenes and walk with it through any art gallery to see how many gestures and types that occur in life can be matched from old paintings. Even Dutch genre paintings that appear to mirror life in all its bustle and variety will turn out to be created from a limited number of types and gestures, much as the apparent realism of the picaresque novel or of Restoration comedy still applies and modifies stock figures which can be traced back for centuries. There is no neutral naturalism. The artist, no less than the writer, needs a vocabulary before he can embark on a "copy" of reality.

Everything points to the conclusion that the phrase the "language of art" is more than a loose metaphor, that even to describe the visible world in images we need a developed system of schemata. This conclusion rather clashes with the traditional distinction, often discussed in the eighteenth century, between spoken words which are conventional signs and painting which uses "natural" signs to "imitate" reality. It is a plausible distinction, but it has led to certain difficulties. If we assume, with this tradition, that natural signs can simply be copied from nature, the history of art represents a complete puzzle. It has become increasingly clear since the late nineteenth century that primitive art and child art use a language of symbols rather than "natural signs." To account for this fact it was postulated that there must be a special kind of art grounded not on seeing but rather on knowledge, an art which operates with "conceptual images." The child—it is argued—does not look at trees; he is satisfied with the "conceptual" schema of a tree that fails to correspond to any reality since it does not embody the characteristics of, say, birch or beech, let alone those of individual trees. This reliance on construction rather than on imitation was attributed to the peculiar mentality of children and primitives who live in a world of their own.

But we have come to realize that this distinction is unreal. Gustaf Britsch and Rudolf Arnheim have stressed that there is no opposition between the crude map of the world made by a child and the richer map presented in naturalistic images. All art originates in the human mind, in our reactions to the world rather than in the visible world itself, and it is precisely because all art is "conceptual" that all representations are recognizable by their style.

Without some starting point, some initial schema, we could never get hold of the flux of experience. Without categories, we could not sort our impressions. Paradoxically, it has turned out that it matters relatively little what these first categories are. We can always adjust them according to need. Indeed, if the schema remains loose and flexible, such initial vagueness may prove not a hindrance but a help. . . . [L]anguage does not give name to pre-existing things or concepts so much as it articulates the world of our experience. The images of art, we suspect, do the same. But this difference in styles or languages need not stand in the way of correct answers and descriptions. The world may be approached from a different angle and the information given may yet be the same.

From the point of view of information there is surely no difficulty in discussing portrayal. To say of a drawing that it is a correct view of Tivoli does not mean, of course, that Tivoli is bounded by wiry lines. It means that those who understand the notation will derive *no false information* from the drawing—whether it gives the contour in a few lines or picks out "every blade of grass" as Richter's friends wanted to do. The complete portrayal might be the one which gives as much correct information about the spot as we would obtain if we looked at it from the very spot where the artist stood.

Styles, like languages, differ in the sequence of articulation and in the number of questions they allow the artist to ask; and so complex is the information that reaches us from the visible world that no picture will ever embody it all. This is not due to the subjectivity of vision but to its richness. Where the artist has to copy a human product he can, of course, produce a facsimile which is indistinguishable from the original. The forger of banknotes succeeds only too well in effacing his personality and the limitations of a period style.

But what matters to us is that the correct portrait, like the useful map, is an end product on a long road through schema and correction. It is not a faithful record of a visual experience but the faithful construction of a relational model.

Neither the subjectivity of vision nor the sway of conventions need lead us to deny that such a model can be constructed to any required degree of accuracy. What is decisive here is clearly the word "required." The form of a representation cannot be divorced from its purpose and the requirements of the society in which the given visual language gains currency.

. . . It is surely no accident that the tricks of illusionist art, perspective and modeling in light and shade, were connected in classical antiquity with the design of theatrical scenery. It is here, in the context of plays based on the ancient mythical tales, that the re-enactment of events according to the poet's vision and insight comes to its climax and is increasingly assisted by by the illusions of art. The records of this development are irretrievably lost, but a Pompeian wall painting of Paris on Mount Ida [92] may illustrate its direction. Here the artist invites us to picture the shepherd dreaming idly by the rural shrine before the quarrel of the goddesses shattered the peace of the scene for ever.

In the whole history of Western art we have this constant interaction between narrative intent and pictorial realism. To ask which came first, the idea of evocation or the means of representation, may therefore seem a rather idle exercise. But where we are confronted with the origins of this entire tradition, the problem of the cause of the Greek revolution, these speculations may at least help to formulate the whole question afresh. What one would like to know is whether the idea of a convincing rather than an effective or lucid image existed in the pre-Greek Orient. Is there any passage in a pre-Homeric text which compares with the description in the *Odyssey* of a gold brooch?

"There was a device on the face of it: a hound holding down a dappled fawn in his forepaws and ripping it as it struggled. Everyone admired the workmanship, the hound ripping and throttling the fawn, the fawn lashing out with his feet in his efforts to escape — and the whole thing done in gold."

We cannot tell what the brooch which Homer's listeners imagined from this description may have looked like. Possibly it would appear less lifelike to us. But in our context it matters more how it was seen: the attitude, or mental set, which enters into the evocation of the scene at the hunt and tries to imagine with the artist how the hound went in for the kill and how the victim struggled. Would not such an attitude inevitably set up that "chain reaction" of which Professor Hanfmann speaks?

I do not want to claim that the existence of Homeric poetry alone can suffice to explain the rise of Greek art. In ancient India, for instance, the development of the epic and drama did not lead to the same consequences, but then India lacked the Egyptian heritage of image making. If one may here apply the scholastic distinction between necessary and sufficient conditions, my hypothesis would be merely that the Homeric freedom of narration was as necessary as was the acquired skill of craftmanship to open the way for the Greek revolution. . . .

...Constable himself...said that an artist who is self-taught is taught by a very ignorant person indeed. But the worship of tradition which he found prevalent among the public sometimes led him to talk as if the artist could ever do without it: "In Art as in Literature, there are two modes by which men aim at distinction; in the one the Artist by careful application to what others have accomplished, imitates their works, or selects and combines their various beauties; in the other he seeks excellence at its primitive source NATURE. The one forms a style upon the study of pictures, and produces either imitative or eclectic art, as it has been termed; the other by a close observation of nature discovers qualities existing in her, which have never been portrayed before, and thus forms a style which is original."

And yet in the very passage with which I began this series of lectures and to which I shall still revert, he makes this confession: "I have endeavoured to draw a line between genuine art and mannerism, but even the greatest painters have never been wholly untainted by manner. Painting is a science and should be pursued as an inquiry into the laws of nature. Why, then, may not landscape painting be considered a branch of natural philosophy, of which pictures are but experiments?"

How did Constable come to link his admission that there is no art without "mannerism" (we would say without traditional schemata) with his plea for experimentation? I think he felt that the history of science presented a story of continuous advance in which the achievements of one observer were used and extended by the next. No scientist would refuse to use the books of his predecessors for fear of becoming a slave to tradition. It so happens we can document the same attitude for Constable. The Courtauld Institute of Art in London possesses a moving testimony which has never been published before because its artistic value is as slight as its psychological significance seems to me great. It is a series of copies by Constable from a drawing book by Alexander Cozens, the eighteenth-century landscape painter who published for the use of his pupils a series of schemata for clouds.

Constable, the bold critic of tradition, sat down and carefully copied these plates, which teach the student a variety of typical skies: "Streaky clouds at the top of the sky"; "Streaky clouds at the bottom of the sky"; "Half cloud, half plain, the clouds darker than the plain or blew part, and darker at the top than the bottom"—and so forth through all manner of combinations and permutations.

We know by now what Cozens teaches Constable. Not, indeed, what clouds look like, but a series of possibilities, of schemata, which should increase his awareness through visual classification. It has recently been pointed out how closely Constable's interest in the most elusive phenomena of the visible world comes to that of his countryman and contemporary Luke Howard, to whom we owe the classification of cloud forms into cumulus, cirrus, and stratus. Goethe, the great morphologist, hailed Howard's effort as a further conquest of the mind "giving form to the indeterminate." Cozens' schemata do the same for the artist who does not merely apply them in his searching study of phenomena but articulates and revises them beyond recognition. There are no more truthful images of clouds than those painted by Constable.

It matters little what filing system we adopt. But without some standards of comparison we cannot grasp reality. Having looked at Constable's creations we may also see clouds in a fresh way. If so, we will owe this heightened awareness to the memory of the images created by art. May it not be argued that when the grand classical manner of narrative painting died a natural death in the eighteenth century, it was this new function of art which brought landscape painting to the fore and compelled the artist to intensify the search for particular truths?

... When Picasso says, "I do not seek, I find," he means, I submit, that he has come to take as a matter of course that creation itself is exploration. He does not plan, he watches the weirdest beings rise under his hands and assume a life of their own. The films which show him at work and his more playful creations, such as his *papiers déchirés*, show that here is a man who has succumbed to the spell of making, unrestrained and unrestrainable by the mere descriptive functions of the image.

It is fitting that a similar claim of discovery through making has been made with much charm and humor by one of the most original of contemporary humorists, James Thurber. Thurber describes how some of his most popular drawings arose unplanned. The drawing "What have you done with Dr. Millmoss?" is a case in point. "The hippopotamus was drawn to amuse my small daughter," Thurber says, "Something about the creature's expression convinced me that he had recently eaten a man. I added the hat and pipe and Mrs. Millmoss and the caption followed easily enough."

But what is an accident in art? Are we right when we speak of random movements and random changes only because the artist did not seem aware of his intention beforehand? It is often thought that such an interpretation would contradict the findings of psychoanalysis, which has warned us against attaching too much importance to conscious intention. The forms and expressions found by twentieth-century artists in the course of their experiments with colors and shapes have been popularly accepted as images arising out of the depth of the artist's "unconscious." But this is, to my mind, a naïve misunderstanding. What psychoanalysis claims is that our conscious and preconscious mind will always tend to guide and influence the way we react to accidents. The inkblot is a random event; how we react to it is determined by our past. No one could predict where the paper which produced Picasso's ghostly mask would tear—what matters is why he kept it. It must have been almost equally hard to know beforehand how the exact position of the eyebrows would affect the expression of Thurber's hippo—what matters is that he knew how to observe and exploit it. The whole vexing question of what we mean by "intention" and how far we are ever in control of our movements is in a state of flux. In a way, perhaps, we always control and adjust our movements by observing their effects, similar to those self-regulating mechanisms that engineers call "feedback." Skill consists in a most rapid and subtle interaction between impulse and subsequent guidance, but not even the most skillful artist should claim to be able to plan a single stroke with the pen in all its details. What he can do is adjust the subsequent stroke to the effect observed in the previous one—which is, after all, precisely what Thurber has done. In this new process of schema and modification, the artist is one controlling fact, the public another. The artist may fear the accident, the unexpected which seems to endow the created image with a life of its own, or he can welcome it as an ally to expand the range of his language, as Leonardo and Cozens did. The more the public wants to join in this game, the less it will be interested in the artist's intention. Those who attribute to modern art the capacity of transcribing the images of our unconscious obviously gravely oversimplify a very complex train of events. We should say rather that it has swept away those restraints and taboos that restricted the artist's choice of means and the freedom of experimentation.

The modern sculptor is free to grope for a global, physiognomic form in shapes which are sisters under their skin to Al Capp's motherly Shmoo. The modern painter may use what he calls "automatic painting," the creation of Rorschach blots, in order to stimulate the mind — his own and those of others — toward fresh inventions. In this new-found freedom the old divisions created by the social idea of decorum have fallen. We hardly ask ourselves whether to pigeonhole the drawings of William Steig as humor or as serious art. No artist is more characteristic of this ultimate fusion of humorous experiment and artistic search than Paul Klee, who described how the artist-creator first builds and shapes the image according to purely formal laws of balance and harmony and then salutes the being that has grown under his hand by giving it a name, sometimes whimsical, sometimes serious, sometimes both.

In turning away from the visible world, art may really have found an uncharted region which waits to be discovered and articulated, as music has discovered and articulated it through the universe of sound. But this inner world, if we may call it so, can no more be transcribed than can the world of sight. To the artist the image in the unconscious is as mythical and useless an idea as was the image on the retina. There is no short cut to articulation. Wherever the artist turns his gaze he can only make and match, and out of a developed language select the nearest equivalence.

Harley Granville-Barker

Included in Granville-Barker's many active interests was his concern for the place of the theatre, as a professional and artistic institution, in the rest of society. He was involved not only in play production, but — in a manner of speaking — in play *reception,* in the very situation of the drama as a part of daily life among people not connected with the theatre in any professional way.

These short excerpts represent the way in which Granville-Barker attended to every detail of his subject. The first series of observations are concerned with the study of dramatic literature — always with an alert eye to the stage life of plays — in terms of modes of theatrical language; the second excerpt deals with that all-important subject, the relationship of a play's structure to its value as an art-work. It is refreshing to find such authority refusing to avoid the question — perhaps too often inhibited in the name of "objectivity" — of the actual *worth* of one play in comparison to another.

from THE USE OF THE DRAMA

THE "EXPLICIT" AND "IMPLICIT" METHODS OF PLAY-WRITING

Take next the question of more and less suitable material for our study. There are roughly—considering both to-day's and yesterday's—two methods of play-writing, that demanding explicit interpretation, and that in which much of the meaning is left implicit, to be conveyed by the actors, not in words nor even in very forthright action, but largely by demonstrating the sort of pattern made in the relations and attitude of the characters toward each other and in the contrasts between them, the dialogue stressing the significance of the design. Marlowe's, for an example, is wholly "explicit" drama, as is more primitive drama than his. So are Shakespeare's earlier plays, and his method in general remains throughout as explicit as the nature of play or character will allow it to be. Chekhov's method, on the other hand, and in quite another fashion Maeterlinck's or Yeats', are "implicit" in the extreme. Yet it is not a difference between modern drama and old. No dramatist could be more explicit than is Bernard Shaw, and others have been returning lately to old forms, while not half the significance in *King Lear* and *Macbeth* finds its way into plain words. But, speaking generally, it is the increased use of the implicit in drama which has marked its more modern developments ("modern" for me, I fear, meaning Ibsen and Chekhov and Maeterlinck; my junior listeners must apply some other epithet), and the demands made on the actors have so far developed as to have all but changed. Romeo and Juliet, for instance, can be acted by a couple of children if they can speak and move as aptly as well-trained choir boys can sing (Shakespeare's Juliet, of course, was so acted, and nobody now thinks of commiserating him upon that; I have even heard him envied). So, indeed, can such a comparatively "implicit" play as *Macbeth* be. In default of great acting for it, simple acting will suffice; impersonal, plastically pleasing, showing as much regard as possible for Shakespeare's share in the business and as little for the actor's own. The tragedy will still yield as much, and its better part. But in Chekhov's *The Cherry Orchard,* unless the actress of Madame Ranevsky brings to her performance not only all she is

From *The Use of the Drama* by Harley Granville-Barker. Reprinted by permission of Field Roscoe & Co. (London).

directed to say and do, but something besides that she must perva-
sively and expressively *be* (and the same thing will be true and truer
of acting in the later plays of that both "explicit" and "implicit"
dramatist Ibsen), there will be left in the place the character should
fill nothing but a very large hole. In most sorts of drama the actor's
personality, animating and clothing the figure the dramatist has
designed, will be a legitimate factor (if only, as we said, the distinction can be kept between personality manifested and ego exploited).
But in this "implicit" sort it is positively needed, and the art of the
dramatist provides for and demands it. And this, in turn, calls on all
that is maturest in the art of the actor. He may need to spend a
professional lifetime making himself into an instrument that, for the
dramatist's benefit, he can so sensitively play upon.

Little or nothing is to be gained from fully filled-in student
performances of this implicit drama, from a Rebecca West or Hedda
Gabler acted by—to put it unkindly, as we soon should—precocious
schoolgirls, or from a Master Builder listening for the younger
generation knocking at the door played by one of that very generation, vaultingly ambitious. On the other hand, the student, remaining a student, nor trying to reach to more than the fullest intellectual
and emotional appeciation of it of which he is naturally capable, will
be less at a disadvantage with this sort of play, however inadequate
his powers over the *expression* of it may be; since—whether for
student or actor—there is the more work to be done at it before
putting it into action, and that dividing line can therefore be drawn
the later. Our class can, in fact, very profitably *study* a play which they
could not hope to *perform* with much benefit to themselves or
pleasure to anybody else.

THE STUDY OF A PLAY PUTS ITS TECHNIQUE ON TRIAL

The classwork by which the students will test and augment their
own knowledge necessarily becomes also something like a test and
trial of the play itself. We consider this first as a whole. Though it
may seldom be planned in any strict obedience to the famous Unities,
some sort of unity it must have. An approximate unity of subject will
be convenient, if the attention of an audience is to be happily held,
and a unity of convention, for the sustaining of the make-believe.
But the conditions of the theatre positively force on the drama
certain limiting disciplines. The actors—for a dominating instance—
are physically limited in what they can do; and this human medium

affects all that touches it. The dramatist will not employ his scenic conventions in a fashion which they, the actors, cannot make convincing. Shakespeare inherits in his theatre, with its platform stage and illocalized balconies and curtains, a seemingly untrammelled freedom in space and time, and his audience would customarily yield to his suggestions a most obedient imagination. But, with his extraordinary "sense of the theatre," he never taxes this aimlessly or too far, never leaves us questioning. Convention in the theatre is a gentleman's agreement between dramatist, actors, and audience. It involves (as do all agreements) consistency, and consideration in the use of it. Shakespeare retains the scenic freedoms of his bare stage, but he uses them considerately. Ibsen, writing for his theatre of scenic illusion, has surrendered them, has, so to put it, anchored himself in space, and, more closely than any of his predecessors, in time. And he cannot arbitrarily resume his freedom. He makes a half-attempt to do so in his last two plays; when John Gabriel Borkman sets off up the snow-bound mountain, in the ending of *When We Dead Awaken* amid avalanches and hymns to freedom. But this does not quite do. The agreement has been broken. The actors may not object to this incontinent reshaping of it; but we, the audience, having first accepted one sort of illusion, will be unwillingly suddenly to change; and against our discomfort neither dramatist nor actors can successfully contend. Audience and actors must be at ease together.[1]

THE QUESTION OF DRAMATIC INTEGRITY

More vital, however, than consistency of convention will be the inner quality of dramatic integrity. A play, as we said, involves

---

[1] It may be argued that an audience, having seen a play given on one night under conditions of scenic illusion, will accept without difficulty Shakespeare and his conventions the next. Yes; but until how recently has Shakespeare not been adapted to the conventions of the contemporary stage? To a degree he still is. To a degree it is because this is "Shakespeare" that an intimidated audience will swallow his stagecraft (nearly) whole. There have lately been, it may be added, various experiments in convention. But they have remained experiments, no general change has developed from them; not, certainly, from one pseudo-Chinese production I remember, nor from a most delightful one out of two projected by Mr. Thornton Wilder. And I doubt whether, in any of the three instances, the parties to the business — author, actors, and audience — were wholly at their ease. A certain self-consciousness, an air of artificial innocence, pervaded it.

Of more importance is Mr. T. S. Eliot's recent *The Family Reunion,* with its modern treatment of the matter of a Greek tragedy. The conventions are mixed: but the actual inclusion of the Eumenides among the characters — mute, but visible both to hero and audience — is for me at once the unlikeliest and the lease necessary of the devices. Mr. Eliot has not yet matured, I think, with perfect certainty, the visually imaginative side of his dramatic art. On the other hand, the verbal treatment of chorus and dialogue, the significant blending of realistic and formal, I find masterly indeed. And while it would be work, truly, for very advanced students, in a testing trial of this play, a distinguishing between its achievements and its shortcomings, we should be dealing with some of the fundamentals of drama.

conflict, outward or inward; this keeps it alive. Its story will be told chiefly by the setting out of differences between the characters. The action develops these and will at last dispose of them, be it, as in comedy, by reconciliation and agreement or by tragic catastrophe – and there are variations enough between these two extremes. The thing to remember is that the differences must always be fairly fought out, each character being allowed to say and do his best on his own behalf. There must be no fraudulent tipping of the scales by the dramatist in favour of this one or that, no lucky but too unlikely accident occurring, no over-opportune conversions from one opinion to another. For the fraud of these will be at once detected, unless the audience is as gullible as the dramatist is dishonest. And characters so indulged will at once lose their dramatic integrity. They will forfeit their seemingly independent status in that mimic world which we have agree to accept for an hour or so as the real world. At the sign of such weakness, such a lapse into puppetdom, we in turn shall weaken in our belief in it, and in them. And it is in this belief – willingly accorded at first, yet to be lost all but unawares – that the maturer art of the drama subsists.

Very much as we feel that a man may be called on to justify his existence in the real world, so must a character's place, speech, and actions in a play be justifiable. And the student temporarily identifying himself with a character or given its interest to defend, will have to make a case for them against whatever devil's advocacy the rest of the class can muster. The brief, on the face of it, may seem but a meagre one. What the character does and says in the short course of the play, what is said *to* the character, what *about* it – in strictness that can be all; and except possibly for certain forms of poetry there is no thriftier kind of writing than the dramatic. A stock curiosity in my youth was the Lord's Prayer written on a threepenny piece. In such a script the whole of Lady Macbeth could, I suppose, be accommodated on a silver dollar, and Hamlet – the part if not the play – on the front and back of a dollar bill. And Shakespeare's was a comparatively verbose school of writing – "explicit" we have called it – delighting in words and their beauty. He had, moreover, to suggest in words such scenery as he might think the play needed, a background for its action; and in every play time must be spared in which to tell the audience all that needs to be known of what has happened before the action begins, in providing it, so to say, with the background of its past; this, from the very little time available. There are simple ways of building up this past, be it of the play as a whole or of a single character; by the Prologue – nothing could be simpler

—bringing the story to the point at which the action begins and can, in the present tense and unencumbered, carry it on; by narrative—a little less simple this—embodied in the action, shaped, perhaps, as reminiscences exchanged between the characters. Familiar devices range from *Romeo and Juliet's* "Two houses both alike in dignity . . ." to the opening of almost any nineteenth-century French farce with its valet and chambermaid, and their "Didn't Master get home very late last night? . . ."[2] But the student will find that, as the art of the drama matures, his brief for a character is reduced more to the dimensions and the stuff of the character itself.

⚓

[2] For the classic burlesque of this method see, of course, Sheridan's *The Critic;* Sir Walter Raleigh to Sir Christopher Hatton: "You know, my friend, scarce two revolving suns . . . You know, besides . . . You also know . . ." and so on, until Dangle interrupts with "But, Mr. Puff, as he knows all this, why does Sir Walter go on telling him?" to be snubbed by a "But the audience are not supposed to know anything of the matter, are they?" Not such sheer burlesque, either!

George Jean Nathan

It is impossible to overestimate the importance of this writer to the development of the American theatre. When he began his work, no plays of real value were being produced. He literally introduced to our theatre the work of almost every important playwright in the first third of the century by brow-beating his public in many magazines and newspapers, by personal contacts, by financial help—in short, by the energy of a supremely dedicated, civilized, and powerful intellect and personality.

He derided what was bad and introduced Shaw, Ibsen, Hauptmann, and Strindberg. In the pages of *The Smart Set* (jointly edited with Mencken), he printed O'Neill, not to mention Joyce, Molnar, Wedekind, Brieux, and many others—in more recent years, for example, O'Casey and Saroyan. He detested the mediocre and fought for quality; he relished eccentricity, never for its own sake but as a possible clue of genius; he published constantly for many years. This essay is concerned with taste in the best sense of that ambiguous word, with audience reception (and perception) of drama.

❧ *from* THE DRAMA AS AN ART

If the best of criticism, in the familiar description of Anatole France, lies in the adventure of a soul among masterpieces, the best of drama may perhaps be described as the adventure of a masterpiece among souls. Drama is fine or impoverished in the degree that it evokes from such souls a fitting and noble reaction.

Drama is, in essence, a democratic art in constant brave conflict with aristocracy of intelligence, soul, and emotion. When drama triumphs, a masterpiece like *Hamlet* comes to life. When the conflict ends in a draw, a drama halfway between greatness and littleness is the result—a drama, say, like *El Gran Galeoto*. When the struggle ends in defeat, the result is a *Way Down East* or a *Lightnin'*. This, obviously, is not too say that great drama may not be popular drama, nor popular drama great drama, for I speak of drama here not as this play or that, but as a specific art. And it is as a specific art that it finds its test and trial, not in its own intrinsically democratic soul, but in the extrinsic aristocratic soul that is taste, and connoisseurship, and final judgment. Drama that has come to be at once great and popular has ever first been given the imprimatur, not of democratic souls, but of aristocratic. Shakespeare and Molière triumphed over aristocracy of intelligence, soul and emotion before that triumph was presently carried on into the domain of inferior intelligence, soul and emotion. In our own day, the drama of Hauptmann, Shaw and the American O'Neill has come into its popular own only after it first achieved the imprimatur of what we may term the unpopular, or undemocratic, theatre. Aristocracy cleared the democratic path for Ibsen, as it cleared it, in so far as possible, for Rostand and Hugo von Hofmannsthal.

Great drama is the rainbow born when the sun of reflection and understanding smiles anew upon an intelligence and emotion which that drama has respectively shot with gleams of brilliant lightning and drenched with the rain of brilliant tears. Great drama, like great men and great women, is always just a little sad. Only idiots may be completely happy. Reflection, sympathy, wisdom, gallant gentleness, experience—the chords upon which great drama is played—these are wistful chords. The commonplace urge that drama, to be truly great, must uplift is, in the sense that the word uplift is used, childish. The mission of great drama is not to make numskulls glad

From "The Drama as an Art" in *The World of George Jean Nathan*, Charles Angoff, ed. (Alfred A. Knopf. Inc.: 1952). Reprinted with permission.

that they are alive, but to make them speculate why they are permitted to be alive at all. And since this is the mission of great drama—if its mission may, indeed, be reduced to any phrase—it combines within itself, together with this mystical and awestruck appeal to the proletariat, a direct and agreeable appeal to such persons as are, by reason of their metaphysical perception and emotional culture, superior to and contemptuous of proletariat. Fine drama, in truth, is usually just a trifle snobbish. It has no traffic with such souls as are readily made to feel "uplifted" by spurious philosophical nostrums and emotional sugar pills. Its business is with what the matchless Dryden hailed "souls of the highest rank and truest understandiing": souls who find a greater uplift in the noble depressions of Brahms' first trio, Bartolommeo's Madonna della Misericordia, and Joseph Conrad's "Youth" than in the easy buoyancies of John Philip Sousa, Howard Chandler Christy and Rupert Hughes. The aim of great drama is not to make men happy with themselves as they are, but with themselves as they might, yet alas cannot, be. As Gautier has it, "The aim of art is not exact reproduction of nature, but creation, by means of forms and colors, of a microcosm wherein may be produced dreams, sensations, and ideas inspired by the aspect of the world." If drama is irrevocably a democratic art and uplift of the great masses of men its noblest end, Mrs. Porter's *Pollyanna* must endure as a work of dramatic art a thousand times finer than Corneille's *Polyeucte*.

Drama has been strictly defined by the ritualists in a dozen different ways. "Drama," says one, "must be based on character, and the action proceed from character." "Drama," stipulates another, "is not an imitation of men, but of an action and of life: character is subsidiary to action." "Drama," promulgates still another, "is the struggle of a will against obstacles." And so on, so on. Rules, rules and more rules. Pigeonholes upon pigeonholes. Good drama is anything that interests an intelligently emotional group of persons assembled together in an illuminated hall. Molière, wise among dramatists, said as much, though in somewhat more, and doubtless too, sweeping words. Throughout the ages of drama there will be always Romanticists of one sort or another, brave and splendid spirits, who will have to free themselves from the definitions and limitations imposed upon them by the neo-Bossus and Boileaus, and the small portion Voltaires, La Harpes and Marmontels. Drama is struggle, a conflict of wills? Then what of *Ghosts*? Drama is action? Then what of *Nachtasyl*? Drama is character? Then what of *The Dream Play*? "A 'character' upon the stage," wrote the author of the last named, "has become a creature readymade—a mere mechanism

that drives the man — I do not believe in these theatrical 'characters.' "

Of all the higher arts, drama is organically perhaps the simplest.
Its anatomy is composed of all the other arts, high and low, stripped
to their elementals. It is a synthesis of those portions of these other
arts that, being elemental, are most easily assimilable on the part of
the multitude. It is a snatch of music, a bit of painting, a moment of
dancing, a slice of sculpture, draped upon the skeleton of literature.
At its highest, it ranks with literature, but never above it. One small
notch below, it ranks only with itself, in its own isolated and generi-
cally peculiar field. Drama, indeed, is dancing literature: a hybrid
art. It is often purple and splendid; it is often profoundly beautiful
and profoundly moving. Yet, with a direct appeal to the emotions as
its first and encompassing aim, it has never, even at its finest, been
able to exercise the measure of direct emotional appeal that is
exercised, say, by Chopin's C sharp minor Nocturne, op. 27, No. 1,
or by the soft romance of the canvases of Palma Vecchio, or by
Rodin's superb "Eternal Spring," or by Zola's *La Terre*. It may, at its
finest as at its worst, of course subjugate and triumph over inexpe-
rienced emotionalism, but the greatest drama of Shakespeare himself has never, in the truthful confession of cultivated emotionalism,
influenced that emotionalism as has the greatest literature, or the
greatest music, or the greatest painting or sculpture. . . .

Art is an evocation of beautiful emotions; art is art in the degree
that it succeeds in the evocation: drama succeeds in an inferior
degree. Whatever emotion drama may succeed brilliantly in evoking, another art succeeds in evoking more brilliantly.

II

Although, of course, one speaks of drama here primarily in the
sense of acted drama, it is perhaps not necessary so strictly to confine
one's self. For when the critic confines himself in his discussion of
drama to the acted drama, he regularly brings upon himself from
other critics — chiefly bookish fellows whose theatrical knowledge is
meagre — the very largely unwarranted embarrassment of arguments anent "crowd psychology" and the like which, while they have
little or nothing to do with the case, none the less make a certain
deep impression upon his readers. (Readers of criticism become
automatically critics; with his first sentence, the critic challenges his
critic-reader's sense of argument.) This constantly advanced contention of "crowd psychology," of which drama is supposed to be at
once master and slave, has small place in a consideration of drama,
from whatever sound point of view one elects to consider the latter.

If "crowd psychology" operates in the case of theatre drama, it operates also in the case of concert-hall music. Yet no one so far as I know seriously maintains that, in a criticism of music, this "crowd psychology" has any place.

I have once before pointed out that, even accepting the theory of crowd psychology and its direct and indirect implications so far as drama is concerned, it is as nonsensical to assume that one thousand persons assembled together before a drama in a theatre are, by reason of their constituting a crowd, any more likely to be moved automatically than the same crowd of one thousand persons assembled together before a painting in an art gallery. Furthermore, the theory that collective intelligence and emotionalism are a more facile and ingenuous intelligence and emotionalism, while it may hold full water in the psychological laboratory, holds little in actual external demonstration, particularly in any consideration of a crowd before one of the arts. While it may be true that the Le Bon and Tarde theory applies aptly to the collective psychology of a crowd at a prizefight or a bullfight or a circus, one may be permitted severe doubts that it holds equally true of a crowd in a theatre or in an art gallery or in a concert hall. The tendency of such a latter group is not æsthetically downward, but upward. And not only æsthetically, but intellectually and emotionally. (I speak, of course, and with proper relevance, of a crowd assembled to hear good drama or good music, or to see good painting. The customary obscuring tactic of critics in this situation is to argue out the principles of intelligent reaction to good drama in terms of yokel reaction to bad drama. Analysis of the principles of sound theatre drama and the reaction of a group of eight hundred citizens of Marion, Ohio, to "The Two Orphans" somehow do not seem to me to be especially apposite.) The fine drama or the fine piece of music does not make its auditor part of a crowd; it removes him, and everyone else in the crowd, from the crowd, and makes him an individual. The crowd ceases to exist as a crowd; it becomes a crowd of units, of separate individuals. The dramas of Mr. Owen Davis make crowds; the dramas of Shakespeare make individuals.

The argument to the contrary always somewhat grotesquely assumes that the crowd assembled at a fine play, and promptly susceptible to group psychology, is a new crowd, one that has never attended a fine play before. Such an assumption falls to pieces in two ways. First, it is beyond reason to believe that it is true in more than one instance out of a hundred; and, secondly, it would not be true even if it were true. For, granting that a crowd of one thousand persons were seeing great drama for the first time in their lives, what reason is there for believing that the majority of persons in the crowd who had never seen great drama and didn't know exactly what to make of it would be swayed and influenced by the minority who had never seen great drama but did know what to make of it? If this were true, no great drama could ever possibly fail in the commercial theatre. Or, to test the hypothesis further, take it the other way round. What reason is there for believing that the majority in this crowd would be moved the one way or the other, either by a minority that did understand the play, or did not understand it? Or take it in another way still. What reason is there for believing that the minority in this crowd who did know what the drama was about would be persuaded emotionally by the majority who did not know what the drama was about?

Theories and again theories. But the facts fail to support them. Take the lowest type of crowd imaginable, one in which there is not one cultured man in a thousand—the crowd, say, at a professional American baseball game—and pack it into an American equivalent of Reinhardt's Grosses Schauspielhaus. The play, let us say, is *Œdipus Rex*. At the ball game, let us say, the crowd psychology of Le Bon operated to the full. But what now? Would the crowd, in the theatre and before a great drama, be the same crowd? Would not its group psychology promptly and violently suffer a sudden change? Whether out of curiosity, disgust, admiration, social shame or what not, would it not rapidly segregate itself, spiritually or physically, into various groups? What is the Le Bon theatrical view of the crowd psychology that somehow did not come off during the initial engagement of Barrie's *Peter Pan* in Washington, D. C.? Or of the crowd psychology that worked the other way round when Ibsen was first played in London? Or of the crowd psychology that, operating regularly, if artificially, at the New York premières, most often fails, for all its high enthusiasm, to move either the minority or the majority in its composition?

The question of sound drama and the pack psychology of a congress of groundlings is a fatuous one: it gets nowhere. Sound drama and sound audiences are alone to be considered at one and the same time. And, as I have noted, the tendency of willing, or even semi-willing, auditors and spectators is in an upward direction, not a downward. No intelligent spectator at a performance of *Ben Hur* has ever been made to feel like throwing his hat into the air and cheering by the similar actions of the mob spectators to the left and right of him. No ignoble auditor of *The Laughter of the Gods* but has been made to feel, in some part, the contagion of cultivated appreciation to *his* left and right. "I forget," wrote Sarcey, in a consideration of the subject, "what tyrant it was of ancient Greece to whom massacres were everyday affairs, but who wept copiously over the misfortunes of a heroine in a tragedy. He was the audience; and for the one evening clothed himself in the sentiments of the public." A typical example of sophisticated reasoning. How does Sarcey know that it was not the rest of the audience — the crowd — that was influenced by this repentant and copiously lachrymose individual rather than that it was this individual who was moved by the crowd?

If fallacies perchance insinuate themselves into these opposing contentions, it is a case of fallacy versus fallacy: my intent is not so much to prove anything as to indicate the presence of holes in the proofs of the other side. These holes seem to me to be numerous, and of considerable circumference. A description of two of them may suffice to suggest the rest. Take, as the first of these, the familiar Castelvetro doctrine that, since a theatrical audience is not a select congress but a motley crowd, the dramatist, ever conscious of the group psychology, must inevitably avoid all themes and ideas unintelligible to such a gathering. It may be true that a theatrical audience is not a select congress, but why confine the argument to theatrical audiences and seek thus to prove something of drama that may be proved as well — if one is given to such idiosyncrasies — of music? What, as I have said before, of opera and concert-hall audiences? Consider the average audience at Covent Garden, the Metropolitan, Carnegie Hall. Is it in any way culturally superior to the average audience at the St. James Theatre, or the Théâtre de l'Œuvre, or the Plymouth — or even the Neighbourhood Playhouse down in Grand Street? What of the audiences who attended the original performances of Beethoven's "Leonore" ("Fidelio"), Berlioz's "Benvenuto Cellini," the original performances of Wagner in France and the performances of his "Der Fliegende Holländer" in Germany, the operas of Händel in England in the years 1733-37, the work of Rossini in Italy, the concerts of Chopin during his tour of England and Scotland?... Again, as to the imperative necessity of the dramatist's avoidance of all themes and ideas unintelligible to a mob audience, what of the success among such very audiences — to name but a few more recent profitably produced and locally recognizable examples — of Shaw's *Getting Married,* Augustus Thomas' *The Witching Hour,* Ibsen's *The Wild Duck,* Dunsany's *The Laughter of the Gods,* Barrie's *Mary Rose,* Strindberg's *The Father,* Synge's *Playboy?* ... Surely it will be quickly allowed that however obvious the themes and ideas of these plays may be to the few, they are hardly within the ready intelligence of what the theorists picture as the imaginary mob theatre audience. Fine drama is independent of all such theories: the dramatist who subscribes to them should not figure in any treatise upon drama as an art.

A second illustration: the equivocation to the effect that drama, being a democratic art, may not properly be evaluated in terms of more limited, and aristocratic, taste. It seems to me an idiotic assumption that drama is a more democratic art than music. All great art is democratic in intention, if not in reward. Michelangelo, Shakespeare, Wagner and Zola are democratic artists, and their art democratic art. It is criticism of Michelangelo, Shakespeare, Wagner and Zola that is aristocratic. Criticism, not art, generally wears the ermine and the purple. To appraise a democratic art in terms of democracy is to attempt to effect a chemical reaction in nitrogen with nitrogen. If drama is, critically, a democratic art since it is meant not to be read by the few but to be played before the many, music must be critically no less a democratic art. Yet the theorists conveniently overlook this embarrassment. Nevertheless, if Shakespeare's dramas were designed for the heterogeneous ear, so, too, were the songs of Schumann. No great artist has ever in his heart deliberately fashioned his work for a remote and forgotten cellar, dark and stairless. He fashions it, for all his doubts, in the hope of hospitable eyes and ears, and in the hope of a sun to shine upon it. It is as ridiculous to argue that because Shakespeare's is a democratic art it must be criticized in terms of democratic reaction to it as it would be to argue that because the United States is a democracy the most acute and comprehensive criticism of that democracy must lie in a native democrat's reaction to it. "To say that the theatre is for the people," says Gordon Craig, "is necessary. But to forget to add that part and parcel of the people is the aristocracy, whether of birth or feeling, is an omission. A man of the eighteenth century, dressed in silks, in a fashionable loggia in the theatre at Versailles, looking as if he did no work (as Voltaire in his youth may have looked), presents, in essence, exactly the same picture as Walt Whitman in his rough gray suit lounging in the Bowery, also looking as if he did no work. . . . One the aristocrat, one the democrat: the two are identical."

III

"Convictions," said Nietzsche, "are prisons." Critical "theories," with negligible exception, seek to denude the arts of their splendid, gypsy gauds and to force them instead to don so many duplicated black-and-white striped uniforms. Of all the arts, drama has suffered most in this regard. Its critics, from the time of Aristotle, have bound and fettered it, and have then urged it impassionedly to soar. Yet, despite its shackles, it has triumphed, and each triumph has been a derision of one of its famous and distinguished critics. It triumphed, through Shakespeare, over Aristotle; it triumphed, through Molière, over Castelvetro; it triumphed, through Lemercier, over Diderot; it triumphed, through Lessing, over Voltaire; it triumphed, through Ibsen, over Flaubert; it has triumphed, through Hauptmann, over Sarcey and, through Schnitzler and Bernard Shaw, over Mr. Archer. The truth perhaps is that drama is an art as flexible as the imaginations of its audiences. It is no more to be bound by rules and theories than such imaginations are to be bound by rules and theories. Who so allwise that he may say by what rules or set of rules living imaginations and imaginations yet unborn are to be fanned into theatrical flame? "Imagination," Samuel Johnson's words apply to auditor as to artist, "a licentious and vagrant faculty, unsusceptible of limitations and impatient of restraint, has always endeavored to baffle the logician, to perplex the confines of distinction, and burst the inclosures of regularity." And further, "There is therefore scarcely any species of writing of which we can tell what is its essence, and what are its constituents; every new genius produces some innovation which, when invented and approved, subverts the rules which the practice of foregoing authors had established."

Does the play interest, and whom? This seems to me to be the only doctrine of dramatic criticism that is capable of supporting itself soundly. First, does the play interest? In other words, how far has the dramatist succeeded in expressing himself, and the materials before him, intelligently, eloquently, symmetrically, beautifully? So much for the criticism of the dramatist as an artist. In the second place, whom does the play interest? Does it interest inferior persons, or does it interest cultivated and artistically sensitive persons? So much for the criticism of the artist as a dramatist.

The major difficulty with critics of the drama has always been that, having once positively enunciated their critical credoes, they have been constrained to devote their entire subsequent enterprise and ingenuity to defending the fallacies therein. Since a considerable number of these critics have been, and are, extraordinarily shrewd and ingenious men, these defences of error have often been contrived with such perusasive dexterity and reasonableness that they have endured beyond the sounder doctrines of less deft critics, doctrines which, being sound, have suffered the rebuffs that gaunt, grim logic, ever unprepossessing and unhypnotic, suffers always. ...

... The art of the drama is one which imposes upon drama the obligation of depicting at once the inner processes of life realistically and the external aspects of life delusively. Properly and sympathetically to appreciate drama, one must look upon it synchronously with two different eyes: the one arguing against the other as to the truth of what it sees, and triumphing over this doubtful other with the full force of its sophistry. Again inevitably to quote Coleridge, "Stage presentations are to produce a sort of temporary half-faith, which the spectator encourages in himself and supports by a voluntary contribution on his own part, because he knows that it is at all times in his power to see the thing as it really is. Thus the true stage illusion as to a forest scene consists, not in the mind's judging it to be a forest, but in its remission of the judgment that it is not a forest." This obviously applies to drama as well as to dramatic investiture. One never for a moment believes absolutely that Mr. John Barrymore is Richard III, so that one may receive the ocular, aural and mental sensations for which one has paid three and one-half dollars. Nor does one for a moment believe that Mr. Walter Hampden, whom that very evening one has seen dividing a brobdingnagian dish of goulash with Mr. Oliver Herford in the Players' Club and discussing the prospects of the White Sox, is actually speaking extemporaneously the rare verbal embroideries of Shakespeare; or that Miss Ethel Barrymore who is billed in front of Browne's Shop House to take a star part in the Actors' Equity Association's benefit, is really the queen of a distant kingdom.

The dramatist, in the theatre, is not a worker in actualities, but in the essence of actualities that filters through the self-deception of his spectators. There is no such thing as realism in the theatre: there is only mimicry of realism. There is no such thing as romance in the theatre: there is only mimicry of romance. There is no such thing as an automatic dramatic susceptibility in a theatre audience: there is only a volitional dramatic susceptibility. Thus, it is absurd to speak of the drama holding the mirror up to nature; all that the drama can do is to hold nature up to its own peculiar mirror which, like that in a pleasure park, amusingly fattens up nature, or shrinks it, yet does not at any time render it unrecognizable. One does not go to the theatre to see life and nature; one goes to see the particular way in which life and nature happen to look to a cultivated, imaginative and entertaining man who happens, in turn, to be a playwright. Drama is the surprising pulling of a perfectly obvious rabbit out of a perfectly obvious, everyday silk hat. The spectator has seen thousands of rabbits and thousands of silk hats, but he has never seen a silk hat that had a rabbit concealed in it, and he is curious about it.

But if drama is essentially mimetic, so also—as Professor Gilbert Murray implies—is criticism essentially mimetic in that it is representative of the work criticized. It is conceivable that one may criticize Mr. Ziegfeld's "Follies" in terms of the "Philoctetes" of Theodectes— I myself have been guilty of even more exceptional feats; it is not only conceivable, but of common occurrence, for certain of our academic American critics to criticize the plays of Mr. Shaw in terms of Scribe and Sardou, and with a perfectly straight face; but criticism in general is a chameleon that takes on something of the color of the pattern upon which it imposes itself. There is drama in Horace's *Epistola and Pisones,* a criticism of drama. There is the spirit of comedy in Hazlitt's essay *On the Comic Writers of the Last Century.* Dryden's *Essay on Dramatic Poesy* is poetry. There is something of the music of Chopin in Huneker's critical essays on Chopin, and some of Mary Garden's spectacular histrionism in his essay on her acting. Walkley, criticizing *L'Enfant Prodigue,* uses the pen of Pierrot. Criticism, more than drama with her mirror toward nature, holds the mirror up to the nature of the work it criticizes. Its end is the revivification of the passion of art which has been spent in its behalf, but under the terms laid down by Plato. Its aim is to reconstruct a great work of art on a diminutive scale, that eyes which are not capable of gazing on high may have it within the reach of their vision. Its aim is to play again all the full richness of the artist's emotional organ tones, in so far as is possible, on the old cerebral xylophone that is criticism's deficient instrument. In the accomplishment of these aims, it is bound by no laws that art is not bound by. There is but one rule: there are no rules. Art laughs at locksmiths.

It has been a favorite diversion of critics since Aristotle's day to argue that drama is drama, whether one reads it from a printed page or sees it enacted in a theatre. Great drama, they announce, is great drama whether it ever be acted or not; "it speaks with the same voice in solitude as in crowds"; and "all the more then"—again I quote Mr. Spingarn—"will the drama itself 'even apart from representation and actors,' as old as Aristotle puts it, speak with its highest power to the imagination fitted to understand and receive it." Upon this point of view much of the academic criticism of drama has been based. But may we not well reply that, for all the fact that Shakespeare would still be the greatest dramatist who ever lived had he never been played in the theatre, so, too, would Bach still be the greatest composer who ever lived had his compositions never been played at all? If drama is not meant for actors, may we not also argue that music is not meant for instruments? Are not such expedients less sound criticism than clever evasion of sound criticism: a frolicsome and agreeable straddling of the aesthetic seesaw? There is the printed drama—criticize it. There is the same drama acted—criticize it. Why quibble? Sometimes, as in the case of *Gioconda* and Duse, they are one. Well and good. Sometimes, as in the case of *Chantecler* and Maude Adams, they are not one. Well and good. But where, in either case, the confusion that the critics lay such stress upon? These critics deal not with theories, but with mere words. They take two dozen empty words and adroitly seek therewith to fashion a fecund theory. The result is—words. "Words which," said Ruskin, "if they are not watched, will do deadly work sometimes. There are masked words droning and skulking about us just now ... (there never were so many, owing to the teaching of catechisms and phrases at school instead of human meanings) ... there never were creatures of prey so mischievous, never diplomatists so cunning, never poisoners so deadly, as these masked words: they are the unjust stewards of men's ideas...."

As they are of men's lack of ideas.

Susan Sontag

Miss Sontag has published critical essays in such magazines as *The Partisan Review*, *The New York Review of Books*, *Film Quarterly*, and *The Nation*. She records, in effect, the reaction over the last ten years to plays, social trends, music and narrative writing, films, and many highly specialized human phenomena—the reaction of a sensibility of these years, highly contemporary, sophisticated, and perceptive of detail.

This piece is from a collection called *Against Interpretation*—a title chosen to argue against the critical act of finding "meaning" when one should try instead to demonstrate how any work of art *is* what it is. Based on an assignment to review the London production by Peter Brook of Weiss's *Marat ... Sade,* this selection discusses the relationships of the play to the work of Artaud, of new narrative values and rules, of the very nature of the drama itself as it appears to be developing in this decade.

❦   *MARAT / SADE / ARTAUD*

"The Primary and most beautiful of Nature's qualities is motion, which agitates her at all times. But this motion is simply the perpetual consequence of crimes; and it is conserved by means of crimes alone."

—SADE

"Everything that acts is a cruelty. It is upon this idea of extreme action, pushed beyond all limits, that theatre must be rebuilt."

—ARTAUD

Theatricality and insanity—the two most potent subjects of the contemporary theater—are brilliantly fused in Peter Weiss' play, *The Persecution and Assassination of Marat as Performed by the Inmates of the Asylum at Charenton under the Direction of the Marquis de Sade.* The subject is a dramatic performance staged before the audience's eyes; the scene is a madhouse. The historical facts behind the play are that in the insane asylum just outside Paris where Sade was confined by order of Napoleon for the last eleven years of his life (1803–14), it was the enlightened policy of the director, M. Coulmier, to allow Charenton's inmates to stage theatrical productions of their own devising which were open to the Parisian public. In these circumstances Sade is known to have written and put on several plays (all lost), and Weiss' play ostensibly re-creates such a performance. The year is 1808 and the stage is the stark tiled bathhouse of the asylum.

Theatricality permeates Weiss' cunning play in a peculiarly modern sense: most of *Marat/Sade* consists of a play-within-a-play. In Peter Brook's production, which opened in London last August, the aged, disheveled, flabby Sade (acted by Patrick Magee) sits quietly on the left side of the stage—prompting (with the aid of a fellow-patient who acts as stage manager and narrator), supervising, commenting. M. Coulmier, dressed formally and wearing some sort of honorific red sash, attended by his elegantly dressed wife and daughter, sits throughout the performance on the right side of the stage. There is also an abundance of theatricality in a more traditional sense: the emphatic appeal to the senses with spectacle and sound. A quartet of inmates with string hair and painted faces, wearing colored sacks and floppy hats, sing sardonic loony songs while the action described by the songs is mimed; their motley getup contrasts with the shape-less white tunics and strait-jackets, the whey-colored faces of most of the rest of the inmates who act in Sade's passion play on the French Revolution. The verbal action, conducted by Sade, is repeatedly interrupted by brilliant bits of acting-out performed by the lunatics, the most forceful of which is a mass guillotining sequence, in which some inmates make metallic rasping noises, bang together parts of the ingenious set, and pour buckets of paint (blood) down drains, while other madmen gleefully jump into a pit in the center of the stage, leaving their heads piled above stage level, next to the guillo-tine.

In Brook's production, insanity proves the most authoritative and sensuous kind of theatricality. Insanity establishes the inflection, the intensity of *Marat/Sade,* from the opening image of the ghostly inmates who are to act in Sade's play, crouching in foetal postures or in a catatonic stupor or trembling or performing some obsessive ritual, then stumbling forward to greet the affable M. Coulmier and his family as they enter the stage and mount the platform where they will sit. Insanity is the register of the intensity of the individual performances as well: of Sade, who recites his long speeches with a painful clenched singsong deliberateness; of Marat (acted by Clive Revill), swathed in wet clothes (a treatment for his skin disease) and encased throughout the action in a portable metal bathtub, even in the midst of the most passionate declamation staring straight ahead as though he were already dead; of Charlotte Corday, Marat's assassin, who is played by a beautiful somnambule who periodically goes blank, forgets her lines, even lies down on the stage and has to be awakened by Sade; of Duperret, the Girondist deputy and lover of Corday, played by a lanky stiff-haired patient, an erotomaniac, who is constantly breaking down in his role of gentleman and lover and lunging lustfully toward the the patient playing Corday (in the course of the play, he has to be put in a strait-jacket); of Simone Everard, Marat's mistress and nurse, played by an almost wholly disabled patient who can barely speak and is limited to jerky idiot movements as she changes Marat's dressings. Insanity becomes the privileged, most authentic metaphor for passion; or, what's the same thing in this case, the logical terminus of any strong emotion. Both dream (as in the "Marat's Nightmare" sequence) and dream-like states must end in violence. Being "calm" amounts to a failure to understand one's real situation. Thus, the slow-motion staging of Corday's murder of Marat (history, i.e. theater) is followed by the inmates shouting and singing of the fifteen bloody years since then, and ends with the "cast" assaulting the Coulmiers as they attempt to leave the stage.

It is through its depiction of theatricality and insanity that Weiss' play is also a play of ideas. The heart of the play is a running debate between Sade, in his chair, and Marat, in his bath, on the meaning of the French Revolution, that is, on the psychological and political premises of modern history, but seen through a very modern sensibility, one equipped with the hindsight afforded by the Nazi concentration camps. But Marat/Sade does not lend itself to being formulated as a particular theory about modern experience. Weiss' play seems to be more about the range of sensibility that concerns itself with, or is at stake in, the modern experience, than it is about an argument or an interpretation of that experience. Weiss does not present ideas as much as he immerses his audience in them. Intellectual debate is the material of the play, but it is not its subject or its end. The Charenton setting insures that this debate takes place in a constant atmosphere of barely suppressed violence: all ideas are volatile at this temperature. Again, insanity proves to be the most austere (even abstract) and drastic mode of expressing in theatrical terms the reenacting of ideas, as members of the cast reliving the Revolution run amuck and have to be restrained and the cries of the Parisian mob for liberty are suddenly metamorphosed into the cries of the patients howling to be let out of the asylum.

Such theater, whose fundamental action is the irrevocable careening toward extreme states of feeling, can end in only two ways. It can turn in on itself and become formal, and end in strict da capo fashion, with its own opening lines. Or it can turn outward, breaking the "frame," and assault the audience. Ionesco has admitted that he originally envisaged his first play, The Bald Soprano, ending with a massacre of the audience; in another version of the same play (which now ends da capo), the author was to leap on the stage, and shout imprecations at the audience till they fled the theater. Brook, or Weiss, or both, have devised for the end of Marat/Sade an equivalent of the same hostile gesture toward the audience. The inmates, that is, the "cast" of Sade's play, have gone berserk and assaulted the

Coulmiers; but this riot — that is, the play — is broken off by the entry of the stage manager of the Aldwych Theater, in modern skirt, sweater, and gym shoes. She blows a whistle; the actors abruptly stop, turn, and face the audience; but when the audience applauds, the company responds with a slow ominous handclap, drowning out the "free" applause and leaving everyone pretty uncomfortable.

My own admiration for, and pleasure in, *Marat/Sade* is virtually unqualified. The play that opened in London last August, and will, it's rumored, soon be seen in New York, is one of the great experiences of anyone's theater-going lifetime. Yet almost everyone, from the daily reviewers to the most serious critics, have voiced serious reservations about, if not outright dislike for, Brook's production of Weiss' play. Why?

Three ready-made ideas seem to me to underlie most caviling at Weiss' play in Brook's production of it.

The connection between theater and literature. One ready-made idea: a work of theater is a branch of literature. The truth is, some works of theater may be judged primarily as works of literature, others not.

It is because this is not admitted, or generally understood, that one reads all too frequently the statement that while *Marat/Sade* is, theatrically, one of the most stunning things anyone has seen on the stage, it's a "director's play," meaning a first-rate production of a second-rate play. A well-known English poet told me he detested the play for this reason: because although he thought it marvelous when he saw it, he *knew* that if it hadn't had the benefit of Peter Brook's production, he wouldn't have liked it. It's also reported that the play in Konrad Swinarski's production last year in West Berlin made nowhere near the striking impression it does in the current production in London.

Granted, *Marat/Sade* is not the supreme masterpiece of contemporary dramatic literature, but it is scarcely a second-rate play. Considered as a text alone, *Marat/Sade* is both sound and exciting. It is not the play which is at fault, but a narrow vision of theater which insists on one image of the director — as servant to the writer, bringing out meanings already resident in the text.

After all, to the extent that it is true that Weiss' text, in Adrian Mitchell's graceful translation, is enhanced greatly by being joined with Peter Brook's staging, what of it? Apart from a theater of dialogue (of language) in which the text is primary, there is also a theater of the senses. The first might be called "play," the second "theater work." In the case of a pure theater work, the writer who sets down words which are to be spoken by actors and staged by a director loses his primacy. In this case, the "author" or "creator" is, to quote Artaud, none other than "the person who controls the direct handling of the stage." The director's art is a material art—an art in which he deals with the bodies of actors, the props, the lights, the music. And what Brook has put together is particularly brilliant and inventive—the rhythm of the staging, the costumes, the ensemble mime scenes. In every detail of the production—one of the most remarkable elements of which is the clangorous tuneful music (by Richard Peaslee) featuring bells, cymbals, and the organ—there is an inexhaustible material inventiveness, a relentless address to the senses. Yet, something about Brook's sheer virtuosity in stage effects offends. It seems, to most people, to overwhelm the text. But perhaps that's just the point.

I'm not suggesting that *Marat/Sade* is simply theater of the senses. Weiss has supplied a complex and highly literate text which demands to be responded to. But *Marat/Sade* also demands to be taken on the sensory level as well, and only the sheerest prejudice about what theater must be (the prejudice, namely, that a work of theater is to be judged, in the last analysis, as a branch of literature) lies behind the demand that the written, and subsequently spoken, text of a theater work carry the whole play.

The connection between theater and psychology. Another ready-made idea: drama consists of the revelation of character, built on the conflict of realistically credible motives. But the most interesting modern theater is a theater which goes beyond psychology.

Again, to cite Artaud: "We need true action, but without practical consequences. It is not on the social level that the action of theater unfolds. Still less on the ethical and psychological levels.

. . . This obstinacy in making characters talk about feelings, passions, desires, and impulses of a strictly psychological order, in which a single word is to compensate for innumerable gestures, is the reason . . . the theater has lost its true *raison d'être.*"

It's from this point of view, tendentiously formulated by Artaud, that one may properly approach the fact that Weiss has situated his argument in an insane asylum. The fact is that with the exception of the audience-figures on stage—M. Coulmier, who frequently interrupts the performance to remonstrate with Sade, and his wife and daughter, who have no lines—all the characters in the play are mad. But the setting of *Marat/Sade* does not amount to a statement that the world is insane. Nor is it an instance of a fashionable interest in the psychology of psychopathic behavior. On the contrary, the concern with insanity in art today usually reflects the desire to go beyond psychology. By representing characters with deranged behavior or deranged styles of speech, such dramatists as Pirandello, Genet, Beckett, and Ionesco make it unnecessary for their characters to embody in their acts or voice in their speech sequential and credible accounts of their motives. Freed from the limitations of what Artaud calls "psychological and dialogue painting of the individual," the dramatic representation is open to levels of experience which are more heroic, more rich in fantasy, more philosophical. The point applies, of course, not only to the drama. The choice of "insane" behavior as the subject matter of art is, by now, the virtually classic strategy of modern artists who wish to transcend traditional "realism," that is, psychology.

Take the scene to which many people particularly objected, in which Sade persuades Charlotte Corday to whip him (Peter Brook has her do it with her hair)—while he, meanwhile, continues to recite, in agonized tones, some point about the Revolution, and the nature of human nature. The purpose of this scene is surely not to inform the audience that, as one critic put it, Sade is "sick, sick, sick"; nor is it fair to reproach Weiss' Sade, as the same critic does, with "using the theater less to advance an argument than to excite himself." (Anyway, why not both?) By combining rational or near-rational argument with irrational behavior, Weiss is not inviting the audience to make a judgment on Sade's character, mental competence, or state of mind. Rather, he is shifting to a kind of theater focused not on characters, but on intense trans-personal emotions borne by characters. He is providing a kind of vicarious emotional experience (in this case, frankly erotic) from which the theater has shied away too long.

Language is used in *Marat/Sade* primarily as a form of incantation, instead of being limited to the revelation of character and the exchange of ideas. This use of language as incantation is the point of another scene which many who saw the play have found objectionable, upsetting, and gratuitous—the bravura soliloquy of Sade, in which he illustrates the cruelty in the heart of man by relating in excruciating detail the public execution by slow dismemberment of Damiens, the would-be assassin of Louis XV.

The connection between theater and ideas. Another ready-made idea: a work of art is to be understood as being "about" or representing or arguing for an "idea." That being so, an implicit standard for a work of art is the value of the ideas it contains, and whether these are clearly and consistently expressed.

It is only to be expected that *Marat/Sade* would be subjected to

these standards. Weiss' play, theatrical to its core, is also full of
intelligence. It contains discussions of the deepest issues of contemporary morality and history and feeling that put to shame the
banalities peddled by such would-be diagnosticians of these issues as
Arthur Miller (see his current *After the Fall* and *Incident at Vichy*),
Friedrich Dürrenmatt (*The Firebugs, The Physicists*), and Max Frisch
(*Andorra*). Yet, there is no doubt that *Marat/Sade* is intellectually
puzzling. Argument is offered, only (seemingly) to be undermined
by the context of the play—the insane asylum, and the avowed
theatricality of the proceedings. People do seem to represent positions in Weiss' play. Roughly, Sade represents the claim of the
permanence of human nature, in all its vileness, against Marat's
revolutionary fervor and his belief that man can be changed by
history. Sade thinks that "the world is made of bodies," Marat that it
is made of forces. Secondary characters, too, have their moments of
passionate advocacy: Duperret hails the eventual dawn of freedom,
the priest Jacques Roux denounces Napoleon. But Sade and "Marat" are both madmen, each in a different style; "Charlotte Corday"
is a sleepwalker, "Duperret" has satyriasis; "Roux" is hysterically
violent. Doesn't this undercut their arguments? And, apart from the
question of the context of insanity in which the ideas are presented,
there is the device of the play-within-a-play. At one level, the
running debate between Sade and Marat, in which the moral and
social idealism attributed to Marat is countered by Sade's trans-
moral advocacy of the claims of individual passion, seems a debate
between equals. But, on another level, since the fiction of Weiss' play
is that it is Sade's script which Marat is reciting, presumably Sade
carries the argument. One critic goes so far as to say that because
Marat has to double as a puppet in Sade's psychodrama, and as
Sade's opponent in an evenly matched ideological contest, the debate between them is stillborn. And, lastly, some critics have attacked
the play on the grounds of its lack of historical fidelity to the actual
views of Marat, Sade, Duperret, and Roux.

These are some of the difficulties which have led people to charge
Marat/Sade with being obscure or intellectually shallow. But most of
these difficulties, and the objections made to them, are misunderstandings—misunderstandings of the connection between the
drama and didacticism. Weiss' play cannot be treated like an argument of Arthur Miller, or even of Brecht. We have to do here with a
kind of theater as different from these as Antonioni and Godard are
from Eisenstein. Weiss' play contains an argument, or rather it
employs the material of intellectual debate and historical reevalua-

tion (the nature of human nature, the betrayal of the Revolution, etc.). But Weiss' play is only secondarily an argument. There is another use of ideas to be reckoned with in art: ideas as sensory stimulants. Antonioni has said of his films that he wants them to dispense with "the superannuated casuistry of positives and negatives." The same impulse discloses itself in a complex way in *Marat/Sade*. Such a position does not mean that these artists wish to dispense with ideas. What it does mean is that ideas, including moral ideas, are proffered in a new style. Ideas may function as décor, props, sensuous material.

One might perhaps compare the Weiss play with the long prose narratives of Genet. Genet is not really arguing that "cruelty is good" or "cruelty is holy" (a moral statement, albeit the opposite of traditional morality), but rather shifting the argument to another plane, from the moral to the aesthetic. But this is not quite the case with *Marat/Sade*. While the "cruelty" in *Marat/Sade* is not, ultimately, a moral issue, it is not an aesthetic one either. It is an ontological issue. While those who propse the aesthetic version of "cruelty" interest themselves in the richness of the surface of life, the proponents of the ontological version of "cruelty" want their art to act out the widest possible context for human action, at least a wider context than that provided by realistic art. That wider context is what Sade calls "nature" and what Artaud means when he says that "everything that acts is a cruelty." There is a moral vision in art like *Marat/Sade,* though clearly it cannot (and this has made its audience uncomfortable) be summed up with the slogans of "humanism." But "humanism" is not identical with morality. Precisely, art like *Marat/Sade* entails a rejection of "humanism," of the task of moralizing the world and thereby refusing to acknowledge the "crimes" of which Sade speaks.

I have repeatedly cited the writings of Artaud on the theater in discussing *Marat/Sade*. But Artaud—unlike Brecht, the other great theoretician of 20th century theater—did not create a body of work to illustrate his theory and sensibility.

Often, the sensibility (the theory, at a certain level of discourse) which governs certain works of art is formulated before there exist substantial works to embody that sensibility. Or, the theory may apply to works other than those for which they are developed. Thus, right now in France writers and critics such as Alain Robbe-Grillet (*Pour un Nouveau Roman*), Roland Barthes (*Essais Critiques*), and Michel Foucault (essays in *Tel Quel* and elsewhere) have worked out an elegant and persuasive anti-rhetorical aesthetic for the novel. But the novels produced by the *nouveau roman* writers and analyzed by them are in fact not as important or satisfying an illustration of this sensibility as certain films, and, moreover, films by directors, Italian as well as French, who have no connection with this school of new French writers, such as Bresson, Melville, Antonioni, Godard, and Bertolucci (*Before the Revolution*).

Similarly, it seems doubtful that the only stage production which Artaud personally supervised, of Shelley's *The Cenci,* or the 1948 radio broadcast *Pour en Finir avec le Jugement de Dieu,* came close to following the brilliant recipes for the theater in his writings, any more than did his public readings of Seneca's tragedies. We have up to now lacked a full-fledged example of Artaud's category, "the theater of cruelty." The closest thing to it are the theatrical events done in New York and elsewhere in the last five years, largely by painters (such as Alan Kaprow, Claes Oldenberg, Jim Dine, Bob Whitman, Red Grooms, Robert Watts) and without text or at least intelligible speech, called Happenings. Another example of work in a quasi-Artaudian spirit: the brilliant staging by Lawrence Kornfield and Al Carmines of Gertrude Stein's prose poem "What Happened," at the Judson Memorial Church last year. Another example: the final production of The Living Theater in New York, Kenneth H. Brown's *The Brig,* directed by Judith Malina.

All the works I have mentioned so far suffer, though, apart from all questions of individual execution, from smallness of scope and conception—as well as a narrowness of sensory means. Hence, the great interest of *Marat/Sade,* for it, more than any modern theater work I know of, comes near the scope, as well as the intent, of Artaud's theater. (I must reluctantly except, because I have never seen it, what sounds like the most interesting and ambitious theater group in the world today—the Theater Laboratory of Jerzy Grotowski in Opole, Poland. For an account of this work, which is an ambitious extension of Artaudian principles, see the *Tulane Drama Review,* Spring 1965.)

Yet Artaud's is not the only major influence reflected in the Weiss-Brook production. Weiss is reported to have said that in this play he wished—staggering ambition!—to combine Brecht and Artaud. And, to be sure, one can see what he means. Certain features of *Marat/Sade* are reminiscent of Brecht's theater—constructing the action around a debate on principles and reasons; the songs; the appeals to the audience through an M.C. And these blend well with the Artaudian texture of the situation and the staging. Yet the matter is not that simple. Indeed, the final question the Weiss' play raises is precisely the one of the ultimate compatibility of these two sensibilities and ideals. How *could* one reconcile Brecht's conception of a didactic theater, a theater of intelligence, with Artaud's theater of magic, of gesture, of "cruelty," of feeling?

The answer seems to be that, if one could effect such a reconciliation or synthesis, Weiss' play has taken a big step toward doing so. Hence the obtuseness of the critic who complained: "Useless ironies, insoluble conundrums, double meanings which could be multiplied indefinitely: Brecht's machinery without Brecht's incisiveness or firm commitment," forgetting about Artaud altogether. If one does put the two together, one sees that new perceptions must be allowed, new standards devised. For isn't an Artaudian theater of commitment, much less "firm commitment," a contradiction in terms? Or is it? The problem is not solved by ignoring the fact that Weiss in *Marat/Sade* means to employ ideas in a fugue form (rather than as literal assertions), and thereby necessarily refers beyond the arena of social material and didactic statement. A misunderstanding of the artistic aims implicit in *Marat/Sade* due to a narrow vision of the theater accounts for most of the critics' dissatisfaction with Weiss' play—an ungrateful dissatisfaction, considering the extraordinary richness of the text and of the Brook production. That the ideas taken up in *Marat/Sade* are not resolved, in an intellectual sense, is far less important than the extent to which they do work together in the sensory arena.

ᴍ

Alan S. Downer

The author of this essay teaches dramatic literature at Princeton University; he has had much experience in the theatre, and his academic control of his subject is given depth and range by an invariably lively sense of the stage and of the craft of playwriting.

Downer's critical question, developed (and answered) in the course of his essay, deals with public perception of drama, particularly the drama of two important playwrights, and involves an incisive discussion of the nature of that drama; why is it that "two... men of such radically different attitudes toward human experience and dramatic technique and the functions of art as Arthur Miller and Tennessee Williams should simultaneously have come into the American theatre and found such success that away from Broadway it often seems as if they *are* the contemporary American theatre...?" While recent years have qualified the unique position of these playwrights—and their theatrical successes, perhaps—Downer's question remains not only fascinating in itself but serves, as his essay expands it, as a splendid example of modern critical writing about the theatre.

❧ THE TWO WORLDS OF ARTHUR MILLER AND TENNESSEE WILLIAMS

Once upon a time a Roman schoolboy, who wanted to impress his teacher with the flattery of an after-lecture question, asked him: "What is the proper definition of a play?" And the teacher, quick as a wink, replied "*Veluti in Speculum.*" I am sure that, as in the case with most teachers, everything the Roman *magister* had said in his carefully prepared lecture vanished into the thin air of his classroom, but his little off-hand simile became immortal—it went from schoolboy to schoolboy, from generation to generation; it turned up in Wittenburg and was duly entered in the tablets of Prince Hamlet: *veluti in speculum,* "the purpose of playing... is to hold, as 'twere, the mirror up to nature." The phrase has, you see, all the requirements for academic immortality: it is short, and vivid; it is even partially true. What goes on the stage does bear some resemblance to the world the audience knows outside the theater; if it did not, the playwright would have to spend so much time explaining what was going on that he would get around to his real action about the time his audience was leaving to catch the last train to Scarsdale.

Indeed there have been times in the history of dramatic art when the little cliché represented the heart of the subject-matter. The drama of fifth-century Athens, of republican Rome, of Elizabethan London, of the court of Louis XIV, did mirror its world pretty accurately; certainly the dramas of many playwrights working in each of those theaters and periods share common attitudes, conventions, even styles and tones. But, it seems to me, a necessary element

Reprinted from *Princeton Alumni Weekly,* Vol. LXII, No. 5 (October 20, 1961) by permission of the author and *Princeton Alumni Weekly.*

in creating the homogeneity of these great periods in the history of playwrighting is the homogeneity of the world they reflect: a shared fund of beliefs, attitudes, values in the audience permits a consistent, single image to appear in the dramatic mirror.

Now, the modern drama is an international art and plays are quickly transplanted from country to country, and find acceptance from audiences for whom they were never intended. New York, this season, has applauded *Beckett* by Jean Anouilh, *Dreigroschenoper* by Brecht, *A Taste of Honey* by Shelah Delaney, *The Hostage* by Brendan Behan. Since these works were first successful in their own countries, presumably they reflect French, German, British, and Irish attitudes; but they do not seem strange or unreasonable to American audiences—if they did, American audiences wouldn't go to them.

The point I am working toward begins as everything theatrical must with the audience. The contemporary American audience is far from homogeneous—America is a federation of fifty states, and no one of its citizens is many generations removed from any one of all the cultures of the world. Therefore, I think it inaccurate to suggest, and foolish to search for, a single image in the American dramatic mirror; there are many mirrors and many images, and the degree to which each one is accurate can only be measured by the degree to which each has been accepted by American playgoers.

All this is by way of explaining something that is essentially inexplicable: why two men of such radically different attitudes toward human experience and dramatic technique and the functions of art as Arthur Miller and Tennessee Williams should simultaneously have come into the American theater and found such success that away from Broadway it often seems as if they *are* the contemporary American theater, and they are frequently referred to as a single phenomenon like Beaumont and Fletcher, Baltimore and Ohio, or Metro-Goldwyn-Mayer. Actually a more unlikely team than Miller and Williams can scarcely be conceived (unless it was Miller and Monroe). They are unlike in every way—in person and personality, in philosophy and aesthetics—unlike in every way except talent and success.

I think I can best indicate the range of difference between them in terms of the worlds they reflect—that is to say, in terms of the worlds they observe and the way in which they present their observed worlds to their audiences.

Here is the world in which Willy Loman, Miller's world-famous salesman, works out his destiny:

Before us is the Salesman's house. We are aware of towering angular shapes behind it, surrounding it on all sides. Only the blue light of the sky falls upon the house and forestage: the surrounding area shows an angry glow of orange. As more light appears, we see a solid vault of apartment houses around the small, fragile-seeming home. . . .

From the right, Willy Loman, the Salesman, enters, carrying two large sample cases. . . . He is past 60 years of age, dressed quietly. Even as he crosses the stage to the doorway of the house, his exhaustion is apparent. He unlocks the door, comes into the kitchen, and thankfully lets his burden down, feeling the soreness of his palms. A word-sigh escapes his lips — it might be "Oh boy, Oh boy."

Like everything else in an art which depends upon visual communication, the setting and the pantomimic action of the opening of *Death of a Salesman* are symbolic. They announce the subject of the play and define Miller's attitude toward it: the exhausted, defeated, bewildered individual finally trapped by the encroaching urban world in which he has lost himself. But if you were experiencing the play in the theater, I do not think it would occur to you that you were being addressed by symbols. Willy is as real as your own father, the apartment buildings are as familiar as your own neighborhood. Miller tells his audience that he is dealing with a real world, a world they recognize, and the very reality and familiarity of that world will affect their involvement in and reaction to the play they are about to experience.

Look now upon this picture. Here is the world of Catherine Holly (or Elizabeth Taylor if you saw the movie), interested spectator in the cannibalism that is the bright particular feature of Mr. Williams' *Suddenly Last Summer:*

The set may be as unreal as the décor of a dramatic ballet. It represents part of a mansion of Victorian Gothic style in the Garden District of New Orleans on a late afternoon, between late summer and early fall. The interior is blended with a fantastic garden which is more like a tropical jungle, or forest, in the prehistoric age of giant fern-forests when living creatures had flippers turning to limbs and scales to skin. The colors of this jungle are violent, especially since it is steaming with heat after rain. There are massive tree-flowers that suggest organs of a body, torn out, still glistening with undried blood. There are harsh cries, sibilant hissings and thrashing sounds in the garden as if it were inhabited by beasts, serpents, and birds, all of savage nature. . . .

A lady enters with the assistance of a silver knobbed cane. She has light orange or pink hair and wears a lavendar lace dress, and over her withered bosom is pinned a starfish of diamonds.

She is followed by a young blond Doctor, all in white, glacially brilliant....

Like Miller, Williams has found a setting that announces the world of his action and his attitude towards that world. Because subtropical gardens and New Orleans aristocrats are considerably less familiar to the mass-audience than suburban apartments and salesmen, the setting takes some adjusting to; and in the process of accepting the realism of the setting, we probably first become aware of its symbolic value. Like Willy, Catherine Holly is trapped by her environment, but it is a special private environment, a primitive jungle enclosed by a Gothic mansion. Williams is telling his audience that her world is just as real as Willy's; it is up to the audience to come to understand just how real (truthful) is his representation of it. But it is not a world that is available to *any* public eye; it is the private vision of the playwright, an inner vision.

I have exhibited these two settings without any intention of saying which is the "better" art. Each is an organic part of its play, each proved acceptable to what was probably the same basic, widely mixed audience. I exhibit these two scenes to illustrate the two worlds of the contemporary American drama, and because all of the qualities, peculiarities, virtues and failings of the two dramatists are announced in them.

While both Miller and Williams have been remarkably consistent in maintaining their attitudes, their visions of the world, the direction in which Williams would develop is scarcely hinted at in his first success. *The Glass Menagerie* (1945) is "a memory play," a subdued, nostalgic, family portrait. Its setting is a cramped urban apartment revealed through the gauzes and unrealistic lighting by which the theater represents dreams. Its hero is a young poet who recalls his mother's desperate, romantic attempt to recreate the atmosphere and graceful formality of the Old South for the purpose of trapping her daughter's "gentleman caller." The mother's character, an exquisite balance of the ridiculous and the noble, is an early indication of the playwright's skill in creating memorable and challenging parts for women; the conflict between the idealistic struggle to recover a dead past and the necessity for survival in an unfriendly present suggests a theme which was to become a preoccupation. But a story in which the most violent action is the accidental breaking of a small glass horse hardly indicated what lay ahead for Mr. Williams' audiences.

The tinkle of shattered glass was to be replaced by the highly articulate cries of shattered souls, and memory by myth. *A Streetcar Named Desire* (1947) contemplates the destruction of a young woman who yearns to live the mythic life of the South before the Civil War, and contemplates her destruction directly, without the gauze of memory. In frustration and despair she is thrust into the life of contemporary New Orleans, is raped by her brother-in-law, and retreats to the security of an insane asylum. In *Camino Real* (1953), which includes a platoon of mythic figures from Don Quixote to Kilroy, the hero's heart is removed and exhibited to the audience. Both *Orpheus Descending* (1957), and *Sweet Bird of Youth* (1959) invoke the legendary emasculation of the ancient bard for a climax. In *Suddenly Last Summer* (1957) the poet-hero is devoured by infant cannibals.

The theatrical world of Williams' plays is not unlike that depicted on an antique map, inhabited by lonely individuals in implacable conflict, hedged in around the edges by unknowable seas blown upon by strange death's heads out of the mapmaker's terrified imagination: cancer on the north, mutilation on the south, the human mob on the east, mendacity on the west. Because of his sympathetic studies of the ruthless destruction of idealists and artists, Williams has often been described as a romantic writer, but it might be more precise to describe him as Gothic. Through his threatened terrain move the lost souls, armed only with liquor or barbiturates. Their lives are Gothic, irregular and aspiring; their dooms are Gothic, massive and uncompromising. And over the whole is cast a prismatic radiance of language like sunbeams spilling through stained glass windows to sweeten the murky interior of a vaulted Gothic cathedral.

Gothic, for example, is the setting of *Summer and Smoke* (1948), a triptych, the heroine's house on the right balanced (or, in this case, unbalanced) by the hero's on the left, permitting either single or contrapuntal actions; between them stands a public garden domi-nated by a drinking fountain in the form of an angel. The statue is always lighted, now brightly, now dimly, a brooding symbol of eternity to enlarge the small romantic story. The hero is a young doctor, and a prominent feature of his office is an anatomy chart on which he challenges the virginal heroine to locate her soul and against which the Other Woman indifferently lounges. When the hero visits the heroine in her chaste parlor, he is pursued by women's voices barking his name from the darkness. *The Rose Tattoo* (1951) is an outspoken comedy of sexuality; at appropriate moments, a goat belonging to the witch-woman next door breaks loose and runs riot in the garden. When the heroine of *Streetcar* is threatened by her brother-in-law, she desperately attempts to make a long-distance phone call. *Lurid reflections appear on the walls. The night is filled with inhuman voices like cries in a jungle.* The back wall of the room becomes transparent and the audience can see a drunk and a prostitute struggling in the street beyond. The scene of *Cat on a Hot Tin Roof* requires only two articles of furniture, standing for the sum of modern culture: a double bed, and combination TV set and liquor cabinet.

Taken together, these plays present a picture of a highly personal world, what one might call an enclosed vision: consistent, terrifying and perhaps terrified. It is a world of little good and great evil. Williams' fascination with evil, directly expressed by the apology of one of his characters, "I'm sorry, I never could keep my fingers off a sore," and indirectly expressed by the vivid colors and sounds with which he decorates his catastrophes, is only too easily transferred to an audience sated by casual entertainment and the domestic problems of conventional realism. Yet neither shock nor problem-solving is the declared intent of the artist. In a stage direction, he observes, *The bird that I hope to catch in the net of this play is not the solution of one man's psychological problem. I'm trying to catch the true quality of experience in a group of people, that cloudy, flickering, evanescent*—fiercely charged!—*interplay of live human beings in the thunder-cloud of a common crisis.* It is a testimony to Williams' seriousness as an artist that in that comment he seems to sense the dangerous nature of his chosen subject matter. For as the Gothic inevitably descends in design and structure from aspiration and vitality to flamboyance, in content it moves from a powerful examination of the wars of the angels in the soul of man to the frenetic.

Williams disclaims interest in individual psychology, professes to search for some general truth of human experience. Arthur Miller also would reject the drama of case-history, but what he would trap in his theatrical net is something more than the truth of human experience, the past. In a clear declaration of purpose he wrote, "The social drama, as I see it, is the main stream and the anti-social drama a bypass. I can no longer take with ultimate seriousness a drama of individual psychology written for its own sake, however full it may be of insight and precise observation. Time is moving;

there is a world to make, a civilization to create, that will move toward the only goal the humanistic, democratic mind can ever accept with honor. It is a world in which the human being can live as a naturally political, naturally private, naturally engaged person, a world in which once again a true tragic victory may be scored."

Such a statement asserts the contemporary vitality of the direction given to the drama by Ibsen a century ago. Miller is aware of his indebtedness to the great Norwegian, and has tried to repay it by adapting one of Ibsen's familiar classics to the uses of the American stage. But Miller's version of *An Enemy of the People* (1950) is crossed with the Marxist impulses of the American drama of the thirties and Ibsen's irony becomes Miller's anger, Ibsen's complex comedy Miller's moral fable. In his preface Miller defends his alterations of the original on the grounds that Ibsen (as an avant-garde thinker who believed that no truth could endure for more than a generation) would have made the alterations himself in the mid-twentieth century. While it is dangerous to hypothesize about the future thoughts of a dead artist, it is plain that Miller is aligning himself with those who believe in the playwright as thinker and the stage as a forum for the discussion of ideas, not in Bernard Shaw's forensic mode, but as the essential part of the dramatic experience for the audience.

Miller's first successful play, *All My Sons* (1947), was so firmly controlled by the idea of individual responsibility to society as a whole that it does not escape from the critical objection of being over-slick, a calculated machine. On the other hand, if *Death of a Salesman* (1949) has in retrospect some defects as a total work of art, they are not the defects of propaganda or argumentation. Some of the symbols of the play, like the setting in which towering apartment buildings cut off the light of the sun from the hero's small house, do suggest a specific social theme. This is reinforced in the exposition which contrasts the hero's father and grandfather, pioneers and artisans, with the hero, an out-of-work, non-productive salesman. But the action of the play is concerned with the fate of a man who has deliberately chosen the wrong goal and who, as a consequence, has ever imperfectly known himself. Such a theme is the beginning of tragedy, and the sympathetic portrait of the hero is the beginning of tragic experience for the audience.

Miller himself recognized that his play, though enormously successful, was taken by the audience as another contribution to the "steady year-by-year documentation of the frustration of man." This he felt was the function of the journalist, not the artist, who must be concerned with man's fate, not with his past or his present, but with his possibilities. In the spirit of *Sartor Resartus,* Miller put negation behind him and set out in quest of the Everlasting Yea. It is characteristic that he should have sought it in an analogue between contemporary events and the past, out of which emerged a theme which spoke with urgency to a world-wide audience.

The Crucible (1953), about the witchcraft trials of colonial New England, was a controversial play. Broadway audiences in that year, aware of newspaper headlines and the televising of un-American investigations, are hardly to be blamed if they saw a more continuous parallel between the Salem tragedy and events in Washington than Miller ultimately intended. For if *The Crucible* had been, as it at first seemed, an exposé of McCarthyism, its focus would have been restricted to the pathos of a man defeated by an unfriendly society, a small subject whose impact would have been lost in the inevitable shifting of the social situation. It was only after the play found acceptance by audiences far removed from the reporting of the American mass-media that its true contribution to the description of man could be appreciated.

Paradox is one of the elements of tragedy, and Miller has found in the story of Salem witchcraft a paradox of peculiar importance to any democratic society. *The Crucible* draws from the hysteria of that ugly summer in 1962 an exemplum of the continuing failure of man successfully to strike a balance between the desire for individual freedom and the necessity for an ordered society. His hero, John Proctor, the cynical observer drawn into the maelstrom through no will of his own, goes to his death rather than compromise with error; a noble decision—but what about the family he leaves behind him? The social order, even though shaken in its convictions, must maintain its stand in the face of reason, or collapse. This is not a case of good versus evil, of black against white; paradox is on both sides. And in the theater the paradox is inescapable, its enduring truth not to be brushed aside by the turn of a particular historical moment.

The Crucible is necessarily directed to a democratic audience, but the paradoxical nature of its theme suggests that, as the play developed in the author's mind, a more timeless tradition than the social drama of Ibsen was beginning to attract him. In *A View from the Bridge* (1955) he turned, as so many of his contemporaries had done, to the dramatic traditions of the classical Greek stage. But his return was in his own character: Miller is not concerned with bringing myth up-to-date, with finding an excuse to readmit kings or heroes to the stage, with seeking shelter in lyric choruses or Freudian symbolism in masks. He sees the Greek repertory as social drama whose ultimate concern is with the destiny of man, but whose immediate strength comes from the public concerns of its own day. To recapture its force for a contemporary American audience, he boldly chooses as his hero a man who never expected to have a destiny, a semi-articulate Brooklyn longshoreman involved in a personal domestic dilemma, and through the action shows that his hero's destiny is a part of the destiny of all mankind.

The original version of the play is in one long unbroken act which in performance captures the swiftness and inevitability of Greek tragedy. Incapable of either rationalization or evasion the hero finds himself caught between an ancestral social code and an individual sexual passion whose remotest implications he cannot begin to sense. Blindly he is driven to break with the primitive code and suffers bloody revenge at the hands of his fellows. Since his passion involves the rejection of his wife for his stepdaughter, a kind of incest, and a shocking scene in which the girl's lover is accused of homosexuality, there is danger that the audience might find more titillation than tragedy in the play.

But Miller employs a striking character, the neighborhood lawyer, as commentator. The lawyer introduces the action, participates in and concludes it to the end that the spectator must understand the play under its universal, not just its temporal aspects. The lawyer is professionally concerned with the codes men live by and with the justice visited upon those who break with the code, but as an old and wise man he remembers that the ancient villains and heroes achieved their pertinence by living beyond the law. *A View from the Bridge* is a reminder that the humblest, the least articulate, the least aware, have that within which no law and no judgment can reach. "Nowadays *we* settle for half," the lawyer declares, but such a settlement is the essence of comedy, not tragedy. Perhaps the spectator may find himself urging the hero of *The Crucible* or of *The Bridge* not to act like a fool, to compromise, to "settle for half." But the lawyer, looking back to the ancient shores of the Mediterranean, recalls the legendary kings who were unable to compromise once they had committed themselves to a position or a line of action and who were, for all their eloquence and skill in argument, the fools of the gods. And their agony and their end, captured in plays time-bound by rigid conventions yet timeless in implication, have become part of the heritage of the human race to such an extent that the most modern scientific attempt to explain man to himself has formed its basic concepts on their ancient tragic actions. To such an end, the explication of man, *A View from the Bridge* is directed. If it does not speak with most miraculous Sophoclean organ, its relative failure may lie in Miller's determination to search out the possibilities for tragic victory in modern life, his refusal to lessen the impact of his discovery with anything that suggests the museum or the library, the repositories of past experience.

In these comments on the plays of our two subjects I have not pretended to analyze their complete works or any one play. But my comments were not quite as random as they may have seemed. They have been made in an attempt to create an (inevitably) impressionistic picture of two very *different* artists.

Their differences do not stem from the fact that one is a poet and the other a reporter, because this is not a fact. Williams may use language in more startling patterns, Miller may turn a more willing ear to the colloquialisms of the enveloping crowd, but in the only way in which it matters in the theater, both are poetic dramatists, manipulating all the elements with which they work — words, to be sure, but also action and scene and color and sound and silence — into organic finality.

Their differences do not lie in the fact that one is a social dramatist working in the mode of naturalism, of Ibsenism, and the other a romantic working in the symbolic mode of Maeterlinck or Yeats, because that is not a fact either. Aside from one or two experimental deviations, which failed, both accept the conditions of contemporary theater-life; that there is as yet, no real escape from the modes established by the founders of the modern drama, no universally acceptable conventions or subject matter aside from those of the loosely named social drama; the drama that begins by reflecting the world around them.

Their fundamental difference, it seems to me, lies not in their subject matter, but in their themes: the attitude they take towards their subject matter, their worlds; or what they see when they look at the external world.

Mr. Williams' theme is perhaps most clearly stated in the moving dialogue between Big Daddy and his son Brick in *Cat on a Hot Tin Roof*. Completely frustrated, Brick has withdrawn from his wife, his family, his world, and sought escape in alcohol. The way of the world, he complains, is *Mendacity,* no one liar and no one lie, but "the whole, the whole — thing. . . ." His father snatches away his glass, and cries,

> What do you know about this mendacity thing? Hell! I could write a book on it! Don't you know that? I could write a book on it and still not cover the subject? Well, I could, I could write a goddam book on it and still not cover the subject anywhere near enough!! Think of all the lies I got to put up with! — Pretenses! Ain't that mendacity? Having to pretend stuff you don't think or feel or have any idea of? Having for instance to act like I care for Big Mama! — I haven't been able to stand the sight, sound, or smell of that woman for forty years now! . . .
>
> Pretend to love that son of a bitch of a Gooper and his wife Mae and those five same screechers out there like parrots in a jungle! Jesus! Can't stand to look at 'em!
>
> Church! — it bores the Bejesus out of me but I go! — I go an' sit there and listen to the fool preacher!
>
> Clubs! — Elks! Masons! Rotary! — *crap!* . . .
>
> I've lived with mendacity! — Why can't you live with it? Hell, you got to live with it, there's nothing *else* to *live* with except mendacity, is there?

That is a pretty explicit speech — and I have tactfully omitted some parts that are even more explicit. The hero's disgust with the world grows out of the world's choice of a way of life — it is not his choice, his way. It is therefore a lie, and the playwright demands our pity for a character so sensitive, so clear-sighted, so defeated. Williams' repeated theme is the way the world has failed the hero.

Miller announces his theme in his first successful play, and while it is hardly accurate to say that he repeats the theme in his later plays, each of the successes after *All My Sons* reconsiders and develops its central idea, *Responsibility.* Here again a father is explaining the world as he has seen it, to his idealistic son who has attacked him for furnishing imperfect airplane engines to the government:

> You're a boy, what could I do! I'm in business, a man is in business: a 120 cracked, you're out of business; you got a process, the process don't work, you're out of business: You don't know how to operate, your stuff is no good: they close you up, they tear up your contracts, what the hell's it to them? You lay 40 years into a business and they knock you out in five minutes, what could I do, let them take 40 years, let them take my life away?

In *Death of a Salesman,* Miller is concerned with the responsibility of man to himself. The hero's only friend makes the point as he stands by Willy's grave:

> Nobody dast blame this man. You don't understand—Willy was a salesman. And for a salesman, there's no rock bottom to the life. He don't put a bolt to a nut, he don't tell you the law or give you medicine. He's a man way out there in the blue, riding on a smile and a shoeshine. And when they start not smiling back—that's an earthquake. And then you get yourself a couple of spots on your hat, and you're finished. Nobody dast blame this man. A salesman is got to dream, boy, It comes with the territory.

A View from the Bridge widens the theme to man's responsibility to the future in the curtain speech of the lawyer:

> *Most* of the time now we settle for half,
> And I like it better.
> And yet, when the tide is right
> And the green smell of the sea
> Floats in through my window,
> The waves of this bay
> Are the waves against Siracusa,
> And I see a face that suddenly seems carved;
> The eyes look like tunnels
> Leading back toward some ancestral beach
> Where all of us once lived.
> And I wonder at those times
> How much of all of us
> Really lives there yet,
> And when we will truly have moved on,
> On and away from that dark place,
> That world that has fallen to stones?

Each of Miller's heroes is as defeated by the world he lives in as any one in the Williams family. But no one of them asks for pity. Understanding, yes, answers to the eternal questions of what and why and how. Miller refuses his audience the luxury of pity, or the evasion of self-pity, and in so doing he fulfills the noblest purpose of a creative artist—to heighten the consciousness of his audience. If the world is out of joint, there is a reason; if there is a reason there is a cure. Miller's repeated concern is with the way his hero has failed the world.

I must insist once again that in comparing these playwrights I am trying to describe but not evaluate their work. If my own preference shows through, let me be the first to acknowledge that the theater is one place where objectivity is both impossible and undesirable. With Blanche duBois and Catherine Holly we grow in feeling, in sensitivity; with Willy Loman and John Proctor and Eddie Carbone, we grow in wisdom. The essential thematic difference for the artist, as always, depends upon the world he sees, and the world he sees depends upon where he looks, and whether he uses a telescope or a stethoscope.

✄

Herbert Blau

These comments and observations form the greater part of a long chapter in Herbert Blau's powerful book, *The Impossible Theatre.* Dealing essentially with two plays in production—Miller's *The Crucible* and Brecht's *Mother Courage*—these excerpts represent a dynamic director's approach to plays vividly seen as mirrors of the outside world or, properly speaking, as projections of the world of which the theatre is itself an important part and from which it removes itself to its peril. Blau's manifesto stems from his experience as co-founder and director of the famous Actor's Workshop in San Francisco. Formerly a director of the repertory company in Lincoln Center, New York, he has taught and published in many fields relative to the drama and on poetry and contemporary social issues as well.

✄   *from COUNTERFORCE I:*
    THE SOCIAL DRAMA

. . . It was another play by Miller . . . that had the most resounding influence on our developing audience. Even to this day, a revival of *The Crucible* will take up slack at the box office. Whatever that may be a sign of, in our theater there was no doubt the reign of McCarthy had a lot to do with its initial success. Miller, however, has tried to minimize the immediate parallel: "It was not only the rise of 'McCarthyism' that moved me, but something which seemed more weird and mysterious. It was the fact that a political, objective, knowledgeable campaign from the far Right was capable of creating not only a terror, but a new subjective reality, a veritable mystique which was gradually assuming even a holy resonance."

The mystique was resonating into an even more subtle shape than Miller had imagined. But while it lacked the terrifying impartiality of greater drama, *The Crucible* had nevertheless the vehemence of good social protest. The play was unevenly cast, put into rehearsal in haste (lest somebody take advantage of the release of rights before we did), the director was replaced after about three weeks, but the actors, upon whom the drama makes no special demands, played it with fervor and conviction if not subtlety. And in our program notes we stressed the McCarthy parallel, speaking of guilt by association and Ordeal by Slander.

The production made us a lot of liberal friends. They are all, all honorable men, but while I have signed the same petitions, that friendship in the theater has always been a little unsettling and subsequent plays have borne out my feeling that if we have the same politics, we do not always have it for the same reasons. While the power of mass psychosis is one of the strongest elements in the play, there is a melodrama in the fervency that always made me uncomfortable. When I brought it up, it made others uncomfortable. But I think it behooves us to understand both the appeal and limitations of those forceful drama—one of those which seems effective so long as it is even middlingly well played, and despite its fate on Broadway.

The Puritan community, as Hawthorne knew in *The Scarlet Letter,* is the ideal setting for a realistic narrative of allegorical dimensions. As Miller puts it, drawing on the annals of the Salem trials: "To write a realistic play of that world was already to write in a style beyond contemporary realism." And there is a powerful admonition beyond that in Proctor's final refusal to be *used.* Like Miller before the congressional committee, he will not lend his name to the naming of names. On this level the play has authority, and it serves as an exemplum. Several critics have pointed out that the analogy between witches and Communists is a weak one, for while we believe in retrospect there were no witches, we know in fact there were some Communists, and a few of them were dangerous. (If Miller were another kind of dramatist, he might claim there *were* witches, but we shall come to that in a moment.) Yet as a generalization, the play's argument is worthy; as a warning against "the handing over of conscience," it is urgent; and to the extent his own public life has required it Miller has shown the courage of his convictions beyond most men—and hence has some right to call for it. One might still wish he were more inventive in form, but in a period where the borders between art and anarchy are ill-defined, we might apply the caution stated in II Corinthians: "All things are lawful, but not all things edify." It is no small thing to say *The Crucible* is an edifying drama.

What the play does not render, however, is what Miller claims for it and what is deeply brooding in the Puritan setting: "the interior psychological question," the harrowing descent of mass hallucination into the life of the individual, where value is deranged, no reason is right, and every man drives his bargain with the sinister. One sees this in *The Brothers Karamazov,* which Miller invokes as that "great book of wonder," and more relevantly in *The Possessed,* where political evil is the reptilian shadow of indecipherable sin. For Proctor, a sin is *arranged,* so that his guilt might have cause. All we can say is: that is not the way it is. For Miller, a psychosis is no more than a psychosis, with clear motive and rational geography. The symptoms are fully describable. His love of wonder is deflated by his desire "to write rationally" and to put a judgmental finger on "the full loathesomeness of . . . anti-social action." The desire is admirable, but the danger is to locate it in advance. Studying Dostoyevsky, Miller had resolved to "let wonder rise up like a mist, a gas, a vapor from the gradual and remorseless crush of factual and psychological conflict." But while that is a good description of the source of wonder in Dostoyevsky, Miller is restive in the mist, which in Dostoyevsky is thickened to nightmare by every wincing judgment and every laceration of meaning, writhing in the imminence of wrong.

By contrast, we know only too well what *The Crucible* means, nor were the issues really ever in doubt. Wanting to write a drama "that would lift out of the morass of subjectivism the squirming, single, defined process" by which public terror unmans us, Miller fills in the record with the adultery of John Proctor and Abigail Williams. He thus provides the rationalist's missing link to the mystery of the crying out. The adultery brings the drama back toward the "subjectivism" Miller was trying to avoid, but its real subjective life remains shallow. Taking up charges of coldness, he says he had

never written more passionately and blames the American theater —
actors, directors, audience, and critics — for being trained "to take
to heart anything that does not prick the mind and to suspect everything that does not supinely reassure."

About the American theater, I think this is exactly so. But my own
reservations have to do with the fact that, while moral instruction
may be a legitimate ambition of the drama, the play *does* reassure —
and it is the *mind* which rebels finally against its formulas while the
emotions may be overwhelmed by its force. A play is privileged to
reconstruct history for its own purposes; but here we have a play
which pretends to describe in realistic terms a community instinctively bent on devotion to God. The Puritans were readers of signs,
and the signs, in daily behavior, were evidences of God's will.
Hawthorne's novel retains the impermeable quality of that experience by accepting completely the terms of the divine or demonic
game. It is yours to choose whose game it really is, according to his
strategy of alternative possibilities. But Miller's play makes the
choices for you, and its hero does not stand — as one approving critic
has said — "foursquare in his own time and place." The records do
show that he considered the inquisition a fraud; but though he is
bound to the community as a farmer, he does not, in Miller's play,
take to heart "all the complex tensions of the Salem community," for
he responds to things like an eighteenth century rationalist with little
stake in established doctrine. Truer to time and place is the Rev-
erend Hale, who knew "the devil is precise" and saw him in the godly,
in himself. He is certainly the more dramatic figure in being compelled to disavow what by instinct and conditioning he has come to
believe. Hale resembles Captain Vere in Melville's *Billy Budd,* where
the drama is truly divested of "subjectivism" by characters who are,
by *allegiance* to retarded doctrine, impaled upon the cross of choice.

One can also see in Melville's Claggart the kind of character that
Miller now wishes he had protrayed in Danforth: evil embodied to
the utmost, a man so dedicated to evil that by his nature we might
know good. Melville saw that to create such a character he would
have to stretch his skepticism toward the ancient doctrine of "de-
pravity according to nature," which alone could explain a Claggart
or an Iago. He does this by a strategy of insinuation. He suggests to
us that there was once such a doctrine, in which intelligent modern
men, of course, can hardly believe. The story virtually drives us back
to the "superstition," as Kafka virtually restores Original Sin. (I
should add that Melville does this in the prose style of the novelette,

which could not always be compensated for in the admirable dramatization by Coxe and Chapman.) Doing so, he takes us back through time, justifying as far as form can reach the eternal intimations of Billy's rosy-dawned execution; a scene which is almost enough to make you believe, with the sailors, that a chip of the dockyard boom "was a piece of the Cross."

Almost. Having proposed to us a possibility just over the edge of reason, Melville writes an ironic coda in which he leaves us to take our own risks of interpretation. Miller, for all his moral conviction and belief in free choice, leaves us none. A master of conventional dramaturgy, with all the skills of building and pacing, he drives past the turbid aspect of social hypnosis to the predetermined heroism of Proctor. Perception yields to sensation and the choice of classical tragedy to its wish-fulfillment. (It is curious that Billy, *typed* down to his stammer, is a more inscrutable character than anyone in Miller's play.) The final irony is that John Proctor, dramatic hero of the populist mind, might even be applauded by members of the congressional committee that cited Miller for contempt. It is no accident, too, that in temperament and general conduct Proctor resembles our true culture hero, John Glenn, who would be perfectly cast for the role if the astronauts were to start a little theater. One may not have the courage to be a Proctor at the final drumroll, nor a Glenn at the countdown, but no one doubts they are worthy of imitation.

This absence of doubt reduced the import of *The Crucible* for those who thought about it, while increasing the impact for those who didn't. You do a play for its virtues, and one devious aspect of the art of theater lies in concealing the faults. Actually, my belief is that if you know what's not there, you can deal more powerfully with what is. Little of what I have said, however, came up during rehearsals of *The Crucible* (which was not so much conceived as put on), but rather in critiques and discussions of plays done later. Whatever its weaknesses, the production was hard-driving in keeping with the play's rhythm, and performance by performance the actors rose to overwhelming approval. Because we would be doing better productions which would not be so approved, it was important to keep our heads. And, indeed, I think this attitude has made it more possible for our actors to sustain their belief through more subtle plays that have not been so vigorously applauded.

At the time we produced *The Crucible,* Miller was already the most powerful rational voice in the American theater. Questioning the play later, I wanted the company to understand that to criticize him was to take his ideas seriously, and to begin to give some shape to our own. The people we often had to question most were those with whom we seemed to agree. Because we were all vulnerable to easy judgments and that depth psychology of the surface which is so inherent in American drama (and acting), it was necessary to see why *The Crucible* was not really the "tough" play that Miller claimed; I mean dramatically tough, tough in soul, driving below its partisanship to a judgment of anti-social action from which, as in Dostoyevsky, none of us could feel exempt. I wouldn't have asked the questions if Miller didn't prompt them with his reflections on Social Drama and the tragic form. But compare the action of Proctor to that of the tragic figures of any age — Macbeth, or Brittanicus, or Raskolnikov: can you approve or disapprove of their action? Can you make the choice of imitating them? Or avoid it? *The Crucible* may confirm what we like to think we believe, but it is not, as Miller says, intimidating to an "Anglo-Saxon audience" (or actors), nor does it really shock us into recognizing that we don't believe what we say we do. Beyond that, the profoundest dramas shake up our beliefs, rock our world; in *The Crucible,* our principles are neither jeopardized nor extended, however much we may fail to live by them anyhow.

As for the inquisitors, Miller wants us to see evil naked and unmitigated. I am prepared to believe it exists (I am certain it exists), and I won't even ask where it comes from. But — to be truer than tough — if you want absolute evil, you've got to think more about witches. Miller wants the Puritan community without Puritan premises or Puritan intuitions (which is one reason why, when he appropriates the language, his own suffers in comparison). His liberalism is the kind that, really believing we have outlived the past, thinks it is there to be used. The past just doesn't lie around like that. And one of these days the American theater is really going to have to come to terms with American history.

Axiom for liberals: no play is deeper than its witches.

The limitations of *The Crucible* as a Social Drama became more apparent to us when we started to rehearse *Mother Courage* about a year later, in December 1955. Brecht's play is far more ironic, ambiguous, and intellectually subtle. That is why, I believe, some "progressives" and members of left-wing groups who were enraptured by our production of *The Crucible,* and who came out in force to support Brecht as a tribal hero, were disappointed. *The Crucible,* aside from the advance publicity of McCarthyism, catches you up at the beginning and, trying to warn and inform, assaults your critical faculties. Its convention is a modulated hysteria. And if the actors can play with minimum thought, it is because they, like the audience, are caught up in the turbulence. If you know what you think before you come, *The Crucible* permits you to exercise your social passion to the limit. You are not, really, a guilty creature sitting at a play, the other guy is guilty. You are a judge, not judging, but biting your thumb at the judges.

But if *The Crucible* gratifies what you already think, *Mother Courage* lets you feel what you think only long enough to make you judge what you feel. Audience and actors. Moreover, though Brecht's captains and colonels are clearly horrors, and his disposition egalitarian, there is no satisfying celebration of the Common Man. True, there is a vigorous humanity in Mother Courage, who has no respect for the historical moment, the death of a great commander or a victory in battle, for whom a worm in the biscuit is a significant event and the injury to her daughter a major tragedy. But Mother Courage and the Commander are similarly corrupted by the same system. And she does not, like Proctor, make the choice all good men would have her make. She capitulates. Like most of us. And sings a song, rehearsing her fall from romantic grace, to tell us why. It is a nonrevolutionary lyric, a kind of advice to the forlorn, with blood knowledge — cultured by long survival — of the Common Man's inexhaustible capacity for compromise and self-preserving cowardice. (Falstaff's battlefield appraisal of honor is an ingratiating progenitor.) It may not be admirable, but it feels more real.

The capitulation is the chief source of the drama's alienating effect. There is of course the apparent detachment in the acting, the historification of the routine, the juxtaposition of great things and small for purposes of reflective irony, the various interruptive devices. But these are the subsidiary, if inseparable, means of Brecht's drama; they say what he wants to say. When we produced *Mother Courage,* these techniques were still novel, and they were disturbing to many. But what was more disturbing was that the ideological intensity was as complex as the emotional center. Brecht's attitude toward his heroine was (and is) ambiguous. *Mother Courage* is a revolutionary play, precisely because it can't be appropriated without misgivings by any particular cause.

Nor is it reducible to a preachment against war, nor to the commonplace "Life is war." Brecht is saying, if anything, that "War is life"—and since he sees life governed by the economic motive, war becomes the widest and most damaging extension of that motive, grotesque and terrible for all the duplicity it really masks. The war, indeed, is not any old war, it is a holy war, "and therefore," as the Chaplain observes, "pleasing unto God."

In the necessary simplifications of our advertising campaign, we described the play as an anti-war drama and were plagued afterwards by those who declared that it was therefore anachronistic, that after Buchenwald, Iwo Jima, and Korea we do not need to be told that war is bad. One might ask: after such knowledge, what forgiveness? But the truth is *Mother Courage* attacks not only war, but all forms of subservience to the ethics of "business as usual"; it attacks, in sum, the kind of economy we still have, structured on the premise that war is, if not our necessity and destiny, what we must prepare for to avoid it. That is what makes it neither dated nor commonplace. It doesn't tell us what we already know; it tells us what some of us don't want to hear. And for some who share its sentiments, it is disturbing because it impugns us all—because there is no final locus for self-exoneration. At the end of 1955, it was not only iconoclastic as to form, testing our beliefs, it was also an anti-trust suit of our commonest emotions, oscillating finally between a Social Drama and an anti-social vision.

What was true for our audience was again true for our company. I have already described the impression of alienation at our first reading—boredom arising from the feeling that the play was static. Only one scene moved the cast, that in which the dumb daughter Catherine beats her drum on the roof to warn the citizens of Halle of an attack. This engaged the actors; this is what they wanted from a play. It was like *The Crucible*. For the rest, it was a lot of talk.

What we soon realized about the play, particularly as it went on its feet, was that its activity is manifold and unceasing. Where it seemed to stand still, there were countless implicit demands for business: where it appeared to be verbose, there were various stratas of relevant irony, disguised and overt. In Scene 6, for instance, Mother Courage, the Chaplain, the Regimental Clerk, and the dumb daughter are spending a rainy afternoon in a canteen tent engaged in conversations on the war, the two women taking inventory. The stage, which previously had been rather bare, is now full of sausages, linens, cheeses, belts, buckles, boots, tins, baskets, and shirts, all the innumerable paraphernalia of Mother Courage's enterprise. For Mother Courage, times are good. But the pre-scene projection announces that the great Commander Tilly has fallen in battle. There is funeral music. The scene opens reflectively. And though nothing "dramatic" happens until late in the long scene, the predominant impression, arising out of a lot of talk, is one of abundance, of a steady throb of counting, checking, sorting, tallying, collecting money for drinks—the business of the actors and business of war forming a single ritualistic image, the business of business, giving point and substance to the conscious ironies of Mother Courage and the ingenuous ones of the Chaplain.

Or take the opening scene, where Mother Courage and her children, traveling with their wagon, are stopped by a Recruiting Officer and a Sergeant, who are interested in her sons, livestock for the war. She identifies herself and, when asked how she got her nickname, explains that she drove through the bombardment of Riga like a madwoman to save some loaves of bread she had in her cart. Her action was not heroic, as some who gave her the name thought (and as some thought when they read our advertising; one woman called for tickets to *Mothers Courageous*). Courage is a pragmatist not a martyr. But the irony is sharper and partially directed against herself. Not only does she discredit the romantic interpretation of her deed, she discredits the deed itself: what a fool, her tone implies, to risk one's life for a few moldy loaves of bread. Business comes first, *except* where it threatens survival. The same attitude prevails in the following scene when, immediately after a surprise reunion, she boxes her son's ears for having too bravely outwitted some enemy peasants. Better always to surrender than to die. (Since for Brecht, this seems to a "positive" action, no wonder he outrages certain intensely anti-Communist socialists.)

Set in the framework of great events, the mundane career of Mother Courage is alienated, then, in the various senses that Brecht intends: estranged, put at a distance, made famous (or infamous), historified. Our critical faculties are trained on that part of history which history slights. Tilly wins a battle at Lutzen; Mother Courage loses four shirts. And in the hectic little scene which juxtaposes these two important events, so much happens so quickly that one can hardly keep up with it: onstage some soldiers, taking respite from the looting, are having a drink at Mother Courage's canteen. Catherine is distraught, running up and down on the periphery. Offstage, a fire is ravaging a peasant's farm. There are cries; wounded people are carried on. The Chaplain runs in, calling for linen. Mother Courage, keeping an eye on the soldiers, one of whom has already stolen a fur coat in the town, tries to protect her goods. She has given all her linen before, she says; she explains to the Chaplain that things are getting worse—taxes, duties, bribes to pay. Furious at her mother's apparent inhumanity, Catherine grabs a stick and rushes at her. Mother Courage shouts her down, but the Chaplain pulls her bodily from the wagon and takes out some shirts which he rips for bandages. There is a cry offstage—a baby is trapped by the fire. Torn between her daughter and her shirts, Mother Courage watches as Catherine dashes off to save the child. Catherine reappears with the baby. Mother Courage, relieved, stalks across the stage to chastise her and tries to take the baby away. Catherine snarls and hugs it fiercely. Meanwhile the soldier with the coat is trying to make off with the bottle of brandy. Mother Courage sees him and, instead of taking back the liquor, snatches the fur coat in exchange, even in the midst of the tumult managing to pull off a deal. The victory music, which had been playing all during the scene, mounts as Catherine joyfully raises the baby over her head.

I have recounted the activity of the scene because so much of it is missed in the reading and because—though it took us hours to work it out—all of it, and a good deal of incidental business that I have left out, happens in approximately one minute.

Thus the initial impression of alienation was mitigated for the actors by the necessity of having to *act* the play. It imposed its will and ways upon them. They could not worry about what they resented when the drama gave them so much to think about and *do*. Gradually they began to realize what Brecht means when he compares Epic theater to the painting of Brueghel. The canvas is large, diffuse, apparently undramatic. But more than in *Galileo,* the minor elements have their unique energy. One looks closer and recognizes that the play is rarely still. The sensation of diversity disappears in the apprehended unity of a common vitality. Degraded and demoralized by the black marketry of war, the people of the play express their consciously rationalized submission with a remarkable vigor. What we have is the caustically robust power of ineffectuality. The stones begin to talk, as one of the projections declares, even before the mute daughter provides the climactic irony with the drum that the war puts in her hands. One feels the rhetorical magic of the contemporary tribunal. A banner with slightly wrenched black (Gothic) letters drops from the flies announcing the place of action: Sweden, Saxony, Bavaria, Saxony, Poland. Why? Because war, like the snow settling over Joyce's Ireland, is general and undifferentiated; it looks the same everywhere. You *need* to be told where you are.

No production we had done until then was so full of discovery. What we all began to sense as rehearsals moved forward was that somehow the diffuse, omnibus, verbal, novelistic character of the play became more active, empathic, concentrated, and dramatic as it approached the end. There was meaning in the graduated contrasts, as in the more obvious interruptions of structure. In the beginning we had the characteristic rhythm and action of apathy and the materialistic vivacity of survival by bargaining. As in Chekhov—so different in general from Brecht—we have continual self-justification and transference of blame by the characters through commentary on public affairs; in Brecht, commentary beyond their scope as people. The songs, with their discreetly sardonic music by Paul Dessau, reflect something of this tendency. Even the Mother Courage ballad suggests with its insistent base the long, tedious way into the war. There is a sustained relationship with the audience: Mother Courage talks through the proscenium and there are frequent interruptions in the narrative. One desires very much to participate in the action, but Brecht makes one stand off and observe it. Later in the play, however, we are made more fully aware of the human relationships, which should have been obvious enough before except that we were distracted by a host of other factors.

Now we pick up events and values by reflexive reference. Back in Scene 3, Yvette, the prostitute, had sung her Song of Fraternization, prompted by memories of her unfaithful lover, Peter Piper. Much later, in Scene 8, the Cook is revealed to be the culprit. The son Eilif reappears, to be executed for a deed for which he had previously been honored. His armor is new and burnished, he dies rich. The Chaplain puts on his robe again and sings the Song of Hours, which suggests the idealistic theological student he must have been.[1] In Scene 12, Mother Courage sings a lullaby to her dead daughter, the only song we did *ohne Verfremdung,* without alienation, although the developing pathos is immediately cut off by the pipes and drums of a regiment on the march, through which we wove a choral reprise of the Mother Courage ballad. And Courage, who learns *nothing* from her suffering, makes the last "deal" of the play, paying a peasant to bury her daughter, and struggles off, bent as she is, to follow the war, which has not, according to the projected narrative, reached its end.

One realizes finally that the play of person on person has not been minimized in the earlier part of the drama (for all the to-do about detachment, the actors had to explore character relations in the usual sense), only it has not been so forcibly brought to our attention. There was much else to say and demonstrate, and it is not until we have accepted through action, gesture, speeches, music, and all the technical elements the unrelenting presence and localized quality of the abstract war that Brecht lets everybody indulge in easier and more rapid dramatic emotions. Hence the preference — at least with our actors and audience, and I think generally — for the latter part of the play. Most of us are still prone to recognize as dramatic mainly that which has uninterrupted momentum, especially if it is fast-paced or violent. But drama exists at the calm peripheries of history as much as in its excited middle, and in the juxtaposition of incongruous elements, such as event, song, legend, rhetoric, or the relaxed flow of ideas.

After the vibrancy of such a play as *The Crucible,* the movement of *Mother Courage* could, indeed, seem too leisurely. But in our anxiety to get on with it, we are likely to skip over a good portion of reality that materializes for a slower pulse. *Mother Courage* was the first of our plays to force us to reconsider the question of Time in the theater, the way it is passed, and the way it gives identity to Action.

At one extreme, there is pure behavior, taking its sweet time; like the bark of a tree, concrete experience in absoluteness. That is the way followed in *The Connection* and certain films of the *nouvelle vague.* The aim: to make tempo disappear in the spatial abstraction of behavior — experience spreads timelessly, becomes graphic, the drama taking on the character of a painting, an Action painting. In Brecht, we also have a spatial form; hence the analogy with Brueghel, whose canvases are mainly outsized compositions of behavior until one examines the parts — or, using incongruously the language of Time, the "events." The eye cannot accommodate it all at a glance (that's life, we may say, and extrapolate from there to the theories behind "pop art"). When we look at a magnified detail of *The Massacre of the Innocents* in an art volume, we are approximating the effect of a scene in *Mother Courage.* The "event" may be violent or casual; two events are united in a total image, not by cause and effect; the whole composition is in repose.

Thus, history diffuses itself through time, resembling space. The dramatist salvages the event from the annals, interpretation, bias, and false report, the mystifications of politics and the decantation of rumor — the obfuscating lens of subjective Time — and places the event before us. In Brecht, the event is not indiscriminately rendered behavior, come what may, life as improvised; but rather, life as judged. The judgment is an aspect of the event, and our emotional predisposition is—in the ideal Brecht performance—redirected by placards, slides, and other appendages that advise us, sometimes ironically, how to take what we see. The event may be named; each scene—as in the ancient Epic—has its argument, which is not a discursive thesis but the logic of narrative. When Weigel is asked about the Method of the Ensemble, she says: "We tell the Story." Story informed by and informing history. The rational intelligence is the chief medium of the telling, and the business of a production is to develop Signs.

The danger . . . is that the Signs, moving into history, are subject to the same errors of misreading and misrepresentation, and to the ever-shifting perspectives of a relativistic universe. (Genet: "It's the reading that counts.")

Now: consider the concrete fact of performance. What is there is there before you, in measured time. You come into the theater at one moment and go out at another. Moored temporarily before a playing space (whether you pay at the box office or not), you are looking for value received. We know that duration in performance is not necessarily proportionate to tempo. A play that speeds by may seem unendurable; a sudden noise may be dramatic, but sustained, it will become the shrill of tedium. But how much time do you take? In *Mother Courage,* we are already dealing with the slow-building omnibus structure I have described. When you play it "cool," doesn't that take more time? The questions point to the trouble we had in our own productions of Brecht, and to my own feelings of laboriousness in certain productions or parts of productions at the Berliner Ensemble. With Brecht's plays over-deliberated performance may not only feel slow, but like a gloss to a Victorian novel, the redundancy of the didactic—so that while True Believers may be edified, the disinterested will not be so much enlightened as anxious to get on with what they already know. One doesn't have to be vain to say this. If Brecht's plays do resemble the chronicles of Shakespeare, it might be well to remember that with a dialectic no less extraordinary Shakespeare was apparently played more nimbly lest the two hours traffic of the stage run into the dark.

While a play like *The Crucible* may blur meaning in momentum, a production of *Mother Courage* may underline it, too much. The task is to *realize* a scene, the whole crisscrossing motion of motives, so that it might be the better alienated. But here is where Time runs back to behavior. I am aware of Brecht's desire for gestural economy such as that of Oriental drama, and there is sufficient ritual in bourgeois life to muster a telling repertoire of gestures, where one motion may do the job of ten. Yet, to the extent the plays have realistic appearances, a single gesture such as Mother Courage's loud mercenary click of her pocketbook is no substitute for the density that comes of varied particulars. (It may even be, as it clicks shut on a "negative" action, what my young actress would call "indicating.") Nor is slowing down an action necessarily more virtuous than speeding it up—it depends on what you see. Critics used to respond to the introspective studies in the acting of the Group by complaining about pace. People who have nothing else to say often will. We know the factitious excitement of overpacing at its best from Kazan, but the aesthetics of pace has never been sufficiently explored. What I have been trying to emphasize is that it has something to do with the mileage of moments—the degree of *illumination* in each instant. Kazan may be the wiser for dazzling us with emptiness, but there is so much substance in Brecht it needn't be labored. The tedious underscoring of points may have been necessary in the *Lehrstück* for uninstructed workers, but as the audiences become, even in the proletarian East Berlin, more bourgeois and informed, one has to be wary that the determined coolness is not that at all, but a rather dispossessed drag in tempo which simplifies motives and ironies alike. Not only forms, but tempos outdate themselves.

The problem is also a cultural matter. If the Noh actor takes all afternoon to turn half a compass and a Russian company takes four hours to play *A View from the Bridge,* it is no wonder that the rhythm of the TNP production of *Mother Courage* was considerably more vivacious than that of the Ensemble. (Actually Brecht recognized and tried to provide for cultural qualifications of tempo. When his company went to England, he advised them to play more briskly, warning against their own tendency to ponderousness.) As for ourselves, when we did *Mother Courage,* the question of Time was very troubling in all its aspects, and I was never able to separate detachment from drag. I have the impression that as a result, within the unhurried structure that Brecht had laid out, some things were pushed in our playing; part of this may have been due to my own natural rhythm of perception, which made me impatient with the sort of underlining I later saw at the Ensemble. As we might expect, however, the general rhythm of our production ended up somewhere between the French and the German.

Fast or slow, let me stress this: there is a difference between an enlightening succession of "events" and a lustreless sequence of "behavior." To those for whom the brilliance of the rational mind remains a supreme value, the catatonic naturalism of such a drama as *The Connection* may be momentarily engaging, but interest is bound to run out. That is why, despite the throwing of the onus on the audience (by the play and its defenders), I refuse to take the blame for boredom as I refuse to accept the moral equivalence of good squares and good addicts. The anesthesia cannot be aestheticized away. As Baudelaire taught us, Ennui is the cardinal sin of modern life, and art cannot be too cavalier about impacting the situation by outdoing it. When I am told the tempo is the tempo of life itself, I understand the quest for pure behavior, the incessant *now,* but there is behavior and behavior, form and form, and there is a world of difference, because of form, between the behavior of *The Connection* and the behavior of, say, *Endgame,* which is involved in the same quest with an even greater sense of stasis.

. . . In the end, [the question of Time] may be the essential question of the contemporary theater. Nevertheless, Time is measured out in the theater in accordance with our feelings about it outside the theater. Today, various kinds of disenchantment, aimlessness, a desire for repose, the influence of the Orient have made us distrustful of Time as we normally understand it. But we can also be too cavalier in smashing our clocks because we have the feeling that some elephantiasis of the time-sense is destroying the Western world. In America, true, we may outrush ourselves in being with it, but being with it is not, in itself, a sin (except perhaps theologically); for we are always stuck with the paradox that the enterprise that is corrupting America also made it. While the serene detachment of the East has produced Zen and Chinese landscapes, it has also produced the misery of millions; and that is a nexus we have to be responsible for in our cultural prejudices, just as we have to be responsible for the atrophying effects of heavy industry based on time study.

The throwing over of Time is concurrent with the throwing over of formal conventions. But in the theater we must still come to terms with the discard of all the traditional equipment of dramaturgy: plot, character, consecutive thought, structure, pacing, pointing, symmetrical rhythms, Time—which are testaments to the form-giving power of mind, not incontestable Signs of debility. Brecht certainly knew this; Beckett knows it. Though he works over an excruciatingly narrowed spectrum, part of his power derives from his transcription of the painful cost of discard—the suicidal impulse of which Melville also knew when he had Ahab throw his log, chart, and compass overboard. No matter what it throws away, a great dramatic form has a long memory; and there is inevitably a little bird, or a bit of cloud, in the immensity of the Chinese sky, to keep the mind from drifting to annihilation.

Influenced as he has been by Eastern art, Brecht's is an obdurate Western mind. The theory of Alienation is a specific instrument of judgment, a rational *critique of behavior* which is socially conditioned. "The social effect of the Peasant Wars," he wrote, "was to take the guts out of the Reformation. Cynicism and business were all that was left." Bowdlerizing the Reformation also deprived it of its sense of comedy. And one of the missions of his drama is to restore a comedy which is virile, critical, Rabelaisian, obscene, a mockery of what is worshiped, as in the satyr plays. (It is a kind of comedy to which our company has become most receptive, and at which it has become increasingly adept.) Here, too, Brecht has affinities with Ionesco, Beckett, and Genet, who want to restore to the ritual of art the propriety of the giant phallus. Separating buffoonery and piety the Protestant ethic domesticated comedy and took away its sting. The comedy of *Mother Courage* is another aspect of Alienation and intensifies the dominant severity of the drama. Unlike *Galileo,* which is similarly witty, *Mother Courage* is restrained neither by the dignity of Science nor the historical eminence of its central character, who is a prototypical nobody. Thus, the comedy is closer to the inn scenes of Cervantes and the chronicles of Shakespeare, with their garrulousness and gallows humor, their juxtaposition of bawdry, bloody slaughters, and affairs of state. And their knowledge that the final comedy is the masque of death, passing beyond social criticism into the terrain of human failure, where comedy and tragedy—for all our enterprise and aspiration—rejoin each other in a common doom.

The most astonishing development of Brecht's play is the aging of Mother Courage, whose energy is hideously wasted after the death of her last child into the baleful abstraction of a Chinese mask. As she pulls the wagon in the finale, the musical themes clashing in the blank distance, Brecht's desire for social change is figured in an image of hopeless changelessness. The stage, made to feel more emptily infinite by the disappearance of other properties (property?), becomes an existential platform. And Mother Courage pulling her wagon, alone against a hostile universe, resembles nobody so much as Sisyphus rolling his stone up the mountain, but with no residue of heroism. In our production her sense of direction was totally destroyed, until her cry after the departing regiments was lost in the twining and imperturbable music, as if in the rhythm of organized nothingness. Still, one can't help being drawn with enormous pathos toward an image of even greater isolation than that of Hamm in the twilight of *Endgame;* for despite the discard of dog and whistle and the complacent terror with which he recovers his face with the bloody handkerchief, Clov remains, however unutterably there.

That final task of the actress also brings into focus all the controversy about acting technique in Brecht's plays. For that mask has to be filled and the emotion of a desperate enterprise that has run down into the mechanical must come all the more from the actress's most secret resources of feeling. If Courage's running after the armies is an emblematic gesture, the most extended image of the play, it is also the inevitable outgrowth of the woman's experience — behavior becoming symbol in a *memento mori.*

The treatment of Courage (played for us by Beatrice Manley) is the traditional crux. The difficulty of preventing compasssion for a woman who is meant to be a negative object lesson has been much mused over, sometimes misleadingly. In Scene 3, for instance, after the long modulated movement leading to the death of the stupid son, we did everything we could to "cool" the grief of Mother Courage — to *show* how, under any duress, she would beat the war at its own game. But the scene was undeniably moving in a conventional way; the more expedient Courage was the more moving, until the ironic pipes and drums of the music cut the emotion. The compassion would seem to be unavoidable; yet there had apparently been conflicts between Brecht and his wife, Helene Weigel, about interpretation of the role, its optimum hardness, and the fine line between compassion granted and compassion solicited. When a critic of the original Zurich production compared Courage to Hecuba, Brecht rewrote the play and made the "heroine" more unsympathetic. That's now part of the Brecht folklore.

As we understood Brecht's revisions, they were designed to show as clinically as possible (less ambiguously than in *Galileo*) that experience is *not* always the best teacher — that certains sufferers from catastrophe continue to woo their ruin. Just before he died, Brecht wrote a program note to the London production, meant to allay again false admiration for Courage: "She believes in the war to the last. It never occurs to her that in a war one needs outsize scissors to get one's cut." A camp-following career woman, she was not to be taken as a symbol of the indomitability of humble folk who, as Esslin puts it, "redeem themselves by their courage in the face of overwhelming odds." Courage is as guilty as the warmongers, and the crafty trade around her wagon is our common petit-bourgeois traffic, the natural freeway of which is war and total devastation.

Now, this view of her *can* be given weight in production or, allowing for more than natural compassion, it can be contradicted. True, unseeing as you make her, an audience may *still* not believe the evidence of its senses. But if, in that final moment (for one example), you have the actress square her shoulders and look steadfastly into the future, hauling her wagon like a resolution to survive, ignoring the fact that she is still following the war blindly, then you play right into the sympathies the Brecht didn't want. (It has been done, I hear.) That final *attitude* is crucial, for as I see it, Courage pulling that wagon is by no means indomitable, but a desperate fool reduced to an unthinking beast of burden.

I am reflecting on a production done some years ago, with fewer resources than we have now. In view of what I've said of our approach to *Galileo,* it might seem that we'd do *Mother Courage* differently. No doubt. If there were changes, however, I think they'd be in the direction of articulating every contradiction in the submission of Courage, her good wit demoralized down to that harrowing vision at the end, so that the chances of evading it are reduced. If there were an empathetic response, I would want that final attitude to arouse shame in the audience so that they went home bent with their own complicity.

To say that the acting of Brecht implies an action plus an attitude toward it is to say that an actor should know, beyond his limited intuitions, what there is to be said, in all its contradictions. In this respect, Brecht's method is not so different from Stanislavski's intentions — the Superobjective, we must recall, had its ethical component, a *reasoned* form. Stanislavski stressed the organic factor between what an actor had to feel and what he had to do to feel it; but he assumed there was something objectively there to be felt. Brecht stressed the objective factor between what might be done and what it could mean; but he had himself practiced the ways of obscurantism and was living in a period when any given action could, if not shaped into definition, mean anything. Actually, one learns in comparing the methods that, like so many theories of modern art, technique points to the same end: truth *imbedded in* experience, not concluded a priori, for all the shaping of Brecht and improvisation of Stanislavski. The image, the action, the totem, the happening carries the weight of meaning. Process is the most of it. Thus, the charges of formalism against Brecht in the Soviet Union (and implications of anarchy) while the stream of consciousness of Stanislavski has become the basis of a very objective art.

As a technique for the actor, the Stanislavski method is good for those who have not yet learned to explore themselves for the materials of their art; it is the depth psychology of the theater—a very necessary therapy for those who are inhibited or artificial in their acting, who have no associational powers, who do not know how to tap their memories, for those who customarily borrow emotion as a result. As I've said, the danger is that going down, you may not care to come up again. The technique of Alienation causes a great deal of consternation for the actor, who suspects he is going to be had, trumped up for a message. He wants to know immediately how to "alienate" his role. But he does not have to alienate anything, by reading his stage directions or exchanging parts with the other players, if by nature and conditioning he is not inclined to sentimentalize his behavior or fondle his feelings or merely play himself or float into irrelevance by association. (When I was at the Ensemble I asked about the "He said, she said" technique, and some of the actors could hardly remember it.) What American acting has little sense of is the thing that astonishes you in the acting of, say, Ekkehard Schall, the young, crew-cut, intensely Communist Marlon Brando of the Ensemble, who played Arturo Ui. He is a political actor. And it is really eye-opening to see somebody get so much out of himself by force of *external* conviction.

When we did *Mother Courage*, what we lacked in political conviction, we made up in part through the enthusiasm of enlightenment —the feeling that the drama was an adventure. It's hard to convey how happily naïve it all became after the initial doubts about the play —the alienation, the politics, the sense of mission; naïve in the best sense. There was a general feeling that with this play the theater might earn an effective social role in the community. Yet our optimism was tempered one rainy night at our Elgin Street warehouse, when morale was soaring in rehearsals and everybody was feeling that we might yet change the world. We were ardently exploring some point in the play when suddenly there was thunder and the rain began to beat heavily on the chicken-wire glass of the skylight; and all together as we were, we felt impossibly alone. The discussion stopped. The sense of isolation spread. And our ardor, momentarily dampened, was revived more realistically when I said the production had to contain the knowledge that we were, after all, but a minority group in a minority form in a country pledged to the protection of minorities, in a period in which they needed such protection. . . .

Kenneth Tynan

Tynan, presently literary manager and advisor to the National Theatre of England, was for many years dramatic critic for *The Observer* (London). His reviews have also appeared in *The New Yorker;* many of them were collected and printed as one volume of criticism entitled *Curtains* (1961).

Beginning with student productions at Oxford, Tynan's experience soon ranged across the continent; his precise and articulate appraisals of performances and productions has brought him a considerable reputation. His critical understanding has always included a deep and probing knowledge of the *making* of a play, and, as the observations reprinted here indicate, his response to performance is itself creative. His grasp of the technique of acting, as well as an understanding of stage design, production management, casting problems, vocal manner, and many other components of performance, make him a valuable critic in the best sense of that word.

He was deeply involved in the National Theatre's plans and rehearsals for its production of *Othello* which opened in 1964 with Sir Laurence Olivier in the title role; the production was immediately described — even by those who disagreed with Olivier's remarkable projection of the part — as one of the most important Shakespearean productions of the century. Reprinted here are Tynan's comments on Olivier as an actor in rehearsal as well as selected reviews by well-known English critics.

❧ *OLIVIER: THE ACTOR AND THE MOOR*

My theme is the growth of a performance, first mooted early in 1963 and brought to birth at the Old Vic Theatre on April 23, 1964, in honour of William Shakespeare's four hundredth birthday. How the performance was received — and the production of which it was the centre-piece — is already history, and amply recorded elsewhere in this book. Let me begin by discussing the performer.

Laurence Olivier at his best is what everyone has always meant by the phrase "a great actor." He holds all the cards: and in acting the court cards consist of (a) complete physical relaxation, (b) powerful physical magnetism, (c) commanding eyes that are visible at the back of the gallery, (d) a commanding voice that is audible *without effort* at the back of the gallery, (e) superb timing, which includes the capacity to make verse swing, (f) *chutzpah* — the untranslatable Jewish word that means cool nerve and outrageous effrontery combined, and (g) the ability to communicate a sense of danger.

These are all vital attributes, though you can list them in many orders of importance (Olivier himself regards his eyes as the ace of trumps); but the last is surely the rarest. Watching Olivier, you feel that at any moment he may do something utterly unpredictable; something explosive, possibly apocalyptic, anyway unnerving in its emotional nakedness. There is nothing bland in this man. He is complex, moody and turbulent; deep in his temperament there runs a vein of rage that his affable public mask cannot wholly conceal. I once asked Ralph Richardson how he differed, as an actor, from Olivier. He replied: "I haven't got Laurence's splendid fury."

Fame, which isolates men from all but their closest colleagues and servitors, has enabled Olivier to preserve in his late fifties the hair-triggered emotional reactions of adolescence. He has never developed the thick social skin of conformity beneath which most of us hide our more violent or embarrassing impulses. With him they are still close to the surface, unashamed and readily accessible. The volcano remains active, the eruption forever imminent. This is an actor ruled by instinct, not a rational being or a patient arguer or a paragon of consecutive thought; and when you ally this intuitive fire with exceptional technical equipment and a long knowledge of

From the book *Othello: The National Theatre Production,* Kenneth Tynan, ed., published by Stein and Day, © The National Theatre 1966. Reprinted by permission of Stein and Day and Rupert Hart-Davis Limited (London).

audience responses, you have something like the theatrical equivalent of the internal combustion engine.

Out of a sense of duty, he has occasionally tried to play what is insultingly known as "the common man"—the seedy schoolmaster, for instance, in the film "Term of Trial." He seldom succeeds. That outsize emotional candour cannot help breaking through, the actor impatiently bursts the seams of the role, and the common man becomes extraordinary. That is why he has spent the greater part of his professional life with his trousers off—playing bare-legged or in tights the great exceptional characters around whom the play-wrights of the past built their tallest tragedies and highest comedies. He has acted in many good movies, but seldom at the height of his talent: partly because the reticence of movie acting is awkward for him, but mostly because his performances need to be seen as flowing, consecutive wholes, not chopped up into long-shots and close-ups and spread over months of shooting. You cannot make love by instalments, and Olivier's relationship with his audience is that of a skilled but dominating lover. He is one of that select group of performers (great athletes, bull-fighters, singers, politicians, ballet dancers and vaudeville comedians are some of the others) whose special gift is to be able to exercise fingertip control over the emotions of a large number of people gathered in one place to witness a single unique event. He can do other things, of course; but that is what he does peerlessly and irreplaceably. His absorption in the hows and ifs and whys of his craft is total. How does he vote? What is his religion? What is his philosophy of life? The questions simply do not arise. Although I have worked quite closely with him in the last few years, I have no idea what his convictions are on any other subject than acting. This separation of work from private beliefs is not necessarily a virtue in him; but I suspect that it contributes to his acting its curious amoral strength. He approaches each character quite unencumbered by pre-conceived value judgments.

The best British actors often come in pairs. A century and a half ago we had John Philip Kemble, all dignity and word-music, and the galvanic rule-breaker Edmund Kean, all earth and fire. People accused Kean of mangling blank verse, but Coleridge said that when he acted it was like reading Shakespeare by flashes of lightning; and Hazlitt's comment on his death-scene in "Richard III" is a set-piece of unforgettably dramatic criticism:

"He fought like one drunk with wounds: and the attitude in which he stands with his hands stretched out, after his sword is taken from him, had a preternatural and terrific grandeur, as if his will could not be disarmed, and the very phantoms of his despair had a withering power."

In modern terms John Gielgud is Kemble to Olivier's Kean—the aesthete, as opposed to the animal. "John is claret," as Alan Dent once put it, "and Larry is burgundy." The difference between them reminds me more of Edmund Burke's famous essay on the Sublime and the Beautiful. According to Burke's definition, the Beautiful (i.e. Gielgud) comprises that which is shapely, harmonious and pleasing; while the Sublime (i.e. Olivier) is irregular, jagged and awe-inspiring, like thunder over the Matterhorn. A dozen or so years ago it looked as if a similar conflict might be stirring between Paul Scofield the poet and Richard Burton the peasant; but Burton went filmwards, and battle was never joined. Incidentally, one of Olivier's most cherished possessions is the sword that Kean used in "Richard III." It was a gift from Gielgud, inscribed with a characteristically generous tribute to his performance.

Young actors trust and venerate Gielgud, but the man they tend to copy is Olivier. What, after all, could be more seductive than performances like his Richard, his Macbeth, his Henry V, his Oedipus, his Coriolanus—acting explosions that opened up new horizons for each of these parts, so that we felt we had never truly seen them before? His mimics are countless, but they always miss his essence. One half of Olivier loves ceremony, hierarchy and ritual—the full panoply of the status quo—and I even suspect that he would not mind being the first theatrical peer. The other half loves eccentricity: he relishes the abnormal, the anti-social, the off-beat, the bizarre. You could see this split in his direction of "Hamlet," the inaugural production of the National Theatre at the Old Vic in October, 1963. It combined, not always too happily, an atmosphere of fanfare and glamour with sharp, gleeful insights into unglamorous quirks of character. Ophelia, for example, behaved in the mad scenes like a suicidal nymphomaniac. In 1944, the two sides of Olivier's nature met and married in one supreme coalition: he played a raging psychotic who adored pomp and circumstance— Richard of Gloucester, multiple murderer and anointed king.

It was not easy to persuade him to play Othello. At least, he made it seem difficult; perhaps, deep in his personal labyrinth, where the minotaur of his talent lurks, he had already decided, and merely wanted to be coaxed. Elia Kazan once told me that the adjective he would choose to sum up Olivier was "girlish." When I looked baffled, he elaborated: "I don't mean that he's effeminate—just that he's coy, he's vain, he has tantrums, he needs to be wooed." It took careful wooing to talk him into Othello, the only major role in Shakespearean tragedy that he had not played. He pointed out that no English actor in this century had succeeded in the part. The play, he said, belonged to Iago, who could always make the Moor look a credulous idiot—and he spoke with authority, since he had played Iago to Ralph Richardson's Othello in 1938. "If I take it on," he said, "I don't want a witty, Machiavellian Iago. I want a solid, honest-to-God N.C.O." The director, John Dexter, fully agreed with this approach. He and Olivier went through the play in depth and detail, at the end of which process the National Theatre had cast its Othello.

Soon afterwards I passed the news on to Orson Welles, himself a former Othello. He voiced an instant doubt. "Larry's a natural tenor," he rumbled, "and Othello's a natural baritone." When I mentioned this to Olivier, he gave me what Peter O'Toole has expressively called "that grey-eyed myopic stare that can turn you to stone." There followed weeks of daily voice lessons that throbbed through the plywood walls of the National Theatre's temporary offices near Waterloo Bridge. When the cast assembled to read the play (on February 3, 1964), Olivier's voice was an octave lower than any of us had ever heard it.

Dexter, dapper and downright, made a bold preliminary speech. After two or three days of "blocking" (i.e. working out the moves), there would be a first run-through with books. Of the text as a whole, he said that "this is the most headlong of the plays"; for the purposes of this production, it would be assumed that the action took place within roughly forty-eight hours—a night in Venice, a night in Cyprus, and a final night during which Desdemona is killed. The settings (by Jocelyn Herbert) would be sparse and simple, with no elaborate scene-changes and almost nothing in the way of furniture except the indispensable nuptial couch. Pride, he said, was the key to all the characters, especially to that of Othello; already he was touching on the theme that was to be the concealed mainspring of the production—the idea of Othello as a man essentially narcissistic and self-dramatising. The germ of this came from a famous essay by Dr. F. R. Leavis, which Dexter and I had already studied with Olivier. "Othello," Dexter told the cast, "is a pompous, word-spinning, arrogant black general. At any rate, that's how you ought to see him. The important thing is not to accept him at his own valuation. Try to look at him objectively. He isn't just a righteous man who's been wronged. He's a man too proud to think he could ever be capable of anything as base as jealousy. When he learns that he *can* be jealous, his character changes. The knowledge destroys him, and he goes berserk. Now let's have a good loud reading this afternoon."

That first read-through was a shattering experience. Normally on these occasions the actors do not exert themselves. They sit in a circle and mumble, more concerned with getting to know one another than with giving a performance. Into this polite gathering Olivier tossed a hand-grenade. He delivered the works—a fantastic, full-volume display that scorched one's ears, serving final notice on everyone present that the hero, storm-center and focal point of the tragedy was the man named in the title. Seated, bespectacled and lounge-suited, he fell on the text like a tiger. This was not a noble, "civilized" Othello but a triumphant black despot, aflame with unadmitted self-regard. So far from letting Iago manipulate him, he seemed to manipulate Iago, treating him as a kind of court jester. Such contumely cried out for deflation. There are moral flaws in every other Shakespearean hero, but Othello is traditionally held to be exempt. Olivier's reading made us realise that tradition might be wrong; that Othello was flawed indeed with the sin of pride. At the power of his voice, the windows shook and my scalp tingled. A natural force had entered the room, stark and harsh, with vowel-sounds as subtly alien as Kwame Nkrumah's; and the cast listened pole-axed. I wondered at the risks he was taking. Mightn't the knockdown arrogance of this interpretation verge too closely for comfort on comedy? Wasn't he doing to Othello precisely what he deplored in the Peter Brook-Paul Scofield "King Lear"—i.e. cutting the hero down to size and slicing away his majesty? Then he came to "Farewell the plumed troop," and again the hair rose on my neck. It was like the dying moan of a fighting bull.

Like the cast, I was awed. We were learning what it meant to be faced with a great classical actor in full spate—one whose vocal range was so immense that by a single new inflexion he could point the way to a whole new interpretation. Every speech, for Olivier, is like a mass of marble at which the sculptor chips away until its essential form and meaning are revealed. No matter how ignoble the character he plays, the result is always noble as a work of art. I realised how vital, for an actor, is the use to which he puts the time available to him before his bodily resources begin to flag. In the last fifteen years Olivier has played more than twenty stage parts, ancient and modern. During the same period Marlon Brando—once, potentially, an American Olivier—has not appeared on stage at all. He had the quality; but quantity is the practice that makes quality perfect.

"Othello" was rehearsed for nine weeks before it opened on tour at the Alexandra Theatre, Birmingham, on April 6. For three of the nine weeks Olivier was absent, suffering from a virus infection which (as he put it) "shook me like a dog shakes a rat." Rather than follow his performance as it evolved day by day, I propose to deal with it scene by scene, using the notes I kept during rehearsals of what was intended and what was achieved.

ACT I/SCENE 2

His first entrance: an easy, rolling gait, enormous sly eyes, and a tender-tigerish smile. It is clear from the start that whatever else this performance may be, it is going to be a closely studied piece of physical impersonation. (Odd how rare this element is in contemporary theatre: modern actors in general—as Max Beerbohm said of Duse—"never stoop to impersonation," wrongly holding it to be a facile and suspect skill.) In the opening exchanges with Iago, Olivier displays the public mask of Othello: a Negro sophisticated enough to conform to the white myth about Negroes, pretending to be simple and not above rolling his eyes, but in fact concealing (like any other aristocrat) a highly developed sense of racial superiority. This will not be a sentimental reading of the part, nor one that white liberals will necessarily applaud.

Note on props: during the early part of the scene he sniffs at and toys with a long-stemmed pink rose. Is this a foreshadowing of the lines in V.2.

"...When I have pluckt the rose,
I cannot give it vital growth again,
It needs must wither..."?

"Keep up your bright swords, for the dew will rust them" is delivered almost affably, with a trace of sarcastic condescension in the second half of the line. Othello's mere presence is enough to silence a brawl. This is a man who does not need to raise his voice to be obeyed.

ACT I/SCENE 3

The Senate scene: a midnight meeting, convened in panic at the impending Turkish threat. Dexter tells the senators to chatter among themselves about what really concerns them—namely, the effect on their own pockets if the Turks seize a trading centre as important as Cyprus: "Look at the economics of the scene. It's not about religion, it's not about politics, it's about money."

Othello, a fully "assimilated" Moor, wears a crucifix round his neck and crosses himself when Brabantio accuses him of having won Desdemona's love with witchcraft. For the great account of the wooing, he is still and central. "Her father—loved me" is directed straight at Brabantio, in tones of wondering rebuke. There is lofty pride in the re-telling of his magical adventures; and when he reaches the line about "the Cannibals, that each other eat,/The Anthropophagi," he utters the Greek word by way of kindly parenthetical explanation, as if to say: "That, in case you didn't know, is the scholarly term for these creatures." He also manages to convey his sardonic awareness that this is just the kind of story that Europeans would expect Africans to tell. (All this in a single phrase? Yes, such is the power of inflexion when practised by a master.) "She wisht she had not heard it: yet she wisht/That heaven had made her such a man" modulates from gentle, amused reminiscence to proud, erotic self-congratulation. "Upon this hint I spake" is preceded by a smiling shrug, the actor dwelling on "hint" as a jocular understatement, and forcing the senators to share his pleasure. On "This only is the witchcraft I have used," Olivier isolates the word "witchcraft" so that you can almost hear the inverted commas, deliberately making the second vowel harsh and African, and pointedly eyeing Brabantio as he delivers it. Throughout the speech, he is at once the Duke's servant and the white man's master. Every time we rehearse it, the room is pin-still. For some of us, this is the high point of the performance.

ACT II/SCENE 1

The arrival at Cyprus, after a hot, wild hurricane that signals our entry into a world quite different from that of super-civilized Venice. Embracing Desdemona, Othello is beside himself with deep, internal joy, wreathed in smiles and barely able to speak. He greets the Cypriots as old friends; they are closer to him in blood than the Venetians.

ACT II/SCENE 3

Contrary to custom, Iago's first song ("And let me the canakin clink") is a home-sick soldier's lament instead of the usual rousing chorus: a perceptive idea of John Dexter's. The Cassio-Montano squabble develops (as Stanislavsky suggested in his notes on the play) into a popular riot, with the mutinous Cypriots rising against their Venetian overlords; thus Othello has something more to quell than a private quarrel. He enters nursing a scimitar; Iago lines the Venetian soldiers up before him, as if on parade.

ACT III/SCENE 3

The great jealousy scene, the fulcrum that thrusts the energy of the play towards tragedy. To Desdemona's pleas for the reinstatement of Cassio, Othello reacts with paternal chuckles, a man besotted by the toy white trophy he has conquered. For the duologue with Iago, Dexter deliberately makes things technically hard for both actors. Othello usually sits at a desk, riffling through military documents while Iago begins his needling; Dexter forbids the desk, thereby compelling the actors to make the scene work without recourse to props. He is swiftly proved right. With no official tasks to perform, Othello ceases to be a sitting target, and Iago must struggle to hold his attention: both actors must find reasons deeper than accidents of duty to keep them together long enough for the deadly duologue to be irrevocably launched. Stroke of genius by Olivier: no sooner has Iago mentioned Cassio than *he* takes the initiative. Iago seems to be hiding something, so Othello determines to quiz him, in order to get a full report on Cassio's character; after all, Desdemona wants the lieutenant reinstated, and the general owes it to his wife to find out all the facts. "What dost thou *think?*", he asks with avuncular persistence, like a headmaster ordering one prefect to tell tales on another. On "By heaven, he echoes me," he is mock-severe, rebuking Iago for talking in riddles. His whole attitude is one of supreme self-confidence. (Query: will the public and critics realise that this is an egocentric Othello, not an egocentric performance?) What he expects is that Iago will disclose a story about a mess bill that Cassio left unpaid, or some similar peccadillo. At this point Othello is cat to Iago's mouse; or, to put it the other way round, Iago is a reluctant matador in danger of being dominated by his bull.

As Othello's interrogation progresses, Iago retreats and hedges, refusing to reveal his thoughts. A show-down is the last thing he wants to precipitate; he is unprepared for anything so drastic. Driven into a corner, he suddenly says: "O, beware, my lord, of jealousy." This is pure improvisation, a shot in the dark. The notion has never before crossed Othello's mind: he thought they were discussing matters of military discipline, and his immediate response is angry incomprehension. When Iago continues:

"But, O, what damned minutes tells he o'er
Who dotes, yet doubts, suspects, yet strongly loves!"

— he replies "O misery!" with a bewildered emphasis that implies: "Yes, it must be miserable to feel like that, but what has it to do with me?"

Next development: Othello explodes in outrage, and Iago is

almost frightened by the ferocity he has inadvertently unleashed. But having gone so far, he must now go further, stressing that a girl unnatural enough to deceive her father and marry a black is capable of anything. Such is Olivier's shame that he cannot face Iago while delivering the treacherous order: "Set on thy wife to observe." Once Iago has departed, his ego reasserts itself: "Why did I marry?" is uttered with the first person singular heavily italicised, as if to say: "I — of all people."

The entry of Desdemona: when Othello complains of "a pain upon my forehead," he places two fingers above his eyebrows, indicating to us (though not to her) the cuckold's horns. At "Come, I'll go in with you," he leads her off in a close, enfolding embrace that will end in bed. During his absence, we have Iago's capture of the handkerchief dropped by Desdemona. Note: in Frank Finlay's interpretation, endorsed by Dexter, Iago has been impotent for years — hence his loathing of Othello's sexuality and his alienation from Emilia.

When Othello returns ("Ha! ha! false to *me?*"), he has been unable to make love to Desdemona; he sniffs his fingers as if they were tainted by contact with her body. He ranges back and forth across the stage for "Farewell the tranquil mind!"; the speech becomes an animal moan of desolation, the long vowels throbbing and extended, and the "ear-piercing fife" rising to an ecstasy of agonised onomatopoeia.

On "Villain, be sure thou prove my love a whore," Olivier locks Finlay by the throat and hurls him to the ground, threatening him with a trick knife-blade concealed in a bracelet. (He will later — in V.2. — use the same weapon to cut his own jugular vein.) This assault leaves Iago hoarse and breathless. From now on Othello is a boundlessly destructive force, needing only to be steered to its target.

Dexter risks a textual emendation to hammer home the hero's egoism. Instead of:

". . . her name, that was as fresh

As Dian's visage, is now begrimed and black

As mine own face." —

he reads: ". . .*my* name, that was as fresh" etc.

The danger with all Iagos is that they make Othello seem too credulous. Unless we find their lies plausible, the play becomes a tale of an oaf gulled by a con man. Dexter asks Finlay to play the whole scene as if he really believed that Cassio was sleeping with Desdemona. Only thus can he create provocation enough to trigger off Olivier's gigantic passion. Approaching the scene in this way (as of course he should; Iago's hypocrisy must be perfect and impenetrable), Finlay almost bursts into tears while recounting Cassio's dream—"In sleep I heard him say, 'Sweet Desdemona,/Let us be wary, let us hide our loves'"—as if he could not bear to think of the general being so vilely deceived. This is a long step towards the true Iago, the one who could fool *us*. As I had expected, Olivier gets through "Like to the Pontic sea . . ."—eight lines of blank verse—with only one pause for breath. His cadenzas hereabouts are hypnotic. After "Now, by yon ma-a-a-arble heaven"—a surging atavistic roar—he tears the crucifix from his neck and flings it into the air. Othello's a Moor again.

Act III/Scene 4

The handkerchief scene. As Othello tells the story of this talismanic heirloom ("there's magic in the web of it"), we get a glimpse of the narrative spell-binder who conquered Desdemona with his tales. She sits at his feet to listen, drawn back once again into the exotic world of the Anthropophagi. These will be their last peaceful moments together. Her rueful comment on the missing handkerchief ("Then would to God that I had never seen't!") produces a sudden, terrific spasm of fury: "Ha! wherefore?"—the words detonate like thunder-claps. Before his exit, Othello repeats "The handkerchief!" three times. Olivier reaches a climax of pointblank intimidation in the first two, but for the third and last he finds a moving new inflexion, uttering the line like a desperate suppliant, whimpering for reassurance, his hands clasped before him in prayer.

Act IV/Scene 1

Othello is now Iago's creature. The new lieutenant is merely a passenger aboard the great plunging ship of Othello's wrath. "All you have to do" says Olivier to Finlay "is toss him a bit of meat from time to time, and he gobbles it whole." Dexter to Finlay: "At this point you're like Lady Macbeth after Macbeth's killed Duncan—there's really nothing left to do except go mad." Iago and the Moor enter together and drift slowly downstage; the sinister responses and repetitions are murmurously chanted, like a satanic litany spoken in a trance:

"Or to be naked with her friend in bed
An hour or more, not meaning any harm?"
"Naked in bed, Iago, and not mean harm . . ."

The two men even begin to sway gently from side to side, locked together in the rhythm of Othello's pain. In the epileptic fit Olivier pulls out all the stops; but, as always, there is science in his bravura.

The symtoms of epilepsy (the long, shuddering breaths; the head flung back; the jaw thrust out) are painstakingly reproduced; and when he falls thrashing to the ground like a landed barracuda, Iago shoves the haft of a dagger between his teeth to keep him from biting off his tongue.

Othello's re-entry after eavesdropping on the Cassio-Iago scene and Bianca's intervention with the handkerchief: he circles the stage, a caged jungle king *in extremis,* with Iago immobile at the centre. Dexter to Finlay: "Think of yourself as a ring-master. Just give him an occasional flick of the whip—like 'Nay, that's not your way'—to keep him in order."

The arrival of Lodovico from Venice: as Dexter points out, this changes the whole situation. Iago's moment of triumph is over, his peak is passed. From "O, beware, my lord, of jealousy" right up to this instant, he is in complete control; from now on he is at the mercy of events. The news of Othello's recall to Venice and Cassio's appointment as governor of Cyprus throws all his plans into confusion; he is forced to improvise, this time with disastrous results—viz. the bungled attempt on Cassio's life.

Othello strikes Desdemona across the face with the rolled-up proclamation he has received from Lodovico. Her reaction (as played by Maggie Smith) is not the usual collapse into sobs; it is one of deep shame and embarrassment, for Othello's sake as well as her own. She is outraged, but tries out of loyalty not to show it. After the blow, she holds herself rigidly upright and expressionless, fighting back her tears. "I have not deserved this" is not an appeal for sympathy, but a protest quietly and firmly lodged by an extremely spunky girl.

"Cassio shall have my place": Olivier turns this line into an ironic *double entente*—hasn't Cassio already usurped his place in bed?

ACT IV/SCENE 2

The interrogation of Emilia (Joyce Redman) and the confrontation with Desdemona, whom Othello now openly treats as a prostitute. The scene is a nightmare of cruelty, and Olivier plays it to the hilt: the superman runs amok, the bull wrecks the china-shop. On lines like:

"... turn thy complexion there,
Patience, thou young and rose-lipt cherubin,—
I there look grim as hell..."

Olivier resorts to shrill and wailing head-notes that savour slightly of self-indulgence. Answer: it is Othello, not Olivier, who is indulging himself emotionally. Question: yes, but will the audience know the difference?

At "O thou weed,/Who art so lovely fair, and smell'st so sweet," he crawls across the stage and lies on top of Desdemona: for a moment, desire almost overcomes disgust: or rather, both emotions co-exist. Othello comes close to committing the crime of which Brabantio accused his daughter: he very nearly "falls in love with what he fears to look on."

Act V/Scene 1

The street scene, including the abortive stabbing of Cassio by Roderigo, and the latter's murder by Iago. Othello's brief and dramatically pointless appearance is cut, in accordance with sound theatrical custom.

Act V/Scene 2

The killing of Desdemona in the bedroom. Entrance of Othello: white-robed and dark-limbed, picked out by a shaft of moonlight through a grille over the chamber door. On "Who's there?", Desdemona wakes up in a convulsion of fear, as if from a nightmare; then says with a sigh of relief: "Othello!" The "murder, which I thought a sacrifice" is accomplished with relentless, implacable precision; honour having been offended, the prescribed penalty must be enforced.

Turning-point of the case against Iago: Emilia can prove that her husband is a dirty-minded gossip-monger, but not until Othello reveals that he has seen Cassio with the handkerchief ("I saw it in his hand") can she prove that Iago is guilty of conspiracy to murder. It takes her a second or two to react to the implications of what Othello has said; but then she bursts out with "O God! O heavenly God!"—and after this clinching double-take it is all up with Iago, since she now reveals that she gave him the handkerchief. The end of Iago: he offers himself masochistically to Othello's sword. "I bleed, sir; but not kill'd" is spoken with quiet satisfaction. The end of Othello: kneeling on the bed, hugging the limp corpse of Desdemona, he slashes his throat with the hidden stiletto we saw in III.3. And slumps like a falling tower.

About six months after the production opened, the Italian director Franco Zeffirelli saw it for the first time. Of Olivier's performance he said: "I was told that this was the last flourish of the romantic tradition of acting. It's nothing of the sort. It's an anthology of everything that has been discovered about acting in the last three centuries. It's grand and majestic, but it's also modern and realistic. I would call it a lesson for us all."

THE CRITICS ON OTHELLO

PHILIP HOPE-WALLACE IN *The Guardian:*

At first consideration, Olivier may not seem ideal casting for Othello. His emanations are not Moorish to put it mildly. His timbre tends to lightness, his grey eyes are rather for the poetry of Macbeth. And yet, what of the evidence of that Coriolanus, that Lear, that Titus Andronicus above all with all the *gravitas* of stark tragedy and where at the height of an unremitting role he cut his hand off before our eyes and then for an eternity of seconds withheld his howl of pain?

In great tragic acting there is always a strong element of surprise. Othello on the rack last night was agonising in the sheer vehemence of his anguish, but it was the inventiveness of it above all, the sheer variety and range of the actor's art which made it an experience in the theatre altogether unforgettable by anyone who saw it. True, it was the noble, wounded professional thrown out of kilter rather than the lumbering bull in Othello that was uppermost; the general self-broken, self-cashiered. "Othello's occupation's gone." We saw it go.

The initial suprise, however, is that it is exactly at first sight that this Othello compels you to accept him, not merely as a coloured man, but as a Negro, with a negroid speech and easy, generous, frank and easily articulated gait and physically imposed authority. It is the breaking down of these and the passing into the torment which is so magnificently taken; slow at first, almost to point of losing rhythm and momentum (it was one hour fifty minutes to "Now by yon marble heaven"), slow, but immensely powerful in building, this Othello caught us, most in the scenes of the second half, overwhelmingly pathetic in the epilepsy, fearful in his scorn ("I took you for the cunning whore of Venice") and at the end cradling his dead wife in his arms. Olivier struck deeper chords than I have ever heard from him: a marvellous assumption of the part which I could write about till morning and after.

John Dexter's production has no fripperies; indeed it is if anything rather short of what is called atmosphere (but that's to the good by and large). Frank Finlay's Iago runs a strangely effective gamut from braggart to whimpering, self-justifying neurotic, plainly deranged by the last scene; an Iago who wanes but seems quite unusually well motivated. Joyce Redman is a sturdy and unaffected Emilia and Michael Rothwell a Roderigo of substance. For Desdemona, Maggie Smith has the dignity and used this quality well; even most originally in her early scenes where she can almost safely skirt comedy. But I didn't find that she easily assumed the pathos of Desdemona in adversity, expecially the voice of simple innocence.

But it was the Othello who carried all before him from the soft laughing assurance of his "My life . . ." to Brabantio, up to the last dying fall. I think this superb performance will be both more homogeneous and even richer as it mellows; certain things — the accent for one — tended a little to "come and go" and though the tirades have a superb surge there is to my ear some loss of pace through broken rhythms elsewhere. But for the greater part it both looks and sounds magnificent.

ALAN DENT IN *The Financial Times:*

The elder Dumas, that very very famous historical novelist, and a playwright too in his day, used to say that he had seen Shakespeare's Othello acted by Talma, Edmund Kean, Kemble, Macready, and Joanny: "Each of these great actors played the part in his own way. Talma played it with his art, Kean with his temperament, Kemble with his mastery of all that the traditions of the stage could do for him, Macready with his physical beauty, Joanny with his instincts." The passage is not at all well-known, and so no excuses need be made for quoting further: "With Talma, Othello was a Moor covered with a varnish of Venetian civilisation; with Kean he was a wild beast, half-man, half-tiger; with Kemble he was a man of a ripe age, violent and uncontrollable; with Macready he was an Arab of the days of the Abencerrages, chivalrous and refined; with Joanny he was — Joanny." (This last, by the way, is now quite forgotten, but he was a fine-looking old French actor who emerged with credit from the riotous first night in 1830 of Victor Hugo's *Hernani*.)

Dumas *père* did not, apparently, live long enough to see the Italian Othello, Salvini, who was by all accounts the most overwhelming of all and who died as recently as 1915, aged 85. Ellen Terry, as good a writer and critic as she was an actress (which is saying much), placed Salvini easily first among Othellos. And that superlative critic, G. H. Lewes, who saw Salvini in London in 1875, compared him not at all unfavourably with our great Edmund Kean whom he saw in his youth, just before the actor's early death in 1833. Dumas *père* might presumably have added Salvini to his list of great Othellos as being an Italian, half-man and half-lion, cutting his own throat in the contrition that followed the jealous frenzy in which he violently and realistically smothered his wife.

Deliberately one mentions all these supreme Othellos of the past since the new one at the Old Vic, Laurence Olivier, unmistakably joins the great traditional line. The performance is a complete thing (as Hazlitt said of the prize fight). It is a highly imagined and already highly developed portrait of a Moor who is black and velvety of voice and who has deep tenderness, charm, authority, and courtesy. But scratch him, as Iago does with his gradual insinuations about his wife's possible infidelity, and you get a dangerous volcano of a man. In the earlier scenes this Othello wins us at once with his civilised virtues. He has a little unexpected smile now and then which he knows how to make very ingratiating and even touching. He is a man deeply in love, and all too soon a man deeply engrossed in that jealously which is so severe a wound to his pride. Note before the crisis of doubt comes to rack him what sweetness he puts into the very name of his wife, Desdemona, and how when they meet again in Cyprus he greets her with the line: "If it were now to die, 'twere now to be most happy" — lingering over that last word as if his happiness were almost an exquisite pain. All this is beautifully played, with the considerable help of Maggie Smith's tall, sweet, and very loving Desdemona.

But considerably less assistance seems to me to come from the Iago, who is that clever comedian, Frank Finlay. His Iago turns out, for me at least, to be a piece of choice miscasting. He makes a furtive slyboots of the character, and this makes nonsense of Othello's regard for him, of his own wife's loyalty, and of the complete trust placed in him by everybody else. Ellen Terry used to say of Irving, her own favourite Iago, that he looked immensely handsome and likeable throughout. How else can Iago make any sense, if he does not *look* amiable or at least honest? . . . Truth to tell, the Desdemona and the Emilia of Miss Smith and Miss Joyce Redman, though both have their moments, are not greatly more than adequate. The production by John Dexter wants some speeding up here and there, though its many bells and great sonorous gongs directly help the tragedy's brooding atmosphere.

This *Othello,* is short, stands and falls by its Moor, and he, as I have said, is fortunately a great one — full of cares, and sighs, and roars, and of utter bewilderment at the foul things he believes about his beloved. He is for all of the second half of the play like a lion caught in a cruel trap. His rages melt the heart, and the wonderful poetry torn from him is over and over again overwhelming in its direct and lacerating impact. Lewes asked: "When shall we see again that lion-like power and lion-like grace — that dreadful culmination of wrath, alternating with bursts of agony, that Kean gave us?" The answer is here and now with the Olivier Othello. The scene-designer Jocelyn Herbert, as if aware of this, gives the sky in the background the colour of a lion in the sun.

ALAN BRIEN IN *The Sunday Telegraph:*

There is a kind of bad acting of which only a great actor is capable. Alone so far among critics, perhaps alone forever among audiences, I find Sir Laurence Olivier's Othello the most prodigious and perverse example of this in a decade.

Sir Laurence can move every muscle at will — I regret he could not move me. To watch him stiffen the sinews and summon up the blood, marshal the corpuscles and stimulate the phagocytes, is to endorse that old newsreel commentator's cliché "the poetry of motion." But it seems to me here the doggerel of emotion.

He is the romantic gymnast of our stage, the noblest Roman wrestler of them all. He can press his own weight in blank verse and hurl a soliloquy like a javelin until it sinks up to the haft in the back row of the gallery. But he is now in danger of becoming overtrained.

In Shakespeare, he begins to anthologise himself — almost as if he were determined to give the casual spectator a medley of footlight favourites.

The long-nosed, breeze-sniffing, fang-licking collie dog of Richard III, the brazen trumpet call of Henry V, the broken-necked, eyeless howl of Oedipus, the sly, nimble old gibbon of Shallow, the anger-drunk, vein-swollen Coriolanus strangling an infinity of invisible snakes — these are only a few of the memorable moments in the Olivier repertory. But one of the reasons they are unforgettable is that we are always being reminded of them.

Olivier is born to action, bred for speed. In the National Theatre

Othello, he runs the gamut on the spot. It is a spectacular demonstration of static exercise like a man racing up a down escalator or
rowing with perforated paddles in a chained skiff.

The standard image for "Othello" is that of a bull fight – the blind,
bewildered beast pricked to death by the cruel agile matador. For
actors like Orson Welles or Frederick Valk, heavily armour-plated
rhomboids churning the mud with their tank tracks in search of the
hidden sharpshooter, this is a natural approach. But W. H. Auden
has supplied us with a new comparison:

Iago treats Othello as an analyst treats his patient, except that, of
course, his intention is to kill not to cure. Everything he says is
designed to bring to Othello's consciousness what he has already
guessed is there.

With an Othello such as Sir Laurence, handsome, commanding,
above all active and energetic, this might have been a promising hint
to a producer. But this interpretation calls for an Iago who is almost
a disembodied intelligence.

I have long admired Frank Finlay, the National Theatre Iago, but
no one could say that his stage presence suggests a cold, penetrating,
scientific intellect. And John Dexter has directed him to be racked
with sobs as he tells of Cassio's dream-confession of adultery, and to
sway shoulder to shoulder with Othello in a kind of mutual hypnosis
as he invents further details.

"Othello" is a curiously balanced play – until the middle of Act III,
Iago has almost three lines to every one of Othello's – so that if the
Moor and his Ancient are not fairly matched, it seems a fixed fight.
With Mr. Finlay's Iago so crude and insecure and rattled, Sir
Laurence must carry the burden of our attention.

He begins as a West Indian dandy flicking a frivolous rose. It is an
impersonation which might have seemed more convincing in the
days when Negroes of all shades and backgrounds were less commonly observed in London streets. Now the combination of a Louis
Armstrong guttural voice and a Stepin Fetchit sway and shuffle
appears rather perfunctory.

Sir Laurence is elaborately at ease, graceful and suave, more like a
seducer than a cuckold. But as the jealousy is transferred into his
blood, the white man shows through more obviously. He begins to
double and treble his vowels, to stretch his consonants, to stagger
and shake, even to vomit, near the frontiers of self-parody. His hips
oscillate, his palms rotate, his voice skids and slides so that the
Othello music takes on a Beatle beat.

Despite the deluge of purple prose from the critics, I cannot believe that Sir Laurence himself counts this as one of the great Othellos. It could be the last splendid fling of a declining style of acting. In Chekhov, he remains a master. But for the Elizabethans, our modern taste is drier, cooler, more precise, less extravagant.

HAROLD HOBSON IN *The Sunday Times:*

The National Theatre production at the Old Vic is not the first time that Laurence Olivier has played in *Othello*. Before the war Sir Laurence appeared as Iago to the Othello of Ralph Richardson. It was a memorable performance, alive with a sophistication unusual in those innocent days when the name of Wolfenden had not yet been heard in the land. Its excess of super-subtlety was such that it may be doubted whether Sir Ralph ever cottoned on to what his mercurial colleague was up to.

The only trace lingering of this interpretation of the play at the Old Vic is a scene in which, when Iago pours poison into Othello's ear, the two men, the African and the European, sway together in a sickening rhythm that suggests a bond uniting them closer than marriage. For the rest, Frank Finlay's convincing and powerful Iago is bluff, provincial, noisy and professionally jealous, sometimes goading himself into hysterical fury, less a Machiavelli than one of those amoeba-minded Southern Senators who still foam at the mouth at the thought of a black man and a white woman getting into bed together.

This is in keeping both with John Dexter's direction and Sir Laurence's sensational performance. Sensational it is: who would have believed that Sir Laurence could make his voice so deep and dark? Who could guess, when in the final scene Othello with one hand claps Desdemona tightly to him, by what a mighty feat of prestidigitation with the other Sir Laurence is going to stab himself, no knife being anywhere in sight? This last is only a decoration to the play, albeit an exciting one. It is one of many touches which show that Mr. Dexter, when with Sir Laurence he has settled the strategy of the production, still has plenty of invention left to make its tactics vigorous and unexpected.

This strategy demands that Iago should be thick-headed. The dominating social and political fact of today, as Arnold Toynbee has pointed out, is that everywhere there is a revolt against the ideals and the faith of the white races. This dynamic schism of our times is recognised in Mr. Dexter's production of "Othello"; in the light of this circumstance, *and the theatre being what it is,* it would be unrealistic to expect that Iago, the persecutor of the blacks, should be shown as a man of high, even if malicious, intelligence.

Sir Laurence's Othello fits into the context of the racial battle as cunningly as Mr. Finlay's Iago. Sir Laurence, challengingly made up as black as darkest night, each Negro characteristic emphasised, begins in a jovial, giggling, flower-twiddling tone. He has the wilful, tense, and nervous frivolity of a man who is not at home with the people among whom he lives. Making his apologia to the Senators, he stands in the midst of them with an uneasy insolence. He speaks with a grave, increasing dignity, but at the end of his account of his courtship he laughs apologetically, like a man trying to ingratiate himself with people he instinctively distrusts.

There is here a concern with the relations between the black and the white races which gives to this production a contemporary urgency lacking in its predecessors. With a curl of the lips, a catlike movement of the body, a roll of staring eyes, an uncomfortable mixture of arrogance and inferiority, Sir Laurence makes this "Othello" a world-drama as well as a tale of individual poignancy and betrayal.

There is little comfort, but much beauty, in Mr. Dexter's interpretation of the play. Before the evil and the cruelty and the unscrupulousness of the white man, the civilisation of Othello is stripped off. In Galsworthy's despairing phrase, it can't stand fire. In one of the tremendous climaxes of which Sir Laurence builds up an astounding series, flinging himself into the theatre of ritual which today commands the best part of our stage, this Othello tears the crucifix from his neck, and on his knees bows his head to the ancient gods of magic, barbarism, and human sacrifice.

The power, passion, verisimilitude, and pathos of Sir Laurence's performance are things which will be spoken of with wonder for a long time to come. Sir Laurence speaks the line "Not a jot" with a casual pain that is extremely moving; there is a tropical storm of energy in his "Othello's occupation's gone"; with Emilia he is extraordinary savage and intense; and to Maggie Smith's candid and rousing Desdemona tender and tormented.

RONALD BRYDEN IN *The New Statesman:*

All posterity will want to know is how he played. John Dexter's National Theatre *Othello* is efficient and clear, if slow, and contains some intelligent minor novelties. But in the long run all that matters is that it left the stage as bare as possible for its athlete. What requires record is how he, tackling Burbage's role for the first time at 57, created the Moor.

He came on smelling a rose, laughing softly with a private delight; barefooted, ankleted, black. He had chosen to play a Negro. The story fits a true Moor better: one of those striding hawks, fierce in a narrow range of medieval passions, whose women still veil themselves like Henry Moore sleepers against the blowing sand of Nouak-chott's surrealistically modern streets. But Shakespeare muddled, giving him the excuse to turn himself into a coastal African from below the Senegal: dark, thick-lipped, open, laughing.

He sauntered downstage, with a loose, bare-heeled roll of the buttocks; came to rest feet splayed apart, hip lounging outward. For him, the great *Richard III* of his day, the part was too simple. He had made it difficult and interesting for himself by studying, as scrupulously as he studied the flat vowels, dead grin and hunched time-steps of Archie Rice, how an African looks, moves, sounds. The make-up, exact in pigment, covered his body almost wholly: an hour's job at least. The hands hung big and graceful. The whole voice was characterised, the o's and a's deepened, the consonants thickened with faint, guttural deliberation. Keep up your bright swords, or de dew will rus' dem': not quite so crude, but in that direction.

It could have been caricature, an embarrassment. Instead, after the second performance, a well-known Negro actor rose in the stalls bravoing. For obviously it was done with love; with the main purpose of substituting for the dead grandeur of the Moorish empire one modern audiences could respond to: the grandeur of Africa. He was the continent, like a figure of Rubens allegory. In Cyprus, he strode ashore in a cloak and spiked helmet which brought to mind the medieval emirates of Ethiopia and Niger. Facing Doge and senators, he hooded his eyes in a pouting ebony mask: an old chief listening watchfully in tribal conclave. When he named them "my masters" it was proudly edged: he had been a slave, their inquisition recalled his slavery, he reminded them in turn of his service and generalship. He described Desdemona's encouragement smiling down at them, easy with sexual confidence. This was the other key to the choice of a Negro: Finlay's Iago, bony, crop-haired, staring with the fanatic mule-grin of a Mississippi redneck, was to be goaded by a small white man's sexual jealousy of the black, a jealousy sliding into ambiguous fascination. Like Yeats's crowd staring, sweating, at Don Juan's mighty thigh, this Iago gazed, licking dry lips, on a black one. All he need do is teach his own disease.

Mannerisms established, they were lifted into the older, broader imagery of the part. Leading Desdemona to bed, he pretended to snap at her with playful teeth. At Iago's first hints, he made a chuckling mock of twisting truth out of him by the ear. Then, during the temptation, he began to pace, turning his head sharply like a lion listening. The climax was his farewell to his occupation: bellowing the words as pure, wounded outcry, he hurled back his head until the ululating tongue showed pink against the roof of his mouth like a trumpeting elephant's. As he grew into a great beast, Finlay shrunk beside him, clinging to his shoulder like an ape, hugging his heels like a jackal.

He used every clue in the part, its most strenuous difficulties. Reassured by Desdemona's innocence, he bent to kiss her — and paused looking, sickened, at her lips. Long before his raging return, you knew he had found Cassio's kisses there. Faced with the lung-torturing hurdle of "Like to the Pontic sea," he found a brilliant device for breaking the period: at "Shall ne'er look back," he let the memories he was forswearing rush in and stop him, gasping with pain, until he caught breath. Then, at "By yon marble heaven," he tore the crucifix from his neck (Iago, you recall, says casually Othello'd renounce his baptism for Desdemona) and, crouching forehead to ground, made his "sacred vow" in the religion which caked Benin's altars with blood.

Possibly it was too early a climax, built to make a curtain of Iago's "I am your own for ever." In Act Four he could only repeat himself with increased volume, adding a humming animal moan as he fell into his fit, a strangler's look to the dangling hands, a sharper danger to the turns of his head as he questioned Emilia. But it gave him time to wind down to a superb returned dignity and tenderness for the murder. This became an act of love — at "I would not have thee linger in thy pain" he threw aside the pillow and, stopping her lips with a kiss, strangled her. The last speech was spoken kneeling on the bed, her body clutched upright to him as a shield for the dagger he turns on himself.

As he slumped beside her in the sheets, the current stopped. A couple of wigged actors stood awkwardly about. You could only pity them: we had seen history, and it was over. Perhaps it's as well to have seen the performance while still unripe, constructed in fragments, still knitting itself. Now you can see how it's done; later, it will be a torrent. But before it exhausts him, a film should be made. It couldn't save the whole truth, but it might save something the unborn should know.

BAMBER GASCOIGNE IN *The Observer:*

A happy birthday indeed. We could hardly have found three finer presents for Himself than the Brook-Scofield "King Lear," now in international orbit, the new "Henry IV" at Stratford, and finally — achieving the almost impossible task of outshining them both — Olivier's *Othello,* directed by John Dexter, at the National Theatre.

In the whole of this production I found only three small grumbles, which we can safely dismiss in the ante-chamber. For some strange reason Brabantio's first speech to the Duke is spoken most irritatingly to Lodovico. In the early scenes Frank Finlay's Iago refuses to rely on his excellent voice to mould and ferret out the meaning of a phrase but backs each speech with a relentless manual geometry of circles and lines and stabs of emphasis; a little of this would be effective; more is both irritating and unnecessary. And there are a couple of passages which Olivier, in his extraordinarily detailed characterisation, seems not yet to have fully digested.

One of the chief qualities of the Moor is his passion for exaggeration. He imagines Desdemona sleeping with the whole army, pioneers included; that Cassio must have tupped her 1,000 times; would he had 40,000 lives and could be nine years a-dying. Olivier rightly plays some of the more bombastic fancies as exhibitionism, mere indulgence, but once or twice it still seems his indulgence rather than Othello's. Those three complaints are all. The slate is clean for sheer critical revelry.

The first amazement about Olivier is his physical transformation. To adapt the song, he walks like a Negro, talks like a Negro: from his hairless shins, drooping eye-lids, the stipulated "thick lips" of the text and a loose hip-rolling walk, which I thought at first might prove a caricature but which remains firmly real, to the uncanny inflections in his voice or the deep-throated chuckle with which he parries Iago's preliminary thrusts.

This Moor has an almost aggressive ease among all those stilted whites. When being accused by Brabantio he strikes a pose of heroic nonchalance, his left hand flamboyantly languishing on the hilt of his sword. Occasionally he crosses himself, chiefly, it would seem, because he does the movement so beautifully. Watching him, you can blink between two fascinating viewpoints. Either, with some difficulty, you peer through the pretence and just manage to make out the familiar figure of Sir Laurence Olivier at work. Or you happily relax and see, as if for ever, Othello himself.

The strong physical aura of this performance extends into Othello's relationships. It makes the actions of Frank Finlay's almost frail Iago seem exceedingly dangerous, as if a young matador were teasing a very large and ferocious bull. And it creates with Maggie Smith's calm and extremely moving Desdemona an atmosphere of the most potent sensuality. In their earlier encounters these two meet only in public and, though they are already married, Shakespeare apparently defers their consummation until the night of triumph in Cyprus. Until that moment they achieve little more than a chaste kiss, but even standing together among soldiers or courtiers the sexual promise between them is electric.

This passionate link continues through all the upheavals until the bedroom scene itself, where it is shattered by Desdemona's sudden moment of realisation and panic; "Kill me tomorrow." And it returns in tragic parody for Othello's great last speech about the base Indian who threw a pearl away, for which Olivier kneels on the bed hugging Desdemona up to him, her head lolling on his shoulder. He achieved the same effect last autumn in his direction of the graveyard scene in "Hamlet," with Ophelia buffeted between her quarrelling men.

For Maggie Smith, up till now famous as one of our very best comediennes, this Desdemona marks a most spectacular triumph. Her stillness, the very opposite of her style of comedy, seemed to make the whole auditorium hold its breath in the willow song scene; even the most ordinary words, such as "Nay, that's not next," when she sings a wrong line, became inexplicably poignant. And Joyce Redman, as Emilia with Desdemona kneeling at her feet, managed brilliantly to speak her polemic about men's infidelity in such a way as even then not to break the mood.

Frank Finlay's most subtle Iago is the only one I have ever seen who comes near to justifying the title "honest, honest." He also makes the perfect touchstone for all the other characters. He seems flimsy beside Othello, power incarnate in his treatment of the foppish but never unreal Roderigo of Michael Rothwell; entirely callous to his wife, Emilia, but an ordinary, rough soldier when with Derek Jacobi's neat Cassio.

Unobtrusive behind all this is John Dexter's exceptionally rich and careful direction. Always a director's real task, far more important than any sweeping re-interpretation, is to help the actors towards the implications (whether by pauses, or glances or whatever) which will spark the life lurking behind the even tread of the lines on the page. Under Dexter's guidance every word breathes. And Jocelyn Herbert's set gives equally tactful support.

In the meteoric rise of this amazingly varied company (no two actors seem even similar) "Othello" makes probably the brightest blaze so far. In the programme there are prints of Kean and other famous Othellos. It was strange to sit in the audience on Tuesday and gradually to realise that the living reality was as historic as those prints.

Robert Brustein

Mr. Brustein was formerly drama critic for *The New Republic* and is presently Dean of the Yale Drama School. His experiences in theatre have been intensely creative and intensely meaningful in any consideration of the development of drama in America. His reviews reveal an understanding of production and acting methods, of directorial intention, and of fields of learning and study related to the theatre. His perceptions of both Brecht and Bolt involve a grasp of history and the importance of plays concerned with society itself. Mr. Brustein is the author of *The Theatre of Revolt,* a study of the major playwrights of the past century.

BRECHT ON THE RAMPAGE

MAN IS MAN *by Bertolt Brecht, translated by Gerhard Nellhaus: Living Theatre;* A MAN'S A MAN *by Bertolt Brecht, adapted by Eric Bentley*

At the conclusion of Shaw's *St. Joan,* when the Maid — long martyred and newly canonized — offers to return to earth as a living woman, all her worshipers blench. "What?" she askes. "Must I burn

again? Are none of you ready to receive me?" Cauchon replies:
"The heretic is always better dead. And mortal eyes cannot distinguish the saint from the heretic." Mortal eyes have had a similar
difficulty, lately, with Bertolt Brecht. A heretic recently sanctified by
Pope Fashion, Brecht is still totally unacceptable as a living being.
For the past year, the dramatist's remains have been on display in a
crypt called *Brecht on Brecht,* where a few trifling pieces of his
anatomy—raised eyebrows, wrinkled nose, twinkling eyes—have
become objects of veneration by a relic-hungry public. But when the
living Brecht, a compound of spleen, horns, and genitalia, rampages
like a maddened bull down our tame, "sophisticated" stage, the
audiences, and the reviewers, begin to scatter in terror. Instead of a
genial Socratic humanitarian with some neat theatrical tricks up his
sleeve, an ugly, brutal, dangerous artist confronts them; and Brecht
must burn again.

Unfleshed, repetitive, and sometimes a little tedious, *Mann ist
Mann* is a minor work of its author, but since this makes it a major
work of any New York season, one suspects the offense lies in its
heresy: it is a savage clown show which uses the devices of farce,
vaudeville, Expressionism, and cabaret theatre to demonstrate the
total insignificance of the individual personality in the modern
world. Located in a fantastic, Kiplingesque India, complete with
Imperial British soldiers, an Oriental bonze, an all-girl orchestra,
and the ubiquitous Widow Begbick (she appears again in that superb
Brecht-Weill masterpiece, *Mahagonny)*, the play follows the metamorphosis of the meek laborer, Galy Gay, into the "human fighting
machine," Jeriah Jip. The real Jip, the fourth member of a machine-
gun unit, has been incapacitated while drunkenly helping to plunder
a Chinese pagoda; his three comrades need someone to conceal their
own part in this hilariously funny crime; and Gay, "a man who can't
say no," looks like the ideal fall guy. The soldiers, however, have to
impress upon Gay the dangers of insisting on one's name; and they
do so in a series of fast circus numbers, during which Gay is
apprehended for selling a phony elephant—tried, convicted, shot
(with blanks), and forced to read a funeral oration over his own
corpse. These tactics of terror are partially effective, but what really
transforms Gay into Jip is the fate of the sadistic sergeant, Bloody
Five. An army-manual martinet when the sun shines, Bloody Five
cannot control his gargantuan lust when it rains; and in order to
remain "myself," he is ultimately forced to shoot away his manhood.
Gay, witnessing the violent consequences of being a "great person-

ality," is finally convinced of the importance of being a cipher, for acquiescence means safety and survival. Wolfing down the rations of his three tormentors, he proceeds to blow up, single-handedly, a Tibetan fortress. Gay equals Jip. Man equals Man. One man's the same as another.

"As has been demonstrated" — so ends a later version of the play — and reviewers have been inclined to criticize the Q.E.D. simplicity of the plot line. But the simplicity lies in them — the play is exceedingly devious, its complexity rooted in the author's ambiguous feelings toward his own demonstration. For Brecht is saying both that the human will is weak and malleable, and that it is savage, brutal, and uncontrollable — that man is forced to conform by a cruel, oppressive society, and that he must conform in order to suppress the murder in his heart. Brecht's horrified awareness of external and internal anarchy accounts for his rejection of Romantic individualism, and it is the subject of all his early, semi-autobiographical work. In *Baal,* for example, he follows the career of a ruthless, bisexual poet who satisfies his instincts without conscience, and finally dies amidst offal and urine, declaring that the world is merely "the excrement of God"; in *In the Jungle of Cities,* he shows the awful consequences of maintaining personal opinions, concluding when his rebellious hero repudiates his idealism in order to escape with his "naked life"; and in *Mann ist Mann,* he rejects altogether the chaos of personal identity, beginning to insist on the complete extinction of the personality. From this, it is only one step either to Communism or to Buddhism; and, as a matter of fact, Brecht commits himself to Communism like a submissive Buddhist monk, trying to lose himself in a process which will satisfy both his impulse to revolt, and his desire to discipline his terrifying aggressive impulses. But no matter how "rational," "scientific," and ideological the surfaces of his plays become, the depths are always rumbling with poetic intensity and Neo-Romantic horror, and those savage aggressions which Brecht could never quite subdue.

The two versions now on view at the Masque and The Living Theatre represent two stages in Brecht's continual revisions of the play. Eric Bentley's free adaptation of an earlier text emphasizes its comic-anarchistic elements, Gerhard Nellhaus' translation of a later variant, its more serious Marxist implications. Those interested in the development of Brecht's thinking will profit from both, for both are excellent. Both productions should also be seen, though for opposite reasons. Neither is excellent; and only between them can one begin to collate a satisfactory interpretation. John Hancock's production at the Masque has the advantage of a strong external concept, aided by Bentley's interpolated additions (including a wicked parody of "Gunga Din"). An amusing prologue and ironic legends introduce the action; the high button shoes, fringed dresses, and ratty fur pieces of the women evoke the smoky decadence of the Berlin cabarets; and the clever use of make-up illustrates first the contrast, then the union, between Gay and the others, as he gradually assumes the pasty white mask that everyone wears.

But the acting at the Masque is too casual and relaxed, not sufficiently ironic or styled. John Heffernan as Gay—too much the corn-fed innocent throughout most of the evening—creates a fine surrealistic concluding scene in which he roars about the stage like a tank stripping its gears, and Clifton James occasionally suggests some of the bloated menace that should be in the soldiers. But the rest of the military seems to have been recruited from the Harvard R.O.T.C. (Bloody Five from the U.S. Marines), and the whores tend to mince like Wellesley girls. At The Living Theatre, the acting is also indifferent; but at least it is not middle-class. Some of the performances are amateurish; some, like Joseph Chaikin's Galy Gay, too screechingly intense. Still, three characters leap from the stage with astonishing life: Warren Finnerty's fierce cockney Bloody Five; William Shari's reptilian Uriah; Benjamin Hayeem's Mr. Wang, a nasal, whining, toothy, obsequious Oriental cartoon. And though Julian Beck's functional bamboo and canvas setting is more impressive than his direction, he does manage to get a harsh, macabre, dirty quality into the play which sometimes startles you into discomforted attention.

Mann ist Mann shows Brecht thumbing his nose at nineteenth-century ideals, which is to say, at the ideals held by most of the twentieth-century West: freedom, heroism, liberalism, and the sanctity of "personal opinions." "An easygoing man can really have two or three different opinions at the same time," notes one cynical character—(if you doubt the truth of this, read a review by Howard Taubman)—and Brecht's agonized perception of the insignificance of the individual in a Copernican universe forms the basis both of his politics and of his art. Mass wars and mass states prove his contention; but his art belies it. For in writings like Brecht's the complicated opinions of a highly gifted individual still find their expression, transformed into an enduring testament of unremitting revolt.

CHRONICLE OF A RELUCTANT HERO

A MAN FOR ALL SEASONS *by Robert Bolt*

After some years of neglect, the chronicle history play has been enjoying a rebirth among the more literary English and French dramatists. Up till now, the results have been rather indifferent, but in Robert Bolt's *A Man for All Seasons* we finally have an effective example of the genre. A faithful account of the martyrdom of Sir Thomas More, this work is too diffuse to be completely successful; yet, compared with more vulgar dramatic biographies like Anouilh's *Becket* and Osborne's *Luther,* it shows remarkable intelligence, historicity, theatrical ingenuity, and good taste. I confess that the work took me by surprise, for nothing in Bolt's last entry, an inept piece of contemporary realism called *Flowering Cherry,* prepared me for the kind of form and substance he handles with such authority here. Yet, I can think of at least two reasons why he and his contemporaries are now turning to history for their subject matter. As Bolt unwittingly demonstrated in *Flowering Cherry,* modern man has become so trivial and uninteresting that he has lost his power to involve us, while modern mass society has inhibited even the superior spirits from expressing themselves through significant action. When human destinies are arbitrated primarily by bureaucrats, "Creon's secretaries," to quote Dürrenmatt's wistfully beautiful insight, "close Antigone's books." In an age without heroes, artists can lament our vacancy and spiritual undernourishment, like Samuel Beckett, or invent subjective heroic fantasies, like Jean Genet, or rake in the embers of the past for adequate human material, like the new dramatic chroniclers. Or, when they have no past, no history, no tradition, they can congratulate us on our triumphant mediocrity, like the Broadway dramatists — but this approach is beneath discussion.

A second reason for the growing popularity of the history play has to do with the influence of Brecht, who brought new eyes to the past and new techniques for putting it on the stage. It is Brecht's spirit, tempered by the spirit of Elizabethan drama and of More himself (whose writings, transcripts, and proverbialisms appear as dialogue in the play), that hovers over Bolt's new work, just as it is the spirit of Teo Otto, Brecht's scenic designer, that inhabits Motley's setting — a handsome unit of simple polished Tudor stairs, located by various signs, emblems, and props dropped from the flies. For the purpose of setting the stage, bridging transitions, and commenting on the action, Bolt has supplied a Brechtian Chorus, who also plays all the lower class characters—a greedy, ironic, calculating opportunist called (with none of the usual Broadway toadying to this type) the Common Man. And just as Bolt's Chorus assumes some of the functions of the Story Teller in *The Caucasian Chalk Circle,* so Bolt's interpretation of More—the great humanist, lawyer, statesman, and saint, who lost his life for opposing Henry VIII's divorce and the English Reformation which followed it—recalls Brecht's concept of Galileo, another historical figure hounded by authorities.

More (whose conversation, according to Erasmus, was "all of jesting and of fun") has usually been treated on the stage as a madcap: the Elizabethan play, *Sir Thomas More,* even has him cracking jokes on the scaffold. Without scanting More's wit, Bolt interprets him more as a melancholy intellectual aristocrat, desperately trying to preserve some corner of private conscience, while preserving his life at the same time. Unlike some of the rasher spirits who surround him, More is prudent and discreet ("Our natural business lies in escaping"), and inclined to protect himself behind legalistic subterfuges. When asked to swear to the Acts of Succession, establishing Henry's divorce and his control over the English Church, he simply maintains silence. Determined not to be a martyr if he can help it, he could probably defend his strategy with the same aphorism as Brecht's Galileo: "Unhappy is the land that needs a hero." More, however, is reluctantly nudged into heroism when all escape routes have been closed. Imprisoned and brought to trial by Henry's minister, a "dockside bully" named Thomas Cromwell, More is goaded to break his silence; but only when he has been convicted on the basis of a witness' perjury does he rise to declare the new Acts "directly repugnant to the law of God." As he delivers himself to the headsman, the Common Man tells the audience, with a salacious wink: "It isn't difficult to stay alive, friends—*just don't make trouble!*" More's death, the wages of integrity, is for the ages; but the moral is for our own time, when the common man ("the master statesman of us all") preserves his skin through compromise and accommodation.

Noel Willman's production is excellent—tight, fluid, graceful, by turns both rowdy and dignified—and the entire cast is impeccable, from George Rose's sardonic Common Man, hastily burrowing in a basket for his various costume changes, through Albert Dekker's Norfolk, played with the robustness of a growling Tudor mastiff, Keith Baxter's Henry, cast against type as a lithe, muscular, egocentric golden boy, and Leo McKern's Cromwell, a pudgy Machiavellian humorist of astonishing dexterity (at one audacious point he leaps backward upon a table). But the play is really a tour de force for Paul Scofield, who superbly endows the leading role with that most elusive of all acting qualities: sheer intelligence. Looking like Holbein's portrait, dowdy, laconic, wry, sweet, mellow, dreamy and humorous (his irony is reminiscent of Oliver's), he tells us almost as much about the quality of More's mind as the play itself, and a good deal more about the quality of More's emotions—especially in one scene where he breaks down quietly over a custard that his wife has brought him in prison. It is a soft expressive moment in a performance of exquisitely subtle modulation (Scofield raises his voice only once in the entire evening); and, if the play tends to fade a little after its initial impact, Scofield's More remains indelibly fixed in your memory.

Nigel Dennis

Mr. Dennis is staff reviewer of *The Sunday Telegraph* (London) and dramatic critic for *Encounter;* while living in the United States, he wrote reviews for *The New Republic* and joined the staff of *Time.* He has written in many forms, including the novel, and his journalistic prose stands head and shoulders above that of most of his colleagues. Taking an aristocratic view of the stage and the purpose of plays, Dennis' piece on *A Man for All Seasons* laments a loss of stature in character portraiture and language which, he suggests, is all too typical of modern drama on historical subjects. Mr. Dennis misses the excitement of "our broad imagination," and his essay applies generally to a particular—and important—form of audience response to theatre.

from DOWN AMONG THE DEAD MEN

... Most actors, today, try their best to be people—and most playwrights, of course, do their best to see that they have parts only

From *Dramatic Essays* by Nigel Dennis. Reprinted by permission of A. M. Heath & Company Ltd. (London), agents for the author, and George Weidenfeld & Nicolson Limited (London).

for people in their plays. Persons are absolutely out: the object is for the people in the auditorium to feel that those who are on the stage are as frankly people as they are themselves. When Mr. Robert Bolt, for instance, writes *A Man For All Seasons,* it is not his intention to let any Tudor person excite our broad imagination. "The action of this play ends in 1535," he notes, "but the play was written in 1960, and if in production one date must obscure the other, it is 1960 which I would wish clearly to occupy the stage." Such a mischievous wish is easily granted by presenting the stage as Tudor and its occupants as people of 1960. Mr. Paul Scofield appears in the costume of Sir Thomas More, but not in the person of Sir Thomas More; his duty is not to let his old-fashioned clothing disguise the fact that he is a very decent QC caught in a tight corner of 1960. That is why we must regard his cloaks and chains as mere whims—comparable to the Regency wallpaper in the modern drawing-room which, far from indicating how far back the owner is in time, announces how well he is keeping up with modern fashions. Mr. Scofield's face, humanely haggard from the start, and his voice, sweetly democratic throughout, declare without any words being really necessary that, unlike Oedipus or Lear, he is going to meet a fate that will be essentially *popular.* In this, he will be helped first by Mr. Bolt, who will see to it that no trace of the ostensible epoch appears in the spoken words, and second by the supporting players, who will guarantee to be only 1960 people, however Tudorially they may be dressed and despite any handles that may be affixed to their names. As Cardinal Wolsey, Mr. Willoughby Goddard fails badly in the above respects, playing the role with style and appearing to be an impressive person; but the rest of the cast understands the modernity of More's problem as thoroughly as could be wished. One sees immediately, for instance, that the Duke of Norfolk is not *really* the Duke of Norfolk: inwardly, he is as much a people as you and me, and his inward will always peep out through his outward. Even Henry VIII, who differed in so many ways from ourselves and might therefore have been portrayed as a person of Tudor times, or even a personage, can be seen to be a pure people, no matter how loud the trumpets or how royal the gestures. The argument here, no doubt, is that if everyone else on the stage is going to be people, it would be unfair to Henry to make him anything so unnatural as a person: this is known, in all artistic matters, as the democratic fallacy, and inflicts mortal injuries upon the stouter figures of the pre-democratic past. Indeed, it injures large figures of any period—as we may see by Mr. Terence Ratti-

gan's *Ross,* wherein the highly exceptional person of Colonel Lawrence is reduced to people's stature as neatly as if an executioner's
axe had taken him off at the neck.

The films are instructive in this matter. When Mr. Spencer Tracy
appeared in Hollywood, his incomparable merits — humility, integrity, decency, loyalty — were seized upon eagerly. It was seen that
his place in a film was one step down from the dramatic top — which
would be filled by Mr. Clark Gable. While Mr. Tracy's honest face
underwent a hundred pangs of unrequited love and long-suffering
loyalty, Mr. Gable's ugly, black mug slew the girls and won the
prizes. It deserved to. Mr. Tracy's virtues were simply not dramatic.
Mr. Gables vices were.

It is this order of precedence that we are changing today. Not
content with being good ourselves, we want to make our dramatic
principals good too. Mr. Spencer Tracy — or Mr. Paul Scofield, or Sir
Thomas More, or whatever we like to call him — is upped into top
place; while Mr. Clark Gable degenerates into a perverted Turkish
pasha or something nasty like Thomas Cromwell. Our heroes bathe
us from the stage in sweetness and decency, and so great are their
efforts not to appear heroic that we scarcely notice that they are on
the stage at all. Because we believe that life and drama should be
synonymous and identical we have forgotten that the wand used to
wave in the opposite direction — that authors like to make their
characters much larger than life, and actors pulled on high boots
and wore tall masks to make sure that their decapitations were of
consequence. Probably it became irritating after some hundreds of
years and may even have seemed artificial. But never, surely, as
artificial as the beheading of Mr. Scofield for no worse crime than
that of struggling to be as undramatic as possible?

If we must have heroes who are good all through, is there no way
in which we can make them more interesting? Aubrey tells an
amusing story of Sir William Roper coming to More's house in
search of a bride and being led upstairs to the bedroom where
More's two daughters were asleep in one bed. More whipped off the
covers; the naked girls whipped over on their stomachs, and Roper,
remarking that he had now seen both sides of them, chose Margaret
as his bride by tapping her on the behind. There was no suggestion
of this in Mr. Bolt's play, presumably because the work is addressed
to 1960, when courtship of the Lord Chancellor's daughter is so
much nicer. But this only shows how careful an author should be
when he summons up the dead to instruct the living. Robbed of the

ginger that made them persons, they are a flaccid people. Deprived of their period poses, stances, and vulgarities, they are wholly dependent on us to give them a style — and style is the one thing we are determined not to supply. We steal the message but reject the person; and it is amusing that a theatre that values the "natural" above all should, by going all out for it, lose in the end not only human artifice, but human nature too.

What the living stage is in danger of losing can be seen by a visit to a good puppet show. The jointed, wooden figures, dependent upon wires for all their movements and upon hidden accompanists for all their utterances, are stylists because they cannot help themselves. No matter how variously they may be dressed and painted they have a unity of style, for however skilfully they are towed across a stage, a certain stiffness impedes their naturalness — which is to say, their limitations give style to their movements just as manners and protocol gave style to the movements of courtiers. A puppet cannot be hurried beyond a certain speed without betraying his inhumanity; and this, too, is a happy limitation, in that it obliges the puppet-master to exploit his actor precisely or not at all. The limbs of a puppet being detachable opens the door to unlimited farce — and when one sees the heads and arms of puppets flying across the stage, one realizes that these civilized little dolls would be exploited as unscrupulously as human actors by their vulgar owners if it were not for their brainlessness and other, blessed, limitations. Puppets, thanks to the very nature of themselves, make unspoken, inflexible demands which must be met: no author can easily give them a message for modern times; no producer can convince them that his own fashionable method of doing something is the very last word in dramatic art. Puppets even demand to be accompanied by strictly-appropriate composers; nothing, for example, will induce them to work with Wagner, whose unbridled romanticism asks too much of their legs. Mendelssohn they can manage very well, having an aptitude for swaying movements and sentimental gestures; but there is no doubt that they are happiest in the world of classical composition, where all is dictated by formality and precision and through which they are able to lead us back to the high severities of the Japanese and Greek theatres. Puppets have been famous for centuries for their playing of harpsichords, pianos, violins, and trumpets; even the slide-trombone can be taken in their stride. But precisely because they are such good instrumentalists, much advantage has often been taken of them, and, in the hands of Italians, they are forced frequently into *opera buffa* in a way that is entirely human and unbecoming. Luminous paints of a garish kind, indefinitely-extensible spring necks, blue-jeans, and the influence of Walt Disney have all helped to corrupt these immaculate little persons, and if ever a means of making them walk properly is found there is no doubt that they will become indistinguishable from living actors and all style lost forever. Many of the male puppets are already tyrannously abused; but the appeal of the long skirt, which hides the jerky stutterings of the feet, is so obvious even to the most ignorant human showman that the future of the lady-puppets is much brighter and they may long continue to recapture the past with an accuracy denied to modern dramatists. Puppets play, of course, on a very small stage that is erected upon the boards of an ordinary stage; seen from the cinders of Rugby they and their stage would seem inordinately small. But this is only an illusion; on leaving the theatre the memory carries away images of life-sized persons, which is again much better than a theatre that starts off with life-sized people but fills the departing memory with recollections of dwarfs. Indeed, any heroic part can always be admirably played by a puppet, since style and heroism, at least on the stage, are inextricably joined; and in the recent production of Podrecca's Piccoli Theatre at the Victoria Palace the puppets showed themselves to perfection even as exponents of bull-fighting. The matador's address to the President, prior to engaging the bull, was a model example of how pride and sobriety commingle in a stage person, and the cries and salutes that greeted each successful pass were no less lusty for being studiedly grandiose. Most of the remainder of the numbers displayed atrociously the vulgarities we have listed above, and yet even they had moments of severity which no amount of degradation and bad script writing could ruin entirely. This would seem to be the difference between the puppet-and the living-stages: no matter how bad the former may be, it is never without style of sorts and, unlike the latter, can never be described as wooden.

Stark Young

The delicacy, nuance, and clarity of perception of Stark Young's theatre reviews have never been surpassed in the United States — and very few English critics have equalled him in these qualities. He began his career on the staff of *The New Republic;* he also wrote reviews for the *New York Times* as well as a number of books on many subjects connected with the theatre. He has translated Chekhov's *The Sea Gull* and several other plays originally written in Italian and Spanish.

Young's remarks on the performances of the Moscow Art Theatre during this company's visit to New York in 1923 remain a hallmark of critical understanding, of *re*creative description of the total effect of a production, never slighting details of technique, of stage setting, or of directorial conception. His personal associations with many of the leading figures of world drama — from Pirandello and Hofmannsthal to O'Neill and Yeats, from Robert Edmond Jones and Reinhardt to Chaplin, Gielgud, and Duse — have enriched his own perceptions and, in turn, those of his countless readers.

❧ *ON PERFORMANCES OF THE MOSCOW ART THEATRE IN NEW YORK*

Jolson's Fifty-ninth Street Theatre. January 8, 1923.

Mr. Oliver Sayler's admirable book, combined with the most intelligent and effective publicity in the course of our theatre, had made us familiar with the Moscow Art Theatre before we ever saw it. And twenty years of criticism have established the main qualities and theories of this group of artists; everyone knows that their method is the representational, which professes the intention of ignoring the presence of spectators and of producing an effect of life as life would be seen going on if the fourth wall of a room were removed; everyone knows by now the phrase "spiritual realism," implying a selection among realistic details that can bring out the inmost spirit of the actual matter. And everyone knows about the exhaustive search for right particulars, the last perfection of illusion in make-up; the spirit of the group working together under Stanislavsky; the competent training that makes it possible to exchange roles among the actors; and the sincerity of approach to the meaning of the dramatist. About the Moscow Art Theatre these are all by now the merest commonplaces; one may see these players through phrases at least if not through the eyes. So that, even more than usual, criticism is free to be a personal affair.

Well, for my part, if I had seen the Moscow company in nothing but their historical poetic drama, *Tsar Fyodor,* I should have been very much disappointed. In this performance I saw that Moskvin was a very fine actor, with an art that was fluid, continuous, pathetic in the deepest sense. I saw that Mme. Knipper-Chekhova was a highly competent actress, and that everyone in the company played carefully, freely, well. The costumes too were superb and evidently correct so far as history goes, the jewels likewise. The palace rooms were plainly authentic canvases of rooms to be found somewhere in Russia, very rich and entertaining. The ensembles were astonishing; as individuals and as a mass the actors in them were convincing and lifelike. And over the whole stage there was—that seven days' wonder of stage directors—a complete air of human beings living there in the familiar ways of men. All these virtues were easy to see in the performance; but, except for bits of pathetic acting and for moments of pictorial beauty of figures and garments, I cared nothing about it. I have no interest in poetry taken as prose, and almost no interest in history taken, but for its mask of antique trappings, as contemporaneous human life. For the truth of history seems to me to be a combination of actuality and remoteness. Of this sixteenth century matter of men, equipage and event, the reality to me is the *idea* of it, and this includes the vista of time as one of its chief elements. In other words, in the performance of an imperial ancient story like this of the *Tsar Fyodor* I should like the style of the acting to achieve not the studied naturalness that we take daily as the ways of men but the form, the magic of distance and scope, the conscious arrangement, the artifice and logic, that would create in my mind the idea. And with jewels and arms and clothes I can see the merely correct history of them in museums if I choose; what I want on the stage is these things translated into stage terms, restated with that luster and relief, to use Coquelin's phrase, that would make them art. In sum, I wanted through all the play less of what that sixteenth century situation may or may not have been and more of what to me it really is. Chaliapin in Boris, then, yes, that was another school of art, that had great style, simplification, removal, magnificent idea; it remained in the mind like music, like great poetry, great abstractions; it was independent of every concern outside its moment, complete in itself. But for this Moscow Art Theatre's fine production of Alexis Tolstoy's historical poetic drama, I was professionally attentive, admiring, but quite unmoved, indifferent. The effort and theory of making the past as natural as if it were the present seems to me only a deficiency in cultural perspective.

As to the décor for *Tsar Fyodor,* I should say that though the device of lowering the richly colored palace ceilings in order to heighten the effect of tallness in those burly knights was a clever one, the décor in general of *The Birthday of the Infanta* knocked this Russian enterprise into a cocked hat. This Russian culture, warmhearted and adolescent, and for us too sweated out with theatre publicity, is not to be taken too seriously.

Of Gorki's play, with its mixture of the dregs of the world, the fallen baron, the fallen actor, the cynical philosopher, the old prostitute, Anna the dying woman, Luka the pilgrim, and the crowd of others, and its remarkable achievement of a kind of heightened and violently crude poetic actuality, the performance seemed to me not wholly convincing but more satisfying than that of the *Tsar Fyodor.* There were passages of fine directing and fine acting all the way through—that last scene of the play, for example, where the lodgers left in the place talk together, with its haunting fervor and ironic desolation; or the scene in the courtyard where the old man and his young wife talk from the window above to the group below, incomparable moment of pure theatre, glittering, bitter and pagan and gay, like two colors laughing together; and most of all the beautiful, faultless scenes where Luka the pilgrim ministers to the dying woman. Fine moments and some fine acting, Moskvin, Mme. Knipper-Chekhova and Kachalov, and stretches of extraordinary poetic realism; and now and then a vast, compelling mood over all, these were the achievements of the Gorki play. But what let me down and left me dashed and disappointed was the broken quality of the performance as a whole. Too often it separated into parts. Character after character stood out to the eye, heavily accented, without a blur. Stanislavsky's Satine was the worst of these—and on this general point there can be no argument, someone was wrong, either Moskvin or Stanislavsky, since Moskvin was exactly the contrary to Stanislavsky. The picture he conveyed was a complete blend without obvious accentuation. Satine's coat, his waistcoat, his shirt, his socks, his shoes, his cap, his beard, he could not turn or move but I ran into more shreds and patches, white stitches, ragged edges, everything insufferably scored—as his speeches, for all their great intelligence, were scored—like the work of a brilliant amateur. And too many of the events in this performance stood as brightly apart as the characters: Alyosha's entrance, for one example, where he danced into the room so delightfully in his rose-colored togs, was quite as much a "number" as anything ever seen in vaudeville. All this spotting and separate rhythm and glare would be well enough so far as I am concerned; I like the effect of pure theatre frankly played as such; and I like the presentation of Gorki's play as high theatricality, which it essentially is rather than naturalism; but the possibilities in this direction were crippled by the Moscow production's working in the opposite, they worked on an assumption of exact realism, and so mixed matters up. On the whole I came away, when the performance was over, stirred and swept and shaken in my memory as after certain great numbers on a concert program, but with no sense of any deep mood or of one single, profound experience, either of art or of poignant life.

The two Chekhov plays were another matter! Here was that rarest of events in the theatre anywhere, the combination of acting, producing and dramatic writing, one proceeding from another and all illuminating one idea. Some of the players were manifestly past their prime — it is only intelligent to recognize that — but it mattered very little; what they did seemed forever right and fine. I saw there on the stage Chekhov's characterizations, so whimsical, pitiful, keen, exact; I saw Chekhov's art come true, all the strange, incessant flux of it, its quivering and exposed humanity, its pathetic confusion of tragic, comic, inane and grotesque. I saw more than ever the likeness between Chekhov's method and Shakespeare's. Shakespeare starting with a fundamental emotion or state of mind, finds facet after facet for the surface of its expression; he makes images, comparisons, ornaments, elaborations of musical cadence, all of them springing from one source and all taken together revealing it. Shakespeare allowed himself every freedom in the poetic method, to use any flight or exaggeration or happy impossibility to secure his end. Chekhov uses only words and actions that are possible in actual daily life that are seen and heard by the eyes and ears. As Shakespeare uses his poetic details Chekhov uses these actualities, throwing together item after item, often seemingly incongruous things, weeping, kissing the furniture, calling on memory and God, asking for water, reproaching a man for trimming his beard, in order to convey the fundamental emotion from which they sprang and which they must reveal. Without using any means that might not be perfectly possible and actual, Chekhov contrives to give us the utmost shock and center of the life he portrays. Shakespeare's scope and power make another discussion; but, though in such diverse regions, this similarity of method between him and Chekhov is full of significance; and it appears unbelievably in the Moscow Art Theatre's interpretation. And out of this modern and realistic art I got something of the same thing that comes off from Shakespeare: the tragic excitement, the vivacity and pathetic beauty, the baffling logic of emotion, the thrill that comes from a sense of truth.

What the visit of the Moscow Art Theatre means to the New York stage seems to be clear enough. It is not that this school or method of production is a new genre; this is in fact what we have had on hand for a generation or more, and tend of late to depart from. It is not that the drama these players bring with them is in any sense new; Chekhov differs only in depth and technical perfection, not in kind, from Cylde Fitch. It is not that we have seen no acting so good as this on our own stage; in single scenes at least I have seen Jefferson, Pauline Lord, David Warfield, Laurette Taylor and others do quite as good realistic acting as any of these Russians. It is not that the scenery of the Moscow Art Theatre can teach us anything; in their present state these settings are battered and much mended, and would, I am sure, have been cast off long ago if the company's finances had permitted; and this scenery belongs to the school that we have seen exhausted by producers like Henry Irving and Belasco; and as exact realism or illusion it has, moreover, been infinitely surpassed by such settings as the Robert Edmond Jones actual barroom in the first scene of *Anna Christie*.

What the Moscow Art Theatre means to our stage—apart from our delight in mere proficiency—is something that is more moral and ethical than aesthetic, in so far as morality can be distinguished from the aesthetic. Chekhov's plays carry realism to an honest and spiritual depth and candor and to a relentless, poignant perfection and truth. These actors can act not only one scene or one play but, through humility and long labor at learning the technique of their art, they are equally competent throughout many parts. They represent a group of sincere artists, created by their art, rich by their intense living in it, and sure of all art's importance and duration. They are artists that have been working together thoroughly and through many years, in an organization, and under a distinguished and sympathetic leader, and for a devoted public. And, most significant of all, they possess a racial or popular life from which they can draw their belief and idea.

Philip Weissman

As in his previous observations on the director of plays (in Part III of this volume), this distinguished doctor and psychoanalyst discusses aspects of personality and creativity relevant here to the "role" of the dramatic critic. Of particular importance — and of interest to any student of theatre or production work — are Weissman's conclusions about those "endowments which enable [the critic or the audience generally] to respond to works of art"; for in such response reside those vital perceptive faculties which enable one to grasp a work on stage as an embodiment of reality. Weissman also discusses the comparative abilities of the critic and the practitioner of an art form as well as reasons why the critical act of perception can be, in its way, entirely creative.

ᴞ *from* THE CRITIC

Creative imagination in the theater is not confined to only those who originate, direct, and perform. Perhaps the most neglected member of the creative world has been the audience for whose consumption the work of art has always been intended. Understandably, the audience must be endowed with some form of creative capacities which lead to aesthetic responses to an artistic communication. The members of any given audience are so numerous and therefore so varied in their individual make-up that the aesthetic endowments of any single member selected at random would not adequately describe the remainder of the group.

Although the critic may not be typical of the audience, he may well be considered its representative. The exploration of the psychology of the critic may tell us much specifically about the creative nature of the critic as well as provide us with some indirect psychological insights into ourselves as members of an aesthetic audience.

Whatever else a critic may or should be, he is minimally expected to be a connoisseur. In any field of human activity, some are designated as critic or connoisseur by society. In preliterate society, the leader or the master was the connoisseur. The step from connoisseur to critic implies progression from knowledge to judgment. Connoisseurship is related to scholarship, and criticism superimposes the factor of judgmental values. Many fields of man's en-

From *Creativity in the Theatre*, by Philip Weissman, © 1965 by Philip Weissman. Basic Books, Inc., Publishers, New York.

deavor call on the critical connoisseur to play the role of historian, evaluator, judge, arbitrator, attributor, and interpreter.

When confined to the fields of artistic creativity, the critic must have a sound knowledge of man's art treasures, past and present. He must have the ability to identify the artist and his works, the skill and the knowledge to attribute unidentified treasures of art to the proper era and the proper artist. Ideally speaking, he should have insight into the nature of the artist and the creative process and how they are integrated. For these functions, it is apparent that psychological intuition or orientation would be desirable.

It is not uncommon for a critic to be devoid of creative powers in the given field of art he is serving. Critics are rarely creative as painters, and creative painters are rarely important as critics. Psychologically speaking, particular requirements are necessary for the function of the critic, since every creative artist would otherwise be the best candidate for the role of art critic. This is not the case. It is as uncommon to find in a single individual the combination of critic and creator as it is to find someone who is both critic and director. This is due to the critic's capacity to identify mainly with the creator's final communication and to his more restricted capacity to share in or identify with the artist's creative capacities which a director must do when he stages a re-creation of the artist's work. Shaw is a rare example of both artist and critic; he was considered a major dramatist but a mediocre drama critic.[1] He was an excellent music critic, and it is not surprising that he was not creative in the field of music. Shakespeare's genius enabled him to transcend the usual limitations of an artist. Only someone of Shakespeare's stature could be both playwright and actor, to say nothing of poet and director. However, even Shakespeare never functioned as critic. These data substantiate the validity of the concept that the critic's capacity to completely experience the artist's work does not extend itself into an equal capacity to be creative in the same art form. As we shall soon see, there are distinctive differences between the artist and the critic in their basic endowments.

There is no question that creative artists have much to tell us about the nature of art and the creative process. Their comments reflect their self-observed creative processes, which are valuable sources of information for other developing artists and their education. However, their criticism excludes consideration of aesthetic communication to the audience, which should be a field of interest to the

---

[1] Eric Bentley, *Bernard Shaw* (New York, 1957).

critic. Arthur Miller, the renowned American playwright, recently remarked (1965), "I never learned anything from critics. They are for the public and not for artists." T. S. Eliot (1942) points out that a poem may have meanings to the reader which differ from those of the author.

The creative artist need not be a connoisseur in his field to be creative. The artist's knowledge of his field may be confined to his awareness of its constituents, but need not be organized into scholarships. The works of his contemporaries or predecessors do not communicate to the artist the usual responses evoked in critics and expert audiences. Along with other experiences in life, the works of other artists stimulate activity in the direction of new creation in a creative person. The artist's subsequent response to his own creation is unique. It does not stir him to a re-creation as it does the critic and the responsive audience. Rather it occupies the position of a past experience subject to all the psychological laws of memories, inclusive of residual instinctual elements, the distortions of screen memories, and typical defenses. When confronted by his own creations, an artist may be able to revive the original creative experience, particularly the inspirational phase, rather than re-create in the manner of the audience. The artist's successive reactions to his creations may be compared to the change from parents' enthusiasm for the newborn to the later feeling for an offspring who has learned to go its own way. Central to the artist's nature is the process of original creation, so that his responses to his creations as well as those of others are quickly redirected to a new creative possibility and do not achieve a full elaboration as in the case of the audience.

Both artist and audience have often expressed the view that they could well do without the critic, who, they feel, frequently functions as an obstructive middleman in matters that are strictly between them. The organized scholarship of the critic, which is or should be greater than that of the artist or audience, is perhaps the crucial factor justifying his existence. A critic, unhampered by the urge to be creative in the given artistic medium in which he functions as critic, is in a better position than the artist to receive the full impact of another person's creative communications. Thus he is better able to evaluate and pass judgment on them. It is not remarkable to find that connoisseurs and critics contribute little to the creative commonwealth of their given art form. They rarely give birth to artistic creation in the same field. Coincidental and unevaluated is the fact that many renowned critics have also been biologically childless.

Samuel Johnson, Pope, Sainte-Beuve, Macaulay, Pater, Ruskin,

Lamb, Berenson, Beerbohm, Shaw, Mencken, George Jean Nathan are some examples. These twelve childless critics emerge from a random sampling of fourteen famous critics. Of the remainder, Emerson had two wives and four children; Addison had one child who appears to have been mentally defective.[2] The biological childlessness of critics is not vital to the present thesis. It merely accentuates the possibility that the childless state of the critic may extend from his personal to his artistic self. It might be fruitful to study the childhood of the childless critic to see if this state was psychologically overdetermined and how it could be correlated with the subsequent choice of becoming a critic. Biographies of critics should be studied to reveal the nature of their oedipal conflicts. One solution which might be predicted is the surrender of their own procreative wishes, which would then permit them to be both curious about and aggressively critical of their creative parents.

According to Kris, it is estimated that the critic's response to an artist's work is a re-creation of a semblance of the artist's original experience.[3] He also suggests that the critic's attitude toward a creator's work may extend in its possibilities from an identification with the creator to rival of the creator, to father and prophet of the creator. These formulations are still deductive suppositions concerning the psychology of the critic; they are derived not from psychoanalytic studies of the lives of critics but rather from clinical hunches which are woven into a theoretical reconstruction of the psychological process in the idealized critic. Critics often behave as if they have incorporated rather than experienced a creative work and subsequently respond as if the engulfed creation is their own and the original work is neither identifiable nor attributable to its original creators. All these reactions on the part of the critic may have their counterpart in the primitive psychological phenomenon of the couvade, in which the male develops the state and feelings of the pregnant female and behaves as if the creative process, biologically impossible for him, is going on within rather than outside himself. In such cases, the sensations, signs, and symptoms of pregnancy are points of departure from the procreative phenomenon with which they are associated; the male has incorporated into himself the female's state of pregnancy at the expense of an empathic reaction to her newly created transformation.

---

[2] I am indebted to Miss Barbara Braun for researching this information.
[3] E. Kris, "Approaches to Art," in *Psychoanalytic Explorations in Art,* (New York, 1952), pp. 13-63.

Other psychoanalytic writers have also suggested that the expert spectator and the critic re-create a semblance of the artist's original experience. Another view is that the artist forces his view on his recipient by identifying with him.[4] There is little doubt that the artist-critic relationship calls for mutual identifications of one with the other. However, to account for all the factors involved in the critic's response to a creative work as an exclusive interchange between artist and critic remains a facile and broad account of more complex phenomena that must be involved. The critic's response to a work of art also partakes of an interchange between the audience and himself.

The connoisseur or critic first makes a preconscious or unconscious identification with the artist, to whom he makes an aesthetic response. His identification with the artist then reaches consciousness. It is my impression that the ultimate function of the critic is his ability to make conscious to the spectator what the latter has experienced preconsciously or unconsciously. To achieve this end, the critic must have an identification with the audience, so that he may actively communicate to them what they have passively experienced.[5] We should bear in mind that, in his historical origin, the critic was a leader of the people rather than of the artists. Professional critics are attuned to a given audience's interests and mode of enjoyment. They make their evaluations in accordance with a specific image of the audience they represent.[6] They attempt to minimize (with varying degrees of success) their very personal responses to a creative work and to serve the collective image of their audiences. The reviewer, such as a music or drama critic of a newspaper, serves the collective image of the audience consciously; the scholarly critic identifies himself unconsciously with his audience.

An estimate of the conscious and unconscious processes of artist, audience, and critic at best can be only roughly achieved. The artist may deliberately permit himself to regress to a lessened state of consciousness in which unconscious derivatives reach his awareness. He then utilizes and elaborates the unconscious content in his creative work.[7] In reverse, the audience proceeds from a conscious

[4] D. Schneider, *The Psychoanalyst and the Artist* (New York, 1954).

[5] The role of the critic, according to Kris, is to explain the process within the artist by means of his interest in the artist's actual experience and biography; such explanation deepens the understanding of the artist's work.

[6] It has been suggested that art is consciously or unconsciously addressed to an expert audience. In urbanized civilization, art lovers are a small, elite group, distinct in social status, mores, and language.

[7] Kris has termed this process regression in the service of the ego.

perception of the work of art to a preconscious elaboration, which subsequently reverberates in its unconscious. Similarly, the critic proceeds from a conscious perception to a preconscious infiltration and unconscious responses. At this point, the ideal critic goes beyond the reaction of the audience. He assimilates and synthesizes his unconscious responses and experiences to the given artistic communication. Viewed from the field of aesthetics, he measures the total communication from standards of correspondence, interest, and coherence for subsequent appraisal of the aesthetic experience. He must also evaluate the degree of completeness and integration of the aesthetic product. A critic approximates the state of optimal functioning when his aesthetic evaluation encompasses and communicates an integrated account of both the artist's and audience's conscious, preconscious, and unconscious participation in a creative experience.

What is the essential equipment for an ideal critic? To detail this may present great difficulties in view of the multiple functions of a critic and the changing emphasis on the major functions of art and criticism. In the latter days of the era of classical art, the function of attribution was emphasized. It was deemed necessary that rediscovered art treasures of earlier centuries be properly identified as to their period and, whenever possible, assigned to the authoritative artists. Psychoanalysis has stressed the similarity between the artist's creative powers and woman's creative powers in childbirth. . . .

Problems of plagiarism and falsification still confront classical connoisseurs of art. In the current romantic era of art, both artist and critic promulgate the view that art shall gratify and express an individual's inner life. Here the critic as well as the artist must be attuned to man's capacity for unconscious communication. For the critic of classical art, attribution is the problem of identifying the proper artist of the past with a remaining work of art. For the critic of romantic art, attribution is the problem of finding the inner part of the artist's life that belongs to the given work under consideration; such criticism can deepen our understanding of the artist and his work.[8]

The critic and the audience must have aesthetic capacities and endowments which enable them to respond to works of art. In the preceding chapters, the basic characteristics of various types of

[8] In the change from classicism to romanticism, psychoanalysis has played an increasingly influential role in the fields of art and art criticism.

creative artists have been detailed. To understand better the differences between artist and critic, it may be useful to specify the line of demarcation between their respective endowments and equipments. For the creative artist, Greenacre[9] has postulated four general characteristics: (1) greater sensitivity to sensory stimuli; (2) unusual capacity for awareness of relations between various stimuli; (3) basic predisposition to an empathy of wider range than average—the empathy to extend from one's own body to external objects and a peculiar empathic animation of inanimate objects; (4) an intactness of sensorimotor equipment, permitting the building up of projective motor discharge for expressive function.

The first part of the third prerequisite is an unusual empathy which extends from one's own body to an external object. This would be a prerequisite for functioning in the romantic concept of art, in which the individual is emphasized. The second part of the third prerequisite calls for a capacity for a "peculiar empathic animation of inanimate objects," which seems to be close to the nature of classical art, in which the external world, as distinguished from man's inner world, is emphasized. Whether empathic for one's own body or for inanimate objects, these traits seem to be prerequisites equally for artist, critic, and audience in both classical and romantic art.

Certainly the fourth prerequisite, projective motor discharge for expressive function, is not essential for the critic, since this represents the specific equipment of the artist's capacity to create original works. Greenacre's first two requirements, which relate to high sensitivity to stimuli and to the relationship between stimuli, are to be found in the expert audience and the critic. The expert critic must have a higher sensitivity than the artist to the interrelatedness of stimuli. The artist must have the ability to create works expressed in aesthetic ambiguities, but often enough only the critic will have the capacity to elaborate the given ambiguities into more variations than the artist could conceive.

Therefore, the critic does not require the highest capacity for projective motor discharge for expression function, but he does require a high degree of sensitivity to sensory stimuli and to the relationships among such stimuli. This capacity must be so developed that he can absorb an artist's communication and disperse its

---

[9] Phyllis Greenacre, "The Childhood of the Artist," *The Psychoanalytic Study of the Child,* Vol. 12 (New York, 1957), pp. 47-72.

contents into the depths of his own unconscious. Then he must reintegrate the unconscious communication into an expert statement of the effects of the artist's communication on the audience. The artist's task is confined to communication to his recipient. He is not responsible for an accounting of what transpires in the audience. With such a status of sensitivity to sensory stimuli, we may well understand that such faculties might be organized in the critic by means of various autonomous functions which promote his curiosity, knowledgeability, and scholarship in a given area of artistic interest.

The manner in which a critic identifies himself with the artist is important, for the effects of such identifications are crucial when the critic is dealing with the biography of an artist. Freud warned of the pitfalls of unconsciously determined idealization of the artist by the critic, which results in an artificial reconstruction of the artist. He writes that

> [B]iographers are fixated on their heroes in quite a special way. In many cases they have chosen their heroes as the subjects of their study because — for reasons of their own personal life — they have felt a special affection for him from the first. . . . They thus present us with what is in fact a cold, strange, ideal figure instead of a human being to whom we might feel ourselves distantly related. That they should do this is regrettable; for they thereby sacrifice truth to illusion, and for the sake of their infantile phantasies abandon the opportunity of penetrating the most fascinating secrets of human nature.[10]

A danger opposite to that of excessive idealization occurs when "the biographer displaces his unconscious hostile feelings on to the subject of his biography — ironically evident in some popular biographies of Freud."[11] Not only are such excessive identifications ("overhostile" and "overloving") pitfalls for the critic, but they are equally hazardous for the artist who may be creating a drama, a novel, an epic poem, a painting, or a sculpture based on the life of a great man.

An inspirational response can reside in the critic for some time and may subsequently be elaborated by him with the aid of his

[10] Sigmund Freud, "Leonardo da Vinci and a Memory of his Childhood," *Standard Edition of the Works of Sigmund Freud* (London, 1957), XI, 59-137.

[11] D. Beres, "The Contribution of Psychoanalysis to the Biography of the Artist," *International Journal of Psychoanalysis* (Vol. 40, 1959), pp. 26-37.

connoisseurship of the given art, the particular artist, his collected works, and the specific work under consideration. Criticism may be as original as art itself. The critic fulfills a creative function when he can transform the audience's immediate implicit responses into a more permanent explicit appreciation and understanding.

Our psychological exploration of the critic views him as unhampered by creative urges in his critical field. While the critic may be limited in his endowments to originate in the areas of his connoisseurship, he may have a greater capacity than the artist for awareness of relatedness among sensory stimuli which reside in and emanate from works of art. Psychoanalytically uninvestigated but phenomenologically suggestive is the speculation that the critic's noncreativity may be rooted in psychological childhood determinants, since critics are often childless in their adult lives. If a critic is blessed with keen psychological intuition, he can enrich us with deeper creative insights into the aesthetic response of the audience of which he is ultimately a member.

The following books are selected because each, in one or more ways, enlarges the subject matter treated in this anthology. This list is by no means intended as an exhaustive bibliography; nor does it "cover" categorically all areas of theatre research, historical and practical. The editor's effort has been to select books, not only important in themselves, but those which suggest new channels of thought; they may then introduce the student of theatre to vital areas of work, hitherto perhaps of no concern to him, or supplement interests already manifested.

Other anthologies are listed only if they are truly basic works in the field, or if they deal exclusively and categorically with single aspects of work in the theatre and thereby become particularly useful to the specialized student. Works from which excerpts are included in this volume are *not* re-listed although other works by the same authors frequently are. Finally, this list pertains — as does this anthology — to theatre of the "modern" period, and standard classical texts are therefore omitted.

Naturally, the works included here reflect the editor's tastes and opinions as clearly as do the selections in this anthology; however, each reader will undoubtedly want to add writings he may consider of particular importance. The list, then, is essentially a browser's guide and can be used most fruitfully if the student, by consulting it, discovers works which lead him towards a richer experience and a more ranging approach to his subject.

Adolphe Appia, *Art Vivant ou Nature Morte?* (Milan: Bottega di Poesia, 1923) (English transl., *Theatre Annual,* 1943).

Adolphe Appia, *The Work of Living Art,* translated by H. D. Albright (Miami: University of Miami Press, 1960).

Antonin Artaud, *The Theatre and its Double,* translated by Mary Caroline Richard (New York: Grove Press, 1958).

John Baird, *Make-Up* (New York: Samuel French, 1930).

George Pierce Baker, *Dramatic Technique* (New York: Houghton, Mifflin, 1919).

Jean-Louis Barrault. *The Theatre of Jean-Louis Barrault* (New York: Hill and Wang, 1962).

Lucy Barton, *Historic Costume for the Stage* (New York: Baker, 1935).

Max Beerbohm, *Around Theatres* (New York: Simon and Schuster, 1954).

Eric Bentley, *The Dramatic Event* (New York: Horizon Press, 1954).

Eric Bentley, *The Life of the Drama* (New York: Atheneum, 1964).

Eric Bentley, *The Playwright as Thinker* (New York: Harcourt, Brace and Co., 1946).

Eric Bentley, *The Search of Theatre* (New York: Alfred A. Knopf, 1953).

Jerry Blunt, *The Composite Art of Acting* (New York: Macmillan, 1966).

Richard Boleslavsky, *Acting: The first Six Lessons* (New York: Theatre Arts Books, 1933).

Bertolt Brecht, "A New Technique of Acting," translated by Eric Bentley (*Theatre Arts*, XXXIII: New York, January, 1949), pp. 38-40.

Robert Brustein, *The Theatre of Revolt* (Boston: Little, Brown and Co., 1962).

Harold Burris-Meyer, *Research in Sound in the Theatre* (Publications of the Stevens Institute of Technology).

Harold Burris-Meyer and Edward C. Cole, *Scenery for the Theatre* (Boston: Little, Brown and Co., 1938).

Huntly Carter, *The Theatre of Max Reinhardt* (London: F. and C. Palmer, 1914).

Barrett H. Clark, *European Theories of the Drama* (New York: Crown Publishers, 1947).

Harold Clurman, *The Fervent Years: The Story of the Group Theater and the Thirties* (New York: Alfred A. Knopf, 1950).

Harold Clurman, *Lies Like Truth* (New York: Grove Press, 1958).

Toby Cole (ed.), *Playwrights on Playwriting* (New York: Hill and Wang, 1960).

Toby Cole and H. K. Chinoy (eds.), *Actors on Acting* (New York: Crown Publishers, 1949).

Toby Cole and H. K. Chinoy (eds.), *Directors on Directing* (New York: Bobbs-Merrill Co., Inc., 1963, rev. ed.).

Jacques Copeau, *Les Fourberies de Scapin de Molière, mise en scène et commentaires,* preface de Louis Jouvet (Paris: Edition du Seuil, 1951).

Edward Gordon Craig, *The Theatre—Advancing* (New York: Benjamin Blom, Inc., 1964).

Edward Gordon Craig, *Towards a New Theatre: Forty Designs with Critical Notes* (London: J. M. Dent and Sons, Ltd., 1913).

Charles Dullin, *L'Avare de Molière, mise en scène et commentaires de Charles Dullin* (Paris: Edition du Seuil, 1946).

Gerald Else, *The Origin and Early Form of Greek Tragedy* (Cambridge: Harvard University Press, 1965).

Martin Esslin, *The Theatre of The Absurd* (New York: Anchor Books, Double-
day, 1961).

Francis Fergusson, *The Idea of a Theater* (Princeton: Princeton University
Press, 1949).

Christopher Fry (ed.), *An Experience of Critics* (New York: Oxford University Press, 1952).

Lewis Funke and John E. Booth (eds.), *Actors Talk About Acting* (New York:
Random House, 1961).

John Gassner, *Directions in Modern Theatre and Drama* (New York: Holt,
Rinehart and Winston, 1965).

John Gassner, *Form and Idea in Modern Theatre* (New York: Dryden Press,
1956).

John Gielgud, *Early Stages* (New York: Macmillan, 1939).

John Gielgud, "Staging *Love for Love*" (*Theatre Arts,* XXVII, November,
1943), p. 632, pp. 662-668.

Douglas Gilbert, *American Vaudeville* (New York: Dover Publications, Inc.,
1940).

Rosamond Gilder, *John Gielgud's Hamlet: A Record of Performance, With notes
on Costume, Scenery and Stage Business by John Gielgud* (New York: Oxford
University Press, 1937).

Mordecai Gorelik, *New Theatres for Old* (New York: E. P. Dutton, 1962).

Harley Granville-Barker, *Shakespeare's Comedy of Twelfth Night; An Acting
Edition with a Producer's Preface* (London: 1912).

Tyrone Guthrie, *A New Theatre* (New York: McGraw-Hill, 1964).

Tyrone Guthrie and Tanya Moisewitsch, "The Production of *King Oedipus*"
in *Thrice the Brinded Cat Hath Mew'd: A Record of the Stratford Festival in
Canada,* Robertson Davies, Tyrone Guthrie and Boyd Neil (eds.) (Toronto:
Clark, Irwin and Co., Ltd., 1955).

Stuart Hall and Paddy Whannel, *The Popular Arts: A Critical Guide to the
Mass Media* (New York: Random House, Pantheon Books, 1965).

Norris Houghton, *Moscow Rehearsals: An Account of Methods of Production
in the Soviet Theatre* (New York: Grove Press, 1962).

Johan Huizinga, *Homo Ludens: A Study of the Play Element in Culture* (Boston:
Beacon Press, 1955).

Louis Jouvet, "The Profession of the Producer" (*Theatre Arts Monthly,* XX,
December, 1936), pp. 942-949, (XXI, January, 1937), pp. 57-64.

C. Koehler and E. von Sichart, *A History of Costume* (London: Harrap, 1928).

Theodore Kommisarjevsky, *Myself and the Theatre* (New York: E. P. Dutton
and Co., Inc., 1930).

Richard Kostelanetz (ed.), *The New American Arts* (New York: Horizon Press, 1965).

Michael Langham, "An Approach to Staging Shakespeare's Works" (A lecture delivered at the Universities of Canada Seminar at the Stratford Shakespearean Festival, Stratford, Ontario, August 16, 1961).

Robert Lewis, *Method or Madness* (New York: Samuel French, 1958).

Kenneth MacGowan, *A Primer of Playwriting* (New York: Random House, 1951).

Kenneth MacGowan, *The Theatre of Tomorrow* (New York: Boni and Liveright, 1921).

Kenneth MacGowan and Robert Jones, *Continental Stagecraft* (New York: Harcourt, Brace and Co., 1922).

Brander Matthews, *Papers on Acting* (New York: Hill and Wang, 1958).

Brander Matthews, *Papers on Playmaking* (New York: Hill and Wang, 1957).

Stanley R. McCandless, *A Method of Lighting the Stage* (New York: Theatre Arts, 1939).

Mary McCarthy, *Theatre Chronicles* 1937-1962 (New York: Noonday Press, Farrar, Straus and Co., 1963).

A. M. Nagler, *A Source Book in Theatrical History,* [originally *Sources of Theatrical History,* Theatre Annual, Inc., 1952] (New York: Dover Publications, Inc., 1959).

Vladimir Nemirovich-Danchenko, "Danchenko Directs: Notes on *The Three Sisters*" (*Theatre Arts,* XXVII, October, 1943), pp. 603-606.

Allardyce Nicoll, *The Development of the Theatre* (New York: Harcourt, Brace and Co., 1958, 4th ed. rev.).

Allardyce Nicoll, *World Drama* (London: George G. Harrap, Ltd., 1949).

Lyn Oxenford, *Design for Movement* (New York: Theatre Arts Books, 1952).

C. B. Purdom (ed.), *Bernard Shaw's Letters to Granville-Barker* (New York: Theatre Arts Books, 1957).

Michael Redgrave, *The Actor's Ways and Means* (London: William Heinemann, Ltd., 1953).

Oliver M. Sayler (ed.), *Max Reinhardt and his Theatre* (New York: Brentano's, 1924).

George Bernard Shaw, *Our Theatres in the Nineties,* 3 vols. (London: Constable and Co., 1932).

Marc Slonim, *Russian Theater* (New York: World Publishing Co., 1961).

Cecil Smith, *Musical Comedy in America* (New York: Theatre Arts Books, 1950).

Viola Spolin, *Improvisation for the Theatre* (Evanston: Northwestern University Press, 1963).

Konstantin S. Stanislavsky, *An Actor Prepares,* translated by Elizabeth Reynolds Hapgood (New York: Theatre Arts Books, 1936).

Konstantin S. Stanislavsky, *Creating a Role,* translated by Elizabeth Reynolds Hapgood (New York: Theatre Arts Books, 1961).

Konstantin S. Stanislavsky, *My Life in Art,* translated by J. J. Robbins (New York: Theatre Arts Books, 1948).

Konstantin S. Stanislavsky, *Stanislavsky Produces Othello,* translated by Helen Nowak (London: Geoffrey Bless, 1948).

Serge Strenkovsky, *The Art of Make-Up* (New York: Dutton, 1937).

J. L. Styan, *The Elements of Drama* (London and New York: Cambridge University Press, 1960).

Jean Vilar, "Murder of the Director," translated by Christopher Kotschnig (*Tulane Drama Review,* III, December, 1958), pp. 3-7.

Jean Vilar, "Secrets," translated by Christopher Kotschnig (*Tulane Drama Review,* III, March, 1959), pp. 24-30.

Percival Wilde, *The Craftsmanship of the One-Act Play* (Boston: Little, Brown and Co., 1932).

John Willet, *The Theatre of Bertolt Brecht* (New York: New Directions, 1959).

Stark Young, *Theatre Practice* (New York: Charles Scribner's Sons, 1926).

Franco Zeffirelli, "Reviving the Dead World of the Classics" (Kenneth Tynan Interviews Zeffirelli; *The Observer,* September 18, 1960), p. 13.

Franco Zeffirelli, "Some Notes on *Romeo and Juliet*" (*Playbill,* February 12, 1962), pp. 19-20.